W9-BBA-617

Harper Dictionary

of Contemporary

Usage

HARPER

DICTIONARY

OF

CONTEMPORARY

SECOND EDITION USAGE

William and Mary Morris

with the assistance of a panel of 166 distinguished consultants on usage

HarperPerennial

A Division of HarperCollins*Publishers*

The Foreword appeared in somewhat different form as an article in a publication of the Cooper-Hewitt Museum, the Smithsonian Institution's National Museum of Design. John Ciardi's poem, "A Withstandee Withstands" was written for the occasion celebrating the first publication of this *Harper Dictionary of Contemporary Usage* and appears here with the permission of the author.

HARPER DICTIONARY OF CONTEMPORARY USAGE (*Second Edition*). Copyright © 1985 by William Morris and Mary Morris. All rights reserved. Printed in the United States of America. No part of this book may be used or reproduced in any manner whatsoever without written permission except in the case of brief quotations embodied in critical articles and reviews. For information address HarperCollins Publishers, Inc., 10 East 53rd Street, New York, NY 10022.

Designer: Sidney Feinberg

The Library of Congress has catalogued the hardcover edition of this book as follows:

Morris, William, 1913–
    Harper dictionary of contemporary usage.

    1. English language—Terms and phrases. 2. English
language—Errors of usage—Dictionaries.
I. Morris, Mary, 1913–   . II. Harper & Row Publishers.
III. Title IV. Title: Dictionary of contemporary
usage.
PE1680.M59   1985   423′.1   83-48797
ISBN 0-06-181606-X

ISBN 0-06-272021-X (pbk.)
92 93 94 95 96 HC 10 9 8 7 6 5 4 3 2 1

Dedication

To WYSTAN HUGH AUDEN, who contributed to this work in its early
stages and who wrote: "For a poet, there is only one political duty
and that is to defend one's language from corruption. And that is
particularly serious now. It is being corrupted. When it's corrupted,
people lose faith in what they hear, and that leads to violence."

And to HENRY LOUIS MENCKEN, who in earlier years, perhaps unwisely,
encouraged us in the first of our lexicographical ventures, and who
wrote: "To the man with an ear for verbal delicacies—to the man who
searches painfully for the perfect word and puts the way of saying
a thing above the thing being said—there is in writing the constant
joy of sudden discovery, of happy accident."

Panel of Consultants on Usage

JANE ALEXANDER, winner of many film, television and stage awards
SHANA ALEXANDER, editor, writer and columnist
CLEVELAND AMORY, writer, radio and TV commentator
DAVID P. "DAVE" ANDERSON, sports columnist, *The New York Times*
BENJAMIN APPEL, writer
MICHAEL J. ARLEN, staff writer, *The New Yorker* magazine
ISAAC ASIMOV, writer; lecturer; professor of biochemistry, Boston University
W. H. AUDEN, poet
SHERIDAN BAKER, educator, professor, University of Michigan
WHITNEY BALLIETT, music critic, *The New Yorker* magazine
THOMAS S. BARBER, writer and editor
JOHN O. BARBOUR, feature writer, Associated Press
STEWART BEACH, editor, writer and historian
ALVIN BEAM, former book editor and columnist, Cleveland *Plain Dealer*
SAUL BELLOW, writer, winner of Nobel Prize for literature and Pulitzer Prize
    in fiction
JULES BERGMAN, science writer
CHARLES BERLITZ, linguist, educator, writer
SIMON MICHAEL BESSIE, writer, editor, publisher, Harper & Row
BARRY BINGHAM, SR., publisher, Louisville *Courier-Journal* and *Times*
ALTON BLAKESLEE, medical and science writer
JULIAN BOND, legislator, civil-rights leader
HAL BORLAND, writer, naturalist, columnist
DAVID H. BRADLEY, writer, associate professor of English, Temple University
JOSEPH A. BRANDT, former president of University of Oklahoma and Henry
    Holt & Co., director of Oklahoma, Princeton, and Chicago university
    presses, founder of UCLA School of Journalism
JOHN BROOKS, journalist and historian
HEYWOOD HALE BROUN, writer, TV and radio commentator
ART BUCHWALD, writer, internationally syndicated columnist
ANTHONY BURGESS, novelist, essayist, linguist
BEN LUCIEN BURMAN, novelist
JAMES MACGREGOR BURNS, political scientist, winner of Pulitzer Prize in
    history
JOAN SIMPSON BURNS, writer, editor
ABE BURROWS, playwright-director, winner of Pulitzer Prize in drama
MELVILLE CANE, lawyer, poet

CASS CANFIELD, SR., senior editor, Harper & Row, author of *The Incredible Pierpont Morgan*

TURNER CATLEDGE, journalist and writer

JOHN CHAPMAN, former drama editor, New York *Daily News*

JOHN CIARDI, poet, columnist and past president, National College English Association

JAMES B. CONANT, president emeritus, Harvard University

ALISTAIR COOKE, essayist, radio and TV broadcaster

GEORGE CORNISH, journalist, former editor in chief, *Encyclopedia Americana*

ROBERT CRICHTON, novelist

ROBERT CROMIE, writer, journalist, radio and TV commentator

WALTER CRONKITE, broadcast journalist and commentator, CBS News

WILLIAM O. DOUGLAS, associate justice, United States Supreme Court

ELIZABETH DOWNIE, musicologist, writer and editor

LEON EDEL, writer, educator, winner of Pulitzer Prize in biography

WILLARD R. ESPY, writer, humorist, light poet

ALEX FAULKNER, C.B.E., former chief American correspondent of the *Daily Telegraph*, London

THOMAS FLEMING, novelist and historian

CHARLES BRACELEN FLOOD, writer, past president of P.E.N.

GEROLD FRANK, author, editor, foreign correspondent

FRANCES FRITCHMAN, writer and editor

STEPHEN H. FRITCHMAN, Unitarian minister, writer

RAY GANDOLF, television sportscaster

ERNEST K. GANN, writer

A. BARTLETT GIAMATTI, president of Yale University

SID GOLDBERG, editor, United Feature Syndicate

HARRY GOLDEN, editor, publisher, writer

ROBERT GOTTLIEB, editor in chief, Alfred A. Knopf

A. B. GUTHRIE, JR., writer, speaker

PETE HAMILL, writer, New York *Daily News* and *The Village Voice*

ELIZABETH HARDWICK, essayist, editor

SYDNEY J. HARRIS, columnist, Field Newspaper Syndicate

RICHARD EDES HARRISON, cartographer, writer, editor

WAKEMAN HARTLEY, columnist, former newspaper publisher and editor

S. I. HAYAKAWA, former U.S. senator, writer and former president, San Francisco State College

GEOFFREY HELLMAN, writer, historian and contributor to *The New Yorker* magazine

PAUL HORGAN, novelist, historian, educator

NORMAN HOSS, editor, managing editor of *The American Heritage Dictionary,* Original Edition

JOHN K. HUTCHENS, journalist, editor, drama and literary critic

ELIZABETH JANEWAY, novelist, critic

DIANE JOHNSON, writer, educator, professor, University of California at Davis

E. J. KAHN, JR., writer, staff writer for *The New Yorker* magazine
HELEN L. KAUFMANN, music writer
WALT KELLY, cartoonist, creator of *Pogo*
ALEXANDER KENDRICK, news correspondent, writer
WALTER KERR, drama critic, *The New York Times*
JAMES J. KILPATRICK, columnist, commentator
CLARK KINNAIRD, editor, historian, biographer
IRVING KOLODIN, music critic
STANLEY KUNITZ, poet
CHARLES KURALT, TV news correspondent and commentator, CBS
LAURENCE LAFORE, writer, professor of history, University of Iowa
DANIEL LANG, staff writer for *The New Yorker* magazine
JOHN LEAR, formerly science editor of *Saturday Review,* science consultant
    for Crown Publishers
ANTHONY LEWIS, columnist, *The New York Times*
ROBERT LIPSYTE, novelist, sports writer and broadcaster, CBS
JULES LOH, journalist and writer
WALTER LORD, writer
RUSSELL LYNES, editor, writer
DWIGHT MACDONALD, critic
HENRY W. MALONE, writer, educator, professor, University of Wichita
BILL MAULDIN, political cartoonist
EUGENE MCCARTHY, former U.S. senator, writer, lecturer, poet
DAVID MCCORD, writer, poet, critic
PHYLLIS MCGINLEY, writer, poet
WILLIAM MCGUIRE, editor, Princeton University Press
SHELDON MEYER, editor, Oxford University Press
JESSICA MITFORD, writer, critic
HERBERT MITGANG, writer, journalist
WILLIE MORRIS, writer
WRIGHT MORRIS, writer
WADE MOSBY, writer, journalist
DANIEL PATRICK MOYNIHAN, U.S. senator, former ambassador, educator
EDWIN NEWMAN, writer, former correspondent, NBC News
URSULA NORDSTROM, editor, writer
STANTON PECKHAM, former editor, book critic
MARGE PIERCY, poet, novelist, essayist
HARRIET PILPEL, attorney, writer and lecturer
FRANCIS T. P. PLIMPTON, lawyer, diplomat
GEORGE PLIMPTON, writer, editor, TV commentator
DAVID POLING, clergyman, columnist
ORVILLE PRESCOTT, writer, literary critic
PETER S. PRESCOTT, book critic, *Newsweek* magazine
F. D. REEVE, poet, novelist, critic
FRANCIS ROBINSON, former assistant manager, Metropolitan Opera

EARL UBELL, science editor, TV commentator, CBS

BILL VAUGHAN, former associate editor, Kansas City *Star*

JOSEPH VERGARA, writer, former editor, Harper & Row

WILLIAM C. VERGARA, science writer

JUDITH VIORST, writer

GEORGE WALD, professor of biology, Harvard University, winner of Nobel Prize for physiology

DOUGLAS WATT, writer and critic

A.B.C. WHIPPLE, writer and editor

CHARLES L. WHIPPLE, former editor of the editorial page of the Boston *Globe*, former editor of the *China Daily*

T. HARRY WILLIAMS, professor and writer

HERMAN WOUK, novelist and playwright

WILLIAM ZINSSER, writer, former professor, Yale University

CHARLOTTE ZOLOTOW, writer and editor, Harper & Row

A Withstandee Withstands

I apathied while she enthused.
She was critiqueing while I rused
How, hopefully, to alibi
My exit soonly. Timewise I
Crawled endless while an ennui
Escalated over me.
Would she never finalize
Her on-goings? "If I rise
And absentee myself, would she,"
I introspected viz-a-viz
Said interminables, "conclude,
Mannerwise, that I was rude?"

Clearly her consensus stood
Unanimous for my own good.
Nor was it unknown to me
How meaningful she meant to be.
She saw herself, conceptually,
As incisively supportive.
That conception was abortive.
The fact that she meant only good
Notwithstanding, I withstood,
But did my best to not infer
How much I had no use for her.

John Ciardi

Foreword

At the start of the twentieth century, language in America—it had not yet become the "American language"—still showed the influence of its largely prescriptive Victorian past. Sentences, both spoken and written, tended to be long and involved and virtually everything that appeared in print was subjected to such neo-Latin "rules" as the ones about never ending sentences with prepositions and never splitting infinitives. Niceties of verbal distinctions were given the force of iron-clad rules. Frank Vizetelley, editor of the Funk & Wagnalls dictionaries and house grammarian for the then-influential *Literary Digest* could thunder: "Raise should never be used of bringing human beings to maturity: it is a misuse common in the Southern and Western United States. Cattle are *raised;* human beings are *brought up* or, in the older phrase, *reared.*"

But then, as always, there were some loudly vocal dissenters—rebels against the status quo. Curiously enough, the same starchy Funk & Wagnalls lexicon was in the very forefront of a movement to radically alter the way the language looked, though not the way it sounded. The Funk & Wagnalls unabridged dictionary was the high-water mark of the Simplified Spelling movement which had its origins late in the nineteenth century but sprang to its fullest flower during the presidency of Theodore Roosevelt.

All presidents have influenced the course of language growth in one way or another. In recent years their influence has been usually detrimental and often inadvertent, like Mr. Eisenhower's mispronunciation of "nuclear" (noo-kyoo-ler) and Mr. Nixon's predilection for expletives deleted.

But Theodore Roosevelt was a great believer in self-improvement, as evidenced by his own development from a rather puny child to an archetypal "he-man," a term popular in his day if not in ours. T.R. found the presidency a "bully pulpit" for championing his favorite causes, one of which was simplified spelling. Its purpose was to convert the nation and its press from such "wasteful" and "unscientific" spellings as *neighbor, through, philosophy,* and *photograph* to *nabor, thru, filosofy,* and *fotograf.* In a remarkable exercise of presidential prerogative, Roosevelt ordered the Government Printing Office to follow the "reformed," or "simplified," spellings. His order was ignored and government publications continued to appear with conventional spellings. Two of the nation's major newspapers, the *Chicago Tribune* and the *New York News,* valiantly attempted for years to promote the new spellings but, except for an occasional "foto" or "thru," the well-intentioned reforms may now be found only in the pages of turn-of-the-century Funk & Wagnalls dictionaries.

One of the founders of the movement, however, left a lasting legacy. He was Dewey of the celebrated Dewey Decimal System, without which our libraries simply could not function. So dedicated was he to the work of the Simplified Spelling Board, of which he was a member, that he performed radical surgery on his own name, lopping the terminal "le" from his first name to become Melvil (not Melville) Dewey.

Despite such radical attempts at reform, the English language, as written and spoken in the United States in the first two decades of this century, differed little from the staid and proper language of the earlier years. The big change was to come in the years following the First World War. Ring Lardner, Ernest Hemingway and Heywood Broun all started as newspaper sportswriters and soon brought a new earthiness and directness to the prose that, before long, began to appear in books, magazines, and in sections other than the sports pages in the newspapers which were then the chief channels of information for the public at large.

During the 1920s radio made its appearance and, by the early thirties, scarcely a home in America was without at least one. Although the early radio announcers were coached in careful speech and were even expected to wear formal clothes when addressing the microphone, advertisers soon learned that "folksy" speech attracted larger audiences, and by the 1940s the calculated semi-literacies of Arthur Godfrey, Herb Shriner, and the like were giving a "down-home" flavor to talk on the airwaves.

The 1930s saw the first strong tendency toward freeing books and the theater from the censorship, both overt and covert, that had carried over from the Victorian era. As late as the 1920s Henry L. Mencken had been arrested in Boston for selling an issue of his *American Mercury* containing a short story about a harlot. Even in the early 1930s plays, including Eugene O'Neill's *Mourning Becomes Electra,* were denied theaters in Boston because of the "immorality" of their themes. But the landmark case (1933) permitting the publication of James Joyce's *Ulysses* by an American publisher foretold increasing freedom in the use of hitherto-taboo language that, by the 1960s and 1970s, threatened to reach epidemic proportions.

Other changes were in the works as well. With the proliferation of governmental agencies during the era of the New Deal, bureaucratic jargon proliferated to the point where one administrator, Maury Maverick, cried out in protest, labeling the language used in government memoranda "gobbledegook." He directed members of his department to "Be short and say what you're talking about. No more 'finalizing,' 'effectuating,' or 'dynamics.' Anyone using 'activation' or 'implementation' will be shot."

Maverick's label—gobbledegook—caught the public's fancy but the rest of his message fell on deaf ears, as a glance at any government memo issued today will attest.

The 1930s also saw the uprooting of thousands of families and their westward migration, so graphically and poignantly depicted by John Steinbeck in *The Grapes of Wrath.* Along with their meager belongings, these Okies brought with them speech patterns and idioms that were profoundly to influence the motion pictures, and the radio and television programs of the years ahead—since the great majority of such programs originated in the place where the Okies landed, California.

World War II—fought on a vastly wider scale than the earlier "War to End all Wars"—brought a proportionally greater influx of new words to the language along with an increasing tolerance of the vulgarisms that are so much a part of the enlisted man's daily conversation. Far and away the most significant development in the world of words, as it was for the world at large, was the impact of the first atomic bomb. Just as it revealed a technology awesome in its immediate power and future potential, it brought with it a new vocabulary. Some of it had been known only to laboratory workers—"fission" and "implosion," for example. With the passing of a very few years, new and perhaps even more menacing words and phrases came into the general language—"hydrogen bomb," "nuclear meltdown," and "China syndrome."

But the years following the war brought not only "cold war," "brushfire wars," and the "Iron Curtain," they also brought America its "baby boom." During the years of the Eisenhower presidency especially, youth and what sociologists labeled "youth culture" seemed to dominate our national interests. Young people, as peer groups often do, developed their own language. Here are a few superlatives popular among teens at that time: "cassy," "cool," "fine," "frantic," "George," "groovy," "the most," "way out," and "real gone." All are long forgotten but, like every new generation of youngsters, from the "Flappers" of the twenties to the "Valley Girls" of the eighties, the fifties teensters evolved their own private jargon which, they hoped, would befuddle what they called the "wardens"—parents and teachers.

The 1960s brought many changes in our ways of life—and each brought its own new language. The Women's Movement gained in numbers and influence, adding "Ms.," "chairperson," and dozens of newly coined or newly oriented words in an effort—generally successful—to eliminate sexism from the language of the media. "Firemen" became "firefighters." The "lady lawyer" became simply "lawyer" and "stewardesses" became "flight attendants."

Just as the Vietnam War brought battle scenes into the living rooms of America, so the Watergate inquiry and the near-impeachment of Richard Nixon brought the pervasive lack of literacy of Washington political figures to general attention. As Barry Bingham, Sr., of the Louisville *Courier-Journal* wrote me at the time: "Whatever one may think of the testimony politically, it seems guaranteed to chill the marrow of the listener who cares about precision in speech."

A characteristic of what came to be called "Watergate language" was the use of several words where one would do ("at this point in time" for "now," and "at that point in time" for "then"), as well as dull metaphors like "go the hangout road" for "tell the truth." Chiefly, though, what Watergate showed besides the utter vulgarity of many high-level ("expletive deleted") conversations was that nothing much had really changed about bureaucratic language since Maury Maverick had made his plea for an end of gobbledegook thirty years earlier.

The new permissiveness of the sixties and seventies was reflected in ways other than the widespread abandonment of traditional moral standards by the young. The publication in 1961 of the unabridged *Merriam-Webster Third International Dictionary* brought cries of outrage from traditionalists who were affronted by its complete abandonment of standards of usage. In partial reaction to Merriam-Webster's "anything goes" approach, American Heritage sponsored in 1969 a comprehensive new dictionary which included several hundred notes on disputed usages ("imply-infer," "biweekly-semiweekly," "ain't," and "like a cigarette should," for example).

Rather curiously, because it was so permissive in other editorial aspects, the Merriam-Webster Third Edition had not entered the taboo words which had received sanction in print in the United States as early as in the 1933 decision involving Joyce's *Ulysses*. The original *American Heritage Dictionary* (1969) included them for the first time since dictionaries of the eighteenth century. Since that date the Merriam-Webster dictionaries have followed suit and the great *Oxford English Dictionary,* in its new supplements, has also entered the so-called four-letter words.

The years since World War II have seen the demise of many major newspapers, especially the once influential evening papers whose role has been preempted by nightly television news. Magazines have changed from the general mix of fiction, light non-fiction, and special features that characterized the *Saturday Evening Post* and similar staples of the early years of the century to publications catering to special interests. Personal letter-writing of the sort that brought us many literary and historical treasures in the past has virtually vanished—replaced by greeting cards for every occasion and, far more significantly, by the omnipresent telephone.

In the near future we may expect an ever-increasing contribution to our general language from science, most especially from the language of space—which has already contributed many new phrases to our general vocabulary —and from the computer, which has already revamped every aspect of publishing from word processors in newsrooms and on authors' desks, to typesetting for the cameras and cold-type printers, which have replaced the Linotypes and metal printing plates of just a few years ago.

· Changes are developing so swiftly in life around us and in the language we use to describe it that one would be mad indeed, in the Orwellian year of 1984, to try to predict the state of the language in 2000.

—WILLIAM MORRIS

Introduction

The *Harper Dictionary of Contemporary Usage* differs in many respects from other handbooks of guidance in the use of our language. First, it reflects the collaborative efforts of some 165 writers, editors, and public speakers chosen for their demonstrated ability to use the language carefully and effectively. Their opinions on scores of the knottiest questions of disputed usage are reported, both in the form of percentages of approval and disapproval and by citation of specific comments from members of the Usage Panel.

Equally important are the contributions, reported here anonymously, of thousands of readers of our syndicated newspaper column. For nearly a third of a century we have maintained a dialogue with people in every part of this country who are concerned about the state of the language and, indeed, with readers of English language newspapers in Mexico and Japan. As a result, many hundreds of questions never before treated in a usage guide are discussed in this dictionary. These are actual problems, put to us by people seriously concerned about the niceties of good speech and writing. Some of the matters discussed will surprise you and some will surely amuse you, but it should be borne in mind that every one of them is genuine and every one of them has at some time posed a problem.

The readers who raise these questions represent a cross-section of the reading public—male and female, young and old, laymen and professional writers, and, naturally, editors of papers carrying the column. As a result, this dictionary treats of virtually every aspect of today's language—idioms, slang, vogue words, and regionalisms, as well as all the vast range of words used in formal speech and writing. Many of the entries in this dictionary record usages regarded as improper or substandard by careful users of the language—"infer" when "imply" is meant, "disinterested" for "uninterested," "irregardless," and the like. Obviously a main purpose of the volume is to call attention to such inaccuracies and thus to correct or eliminate them.

A second purpose of this dictionary is to show by discussion and example the standards of linguistic usage adhered to by those who use the language well. In this undertaking we make every effort not to be dogmatic and, most assuredly, not dictatorial. Even had we been so inclined, the reactions of our panelists and consultants would have convinced us otherwise for, of the many scores of questions put to these panelists, only a very few received unanimous verdicts. On every other point, we had yea-sayers as well as nay-sayers. Inasmuch as all the panelists have amply demonstrated their ability to use the language effectively, this lack of unanimity is proof that language is no static thing to be fixed by rules. Rather it is ever-growing, ever-changing, and the often-expressed hope of the panelists as well as of the editors is that the changes may be influenced only for the better.

A word on the history of the panel may be in order. The fundamental idea behind it is, of course, that the day when one person—be he H. W. Fowler or Frank Vizetelley—could dictate the rights and wrongs of language is long past. Changes in the language are too many and too rapid for any one person to pass judgment on all the matters involved. The idea of gathering opinions from a variety of qualified users of the language was first suggested to your editors by a monograph of the National Council of Teachers of English—*Facts About Current English Usage* by Albert H. Marckwardt and Fred G. Walcott, published in 1938. This pioneering survey was "an attempt to find out what various judges have observed about the actual use or non-use by cultivated persons of a large number of expressions usually condemned in English textbooks and classes." The authors submitted questions to a group of judges including linguistic specialists, editors, authors, businessmen, and teachers of English and of speech. The last-named group, not surprisingly—considering the sponsor of the project—outnumbered all other participants combined.

It seemed to us, in organizing the panel of consultants for the *Harper Dictionary of Contemporary Usage,* that the general user of the language would be better served by a panel with many fewer teachers—though we do have some very distinguished members of that profession on the panel—and relatively more writers and editors. So in April 1971 and again in 1980 we invited a number of the leading authors and editors—men and women who had demonstrated their ability to use the language well—to participate in our work to the extent of answering queries put to them on a series of ballots continuing, as matters turned out, over several years. Response was immediate and enthusiastic, as you will see from the comments quoted in many of the entries in the body of this dictionary. Their interest and dedication is perhaps even more remarkable in light of the fact that all were serving as unpaid consultants. Their reward, as we noted in our letter of invitation, "chiefly lies in the realization that they will have played an important role in recording the standards of usage respected by today's foremost writers."

Many of the panelists had strong opinions about the state of the language today. Here is a sampling of their comments.

SHANA ALEXANDER: Thank you for service to language and fun for me.

BENJAMIN APPEL: Language is language, for better or for worse; shaped and molded by many hands and mouths (particularly mouths). A great civilization makes its own language; a corrupt one. . . . Well, all of us know only too well what has happened and what is happening to this country of ours. As writers, we should see to it that our words serve as a delaying action.

ISAAC ASIMOV: The English language is the finest tool for communication ever invented. Since it is used indiscriminately by hundreds of millions, it is no wonder that it is badly misused so often. All the more reason for those who can to hold the standard high.

JOHN O. BARBOUR: The test is whether or not words reach their intended targets in the mind of the reader—engendering, beyond dictionary meaning, tone, mood, accent. Even then, as precisely aimed as a word is, the target may move unless restrained by context. And all of that fails if the writer's idea was murky in the first place.

STEWART BEACH: I hope the panel will overwhelmingly flout the incorrect and flaunt the correct.

SIMON MICHAEL BESSIE: It becomes increasingly clear to me that I am becoming freer in my acceptance and use of changes in language. Aren't we all?

BARRY BINGHAM, SR.: We are constantly in your debt for your gallant fight on behalf of the English language.

ALTON BLAKESLEE: Language, like people, should keep breathing, changing, aging, mellowing. Some new words and usages enrich our language and us. Others debase. Let a careful jury continue watch.

HAL BORLAND: The spoken language is supposed to be the testing ground for new words to enrich the language, but I find that Madison Avenue, TV, and too many of the high-school crowd don't even know the old words. How can they give us new and better ones? I have no choice but to hold on to the old, precise language and hope it survives.

JOSEPH A. BRANDT: New words are like strangers you meet for the first time. Usually your first impression is one that lingers; however, you may change your mind. So the use of words remains in the last analysis a choice of dropping the words that annoy or continuing the new ones which somehow do fuse vitality into the sponge which we call the English language. If a sponge picks up an abrasive, it hurts when you squeeze the sponge, just as an objectionable word or usage lowers your sense of dignity of the language.

JOHN BROOKS: I don't feel that the language is necessarily disintegrating or being irrevocably debased. It is widely misused, and the misuse is disseminated by the media. But eventually, as in the past, the valuable neologisms will survive and the worthless ones will disappear.

HEYWOOD HALE BROUN: It apparently needs saying again that language should be, ideally, as accurate as it is beautiful—a mixture of art and arithmetic.

BEN LUCIEN BURMAN: I am anything but a snob in my social relationships. But I'm a terrible snob regarding language. I can't abide words that through debased usage by adolescents, commentators or careless authors appear overnight in our literature and, like nouveau riche Southern rednecks who have found oil on their property, try to make ugliness and ignorance fashionable.

ABE BURROWS: The word Grammar is the etymological parent of the word Glamour. That is, glamour in its original meanings: magic; a spell or charm. Those wicked criminals who commit high crimes against grammar, i.e., saying "between you and I" or "He invited she and I to a party," shall have an evil spell cast over "they" for all of their miserable lives. Outside of simple grammatical errors and solecisms, my objection to some "newly accepted usages" is based on my ear. Perhaps it's because most of my work is in the theatre. Obviously language can't be rigid. I feel, however, that "good grammar" has to be "good sound."

MELVILLE CANE: The language needs to be refreshed. What I object to is not the addition of new words, but the misuse of old words. My favorite example is the word *demean,* which is generally accepted as signifying disgrace, while in reality its derivation connotes behavior, demeanor which has no adverse connotation, but simply represents an attitude or state of mind.

JOHN CIARDI: Are there any enduring standards of English usage? I think there are only preferences, "passionate preferences," as Robert Frost used to say, the level at which any English speaking person chooses to engage the instrument—the orchestra—of the language. In the long run the usage of those who do not think about the language will prevail. Usages I resist will become acceptable. It is worth remembering that Swift inveighed against "mob" as a vulgar corruption of "mobile vulgus." He thought he was right to resist—"mob" must have sounded to him as "rep" for reputation sounds to me today—yet English speaking people decided that he was wrong. It will not do to resist uncompromisingly. Yet those who care have a duty to resist. Changes that occur against such resistance are tested changes. The language is better for them—and for the resistance.

ROBERT CRICHTON: The challenge to the language is the inclination and desire of institutions and government and persuasive people to turn the concrete into the abstract. When that happens language dies, which is probably the unconscious desire of these groups. This is the killing wound; all the rest is mere stuff for Band-Aids.

WALTER CRONKITE: Language has many functions from simple communication to the emotional stimulation of great literature and it is not necessary that the rules should be the same for all forms. However, for those who write and speak formally—presumably setting the standards of proper usage—there must be exercised the utmost care to prevent debasement of the language through too hasty acceptance of the vernacular.

LEON EDEL: The media are changing our language and ritualizing it. "Have a good day"—now universal—is a TV gift to America and has become meaningless. . . . If TV speech could be improved, our young would speak more accurately. But I suppose that isn't your problem. [NOTE: One very important reason for the creation of the *Harper Dictionary of Contemporary Usage* is the hope that it will influence all users of the language to a greater accuracy and precision in its use. To that extent it *is* our problem and the problem of all contributors to this dictionary.]

ALEX FAULKNER: When all is said and done, the geniuses will make their own rules. What journalists, not as a rule being geniuses, can do is to try (not too slavishly) to keep the Pierian Spring undefiled and to yelp loudly whenever they catch the careless, the commercial, the bureaucratic, and the technological making a mess of the language.

GEROLD FRANK: I am appalled by what is happening to written English and feel it affects me almost subliminally, and for the worst. Carelessness and letting go of standards seem to have their own almost magical quality as precedents. The thing to do is fight, and be aware.

STEPHEN H. FRITCHMAN: As one whose craft demands the use of language I shall join the long march of protest against its disfigurement, corruption and betrayal, however long it takes. I believe in evolution, in change and in flexibility, but none of these transformations calls for the butchery now going on. I am neither paranoid nor paleolithic, just a freedom fighter for clarity, beauty and joy. Is this too much to ask for?

A. B. GUTHRIE, JR.: The English language is so fine a tool that misuse of it seems to me shameful. It has room for growth, of course, but allows no smudging as people smudge it who equate "imply" and "infer" and "comprise" and "compose." Exactitude should be the rule of all who speak or write for audiences or readers.

GEOFFREY HELLMAN: The state of the language is a shambles, just to give an illustration.

PAUL HORGAN: As never before, language is the servant of commercial interests, chiefly through advertising and its most powerful arm, television. Catering to a huge indiscriminate public, the medium must resort to the lowest vulgate, and even, in effect, invent a new and more debased set of verbal signals, to entertain in order to sell. Like children learning to speak, the pop audience uncritically repeats what it hears; and, so, popular usage is created and soon has the force to corrupt immediately a language hitherto more slow to change and develop. Solecisms deliberately appealing to the illiterate, imprecision and exaggeration to the point of mendacity, along with governmental and academic jargon (v. "parameter" commonly used now by learned panels to mean "perimeter"), all create with irresistible swiftness a new language largely useless for serious purpose, including the aesthetic. Perhaps we are seeing something new for English—a language divided into two levels of taste, form, and meaning: Low English, created by commercial education, and High English, the survival of evolving traditions based on decent literacy unaffected by the commercial motive.

ELIZABETH JANEWAY: Since language is a tool of communication (*the* tool, if you wish) it should be precise. It will never be utterly so, for individual experiences will never quite match each other, and the expression of this individuality creates a tension within language which (I suppose) is a cause of vitality and richness. Nevertheless, we must strive for precision on pain of losing our ability to talk together at all.

HELEN L. KAUFMANN: New words are bound to creep into the language; that's the way it grows. The trick, for writers especially, seems to be to winnow the wheat from the chaff, to bestow their blessing only on what words appear meaningful, euphonious, and enduring, and hope that the others will die a natural death. The English language is constantly in flux, probably no worse today than it was when Chaucer took it in hand and Shakespeare improved on it.

ALEXANDER KENDRICK: Everybody talks about the state of the language, but nobody seems to do anything about it.

CLARK KINNAIRD: We should all be aware that language is one of the last forms of popular expression. People at large still have the right to adopt, simplify, or transform meanings.

STANLEY KUNITZ: The English language is a remarkable instrument, equipped to name and describe everything imaginable and to register the most evanescent thoughts and feelings. Poets know that the exact words are there, if only they have the patience or cunning or luck to find them; they even believe, given the riches at their disposal, in the possibility of marrying sense to sound in the most complex and satisfying of harmonies. They also know that the language is not a fixity but a changing phenomenon, attached to its ancient roots but forever seeking augmentation and renewal. A society indifferent to right words is a society grown careless of its life-giving values.

LAURENCE LAFORE: I am inclined to think that my notion of what is and what is not proper is largely formed by age: I accept the usages which were general in my adolescence, when I first began to write with any consciousness of form. I am strongly averse to most habits of speech which have developed since—but I am aware that if I had been born thirty years earlier I should have written "averse from" instead of writing "averse to." I think, however, that there is a reasonable defense to be made, a sort of program of planned obsolescence, of this attitude. It is worthwhile, perhaps, to postpone acceptance of new forms for a generation, since a good many of them will disappear into the oblivion of dead slang. Some usages that seemed on the verge of acceptability when I was growing up are now forgotten. I think, for example, of the usage of "capable" in the sense of "able" or "competent." No one says nowadays, "She is a very capable person." To be old-fashioned today is to avoid having one's writing appear old-fashioned tomorrow. I decline to use words like "meaningful" or "life-style" or "hopefully" and "presently" in their current, distorted meanings. I hope and believe that my refusal may mean that, ten years from now, my writing will be less dated.

JOHN LEAR: That TV and radio performers are debasing the language is as obvious to me as it is deplorable. But the spoken word and the written word are and ought to be distinct. So the distortions of usage committed by magazines and newspapers are a deeper and more lasting threat.

ROBERT LIPSYTE: During a recent school board election in my town, the candidate I supported used the sound "prioritize." Agonizing, I voted for her, then threw away my Word Sheriff's paper star and went back to work in debasement.

JULES LOH: A writer ought to regard the language as a sailor the sea. The tried and familiar routes are the surest. Innovation is risky.

WALTER LORD: Good usage is whatever a panel like this says it is, and the only thing that makes this preposterous situation tolerable is that people can always, anytime they choose and by sheer weight of numbers, veto our decision!

EUGENE MCCARTHY: The integrity of language is always threatened, most seriously by those who have difficulty explaining themselves or who don't want to explain. The English language, as used in the United States, has survived the assaults of the Pentagon and of the Johnson and Nixon administrations, as they attempted to justify and explain the Vietnam War. We must now look to new threats.

PHYLLIS MCGINLEY: I said I am a purist and I am. I hold the line as firmly as I can, although it's a losing battle. But it is a pleasure to take up the sword in defense of the language and against its impoverishment.

HERBERT MITGANG: Slanguage isn't language until mellowed by time; permanent written words should remain purer than spoken words. Consider the sentences of all advertisers, broadcasters, and presidential speechwriters "guilty" until proven innocent.

WRIGHT MORRIS: In the vernacular, usage and abusage are inseparable.

WADE MOSBY: We should relish the vigor brought to our language by the changing times—and at the same time retain the integrity to recognize the difference between casual intrusions and welcome additions.

HARRIET PILPEL: It is important that students at high school and grammar school learn grammar, not only for the obvious reasons, but also because grammar can be fun. I am in frequent contact with many young people and it is clear that they have no notion of what used to be taught under the heading of "grammar." Their language is replete with "between you and I" and "I went down the road with Tom and he." If it is enjoyable as well as useful to parse a sentence (for example), shouldn't something be done about this special and apparently widespread deprivation?

DAVID POLING: There are so many forces in opposition to clear and precise language: perhaps the age of multi-media and the expansion of the graphic arts is to blame. Alas, this boom has placed many in new positions of reporting and comment where they are unfamiliar with the written word and uneasy in a library. And some in creative writing are brilliant but lazy; their excellence of idea and imagination are punctured by poor grammar and the unwillingness to reach for a dictionary. But with this new usage dictionary there is hope.

PETER S. PRESCOTT: There are areas where our language is disintegrating. I am quite serious when I say I am angry about this; as a writer I feel I have fewer tools with which to work. I wonder whether the increase in energy which our language has acquired in recent years (general acceptance of the vernacular in more formal modes of writing) is worth the loss of so many words of precision, such as *flout* and *disinterested.*

F. D. REEVE: I've found that young people, minority groups, regional groups develop speech patterns to express their separateness and unity; that the schools teach only formal grammar, never usage; that consequently the responsiveness of language lies in colloquial speech, not in "standardized," falsely imitative pap of the schools and TV. To a trusted audience most people will speak readily and idiomatically, even "correctly," although they will insist that (because usage and grammatical norms do not go together for them) they cannot write. Indeed, what we need *any more** is not a Dictionary of Spelling (and you have to know how to spell it before you can find it) but a Dictionary of Usage.

LEO ROSTEN: I, for one, find the options for oral English as against written English quite useful—indeed, invaluable. Let oral English be the proving ground on which some succeed and others are slaughtered. Much cant and kooky stuff from the 1960s has already been beaten back.

BERTON ROUECHÉ: It isn't slang that most threatens the well-being of our language, or even the violation of the accepted rules of grammar; it is the simple ignorance of the true meaning of words that is "presently" abroad among those too "disinterested" to care.

VERMONT ROYSTER: Looking back on the experience, I find that I frequently modified my instinctive purist's reaction when I forced myself to think about my actual usage. In some areas I found myself becoming increasingly tolerant of usages not found in dictionaries or grammars. For example, I am inclined to accept new and useful words—e.g., "staffer" instead of having to say "member of a staff," and even the transmutation of nouns into verbs or adjectives into adverbs when the resulting word fills a gap or avoids circumlocution. After all, we have long accepted the idea that a ship sails from port, even though it has no sails at all. We are indebted to slang and journalese for enriching the language in this way. The new coinages that fall by the wayside are those that fail. What I deplore is the debasement of the language, whether from violation of the simple and logical rules of grammar or from using a good, useful word wrongly. In both cases the fault is ignorance. In both cases the consequence is a breakdown in communication. Not only are all subtleties and shades of meaning lost, but in some cases there is actual misunderstanding between writer and reader. This occurs no matter whether it is the writer or the reader who is using the language wrongly.

HARRISON SALISBURY: The wonderful thing about language is that it is always changing and always growing.

DAVID SCHOENBRUN: I do not know how to arrest and correct the debasement of both written and spoken English except to take a vow not to contribute

---

*"Any more" in the sense of "now" was one of the questions put to the Usage Panel of this book.

to the degradation myself. A great rabbi said centuries ago, "Perhaps I cannot change the world but I will try anyway and take care that the world not change me."

HAROLD SCHONBERG: New words make their way into the world. But improper grammar and incorrect usage are examples of intellectual sloppiness and must be fought. Language must be precise or it is not language.

DANIEL SCHORR: I accept the enrichment of language through change in the meanings of words through usage. But I do not accept simple confusion between words. *Flair,* as a bent or talent in some direction, sounds like but is not the same as *flare,* which is a matter of combustion. Let the language grow, but not get all mixed up.

ERICH SEGAL: Homer distinguished between wingèd and unwingèd words. So should we. Dammit.

ROBERT SHERRILL: The really serious threat to our language comes from government functionaries and politicians who systematically use it to mislead and falsify. When a Kleindienst can avoid a perjury rap by slip-streaming a phrase or two, then people begin to think of language itself as being part of the sham. When they feel they cannot believe what they read or hear, then they will stop reading and stop listening, and that's when the language will start getting flabby indeed.

WALTER W. "RED" SMITH: In usage I accept what I have come to accept and reject what I don't accept. It is that subjective. In my lifetime, "hectic" has come to have newer meanings and this seems perfectly reasonable to me. But to make a verb of a noun like "gift" or "host" offends me to the soul. Why? Probably because these usages are newer than, say, "hectic" and because I'm older. In short, I rule from prejudice. . . . Speaking as a curmudgeon, I insist that "presently" means "soon," rather than "at present," that "hopefully" means "in a manner full of hope" and not "I hope" or "they hope" or "it is to be hoped," and that "momentarily" means "for a moment," not "in a moment." That is, "briefly," not "soon."

JEAN STAFFORD: It is with passionate delight, and with sober responsibility, that I accept your invitation. On my back door there is a sign with large lettering which reads: THE WORD "HOPEFULLY" MUST NOT BE MISUSED ON THESE PREMISES. VIOLATORS WILL BE HUMILIATED. My friend and neighbor Berton Roueché and I several times a week on the telephone mourn the infusion of hogwash into the bloodstream of the American language: the tough and dandy darling is going into paresis. Do count on me as a dedicated physician who will even pay house calls in the middle of the night.

ELVIS STAHR, JR.: Contributing to this dictionary has been a special joy because of the sharing of panelists' comments. These I am sure will also delight many readers, and it is certainly encouraging to know that so many of the ablest users of words in our country react as I do to shoddy usages.

REX STOUT: Changes made by the genius and wit of the people are inevitable and often desirable and useful. Those imposed by ignorant clowns such as advertising copywriters and broadcasters are abominable and should be condemned by all lovers of language.

FRANK SULLIVAN: Some things grate on one, just as a personal reaction. Nothing would ever reconcile me to "like" as a conjunction, especially after those dreary television commercials. On "most unique" I always remember one time when I used it in something I wrote when on the *World* and that old precisionist, FPA, called me down. So I never made that mistake again. . . . "Contact" and all the nouns made into verbs, usually by Madison Avenue, grate on me, and so does the suffix "wise," also a contribution of the hucksters.

HOWARD TAUBMAN: What can one do but write with as much precision and clarity as one can command? There is no beating back the tide of "like" as a conjunction. I read a number of British publications, and I find Oxford dons using "like" in that jarring way. Lately I have run into the locution "and nor" perpetuated by well-known British writers. We may not be able to change the world back to rectitude of usage, but we can be right.

DAVIDSON TAYLOR: If I could persuade people, *any* people, to discriminate between the words "precipitate" and "precipitous," I would not have lived entirely in vain.

HAROLD TAYLOR: I like the way the American language keeps on inventing itself but I hate the fact that some of the most dreadful words ("hopefully," "meaningfully," and words like that) get into the public discourse.

LIONEL TRILLING: I find righteous denunciations of the present state of the language no less dismaying than the present state of the language.

EARL UBELL: I love our American language as if it were my own child. I watch it grow, adding words from the streets and the sciences. I wince with pain when I see or hear a good old word being broken on the wheel of ill usages. It's as if my own child were having a finger snapped.

JUDITH VIORST: I find that my standards are impure and utterly subjective. Some things simply make me wince; others I feel comfortable with—and that's that. I love splitting infinitives, for instance, but "performancewise" gives me pains in my stomach.

DOUGLAS WATT: The English language began to curl up and die, instead of being regenerated, sometime after the Second World War, until now it has become like, wow!, you know.

A.B.C. WHIPPLE: Though some of us may sound like a chorus of Neanderthals, my impression is that most of us do recognize that a living language has to grow and change. I hope that your dictionary provides that essential order.

T. HARRY WILLIAMS: I love the language but I fear for it. It is being debased by the bureaucrats, the jargonists of the advertising community, and the social scientists. And the debasements get instant exposure on the media and so pass into instant usage. Even academicians, who should know better, are taking up the awful "hopefully."

HERMAN WOUK: In writing, especially in fiction—but often in essay writing, too—one can deliberately traverse the spectrum from tasteless boorishness to the best elegance one can produce, depending on the tone of voice and the impact desired. But the author's underlying voice should speak the best (not the fanciest or most rigidly traditional) English.

In addition to the panel of consultants on usage, many people have been of great help to us in the creation of this dictionary. Perhaps the earliest influences were Francis Wayne MacVeagh, William's tutor in English at Harvard, who first introduced him to the delights of Fowler's *Modern English Usage,* and Elizabeth Jones Davis, Mary's mother and extraordinary teacher of English, who instilled in her daughters and sons a deep love of and respect for the language. During the years since then, scores of educators, editors, and members of the general public have made their contributions, for the most part unwittingly, to what has become the *Harper Dictionary of Contemporary Usage.*

A few names must be singled out for special thanks. Joseph Vergara, William Davies, Dolores Simon, and William Monroe supplied for the first edition the most conscientious and helpful editing and copyediting we have ever been fortunate enough to receive. We want also to thank Sidney Feinberg and Joseph Montebello for collaboration on the design and composition of a handsome and eminently practical type page and format. For this second edition we express thanks to Bitite Vinklers, Lucy Adelman O'Brien and, especially, Carol Cohen, whose contributions were far beyond the call of duty. Also our special thanks to Marie Longyear and Mimi Morris for their special help.

Now that the work is completed we share with Samuel Johnson the certain knowledge that while "every other author may aspire to praise, the lexicographer can only hope to escape reproach."

WILLIAM AND MARY MORRIS

Old Greenwich, Connecticut
January 1985

Glossary of Terms Used in Evaluating Levels of Usage

standard—word usage occurring in the speech and writing of literate, educated users of the language.

substandard—word usage considered unacceptable in speech or writing by literate speakers and writers. This category may include regional dialect or folk idiom (for example, *mought* for *might*: "Looks like it *mought* rain") and range to the clearly illiterate (for example, *irregardless*: "She plans to come *irregardless*").

formal—words and phrases usually found in such contexts as diplomatic messages, legal briefs, and sermons by divines of the traditional persuasion.

informal—casual colloquial speech and writing, appropriate in all contexts save those indicated in the category *formal*.

slang—topical and often ephemeral idiomatic expressions, often derived from the private language of some trade, profession, or culture. *Slang* is often used to add color and topicality to speech and writing but one should exercise caution in its use because it can have an awkward or even embarrassing impact on the listener or reader.

vulgar—words and phrases generally considered taboo in the speech and writing of careful, literate users of the language. Many *vulgar* terms, notably the so-called four-letter words, are not truly *slang* but are definitely regarded as *substandard* by the vast majority of speakers, writers, and, perhaps most significantly, publishers. Other terms such as poetic, archaic, and obsolete may be used but their meanings are obvious.

A

a/an One of the most common mistakes, both written and oral, is the use of *an* before "historical" or "historic." Even the guide to the White House, published in 1965, was titled *The White House: An Historic Guide.*

When the word following the article begins with a consonant sound, the article used is *a.* When it begins with a vowel sound, the article used is *an.*

Note that the word "sound" is used twice in that paragraph. A word may in fact begin with a consonant, yet have an initial vowel "sound." The word "honest" is a case in point. Say it aloud and you will see what we mean. The initial consonant "h" is silent, so the word has an initial vowel sound. Hence: "*an* honest man," "*an* hour ago," "*an* heir to the throne," and "*an* honorable peace."

However, when a word begins with an aspirated "h," correct usage is "*a* hotel," "*a* house," "*a* hill," "*a* hymn," and "*a* honeycomb."

There are also words beginning with vowels which have a consonant sound. Say "unique" aloud and you will hear that it contains in its first syllable a consonant "y" sound as well as the vowel "oo" sound. You are saying (phonetically) yoo-NEEK. Similarly, "union," "use," and "eulogy" begin with a consonant "y" sound and call for the article *a.*

It is true that, in the King James version of the Bible, you will find references to "*an* house," "*an* hill," "*an* hymn," and "*an* honeycomb."

However, the pronunciation of many words beginning with "h" has changed in the centuries since the King James Bible was translated. At that time the initial "h" in virtually all words of French origin was not sounded, so *an* was used in such phrases as "*an* hotel." Today the only words in American speech with the silent "h" are "heir," "hour," "honest," "honor," "herb," and variants of these.

Correct British usage now also calls for sounding the initial "h" in all words except those mentioned in the paragraph above. Indeed, "dropping your haitches" has become characteristic of cockney dialect—the same that gave Eliza Doolittle so much trouble when Professor Higgins was trying to teach her that "The rain in Spain stays mainly in the plain." Next time you hear that delightful song, note especially the lines "In Hartford, Hereford and Hampshire, hurricanes hardly happen." When Eliza managed to articulate each of these "h's," the professor knew once and for all that "She's got it!"

a (before the name of a person)   The use of the article *a* before the name of a particular person as a means of indicating a type of person is both tiresome and inaccurate, since it implies that many people may have qualities unique to one. Panelist Shana Alexander writes: "My least favorite usage is the hideous, tiny 'a,' as in 'President Ford could use a Harry Hopkins' or 'A Red Smith would not have expressed himself so tendentiously.' 'A Red Smith' did not exist. Happily Red Smith did."

If it is necessary to use an individual's name for purposes of comparison, at least phrase it "*a* writer such as Red Smith" or "*a* writer like Red Smith."

abbreviations   Generally speaking, *abbreviations* are to be avoided in formal writing, except for such inescapable *abbreviations* as "Mr.," "Mrs.," "Dr.," and the like. *Abbreviations* are still commonly found, and in profusion, in scholarly papers, especially in footnotes. Reference books formerly used many such abbreviations as "e.g.," "i.e.," and so on. The tendency today is to avoid such cryptic shorthand in copy, even of a fairly technical nature. For example, the original edition of the *American Heritage Dictionary,* in which we take justifiable pride, entirely eschews this sort of lexicographical shorthand in its main-entry section. So, indeed, does this volume.

Abbreviations are still often heard in casual speech. One doesn't hear "disc jockey" nearly as often as one hears "d.j.," for instance. Shop talk and jargon abound in similar casual *abbreviations.* In medical circles obstetrics is always simply "O.B." and the minor operation known as "dilation and curettage" is simply "D. and C." Likewise in police trade language "dead on arrival" is invariably "D.O.A." Sometimes these common informal sets of initials are written without periods. Thus what first was T.V.A. (Tennessee Valley Authority) has long since become TVA. Still other such *abbreviations* as Anzac (Australian and New Zealand Army Corps) in time are written solid, without periods, and are called *acronyms* (which see).

Some dictionaries give lengthy lists of *abbreviations,* though the current tendency (again as exemplified by the original *AHD*) is simply to enter the abbreviations in the normal alphabetical sequence of entries. For anyone wishing to pursue the matter further, there are several special dictionaries of *abbreviations* and acronyms.

abdicate. *See* ABROGATE/ABDICATE

abdomen   *Abdomen* may be pronounced either AB-doh-men or ab-DOH-men.

ability The idiom is *ability to,* not *ability of,* and it is followed by an infinitive rather than a gerund or verbal noun. So "*ability* to function effectively," not "*ability* of functioning effectively."

abjure/adjure These two look-alike words are sometimes mistakenly used each for the other, though they can't be by anyone who knows their meanings. *Abjure* means to swear off or renounce: "The new President *abjured* the use of violence." *Adjure* means to warn solemnly or admonish: "He *adjured* the maiden to remember her vows."

able This customarily is followed by an infinitive in the active voice but not in the passive: "He was *able* to hear the engine" but not "The engine was *able* to be heard"—rather, "The engine could be heard."

-able. *See* -IBLE/-ABLE

aborning This simply means "in the state of being born, either figuratively or literally." The prefix "a-" occurs fairly often in such words as "awake" or "asleep" or in such lines as "The frog he would a-wooing go." Notice the hyphen in "a-wooing." This may be because the nursery rhyme of which it is a part goes back at least to the seventeenth century, when rules of hyphenation were somewhat different.

about to/not about to *About* in the sense of ready or prepared for something is standard English: "The wedding party is *about to* depart." The phrase *not about to,* implying resolute determination not to perform some action, is a commonplace of regional speech, especially in the Southwestern U.S.: "Sally's *not about to* try to drive a car." During the presidency of Lyndon Johnson this formulation was used at least once in a formal address: "Peace is the mission of the American people and we are *not about to* be deterred." Despite this example, *not about to* should be avoided in all formal contexts, though it is quite permissible in casual speech.

above *Above* as an adjective meaning "previously mentioned" or "appearing earlier" has a certain value in business correspondence and is, indeed, indispensable in some legal briefs. However, its frequent use adds a note of stuffy formalism to any prose and it may well be avoided in favor of either of the phrases given above as synonyms. Even more to be avoided is the use of *the above* as a noun phrase, as in "Pay attention to *the above.*"

abridged/unabridged Technically, any dictionary—even a child's elementary dictionary—is an *unabridged* dictionary if it has never been *abridged,* that is, cut down from a larger into a briefer edition. In actual practice, however, we think of an *unabridged* dictionary as being one that contains as broad a sample of our vast language as it is possible to fit between two covers. Usually this means a dictionary of approximately 400,000 entries. *See also* ENTRY, DICTIONARY.

abrogate/abdicate   These two verbs are sometimes confused, as in the following statement quoted in a newspaper story on labor relations: "We as contractors have *abrogated* our responsibilities to the unions by allowing them in effect to do the hiring." This is, of course, in error. *Abrogate* means to abolish or annul. The correct word would have been *abdicate,* meaning "to abandon." The sentence should have read: "We as contractors have *abdicated.* . . ."

absent

USAGE PANEL QUESTION

"Absent" as a preposition synonymous with "without" has recently appeared in the writings of a few rather pretentious columnists. Example: "Absent new evidence to the contrary, the verdict must be judged correct."
Would you use "absent" this way in writing?
Yes: 8%. No: 92%.
In speech? Yes: 5%. No: 95%.

ISAAC ASIMOV: "Absent any trace of literacy, I might use it."
WHITNEY BALLIETT: "Awful."
ALTON BLAKESLEE: "Is our language to be bastardized by pretentions?"
JOHN BROOKS: "A legalism but not really offensive to me."
HEYWOOD HALE BROUN: "Often we are asked to condone a popular vulgarity. A popular incomprehensibility seems too much."
JAMES MACGREGOR BURNS/JOAN SIMPSON BURNS: "Joan says 'no' to both uses; Jim might use in speech. What's wrong with 'without'?"
ROBERT CROMIE: "Not unless I become much more absent-minded than I am now."
WILLARD R. ESPY: "Absent premature senile dementia, certainly not."
GERALD FRANK: "I always do a double-take when I come across this use of absent."
FRANCES FRITCHMAN: " 'Pretentious' is the word, all right."
PAUL HORGAN: "Despite George Will."
JOHN K. HUTCHENS: "Another silly term. Why not use, for instance, 'lacking'?"

ELIZABETH JANEWAY: "Horrible. I suspect some sinister Pentagonal influence here."

JULES LOH: "Too pretentious for my taste."

DWIGHT MACDONALD: "What possible point here? Just the itch for variety?"

EDWIN NEWMAN: "I would not use it, but it is a helpful term, again if not overdone."

PETER S. PRESCOTT: "In law, where the language is generally mangled, this term may be used—nowhere else."

ANDY ROONEY: "I wouldn't, no, and I'm a pretentious columnist, too."

LEO ROSTEN: "Absent a rationing of ink, I would continue to say 'in the absence of.' "

VERMONT ROYSTER: "I may be a pretentious columnist but I'm not *that* pretentious."

JACK SMITH: "I see no reason for this queer one at all."

ELVIS STAHR, JR.: "Why not? It's simply quicker than 'in the absence of.' "

WALLACE STEGNER: "An indictable offense."

KARL V. TEETER: "Again, a modish borrowing from jargon (legal jargon in this case)."

EDWARD TRIPP: "I believe this is a legal usage, but who would wish to copy a lawyer's language? Unnecessary and self-conscious."

BARBARA TUCHMAN: "Awful."

A.B.C. WHIPPLE: "Mere pretentiousness."

HERMAN WOUK: "Pedantic."

absolutely *Absolutely* as an affirmation of strong and enthusiastic approval is entirely acceptable in both speech and writing. However, *absolutely* as a simple adverbial modifier should be used with caution since it implies no conditions whatever. If you say that something is *absolutely* correct, it must be just that—with no ifs, ands, or buts about it.

absolutist *Absolutist* and *absolutism* are nouns relatively rarely encountered. They refer to a form of government in which absolute power is vested in a monarch and his advisers. The word gained a brief vogue during the Watergate episode of the second Nixon presidency, with several commentators referring to the *absolutist* tendencies of the White House incumbents of the time.

academic tenure. *See* TENURE/ACADEMIC TENURE

academicals The British equivalent of the American "cap and gown." To the best of our knowledge, the English have not yet followed the American example of having kindergarten graduates clad in *academicals*.

a cappella   This expression (from the Italian, meaning "from the chapel or choir") is a musical notation meaning "without accompaniment," especially "without instrumental accompaniment."

accent marks. *See* RESUME

accept   *Accept* should be pronounced ak-SEPT, not uh-SEPT.

accessible   *Accessible* should be pronounced ak-SESS-ih-b'l, not ass-SESS-ih-b'l.

accessorize   *Accessorize* is a bastard offshoot of the noun *accessory.* It has appeared in advertising copy like the following: "The new kitchen range is *accessorized* with stainless steel." This says nothing that "trimmed" doesn't say better and more simply. Avoid *accessorize.*

accessory   *Accessory* should be pronounced ak-SESS-uh-ree, not uh-SESS-uh-ree.

acclimate   *Acclimate* may be pronounced either AK-lih-mayt or uh-KLY-mit.

accommodate. *See* SPELLINGS, TRICKY

accompanist   *Accompanist* should be pronounced uh-KUM-puh-nist, not uh-KUM-pu-nee-ist.

accumulator   British equivalent of the American "battery," especially in reference to the storage "battery" used in automobiles, boats, and the like.

accusative case/objective case   The terms *accusative case* and *objective case* are synonymous, with the latter somewhat more common in English and the former standard in discussions of Latin, where case distinctions in nouns and pronouns are vital. By contrast, English nouns do not vary in form no matter what their grammatical function. For example, in the sentences "The man hit the boy" and "The boy hit the man" the forms of the nouns do not vary, though their functions change from subject to object.

    NOTE: Certain nouns, notably those which retain their older English plural forms (like "children," "geese," and so on), do change form between singular and plural, but this is not a matter of changing or inflecting forms because of differing functions of cases of the nouns.

    The *accusative* or *objective case* changes in form occur only in the personal pronouns ("I"/"me," "he"/"him," "she"/"her," "we"/"us," and "they"/"them.") "You" and "it" are unchanged in the *accusative* or *objective case.* The relative pronoun "who" does have a relatively little used *accusative* or *objective case:* "whom." *See also* WHO/WHOM/WHO-EVER/WHOMEVER.

accused, the   *The accused* is the common way of referring to the defendants in a criminal legal action. They are *accused of,* not *accused with,* a crime.

acme/epitome   You will occasionally find *epitome* used as a synonym for "ideal" or *acme* but there is a distinction to be made and careful users of the language make it.

 Epitome literally means a part representative of the whole. It may be either a summary or a sample section characteristic of the whole. In correct usage, *epitome* has no qualitative implications. For instance, a piece of text can be the "*epitome* of graceless prose" just as another may be the "*epitome* of brilliant writing."

 Acme means "peak" in the sense of utmost attainment. A U.S. Senator, when asked if he had any presidential aspirations, replied, "I would love to be President. Who wouldn't? It's the *acme.* It's the top."

 If you wish to refer to a person or thing as the peak, pinnacle, or apex of perfection, say so—and reserve *epitome* for the more restricted and particular use.

acoustics is/are   *Acoustics* is singular when used in referring to the science of sound: "*Acoustics is* an increasingly important branch of physics." It is plural when you refer to the sound-reflecting or absorbing qualities of a room or auditorium: "The *acoustics* of the old Metropolitan Opera House *were* second only to those of Boston's Symphony Hall."

acquiesce   The proper preposition to use with *acquiesce* (to consent without protest) is "in": "All parties to the debate *acquiesced* in the decision."

acronym   An *acronym* is a word made up of the initial letters or syllables of a phrase. Since about 1940, and doubtless because of the earlier New Deal practice of calling government projects by initials (TVA, WPA, etc.), there has been a vast proliferation of *acronyms,* especially in scientific fields (for example, "radar" for Radio Detection and Ranging) and in the areas of social and political action (CORE for the Congress of Racial Equality and CREEP for Committee to Re-Elect the President). Some singularly infelicitous coinages have resulted from this activity, notably MOUSE for Minimum Orbital Unmanned Satellite of Earth. Most *acronyms* of this order, of course, are nonce words, quickly forgotten and happily so. Others, such as the aforementioned "radar," are well established as standard English. It is perhaps worth noting that one of the early *acronyms* (coined by C. K. Ogden in 1925 or thereabouts) was the

BASIC in Basic English. Translated, it is British-American Scientific International Commercial English.

Computers have brought with them a number of innovative expressions, as noted under the entry COMPUTERESE. Many of the terms lend themselves to abbreviation in the form of *acronyms*. Interestingly, one of most widely used of these acronyms is the same BASIC mentioned above, though now the letters stand for different words. Here are some of the *acronyms* currently used in the world of computer programming:

> BASIC—Beginners' All-purpose Symbolic Instruction Code
> EFTS—Electronic Funds Transfer System
> FIFO—First In, First Out
> GIGO—Garbage In, Garbage Out
> ICE—In-Circuit Emulator
> JOVIAL—Jules' Own Version of International Arithmetic Language
> LIFO—Last In, First Out
> PROM—Programmable Read Only Memory
> SOS—Silicon on Sapphire
> TICTIT—Time-shared Interactive Computer Controlled Instructional TV
> WATS—Wide Area Telephone Service

See COMPUTERESE.

across   *Across* should be pronounced uh-KROSS, not uh-KROST.

action   *Action* has acquired an extended sense of any sort of spirited activity, not merely the physical combat implied in the traditional phrase "send troops into *action.*" During broadcasts of such disparate events as the World Series games and Senate hearings, announcers will note "a break in the *action.*" Similarly, the desire is often voiced to be "where the *action* is." Both of these extended usages may be regarded as perfectly O.K. in casual speech but probably to be avoided in formal writing. Still more remote from the basic meaning is the slang sense of *action* as the spoils of gambling or other slightly or completely nefarious business activity: "Be sure that I get a piece of the *action*—or else."

action replay   *Action replay* is the British television equivalent of the American "instant replay."

activation. *See* EUPHEMISM

ad   *Ad* as a shortened or clipped form of "advertisement" is now suitable for use in all save the most formal contexts. Indeed, in this very volume you will find an entry labeled "admen's jargon," indicating that even the clipped "adman" version of "advertising man" has our approval in informal contexts.

adage Since an *adage* is defined as an "old saying," it is redundant to speak or write of an "old *adage.*"

Adam's off ox A regional dialect expression, originally found in New England but now in many parts of the country, especially in rural areas. Its meaning is clear from the version in which it is most often heard: "I don't know him from *Adam's off ox,*" meaning "I don't know him even the slightest bit." The *off ox* is the far or right-hand ox.

adapt/adopt *Adapt* (to adjust oneself to a new or changed situation) is sometimes confused with *adopt* (to choose and follow a new course of action). A case in point was the query of a column reader about this sentence: "Strangers in town should *adapt/adopt* their habits to those of their neighbors." The proper word, of course, is *adapt* in this instance.

Addisonian termination The *Addisonian termination* is simply the ending of a sentence with a preposition. The Addison involved is Joseph Addison, co-author of the famous Addison and Steele essays and, it would appear, a writer addicted to the ending of sentences with prepositions. According to the classically oriented pundits of his day, this was an unthinkable practice, the more so since Addison had long since demonstrated his ability to write both well and persuasively. Since Latin virtually never tolerated sentences ending in prepositions (most Latin sentences ended with verbs), the received wisdom was that English should be hammered into the same mold—a proposition that Addison took a dim view of. As do we.

The creator of the term *Addisonian termination* was, perhaps not surprisingly, an Anglican bishop, Richard Hurd. His other contributions to literature, if any, are long forgotten, while Addison is still read. So it would appear that the Hurdian termination was rather more final than the *Addisonian termination. See also* PREPOSITION AT END OF SENTENCE.

additional. *See* ANOTHER/ADDITIONAL/MORE

address *Address* as a noun ("My *address* is 316 Main Street") is pronounced with the stress on the first syllable: ADD-ress. However, in the sense of a formal speech ("He gave an *address* to the Congress") the stress is on the second syllable: uh-DRESS. As a verb ("She *address*ed the crowd"), the stress is always on the second syllable: uh-DRESS.

adhere A Pittsburgh firm which sells acoustical ceilings and interiors once asked us if the verb *adhere* could be used in the passive voice as in "This material will be adhered to the existing plastered ceiling."

Adhere, an intransitive verb, cannot be used in the passive voice. It would be correct to say, "This material will *adhere* to the existing plastered ceiling." Better yet would be: "This material will be fastened (or attached or affixed) to the existing ceiling."

ad hoc *Ad hoc* is a Latin phrase literally meaning "toward this" but used in the sense of "for this special purpose." An *ad hoc* committee is one organized to direct attention to a single particular situation, usually without regard to the broad picture. Thus, members of a university faculty might organize an *ad hoc* committee for the defense of one of their number who they feel has been unfairly discharged, without regard to the general problem of academic freedom or tenure or whatever broader concept might be involved. When the problem is solved, the committee goes out of existence.

Because many such committees are formed spontaneously and without any parent body, the phrase is sometimes interpreted to mean "unofficial" or "informal." This is not necessarily the case, however. An organization with standing committees may form an *ad hoc* committee to deal with a particular situation.

adjacent (to) Etymologically speaking, *adjacent to* is a redundancy since the "ad" in *adjacent* means *to.*

However, the idiom is clearly *adjacent to,* if only because the word *adjacent,* being an adjective, cannot take an object and needs the preposition *to,* which can. If it bothers you to say, "The park was *adjacent to,*" simply rephrase it to "The *adjacent* park."

adjective An *adjective,* in the words of Noah Webster's original *American Dictionary of the English Language* (1828), is "a word used with a noun to express a quality of the thing named or something attributed to it, or to limit or define it, or to specify or describe a thing as distinct from something else. Thus in the phrase a *wise ruler, wise* is the adjective or attribute, expressing a particular property of *ruler.*" A century and a half later, that stands as a good definition of *adjective.* Later generations of linguists have tended also to classify nouns used attributively (for example, "school" in "school year") as *adjectives* on the ground that any word modifying it (say, "entire" in "entire school year"), would necessarily be an *adjective.*

It is desirable in choosing *adjectives,* as in choosing any other word, to be as precise and exact as possible. It is also desirable to avoid the use of trite *adjectives* like "cute" in "cute girl," "bloodcurdling" in "bloodcurdling yell," and "bored" in "bored to death." And nothing is gained by piling *adjective* upon *adjective.* One or two precise and carefully chosen *adjectives* will make the point far better than the sonorous series of platitudinous descriptives ("one of the finest, most loyal, most devoted, most patriotic . . .") beloved of politicians and just about anyone making a nominating speech. Henry Luce had one thing right when he laid down the law to early *Time* magazine editors: "Be curt, clear, concise." That's a good plan for any writer to follow—including your editors.

adjectives, comparison of *Adjectives,* unlike nouns and most pronouns, change form to indicate a greater degree of the quality of the thing being described. The adjective "hot," for example, changes in the comparative degree to "hotter"; in the superlative degree to "hottest." Some *adjectives* achieve the comparative and superlative degrees not by changing their endings but by being preceded by either "more" ("more interesting") or "most" ("most interesting"). Which form is to be followed is a matter of according with the idiom. It is not easy for a speaker or writer—especially for one whose native language is not English—to determine whether the inflected forms ("-er," "-est") or the "more," "most" version should be adopted. Fortunately, most contemporary dictionaries offer sound guidance in determining which formulation is the idiomatic one. If the adjective entry is followed by the comparative and superlative forms ending in "-er" and "-est," these are the forms to follow. Thus one finds, in *Webster's New World Dictionary,* for example, "*early,* adj. & adv. (earlier, earliest). . . ." On the same page, one notes "*eager,* adj." with no indication of comparative or superlative forms. This means that "eager" forms these other degrees by the addition of "more" or "most."

A handful of *adjectives,* notably *unique* (which see), are held to be incapable of being compared, since they are absolute. One blow cannot be "more fatal" than another, nor can one task be "more impossible" than another. Perhaps the most notable exception to the general prohibition against comparison of these *uncomparable adjectives* (which see) is in the preamble to the U.S. Constitution, in which the goal of the drafters is to "create a more perfect union." The reason for this particular phrasing is discussed under *more perfect.*

Objection is often raised—and properly so—to the use of the superlative degree of an *adjective* when only two elements are to be compared. However, here again the popular idiom dictates acceptance, at least on an informal basis, of "May the best man win," rather than the more precise and formal "May the better man win."

adjectives, idiomatic placement of Nit-pickers often complain about expressions like "a hot cup of coffee" and "a new pair of shoes," claiming that it's the coffee that's hot, not the cup, and the shoes that are new, not the pair. This sort of thing is both pretentious and downright silly because it flies in the face of established idiom. In theory, of course, *adjectives* should be in close proximity to the nouns they modify, but to try to convert this theory into a strict rule is to play fast and loose with established idiom. So, especially in speech, feel free to order up a "hot cup of coffee" or bewail the loss of an "old pair of glasses." You will have plenty of literate company.

adjectives into nouns

USAGE PANEL QUESTION

We have seen many examples of bureaucracy's tendency to use nouns as verbs ("The recession impacts our economy"). Advertising copywriters have lately been having a field day with the forced conversion of adjectives to nouns. According to the latest dictionaries "delicate" is an adjective and only an adjective. "Clean," similarly, is an adjective, though it may sometimes be used as an adverb, and often as a verb. *Neither is a noun.* Still we see and hear many times a day "The clean in your mouth is Colgate," "Get lemon-fresh Joy for a lemon-fresh clean," and even the suggestion that "you wash your delicates in the small-load basket of Brand X washing machine."

Do you think that these calculated illiteracies will influence the speech patterns of educated Americans? Yes: 21%. No: 79%.

Do you feel that these are *not* solecisms but accurately reflect the speech of most Americans? Yes: 8%. No: 92%.

ISAAC ASIMOV: "Yes. It will affect all the stupids even if they are educateds as well. The usage is an example of the horribles."

BARRY BINGHAM, SR.: "No, if those who care for English keep fighting back."

ALTON BLAKESLEE: "Pray God, No" (in answer to second question).

ANTHONY BURGESS: "If Caliban can use 'fresh' as a noun, anything goes."

BEN LUCIEN BURMAN: "This use of 'clean' makes me feel like washing my mouth with Listerine."

JAMES MACGREGOR BURNS: "Yes (on influence speech patterns) but I prefer not."

JOHN CIARDI: "If 'educated' means 'aware of at least one other language' . . . no; if it means 'product of U.S. schools' . . . yes."

GERALD FRANK: "Awful!"

PAUL HORGAN: "Advertising at its most corrupt."

JOHN K. HUTCHENS: "This use of nouns as verbs is, I hope, a minor current atrocity and, I hope, will not be with us for long. Ditto the use of adjectives as nouns."

ELIZABETH JANEWAY: "I don't really know how we can tell what will influence speech patterns. I'd say the chance of these follies doing so is minimal."

WALTER KERR: "Oh, temporarily, but fast-fading."

STANLEY KUNITZ: "Cheap advertising lingo—forget it!"

JULES LOH: "They are too 'cute' to come naturally. They have to be thought up, for heaven's sake."

DWIGHT MACDONALD: "Can't imagine anyone but a TV copywriter using such fantastic lingo."

WILLIAM McGUIRE: "Unfortunately, they'll be influential on the millions whose speech is being affected by TV Newspeak—though they're not quite normal, morphologically, like 'the rich and famous,' 'the poor,' etc."

MARGE PIERCY: " 'The clean of your body excites me, Theresa,' he murmured. I think not."

PETER S. PRESCOTT: "These are footling examples of the ad man's power of corruption. None has the malefic effect of 'like a cigarette should.' "

LEO ROSTEN: "These are not only illiteracies. They are examples of 'cute' and fraudulent neologisms."

VERMONT ROYSTER: "Your examples are not yet part of American speech— but I fear they will be if they are spread by illiterates, calculating or otherwise."

HAROLD SCHONBERG: "Of course some poets—E. E. Cummings, for one— always were using nouns for verbs and vice versa. But they could get away with it. I must say that I admire 'wash your delicates.' It creates, as poetry does, a host of interesting implications."

ERICH SEGAL: "These are not 'calculated illiteracies,' but legitimate evolutions in language. By your standards Shakespeare teems with 'calculated illiteracies.' "

I. F. STONE: "Maybe but horrible."

HOWARD TAUBMAN: "No, but I am not sure. It is remarkable how many solecisms come into wide usage, even by educated Americans."

KARL V. TEETER: "This is the centuries-old manner of word formations in English, typical of the language."

EDWARD TRIPP: "I don't think most people feel that such words are natural enough to be comfortable with them for long, if at all. Some squeamish types might use 'delicates' as a euphemism for underwear."

BARBARA TUCHMAN: "I certainly hope not."

JOSEPH VERGARA: "These copywriters give me the angries."

DOUGLAS WATT: "Horrible!"

A.B.C. WHIPPLE: "My God, I hope not."

adjectives/participles (verbal adjectives). *See* VERY PLEASED (INTERESTED)/VERY MUCH PLEASED (INTERESTED)

adjectives, uncomparable Some adjectives, notably *unique* (which see), are considered to be absolute in their meanings and, hence, not capable of having comparative or superlative degrees. Some which certainly meet this test include "inevitable," "incessant," "simultaneous," "eternal," and "universal." No noise can be "more incessant" than another. And if something is inevitable, it's inevitable. There is no such thing as "most inevitable." Beyond these words, however, there is a substantial group including "perfect," "dead," "impossible," and "black," which—at least in casual speech—are heard in the comparative and superlative degrees. One hears expressions like "Indianapolis is the deadest city I ever visited." And, to our own knowledge, there are shades of black, for an old friend of ours was once famous in the fabrics field for his ability to "match blacks." Some blacks are blacker than others. So there are degrees of difference among these *uncomparable adjectives.* The ones in the first group should be held inviolate. The ones in the second group should be handled with extreme caution. *See also* UNCOMPARABLE.

adjudicate. *See* ARBITRATE/MEDIATE/ADJUDICATE

adjure. *See* ABJURE/ADJURE

admen's jargon   The calculated assault on literacy and even on common sense by some radio and television advertisers—and some in the print medium as well—continues unabated. Long past are the times when they were content merely to create transitive forms of intransitive verbs, as in the slogan about the cigarette that "travels the smoke further." Now we hear exhortations to "tall up" with a certain brand of cornflakes and the claims for a toothpaste that guarantees its user will have "less" (not "fewer") cavities.

It's not a new trend, of course. Many years ago automobile makers showed their contempt for the intelligence of their customers by labeling the cheapest mass-produced car in the line "custom"—a word that for many decades had meant "made to special order, to individual specifications." The same simple distortion of fact is evident in the claims of several brewers that they produce "draft beer in cans." Beer in a can is beer in a can. It is not beer drawn from a tap. And coffee cooked in a percolator is the only coffee properly labeled "perked," despite the claim of one packer of so-called "instant coffee" that his product is "real perked coffee in a bottle." And now there is an ice-cream maker who advertises "real hand-packed flavor" for his brand of prepackaged supermarket ice cream. Truly America's admen seem to believe in the gospel according to Humpty Dumpty: "When I use a word, it means just what I choose it to mean—neither more nor less." *See also* EUPHEMISM.

admittance/admission   The distinction between *admittance* and *admission* has become so blurred in recent years that it seemed unusual to see a cutline in the *New York Times* which read: "Relatives and friends of

Attica inmates wait for *admittance* to the state prison." Both words have the basic meaning of admitting or allowing to enter, and are interchangeable to some degree. However, *admittance* is restricted to the physical act of entering, while *admission* may refer to a privilege or right by virtue of qualification, such as *admission* to a club (by virtue of approval and payment of dues) or *admission* to a theater (by virtue of paying the price of *admission*).

Admission also has a figurative sense, as in "*admission* of hearsay as evidence." It is also used in the phrase "*admission* of guilt." In neither of these examples can *admittance* be substituted.

USAGE PANEL QUESTION

Panelist BILL VAUGHAN raised the following question: "Should we continue to make a style-book distinction between 'admittance' for 'admittance to the theater' and 'admission' as in 'admission of guilt'?" The panel was asked: "Do you observe this distinction in your own speech?"
Yes: 46%. No: 54%.
Do you observe this distinction in your writing? Yes: 59%. No: 41%.

The panel, though quite evenly divided, indicated substantially greater adherence to this "style-book distinction" in writing than in speech. Here are typical comments of panelists.

ISAAC ASIMOV: "No. I virtually never use 'admittance' or 'permittance,' either."
JOHN O. BARBOUR: "No—and that's an admission of guilt, if I've ever seen one."
STEWART BEACH: "Yes, but it should be noted that all theaters use 'admission' when referring to the price of 'admittance.' "
HEYWOOD HALE BROUN: "It is, in editing, allowable to make this distinction. We should all forgive in others what we won't in ourselves."
STEPHEN H. FRITCHMAN: "I observe the distinction—when I remember it."
S. I. HAYAKAWA: "No. But there are other distinctions. A college has a 'Director of Admissions.' "
JOHN K. HUTCHENS: "No. This is a silly bit of nit-picking."
ALEXANDER KENDRICK: "No. I believe this has become a distinction without a difference."
WALTER KERR: "Yes. Would anyone use 'admittance of guilt'?"
NANCY MITFORD: "I would use 'admission' in the sense of the price of a ticket. 'Admittance' would imply difficulty, as 'gained admittance to the closed meeting.' "
EDWIN NEWMAN: "No—but I should."

RICHARD H. ROVERE: "I'd forget it and settle for 'admission' in both cases."

HARRISON SALISBURY: "I *never* use 'admittance.' It sounds too prissy and uptown."

MARK SCHORER: "No. Who *would* say 'admittance of guilt'? Yet one would say, 'I admit my guilt.' "

WALTER W. "RED" SMITH: "Yes. Of course—unless we're talking Swahili."

DAVIDSON TAYLOR: "Yes, but it's automatic, not logical."

BARBARA TUCHMAN: "No. Nobody ever says or writes 'the price of admittance.' "

BILL VAUGHAN (who raised the question originally): "Yes. It's a conditioned reflex."

adopt   The British equivalent of our "nominate," in the political sense. In America candidates for political office are nominated at conventions or in primary elections and subsequently "run" for office. In England a party caucus *adopts* its candidates, who then "stand" for office. *See also* CAUCUS and ADAPT/ADOPT.

adopted/adoptive   A child taken to be reared legally as one's own child is an *adopted* child and the adopting couple are called *adoptive* parents.

adult   *Adult* may be pronounced uh-DULT or AD-ult, with the former slightly preferable.

advance/advanced   *Advance* and *advanced,* as adjectives, differ in that *advance* is used literally to designate a forward position in place (*advance* party) or time (*advance* payment). *Advanced* is used figuratively to indicate a position somewhat beyond an accepted norm (an *advanced* program of social legislation).

   NOTE: *Advance* in the commonly heard phrase "*advance* planning" is clearly redundant and should be omitted. All planning, by definition, is done in *advance*. *See also* REDUNDANCY.

adverb   An *adverb,* in the textbook definition, is a part of speech that modifies a verb, an adjective, or another adverb. Most of the strictures set forth in the entries *adjective* and *adjectives, comparison of* apply also to *adverbs.* Most *adverbs* end in "-ly"; indeed, most *adverbs* are merely adjectives with "-ly" added ("hotly," "fairly"). For this reason many speakers and writers mistakenly assume that all *adverbs* must end in "-ly." The fact is that there are dozens of words that function as *adverbs* but have precisely the same form as their adjective counterparts. The one which causes the most trouble is "slow" (as in "go slow"). Either "slow" or "slowly" is correct.

   As is the case with adjectives, one should take care not to overuse and hence abuse *adverbs.* Often they are unnecessary. A careful writer will review his copy to see whether such a sentence as "The speeding car careened (or careered) wildly out of control" really needs the "wildly" or whether the idea isn't inherent in the verb used.

Some years ago a group of fashionable writers—among them Alexander Woollcott and Lucius Beebe—operated on the assumption that one should never use an adjective without a modifying *adverb.* Thus a movie actress was never simply "charming" but "radiantly, rapturously charming" (using *two adverbs* scored extra points) and a locomotive was not merely "majestic" but "superbly majestic." The result of this proliferation of *adverbs* modifying adjectives was a luxuriance of prose that many— including us—found stifling. Happily the style seems to have died with its most eminent practitioners and it is one style that we devoutly hope will never be revived.

adverse. *See* AVERSE/ADVERSE

advertisement   There are three acceptable pronunciations of this much-used word: ad-ver-TIZE-ment, ad-VER-tis-ment, and ad-VER-tiz-ment.

advise/inform/write   *Advise,* in the sense of *write* or *inform,* is greatly overused in business correspondence and adds an extra touch of stuffiness to letters that are usually already dull. *Advise,* in this sense, should be restricted to such usages as "The officer *advised* the suspect of his rights." The use of *advise* in the sense of "to give advice" is unquestioned.

Such usage as "he *advised*" when quoting a person making a simple statement is pretentious. "He said" is sufficient.

adviser/advisor   Both spellings of this word are listed as acceptable although most dictionaries give *adviser* first, indicating that it is preferable. At one time, *advisor* was considered to be a British spelling. In recent years the trend in America has been toward *advisor,* probably by analogy to the adjective "advisory." So use whichever looks right to you.

aeroplane   *Aero* is still the more common prefix in England for words relating to aviation, such as *aeroplane, aerodrome,* and *aero club.* However, the influence of the American *airplane* and *airport* has been powerful and the Supplement to the *Oxford English Dictionary* (1972) lists several pages of such *air-* compounds, indicating that that prefix is quite as acceptable as *aero-.*

aesthetic/esthetic   *Aesthetic* comes from the Greek "aisthetikos," meaning "perceptive." Thus an aesthete is one who perceives. Today it is applied chiefly to a person with a keen appreciation and love of the beautiful, especially in art, music, and poetry.

There has been a marked tendency over the past few decades to spell words from the Greek with "e" rather than "ae." "Anesthesia" has replaced "anaesthesia," for example. However, a survey by linguists at Brown University shows that the spelling *aesthete* appears at least four times as often as *esthete* in American books and magazines. So, while *esthete* is certainly acceptable, *aesthete* is still the preferred spelling.

afeard This variant spelling of "afraid" was once standard English. Shakespeare used it in Macbeth ("Fie, my lord, fie! a soldier, and afeard?") and the *OED* traces it back to Middle English, the language spoken in England roughly between 1150 and 1500. However, it is now considered either regional dialect or archaic. In several parts of the U.S., notably in mountain regions of the Carolinas, West Virginia, and Kentucky, dialects have changed very little over the centuries because people there resident have been quite isolated from influences affecting speech patterns in other parts of the country. Indeed, the claim can be made that, since terms like *afeard* were common in Elizabethan England, the speech of some mountain folk is closer to "true" English than the language most of us commonly use. However, the warning implicit in the label "dialect" still stands: avoid *afeard* except when using it consciously in dialogue to establish character or locale.

affect/effect Confusion concerning the use of these two words stems from the fact that anything that *affects* something else has an *effect* on it.

The verb meanings of the two words differ widely. Perhaps one way to determine proper usage is to think of to *affect* as meaning to bring about partial results; to *effect* as meaning to achieve complete results. "The cost of the farm program *affects* all our pocketbooks"; "Arbitration was necessary to *effect* a settlement of the strike."

There is, of course, another meaning to the verb *affect:* to pretend or feign something in order to influence: "She *affected* a passion for sports because she loved college weekends."

Effect is the only one of these words in common use as a noun; *affect* (noun) is used only in psychology and literary criticism.

affidavit. *See* SPELLINGS, TRICKY

affluence/affluent *Affluence* should be pronounced AFF-loo-enss, not uh-FLOO-enss. Similarly, *affluent* (the adjectival form) should be AFF-loo-ent, not uh-FLOO-ent.

aficionado A voguish borrowing from Spanish is *aficionado,* meaning an enthusiast or devotee: "The new mayor is an *aficionado* of jazz." It is pronounced uh-fee-see-uh-NAH-doh, with the Spanish version sounded as ah-fee-thee-uh-NAH-thoh.

Afro *Afro* originally referred to a hair style adopted by American blacks in imitation of African modes. It also refers to a quasi-African style of dress, including the dashiki, a loose and often brightly colored tunic worn originally in Africa by men but in the U.S. by black men and women.

afters British informal for "dessert." "Mum, what are we having for *afters*?"

afterward/afterwards Both of these words have the same meaning of "at a later time" and in America they are used interchangeably. In Britain, however, you'll usually hear *afterwards.*

again/against The standard American pronunciation of these words is "uh-GEN" and "uh-GENST," while the British pronunciation is "uh-GAYN" and "uh-GAYNST." One notable exception among American speakers, however, was President Franklin D. Roosevelt, who *again,* and *again,* and *again* used the British pronunciation in a series of three *agains,* whether for emphasis or because it was natural to him is not clear. The characteristic British pronunciation is well illustrated in the verse from *Alice's Adventures in Wonderland* telling why Father William everlastingly stood on his head: " 'In my youth,' Father William replied to his son,/'I feared it might injure the brain;/But now that I'm perfectly sure I have none,/Why, I do it again and again.' "

agenda *Agenda* (from the Latin "things to be done") was plural in form in the original Latin but now has been fully accepted as singular in English, in the sense of "list," and followed by a singular verb: "The *agenda* for today's meeting contains [not contain] the following items." So thoroughly established is *agenda* as a singular that the plural *agendas* is now commonly heard and seen: "The *agendas* of the various meetings of the convention contain more than a hundred topics." *See also* MEDIA.

aggravate

USAGE PANEL QUESTION

Aggravate originally simply meant to make worse, as "The fever *aggravated* his already weakened condition." It is also widely used in the sense of "to exasperate" or "to vex," as "The loudness of the music *aggravated* him." Do you accept this second sense?

In writing   Yes: 43%. No: 57%.
In speech   Yes: 53%. No: 47%.

The panelists were very nearly equally divided, with a slight majority opposed to acceptance of *aggravate* in this sense in writing and an even more modest majority favoring its acceptance in speech. Here are typical opinions.

ALEX FAULKNER: " 'Aggravate' for 'annoy' seems to be too firmly established to fight—alas."

ELIZABETH JANEWAY: "I don't like it but I think it's too late to stop it."

WALT KELLY: "Here the original meaning has been discarded for modern use. It is so common that the purist must look the other way."

CHARLES KURALT: "No down-east North Carolinian like me can be 'aggravated' by this use. It is the authentic music of home."

EUGENE MCCARTHY: "No. For some reason 'was aggravated by' is more acceptable, or the adjectival use as in 'aggravating child.' "

ORVILLE PRESCOTT: " 'Aggravate' has been used in this sense for generations. There is no point in not accepting it."

BERTON ROUECHÉ: " 'Aggravate' in its proper sense is a needed word—we have enough words meaning vexation."

ROBERT SHERRILL: "I believe I can speak for Southerners when I say that we *only* use 'aggravate' in the sense you're asking about. At least that's true of us red dirt Southerners."

EARL UBELL: "No. I'm reacting to having been born and brought up in Brooklyn, where children, butchers, in-laws, and everything else aggravated everyone."

agnostic/atheist   An *agnostic* is a person who neither affirms nor denies the existence of God. The word was coined by Thomas Henry Huxley, the eminent British biologist. Since he felt that the existence of God was a proposition that could not be proven scientifically, he combined the Greek words "a" (without) and "gignoskein" (to know). So an *agnostic* says, in effect, "This may be true. As for me, I do not know."

An *atheist,* on the other hand, denies the existence of God. *Atheist* is likewise derived from Greek—from "a" (without) and "theos" (god).

ago   *Ago* should be followed by *that,* not *since.* Though commonly heard, expressions like "It was two years *ago* since we saw each other" are redundant. The time element expressed in *ago* is already present in "since." The proper formulation is: "It was two years *ago* that we saw each other."

agree about/agree to/agree with When a consensus is reached on a matter, the participants *agree about* the details. When a proposition is presented to which no objection is raised, the participants *agree to* the proposal. When two or more people find themselves in harmonious accord on a proposition, they *agree with* each other.

agreement of pronoun with antecedent. *See* PRONOUN, AGREE-MENT WITH ANTECEDENT

agricultural labourer Here is one of the relatively few instances in which the American designation for a person following a certain trade or profession is simpler than the British. In America an *agricultural labourer* is simply a "farmhand."

aide *Aide,* properly speaking, should be restricted to the meaning of "assistant": "Presidential *aides* face subpoenas." In actual newspaper practice, however, it is widely used to label practically anyone on the secondary levels of government—especially by newspaper headline writers, to whom short words, however inaccurately used, are a boon.

ain't It is doubtful that any word in English has been more discussed and denounced than *ain't.* First recorded as appearing in print in 1788, it was labeled by the *OED* "illiterate or dialect" and a variant of the earlier "an't," which was similarly labeled. Noah Webster ignored its existence in his first (1828) *American Dictionary of the English Language.* A century later the *Webster New International, Second Edition,* was recording the word with the same pejorative labels used by Oxford. *Funk & Wagnalls Unabridged* (1913) was taking a somewhat more tolerant view, recording *ain't* in the sense of "am not" as "colloquial but inelegant," but adding that *ain't* in the second or third persons (you *ain't,* he *ain't,* and they *ain't*) was "illiterate and ungrammatical."

A somewhat similar but even more tolerant view was expressed by Henry W. Fowler in *Modern English Usage* (1926) when he noted that "*ain't* used for 'isn't' is an uneducated blunder . . . but it is a pity that *ain't* used for 'am not,' being a natural contraction and supplying a real want, should shock us as though tarred with the same brush." But nobody seemed to be listening, least of all America's schoolteachers, who, virtually unanimously, condemned *ain't* whether in the first, second, or third persons, singular or plural, as "ungrammatical."

The prevailing attitude of teachers was voiced in rhyme by Gelett Burgess (1900): "Now *ain't* is a word/ That is very absurd,/ If you use it for 'isn't' or 'aren't'/ Ask teacher about it,/ She'll say 'Do without it!'/ I wish you would try if you can't."

That's the way matters stood when, in 1961, *Webster's Third New*

International Dictionary appeared, entering *ain't* with the comment that "it is used orally in most parts of the United States by many cultivated speakers." This aroused howls of indignation in most parts of the United States and led one wit to remark, "We don't know where Webster cultivated those speakers."

That *ain't* is still regarded as substandard both in speech and writing is amply demonstrated in the responses of the Usage Panel.

USAGE PANEL QUESTION

In balloting for the first edition of the *Harper Dictionary of Contemporary Usage* we asked this question: "*Ain't* has been stigmatized by generations of schoolteachers as illiterate or worse. Yet it has its defenders, including H. W. Fowler and other writers, especially when used in the first person singular. Would you accept 'I *ain't* the least bit interested'?" Only 4 percent of the panelists at that time approved the use of *ain't* in writing and several of them indicated that they were referring to its use in fictional dialogue to establish characterization. Sixty percent rejected its use in speech.

Recalling the famous dictum of *Merriam's Third International* (1961) that *ain't* is "used orally in most parts of the U.S. by many cultivated speakers," would you today approve *ain't* in speech?

Yes: 19%. No: 81%.

In writing not fictional in nature? Yes: 6%. No: 94%.

SHANA ALEXANDER (voting "yes" to its use in writing): "But only if used for some reason of style."

MICHEL J. ARLEN: "No. It has always seemed affected—especially when the British use it. For example, Harold Macmillan's 'There ain't going to be any war.' "

ISAAC ASIMOV: "I use it in speech freely, but I am a certified eccentric."

W. H. AUDEN (voting "no"): "I would accept 'ain't' in certain contexts, but not this one."

SHERIDAN BAKER: "Only as humorous (and snooty) slumming. Even my cultivated Southern friends glance around if it slips out when Yankees are present."

STEWART BEACH: "Any dictionary of usage should frankly state that 'ain't' is improper in speech and writing among educated people."

ALVIN BEAM: "My conscience bothers me a little when I say I wouldn't 'accept' the 'ain't' usage. My father commonly used 'ain't'—it was quite natural with him—and I'm saddened now that this grated on me as I moved into my teens. Of course, I 'accept' 'ain't' from many people. But

I wouldn't *approve* of it in a child under my tutelage and it's in that sense that I vote 'no' here."

CHARLES BERLITZ: (In speech) "No except in dialectal *bon mots*—'If it ain't broke, don't fix it.' "

BARRY BINGHAM, SR.: " 'Ain't' is often met as a conscious bit of folksy speech by those who know it is incorrect. Used in that way in casual speech, it seems to me harmless."

DAVID H. BRADLEY: "C'mon. We *gotta* have *some* standards."

JOSEPH A. BRANDT: " 'Ain't' is as permissible as saying 'Hi, Betty!' on being introduced to Queen Elizabeth. However, it's permissible in writing to indicate a character's class or status."

JOHN BROOKS: "Yes. I'd accept but in most cases consider it an affectation."

HEYWOOD HALE BROUN: "One usage (in writing) is simple ignorance; the other (speech) a sleazy hope of folksiness."

ANTHONY BURGESS (voting "no" re writing, "yes" re speech): "But 'ain't' will always be facetious in British English, apart from cockney."

ABE BURROWS: "I'll accept 'ain't I?' instead of 'am I not?' That's useful."

JOHN CIARDI: " 'Ain't' is the right and inevitable contraction the language demands and will have. No amount of schoolmarming will suppress it. It is about time to end the conspiracy against it."

GEORGE CORNISH: "Few literate people use 'ain't' except in attempts, usually unsuccessful, to be 'folksy.' "

GEROLD FRANK: "To my mind and ears, 'ain't' jars whenever and wherever used."

FRANCES FRITCHMAN: "Yes, in informal speech with humorous overtones—as in 'Ain't it the truth!' "

A. B. GUTHRIE, JR.: "Yes (in speech) but only as a bit of indifferent humor."

RICHARD EDES HARRISON: " 'Ain't' in speech is useful for emphasis on occasion."

WAKEMAN HARTLEY: "Provided it's written with a twinkle."

PAUL HORGAN: "Deliberate archaisms sound 'cute.' "

JOHN K. HUTCHENS: "I believe that its sole legitimate use is for purposes of characterization in fiction—or for purposes of humor."

ELIZABETH JANEWAY: "I would accept it in dialogue, as indicative of character, status, etc."

WALT KELLY: " 'I'm not' is easier to say."

WALTER KERR: "It's still coarse and back-country."

STANLEY KUNITZ: "Acceptable in literate speech or writing only for jocose emphasis or as a mock vulgarism.' "

CHARLES KURALT: "When used by one who knows better, 'ain't' is not ignorant, merely colorful. Therefore I suppose we have to accept its use in speech by anyone."

JULES LOH: "I vote no to its use as a casual contraction, even in the first person singular. But it makes an effective intensifier in rare and appropriate in instances, including nonfiction.''

WALTER LORD: "In research I find 'ain't' is sometimes used in formal, even official, letters in 1812–1814, but that doesn't excuse it today. Just as words come into usage, they can go out of usage, too."

DWIGHT MACDONALD: "I think 'ain't' is historically good English and practically necessary. But the schoolmarms have made it impossible, alas."

DAVID MCCORD (voting "yes" to 'ain't' in speech): ". . . when used by a person known to be literate. Beerbohm could have said 'I ain't.'"

PHYLLIS MCGINLEY: "'Ain't' is now obsolete or at least archaic."

WRIGHT MORRIS: "'Ain't' is an ugly sound and we should preserve it *as* ugly."

DANIEL PATRICK MOYNIHAN: "'Ain't' is archaic, i.e., eighteenth-century English."

EDWIN NEWMAN: "'Ain't is acceptable only as a rather coy joke."

MARGE PIERCY: "*Ain't* is still useful in dialogue but unacceptable in any but the most casual usage. When used in public speech, it generally aims to give a folksy hue."

DAVID POLING: "I feel that 'ain't' is on a sharp decline in usage."

ORVILLE PRESCOTT: "'Ain't' is still used only by the uneducated. It is still offensive to the eye and ear."

PETER S. PRESCOTT: "The word might be useful in the first person singular, but it is irredeemably associated with the illiterate and is therefore unusable."

F. D. REEVE: "It's in Shakespeare. I'd vote to see it come back. ('Amn't' is impossible)."

VERMONT ROYSTER: "When 'I'm not' is so easy to use, why not?"

HARRISON SALISBURY (voting "yes" to both questions): "But 'ain't' is rapidly becoming obsolete, alas, due to generations of excoriations by schoolteachers."

LEONARD SANDERS: "Fowler laments that 'ain't' has not won acceptance; in so doing, he confirms that it has not."

DAVID SCHOENBRUN: "I prefer 'I'm not' to 'ain't' in this case. I like to use 'ain't' for emphasis: 'Say it *ain't* so' or '*Ain't* it the truth!' but not just for sloppy speech."

MARK SCHORER: "'Ain't' is acceptable in speech, if the speaker is being funny."

ROBERT SHERRILL: "I favor 'ain't' in the first person, but even Fowler seems to acknowledge its death from second- and third-person abuse."

WALTER W. "RED" SMITH: "Though I use 'ain't' habitually in speech, I would write it only in the vernacular or in a jocular tone."

ELVIS STAHR, JR.: "Subcultures are important here—but 'ain't' is acceptable (to me) only when one is sure that the user is conscious of using it."

DAVIDSON TAYLOR: "I might use 'ain't' in speech when speaking to friendly illiterates."

LIONEL TRILLING: "Clearly some such form is needed, but I can't bring myself to accepting this one."

EDWARD TRIPP: "Disapproving of 'ain't' when no good substitute contraction exists seems stuffy but childhood brainwashing is hard to overcome."

EARL UBELL (voting "yes" to both questions): "But only ironically, i.e., to imply that I'm talking with a voice not my own."

JOSEPH VERGARA: "Can't bring myself to use it—except of course when I put it in someone else's mouth."

JUDITH VIORST: "It sounds rotten."

GEORGE WALD: "When I do use 'ain't' it's caricature: 'It ain't nuthin!' "

DOUGLAS WATT: "Only colloquially or for particular emphasis."

A.B.C. WHIPPLE: "No, except as intentional slang."

CHARLES L. WHIPPLE: "Only when deliberately used for comic or other effect."

HERMAN WOUK: "In writing I would use 'ain't' for a character who talks so. Its use in speech would be waggish or jocose, for me."

See also AREN'T I?

air   *Air* has long been established as a transitive verb in such expressions as "*airing* one's grievances" and "*airing* the room." It has recently acquired a new intransitive use as part of the jargon of broadcasting: "The new program will *air* Tuesdays at 8 P.M." or "will be aired."

air-/aero-. *See* AEROPLANE

Alabaman/Alabamian   Panelist George Cornish commented: "I came originally from Alabama and we used to call ourselves *Alabamians.* However, I often see *Alabaman* in print. Which is correct?"

Adaptations of place names to designate residents of various towns and cities follow no special rules, though attempts have been made to codify them. Some years ago, George R. Stewart, author of *Names on the Land* and the more recent *American Place Names,* reported that "if a name ends with '-i,' '-an' is added; if it ends in '-a,' not preceded by '-i,' the common rule is to add '-n.' " According to this, *Alabaman* would be preferred.

But the fact of the matter is that natives of Alabama overwhelmingly prefer *Alabamian.* Indeed, the editor of the Dothan (Alabama) *Eagle* went on record with this statement: "If there is any merit in the rule of spelling a proper name just as the possessor spells it, then we are *Alabamians.*" So you'll not be wrong whichever you choose, but the advice from here is "When in Alabama, do as the *Alabamians* do."

alarm   *Alarm* is a transitive verb but, like many other verbs, it is occasionally abused. On a stairwell door of a building occupied by a major New York publisher is a large sign: "This door electrically alarmed."

alibi

USAGE PANEL QUESTION

Alibi in law means a defense based upon proof that the accused was not at the scene when the crime was committed. Many writers and speakers use it in the broader sense of any kind of excuse. Ring Lardner used it thus in naming his character Alibi Ike, about whom he wrote: "This baby can't even go to bed without apologizing, and I bet he excuses himself to the razor when he gets ready to shave." Do you approve the use of *alibi* in this sense?

In writing   Yes: 55%. No: 45%.
In speech   Yes: 68%. No: 32%.

The Usage Panelists were quite evenly divided on this question, with a slight majority favoring the extended use of *alibi* in writing and more than two-to-one in favor of its use in speech. Typical comments follow.

HAL BORLAND: "No, I will cling to it to the end, though it's a lost cause."

HEYWOOD HALE BROUN: "Yes. Anything which is okay with Ring Lardner is okay with me."

ANTHONY BURGESS: "No. 'Alibi' means 'somewhere else' to me. It can't mean one thing in Latin and law and another thing in nonlegal English."

ABE BURROWS: "Yes. Once 'alibi' got out of the courtrooms, it belonged to the world."

WILLIAM O. DOUGLAS: "Yes to the use of 'alibi' in the extended sense, both in speech and writing."

GEROLD FRANK: "No. The word has such a strong legal flavor that to use it too broadly gives an almost grotesque quality."

JOHN K. HUTCHENS: "No [to 'alibi' in writing], because as a newspaperman I was taught to be careful about this word. Yes [to it in speech], because there's nothing to be done about it."

ELIZABETH JANEWAY: "I'd accept the usage in speech. As for writing, it depends on what you're writing. At times precision is absolutely necessary. Not always? Well, I think Lardner's extended use is O.K."

ALEXANDER KENDRICK: "In speech at least, usage, aided by the right of free translation, wins over strict meaning."

STANLEY KUNITZ: "Yes, with reservations. This battle has, I fear, already been lost."

CHARLES KURALT: "No—except for Ring Lardner."

PHYLLIS MCGINLEY: "I might as well give in on this one. 'Alibi' has for so long been used in the meaning of 'excuse' that even we purists might as well admit defeat."

FRANCIS T. P. PLIMPTON: "No."

GEORGE PLIMPTON: "Yes."

PETER S. PRESCOTT: "No. I'll bet Ring Lardner knew that 'alibi' in the sense he used it here was vernacular. His book was written with a sure ear for speech patterns. I don't think people who care for the language can use 'alibi' in the broad sense without irony."

RICHARD H. ROVERE: "On this one occasion [Alibi Ike], yes."

VERMONT ROYSTER: "The example offered is not too good. The nickname is appropriate in the Ring Lardner subculture. Who expects Huck Finn to be grammatical, however learned Mr. Twain?"

ROBERT SHERRILL: "If I understand the example, it is too broad for me. I do use 'alibi' to mean a covering-up type of excuse for not doing something that should have been done, or for otherwise fouling up."

WALTER W. "RED" SMITH: "I avoid it, but it's firmly established."

ELVIS STAHR, JR.: "Yes, but only because the battle was lost before I could protest."

BILL VAUGHAN: "Generations of newspaper editors have waged this battle. I'm sorry but it's probably lost."

HERMAN WOUK: "This new meaning has simply emerged as a secondary one, like it or not."

all An increasingly common use of *all* is in expressions like "He's not *all* that good" and "It's not *all* that certain that he'll be elected." This adverbial use of *all* is pleasantly folksy sounding and, if it comes naturally to you, is certainly unobjectionable in casual speech. It should, however, be carefully avoided in writing, especially writing of a formal nature.

all/all of In formal contexts, use simply *all*: "*All* Britain stands mute, awaiting your words of inspiration." In informal contexts, *all of* is more commonly encountered: "*All of* the members of Joe's Service Station bowling team paused for beers after the match." When a personal pronoun is involved, the idiom is invariably *all of*: "*All of* me, why not take *all of* me?" and "The leaders who held the power relinquished *all of* it."

all-. *See* PREFIXES AND SUFFIXES, WITH AND WITHOUT HYPHEN

allergic/allergenic Correspondents in Chicago and Omaha have reported purchasing pillows labeled "nonallergic." An allergy, as all sufferers from hay fever know, is sensitivity to a substance such as pollen or dust, which, in similar quantities, is harmless to other people. Obviously, an inanimate object such as a pillow cannot have an allergy. It can, however, be made of *allergenic* (allergy-inducing) substances such as feathers.

The labels should have read "nonallergenic."

all in   This is a British informal phrase, short for "all inclusive" in reference to costs of holiday tours and the like. It's worth noting that the British version of the phrase has nothing whatever in common with the American *all in,* meaning worn out or exhausted.

alliteration   *Alliteration* is simply the repetition of the same sound at the start of a series of words, usually three or more. It has often been used with effect both in prose and poetry and is a favorite device of political orators. Speechwriters for unfrocked Vice President Spiro Agnew used the device so often that it became a somewhat boring characteristic of his stump speeches. Perhaps the most memorable, or at least most quoted, example from the Agnew collection is William Safire's "nattering nabobs of negativism," a term that presumably included everyone who did not see eye to eye with the Nixon administration. Your editors, in a rather outspoken newspaper interview critical of the prose coming from Washington during this period, specifically marked out this type of *alliteration* as something we'd be happy to see abandoned. "But," commented the interviewer, pinking us neatly, "if you disapprove the use of *alliteration,* why have you for more than a score of years called your column 'Words, Wit and Wisdom'?"

All my eye and Betty Martin!   This is roughly the British equivalent of "baloney" or "bosh." It's an expression of unknown origin but quite commonly heard and found in literature all the way back to Oliver Goldsmith. It is often heard in the abbreviated form of *All my eye* and is slang in any context. *See also* BOLOGNA.

all ready/already   A question put by a column reader asks: "Which is correct in this sentence: 'By midnight the cartons were all ready/already to seal'?" The answer is, of course, *all ready* because the reference is to the cartons collectively. *Already,* an adverb, has the meaning of previously or before.

all right/alright

USAGE PANEL QUESTION

One usage authority has written: "*All right* is the spelling of both the adjective phrase (He is *all right*) and the adverb phrase meaning 'Yes, certainly' (*All right,* I'll come). *Alright* is a natural analogy with *altogether* and *already* but at present is found only in advertising, comic strips, unedited writings, and, rarely, in fiction. It will be worth watching to see if *alright* makes its way into General English"—which he defined as "the speaking and writing of educated people in their private or public affairs." Would you use *alright* without restriction as a substitute for *all right*?

Yes: 14%. No: 86%.

Would you use *alright* in the sense of "Yes, certainly"? Yes: 25%. No: 75%.

ISAAC ASIMOV. "No. 'Alright' looks funny."

W. H. AUDEN: "I might use it—but I don't."

HAL BORLAND: "Follow that analogy and you get 'alwet,' 'alwrong,' 'alinclusive,' etc. ad infinitum."

HEYWOOD HALE BROUN: "For those who wish a simplified form, may I suggest 'O.K.'?"

STEPHEN H. FRITCHMAN: "No, but this negative reaction may be a result of early conditioning. I cannot clearly explain why the 'alright' version so much annoys me."

ELIZABETH JANEWAY: "No. Why in hell should I? My understanding of 'alright' is that it is a cant adjective: He's an 'alright' kid."

ALEXANDER KENDRICK: " 'Alright' has become all right in most cases. However, I would not like to use even 'all right' for 'Yes, certainly.' "

CLARK KINNAIRD: "Yes to 'alright' but *not* 'alrighty,' now often heard in colloquial speech."

LAURENCE LAFORE: " 'No' to 'alright' in both contexts—but I should not correct it when used in an adjectival sense."

EDWIN NEWMAN: "No. Incidentally, your usage authority should have said, 'see *whether alright* makes its way into General English,' not 'if' it would." (NOTE: He also should have said "analogue," rather than "analogy"—but let it pass.)

VERMONT ROYSTER: "No, except in dialogue to indicate slurring in pronunciation."

HARRISON SALISBURY: "No—but it is here to stay, alas."

MARK SCHORER: "No to both queries. But I wouldn't object. Habit again."

WALTER W. "RED" SMITH: "I don't happen to use 'alright' at all. Is that all right, meaning O.K.?"

HOWARD TAUBMAN: "No, but it wouldn't disturb me if someone else used it."

BILL VAUGHAN: "No. When it comes to 'alright' in the sense of 'Yes, certainly,' I prefer 'All-righty' or even 'Okey-dokey.' "

JUDITH VIORST: "No. But I've been brainwashed. I'd like to see the change made, after which I'd probably start to use it—eventually."

---

all-round/all-around *All-round* as an adjective meaning versatile or talented in many areas of activity is preferred to *all-around.*

allude/elude/refer *Allude* and *refer* have basically the same meaning of making reference to something. The difference, which should be observed but often is not, is that *allude* implies indirect reference ("His letter *alludes* to some unspecified difficulties"), while *refer* implies direct reference ("The judge *referred* to ten specific violations of the Constitution").

Elude, of course, has nothing whatever in common with *allude,* except a similarity of sound which sometimes causes confusion. To *elude* something or someone is to escape or avoid it or him or her.

allusion/illusion These words, not related at all in sense and only distantly in etymology, are sometimes confused because of their similar sound. A reader asked for the correct word in this sentence: "The president made several *allusions/illusions* to his earlier speech." The correct word is *allusion,* meaning "an indirect reference." *Illusion* means a false concept or impression: "He had the *illusion* that the setting sun was actually sinking into the ocean."

almond *Almond* is pronounced AH-mund or AM-und, not AL-mund.

almost/most *Almost* and *most* are synonymous in meaning, with the former suitable in any context. *Most,* which often in years past was written *'most,* is an informal contraction of *almost* especially common in the speech of young people: "*Most* anyone can do this dance."

almost never This item appeared in a Washington, D.C., newspaper: "It is strange when we think of it that we *almost never* hear anyone mention the size of the bed on which we sleep as a factor (in insomnia)."

There are those who would be happier if the writer of this sentence had written "seldom" or "hardly ever" in place of *almost never.* "Almost" means "very nearly" and "never," of course, means "not at all." If the writer meant to indicate that this factor is mentioned very rarely indeed, there is no reason to object to *almost never.*

alongside/alongside of *Alongside* is entirely correct and adequate in and of itself: "The ship was moored *alongside* the dock." However, *alongside of* is considered an acceptable prepositional idiom, especially in casual conversation.

also *Also* should not be used as a connective in place of *and.* One should not say: "He ordered beer, frankfurters, *also* rye bread." Say rather, "... and rye bread" or "... and *also* rye bread." Many careful writers disapprove of the use of *also* to start a sentence in order to link it with the sentence preceding. Example: "We went to France and England. *Also* we toured Wales." Preferable would be: "We went to France and England and *also* toured Wales."

alternate press. *See* UNDERGROUND PRESS/ALTERNATE PRESS

alternative   Strictly speaking, an *alternative* is one of two possibilities, often mutually exclusive opportunities: "the *alternative* to life is death." To the purist one should never speak of three *alternatives,* rather of three "choices" or three "possibilities." However, the expressions "three *alternatives*" and "a third *alternative*" appear often in the speech and writing of careful users of the language. One reason for this is that *alternative,* unlike "choice," carries a certain imperative connotation. When faced with three *alternatives,* a person must choose one of the three. However, faced with three "choices," he may choose to ignore all of them.

although/though   *Although* and *though* are practically interchangeable as conjunctions introducing subordinate clauses in the sense of "disregarding the fact that . . ." *Although* usually appears in clauses preceding the main or independent clause and, in general, is used in sentences of a more formal nature ("*Although* the ministers had agreed to defer the action, the king ordered otherwise"). *Though* usually appears introducing subordinate clauses following the main clause ("The team chose to play the game anyway, *though* they had nothing to gain in the league standings").

alumna/alumnus   An *alumna* is a female former student of a school or college. An *alumnus* is a male former student of a school or college. They may also be graduates of the institutions they attended, but this is not essential. In other words, a person who falls short of completing the graduation requirements of an institution is nonetheless an *alumnus* or *alumna* of it. Graduates and former students of a coeducational institution are generally referred to by the masculine plural form *alumni.*

A.M./P.M./N./M.   The designations "A.M." for the period between midnight and noon and "P.M." for that between noon and midnight are indisputable and never confused. Some persons are confused, though, as to how to write "12 noon" and "12 midnight."

The abbreviation 12 M. is sometimes used to denote noon (M. denotes "meridian"). However, 12 M. is likely to be interpreted as an abbreviation for midnight. Hence, 12 M. should not be used either.

The following are three solutions to the problem of designating noon and midnight unambiguously:

(1) Use the complete words "noon" and "midnight." If midnight is used give the two dates between which it falls. Thus, for example, "midnight of 7 October" is ambiguous but "midnight of 7/8 October" is specific.

(2) Prepare schedules with times other than noon and midnight. Use times such as 12:01 A.M., 11:59 P.M., etc. This is done by railroads.

(3) Use the 2400 system, which is used by international airlines and the military services. The first two digits give the hours past midnight and the second two give the minutes. Noon is designated by 1200. Midnight is designated as 0000 of the new date, i.e. midnight of 7/8 October is 0000, 8 October.

-ama The suffix *-ama,* a shortened form of "-orama," from the Greek *horama,* meaning sight, has obviously been around for a long time. As part of *cyclorama* and *panorama,* it has long been part of standard English. At the time of the 1939 New York World's Fair, however, General Motors, drawing on the theme of the fair ("The World of Tomorrow"), named its exhibit "Futurama." It was the big hit of the show and spawned hundreds of imitative names, most of them now forgotten. *Cinerama,* a spectacular wide-screen motion-picture technique, is a term still in use. Among the candidates for oblivion, however, we propose *sporterama, bowlerama, chickenerama* (fried-chicken stand), and, a New York City favorite, *bagelorama,* where gourmets may stock up on bagels, lox, and, one supposes, cream cheese.

ambiance/ambience In the late sixties, *ambiance* became one of the vogue words which many writers and speakers overused extensively. A simpler word is "environment," for that is all that is usually meant when the word is used. *Ambiance* is a borrowing from the French and is pronounced AM-bee-unss.

Literally it means "that which goes around or encompasses on all sides," from which comes its literary and artistic sense of the totality of patterns surrounding and enhancing the central element of a design. There is also a perfectly good (though more uncommon) spelling, *ambience.*

ambivalence/vacillation These two words are sometimes confused, with careless writers regarding *ambivalence* as a fancy synonym for *vacillation.* Actually, *ambivalence* reflects a sense of having two minds about a matter, having two conflicting emotions—such as love and hate—simultaneously. *Vacillation,* by contrast, implies shifting between opinions or emotions, wavering from one to another irresolutely.

ambivalent. *See* VOGUE WORDS

amenities In America *amenities* take the form of social courtesies or pleasantries, as when two heads of state exchange *amenities* before proceeding to the business at hand. In England, by contrast, *amenities* usually refer to physical conveniences, as when a hospital offers special *amenity* beds available to patients willing to pay higher rates, and a town boasts of its "*amenity* centre comprising a clubroom with cinema and a playing field."

American It can hardly be denied that this word in all the languages of the world is interpreted as referring to a citizen of the United States. This is not to say that other peoples of the Western Hemisphere are overjoyed that this is the case.

Canadians, in particular, resent the somewhat chauvinistic attitude taken thoughtlessly by most United States citizens that they and they alone should be called "Americans." Mexicans, while understandably proud to be called "Mexicans," sharply resent hyphenated labels like Mexican-American and Latin-American and have been known to make the point that the first land to be known as America (after Amerigo Vespucci) was in their latitude, not farther north, where today's self-styled *Americans* reside.

So tact, if not general linguistic practice, suggests that we consider our neighbors to the north and south just as *American* as we are.

Americana The pronunciation uh-mehr-ih-KAY-nuh was, until fairly recently, the indicated preferred pronunciation in most American dictionaries—though it is reasonable to doubt that any dictionary editor ever heard the word pronounced that way outside the dictionary office. Here's how this came about. Those earlier dictionaries, including both the Merriam-Webster Second Edition and the Funk & Wagnalls Unabridged, followed British patterns of pronouncing terms derived from Latin. This is in contrast to the "classical" Latin pronunciation taught in such of our schools as still teach any Latin at all. For example, when Congress adjourns "sine die" (without setting a date for reconvening) the phrase is rendered SIN-eh DEE-ay in "classical" Latin but SY-nih DY-ee in British or legal Latin. By these same principles, the "-ana" suffix is supposed to be pronounced AY-nuh. Hence the traditional lexicographers' uh-mehr-ih-KAY-nuh. But the newer dictionaries have editors who listen to actual speech, so you will find the pronunciations given as uh-mehr-ih-KAH-nuh, uh-mehr-ih-KAN-uh, and the traditional uh-mehr-ih-KAY-nuh trailing in third place.

America's Cup After an interruption by World War II, the leading yachtsmen of Great Britain, Australia, and the United States have been competing at irregular intervals for an ancient mug that symbolizes international supremacy in yacht racing. Many a sportswriter and many a proofreader had to learn anew that the cup at stake is not the "American Cup" but *America's Cup.*

To know the significance of that particular " 's," we have to go back more than a hundred years to the time when the cup was known as the "Hundred-Guinea Cup" and was offered by the Royal Yacht Squadron as the trophy for the winner of an international yacht race. None of the proud members of the squadron dreamed that an upstart American could successfully challenge craft of the empire that had for centuries ruled the waves.

But that is just what the yacht *America* did. She sailed the broad Atlantic, bested the finest British yachts, and brought the coveted cup back with her. Then, compounding the chagrin felt by the vanquished British, the cup's new owners proudly renamed it the *America's Cup.*

The original *America,* incidentally, went on to an illustrious career after her original triumph. During the Civil War she served as a dispatch carrier for the Confederate forces, was seized by the Union Navy, and was sent to Annapolis, where she served as a training vessel. Refitted for racing after the war, she competed for her cup in 1870 but came in fourth. Eventually she was berthed at Annapolis and finally was broken up during the 1940s.

amid/amidst   One fact of language growth is its continual change. Words fall out of fashion and others take their place. *Amidst* and *amid* are cases in point. While they were common in the writings of the nineteenth century and earlier they are now considered "literary words" which can best be stricken in favor of "among" or "in."

amnesty   Proponents of *amnesty* for draft evaders, deserters from the armed services, and the like often make the argument that the true meaning of *amnesty* is "forgetting," not "forgiving," the theory being that it should be easier for governmental authorities to forget than to forgive. There is some basis, etymologically, for this argument. *Amnesty,* after all, came from the same Greek root as *amnesia,* the medical term for total or partial loss of memory. However, though *amnesty* originally meant "forgetting" or, more precisely, "a deliberate act of not remembering," it has now been formalized into a legal term meaning a pardon given by a government to persons who have been convicted of violating a law. So *amnesty* now means "forgiving."

amok/amuck   A headline on a book review reads RADICALISM RUN AMOK and a correspondent questions whether it is an error. While this is a variant spelling of *amuck* and, as such, less preferable, it is actually closer to the Malayan word "amoq" from which it is derived. The word was originally used to describe the actions of Malayan tribesmen who, frenzied by hatred and hashish, would rush furiously into combat. In the instance of this headline, *amok* was undoubtedly chosen because it took less space.

among/between The distinction between *among* and *between* is regarded by many purists as simple and direct: *among* is used in referring to groups of three or more ("The lottery prize was divided *among* the members of the pool of bettors") and *between* is used in referring to two persons or things ("the difference *between* men and women" or "the choice *between* wealth and poverty"). One exception to this practice may be noted: when three or more entities are considered individually, albeit closely associated, *between* may be preferable ("There was a binding treaty of confederacy *between* the five tribes of the Iroquois nation"). The questions on the ballot sent to Usage Panelists explored these aspects of *among/between*. Here are the percentages of affirmative and negative replies to each part, followed by the comments of various panelists.

USAGE PANEL QUESTION

The distinction between *among* and *between* is, according to traditional precepts, simple: *between* is used when two persons or things are concerned, *among* when three or more are under consideration. Exceptions to this "rule" are often noted in the press, however, and are defended in instances where three or more parties are considered to be in close relationship. Would you consider the following acceptable:

(a) "Negotiations affecting the entry of Great Britain were going forward *between* members of the European Common Market"? Yes: 28%. No: 72%.

(b) "Pressed for ransom, the three parents could raise only $5,000 *between* them." Yes: 22%. No: 78%.

SHERIDAN BAKER: "This seems clearly to call for 'among.' I think I would write 'between several members' to suggest a number of pairings simultaneously and in succession both, but always between two negotiators, as it probably would be."

STEWART BEACH: "I have always followed the traditional distinction in speech and writing. This is a borderline case: the negotiations might easily be carried out by two diplomats rather than in plenary session."

STEPHEN H. FRITCHMAN: "When the origin of a word ('between,' by twos) helps clarify the usage, let's keep it that way as long as possible, especially when we have 'among.'"

PAUL HORGAN: "Dread familiarity has forced this into acceptability."

ALEXANDER KENDRICK: "Yes, since there is also considerable bilatera-
lism."
ORVILLE PRESCOTT: "Yes. But 'among' is preferable."
PETER S. PRESCOTT: "No. Let's preserve the distinctions we have and change
language only to make it stronger."
VERMONT ROYSTER: "It depends. If referring to bilateral negotiations among
the members (which could be the fact), Yes. Otherwise, No."
LEONARD SANDERS: " 'Between' is so specific in meaning that the word simply
cannot be warped—not in good conscience."
ELVIS STAHR, JR.: "Yes, but only because the negotiations may have been and
probably were going on in a series of bilateral talks."
BENJAMIN APPEL: "Yes, because the three parents are in the same boat."
ALEXANDER KENDRICK: "No, this is stretching proximity."
ORVILLE PRESCOTT: "This is acceptable, but 'among' is preferable."

among/in   During the lifetime of Dr. Martin Luther King, Jr., a television newsman, reporting the burning of a church, spoke of Dr. King
as having "held a prayer meeting among the debris left after the burning." The question is raised as to whether *among* may be used with a
singular noun, and the answer is "yes." The line quoted is not wrong
grammatically; it is just not idiomatic. In the Bible, for instance, you
find references to Jesus passing "*among* the crowd." In the instance
quoted, however, "*in* the debris" or "*among* the ruins" would be preferable.

amoral/immoral   "A-" as a prefix means "without," so *amoral* is applied
to someone who neither knows nor cares about the mores of society or
standards of right and wrong. An *immoral* person is one who, while
knowing the difference between right and wrong, willfully disregards
standards and principles.

amount/number   *Amount* is used to refer to quantities viewed in bulk
("The *amount* of sugar used in this recipe"). *Number* refers to quantities
or things that are counted in individual units ("The *number* of spectators
exceeded fifty thousand"). *See also* LESS/FEWER.

ampersand (&)   The *ampersand (&)* is the sign everyone recognizes and
whose name almost nobody knows. The British sometimes call it "short
and" but that seems to us certain to cause confusion with the more widely
used "shorthand." In any event, the *ampersand* is a very useful device in
shorthand or any kind of terse note taking. It is also commonly seen in
corporate names like the lamented Merrill Lynch, Pierce, Fenner &
Beane, though some firms have seen fit to delete it in recent years, "Bat-
ten, Barton, Durstin & Osborne" having decided to become simply "Bat-
ten, Barton, Durstin, Osborne," thereby deleting part of the charm which

led Heywood Broun to say that the corporate name sounded to him like a "beer barrel rolling down a flight of steps." In any event, avoid the *ampersand* in writing of a formal or semiformal nature, save for the most impromptu personal notes.

amuse/bemuse   Centuries ago these words were synonymous, but no longer. To *amuse* means primarily "to give pleasure to others," especially by causing them to laugh or smile: "The comedian *amused* the crowd with his one-liners." One is *bemused* when he is confused, preoccupied, or even stupefied: "A man *bemused* by overindulgence in strong liquor."

analyst/analysand   In these days of widespread use of psychoanalysis, there is a need for a word other than "patient" to designate the client of an *analyst.* He or she is the *analysand,* pronounced uh-NAL-iss-and.

ancillary   This is not a new word but one that has recently been very much in vogue, especially among Washington bureaucrats, some of whom cannot pronounce it correctly. One of our top-ranking senators recently mystified his auditors more than he realized by repeatedly referring to the an-SILL-er-ee aspects of a particularly messy scandal. He should, of course, have said AN-sill-er-ee. And what does *ancillary* mean? Originally it meant "subordinate to" or "auxiliary." Now, especially in Washington, it's used as a fancy substitute for "related."

and, beginning sentence with   Many years ago schoolteachers insisted that it was improper to begin a sentence with *and* but this convention is now outmoded. Innumerable respected writers use *and* at the beginning of a sentence. It is wise not to overdo this practice and to keep such sentences short. *See also* BUT.

and/or   *And/or,* a phrase that should be used with precision, is applicable only when a choice of three alternatives, involving two elements, is concerned: "The crime is punishable by a fine and/or prison term," meaning that the guilty party may be given a fine, sentenced to prison, or both. *And/or* is suitable chiefly in legal or business communications.

ane. *See* LOST POSITIVES

anesthesia/anaesthesia. *See* AESTHETIC/ESTHETIC

angst   This is voguish borrowing from German. It means "anxiety, combined with a feeling of depression and neurotic gloom." As panelist Harold Schonberg notes: "*Angst* is, I think, both nouveau and faddish—and adds naught to the flexibility of our tongue." We agree.

annex *Annex* as a verb is preferably pronounced with the stress on the second syllable: uh-NEX. However, AN-ex is also considered acceptable as a pronunciation of the verb. The noun *annex* is always pronounced with the stress on the first syllable: AN-ex. Nevertheless—and we can give personal ear-witness testimony to this—during the 1930s school administrators in New York City invariably referred to high-school annexes as an-NEXES. Whether this particular illiteracy persists to this day we do not know. We hope not, but we wouldn't bet on it.

Annie Oakley An *Annie Oakley* (sometimes simply *annie* or *oakley*) is theatrical jargon for a free pass to a show. Such free tickets (also sometimes called "freebies") usually have a hole punched in them to prevent their being returned to the box office for refund. The original *Annie Oakley* was a famous sharpshooter who toured with Buffalo Bill and other Western stars. Her ability to shoot holes through any target gave rise to the use of her name for the free tickets.

anno Domini In formal style the initials A.D., usually in small capital letters, meaning "in the year of our Lord," precede specific dates in the Christian era: A.D. 746. Dates prior to the birth of Christ are usually given with the initials B.C. following the date. Thus: 44 B.C. In informal use the initials A.D. sometimes follow the date, especially when the date is general, rather than specific. Thus: "during the third century A.D."

annual. *See* FIRST ANNUAL

another/additional/more *Another* means "one more" and should not be used in such statements as "Another seventy delegates . . . are to arrive." A better phrasing would be "Seventy *more* . . ." or "Seventy *additional* . . ."

antagonist. *See* PROTAGONIST/ANTAGONIST

ante-/anti- *Ante-* is a prefix meaning "before," as in "*ante*bellum," before the war. *Anti-* is a prefix meaning "against," as in "*anti*-fascist," against fascists and fascism. *See also* PREFIXES AND SUFFIXES, WITH AND WITHOUT HYPHEN.

antenna *Antenna* has two plural forms, *antennae* taken direct from Latin, and *antennas.* The former is used exclusively in biological or zoological contexts. The latter is used in reference to *antennas* or "aerials" used with radio, television, and the like.

anthem/song We speak of a "national *anthem*" but a "state *song.*" The distinction between *anthem* and *song* is a precise one, worth preserving.

An *anthem* is a hymn, usually one pledging loyalty to a religion, people, or nation. As such it is sung with earnest solemnity. The exceptions are rare—as when José Feliciano gave a rock-accented version of "The Star-Spangled Banner" at a World Series game and brought upon himself screams of anguish from just about every patriotic organization in the country.

A *song,* by contrast, is rendered in a more lighthearted way, expressing more of joy than solemn devotion. A good example of a state *song* is the Rodgers and Hammerstein "Oklahoma," first the hit of Broadway for years and now the official *song* of the state.

anticlimax   An *anticlimax* is a sort of failed figure of speech—a series of statements seemingly building to a climax whose effect is spoiled by a concluding item of trifling importance or ludicrous incongruity. Perhaps the most celebrated American *anticlimax* is "For God, for Country, and for Yale!"

antonym   An *antonym* is a word that means nearly the opposite of another word. As is the case with *synonyms* (which see) there is no such thing as an absolutely precise *antonym,* though broadly opposing categories ("good" as an *antonym* for "bad," for example) are commonly encountered. Dictionaries of synonyms and many general-purpose dictionaries enter *antonyms* as well as synonyms.

anxious/eager   *Anxious* and *eager* are somewhat analogous in meaning but careful speakers and writers use *anxious* when some doubt or worry exists ("She is *anxious* because the plane is long overdue") and *eager* when the mood is one of joyous anticipation ("I am *eager* to hear the awards announced").

any   The pronoun *any* may be followed by either a singular or plural verb, depending on the context in which it appears. *"Any* of the boys is suitable for the post" is correct, since the *any* stands for *any one.* *"Any* of the books submitted are likely prize winners" is correct because *any* stands for "several" or "some."

Any, as an adjective, is sometimes found with a singular noun: "The Rolls-Royce is the most expensive of *any* standard-make car." This is at best barely tolerable in folksy speech and most certainly inadmissible in writing. The correct formulation is: "The Rolls-Royce is the most expensive of standard-make cars."

any more   *Any more* as a synonym for "nowadays" has been reported in regional dialects for more than seventy-five years. Harold Wentworth in his *American Dialect Dictionary* reported hundreds of examples in areas as remote from each other as Iowa and West Virginia. Usually it was heard in semi-literate context. Here are two examples from West Virginia: "So many strange automobile plates are seen *any more* that when we see one from West Virginia it almost makes us homesick" and "There's getting to be so much money talked about in big figures *any more* that panhandlers ain't satisfied unless they're given paper money."

When Wentworth compiled his dictionary (1944) he noted that although *any more* was mostly heard in rural areas, it "is not confined to the illiterate." During the past decade we have had reports of its appearance in the speech of relatively literate users of the language in places as widely scattered as Columbus, Ohio; Tacoma, Washington; and San Bernardino, California. Webster's Third International (1961) labeled it as "dialect," just as Wentworth did, and, indeed, gave an amusing illustration, obviously from a hillbilly source: "Used to be I had to carry my own whiskey out of the hollow, but *any more* I'm such a good customer they tote it up here for me." Still, *any more* seems to be emerging from the status of semi-literate dialect speech and is appearing with greater frequency in print. To help establish its level of usage, we put the following question to members of the Usage Panel.

USAGE PANEL QUESTION

In a *Newsweek* article, Bob Greene wrote: "Nothing is forbidden. We cannot be shocked in the United States any more. We are so cool and so hard and so hip any more . . . that there has grown a large dead spot inside us all." His first use of *any more* is, of course, standard usage. His second *any more,* however, represents a new sense, synonymous with "nowadays" or "at this time." Though seldom seen in print, this usage is heard with increasing frequency, especially in the speech of young people. Do you approve this extension of meaning of *any more*?

Would you use it in speech   Yes: 9%. No: 91%.

In writing   Yes: 4%. No: 96%.

The overwhelming rejection of *any more* in this new or semi-dialect sense reflects two factors: (1) a profound belief on the part of most panelists that the formulation makes no sense at all, and (2) a refusal on the part of some panelists, since they themselves have never heard the expression, to believe that it even exists. Here follows a sampling of comments.

ISAAC ASIMOV: "You mean the speech of *uneducated* young people, I presume."

JOHN O. BARBOUR: "Sounds wrong to the ear without the negative. The word 'any' implies a negative or lack. Thus we don't say 'we have any,' we say 'we don't have any.' "

ALVIN BEAM: "It isn't natural to me, but I do rather like the sound from others."

BARRY BINGHAM, SR.: "I don't object to new words and phrases when they fill some need, perhaps a new or changing one in relation to a rapidly changing world. I can see no purpose, however, in the use of 'any more' to replace 'now,' a shorter and simpler form. Furthermore, I want to utter a loud protest at the cliché phrase 'at this time' as yet another substitute for 'now.' It is much in use by public speakers of the less talented order, who appear to employ it as a means of extending the introduction of the guest of honor by another moment—'At this time I am happy to introduce Mayor Zilch!' " (NOTE: This comment on "at this time" was written before the Senate Watergate hearings conferred a sort of immortality on the phrase "at this point in time." For Mr. Bingham's comments on the latter, see *Watergate language*.)

HAL BORLAND: "If this continues, there won't be any more anymores to use by lazy anymorons."

HEYWOOD HALE BROUN: "No, but then I don't much approve of the speech of young people."

ANTHONY BURGESS: "It has no meaning in this positive form. It adds nothing."

ABE BURROWS: "Quoth the raven: 'Never any more.' "

JOHN CIARDI: "Barbaric patois."

LEON EDEL: "It tends to weaken accuracy. He means 'nowadays.' "

THOMAS FLEMING: "Yes—but I wouldn't use both in the same sentence."

PAUL HORGAN: "It sounds like unsure immigrant speech."

HELEN L. KAUFMANN: "This usage is completely unfamiliar to me, nor can I see any grammatical reason for it."

ALEXANDER KENDRICK: "We can, too, be shocked and this use is one way to do it. 'Any more'? NEVERMORE!"

LAURENCE LAFORE: "It was common in the rustic vernacular in Pennsylvania fifty years ago. It is still a common usage among old people in the Midwest."

JULES LOH: "Me hip enough to accept this usage? No way!"

DWIGHT MACDONALD: "Never heard this—thought it was a typo. Can't see how 'any more' could ever mean 'nowadays.' "

WADE MOSBY: "This is the most awkward thing I ever heard of."

ORVILLE PRESCOTT: "This is illiterate and without meaning."

LEO ROSTEN: "It is silly and probably a boner to which Greene would admit."

RICHARD H. ROVERE: "This usage is standard in Dutchess County, N.Y. I have never been able to learn why."

DAVID SCHOENBRUN: "When words lose all meaning, communication and thought itself cease."

MARK SCHORER: "It is simply confusing."

ROBERT SHERRILL: "(1) I have never heard it used this way. (2) I am unable to see the logic of its use in this way."

WALTER W. "RED" SMITH: "This is a barbarism in common use thirty-five years ago in South Philadelphia and may be still. In Philadelphia small boys address all adults as Bud. 'Paper, Bud?' 'Watch your car, Bud?' And all redheads are plural: 'Reds.' "

BILL VAUGHAN: "This use of 'any more' has always been common among Midwest plain folk."

USAGE PANEL QUESTION—Second Edition

In balloting for the first edition we quoted from a *Newsweek* article by the columnist Bob Greene: "Nothing is forbidden. We cannot be shocked in the United States any more. We are so cool and so hard and so hip any more . . . that there has grown a large dead spot inside us all." We noted that his first use of *any more* was standard but that his second *any more* represented a new sense, synonymous with "nowadays" or "at this time." We added that, while this use of *any more* had been common in rural dialects for many years, it was just beginning to be heard generally, especially in the speech of young people. We asked if the panel approved this extension of any more.

The verdict was overwhelmingly in the negative, with some panelists saying they had never heard it and hoped they never would, although "Red" Smith labeled it "a barbarism in common use thirty-five years ago in South Philadelphia" and Bill Vaughan said it was "common among Midwest plain folk."

That is precisely what we are now doing.

Have you noticed *any more* in the sense of "nowadays" in speech or writing of a literate nature? Yes: 13%. No: 87%.

In semi-literate or illiterate contexts? Yes: 36%. No: 64%.

JOHN CIARDI: "It is common, alas. I have even heard it from the mouths of English professors. It is proper in negative constructions: 'We don't go there any more.' Whence it has been slovened out of the negative to mean 'nowadays.' It is, I believe, a conquering illiteracy."

RAY GANDOLF: "As one of the late Bill Vaughan's 'Midwest plain folk,' I recall the usage. It does seem to be passing out of vogue. When it disappears I won't mourn but I will tip my hat."

JOHN K. HUTCHENS: "Only occasionally and it still seems a barbarism."

WALTER KERR: "It may be disappearing."

JAMES J. KILPATRICK: "I wouldn't use 'any more' in the sense of 'these days' and I haven't come across any tolerably literate composition in which I've seen it. But the fellow who runs our country store in the Blue Ridge Mountains uses it all the time: 'Any more it's hard to get good vegetables.' "

JULES LOH: "Now for the larger question: semi-literate or not, is it one word or two?"

WILLIAM MCGUIRE: "It's dialect creeping up into standard—a time-honored phenomenon. But the locution is still stigmatized by its 'lower class' origin."

MARGE PIERCY: "My problem with that phrase is that I grew up a street kid in Detroit and did not learn till I had been to college a while that there was anything wrong with it. It has emotional connotations to me that 'any longer' can't carry in ordinary speech. I would not use it myself in a passage in my own style but would use it in preference to 'any longer' in many passages of conversations. In conversation 'no more' and 'any more' have a power for me that the sound of 'any longer' simply can't convey."

F. D. REEVE: "I've even seen it in poems."

HAROLD SCHONBERG: "First time I've come across it."

ELVIS STAHR, JR.: "One continues to hear it and this one continues to abhor it. I'm not sure that I hear it more often than I did a decade ago, so maybe it will die out."

KARL V. TEETER: "It's colloquial. It's striking and has character."

JOSEPH VERGARA: "I've heard it in Arizona and I've heard it in N.Y. . . . I'm shaken a bit by it. Any way to head it off?"

JUDITH VIORST: "Never."

DOUGLAS WATT: "No, but then I don't get around much *anymore,* at least not in South Philly."

A.B.C. WHIPPLE: "No, and I hope my children don't."

anyone/anybody *Anyone* and *anybody* are often and mistakenly used with plural pronoun references in the predicate: "*Anyone* who tries to descend the Grand Canyon on foot must be out of their mind." "Their" should be singular—"his" or "her."

ape, go One who *goes ape* is one who gets wildly excited or enthusiastic over something or someone. It is slang.

aplomb *Aplomb,* meaning "poise, assurance, or self-confidence," was until fairly recently given only one pronunciation by the major dictionaries: uh-PLOM. However, more recent lexicons have acknowledged that the pronunciation uh-PLUM is at least as widely used and now grant it equal recognition. Say whichever comes more readily to your tongue.

apostrophe The apostrophe is the superscript sign (') used primarily to indicate possession (*John's* briefcase), the omission of a letter or letters from a word or phrase ("I'm" for "I am"), and, though less commonly of late, in the writing of numerals ("the fads of the 1960's"). However, amateur sign painters seem addicted to scattering apostrophes where they do not belong. A reader in Wisconsin reported that in one short Sunday drive he saw these signs: "Egg's for Sale," "Auto Repair's," "Fresh Strawberry's," and "The Smith's." These are, of course, sheer illiteracy. We wish we knew the cause and cure—but we don't (for "do not"). *See also* QUOTATION MARKS.

Appalachia *Appalachia,* strictly speaking, refers to a mountain range in the Eastern United States ranging from southern Quebec to northern Alabama. However, because parts of that region have become famous or infamous as pockets of poverty of the grimmest order, the term *Appalachia* has become almost synonymous with poverty-stricken backwoods mountainous areas.

appear. *See* LINKING VERBS

apple-pie order This informal, folksy expression is actually a borrowing from the French "nappe plié," meaning "folded table linen." The process of linguistic change which converted "nappe plié" into *apple-pie order* is known as folk etymology, the tendency to change unfamiliar words into more familiar combinations, as "demijohn" into "Jimmy John." *See also* FOLK ETYMOLOGY.

applicable With radio and television so much a part of our daily lives, questions of pronunciation (and mispronunciation) are frequently raised by our correspondents.

A case in point is that of the correct pronunciation of *applicable.* The question was: "Is it permissible to pronounce the word *applicable* with the accent on the 'lic,' so it sounds like uh-PLIK-uh-b'l?"

The answer is: "Yes, it is. Pronunciation with the stress on the first syllable is considerably more common, but uh-PLIK-uh-b'l is also accepted."

appraise/apprise/apprize Far too often, the word *appraise* is used when *apprise* is meant. A radio announcer reported that he would keep his listeners *appraised* of developments in a hotly contested election.

To *appraise* means "to set a price or value on (something)." To *apprise* means "to inform or notify (somebody) of something."

Apprize is simply a variant spelling of *apprise* and is seldom seen except in British publications.

appreciate *Appreciate* in the sense of "being sensitive to or understanding of" is well established in both speech and writing: "We *appreciate* the gravity of your situation." There is a feeling on the part of some careful writers that its use in less serious contexts is somewhat affected, bordering on Elegant English: "It is *appreciated* that you could not concern yourself with a matter of this trivial nature." *Appreciate* also has the standard business sense of increase in value or price: "The stock *appreciated* steadily in value over the years we held it," and is also very commonly used for "We are grateful for what you have done."

apt/likely/liable   When followed by an infinitive, *apt* and *likely* are considered by many to be interchangeable. This is true when used in the sense of "probable" or "tending toward": "*Apt* to fail/*likely* to fail."

However, *apt* has a further meaning: "to have an inherent inclination toward." (Note the related word "aptitude.") For example, "She is an *apt* pupil of languages."

Liable is still another matter. It is (in this sense) considered suitable only in informal contexts and, even then, used only in speaking of unpleasant possibilities. "You are *liable* to get hurt if you step out into traffic without looking." In formal use, *likely* would be preferable in this instance. *Liable* in careful usage appears in sentences like "You are *liable* to be arrested if you trespass." Strict legal phrasing would be "*liable* to arrest."

arbitrate/mediate/adjudicate   An important distinction should be observed between *arbitrate* and *mediate,* both terms much used in reports about labor negotiation. One who *arbitrates* hears evidence from all people concerned, then hands down a binding decision on the issues raised. One who *mediates* listens to arguments of both parties and tries by the exercise of reason and persuasion to bring them to an agreement. But he has no power to enforce a final judgment. One who *adjudicates* hears evidence and settles a dispute by judicial procedure.

arcane words   Among the *arcane words* which have surfaced and found their way back into fairly widespread use in recent decades is, appropriately enough, *arcane* itself. Back in the early 1950s we were chatting with old friends, a magazine editor and a college professor of English among them, when one noted that the word *arcane,* though known to all of us from its Latin root (*arcanum,* something closed or hidden), was not to be found in his "college" dictionary. A later check through our files showed that, though the word was entered in the unabridged dictionaries, it was absent from nearly all of the so-called desk dictionaries.

As a sort of automatic reflex, we wrote a column about this odd fact and later incorporated the story in a book about vocabulary enrichment. Since the latter sold many hundreds of thousands of copies, we may just possibly have played a role in restoring *arcane* to more widespread use.

But this case is far from unique. One of the oddest things about our language is the way words will flourish for a while, then seem to die— or, at least, to pass from general use—only to enjoy a sudden lively rebirth. During the past few decades, such long-established words as "ecumenical," "charisma," and, yes, *arcane* have enjoyed such revival.

They had all been resting in the limbo of the small type in unabridged dictionaries, but it took the research of scholars and then a sudden quirk of popular fancy to bring them back into vogue.

An even odder case is that of "couth." This word had appeared in our column in a list of "lost positives," along with "kempt," "sheveled," and others. When word play about "lost positives" became popular in the early 1950s, John Crosby, then writing a TV column for the lamented New York *Herald Tribune,* and Richard Maney, the legendary theatrical press agent, did much to popularize the quest for words like "sidious," "nocuous," "gruntled," and "ept." Our column did its bit in furthering the fad, though we were careful to note that "ept" was never really lost. It was simply spelled "apt."

Be that as it may, "couth" made such a comeback that the seventh edition of Webster's Collegiate soberly recorded it as a "backformation from uncouth." So far so good. But "couth" is really one of those *arcane* words restored to life, not at all a "backformation from uncouth." It appeared in Old English as "cuth," meaning known or familiar. In fact, the word—now spelled "couth"—was listed in the Fifth Edition of the Collegiate (1936) but labeled "obsolete." During the Middle Ages the negative form "uncouth" appeared, at first in the sense of "unfamiliar" or "unknown." Since people tend to fear the unknown and since much of the unknown bordered on the barbarous in those days, "uncouth" soon came to mean outlandish, repellent, and boorish—meanings it still has.

But, nit-picking aside, mark "couth" as a word restored to full and correct usage in such senses as "knowledgeable," "suave," "well-mannered," and "civilized." You'll probably find yourself using it primarily, as Crosby and Maney did, in humorous contexts. *See also* LOST POSITIVES.

aren't I?

USAGE PANEL QUESTION

The expression *aren't I?,* more common in England than in the United States, is used by some to avoid "ain't I?" Would you accept, in casual speech, "I'm afraid I'm late, *aren't I?*"
Yes: 54%. No: 46%.

ISAAC ASIMOV: "This is impossibly cute!"
W. H. AUDEN: "Yes, though I would avoid it myself."
SHERIDAN BAKER: "Both 'ain't I?' and 'aren't I?' are usually avoided in the upper Midwest by taking another tack, usually 'don't you think?'

Most people in these parts would simply come to a full stop after 'late.' "

ALVIN BEAM: "Yes. I sometimes use it myself, for variety."

SAUL BELLOW: "I stop at 'late.' "

ALTON BLAKESLEE: "Yes, but I would prefer 'am I not?' "

HAL BORLAND: " 'Aren't I?' sounds pretentious and stilted."

HEYWOOD HALE BROUN (voting "yes"): " 'Am I not?' sounds a little stuffy."

ANTHONY BURGESS: "Yes. This is normal British usage."

GEORGE CORNISH: "It doesn't travel well. Why not let the British keep it?"

ROBERT CRICHTON: "My father (NOTE: Kyle Crichton) always said: 'Never say the obvious.' This is a British nicety."

WALTER CRONKITE: "I accept 'aren't I?' reluctantly. It sounds strained and is frequently redundant."

PAUL HORGAN: "Yes—with a comic inflection."

JOHN K. HUTCHENS: "But why not simply say, 'Am I not?' "

WALTER KERR: "I don't expect to hear it much, but I'd accept it."

IRVING KOLODIN: " 'Aren't I?' sounds affected. I would favor, if anything, 'Am I not?' "

ROBERT LIPSYTE: "If your pinky sticks out that far, say, 'Am I not?' "

HENRY W. MALONE: "I'd accept 'Am I not?'—with mental reservations about the speaker!"

PHYLLIS MCGINLEY (voting "yes"): " 'Am I not?' is too prim for conversation."

ORVILLE PRESCOTT: "Yes, but only in casual speech. In writing it should be 'Am I not?' "

HARRISON SALISBURY: "No! This is too arch."

DAVID SCHOENBRUN: "The thing to say after 'I'm afraid I'm late' is 'Sorry.' Not 'Ain't I?' and God! not 'Aren't I?' How prissy!"

WALTER W. "RED" SMITH: "As for that Nice Nellie usage 'Aren't I?,' I'd rather commit adultery."

REX STOUT: "I'd accept 'Aren't I?'—but not with glee."

DAVIDSON TAYLOR: "This is simply not U.S. style."

LIONEL TRILLING: "Even in England, where I have heard it very seldom, it sounds whimsical or coy or arch, even rather girlish. In America it sounds hopelessly affected—a conscious Briticism."

argy-bargy British slang term for argument, especially one that degenerates into a squabble. The Supplement to the *Oxford English Dictionary* prefers *argle-bargle* and notes that it is of Scottish origin. However, both versions qualify for the classification of "ricochet words," treated at greater length in *Morris Dictionary of Word and Phrase Origins* by the editors of this dictionary. *See also* RICOCHET WORDS.

arise. *See* RISE/ARISE/GET UP

arm-twisting *Arm-twisting,* used both as noun and adjective, is informal for "applying pressure": "It took lots of presidential *arm-twisting* to get the revenue bill past the House."

aroma. *See* STINK

around. *See* ROUND/AROUND

arrive/depart *Arrive* and *depart* are two items from the semi-literate lingo of airline dispatchers. By elimination of the simple prepositions *at* and *from,* they have converted these verbs from intransitive to transitive. Now in their hybrid tongue planes no longer *depart from* La Guardia, they *depart* La Guardia. The planes subsequently do not *arrive at* O'Hare, they simply *arrive* O'Hare. Another lost cause.

arterial road England has until recently happily been spared the multilane freeways, thruways, and interstates which crisscross the American land-scape. Their main roads are much more modest than America's, though just as jam-packed at rush hours. The major highways are known as *arterial roads.*

arthritis *Arthritis* has only three syllables and has nothing to do with anyone named Arthur. It is pronounced ar-THRY-tis and *not* ar-thur-EYE-tis.

as. *See* EQUALLY AS

as . . . as/so . . . as When the sense of a sentence is positive, the preferred correlatives are *as . . . as:* "He is *as* tall *as* I." When the sense is negative, *so . . . as* is deemed preferable by traditional grammarians: "She is not *so* heavy *as* I." However, both forms are now considered acceptable in the negative and we find "She is not *as* heavy *as* I" entirely O.K., especially in informal contexts.

as/because *As* used in the sense of *because* may well be completely correct syntactically, yet possibly confusing to the reader. Here is a case in point, as reported by a column reader. "Although I can't point to a rule of grammar to explain why I object to the use of *as* in the following sentence, something about it sounds stuffy," she writes, "something I can't quite put my finger on: '*As* you were not entitled to benefits at that time, your claim was denied.' I would have said 'Your claim was denied because you were not entitled to benefits.' "

We pointed out that, while there is nothing wrong with the first sentence, the second is much more direct and effective. We noted further that confusion may arise because *as,* besides being used in the sense of *because,* may also be used in reference to events in time. For instance, the sentence "I did not hear the noise *as* I was reading" could be interpreted to mean "because I was reading" or "at the time I was reading." For this reason *because* seems less capable of misinterpretation.

as far as

USAGE PANEL QUESTION

Increasingly in recent years public figures speaking on radio or TV omit the concluding words of phrases beginning *as far as.* . . . For example, the Mayor of Portland, Oregon, speaking of the plight of homeless men and women in his city, said: "Many of them are irresponsible as far as their behavior and decorum." Most careful speakers would conclude with ". . . are concerned" or, simply, "go."

Do you regard such truncated statements as acceptable in speech? Yes: 10%. No: 90%.

In writing? Yes: 1.25%. No: 98.75%.

MICHAEL J. ARLEN: "Better still: '. . . irresponsible in their behavior and decorum.' "

ISAAC ASIMOV: "I would throw the Mayor of Portland as far as. . . ."

WHITNEY BALLIETT: "Simply another step toward the mass ellipsis that threatens to send us all back to cave speech."

SAUL BELLOW: "The mayor's 'carelessness' is unforgivable. But everybody's doing it, as far as. . . ."

ALTON BLAKESLEE: "Why not just say 'in' for 'as far as'? Much more economical."

HEYWOOD HALE BROUN: "What is acceptable from mayors is not necessarily acceptable from the educated part of the population."

BEN LUCIEN BURMAN: "The Mayor of Portland should go back to high school."

ROBERT CROMIE: "Bet the Mayor never drops that other shoe."

WILLARD R. ESPY: "Only those will accept this who are irresponsible as far as their grammar . . ."

ALEX FAULKNER: "A good rule in writing (if you are not an Anthony Burgess or a James Joyce) is to keep it as simple as you can."

RAY GANDOLF: "The incomplete 'as far as' is the most egregious misuse of the language today. It is dangerous. And it is epidemic. Preschool teachers and parents must whisper 'as far as (such and such) is concerned' into children's ears even as they sleep. The truncation must be stamped out. Users should be condemned to a life of coitus interruptus."

ROBERT GOTTLIEB: "Horrible, because clearly ungrammatical and ugly."

ELIZABETH HARDWICK: "The example quoted doesn't make sense. It isn't asking too much to complete the sentence and no special refinement is required to do so."

SYDNEY J. HARRIS: "Illiterate."

JOHN K. HUTCHENS: ". . . a form of mere laziness."

DIANE JOHNSON: "Horrors!"

WALTER KERR: "Terrible—meaningless."

JAMES J. KILPATRICK: "Absolutely unacceptable."

JULES LOH: "It's silly to use a period until you come to the end of the."

DWIGHT MACDONALD: "Sentence could easily read 'irresponsible in their behavior' and avoid both bad grammar and clumsy style."

EDWIN NEWMAN: "The mayor could have said 'irresponsible in behavior and decorum.' "

PETER S. PRESCOTT: "I find such a usage, or perhaps I should say non-usage, incredible. Another example of laziness nudging our language toward entropy."

LEO ROSTEN: "I would not write or say 'He is intelligent, as far as his brain' either."

BERTON ROUECHÉ: "Makes me think of 'graduate college.' "

VERMONT ROYSTER: "They are irresponsible *in* their behavior and decorum, as the mayor is in his use of language."

DAVID SCHOENBRUN: "It is part of the lazy speech and writing that is deplorable. It does not enhance or enrich communication, it obscures and impoverishes it."

JACK SMITH: "Why not say, 'as for Reagan . . .' instead of 'as far as Reagan is concerned'?"

ELVIS STAHR, JR.: "It's sloppy; it almost reduces the sentence to gibberish. Why not just 'in' or 'with respect to' instead of 'as far as'?"

KARL V. TEETER: "Semi-literate speech."

EDWARD TRIPP: "This habit seems to me to result from (1) confusion with 'as far as . . . go' or just 'as for . . . ,' which means ignorance of the fact that such phrases are not mere formulas but have a precise grammatical structure and meaning, or (2) sheer laziness, or more likely (3) both."

JOSEPH VERGARA: "Clumsy—says nothing that 'in' alone doesn't."

GEORGE WALD: "Like 'you're entitled!'—a wry, sometimes ironic New Yorkism."

DOUGLAS WATT: "Keep it in Portland."

A.B.C. WHIPPLE: "If he wants brevity, he need only say 'As for. . . .' "

CHARLOTTE ZOLOTOW: "Leaves an unfinished feeling in the mind."

as follows

We are all familiar with *as follows* in constructions where it is preceded by both singular and plural constructions ("His answer is *as follows*" and "The contestants were listed *as follows*"). However, some speakers use *as follow* when a plural noun precedes ("The winners of the lottery are *as follow* . . ."). Do you approve *as follow* when a plural noun is involved?

Yes: 13%. No: 87%.

ISAAC ASIMOV: "This may be correct in theory, but it sounds funny."

SHERIDAN BAKER: "No. I delete the whole thing whenever I can, just putting a colon after 'are.' "

STEWART BEACH: "No. I suspect the sociologists have been at work here again in their silly way."

ALTON BLAKESLEE: "No. It is a listing (singular) that follows."

HAL BORLAND: "Why not say, 'The names of the winners are . . .'? The 'as follows' is one of the excess-word tribe that are a damned nuisance. This brings up a whole list of words and phrases that are no more than space fillers and time killers. They include 'by means of,' 'in order to,' 'for the purpose of,' 'in the nature of,' 'in the case of ' (except in a court of law), and so on. They are inconclusive generalities that merely delay a clear, concrete statement. Still another is 'make use of ' for 'use.' "

HEYWOOD HALE BROUN: "No. I'm a purist but not a puritan."

ANTHONY BURGESS: " 'As follows' refers to a phrase, a list, a single entity. The plural would be wrong."

JOHN K. HUTCHENS: "Yes. It does make sense, though I wouldn't swear I use it."

LAURENCE LAFORE: "No. Of course not. This arises from a misunderstanding of syntax."

DWIGHT MACDONALD: "Isn't this just wrong? Who ever wrote or said 'as follow'?"

ORVILLE PRESCOTT: "No. It's unnecessary. 'The winners were . . .' is sufficient."

LEO ROSTEN: "No! The total group (therefore singular) follows."

BERTON ROUECHÉ: "No. This sounds prissy to me."

VERMONT ROYSTER: "No. It just sounds awkward to my ear."

WALTER W. "RED" SMITH: " 'As follow' is Nellie usage and probably incorrect. To me the construction means 'as in the list which follows.' "

as good or better than This common error can be very easily corrected: simply insert a second *as* before the "or." "My piano playing is *as good as or better than* his."

Asian/Asiatic flu When a new form of influenza first swept this country, it was called *Asiatic flu*. Then it was pointed out that Asians prefer to be called that—*Asians*—rather than *Asiatics,* a term which many regard as derogatory. So the official medical terminology was changed to *Asian flu.*

as if/as though *As if* and *as though* are interchangeable. However, opinion is divided on whether to use the subjunctive or indicative form of the verb in the clause which follows.

A news story included the sentence: "The place was being operated much the same *as if* it *was* a private country club." The preference in formal usage would be "*as if* it *were* a private club." However, in informal usage, the indicative ("was") is entirely acceptable.

as is/as are Used most frequently in connection with the sale of goods, *as is* is the generally accepted idiom for "to be sold in damaged condition —let the buyer beware." Since it is used adjectively or adverbially, it does not vary in form. Goods are always *as is,* never *as are,* whether a single item or many items are involved.

asphalt The proper pronunciation of asphalt is ASS-folt. The pronunciation ASH-folt is admissible only in jest.

assassin/murderer Anyone who unlawfully, maliciously, or with premeditation takes the life of a fellow human being is a *murderer.*

An *assassin* is politically motivated in his deed and his victim is a public official or otherwise prominent person. Thus Lee Harvey Oswald was not merely the *murderer* of John F. Kennedy, he was his *assassin.*

The first *assassins,* incidentally, were members of a Muslim sect who, fired up with the drug hashish, set upon the Crusaders and killed them.

assassination, date of If a public figure is shot one day and dies the next, was he *assassinated* on the day he was shot, the day he died, or during both days? That's an intriguing question and one of concern to newspaper editors and historians. The answer, judging by most authoritative sources checked, is that he is *assassinated* on the day he is attacked, even though death may occur days or weeks later. A case in point is President James A. Garfield, who was assassinated on July 2, 1881, but did not die until September 19, 1881.

assault and battery The expression *assault and battery* is often reported in the press as part of a single charge against an offender, so that many readers think of it as a single crime. However, *assault* in the legal sense is an act that leads a person to think he is in imminent danger of attack. *Battery* is the actual attack. One can take place without the other. For instance, a person can aim a loaded gun at another, thus being guilty of *assault,* without firing it, and thus remaining innocent of *battery.*

assistant or shop assistant   This is standard British for a worker in a retail shop, the sort of person that in America would be called a "clerk." In Great Britain "clerk" (pronounced KLARK) is usually used to refer to an office worker, rather than one working in a store.

associate   Preferred pronunciations for *associate* are uh-SOH-shee-ate for the verb and uh-SOH-shee-it for the noun and adjective. However, uh-SOH-see-ate and uh-SOH-see-it are also widely· heard in the speech of careful users of the language. So feel free to use whichever comes more naturally to your tongue.

assume. *See* PRESUME/ASSUME

assurance. *See* INSURANCE/ASSURANCE

asterisk   The *asterisk* (*) is used in typed and printed matter to indicate that a footnoted item will add information, such as source material, of value to the reader. Formerly it was commonly used to indicate material, such as profanity or obscenity, omitted. Nowadays the ellipsis (. . .) or dash as in "f——" performs this function, although more and more often the hitherto taboo material is simply printed in full.

as though. *See* AS IF/AS THOUGH

astonish. *See* SURPRISE/ASTONISH

as to whether   This formulation occurs frequently in the speech and writing of those who will never use a single word where three can be found. Example: "There is some question *as to whether* the bill will pass." The *as to* can simply be deleted. *Whether* says it all.

astronaut   *Astronaut* has been in the learned lexicons since 1956, when it was entered in the *Air Force Dictionary.* Although no one has laid claim to its invention, it is a perfectly logical blend of "astron," Greek for "star," and "nautes," a sailor.

at   The unnecessary addition of the word *at* in a question such as "Where is it *at*?" is a redundancy common in folk and dialect speech. Harold Wentworth, in his *American Dialect Dictionary,* lists dozens of such examples, with such labels as "painfully common" or "usually dialect, sometimes deliberately jocose or humorous."

at first blush. *See* FIRST BLUSH, AT

atheist. *See* AGNOSTIC/ATHEIST

athlete/athletics *Athlete* should be pronounced ATH-leet, not ATH-uh-leet. Similarly, it should be ath-LET-ix, not ath-uh-LET-ix.

at long last On the face of it, this idiom does not make much sense. *At last* by itself means "finally" or "at the end," so how can "long" add to the sense of finality?

It does, however, add the sense that a period of long duration has been endured before the hoped-for or anticipated conclusion has been reached. When a nation's leader says, *"At long last,* victory is ours," the implication of a protracted struggle is much stronger than if he said merely, *"At last* victory is ours."

at that point in time During the early 1970s when a special committee of the U.S. Senate (known as the "Watergate Committee") held public and televised hearings of its investigation into certain political activities of the time, the phrase *at that point in time,* used by numerous witnesses before the committee, became an instant cliché. Although used in seriousness by those testifying, it was mocked by the public. *See also* WATERGATE LANGUAGE.

attorney/attorney at law The former is a term that includes all kinds of lawyers. The latter specifically refers to a lawyer who is qualified to represent his clients in a court of law.

attorney general The correct form of the plural is *attorneys general,* and because lawyers are involved, the propriety is generally observed in all legal papers. However, there has been a marked tendency on the part of the press to make it *attorney generals.*

attributive nouns and adjectives A noun modifying another noun ("sports arena") is referred to as a *noun* used *attributively.* In like fashion an adjective standing next to the noun it modifies ("handsome man" or "gifts galore") is called an *attributive adjective.* This is in contrast to the predicate adjective, separated from the noun it modifies by a copulative, or linking, verb ("The man is bad").

aud *Aud* (NOT audit) is a word from the strange jabberwocky of educational journals that we simply wouldn't believe if we hadn't seen it in a Ripon,

Wisconsin, high-school newsletter. The message, from teachers to parents, ran like this: "We hope you will note improvement in your child's auding at home." We suspect that *auding* is supposed to mean "listening with attention and comprehension" but, not being privy to the inner workings of the minds that create the curious half-language known as "educationese," we can only speculate.

audience/spectators/congregation An *audience* is made up of those who come to hear; *spectators* are those who come to watch; and a *congregation* is made up of those who have come to worship together. Of course, an *audience* may also watch a performance but the main purpose is to hear words or music.

aunt *Aunt* is commonly pronounced AHNT by speakers in the Eastern United States, especially in New England. Elsewhere ANT is the standard pronunciation.

au pair girl This is a borrowing from French via English and one still little heard in America. It refers to a young woman, usually of foreign birth, who trades her services as baby-sitter or housekeeper in return for food, lodging, and, occasionally, a modest fee. It should be considered standard English and, in time, may become standard American, as well.

author (as a verb)

USAGE PANEL QUESTION

The conversion of nouns to verbs is a form of linguistic change as old as the language itself. Such changes often meet resistance from careful users of the language, especially if they seem to duplicate an established verb. One recent instance of such noun-to-verb conversion is found in the word *author*. Would you accept "He *authored* three books in a single year"?
In writing   Yes: 10%. No: 90%.
In casual speech   Yes: 22%. No: 78%.

The Usage Panelists overwhelmingly disapprove the use of *author* in place of the long-established "write" both in writing and in speech. Here are typical comments.

MICHAEL J. ARLEN (voting "yes" in both categories): "Why not? You say 'He homered' instead of 'He hit a home run.' 'Author' is clear and strong."

ISAAC ASIMOV (voting "no" to both queries): " 'Wrote' is one syllable less."

JOHN O. BARBOUR: "I guess if you can father three sons and mother them as well, you can *author* a book once in a while."

STEWART BEACH: "Without meaning to freeze the language, I dislike this sort of noun-to-verb switch. It isn't the least necessary and I can only regard it as cute."

SAUL BELLOW: "No, nor the word 'crafted.' Abominable!"

HAL BORLAND: "This is downright stupid because it is far better to say, 'He wrote three books.' You wouldn't say, 'He poeted three poems.' "

JOHN BROOKS: "Phony elegance. Why not 'He wrote'?"

HEYWOOD HALE BROUN: "Why even consider it when 'wrote' is available?"

ANTHONY BURGESS: "No. Otiose here. It adds no new nuance to the ordinary 'wrote' verb."

WALTER CRONKITE: "Nouns into verbs are not necessarily bad but this is unnecessary."

SYDNEY J. HARRIS: "It fills no real need."

WAKEMAN HARTLEY: "I intensely dislike this sort of butchering."

PAUL HORGAN: "This is falsely economical journalese."

JOHN K. HUTCHENS: "This is a fake verb. Why not say, 'He wrote'?"

WALTER KERR: "There's a simpler word available—and 'author' sounds terrible."

IRVING KOLODIN: "Like most innovations, this is a slipshod substitute for approved usage."

CHARLES KURALT: "Emphatically not. I have lately seen 'The bride was gifted with a silver service' and even 'The new missile obsoletes its predecessor.' This is an infuriating misuse by an ignoramus who thinks 'authoring' three books is somehow a grander achievement than writing them. It ain't."

ORVILLE PRESCOTT: "This is an abomination."

PETER S. PRESCOTT: "No, because it serves no useful purpose, weakening rather than strengthening the language. Why not 'He surgeoned four patients today'?"

RICHARD H. ROVERE: "Books are written, not authored."

HARRISON SALISBURY: "This is the worst of usages, though just yesterday I saw 'surveill' as a verb. Ye gods!"

LEONARD SANDERS: "The fact that he wrote three books in a year does not necessarily mean that he 'authored' three books in a year, unless he has a speedy publisher."

DAVID SCHOENBRUN (voting "yes" to *author* in casual speech): "I would accept it without cringing but I would not use it."

WALTER W. "RED" SMITH: "No, unless we add 'and I readered all three.' "

FRANK SULLIVAN: "Why use 'author' when there's a perfectly good word— 'write'?"

EARL UBELL: " 'Author' offends the ear."

automatic. *See* PISTOL/AUTOMATIC/REVOLVER

avenge/revenge   *Avenge* differs from *revenge* in that the person *avenging* a wrong is usually not the person wronged: "Hamlet sought to *avenge* his father's murder." By contrast the person seeking *revenge* is usually the person wronged: "The broker sought to *revenge* himself by sending the embezzler to jail."

averse/adverse   The extra consonant ("d") in the second of these words marks the distinction between their meanings. Both words express opposition. *Averse* is applied to a person who is opposed to something, usually on a personal basis. "She is *averse* to shopping in the city because she dislikes crowds." *Adverse* applies to that which is in opposition to or working against a person or program, as "*adverse* circumstances," "*adverse* criticism," or "*adverse* comments."

   The usual formulation as far as the accompanying preposition is concerned is *averse to* and *adverse to,* although *averse from* is occasionally found.

avert/avoid   These verbs differ basically in that *avert* means to ward off or to turn away: "*avert* the tragedy" or "*avert* one's eyes," while *avoid* simply means to keep clear of something, to shun it completely: "*avoid* the chance of danger by staying indoors."

awesome

USAGE PANEL QUESTION

Awesome is defined as "inspiring awe," which is "an emotion of mingled reverence, dread and wonder, inspired by something majestic or sublime." At the present time *awesome* is enjoying considerable favor among radio and TV commentators or their ghostwriters. For example: "Gossage's fast ball has been good this season but it hasn't been awesome."
Would you approve this extension of meaning in speech?
Yes: 46%. No: 54%.
In writing?   Yes: 44%. No: 56%.

ISAAC ASIMOV: "It has a certain humorous quality I don't object to."
BARRY BINGHAM, SR.: "This is just another dilution of a strong, expressive word."
JOHN BROOKS: "Well, I wouldn't write it."
ANTHONY BURGESS: "Let's avoid inflation."

BEN LUCIEN BURMAN: " 'Awesome' here is loathsome."

JOHN CIARDI: "It is a weakened sense extension. Such extensions are a farce."

ROBERT CROMIE: "Reverence, dread and wonder seem the perfect reaction to Mr. Gossage's fast ball."

WILLARD R. ESPY: "The trivialization of language is unforgivable. Within weeks after the mass suicides at Jonestown, political reporters in this country were using 'Jonestowned' to describe the defeat of one candidate for office. This sort of thing gives me an awesome headache."

FRANCES FRITCHMAN: " 'Overwhelming' is what they are trying to say."

RAY GANDOLF: "I approve the extension of the meaning but deplore its over-usage. Gossage, however, *is* awesome."

PAUL HORGAN: "Fancy nonsense."

JOHN K. HUTCHENS: "No, its original definition should stand as it is, too majestic for a pitcher's fast ball."

ELIZABETH JANEWAY: "But then, I don't awe easily. It seems merely a colorful usage and if it reduces the general tendency to fall into fits of awe, so much the better."

WALTER KERR: "Forced."

JAMES J. KILPATRICK: "I see nothing wrong with using 'awesome' to describe Gossage's fast ball. The meaning is exact: inspiring mingled reverence, dread, and wonder. Ask any batter who ever faced him."

STANLEY KUNITZ: "Lucid and cogent usage, a natural extension of meaning."

ROBERT LIPSYTE: "When it's right, Gossage's fast ball *does* inspire reverence, dread, etc., especially by those trying to hit it."

JULES LOH: "But only when the hyperbole is intended and obvious."

WADE MOSBY: "This has become a cliché of awesome proportions."

WILLIAM McGUIRE: "What must have started as an attempt at vivid writing has become plain silly."

EDWIN NEWMAN: "This word is being grossly misused and cheapened."

MARGE PIERCY: "We lost 'awful' so then we needed 'awesome.' We're running out of ways to say 'causing awe.' "

ORVILLE PRESCOTT: "Permissible because one of the three words, 'wonder,' applies and one is enough."

PETER S. PRESCOTT: "I don't see it as an *extension* of its meaning. Gossage's fast ball can be awesome."

LEO ROSTEN: "The usage can no longer be stopped. 'Awesome' is more economic than 'awe-inspiring.' "

VERMONT ROYSTER: "Gossage's fast ball may inspire dread and wonder in a batter but hardly reverence."

HAROLD SCHONBERG: "Another modish word. Kids use it all the time."

JACK SMITH: "Just another instance of trivializing a good word."

ELVIS STAHR, JR.: "Extension!!?? Why, Gossage's 1980 fast balls fit the definition to a tee! However, far too often these days 'awesome' is misused by people trying to puff up the importance of something."

KARL V. TEETER: "Already established."

EDWARD TRIPP: "Isn't this just hyperbole? Should one also try to rehabilitate 'awful,' which means the same thing?"

JOSEPH VERGARA: "Overblown and overused."

JUDITH VIORST: "Who is to say that an awesome fast ball isn't majestic or sublime?"

GEORGE WALD: "Once in a great while as hyperbole."

A.B.C. WHIPPLE: "I also don't approve of the rest of their exaggerations."

WILLIAM ZINSSER: "Very big with college kids."

awful As noted in the entry *awfully good,* the primary meaning of *awful* is "inspiring awe or reverence." However, it has long had an informal sense of bad, unpleasant, dreadful, and—to use another word that has strayed from its original meaning—*terrible* (which see).

awfully good The first meaning of "awful" is not "bad" or "ugly," as most people seem to think. It is "inspiring awe or reverence." Thought of this way, the expression *awfully good* is not at all inconsistent. However, it has come to be accepted as an informal expression simply meaning "very good" or "extremely good."

awhile/a while Some copyeditors, and writers, especially those afflicted with an incurable tendency to fuse words whenever possible, routinely "correct" *a while* in phrases like "*a while* ago" to "*awhile* ago." *Awhile* as an adverb is properly written solid in expressions clearly adverbial, such as "linger *awhile.*" However, in the example first noted, we regard *while* as a noun and insist that it keep its distance from the article *a.* The proper analogy would be to expressions like "an hour ago" or "a month ago."

ax *Ax* is musicians' slang for any musical instrument, even the piano or organ, especially when employed in jazz or rock contexts.

ax/axe *Ax* is the preferred American spelling but it is, as the Supplement to the *Oxford English Dictionary* states, "now disused in England" where the preferred spelling is *axe.*

ax (axe) to grind A person with an *ax (axe) to grind* is one pursuing a selfish course, acting solely out of self-interest. The expression has been so long used and abused that it has assumed the status of cliché and is best avoided. *See also* CLICHÉ.

B

bachelor A *bachelor* is any unmarried man, whether divorced or never married. Concern has been voiced, especially by members of the Women's Movement, that here, as in other areas of the language, the scales seem tilted in favor of the male. A woman who has been married and divorced is labeled a "divorcee," while a man under similar circumstances is a *bachelor* and enjoys all the prerogatives that carefree label carries with it. There is, of course, the masculine form "divorcé" (pronounced the same as the feminine div-or-SAY) but we have never seen it used in print because of the obvious likelihood of confusion with the other "divorce" (pronounced dih-VORSS). The whole matter may become academic, since there seems a marked trend to label any unmarried person of either sex a "single."

back-formations *Back-formation* is a linguistic term describing the creation of a new word by the deletion of a prefix or suffix so that the resulting word appears to be the word from which the longer word was derived. Thus "enthuse" is actually a *back-formation* from "enthusiasm," though a glance at the two words might lead an uninformed person to deduce precisely the opposite—that "enthusiasm" had been formed from "enthuse." Other common *back-formations* include the verbs "buttle" from "butler," "laze" from "lazy," and, one that still distresses many careful users of language, "burgle" from "burglar."

backgrounder A *backgrounder* is newspaperman's slang for a press conference in which a government official releases data of interest to the press but without any official attribution to the spokesman giving the data.

backlash *Backlash* is informal for "reaction," especially reaction of a violent order: "The anti-busing *backlash* was much greater than had been expected."

bad/badly It sometimes seems as if the vast majority of Americans simply cannot believe that a verb can be modified by anything other than an adverb ending in "-ly." But there is a distinction between "feeling *bad*" and "feeling *badly*."

One frequently voiced opinion runs like this: If you want to say that you are unhappy about something or that your health is impaired, say, "I feel *bad*." "Feel" in this use is what grammarians call a "linking verb" and takes a predicate adjective. However, if you mean to say that you have lost your sense of touch, go ahead and say, "I feel *badly.*" As Clifton Fadiman once observed: "Don't feel bad when you hear the broadcaster say he feels badly. Just remember that all men are created equally."

USAGE PANEL QUESTION

When referring to your mental or physical state, do you say, "I feel *bad*"?
Yes: 77%. No: 23%.
"I feel *badly*"? Yes: 26%. No: 74%.

The clear majority of panelists agrees with the position given in the usage note preceding the panel question. However, as always, there were pithy comments from panelists on both sides of the issue. Here are some typical comments.

CLEVELAND AMORY (rejecting "feel *badly*"): "And I feel terrible when someone else says it!"

ISAAC ASIMOV: " 'Feeling badly' is the mark of an inept dirty old man."

STEWART BEACH: "I avoid both. I would simply say, 'I don't feel well.' "

BEN LUCIEN BURMAN: "Sometimes I use one, sometimes the other. When I feel really terrible, I say 'bad.' "

ROBERT CRICHTON: "I say 'feel bad.' You don't feel 'goodly,' do you?"

ROBERT CROMIE: "I avoid the issue by saying, 'I feel lousy.' "

ALEX FAULKNER: " 'Badly' in this use seems a bit pedantic, but I would say, 'I feel badly about letting you down.' "

GEROLD FRANK: "Both sound awkward to me. I'd say, 'I don't feel well.' "

WAKEMAN HARTLEY: "My sense of touch is good—so I don't 'feel badly.' "

ELIZABETH JANEWAY: "I generally say, 'I feel like death, awful, etc.' But 'bad' is the answer to the question."

WALT KELLY: "I say 'I don't feel good.' "

CLARK KINNAIRD (voting "no" to both): "I particularize the symptoms. That's much more impressive."

DWIGHT MACDONALD (voting "yes" to *badly*): "But what I really say is 'I feel terrible' (or 'lousy')."

DAVID MCCORD (voting "no" to *badly*): "Yet 'I feel poorly' *does* distinguish between health and poverty."

JESSICA MITFORD: "No to both. I should say 'I feel ill' or 'depressed.' "

DANIEL PATRICK MOYNIHAN: "I distinguish. Some situations seem to call for 'bad,' others for 'badly.' "

BERTON ROUECHÉ: " 'Feel badly' is a dainty-ism used by people who think 'bad' is too blunt and crude."

DAVID SCHOENBRUN: "I use 'I feel bad' to express a physical condition, but 'I feel badly' to express an emotional response."

WALTER W. "RED" SMITH: "If my tactile sense were so blunted that I felt badly, I'd feel po'ly about it."

ELVIS STAHR, JR.: " 'I feel badly' is godawful because it signifies an effort to be elegant by one obviously ignorant."

FRANK SULLIVAN: "I'm sure I'd really say, 'I feel lousy.' "

BARBARA TUCHMAN: "Neither. I'd say, 'I don't feel well' or 'I feel awful'— which in principle, I suppose, is the same as 'I feel bad.' "

badly in need of *Badly,* in the sense of "very much" (*"badly in need of* sleep") has been criticized by some grammarians as substandard. However, the Usage Panelists overwhelmingly voted to accept it as standard American. Herewith the question put to the panel, with percentages of their replies and typical comments.

USAGE PANEL QUESTION

Leaving political considerations to one side, would you approve of this use of *badly* in a recent newspaper story: "The Democratic party is *badly* in need of new leadership"?

Yes: 77%. No: 23%.

HAL BORLAND: "No. Not unless you can also say 'The Republicans are goodly in luck.' "

HEYWOOD HALE BROUN: "Yes. It has the virtue of clarity."

STEPHEN H. FRITCHMAN: "No. I prefer 'greatly' or 'much.' These have no moral overtones and more elegance."

ORVILLE PRESCOTT: " 'Badly' has long been used in the sense of acutely. It is unobjectionable."

LIONEL TRILLING: "Why not, since this is an established idiom."

badmouth *Badmouth,* meaning "to speak ill of or to disparage [a person or thing]," is a fairly recent borrowing into general slang from regional and black dialect. James Thurber used it in a short story as long ago as 1941 and E. B. White, thirty years later, wrote: "Geese are friends with no-one. They *badmouth* everyone and everything." Despite this evidence of the use of *badmouth* by writers of rare taste and talent, it should be treated warily and used only in appropriate contexts.

Bad show! British slang for "Tough luck!" or "Sorry you didn't do better!"

bag Slang for an old or unattractive woman: "The old *bag* went on and on about the high prices." Formerly also slang for a prostitute. Also Australian slang for a hobo or tramp who carried his belongings in a bag; a swagman.

bag   *Bag* in the sense of special interest, enthusiasm, or hobby ("Finding new words is my *bag*") is a relatively recent addition to popular slang. Originating in the argot of black musicians, it remains inappropriate in formal contexts.

bag/sack/poke   *Bag* is the generic term for all sorts of containers from suitcases to plastic refrigerator "Baggies," but in many parts of the country you will find the regional term *sack* used for a paper *bag*. At the same time, *sack* is used universally to mean a burlap *bag* or a gunny *sack*.

   Another item of regional dialect now seldom heard is *poke* for a small *bag* whether made of cloth or paper. In Gold Rush times, a miner's stake was always kept in his *poke*, which is why Robert Service once wrote: "the woman who kissed him and pinched his poke was the lady that's known as Lou."

bagman   In American slang, a *bagman* is a person who collects the bribes or "pay-offs" for illicit operations. *Bagman* in standard British English is simply a traveling (or, as the British would put it, "travelling") salesman.

bags   British term for men's slacks, especially those of the 1920s vintage, known in America as the "Harold Teen pants" (after a comic strip character of the time) which featured very wide bottoms of the trouser legs.

baker-legged/baker-kneed   British slang for "knock-kneed."

bakery   The use of the word *bakery* to refer to baked goods is fairly widely heard in dialect and folk speech, particularly among people of German descent. This use of *bakery* is substandard. *Bakery* should be used only in two senses: a place where food items such as bread, cakes, and pastry are baked or a store which sells such items.

balance   *Balance*, in the sense of "remainder" or "rest" ("the *balance* of the season remains to be played") is frowned on by some careful speakers and writers, who would restrict *balance* to the bookkeeping sense of the difference between credit and debit sides of an account. However, this extended sense of *balance* is certainly acceptable in all informal contexts.

balance, on. *See* VOGUE WORDS

balance was/were *Balance* as a collective noun poses a special problem in this sentence from a newspaper account of the closing of an army camp: "Since the closing order, 350 trainees have been graduated, 130 withdrew, and the *balance* was sent to other centers." The rule governing collectives in such cases is this: if the collective noun refers to a group as a whole or as a unit, it takes a singular verb; if it refers to the individuals of the group, it takes a plural verb. Since the *balance* in this instance did not go as a unit to a single center, but were sent to "other centers," the plural "were" should have been used.

balding

USAGE PANEL QUESTION

"Balding" was one of the early coinages of *Time* magazine editors, along with "tycoon" and "socialite." Unlike most *Time*style inventions which have already dropped into obscurity, *balding* seems to many writers to serve a useful purpose, though others object to it on the ground that it is a hybrid blend of adjective ("bald") and participial ending ("-ing"). Would you approve "His *balding* head was sprinkled with gray hairs"?

In writing Yes: 71%. No: 29%.
In speech Yes: 69%. No: 31%.

Although a clear majority of panelists approve *balding* both in writing and in speech, a slightly larger percentage approves it in writing than in speech, a surprising finding in that patterns of speech are usually more casual than those of writing. Here are the comments of some of the panelists.

SHANA ALEXANDER: " 'Balding' is useful because I know no other word which means half-hairy."
ISAAC ASIMOV: "Yes. I can't think of a decent substitute, so why not?"
W. H. AUDEN: "No, but in certain contexts 'balding' seems to me possible."
SHERIDAN BAKER: "Yes. An accurate word for an acute phenomenon."
STEWART BEACH: "Though I never expect to use the word, I see no objection. It describes a condition clearly not covered by any other word. There is a precedent in 'graying' which has full acceptance."
HAL BORLAND: "Yes. I would also say, 'His graying head is turning bald.' "
JOSEPH A. BRANDT: "Why not? We are an inventive people and our language can afford being hirsute rather than bald—but not to the point of being obscure."

HEYWOOD HALE BROUN. "No. In your sentence 'bald' would seem more accurate."

ANTHONY BURGESS (voting "no" to *balding* in writing, "yes" to it in casual speech): "It always carries a *Time* flavor. I wrote in *Enderby:* '. . . desperately balding, as if to get into *Time* magazine.' This is the only way it can be used in writing."

JAMES MACGREGOR BURNS: "Yes. 'Thinning hair' is more descriptive, though."

ABE BURROWS: "*Time* once called me 'balding.' They said I should be pleased they did. If they didn't like me, they said, they would call me 'egg bald.' My hair is past the participle."

GEORGE CORNISH: "Surely no one uses 'balding' except as a joke at the expense of *Time* style."

ROBERT CRICHTON: "The 'balding' works. It's the 'sprinkled' that bothers me."

THOMAS FLEMING: "Yes. It's part of the language now."

RICHARD EDES HARRISON: "If 'graying' is acceptable, why not 'balding'?"

PAUL HORGAN: "No. I would prefer even 'baldening.' "

JOHN K. HUTCHENS: "In writing, yes, because it has a certain precision. In casual speech, no—because it's not at all 'casual' then."

ALEXANDER KENDRICK: "Despite the mixed parentage, I can see no objection since it does fill a need."

STANLEY KUNITZ: "Yes. A useful neologism. What can we say in its place?"

CHARLES KURALT: "I don't have much hair but I'm not quite bald, either. Seems to me *Time* invented a useful word here, not just a cute one."

EDWIN NEWMAN (voting "yes" to *balding* in writing, "no" in speech): "Though it is affected writing, where used."

ORVILLE PRESCOTT: "Yes, because it has acquired the meaning of becoming bald but not yet bald."

PETER S. PRESCOTT: "Yes. Since the only other way to say it involves many more words, it is a useful addition to the language."

BERTON ROUECHÉ: "Yes. There is no other word to describe a balding head."

VERMONT ROYSTER: "Yes. A useful coinage for balding, graying writers!"

DAVID SCHOENBRUN: "I object most to the use of 'sprinkled' in this barbarous sentence. No real objections to 'balding.' It's a useful descriptive, not otherwise available."

HAROLD SCHONBERG: "Yes. One of the few useful *Time* coinages. What's the alternative? 'His beginning-to-get-bald head'?"

MARK SCHORER: "No. I dislike 'balding' but 'sprinkled' is just as bad, though for different reasons."

HOWARD TAUBMAN: "Yes. It grates on my ear but it does offer a useful distinction between 'bald' and the sad process of becoming."

LIONEL TRILLING: "Although I would probably not use it, it seems a reasonable and useful word."

CHARLES L. WHIPPLE: "Yes. A needed word to show growth or its lack."

ball game, whole new A *whole new ball game,* meaning a complete revision of an existing situation, became an instant cliché during the 1960s: "After Kissinger arrived in the Middle East, it was a *whole new ball game.* "

ball's in your court, the Slang expression meaning "It's your move now" or "Now the problem is for you to solve."

bandwagon, climb on the *Climbing on the bandwagon* is a well-established item in the language of American politics. The original bandwagons were wagons large enough to hold a band of musicians and be drawn through the streets of a town to gain publicity for a coming event, such as a political rally. Candidates for office would ride the bandwagon and those who wished to show their support for the candidate would *climb on the bandwagon.* Often there was a desire for personal benefit behind such public expression of support. The one who *climbed on the bandwagon* hoped that his action would mean that the candidate, if elected, would be in his debt. Today the phrase is used almost exclusively in the figurative sense, and not always in the context of politics.

banger The British *banger* is a culinary delight, quite unlike any so-called sausage to be found in America. A staple of pubs, it may be served hot or cold, and a brace of *bangers* with a pint of bitter makes a delightful light lunch. The *OED Supplement* labels *banger* slang and another source claims that the *banger* got its name from a slight explosive sound it makes when being fried. This may well be, though we must confess never to have heard the sound despite many watchful moments spent inspecting *bangers* in preparation at our favorite pubs.

bank holiday These are the most important legal holidays on the British calendar, excepting Christmas, Boxing Day, and New Year's, of course. Unlike so-called legal holidays in the United States, which may be celebrated on the anniversary of the date commemorated or on the nearest Monday, depending on the state one is in, Britain's *bank holidays* fall on schedule (pronounced SHED-yool, of course) and are inflexible. What's more, everything of a business nature—short of essential services—closes down and there is no nonsense like the American Washington's Birthday sales and the like. At this writing there are five *bank holidays* in Britain and the visitor from foreign lands is well advised to know about them in advance and plan accordingly.

bant/banting These are British terms for the international practice of dieting. *Banting* got its name from a nineteenth-century London cabinetmaker named William Banting, who popularized a method of "reducing corpulence," as he put it, by restricting the intake of fat-producing foods, sugar, starches, and the like. The verb to *bant,* which the original *OED* labeled "humorous" but now is standard English, is a back-formation from *banting*, which some people, apparently unaware of Mr. Banting's existence, thought was the present participle of a verb to *bant.*

barbiturate   The name of this category of sedative drugs was originally pronounced bar-bih-TYOOR-it or bar-bih-TYOOR-ate when the drugs were first introduced in the early part of this century. However, just as the pronunciation of "penicillin" changed from the original pen-ISS-ih-lin to pen-ih-SIL-in, so the accent in *barbiturate* gradually shifted in popular use. Now the pronunciations bar-BICH-oor-it and bar-BICH-oor-ate are most commonly heard, though the earlier pronunciation is still favored by many members of the medical profession.

barge pole   The *barge pole* is the device with which the British will not touch the same stuff Americans will not touch with a "ten-foot pole."

barman   *Barman* is standard British for the man most Americans call bartender. However, the owner or manager of the public house in which the *barman* plies his trade is usually known as the "publican," though he may put in time behind the bar as *barman.* More often than not, though, especially in urban areas, the person behind the bar will be that uniquely British creation known as the "barmaid."

barrister/solicitor   *Barrister* is the British term for an attorney who specializes in trial law, pleading in the superior courts. The attorney retained by the client is a *solicitor,* who pleads in the lower courts and retains the *barrister* for court appearances in the higher courts. Somewhat the same relationship obtains in the U.S., where attorneys represent clients in business matters but a counselor or a trial lawyer represents the client in court. It should be noted, however, that the distinction is by no means as clear-cut in the U.S. as in England and that attorneys do often make courtroom appearances for their clients, especially in matters of modest importance.

basal/basic   One curious item of educationese during the 1960s was the substitution of *basal* for *basic,* apparently on the assumption that it sounded more impressive. We learned of this when a young correspondent in, of all places, Broken Bow, Nebraska, wrote us: "Today our senior English class was picking out basal parts in sentences and came across this sentence: 'Everybody was once interested in mining.' We had quite a discussion over whether 'interested' was part of the verb or whether it was a subjective complement." We replied that, in our English-teaching years, life and language were much simpler. When we wanted to say *basic* we said *basic.* We didn't trick it up with a different ending to make it sound more impressive—and more confusing. We noted further that, in those simpler days, we didn't worry about "subjective complements." We simply would call "interested" a predicate adjective modifying "everybody." And that's what we would still call it today.

Basic English *Basic English* is a list of 850 words compiled during the 1920s by a committee headed by C. K. Ogden and including I. A. Richards. It was designed as an introduction to English for the foreign-born and as a simple means of communication among members of the scientific and business communities. *Basic* is an acronym for British-American Scientific International Commercial.

bastille *Bastille* has enjoyed some popularity as an item of youthful slang, used primarily to refer to schools which the young people believe to be too strict in rules of conduct. The original *Bastille* was the famous prison in Paris that figured prominently in the early days of the French Revolution.

bath chair *Bath chair* is the British equivalent of the American wheelchair. The first *bath chairs* (then spelled with a capital "B") were devised at Bath for the convenience of invalids who came there to partake of the allegedly curative waters at that famous spa.

bathos. *See* PATHOS/BATHOS

batman *Batman* is British armed service slang for an officer's manservant.

be. *See* LINKING VERBS

beastly British slang for damnably unpleasant or gravely unkind. Noel Coward's satiric wartime ballad "Let's Not Be Beastly to the Germans" nicely underscored the traditional British stiff upper lip and sense of humor in the face of overwhelming odds.

beat/beaten The use of *beat* where *beaten* is called for, as in "The local team was badly *beat* last night," is illiterate.

beatnik/hippie *Beatnik,* meaning an unconventional devotee of the arts, is a word which enjoyed great popularity in the late 1950s and early 1960s but has virtually disappeared from the general vocabulary of America. A *beatnik* was what an earlier generation would have called a "Bohemian."

The coinage of the word came after October, 1957, when the Russian sputnik flashed across the heavens and, as a minor side effect to man's entry into space, added the suffix "-nik" to the already well-established "beat."

Back in the 1930s, "beat" in the sense of "exhausted" was part of the jargon of jazz musicians. After a long night of work or an arduous recording session, a jazzman might say he was "beat."

In the late 1940s a group of West Coast self-styled intellectuals adopted the term "The Beat" to describe themselves and their activities. Jack Kerouac, one of their number, had the audacity to claim that the word "beat" was a shortened form of "beatified." This suggestion didn't quite get him laughed out of the lodge but no one with an understanding of the evolution of the language took him seriously.

In recent years a much more commonly heard word is *hippie.* While it is used to refer to a nonconformist or rebel against traditional mores, it has a broader application than the almost forgotten *beatnik.*

beau Now obsolescent, if not obsolete, for "boy friend," *beau* forms its plural regularly by adding "s": *beaus.* The French plural *beaux,* formerly used in formal contexts, is now entirely obsolete in this country.

beauteous/beautiful There is no difference in meaning between these two words but a decided difference in use. *Beauteous* is used chiefly by people seeking a bit of "elegance" in their speech or writing. *Beautiful,* on the other hand, is quite at home in any context.

because/for/since/as *Because* is used as a conjunction introducing a subordinate clause stating the reason or reasons for the action reported in the main or independent clause: "He claimed victory *because* the polls were running heavily in his favor." *For, since,* or *as* may be used in similar constructions, but *because* is the most emphatic of the possibilities, with *since* and *as* rather more informal and *for* somewhat more formal. Though often heard, especially in informal contexts, the formulation "The reason is *because* . . ." is best avoided as somewhat redundant. Say and write rather: "The reason is that . . ." or simply "The reason is . . ." *See also* REASON IS . . . THAT/BECAUSE and ON ACCOUNT OF (BECAUSE).

because of. *See* DUE TO/BECAUSE OF/OWING TO

become. *See* LINKING VERBS

bed-sitter British term for what Americans call a studio apartment: a combination sitting room (when the folding bed or couch is made up) and bedroom (when it is opened out).

been The standard American pronunciation of *been* is BIN. The British pronunciation BEAN is regarded as an affectation when used by one of American birth.

beer and skittles   *Beer and skittles* is the British equivalent of a casual, friendly good time. *Skittles* was an early form of bowling, in which a flattened disk was hurled or slid across a green toward the ninepins. The average medieval yeoman's idea of paradise enow was not a "jug of wine, a loaf of bread and thou" but a pint of *beer,* a game of *skittles,* and "thou" staying somewhere out of the way. Today the term is used mainly in the well-known negative cliché: "Life is not all *beer and skittles.*"

before. *See* PREPARATORY TO/BEFORE

behalf, in/on   A person acting *on behalf* of another is acting in his place or as his representative or agent. "*On behalf* of the company, I wish to present you this gold watch in appreciation." One acting *in behalf* of another is acting for his benefit or his interest: "*In behalf* of my client I ask that you consider his limited income."

beholden   *Beholden* in the sense of "obligated" or "indebted" ("I don't want to be *beholden* to anyone") has a pleasantly old-fashioned flavor. It is, however, completely proper in any context.

bemused   Care should be taken not to confuse *bemused* with *amused.* A person *bemused* is deep in thought, sometimes to the point of stupefaction. He most definitely is not laughing.

bench mark. *See* VOGUE WORDS

benefactor/beneficiary   Both *benefactor* and *beneficiary* have to do with the bestowing of gifts or help. They differ in that the *benefactor* is the giver or donor, while the *beneficiary* is the receiver or donee.

bennies. *See* DOWNERS/UPPERS

beside/besides   *Beside* and *besides* obviously overlap considerably in use. *Beside* is more often used in the literal sense of "located at the side of": "I stood *beside* the president as he took his oath of office." *Besides* is the preferable choice when the concept of "in addition to" is the sense of the sentence: "He ordered up three magnums of champagne, *besides* ordering filet mignon for the group."

bespoke   *Bespoke* in such expressions as "*bespoke* shoes" and "*bespoke* suits" is a British word meaning "made-to-order." It derives from the fact that one must make oral arrangements in advance—that is, one must bespeak the merchandise before it can be made to your order and specifications.

best/better   "May the *best* team win" is a common exhortation but there is some controversy as to whether "*best* team," when referring to one of only two teams, is an error.

As distinguished a grammarian as Professor C. C. Fries has said: "The use of the superlative instead of the comparative for two, thus ignoring a dual as distinct from a plural, is standard English usage and not limited to vulgar English." *See* ADJECTIVES, COMPARISON OF

better than/more than   *Better than* in the sense of *more than* ("She took *better than* an hour to complete the job") is inadmissible in careful writing, though acceptable in casual speech.

better than I/me   Which is correct, queries a reader, "He can sing *better than me*" or "He can sing *better than I*"? Formal use would certainly insist upon the latter, regarding *than* as a conjunction introducing a clause with the verb omitted: "He can sing *better than I* (can)." However, in informal use, especially in speech, *than* is regarded as a preposition and followed by the objective case: "He can sing *better than me.*" So the verdict depends on the context in which the expression occurs.

between/among. *See* AMONG/BETWEEN

between you and I

USAGE PANEL QUESTION

The phrase *between you and I* is often heard, even from otherwise literate speakers. Do you accept this in casual speech?
Yes: 3%. No: 97%.
In writing   Yes: 2%. No: 98%."

W. H. AUDEN: "Horrible!"
SHERIDAN BAKER: "I wince and grind my remaining teeth."
JOHN O. BARBOUR: "Yes—but don't let it get around."
BARRY BINGHAM, SR.: "It is no easier to say than 'between you and me' and serves no purpose whatever."
HAL BORLAND: "Pretentious—as well as sloppy English."
HEYWOOD HALE BROUN: "Why!"
ANTHONY BURGESS: "Not yet. Only when 'give it to I' is also used."
GEORGE CORNISH: "One has to make a stand somewhere. If not against this phrase, then where?"

GEOFFREY HELLMAN: "Yes. This is an upperclass affectation. Maybe lower-class too, but I don't know the lower classes."

PAUL HORGAN: "Never heard a literate person use it."

ALEXANDER KENDRICK: "Never."

CLARK KINNAIRD: "Politeness may require acceptance, but I don't believe it."

IRVING KOLODIN: "Probably. But not pridefully."

RUSSELL LYNES: "I overheard recently a man say to another: 'Just between you and me . . . or I should say "I." ' This on the very doorstep of Harper & Row."

EDWIN NEWMAN: "There is no reason to accept this."

ORVILLE PRESCOTT: "Another abomination!"

FRANCIS ROBINSON: "God forbid!"

VERMONT ROYSTER: "Between you and me, I rarely hear it from literate speakers."

HARRISON SALISBURY: "No, no, no!"

DAVID SCHOENBRUN: "It is just as easy to be correct and say 'me.' "

WALTER W. "RED" SMITH: "A thousand times no! Nor that cowardly evasion 'myself' neither."

ELVIS STAHR, JR.: "This one, above all, chills me. It signifies an effort to be elegant by one obviously ignorant."

beyond the pale. *See* PALE, BEYOND THE

bi-. *See* PREFIXES AND SUFFIXES, WITH AND WITHOUT HYPHEN

Bible/bible
Bible, with a capital "B," is preferred when the reference is to the Holy Bible of the Christian faiths: "He read two verses from the King James version of the Bible." *Bible* with a lower-case "b" is the preferred form when one is referring to a standard and highly respected book or other publication of reference: "*Variety* is widely considered the *bible* of show business."

bibliomania. *See* MANIA

bid
Bid in the sense of attempt or effort ("He made a strong *bid* for the Senate seat left vacant by the incumbent's death") is now standard English, admissible in any context.

b.i.d./t.i.d./Rx
Doctors still write their prescriptions in Latin not only because this has been the language of medical scholarship since the Middle Ages but also because it provides a convenient shorthand for instructions to the pharmacist.

Thus writing "Sig.*b.i.d.* (or *t.i.d.*)" is much simpler than spelling out, "Mark: twice (or three times) a day." Similarly, *Rx* (actually the capital

"R" with a slant bar across the leg of the "R") is simpler than "recipe," which literally means "take ye." Until early in this century the term "recipe" was generally used throughout the medical profession. It has now been replaced by "prescription," though the symbol remains.

bilk *Bilk* as a verb meaning to cheat or defraud is now standard English ("The get-rich-quick scheme *bilked* many people out of their life savings"). *Bilk* also exists as a noun meaning either one who manipulates such a swindle or the swindle itself. The noun use is, however, relatively rare.

billet-doux This is a slightly old-fashioned borrowing from the French. Pronounced bill-ay-DOO, it means love letter. It should be noted that the plural form, following the French, is *billets-doux,* not *billet-douxes.*

billion In the United States a *billion* is the number one followed by nine zeros or one thousand million: 1,000,000,000. In Britain this is called a "milliard." The British *billion* is the number one followed by twelve zeros or one million million: 1,000,000,000,000.

bimonthly and semimonthly

USAGE PANEL QUESTION

Some American dictionaries enter *bimonthly* and *semimonthly* as synonymous —thus implying that *bimonthly* may mean both "twice a month" and "every other month." Do you use these words interchangeably?

In your writing   Yes: 8%. No: 92%.
In casual speech   Yes: 9%. No: 91%.

SHANA ALEXANDER: "They have entirely different meanings, as any writer of a semimonthly column knows. Semimonthly and biweekly are synonyms."

MICHAEL J. ARLEN: "I've never really known what either of them meant."

ISAAC ASIMOV: "I wrote for magazines for many years and I well know the difference between one published bimonthly and one published semimonthly."

STEWART BEACH: "I think it is shocking that dictionaries should approve this nonsense. 'Bimonthly' means every two months, 'semimonthly' twice a month."

HEYWOOD HALE BROUN: "If you do, you spend a lot of time waiting for your bimonthly magazine."

ANTHONY BURGESS: " 'Bimonthly' means 'every two months' and can mean nothing else. 'Every fortnight' is preferred [to *semimonthly*] in my usage."

JAMES MACGREGOR BURNS: "Let's keep these words clear!"

JOHN CIARDI: "I simply avoid 'bimonthly' as an incurable confusion."

RICHARD EDES HARRISON: "I hope not."

PAUL HORGAN: "How can distinct differences in meaning be merged without resultant confusion?"

HELEN L. KAUFMANN: "Definitely not."

ALEXANDER KENDRICK: "I have to pause to calculate, but usually wind up correctly."

STANLEY KUNITZ: "Let's preserve the distinctions when we can!"

WALTER LORD: "Never—but for twelve years the distinction was brought to my attention by a biweekly school report card."

JESSICA MITFORD: "I don't say 'bimonthly' at all, as I am uncertain of what it means. I'd write 'semi-monthly' with a hyphen."

HERBERT MITGANG: "Let's not break down two different words with clear prefixes."

DAVID POLING: "Yes. This is confusing—and I fear that as a writer and speaker, I have added to the confusion."

PETER S. PRESCOTT: "Again—this kind of deterioration weakens, rather than strengthens, the language. We need both words, with their very different meanings."

HAROLD SCHONBERG: "Words have to have *some* meaning. Bimonthly— every other month, and that's it."

MARK SCHORER: "I try not to, but I can't always keep them straight."

DANIEL SCHORR: "Yes, however confusing, one has come to mean twice a month, the other—every half month."

ROBERT SHERRILL: "Yes—that is, if I use 'bimonthly' at all. It is confusing to the point of being useless to me."

EARL UBELL: "I avoid both words because I know that the meaning is totally unclear to most readers. So I will say 'every other month' or 'twice a month' to be perfectly clear."

JUDITH VIORST: "I attempt to use these words properly, but wish they were interchangeable."

GEORGE WALD: "It's the difference between 2 and ½! Don't toy with it."

A.B.C. WHIPPLE: " 'Fortnightly' seems to me O.K. It's no longer too British."

bindle stiff/grifter/hobo   *Bindle stiff* is an item of underworld or hobo slang now bordering on the archaic. A *bindle stiff* was a migrant worker who carried his own bedroll with him. The *bindle* is a variant of "bundle," a reference to the bedding he carries. Jim Tully, an ex-prizefighter and hobo, whose writings were popularized by H. L. Mencken in the 1920s, once explained the various classes of men who chose a life "on the road." Said Tully: "I was a *bindle stiff*. That's the class that will do some work once in a while. The *grifters* are the desperate characters; the *hobos* are the philosophers."

biodegradable   *Biodegradable* is a term from science recently arrived in the general language thanks to the campaign for improving our environment. A *biodegradable* substance is one that can be decomposed by natural biological processes. *Biodegradable* is standard English usable in any context.

bird   British slang for an attractive young girl. It has had some vogue in America, especially in the wake of the invasion of English pop and rock singers, most of whom seemed to be amply accompanied by *birds.* Centuries ago the word "burd" was used to refer to an unmarried girl or maiden. By the process of *folk etymology* (which see), "burd" was altered to the more familiar spelling *bird. See also* BROAD.

biro   *Biro* (pronounced BY-roh) is the British term for ball-point pen. Originally a trademark, it has now become the generic term for the instrument and even appears as a verb ("Most poems are no longer penned but *biroed*"). The word comes from the name of the Hungarian inventor Laszlo *Biro.*

birthdays, dating of   Logically the day of one's birth should be one's first *birthday* and the first anniversary of that day would be one's second *birthday.* That, however, is not the way such matters are managed in our Western civilization. Perhaps in an unconscious effort to keep the number as low as possible, we name the first anniversary of birth the *birthday.* One may, of course, speak of being in one's sixty-first year immediately after celebrating one's sixtieth *birthday*—and this is not uncommon in England, though rare in the U.S. When we visited C. T. Onions, the last of the original editors of the *Oxford English Dictionary* back in 1964, he announced quite proudly that he was "in his 91st year." At the time of his death, a few months later, he had passed the next milestone and the obituary notices recorded his age as 91 years.

The Occidental method of recording age is not followed in Japan or China. Those countries follow the same custom used for recording the age of thoroughbred race horses. Each one's age is computed from January 1 of the year of his birth and everyone born in the same year is considered to be the same age. Since the Chinese and Japanese also regard a child to be a year old at birth (that is, having its first *birthday* on the day of its birth, not a year later as we do), a child born December 31 is two years old the following day. Ah, the inscrutable Orientals—but how much more logical than the ineffable Occidentals!

bit

USAGE PANEL QUESTION

Bit in the sense of small or insignificant ("*bit* part") seems well established. A somewhat analogous noun use of *bit,* in the sense of "specialty" or "distinctive behavior," has been in vogue of late. Do you accept: "He does the intellectual critic *bit* whenever he can find an audience"?

In writing   Yes: 32%. No: 68%.
In casual speech   Yes: 66%. No: 34%.

ISAAC ASIMOV: "Yes. Another case of graphic and worthy slang."

CHARLES BERLITZ: "Yes—a question of what style is being followed."

ALTON BLAKESLEE: "Yes, reluctantly."

JOHN BROOKS: "Horrible—and passé too."

BEN LUCIEN BURMAN: "Speech, yes. But a bit too much for writing."

JAMES MACGREGOR BURNS: "Yes. My wife disagrees."

JOHN CIARDI: " 'Tis but temporal cant."

ALEX FAULKNER: "If humorous, yes."

RICHARD EDES HARRISON: "No. Fad."

PAUL HORGAN: "No, no, no. Also: down with 'the whole bit.' "

JOHN K. HUTCHENS: "Yes, but only if the sense of it is comic."

STANLEY KUNITZ: "Yes. More effective and metaphorically precise than any alternative construction I can think of."

LAURENCE LAFORE: "No. Except as part of a quotation."

RUSSELL LYNES: "No—in writing; yes—in speech. Pure slang."

LEO ROSTEN: "Yes, when calculated to be colloquial, though I don't like faddist conformities."

BERTON ROUECHÉ: "Sounds dated already."

VERMONT ROYSTER: "That usage annoys me—the writer is being cute."

HARRISON SALISBURY: "Maybe, but I don't like it."

JEAN STAFFORD: "I would accept this use in both speech and writing if the intention is ironic or contemptuous. I very much like the sample offered: it puts me in mind of quite a number of stuck-up boobs I know who still use the word 'Zeitgeist' and habitually misuse the word 'dichotomy.' "

ELVIS STAHR, JR.: "Very casual speech! But: it's coming—it's coming—maybe it's here!"

BARBARA TUCHMAN: "No. Detestable—might as well allow 'like' in the vogue sense—'It's like October.' "

BILL VAUGHAN: "No. Funny at one time; now tiresomely overworked."

JUDITH VIORST: "Depends on use."

bitch   *Bitch* is, of course, standard English as a term for a female canine. As a term for a female of the human species it is derogatory slang, bordering closely on the vulgar. As a verb *bitch* also has the slang sense of complain, grouse, and grumble. A further slang sense of the verb, with "up," means "to bungle" ("He didn't follow instructions and so he *bitched* up the play").

bite/bitten/bit   *Bite* has two past participles, *bitten* and *bit,* but only the former is now acceptable in the passive voice. You can say, "He has *bit* (or *bitten*) into the cake," but you can only say, "The cat was *bitten* (not *bit*) by the dog."

bite the bullet   *Bite the bullet* is a presently voguish expression meaning about the same thing as the earlier "face the music." It means that an unpleasant prospect awaits and one must summon up his courage to face it bravely. The expression is apparently borrowed from British and was probably originally an armed services expression from the practice, during the nineteenth-century pre-anesthesia days of medicine, of having a wounded infantryman *bite the bullet* to distract his attention from the pain of surgery or amputation.

bit of goods   British slang for a pretty girl. "A neat *bit of goods*" is the sort of expression that might be used in admiring comment when an attractive girl comes into view.

bitter/bitterly cold   In choosing between *bitter cold* and *bitterly cold,* some might argue that since "cold" is an adjective and since the word which modifies it has to be an adverb, *bitterly* is the only correct form. Not true. *Bitter* is an adverb as well as an adjective, so *bitter cold* is as correct as *bitterly cold.*

bitter end   *Bitter end* has nothing to do with "bitter" in its usual sense but was originally a nautical phrase. Aboard ship, a bitt is a post around which cables and ropes are wound. The end of the rope which is nearest the bitt is the *bitter end.* If the anchor cable is let out to the *bitter end,* the ship is more subject to misfortune and possible shipwreck. Hence the phrase came to mean "to the very end" or even "until death." It is so overworked a cliché, though, that it is best to avoid it.

black/Negro   In the 1960s and 1970s we witnessed an effort to effect the abandonment of the word *Negro* in favor of *black.* An interesting and almost forgotten sidelight to this effort is that earlier *Negro* educators and leaders fought a long and finally successful battle to get themselves referred to as *Negroes* with a capital "N."

As recently as the 1930s, many dictionaries and newspaper style books listed *negro* with a lower-case "n" as acceptable. Steady pressure on editors of newspapers and magazines resulted in a gradual change to the upper-case "N."

Now we are told, in the words of one articulate spokesman, that " 'Negro' is just the white man's word for 'nigger' and must be eliminated in favor of 'black.' "

This development is reflected in the instructions in *The Boston Globe Stylebook* which says: "Use 'black' (lower case) as a racial designation. 'Negro' (upper case) only in direct quotes. But 'Black Power.' "

black-coat worker   *Black-coat worker* is the British equivalent for the American "white-collar worker," in reference to professional and clerical workers as distinguished from industrial laborers and the like, known in the United States as "blue-collar workers."

blame on/blame for   In 1913 the editors of Funk & Wagnalls Unabridged stated flatly that "to *blame* a fault *on* a person is incorrect. We *blame* a person *for* a fault or lay the *blame* upon him." This prescription is now completely out of date and the idiom *"blame (something) on (someone)"* is now entirely acceptable both in speech and writing: "The mayor *blamed* his defeat *on* himself and *on* the ineptness of his campaign."

blatant/flagrant   *Blatant* and *flagrant* are frequently confused, in part because of the slight similarity of their spelling but more because each describes antisocial behavior. *Blatant* implies outrageous exaggeration, especially when accompanied by noisy bluster: "The *blatant* exaggerations of the picketing strikers did nothing to help their case." *Flagrant* implies conduct far beyond the accepted standards of propriety: "The attorney's impassioned summation was a *flagrant* breach of legal ethics."

blazes. *See* SAM HILL

blend words/brunch words/portmanteau words   Words that are combinations of two words are generally called *blend words* or, occasionally, *brunch words,* the latter label reflecting the popularity of one of the most widely used of the *blends.* The most famous creator of such words called them *portmanteau words.* He was, of course, Lewis Carroll, whose pages sparkled with such inventions as " 'Twas brillig and the slithy toves did gyre and gimble in the wabe."

In *Through the Looking-Glass,* Carroll explains that he chose the word *portmanteau*—then a fashionable term for suitcase—because there are two meanings "packed up" in such a word. Among his most vivid concoctions were "slithy," a blend of "lithe" and "slimy," and "mimsy," from "miserable" and "flimsy."

Some of Carroll's other coinages have become part of standard English. For example, "squawk" from "squeak" and "squall," and "chortle" from "chuckle" and "snort." But the native American genius for creation of *blend words* has been in evidence at least since 1813, when "gerrymander" (from Elbridge "Gerry" and "salamander") was coined. The dreadful extremes to which this tendency can be pushed were often on display in the Broadway columns of the now nearly forgotten Walter Winchell era ("cinemactress," "hemotion," "infanticipation," "snoopervise," and so on). A few happy coinages seem likely to prove hardy perennials—"happenstance" and "guesstimate," for example.

As mentioned earlier, "brunch" seems the hardiest of all *blend words*. Mencken reported in *The American Language* that it first appeared in England around 1900 "and it was thirty years later before it began to make headway on this side of the water." Since Mencken was one of the notable New York bon vivants of the 1920s era, he would certainly have known if anyone had been offering brunches during that period. Your editors can attest, however, that it was widely used in New York and elsewhere, especially in the phrase "Sunday brunch" at restaurants and hotel dining rooms, during the 1930s. In support of Mencken's dating and attribution of "brunch" to England at the turn of the century, *OED Supplement* cites it as appearing in *Punch* in 1896 and labels it "University Slang" and "an excellent portmanteau word."

blighter British slang, roughly equivalent to the American "pain in the neck," used in reference to an unpleasant or troublesome person. In recent years it has meliorated somewhat and is now not solely a term of disparagement. Occasionally one may hear an expression like "He's an accommodating *blighter*," where *blighter* means little more than "chap."

blighty British slang for "home" or "homeland," meaning, of course, England. It's derived from the Hindi "bilayati," meaning "English," and originated as service slang among British soldiers posted to India, to whom a trip "back to *blighty*" was the fulfillment of their fondest dreams. During World War I, *blighty* was also used by soldiers as a term for a wound which would require their return to England.

Blimey! This is a British slang corruption of "Blame me!" or perhaps "Blind me" and may, in turn, be a shortened form of "Gorblimey," which represents the preceding phrases prefaced by "God." For reasons that are at best unclear to these American ears, the expressions are both considered quite vulgar.

blimp British equivalent of the U.S. "stuffed shirt," an expression derived from the cartoon character "Colonel *Blimp*" created by David Low in World War II.

blind robin   Regional dialect term once common in Pennsylvania and Ohio. The *blind robin* is a dry smoked herring of the sort sold with beer in saloons. One correspondent reports it as common as long ago as 1892, while another traces it to the saloons and speakeasies of the 1920s. It's similar to the British "bloater."

blink   Besides its first and commonest meaning of "to open and shut the eyes quickly" (or a single eye—though this eye motion is more often expressed by "wink"), the verb *blink* has two special senses. As a transitive verb, usually in the negative, it has the sense of "avoid": "You simply can't *blink* the unpleasant facts of the matter." With "at" *blink* implies calculated disregard or condoning: "The teacher *blinked* at the misconduct in the school corridor."

blizzard   Although almost any wild and windy snowstorm that piles up a lot of snow is popularly called a *blizzard,* weather experts have a special set of specifications that a storm must fit before it rates the name *blizzard* officially. According to the Weather Bureau, a *blizzard* must be characterized by sustained high winds—not just gusts—of at least thirty-five miles per hour and sustained temperatures of less than ten degrees above zero.

bloc/block   A *bloc* is a coalition of persons, organizations, or nations with a common goal or purpose. *Block* can mean several dozen other things but it does not have the special meaning of *bloc.*

blockbuster   In World War II *blockbuster* was a term used to describe an aerial bomb powerful enough to destroy an entire city block. It has acquired a new sense in the language of urban politics and, particularly, real-estate-related politics. The *blockbuster* today is an operator—in the business sense—who moves several families made up of members of racial minorities into previously all-white blocks in order to lower property values, so that property owners will sell to him at a loss. Also used attributively: "blockbuster novel."

block of ice   British barman's phrase meaning the same as the American "ice cube."

blond/blonde   *Blond* and *blonde* as adjectives may be applied to members of either sex, though *blonde* is more commonly applied to females. *Blond* as a noun is exclusively used for males, *blonde* exclusively for females.

blood money. *See* POTTER'S FIELD/PAUPER'S FIELD

bloody   *Bloody,* in British informal use, is chiefly employed as an intensive adjective (*bloody* fool) or adverb (*bloody* awful). G. B. Shaw created a sensation in 1914 when, in *Pygmalion,* he had Eliza Doolittle say: "Walk! Not *bloody* likely!" At the time *bloody* was considered the most vulgar of vulgarisms. In the half-century or more since Shaw violated the taboo, however, it has meliorated somewhat and is now sometimes heard in the speech of people of some refinement. Americans, however, are wise to avoid its use for fear of offending.

blower   British informal for "telephone." It probably originated in Navy and Merchant Service slang describing the tube used for voice communication between the bridge and the engine room and between the bridge and the radio shack. The device is actuated by blowing through the tube to create a whistling noise at the other end.

blue-eyed boy   *Blue-eyed boy* is the British informal equivalent of the U.S. "fair-haired boy."

boast

USAGE PANEL QUESTION

The idioms *"boast* of" and *"boast* about" are well established. However, some careful users of language question the propriety of *boast* as a transitive verb in the sense of taking pride in the possession of some attribute. Would you accept: "The new JFK auditorium *boasts* the finest acoustics of any American concert hall"?
Yes: 56%. No: 44%.

SHANA ALEXANDER: "Yes, I would accept it; but I would never write it."
BENJAMIN APPEL: "Yes. Both usages have established themselves in the language."
HAL BORLAND: "No inanimate object can boast, ever."
ROBERT CRICHTON: "Yes, reluctantly."
WALTER CRONKITE: "I'm afraid of inanimate objects that talk."
THOMAS FLEMING: "Cheap use of the word."
A. B. GUTHRIE, JR.: "Not the real question. An auditorium can't boast about anything."
RICHARD EDES HARRISON: "Only people boast."
WALT KELLY: "Used as in the sentence, 'boasts' has come to mean something like 'displays' but probably started as a mildly funny critique."
WALTER KERR: "Yes . . . established as journalese, at least."
CLARK KINNAIRD: "An inanimate uncommunicative object cannot boast of anything."

ROBERT LIPSYTE: "No . . . only if used as a substitute for 'claims' in the PR sense."

PHYLLIS MCGINLEY: "I think these words have become so firmly fixed in the language that the fight is useless."

EDWIN NEWMAN: "Yes, but it is a banal way to put it."

PETER S. PRESCOTT: "Again, reluctantly. I like particularly the use of 'boast' as a term for a particularly difficult serve in squash."

BERTON ROUECHÉ: "Why not 'has' the finest'?"

VERMONT ROYSTER: "How can an auditorium boast—or wail, or lament?"

LEONARD SANDERS: "An auditorium should leave all boasting to its paid publicists."

LIONEL TRILLING: "Yes, a little wearily."

JUDITH VIORST: "I'd try not to use it but I'd accept it."

HERMAN WOUK: "This is common informal usage now."

boat/ship   There is a distinction between these two words that no old salt could ever forget and no landlubber ever seems to learn. The basic distinction is that a *ship* is big and travels the sea lanes. A *boat* is relatively small and stays mostly in shallow or sheltered waters. The traditional Navy version runs: "It's not a *boat* unless you can hoist it aboard a *ship.*" The only exceptions are submarines and Great Lakes ore carriers. Those are *boats,* also.

boater   *Boater* was originally British for the hard-rimmed straw hat with a flat crown which American businessmen used to don religiously on May 15 and wear until after Labor Day, when they returned to felt hat or derby for the cooler months. This pleasant custom has long since passed and with it most of the *boaters,* which are now regarded as badges of eccentricity rather than conformity, as was formerly the case.

bobby   Though still labeled slang, *bobby* is virtually the standard name for policeman in England, especially in London. Occasionally one hears "peeler" in the same sense. Both names come from Sir Robert Peel, who created the first modern constabulary in London in 1828.

bodacious   A dialect term popularized in America in the "Barney Google and Snuffy Smith" comic strip. It means bold, audacious, daring, even arrogant. It may well be a blend of "bold" and "audacious" and originally appeared in British slang centuries ago as *boldacious.* However, the Supplement to the *Oxford English Dictionary* credits the present version as an Americanism.

body, dead   In any report of or reference to death, it is unnecessary to refer to a *dead body.* In such instances, the word "dead" is redundant. Also, according to *The Boston Globe Stylebook*, "Bodies are taken, brought, flown or sent. They are not shipped."

boff/boffo   This is show-business slang for "hit." Originally a *boff* was a belly laugh—a comedian's finest reward. Then it came to mean any kind of success: "The new musical is a *boff.*" *Boffo* is the adjective form and "*Boffo* at the B.O." is a *Variety* magazine superlative for "very successful at the box office."

boffin   *Boffin* is an odd item of British slang that originated in the services early on in World War II. It may mean an "over-age" naval officer—that is, one over thirty-two years of age—or a research scientist, also sometimes called a "back-room boy." There are a number of theories of how the RAF fliers engaged in research in the development of radar came to call their scientific counterparts *boffins.* Many of the stories claim to be based on an actual Mr. *Boffin* or Colonel *Boffin,* but Sir Robert Watson-Watt, who should know (he invented radar), says these stories are nonsense. The *OED Supplement One* reports that "numerous conjectures have been made about the origin of the name but all lack foundation."

bog-trotting Irish. *See* IRISH, BOG-TROTTING/LACE-CURTAIN/ SHANTY

bologna   The city *Bologna* in Italy is properly pronounced buh-LOHN-yuh. The sausage product is properly pronounced buh-LOH-nee. The latter is also sometimes spelled phonetically "baloney."

bomb   This term in its slang use has two quite contrasting meanings: (a) a smashing success and (b) a disastrous failure. The former meaning is standard (though still slang) in the United Kingdom and on the Continent. Indeed, "Ein Sexbombe" is the common German expression for a young woman of devastating sex appeal. By contrast, when Joseph Heller wrote a play titled *We Bombed in New Haven,* no American had any doubt that he was referring to failure in New Haven.

bonkers   British slang for "addled," "nutty," "crazy in the head," or "*crackers*" (which see). Eric Partridge reports its first appearance in armed forces slang during World War II and says that it may be derived from "bonk," a blow to the head—which might well result in the condition described.

bonnet   British equivalent of the American automobile's "hood."

boob   *Boob* in U.S. is slang for a stupid fellow and the female breast. In Great Britain it is slang for a trivial mistake, much the same as the American slang "boo-boo."

boob tube. *See* RICOCHET WORDS

bookie/bookmaker. *See* TURF ACCOUNTANT

boondocks This borrowing from service slang has become quite widely used in recent years in referring to wild back country. It was originally a word in the Tagalog dialect spoken by some Filipinos and was picked up by American marines during our long occupation of the Philippines following the Spanish-American War.

boondoggle. *See* VOGUE WORDS

boot British equivalent of the American automobile's "trunk."

borax *Borax* is a Yiddishism common in retail trade to indicate shoddy merchandise. It is especially commonly used in the furniture business to describe gaudy but meretricious merchandise. *See also* YIDDISHISMS.

born/borne As past participle of the verb "to bear," in the sense of "to give birth to," *borne* is preferred in the active voice ("She has *borne* three children") and in the passive when followed by "by" ("Three children were *borne* by her"). Other passive constructions require *born* ("He was *born* with the gift of laughter and the sense that the world was mad").

born to the purple This expression is loosely used to indicate any person born into a royal family or even, by a sort of democratic extension, born into a family of great wealth and power, as one might say, "David Rockefeller was *born to the purple.*" However, there is one distinction observed by aficionados of the lore of royalty: a person *born to the purple,* precisely speaking, is one born while his parents are on the throne, as distinguished from those of royal birth whose parents were not reigning at the time of their birth.

borstal *Borstal* is the British term for a reform school. The name comes from the town of Borstal, where the first of these institutions was located. Americans know the term best through Brendan Behan's autobiography, *Borstal Boy.*

boss *Boss,* whether in the sense of a head of a business or as a political leader, is standard English, not slang. Indeed, it has been part of American English ever since Peter Minuit landed in New Amsterdam. The word "baas" was already common among the Dutch in the sense of "master" or "uncle." Any expert craftsman, especially one who guided a number of apprentices, was known as "baas." As Dutch influence diminished and English-speaking people took over the political destinies of the colony, the word *boss* was soon adopted in the sense of anyone supervising a project involving a number of employees. From this it was a short step to *boss* in the sense of one who runs a political machine. During the 1960s *boss* had a brief vogue as a teen-age slang term meaning excellent, fine, or top-notch.

both   Properly used, *both* should be used only in reference to two people or things. "*Both* Morris and Peter qualified for membership," but not "Among their qualifications were *both* height, reach, and power."

bottom line/bottom-line man   Slang terms for "ultimate reckoning" and "person who determines the ultimate reckoning." These expressions were much in vogue in Washington circles during the Watergate and impeachment hearings of the early 1970s. They originated in the business community and obviously refer to the fact that any business statement has its pluses and its minuses but all are finally resolved favorably or unfavorably at the *bottom line*.

boughten   *Boughten* is a variant dialect past participle of "buy." While commonly heard in folk speech in rural regions of the U.S., it should be avoided in writing of either formal or informal nature.

bouillabaisse   The correct pronunciation of the name of this French seafood dish is boo-yuh-BASE. Some fairly appalling pronunciations have been heard on broadcasts, even from cooks who should know better. One such was bull-yuh-BEZ from the lips of one of the highest-priced "talents" on the air. Ah, well.

boutique   *Boutique* is a relatively recent borrowing from French and is now acceptable in all contexts, written and spoken. It describes a small retail specialty shop.

bovine   *Bovine* is usually used as an adjective meaning "pertaining to the genus *bos*"; hence, any ox or cow. It also is a noun, so if one wishes to refer to a single such animal without regard to its sex (either "bull" or "cow") one can simply say "a *bovine.*"

bowler   British name for the stiff rounded-top man's hat known in America as the "derby." It is supposed to be a corruption of "Beaulieu," the name of the French designer who created the first *bowler* for a huntsman weary of having his topper knocked off as he rode under low-lying branches.

Boxing Day   British name for the day after Christmas, unless Christmas falls on a Saturday, in which case *Boxing Day* is the Monday following. It is observed as a legal holiday. The rather odd name is supposed to have originated in the fact that in Victorian times well-to-do families would distribute boxes containing gifts to the family retainers on this day.

boy friend. *See* GIRL FRIEND/BOY FRIEND

brain trust   This term, coined by a *New York Times* political reporter, James M. Kieran, to describe President Franklin D. Roosevelt's unofficial cabinet of advisers, was originally "brains trust." However, popular use and the ever-present need of headline writers to economize on the number of letters used in their heads soon reduced the label to *brain trust.* It has since been used to describe any unofficial group of expert advisers and planners, especially one involved in governmental affairs.

brass, the   This was originally military slang for "high-ranking officers." It was used in British military circles back in the 1890s and picked up by the U.S. military during World War I. The allusion is to the gold braid worn on the cap visors of top-ranking officers as insignia of rank. The term has long since been borrowed into civilian slang, and heads of business enterprises are commonly known to their underlings as *the brass.*

bread   Long used by extension to mean food in general, *bread* has acquired the slang sense of "money." Like many other items of current slang, this originated in the argot of black musicians: "Man, how much *bread* do we get for this gig [job]?"

break a leg   This is show-business jargon for "Good luck!" and is customarily said to an actor or entertainer just about to go on stage or before the cameras. It is a translation of an expression once common in the Yiddish theater.

bring/take   The distinction between *bring* and *take* is one that today is honored in the breach almost as often as in the observance.
      Simply put, here is the difference: *Bring* means to transport, carry, or lead a thing from a distance to where the speaker is. So you might say, "*Bring* the dishes from the kitchen so that I may set the table." *Take* implies transporting something away from where the speaker is. For example: "Please *take* these flowers to the hospital." Most dictionaries observe this distinction, but *Webster's Third New International Dictionary* unfortunately ignores the difference. In fact, one of the definitions given there for *bring* is "to take or carry along with one." This is

a debasement of our language in which a careful writer or speaker will not concur.

USAGE PANEL QUESTION

Purists emphasize a distinction between *bring* and *take*. *Bring* implies transporting something from a distance to where the speaker is. *Take* means transporting something away from where the speaker is. Do you observe this distinction?

In your writing   Yes: 91%. No: 9%.
In casual speech   Yes: 84%. No: 16%.

STEWART BEACH: "Yes. But I doubt this distinction can be ironclad. It would depend on situation and context."

HAL BORLAND: " 'To bring' means to fetch. 'To take' means to tote. If the ear doesn't make the distinction, the writer is deaf as well as dumb."

HEYWOOD HALE BROUN: "Yes. The loss of any shade of meaning is to be deplored."

ANTHONY BURGESS: "Purists, for God's sake? The distinction is in the very roots of the language."

GEORGE CORNISH: "Such distinctions were once made to give employment to high-school English teachers."

THOMAS FLEMING: "Yes. But not consciously. I had to think about how I used these words."

RICHARD EDES HARRISON: "Yes—certainly."

CHARLES KURALT: "Yes. A third-grade distinction which seems elementary to me."

WALTER LORD: "Yes. Except when I bring something to your attention!"

HERBERT MITGANG: "Yes. Hold the fort in writing."

ORVILLE PRESCOTT: "You can't bring something away from you, but you can bring it with you."

PETER S. PRESCOTT: "I am astonished anyone confuses these. Do people really say, 'Take it here'? and 'Bring it there'?"

RICHARD H. ROVERE: "In writing—yes. In speech—no. (Wish I did.)"

VERMONT ROYSTER: "A vital distinction. The IRS takes but never brings."

LEONARD SANDERS: "Lord knows I am not a purist, but I did not know one was required to be in this instance."

DAVID SCHOENBRUN: "If writers do not respect the meanings, shadings, precisions, and distinctions of words, then who will? We may all end up grunting to one another, but, at least, we ought to have clear, correct, precise texts to read."

BARBARA TUCHMAN: "Yes. 'Take' has many other meanings, too."

JUDITH VIORST: "I would love to observe this distinction in my writing but I keep forgetting what it is. . . ."

brinkmanship *Brinkmanship,* coined by Adlai Stevenson to describe the policies of John Foster Dulles, who, when Secretary of State, boasted of "taking us to the brink of war" to preserve peace, seems to have found a lasting niche in the lexicon of diplomats and commentators. It was coined in the tradition of Stephen Potter's "gamesmanship," "one-upmanship," and "lifemanship."

British-American spelling variations There are many hundreds of differences between British spelling and American. The most commonly seen, we suspect, are the "-our" endings on such words as "labour," though Americans have retained a few such endings, notably on the word "glamour." A rather special case in point is discussed under the entry *gaol* (which see). However, other such differences are noted at their appropriate alphabetical positions in this dictionary and we shall merely note a few here in passing: "enquire" for "inquire," "cheque" for "check," and "organisation" for "organization."

British collective nouns A column reader queried these statements by Sir Anthony Eden: "I am sure Her Majesty's government were right to do that" and "I would suggest to the government that they should consider an approach to the French government." "Are these plural verbs with singular subjects peculiar to English grammar?" he asked.

   The answer is that the British regard collective nouns like "government" as collections of individuals, rather than as units as Americans do. For this reason they are followed by plural, rather than singular, verbs. That's why, incidentally, Americans new to England are frequently jolted by such headlines as EAST ANGLIA CRICKET TEAM ARE DEFEATED.

British English/American English The evolution of a separate strain of English in America as a result of the distance from England, the influences of very different climate, topography, political and racial conflicts, and a myriad of other factors has been a topic of interest almost since the first colonists arrived. Mencken on this side of the Atlantic and Shaw on the other commented frequently on the differences between *American English* and *British English,* and the topic continues to this day to attract the attention of scholars and laymen alike. In this dictionary the reader will find many examples of these differences, most of them entered in their logical alphabetical location and bearing such labels as "standard British," "British slang," "British informal," and so on.

   Someone—perhaps G. B. Shaw—once described the English and the Americans as "one people divided by a common language." The truth of this observation is apparent to the language-conscious American as soon as he sets foot on Britain's shore. You're scarcely off the plane before you find yourself being urged to stow your bags in the boot of your hire-car, advised that you will find your first important turn just beyond the second double-bend and that you should mind the windscreen for it might mist up a bit with fog coming on. However, you needn't worry about speed, for your car has already been run in.

All clear? Well, it certainly wasn't to us—especially since the matter of driving on the "wrong" side of the road while thousands of cars and minicars whirled past (all on the "wrong" side, of course) required a little concentration in itself.

But, about the time we had negotiated the third double-bend ("S-curve" to Americans), the catalogue of word variations was beginning to fall into place. The "boot" is the trunk of the car. A "hire-car" is simply a rental car, though one bought on "hire-purchase" would be one bought on the installment plan. The "windscreen," usually simply "screen," is the windshield and, logically enough in Britain's climate, a car doesn't have a defroster but a "demister." And a car that has been "run in" may or may not be a car that has been run into. It's simply a car that has been through what Americans call the breaking-in period.

Cars in Britain are not parked on the street, though there are "town car parks" available for the purpose. The word for short-term parking at the "kerb" ("curb" in America) is simply "waiting" and one finds many signs reading "No Waiting This Side Today." Sometimes these signs are designed so that they may be simply flipped, as the occasion or local regulations may warrant, to read, "Waiting Limited to Thirty Minutes" and so on. Fortunately for the green American driver, the lorry drivers —unlike their American counterparts—are unfailingly courteous and helpful. "Lorry"? Oh, pardon our English. We meant "truck," of course.

Briton/Britisher   *Briton* is the formal term for a native of Great Britain and one which he would use to describe himself. *Britisher* is an informal term for the same person.

Britisher became popular in America shortly after the Revolution and originally was a somewhat derisive term. However, by now it has lost all its derogatory or comic overtones and is regarded by most careful writers as just a synonym for "Englishman."

broad   *Broad* is a slang term for a woman. Originally it referred primarily to women of low repute or prostitutes. During the past two decades, though, it has meliorated and now is used, often with affection and admiration, in reference to any attractive young woman. Partly responsible for this change was the use of the term in the Oscar Hammerstein song in *South Pacific* referring to a girl "who was broad where a *broad* should be broad." Many regard it as a sexist term.

brodie The expression "the act *brodied*" is straight from the show-business lexicon of *Variety* magazine. It means that the act was a failure. The expression comes from the famous exploit of Steve Brodie, who either did or did not jump off Brooklyn Bridge in 1886. He claimed that he did and achieved instant fame for the deed. However, since he had no witnesses to prove his claim, skeptics soon voiced their doubts about the feat. So it was certainly less than an unqualified success.

broke *Broke* is informal for "without funds." It appears also in the slang expression "Go for *broke*," meaning "to put all one's energy or funds into one desperate effort." *Broke* is also incorrectly used as a past participle for "break." "His leg was *broke*" should be "His leg was broken." *Broke* is also the standard past tense of break: "She *broke* the cup."

brolly *Brolly* is what the *OED Supplement One* labels a "clipped and altered form of umbrella" and notes that it first appeared in British university slang around 1870. Today it is labeled informal but is virtually the standard British word for the umbrella.

Brontë This is a real oddity and a copyeditor's delight—the only proper name in English employing an umlaut or dieresis. The real family name of the father of the *Brontë* sisters—Charlotte, Emily, and Anne—was Brunty. The son of an Irish farmer, he enrolled in 1802 at Cambridge and signed himself Patrick *Brontë*. The great British naval hero, Horatio Nelson, had recently been given the honorary title of Duke of Bronte (no dieresis) in Sicily and this apparently influenced Brunty's name change. But the added fillip of the dieresis was all his doing.

brother-in-law The plural of *brother-in-law* is *brothers-in-law*. *See also* PLURALS OF COMPOUND WORDS AND PHRASES.

brownout This term for the partial reduction of lights through lessening of electrical power was coined during World War II to describe the partial blackout of coastal cities as defense against possible bombing raids. After a couple of decades of disuse, it has returned as a part of standard English in the new sense of deliberate curtailment of electric power to avoid too heavy a drain on generators and other sources of power.

browse/graze An animal *grazing* is eating growing greens, while an animal *browsing* is eating twigs, shoots, or leaves of shrubs and small trees.

brunch/brunch words. *See* BLEND WORDS/BRUNCH WORDS/ PORTMANTEAU WORDS

bug/irritate

USAGE PANEL QUESTION

The word *bug* has acquired the sense in recent years of "to irritate, vex, or
exasperate." Would you accept this: "His habitual lateness for appointments really *bugs* me"?
In writing   Yes: 29%. No: 71%.
In casual speech   Yes: 83%. No: 17%.

ISAAC ASIMOV: "Yes. Short and graphic."
STEWART BEACH: "No. This is a vague expression which I am sure will not be long for this language."
CHARLES BERLITZ: "Yes—depending on the style."
HEYWOOD HALE BROUN: "No. The purpose of slang is to add color."
BEN LUCIEN BURMAN: "No! No! No! There are too many other bugs around without adding any more."
JOHN CIARDI: "Depends on context. I am not against slang. 'Bugs me' is, I think, the part of slang that does for one decade of the young but not for the next decade."
ROBERT CRICHTON: "I wouldn't use it because it would serve to date the hell out of me five years or more from now."
WALTER CRONKITE: "Yes, but not in a formal paper or speech, of course."
GEROLD FRANK: "Only in casual speech—reluctantly."
RICHARD EDES HARRISON: "No. They're overdoing it."
JOHN K. HUTCHENS: "Yes. I think this has won its way through usage."
ELIZABETH JANEWAY (voting "yes"): "There's an overtone of 'create a feeling of frustration and resentful impotence' in 'bug.' Thus it applies succinctly to a situation which has no other simple, single verb to express it."
HELEN L. KAUFMANN: "In speech—yes—as slang."
PHYLLIS McGINLEY: "It is slang but we are not trying to eradicate that. It would be hopeless. The same goes for 'bit.' Neither word is a matter of grammar."
WRIGHT MORRIS: "Yes. The vernacular has given a further and more expressive twist to the term."
GEORGE PLIMPTON: "Yes—depending on style."
PETER S. PRESCOTT: "Yes, because I support strong colloquialisms when used for conscious effect. In the most formal prose—no."
LEO ROSTEN: "Yes, as humor."
VERMONT ROYSTER: "No, because we have a perfectly good word in 'annoy.'"
JUDITH VIORST: "Maybe in speech—depends on use."

HERMAN WOUK: "In this sense it should be used only when the narrator assumes a 'Huck Finn' voice."

bug/wiretap

USAGE PANEL QUESTION

In recent years the verb *to bug* in the sense of "to wiretap" or "to listen clandestinely with electronic devices" has appeared with considerable frequency in the press. Would you approve "The bureau has authorized only two hundred orders to *bug* this year" in the context of a formal report to Congress?
Yes: 43%. No: 57%.
In casual speech   Yes: 84%. No: 16%.

ISAAC ASIMOV: "Yes. The word 'bug' is short, graphic, and expresses the proper insect mentality of those who eavesdrop."

SHERIDAN BAKER: "Yes. Since the context would have been established."

STEWART BEACH: "No. I think 'wire taps' is better."

HEYWOOD HALE BROUN: "Not in a formal report. Writing in matters of law should be more specific than slang allows."

BEN LUCIEN BURMAN: "Yes. It bugs me, but it's one of those new technical words for which there's no substitute."

ROBERT CROMIE: "Yes, because it's so damned descriptive and useful."

WALTER CRONKITE: "Yes. It's a whole new language of eavesdropping. We can make our own rules."

RICHARD EDES HARRISON: "In journalism you will certainly accept 'bug' over 'concealed electronic listening devices.' "

JOHN K. HUTCHENS: "Yes, but perhaps in quotation marks, indicating that it didn't mean a Volks."

ALEXANDER KENDRICK: "These all seem to me not only acceptable, but colorful colloquialisms."

JULES LOH: "A precise and colorful coinage . . . but slangy at times."

RUSSELL LYNES: "Slang and good slang."

PETER S. PRESCOTT: "Yes, but be careful: bug does *not* mean wiretap: there is a clear and crucial difference in law and ethics. 'Bug' is electronic, not a phone tap."

VERMONT ROYSTER: "Yes. It's a useful new coinage for 'listening devices'—clear and expressive."

LEONARD SANDERS: "Yes. In this usage, the word fulfills a new, electronically created need."

ROBERT SHERRILL: "Sure. They mean 'bugging arrangement' when they use 'bug' in this way. They don't mean 'bug' as a verb or as a device. They mean a combination of both, plus the formality of setting up the job."

JEAN STAFFORD: "I dislike 'bug' as I dislike 'to rap' in the sense of 'to talk,' and as I dislike a good deal of other contemporary slang. Good slang is nifty; I love slang that packs a wallop and is informed with razzmatazz, but I hate flabby slang and I hate peevish slang."

GEORGE WALD: "Yes—if previously defined."

HERMAN WOUK: "No. It is an informal word."

bum *Bum,* in British slang, means the buttocks. It is considered a vulgarism and Americans would be wise to avoid it.

bummer Recent slang for "serious disappointment" or "letdown." "Despite the favorable reviews, the new novel was a *bummer.*"

Bummer also appears in the jargon of drug users as synonymous with "bad trip" or unhappy experience.

bum-rap A recent slang conversion of the noun phrase "a bum rap," meaning an unjust accusation, into a transitive verb: "You can't *bum-rap* the Senator on that issue." Though "rap" in the sense of accusation or rebuke has been in the language since 1777, the expression *bum-rap* should be avoided in all save the most casual contexts.

bunk/bunkum/buncombe While *bunk* is often heard, the more formal version of the word is the seldom-heard *bunkum.* Both, of course, mean "talking nonsense," but *bunk* is slang, while *bunkum* and *buncombe* are standard American.

bunked/bumped "I *bunked* into him" is a dialect expression which is local to New York City, perhaps even to the borough of Brooklyn.

bureaucratic barbarisms Mutilation of the language by bureaucrats is nothing new, nor is it confined to U.S. bureaucrats, as a reading of Sir Ernest Gowers' *Plain Words,* a survey of the linguistic transgressions of British bureaucrats, amply attests. Attacks on the artificial pomposities of highfalutin bureaucratese have been mounted, in this century, by Theodore Roosevelt, Woodrow Wilson, and many others in high places, politically speaking. None have had much effect. Perhaps the most dramatic instance was Maury Maverick's slashing attack on gobbledygook in the 1940s—again to little avail. The tendency of bureaucrats to use two or three elaborate words or phrases when a simple word would suffice was never more in evidence than during the final months of the Nixon administration, with the proliferation of what came to be called *Watergate language* (which see). "At this (or that) point in time" became an instant

cliché, to be replaced—at a later point in time—by "in this time reference" or "that time frame" or "in the context of hindsight." The mutilation of our tongue extends, among bureaucrats, to "grevious" mispronunciations, as well. *See also* EUPHEMISM.

burgeon The widespread use of *burgeon* is a source of concern to the
careful user of the language. To *burgeon* is "to bud," either literally or
figuratively. It does *not* mean "to mushroom or expand rapidly," a sense
in which it is used by many speakers and writers.

The New Yorker, in its "Talk of the Town" of July 24, 1971, makes
the distinction in this statement: "On every hand, one finds slack, demor-
alized citizens and legislators, increasingly willing to turn over their destinies to eager executive-branch management teams, who are bursting with
energy and organizational skill but have only the most sadly diminished
and debased ideas about what to do with their burgeoning power and
mushrooming organizations."

Burgeoning should in the view of precisionists be restricted to something which is new or just beginning and not applied to something well
on its way to great size.

USAGE PANEL QUESTION

In recent years the verb "to *burgeon*" has been, in the opinion of purists,
widely misused. Its primary sense is simply "to bud," yet it has been
widely used as synonymous with "to mushroom." Would you accept "the
rapidly *burgeoning* city of Dallas"?
In writing   Yes: 39%. No: 61%.
In speech   Yes: 46%. No: 54%.

MICHAEL J. ARLEN: "It's bad enough that people use words such as burgeon
  because they think they're sexier than 'grow.' At least let them use an
  accurate word."
ISAAC ASIMOV: "This is false elegance. 'Growing' is much better."
STEWART BEACH: "I'm afraid the incorrect meaning has gained so much
  acceptance it will be hard to stop."
JULES BERGMAN: "The meaning is clear in writing but vague and affected
  when spoken."
HAL BORLAND: "This is another example of pretension. What's wrong with
  saying, 'Dallas *grew*'? Or '*rapidly growing* Dallas.' "
JOSEPH A. BRANDT: "It's too journalistically acceptable to kill."
HEYWOOD HALE BROUN: "One is careful about writing, or should be. The
  purpose of speech is simply to be understood and most would understand."

ANTHONY BURGESS: "Yes. The sound and adventitious associations ('burg,' e.g.) make it suggest something bigger than mere budding."

ABE BURROWS: "Only if Dallas were a brand-new city."

WALTER CRONKITE: "I would not use it now that the definition has been called to my attention."

RICHARD EDES HARRISON: "Its meaning has always been broader than *bud* and not confined to botany. Its old use in cutaneous diseases makes it highly appropriate for Dallas, at least."

JOHN K. HUTCHENS: "I think the purists are too insistent about this, as they are when saying 'agenda' must be used as a plural noun."

CLARK KINNAIRD: " 'To mushroom' is as inept a usage as 'meteoric rise'; mushrooms either droop or get plucked quickly."

STANLEY KUNITZ: "This usage should be nipped in the burgeoning."

ROBERT LIPSYTE: "Burgeon has burgeoned out of old usage."

EDWIN NEWMAN: "I accept this because it is a misuse of which I am guilty, on the rare occasions on which I use the word. A poor reason."

PETER S. PRESCOTT: "No. Incidentally, my editor would not let me use 'mushroom' on the grounds that it now evoked a cloud, not a vegetable image. I think he is wrong."

DAVID SCHOENBRUN: "Yes, I would use the term, not in the sense of mushrooming, but in the sense of growing new buds."

WALTER W. "RED" SMITH: "Here massive usage overwhelms strict translation."

REX STOUT: "But I wouldn't accept Dallas even disburgeoning."

A.B.C. WHIPPLE: "It's probably better than the 'mushrooming city of Dallas.' In fact, it's probably better than Dallas."

HERMAN WOUK: "This one's getting there."

burglary/robbery *Burglary* and *robbery* are not interchangeable. *Burglary* is breaking and entering, with the intent of theft. *Robbery* means "taking the property of another person by threat or use of force." You can "rob a bank" but that which is taken is not "robbed." It is stolen.

burgle *Burgle* is a back-formation from the noun "burglar." As such it was long frowned upon by careful speakers and writers but now is considered acceptable in informal contexts. *See also* BACK-FORMATIONS.

burn-out

USAGE PANEL QUESTION

With the coming of the space age *burn-out,* describing the termination of a rocket operation because of fuel exhaustion, became a commonplace euphemism for a condition of exhaustion resulting from overwork. Psychologists object to this casual use of *burn-out* and say that it should be limited to describe the condition of people in their middle years who "perform at high level until stress and tension get to be too much for them." Do you think the use of *burn-out* should be limited to its scientific and quasi-scientific senses? Yes: 46% No: 54%.

Would you use *burn-out* as a synonym for "exhaustion," in speech? Yes: 45%. No: 55%.

In writing? Yes: 37%. No: 63%.

ISAAC ASIMOV: "I can just see 'burn-out' becoming a synonym for 'slightly tired.' "

BARRY BINGHAM, SR.: "This is a good, strong expression, and should be reserved for appropriate purposes, not for trivial expressions of tiredness."

ALTON BLAKESLEE: "It is a cute cop-out."

HEYWOOD HALE BROUN: "I am often exhausted, but need a special phrase for the coming burn-out."

ANTHONY BURGESS: "No. 'Burn-out' has a technical meaning in leprosy (e.g. 'A Burnt Out Case')."

BEN LUCIEN BURMAN: "No. But 'burnt-out' seems acceptable and good. Why change?"

JAMES MACGREGOR BURNS/JOAN SIMPSON BURNS: "We are divided on this. Joan would use it in both writing and speech; Jim only in speech."

JOHN CIARDI: "Words are constantly acquiring extended senses, but I prefer 'burned out.' "

ROBERT CROMIE: "Language should be protected from poachers. 'Burn-out' has (or had) a good solid meaning and should not be diminished."

WILLARD R. ESPY: "It is scarcely cricket for the psychologists, who borrowed this term from the engineers, to complain when others borrow it in turn. But do not consider it a synonym for temporary exhaustion; the exhaustion would have to be inexhaustible."

THOMAS FLEMING: "No, except as part of an obviously slangy sentence or phrase."

FRANCES FRITCHMAN: "Not a true synonym for exhaustion. It means finished —dead—not merely just extremely tired."

RAY GANDOLF: " 'Burn-out' is no less accurate, and far more colorful, than exhaustion or nervous breakdown. I would prefer a revival of 'the vapors' or 'the fantods' but I'll settle for 'burn-out.' "

PETE HAMILL: "The word (burn-out) suggests finality, while exhaustion might be only a temporary condition. It's a hyperbolic usage."

JOHN K. HUTCHENS: "I think it may well be applied to any age."

JAMES J. KILPATRICK: "I am of two minds on 'burn-out.' At the time of the PATCO strike we heard the word every day, but always in the sense defined by the psychologists. I see no great objection to its casual extension but it strikes me as the kind of hyperbole we witness in the teen-ager's room that has become a 'disaster area.' "

IRVING KOLODIN: "Not yet. I am only 74."

STANLEY KUNITZ: "Acceptable as a striking metaphor, but too intensive for casual usage."

JULES LOH: "Vogue words—being used to exhaustion and likely to burn out soon."

DWIGHT MACDONALD: "Why not? A vivid metaphor—enriches the language."

WILLIAM MCGUIRE: "Seems more acceptable in the participial adjective form, 'burnt out'—cf. Graham Greene."

EDWIN NEWMAN: "No. It seems to me that 'exhaustion' serves—or weary or tired or bored or exhausted or worn out to describe the person affected."

PETER S. PRESCOTT: "This is a case of our language being strengthened by scientific terminology. We must never allow psychologists to define how language is to be used."

VERMONT ROYSTER: "Yes (on use), perhaps because I already feel 'burnt-out.' "

DAVID SCHOENBRUN: "Right now I really am burned out after a busy season of writing and broadcasting."

HAROLD SCHONBERG: "This seems legitimate to me—a very accurate and descriptive modern coinage."

JACK SMITH: "I'm for the limited 'burn-out.' There isn't much chance, though, of saving this useful term from burn-out."

ELVIS STAHR, JR.: "Actually, in resigning the presidency of Indiana University, as far back as the late 60s, I not only stated that I had 'presidential fatigue' but that my bearings had worn so thin that I feared they would burn out if I didn't get out."

WALLACE STEGNER: "In some kinds of writing. It's more vivid than 'exhaustion.' "

HAROLD TAYLOR: "It's used too much in these ways and I wouldn't care to join in spreading the cliché more widely."

KARL V. TEETER: "Prefer 'burnout' no hyphen—already an established form."

EDWARD TRIPP: "If psychologists use such non-specific words for specific conditions, they have to expect their meaning and force to be diluted in popular parlance."

JOSEPH VERGARA: "Why are psychologists defining scientific terms? They have enough trouble defining their own jargon."

DOUGLAS WATT: "In 'A Burnt Out Case,' Graham Greene gave a partial or temporary legitimacy to a similar usage, but actually with a very different point of reference."

HERMAN WOUK: "Slovenly use of popularized jargon, in an effort to sound

up-to-the-minute, characterizes much banal and dull writing and speech."
WILLIAM ZINSSER: "Yes, without the hyphen."

burst/bust *Burst,* "to fly apart suddenly or to come forth in full force"
(*burst* into song), is standard English in all contexts. *Bust,* originally a
variant spelling and pronunciation of *burst,* is still considered slang in
virtually all senses, whether used as a noun or verb.

bush/bush league *Bush* and *bush league,* borrowed from the language
of baseball, have the connotation of amateurish incompetence. The original *bush leagues* were the very lowest order of professional and semi-
professional baseball. Anyone working in these leagues was either a rank
beginner or a worn-out old timer, so the standards of performance were
far from truly professional. Neither expression should be used in formal
contexts.

busing/bussing As a result of the attempts toward racial integration of
the nation's schools, the practice of transporting pupils by bus became the
center of controversy in many communities. Thus the word *busing* appeared in headlines across the nation.

This raised the question whether, in view of rules of pronunciation,
it should not be *bussing* instead.

Generally speaking, American preference is opposed to doubling the
final consonant in forming plurals or variant forms of verbs (for example:
travel, traveled, traveling). British usage favors such doubled consonants
(busses, travelled, travelling). But you cannot draw any hard and fast line;
you will find both styles in both countries.

In the case of *busing* vs. *bussing,* it is obvious that headline writers
would prefer the single-consonant form, if for no other reason than that
it takes up less space. Whatever the reason, *The Boston Globe Stylebook*
states flatly: "The plural of bus is buses." By extension, the present
participle of "to bus" would be *busing,* not *bussing.*

but *But* is a coordinating conjunction connecting two equal but opposite
elements: "He planned to go home *but* his wife said he had to stay." This
is an instance of *but* coordinating two independent clauses. It may also
be used to connect equal but opposite adjectives ("not handsome *but*
homely"), adverbs ("not gaily *but* morosely"), phrases ("not in the line
of duty *but* exceeding all expectations"), and to establish the relationship
between independent sentences ("Churchill painted a gloomy picture. *But*
the British people rallied to the challenge"). *But* may, as the previous
example indicates, be used to start a sentence, a practice deplored by
Victorian grammarians. *But* is a strong, forceful word by itself. It should
not be weakened by the addition of a redundant "however" ("She demanded a refund but [no 'however'] the store refused to comply").

but (in the sense of "except")   When *but* is used in the sense of "except" it may function as either a preposition or a conjunction, depending on context. When it falls near the end of a sentence and is followed by a personal pronoun, it should be construed as a preposition and followed by the objective case: "Nobody was left in the parking lot *but* me." When it is part of a compound subject, it is construed as a conjunction and is followed by a pronoun form in the nominative case: "Nobody *but* I was left in the parking lot." The use of "me" in the sentence immediately preceding, though often heard, is considered substandard.

but that/but what   *But that* is preferable in writing and careful speech: "He was not sure *but that* the train had already left," not "He was not sure *but what* . . ."

buttle/butler. *See* BACK-FORMATIONS

buy   *Buy* as a noun meaning an item purchased ("That car is a good *buy*") should be used only in informal or business contexts. *Buy* as a verb indicating acceptance ("I'll *buy* that idea") is slang and should be avoided in formal contexts.

by and large   *By and large,* in the sense of "generally speaking" or "on the whole," is a borrowing from the jargon of seafaring men when ships were still powered by sail. It was an order to the helmsman which would put the ship on a tack that would leave him in slight danger of being "taken aback." The original sense of the phrase has long been forgotten, but the expression in its present meaning is perfectly standard English.

C

cab rank   *Cab rank* is the British equivalent of the American "taxi stand."

café. *See* SALOON

calculate   *Calculate,* used precisely, means "to compute, reckon, or evaluate." However, it is also much used in regional speech in the sense of "think" or "suppose": "I *calculate* it's going to rain." Pronounced KAL-kyoo-layt in its more formal use, *calculate* is often rendered KAL-klayt in its regional dialect use.

call a spade a spade This often-heard injunction against the use of *euphemisms* (which see) led a reader to inquire, perhaps jestingly, why the admonition did not read "call a shovel a shovel," on the ground that that implement is more widely used. True enough, but the fact is that "spade" has been in the English language longer than "shovel," so it was readily at hand when the time came to translate the expression from the original Latin "Ficum ficum, ligonem ligonem vocat"—"He calls a fig a fig and *a spade a spade.*"

call-box *Call-box* is the British equivalent of the American telephone booth. Incidentally, British *call-boxes* posted prominently on streets and highways were common long before American telephone companies adopted them.

callous/callus *Callus* is a noun meaning a small area of skin which has hardened and thickened. It is also a verb meaning to so harden and thicken.

    Callous as an adjective means insensitive emotionally. As a verb, it means to make or become emotionally insensitive. Confusion as to usage arises frequently, however, because both *callus* and *callous* can be correctly used in the literal sense (in reference to skin) but only *callous* can be used in the figurative sense (in reference to emotions).

Camelot. *See* VOGUE WORDS

camp, high and low *Camp* was, in the 1930s, an item of homosexual argot, meaning "exaggeratedly effeminate behavior," especially in an effort to attract attention of persons of like interests. By the 1960s *camp* had meliorated, linguistically speaking, and had acquired the adjectival sense of "exaggerated, banal, trite, and pretentiously vulgar or mediocre." *High camp* means "the knowledgeable, sophisticated use of tawdry or vulgar elements in art or entertainment," while *low camp* refers to the unwitting use of the same elements.

camper While *camper* retains its basic meaning of "a person who lives in a temporary shelter out in the open," the word has acquired a new meaning of a vanlike vehicle equipped with facilities for eating and living which can either be parked at a campsite for a length of time or used as living quarters while making long trips. One version of a *camper* is a boxlike unit which rests on the bed of a pickup truck. *See also* CARAVAN.

can/may In formal English a distinction is drawn between *can* and *may*. *Can* is used when indicating physical ability to do something: "I *can* jump more than five feet." *May* is used when indicating permission to do something: "You *may* stay home from school tomorrow." However, it is only fair to say that the distinction is often ignored, especially in informal speech and writing. That's rather a pity, for the distinction is a nice one —and not really very hard to remember.

cancel out   This expression is commonly heard, especially among bureaucrats who never say anything simply if a more complicated way is available. It is clearly redundant. *Cancel* alone expresses the thought effectively.

Cantabrigian   A *Cantabrigian* is a person native to or resident in Cambridge, England, or Cambridge, Massachusetts. In the latter instance *Cantabrigian* (often shortened in newspaper style to *Cantab*) may be used in special reference to students and graduates of Harvard College and of Cambridge High and Latin School. *Cantabrigian* is pronounced kan-tuh-BRIJ-ee-un, though the penultimate syllable is often slurred or omitted entirely.

can't hardly   *Can't* and *hardly* are contradictory, and hence ungrammatical, in statements such as "I *can't hardly* accept that as a fair price." With *hardly* used here in the sense of "probably not," the result amounts to a double negative. Depending on the degree of probability, it should be changed to "can hardly accept" or "can't accept." *See also* NEGATIVE, DOUBLE.

can't help but   Formulations such as "I *can't help but* wonder why" should not be used in formal speech or writing. Make it "I cannot help wondering why" or "I wonder why." *Can't help but* is a double negative. *See also* NEGATIVE, DOUBLE.

cant words   In the eighteenth century *cant words* or "canting words" were terms used by dictionary editors to designate a variety of vulgar words, including the so-called four-letter words. Several dictionaries of the period, notably that of Nathaniel Bailey (from which Dr. Johnson borrowed heavily) and one by the Reverend John Ash, published in 1775, included such words. During the nineteenth century, under the influence of Bowdler (who published the expurgated Shakespeare) and Queen Victoria, such words were taboo. They have only recently begun to reappear among dictionary entries. The *American Heritage Dictionary,* the first in this country to include all the *cant words,* labels them "vulgar slang."

Johnson, incidentally, did not include them in his dictionary. They say that a pair of very proper ladies approached him at a literary tea and declared: "We see, Dr. Johnson, that you do not have those naughty words in your dictionary." To which he replied: "And I see, dear ladies, that you have been looking for them."

Canuck *Canuck,* meaning a Canadian-American, especially one of French-Canadian ancestry, is an oddity. In some areas of eastern Canada and in the former mill towns of New Hampshire, it is considered a derogatory racial label. However, in many other parts of Canada it is regarded as an affectionate nickname, and many Canadians, notably those in the western provinces, accept it cheerfully. Indeed, the professional hockey team in Vancouver rejoices in the name *Canucks.* The advice from here is to use the term carefully, if at all, unless you are of Canadian ancestry and aware of the semantic implications of its use.

canvas/canvass *Canvas* is a cloth; *canvass,* as a verb, means "to solicit or poll," and, as a noun, means "the act of soliciting or polling."

capital/capitol The place where a government is located is a *capital;* the building housing the seat of government—whether state or federal—is a *capitol.*

capital/seat of government The *capital* and the *seat of government* of a country are not necessarily the same. The *seat of government* simply means the city in which most government functions are carried on. It is sometimes also called the "de facto *capital*" or "administrative center." This situation can occur for a number of reasons: tradition, the historical role played by the city, accessibility, more favorable year-round climate among them.

In the case of the Netherlands, Amsterdam is the constitutional *capital,* in which the principal governmental activity is the swearing-in of the Parliament. The *seat of government* is The Hague and there also are located the headquarters of the National Supreme Court and the royal residence. In addition The Hague has been the site of several international meetings of great historic importance.

In Bolivia the *capital* is Sucre and the *seat of government* is La Paz. In this case it is purely a matter of accessibility that resulted in most of the government functions being centered in La Paz.

capitalization Elsewhere we quote the comment of a famous copyeditor that he who takes hyphens seriously must surely go mad. Almost the same thing may be said about *capitalization* or the lack of it in published material. One of the remarkable innovations of the much-discussed *Webster's Third New International Dictionary* was its entry of virtually all words with lower-case initial letters. The sole exception to this practice was the word "God." In many thousands of instances entries like "floridian" and "menckenian" were followed by the notation "usu cap," which regular users of the dictionary soon learned should be translated as "always capitalized," while its fellow label "often cap" actually meant "usually capitalized." But, Merriam aside, there is general agreement that proper names should be capitalized, as well as adjectives derived from them ("Shavian," "Georgian," and so on). It is also generally agreed—with only e.e.cummings and Don Marquis dissenting—that a sentence should start with an initial capital.

But there is nothing like unanimity in the use of capital letters other than in these two instances. The *Associated Press Stylebook* devotes four and a half pages to the subject and the *Los Angeles Times Style Guide* gives it almost as much space. Clearly, then, there is much that could be said on the subject.

One view was voiced in a letter we received from a Milwaukee reader of our column. "How can an otherwise reputable newspaper consistently ignore the basic rule of grammar which states that every word of a proper name be capitalized? The newspaper is the Milwaukee journal (to use the form of capitalization they use for everything except newspapers). Their fanciful capitalization results in the Thames river, the Indian ocean, Rand mountain, the Huntington library, Ohio State university, and many more. These deliberate illiteracies affect more people and confuse more students than any Madison Avenue-ese, since the newspaper is widely and carefully read and is generally regarded as being a model of correctness. What possible reason can a widely read newspaper have for its continued assault on accepted practices?"

It happens that we subscribe to those sentiments, though we should not state them quite so strenuously, and we would readily concede that many publications, especially newspapers, lower-case what they regard as the generic element in such names and titles. Our position is well stated in the *Style Manual* of the U.S. Government Printing Office, which states: "A common noun or adjective forming an essential part of a proper name is capitalized: Massachusetts Avenue, North Platte River, etc." The *Los Angeles Times Style Guide,* noting that it follows a "modified up-style of capitalization," says pretty much the same thing: "Capitalize common nouns or generic terms when part of a name: Occidental College, Los Angeles County, Union Station, Federal Building, Imperial Valley, World War II. Do not capitalize common nouns in plurals: Los Angeles and San Bernardino counties."

Those statements represent our sentiments, though we feel it our duty to report that a very great number of newspapers differ with our views and the day may not be far removed when we shall find in the press references to "Central park," "Rockefeller center," or even, heaven forfend, "sierra Madre."

capital letters   *Capital letters* are customarily used at the start of sentences ("The train will be early"), as initial letters in proper names and adjectives derived from proper names ("Morgan Library," "Shavian irony"), when printing trademarked names ("Coca-Cola"), when citing the titles of books, articles, and the like *(The Winning of Barbara Worth),* when referring to the first person singular ("I"), to the deity ("God"), and to the President of the United States. *See also* TRADE MARK/TRADEMARK.

caravan *Caravan* is the British equivalent of the American "camper" or "house trailer." A *caravan park* or *caravan site* is the equivalent of the American "trailer court," a place where *caravans* are parked, sometimes permanently. *See also* CAMPER.

careen/career *Careen* has several meanings in nautical usage, all having to do with causing a boat to tip on its side, to heel over, especially for repairs or cleaning its bottom, or, when afloat, to heel (not keel) over in a strong wind. *Career,* according to traditional dictionary definitions, means to move at high speed with a headlong motion, "at full tilt," as the popular idiom has it. However, for the past several decades, *careen* has seemed to assimilate the meaning properly attributed to *career* and statements like "The car lurched out of control and *careened* crazily down the hill" are commonplace in the press. Fowler, second edition, reports this change as evident midway through the twentieth century in U.S. fiction but, judging by the results of the poll of our Usage Panelists, it is well established in nonfiction as well. It would appear that we have here an instance, not of changing usage, but of changed usage.

USAGE PANEL QUESTION

A newspaper report says, "The car *careened* wildly down the street." Do you accept this use of *careen* in the sense of to move fast with a lurching or swerving motion?
In writing   Yes: 87%. No: 13%.
In speech   Yes: 88%. No: 12%.
Would you prefer *career* in the sentence quoted above?
Yes: 20%. No: 80%.

ISAAC ASIMOV: " 'Career' has too prominent a meaning, in another sense."

STEWART BEACH: "Only a grammarian would prefer 'career,' which means something quite different in our language. The British, by the way, as a result of careening when one car hits another speak of it as 'cannoning off.' "

HAL BORLAND: " 'Careen' is utterly wrong, and we have abandoned 'career' in this sense, though right. About all we have left is 'lurch.' "

HEYWOOD HALE BROUN: "Careening is never done wildly. This quiet job of ship repair is usually done in the lee of a tropical island while all hands enjoy fresh fruit."

BEN LUCIEN BURMAN: "Absolutely. It gives a perfect feeling of giddy speed."

[As to the use of "career"] "Good heavens, no! I'd think it as pompous as a career man of the State Department."

ABE BURROWS: "I'll accept 'careen' in the hope that the car looked as though it were *on two wheels*. In speech, 'careen' is too vivid for me. So is 'career' in speech *or* writing."

ALEX FAULKNER: " 'Careened.' When a word has a definite connotation, in this case nautical, it seems a pity to water it down by using it carelessly to describe something else. Since a wildly zig-zagging car and a careened boat have nothing in common, this strikes me as a simple misuse of the word."

A. B. GUTHRIE, JR. "[I would prefer 'career'] but I yield to the common usage."

SYDNEY J. HARRIS: " 'Career' is obsolete."

RICHARD EDES HARRISON: "Lurch, sway, swerve seem to require qualification ('from side to side') before they can substitute for 'careen' even though it has a more restrictive technical meaning."

PAUL HORGAN: "No. To find a synonym is not too difficult."

ALEXANDER KENDRICK: "Yes, even onomatopoetically, 'careen' wins, especially since 'career' has a special human application."

WALTER KERR: "Not any longer—'careen' has taken on the color of the meaning."

CHARLES KURALT: "I wouldn't object to 'career,' but it seems out of date."

JULES LOH: "This fight is long lost."

PHYLLIS MCGINLEY: "Of course 'careened' means 'heeled over' although some dictionaries now give that 'lurching motion' definition. I have even had editors change my 'career' to 'careen' in copy."

WADE MOSBY: "Most newspaper readers (and too many editors) are unaware of 'career' in this sense. I'd prefer to let them have their way instead of making them stumble over the truth."

EDWIN NEWMAN: "Yes. But now I realize I have been wrong."

BERTON ROUECHÉ: "I think this is a case of a word whose meaning has altered for the good. Besides, 'careened' sounds more like the action than does 'career.' "

LEONARD SANDERS: "Lord, the hours I have spent in newsroom arguments on this one. If a car is careering wildly, undoubtedly it will careen. With no evidence to the contrary, 'careen' perhaps is a more apt description."

DAVID SCHOENBRUN: " 'Careen' has achieved general usage. 'Career' has become pedantic, and 'careen' does not jar."

JEAN STAFFORD: "Prefer 'career' . . . maybe."

care of, symbol for. *See* PERCENT/IN CARE OF, SYMBOLS FOR

Caribbean   The preferred pronunciation is Kar-ih-BEE-un but Kah-RIB-ee-un is also acceptable.

carousel/carrousel   Many Americans mistakenly think *carousel* and *carrousel* are British terms for the American "merry-go-round." Not so. The standard British name for this amusement-park delight is "roundabout."

carriageway   British motoring equivalent of the American "highway." A "dual *carriageway*" is, obviously, a dual highway.

carrier salesman   Journalistic euphemism for "newsboy," chiefly business-office use.

case, grammatical   In an inflected language like Latin, *case* is vitally important in the construction of sentences and each *case* clearly differs from the others by different *case* endings or, occasionally, by position in the sentence. Latin nouns customarily appear in one of six *case* forms: nominative, genitive, dative, accusative, vocative, and ablative. English, as a non-inflected language, has really only three different forms for nouns: the basic, all-purpose forms (singular "nightingale" and plural "nightingales") and the possessive form made by adding "'s" to the singular and an apostrophe or " 's" to the plural. Adjectives do not change form. Personal pronouns sometimes have three forms: "I," nominative; "my," genitive or possessive; and "me," objective or accusative. In the plural these become "we," "our," "us." The relative pronoun "who" has the little-used objective *case*, "whom." *See also* WHO/WHOM/WHO-EVER/WHOMEVER.

cashier   In the sense of "to fire or dismiss from a position of command or responsibility for disciplinary reasons," *cashier* is not slang but standard English.

casket/coffin   *Casket* has become a euphemism for *coffin* and we suspect it happened about the same time that an "undertaker" became a "mortician" or "funeral director." The basic meaning of *casket* is "small box for holding jewelry or other valuables" and *Webster's New World Dictionary* gives a clue as to why it became a euphemism for *coffin* when it gives as the second definition of *casket* "a coffin, usually an expensive one."

castor (caster) sugar   British equivalent of the American "superfine" sugar, though more finely ground. It gets its name from the fact that it is ground finely enough to be shaken from a *castor* (British spelling) or *caster* (American spelling).

casualty/death   A *casualty* in time of war is a person killed, injured, captured, or missing in action. Thus the *casualty* figure is always substantially higher than the *death* list. Nonetheless, during the Indochina War, the semantically more acceptable word *casualty* was used many times by leading spokesmen, including the President, when the *death* count was what was actually being stated. Thus a much lower and presumably more acceptable figure was arrived at.

catalogue/catalog   Both spellings are acceptable, with the *catalogue* spelling slightly more commonly found.

cater-corner/cater-cornered/catawampus   On the diagonal. *Cater-corner* and *cater-cornered* are the standard forms of this expression, but there are any number of informal and dialect variations, the most common being "kitty-corner" and "catty-corner." The word originally came from the French "quatre" (four) and merely meant "four-cornered." But users of the term detected a fancied resemblance to the domestic feline and, through folk etymology, made the transition to "kitty" and "catty," in place of "cater." There are some still more remarkable variants, including one common in Southern folk speech, *catawampus* or *cattywampus:* "The policeman gave him a ticket for crossing the street *cattywampus.*" According to perhaps dubious legend, one eminent geometry professor at the University of Tennessee used to make a point with his pupils by explaining that "you might call a rhombus a *catawampus* square."

catsup. *See* KETCHUP/CATSUP

caucus   In the United States a *caucus* is a private meeting of leaders of a political party or faction, usually to plan strategy or a program to be presented before an open meeting of the party or faction. In England, a *caucus* is the controlling organization, usually elected, of a political party.

caused. *See* RESPONSIBLE/CAUSED

-cede/-ceed/-sede   Since there is only one English word which ends in *-sede* ("supersede") any confusion is between *-cede* and *-ceed.* Try to remember that only three words have the *-ceed* ending: "exceed," "proceed," and "succeed." All others of the like-sounding endings are spelled with *-cede,* as "accede," "concede," "precede," and so on.

celebrant/celebrator   The traditional meaning of *celebrant* is "a person who performs a religious ceremony or rite," but it is now frequently used as a synonym for *celebrator,* "one who takes part in a celebration." In formal writing it is best to restrict *celebrant* to its original meaning.

celebrate. *See* COMMEMORATE/CELEBRATE

cemetery   The standard American pronunciation of *cemetery* includes all four syllables, SEM-eh-ter-ee. The slurred pronunciation SEM-eh-tree is either British or an affectation, like DIK-shun-ree for "dictionary" and MIL-ih-tree for "military."

center on/around While *center around* is a very common idiom and is completely understandable by anyone with an ear for the rhythms of colloquial speech, *center on* is surely preferable. Another possibility is "revolve around."

centuries, numbering of Confusion occasionally occurs because of the rather odd practice of naming a century by the date of its end rather than of its beginning. Thus the nineteenth century began in 1800 (some would say 1801) and ended in 1900. To avoid any possible confusion, it may be preferable to refer to the present century as "the 1900s" rather than the "twentieth century." Both formulations are entirely acceptable on any level of usage.

centurion Dictionaries define a *centurion* as a man who commanded a Roman army unit called a "century," a troop unit believed to have numbered one hundred men. Now, with social security, Medicare, and miracle drugs the order of the day, more and more of our citizens are reaching the age of one hundred and the word is acquiring the extended sense of "a person of one hundred years of age or more."

The term is used, semi-facetiously, in still another sense by members of one of the nation's most exclusive assemblages of literary, artistic, educational, and political leaders, the Century Association of New York City. Members of this august group, which includes many university presidents and professors, delight in calling themselves *Centurions.*

cerebral Two pronunciations are acceptable for *cerebral:* seh-REE-brul or SEH-reh-brul, with the former rather more commonly heard.

ceremonial/ceremonious Both of these adjectives are derived from the noun "ceremony" but there is a distinct difference in their meanings. *Ceremonial* means "pertaining to or consisting of ceremony" and is applied primarily to things, as in *"ceremonial* robes." *Ceremonious,* on the other hand, can be applied to either persons or things, and means "full of ceremony or formality," as in *"ceremonious* occasion."

certain Since *certain* means "inevitable" or "unquestionable," it would seem not to require a qualifying modifer or to be subject to comparison, but it is often preceded by words such as "more," "most," "fairly," or "reasonably."

chair As a verb meaning "to preside over (a meeting)," *chair* is widely used and generally accepted as suitable in formal usage. This use of *chair* contrasts with its older meaning of "to place in a position of authority or to elect as chairman."

chair/chairman/chairwoman/chairperson   Until the growth of the Women's Movement, the word *chairman* was used as a matter of course to designate anyone who is in charge of a meeting or a committee, although the term *chairwoman* was not unknown. Because of the protests of feminists to the use of *chairman* for both men and women, many publications adopted the term *chairperson* when the sex was unknown and used *chairman* only when appropriate.

With the feeling that *chairperson* is an awkward word, we suggest the use of the simple word *chair* to cover all situations.

chaise lounge

USAGE PANEL QUESTION

Panelist GEORGE WALD, among others, deplores the appearance of *chaise lounge* in furniture advertisements and in popular speech.
Would you use it in writing   Yes: 9%. No: 91%.
In speech   Yes: 12%. No: 88%.

ALVIN BEAM: "No. But I don't deplore. I hope *lounge* wins in the long run —or just 'long chair' or 'reclining chair.' "
BARRY BINGHAM, SR.: "I see no excuse for chaise lounge. If we are to use the French word 'chaise,' why boggle at its French adjective 'longue'? I think we have a choice of 'chaise longue' or 'long chair.' Chaise lounge is a bastard phrase."
ABE BURROWS: "This horror, which has bothered me for years, is not a simple error. It is based on a mighty optical illusion. People who have no French look at the word 'longue' and automatically their optic nerves move the 'u' to a more logical spot. They don't know what a 'chaise' is but they can see an object that looks like a lounging thing so it's a 'lounge.' Perhaps Mr. Chaise is the man who invented it. 'Sam Chaise and Co. Fine Furniture.' "
JOHN CIARDI: "It is taking over with people who sell bedroom suits. I think they really mean 'chair lounge' as 'lounging chair' and certainly the thing described by either of these terms is different from the thing described by 'chair.' "
HELEN L. KAUFMANN: "If we're going to ingest foreign words into English, we should take them 'as is,' e.g., *flair* and *chaise longue*. Chaise lounge has been creeping insidiously into usage, and I shudder when I hear it."
CLARK KINNAIRD: "There's scant excuse for this usage in any writing or

speech. When was the last time you saw one actual 'chaise longue,' not a divan or sofa?"

PETER S. PRESCOTT: "But surely this is simply a matter of ignorance—it is *wrong,* that's all, not a useful attempt to make our language more flexible."

DANIEL SCHORR: " 'Chaise lounge' is simply an error made by persons who do not know the French origin of 'chaise longue.' "

HAROLD TAYLOR: "Haven't heard anybody say that and hope I never will. I would figure that he was making some kind of joke."

BARBARA TUCHMAN: " 'Lounge' is simply an error."

chambers In American usage *chambers* is the name for a judge's office, usually adjacent to his courtroom. In England it refers to the private office of a barrister.

champion In American usage a *champion* is the person who excels all others in any particular activity, especially in sport. *Champion* is sometimes used attributively but always with the implication of superlative excellence. In England it may also be used to indicate the equivalent of "splendid," as in "He's a *champion* companion on a hike."

chargé d'affaires Like "fiancé" and "chaise longue," *chargé d'affaires* has been borrowed from the French and should retain the French pronunciation, including the pronunciation of the final accented "e" on the first word of the phrase. It literally means "(one) entrusted with business" and should be pronounced shar-ZHAY duh-FAIR. The plural is *chargés d'affaires.*

charisma Originally, *charisma* meant, literally, "a gift from God"—"a special favor, talent, or grace granted by God." In this sense it went unchanged for twenty-five centuries from its Greek origin. It and its adjective "charismatic" were used during the 1930s by followers of Adolf Hitler and Benito Mussolini to indicate their belief that these men were divinely inspired. During the 1950s the term suddenly achieved wide use to describe a person of great personal appeal and charm, especially a political leader with these qualities. During the brief administration of John F. Kennedy, the term was frequently applied to him and Mrs. Kennedy. Since that time the word *charisma* has become so widely abused that one television commentator has defined it simply as "star quality."

In the 1984 presidential campaign, *charisma* was widely used in describing the appeal of Rev. Jesse Jackson. A major work on *charisma* titled *The Spellbinders* was published by Yale University Press. *See also* VOGUE WORDS.

chauvinist

USAGE PANEL QUESTION

Panelist LEONARD SANDERS noted that the word *chauvinist* has come into general use in the sense of "male *chauvinist.*" In Women's Liberation discussions, he reports, the adjective is often dropped and the simple statement "He's a *chauvinist*" is made. Would you agree that the truncated term serves as well as the original "male *chauvinist*"? Would you use the shorter form?

In speech   Yes: 11%. No: 89%.

In writing   Yes: 8%. No: 92%.

JOHN O. BARBOUR: "No. The ultimate in feminine chauvinism would be to deprive other chauvinists of their special chauvinisms."

BARRY BINGHAM, SR.: "The word 'chauvinist' still retains for me its classic meaning of 'one who exhibits exaggerated or bellicose patriotism.' When used alone, I would assume this meaning was intended. When modified by another word, as in 'male chauvinism,' it is clear that the thought has been extended in a certain direction. But 'chauvinist' by itself should be allowed to fill its traditional place in the language, to express a thought that still requires precise expression."

HAL BORLAND: "If there really is an all-male nation somewhere, there it is quite correct. Elsewhere, no."

HEYWOOD HALE BROUN: "How often zealotry leads to inexactitude!"

ANTHONY BURGESS: "It would be a pity to lose the primary meaning, which we still need."

WILLIAM O. DOUGLAS: "Yes—one may say 'she's a chauvinist.' "

ALEX FAULKNER: "No. Only if you mean he's a chauvinist, period, in the traditional sense."

STEPHEN H. AND FRANCES FRITCHMAN: "It *has* to be qualified to retain any useful meaning at all. There are, alas, many kinds of chauvinists."

HELEN L. KAUFMANN: "Why narrow the use of a fine musical-sounding word like *chauvinist* which applies to men, women, children, politicians, nationalists, or what have you?"

ALEXANDER KENDRICK: "I wouldn't use 'chauvinist' at all, in matters of gender. It's not what M. Chauvin had in mind."

JULES LOH: "I might use 'chauvinist' without the modifier if the context clearly indicated sexist zealotry. But chauvinists of all stripes, sadly enough, will be with us forever and need to be identified by craze."

RUSSELL LYNES: "No. What would become of all those other kinds of chauvinists, including female chauvinists?"

DWIGHT MACDONALD: "No. 'Chauvinist' means a super patriot and still does

—and if we make it mean just one kind, then what about 'social chauvinist' once common? Such a change would make language more ambiguous."

DAVID SCHOENBRUN: "I know many male chauvinists who are not chauvinists."

MARK SCHORER: "The original sense of ugly nationalism should be preserved."

EARL UBELL: "No, because the word has other meanings without male."

BILL VAUGHAN: "No. Unless context makes 'male' obvious."

DOUGLAS WATT: "Only when discussing excessive patriotism."

A.B.C. WHIPPLE: "Why limit the use of such a helpful word?"

check/cheque *Check* is the standard American spelling; *cheque* the British. When *cheque* appears in American writing it is either an affectation of the writer or an attempt to impart British flavor, for example: "American Express Travelers' cheques."

checkoff The passage of Section 7A of the Wagner Labor Relations Act made *checkoff* familiar to both labor and management as plants and industries became organized by labor unions. It is the system by which union dues, fees, and assessments are withheld from a worker's pay with his approval and turned over to union officials, thus eliminating a great deal of paperwork on the part of union representatives. It has become such a common practice that such sums are now simply listed under "deductions" along with social security, withholding tax, and other check-shrinking items.

Cheers! British toast, equivalent to "Here's to you!" or "To your good health!," now common also in the U.S.

cheese-paring Despite the informality of its appearance, the British term *cheese-paring* is indicated as standard by the *OED*. It means stingy or parsimonious. A *cheese-paring* fellow is the equivalent of the American "penny-pincher."

chemist The *chemist* is the British equivalent of the American "druggist" or, less frequently, "pharmacist." The "*chemist*'s shop" is the same as the American "drugstore," right down to the fact that the *chemist*'s shops in metropolitan areas sell just about everything under the sun, including medicines almost as a sideline.

chicanery. *See* MENDACITY/DUPLICITY/CHICANERY/CORRUPTION

Chicano Americans of Mexican descent used to be known as Mexican-Americans but today many of them prefer to be known as *Chicanos,* in much the same way that many Negroes prefer to be identified as *blacks*. *See also* BLACK/NEGRO.

Chief Justice   There is a distinction between the title *"Chief Justice* of the United States" and *"Chief Justice* of the Supreme Court," though traditionally the same man has held both offices. As *Chief Justice* of the United States, he is charged with the direction of all federal courts. As *Chief Justice* of the Supreme Court, he is "primus inter pares," the first among equals.

childish/childlike   When used in speaking or writing about adults, *childish* denotes disapproval inasmuch as it indicates something which is immature and of which an adult should not be guilty. *Childlike,* on the other hand, denotes approval, as in *"childlike* faith."

While *childlike* should never be applied to a child, it is proper to use *childish* to describe characteristics or actions of a child, as in *"childish* laughter" or *"childish* pretending."

Chino-. *See* SINO-

chintzy   Chintz is a glazed cotton fabric with brightly colored floral print. The adjective *chintzy* originally meant pertaining to or decorated with such fabric but it also has an extended meaning of "tawdry" or "cheap." In this extended sense it is not slang but informal and should be avoided in formal writing or speech.

chit-chat. *See* RICOCHET WORDS

chocolate   *Chocolate* has almost as many pronunciations as there are brands of it on the market. The *Pronouncing Dictionary of American English* lists seven different and acceptable pronunciations. The four most common are CHOK-lit ("o" as in "lot"); CHAWK-lit; CHOK-uh-lit; and CHAWK-uh-lit. Since so many *chocolate* lovers pronounce its name with differing regional emphasis, it is correct to use any of these four versions. Purists, however, will continue to sound all three syllables.

choice. *See* ALTERNATIVE

chortle. *See* BLEND WORDS/BRUNCH WORDS/PORTMANTEAU WORDS

chow   *Chow* is now considered slang when used as a generic term for "food." For such a lowly word, it has rather remarkable antecedents. In Mandarin Chinese there is a word "ch'ao," meaning to cook or fry. This is probably the word from which we get *chow* and here's how it came about. At and after the time of the California Gold Rush, many thousands of Chinese were imported to work on the transcontinental and other railroads then under construction. One of their early contributions to American cuisine was a preserve of ginger and various fruits in heavy syrup which they called *chow-chow*. Later this expression was applied—as it still is—to a variety of pickles in mustard sauce. And then, of course, there is *chow* mein, an authentic Chinese dish. In any event, with all these influences, it is not surprising that *chow* became broadened in meaning and, by 1880, was widely used in slang contexts to mean food of any kind.

Christmas/Xmas. *See* XMAS

chucker-out The *chucker-out* (marvelously descriptive phrase) is the bouncer in a British pub.

chutzpah This word, borrowed from the Yiddish, is becoming more and more common in informal speech. It is pronounced HUTZ-puh, with the initial "h" sounding as if you were clearing your throat. It has been defined as "gall, moxie, nerve and audacity compounded with brazen assertiveness and a complete disregard for the sensibilities of others." It was *chutzpah* that Made Sammy Run and resulted in his being one of the most colorful characters in modern fiction.

A well-known example of *chutzpah* is this: a lad with real *chutzpah* is one who would kill both his parents and then demand leniency from the court on the ground that he is an orphan. *See also* YIDDISHISMS.

cigaret/cigarette *Cigarette* is the preferred spelling, though *cigaret* is acceptable.

circadian rhythm *Circadian rhythm* is the technical term for a phenomenon sometimes loosely called the "human body clock," disruption of which leads to "jet lag." It is the pattern or rhythm that each of us sets up for governing the routine of working, sleeping, and eating through a normal twenty-four-hour period. Most of us are not aware of the degree to which we have routinized our lives until we take an overnight flight to Europe or the Orient with little or no sleep en route. If we then try to conduct our normal activities on the day we arrive, the resulting mental and physical dislocation can be so severe that extreme fatigue or blackout may result.

circle/cycle. *See* VICIOUS CIRCLE/VICIOUS CYCLE

circus In America the *circus* is the entertainment, primarily for children, featuring clowns, animals, trapeze artists, and the like. In England a *circus* is simply a rotary intersection. It may be as simple as the kind known in

America as a traffic circle—indicated by a road sign reading "*circus ahead*"—or it may be a major intersection like London's Oxford Circus and Piccadilly Circus. In recent years most road signs in rural areas have been changed to "roundabout ahead."

cities, famous The names of internationally celebrated cities need not—indeed, should not—be accompanied by the names of the countries in which they are located. There is only one internationally famous Paris and there is no need to add that it is in France. The same goes for London, Rome, Hong Kong, Tokyo, and Cairo. It is important, however, to add the clarifying geographical tag on namesake cities like Cairo, Illinois; London, Ontario; and Paris, Maine.

City, the British name for the equivalent of the American "Wall Street" or financial district. For this reason, the City editor of a London newspaper is its financial editor, not—as in the U.S.—the editor responsible for local news coverage.

claim *Claim* has an element of expected opposition or doubt which verbs such as "assert" or "state" do not. If a person *claims* that the boat he is selling is watertight, he may well believe this to be true but it is also possible that he may be proven wrong.

classic/classical While these two adjectives are technically interchangeable in some senses, *classical* is preferred for anything pertaining to Roman and Greek culture and literature or to an established, authoritarian method, as a "classical education."

Classic also has a meaning not attributed to *classical:* that of "outstandingly important" or "the very best."

cleanse/clean While both mean "to rid of impurities or dirt," *cleanse* is used primarily in a figurative sense, as in "*cleanse* my soul," while *clean* has a more literal sense, as in "*clean* the garage."

cleave Many people are puzzled as to how the word *cleave* can mean "cling to" and "separate from." Even the Bible perpetuates the confusion. There we find (Job 29:10) "their tongue *cleaved* to the roof of their mouth" and (Genesis 22:3) Abraham "clave the wood for the burnt offering." Here we have the cause of the trouble, for these are actually two different words.

In Middle English the first word ("cling to") was spelled "clevian" and came from the Old English "cleofian." At the same period the second word ("separate from" or "split") was spelled "cleven" and came from the Old English "cleofan." The scholars who translated the King James version of the Bible decided, rightly or wrongly, to ignore the single letter "i" that marked the difference between the two words in their earlier forms. Both were rendered as *cleave* and that's how the confusion began.

clench/clinch   While either may be used in the sense of "to fasten or secure a nail or rope," each has its own uses in other respects. A person *clenches* hands, fists, teeth, or jaw, or an object held tightly in his or her hand. He or she *clinches* an argument or an agreement and boxers *clinch* when they hold each other so that neither can strike.

clerihew   A four-line humorous verse about a person—usually famous—who is named in the first line. It gets its name from its inventor, E. *Clerihew* Bentley. Here is an example: "It was a weakness of Voltaire's/To forget to say his prayers/And one which, to his shame,/He never overcame."

cliché   *Cliché* is a direct borrowing from the French word for stereotype plate. So its basic meaning is the same as our word "stereotype" when used to mean something everlastingly repeated in the same form. We have all been forced to sit through long, *cliché*-ridden speeches and we have been bored to tears (and that's a *cliché* for you!). So we would be the last people to make a strong defense of the *cliché*. It's worth remembering, however, that very often—most often, indeed—a *cliché* became a *cliché* because it expressed a thought more clearly and precisely than any other combination of words. Sometimes a speaker or writer, trying to avoid the obvious *cliché,* ends up using a lot more words and impressing his listeners or readers as being far more windy than he needs to be. So the advice from here is to avoid the *cliché* when an equally apt phrasing comes readily to mind. However, if the tried-and-true (ah, there, another *cliché*) expression says what you want to say and says it well—go ahead and use it. Remember Mark Twain's advice about words—"The difference between the right word and the almost right word is the difference between lightning and the lightning bug." And that advice has been quoted so often that it's close to *cliché* status itself by now.

The great authority on *clichés* is, of course, Usage Panelist Frank Sullivan, author of the unforgettable Mr. Arbuthnot essays in *The New Yorker* magazine. On the eve of his eightieth birthday, Alden Whitman of *The New York Times* interviewed Sullivan and he described himself as being "fit as a fiddle, although not as spry as I used to be. The spirit is willing, but the flesh is weak. Otherwise I'm in the pink." And he adds his advice to a young man starting out on a career as a humorist: "The neophyte, the tyro, must start from the time he is knee-high to a grasshopper to guard his own funny lines while stealing every quip he can lay his hands to. . . . He should seek out the foibles of his times and hold them up to gentle ridicule. He should provoke laughter but never forget that mirth has a serious side. Just as there should be a pearl in every oyster, there must be a rock in every snowball." And that, it seems to us, is stealing enough of Mr. Sullivan's quips to illustrate our proud boast that nobody knows *clichés* like Frank Sullivan. And in the hands of a master humorist the *cliché* is certainly not to be avoided.

climb on the bandwagon. *See* BANDWAGON, CLIMB ON THE

clinch. *See* CLENCH/CLINCH

clinic   "Clinicus," the Latin word from which our *clinic* comes, originally meant a person confined to bed by illness. Then it came to mean a doctor whose practice was largely made up of visiting bedridden patients. In time it described a technique of teaching medicine by examining and treating patients in the presence of medical students. A further refinement was the development of *clinics* as places where groups of doctors practiced, either each in his own specialty, as at the Mayo *Clinic,* or specializing in treatment of a single disease, as a cancer *clinic.* It is also applied to the section of a hospital or medical school where outpatients are treated.

All of these meanings of *clinic* had some relation to the original meaning. In recent years, *clinic* has come to also mean any institution or organization offering treatment or advice or practice. Now we hear of sales-promotion *clinics,* job-finding *clinics,* domestic-relations *clinics,* and even Little League baseball *clinics.*

clique   All current dictionaries now list both KLEEK and KLIK as acceptable pronunciations for *clique.* The late Frank Colby in his *American Pronouncing Dictionary* claimed that most Americans prefer KLIK, but we suspect that his ear was attuned to Western American speech, rather than to the speech patterns of the country as a whole. Those who are aware of the French origin of the word are more likely to pronounce it KLEEK.

clone/cloning   *Clone,* an intransitive verb, and the noun *cloning* are fairly recent additions to the body of standard English, borrowings from the language of science. *Cloning* is asexual reproduction or propagation. At first it was confined to bulbs, cuttings, and the like. More recent laboratory experiments have duplicated frogs, for instance, without the customary cooperation of a member of the opposite sex. Whether *cloning* of the human animal is within even the remotest range of possibility is something only science can answer. The product of cloning is a *clone.* And *clone* may be used figuratively—"He is a *clone* of his professor."

close proximity A *redundancy* (which see). *Proximity* is closeness; delete *close*.

clout This is a *vogue word* (which see) which became popular in the early 1970s especially in business and political circles. Originally meaning "a strong blow," it was extended to mean "great and effective influence," or "sufficient pressure to achieve a desired end."

club. *See* SALOON

club (its/their) *Club* is a collective noun and, in American usage, is followed by a singular verb, as is "committee." Despite the fact that each is made up of individuals, it is not proper to say that "the *club* (or committee) will hold *their* annual meeting on Tuesday." Say rather: ". . . *its* annual meeting."

clunker This is slang for something that is inferior or worthless, especially a car or other vehicle. A *clunker* may be a "lemon," a new or fairly new car which has everything wrong with it, or it may be a dilapidated, worn-out car which is equally worthless. *Clunker* is also used in show business jargon.

co-. *See* PREFIXES AND SUFFIXES, WITH AND WITHOUT HYPHEN

co-author. *See* AUTHOR and CO-COMMENTATE

COBOL A computer programming language, similar to English, that is used in data processing. It is an acronym of CO(mmon) B(usiness) O(riented) L(anguage). What's more, it was devised by CODASYL, the C(onference) O(f) DA(ta) SY(stem) L(anguages).

cockamamie Slang for "silly," "foolish," "inconsequential," "valueless": "What a *cockamamie* notion!" The word has its origin in children's mispronunciation of "decalcomania," the name of dye transfers that youngsters used to put on their hands and arms. Since they were very cheap and soon wore off, *cockamamie* came to be applied to anything trifling or second rate. More recently it acquired the meaning of "silly" or "ludicrous."

cock a snook British expression, enjoying something of a vogue in the Eastern U.S. as well, for "thumb one's nose."

cocktail, to Madison Avenue advertising writers do not have a corner on abuse of the language by converting nouns into verbs. In the columns of classified advertising in a Wausau, Wisconsin, newspaper the following appeared: "Bartender and cocktail waitress. Must be able to tend bar 5 days a week over the noon hour, 3 hours a day. Must be able to *cocktail* 2 nights a week. Guaranteed Sundays off."

cocktail lounge. *See* SALOON

co-commentate   Although widely used in reference to television coverage of news events, *co-commentate* is still a singularly graceless verb, almost as irritating as "co-author" and "co-host." At least, *commentate* is a verb form, while "author" and "host" are nouns being converted to verbs. *Commentate* is listed in the *Oxford English Dictionary* as going back as far as 1794 but is labeled "rare." Present-day dictionaries list all three words as verbs, but literate people find them awkward and unappealing. If these words continue as verbs, it is to be hoped that the "co-" forms at least retain the hyphen so that they can be pronounced correctly. *See also* AUTHOR and HOST/CO-HOST.

coffin. *See* CASKET/COFFIN

cohese   *Cohese* is an illiterate back-formation from "cohesion" that merits attention only because it was used by one-time White House adviser Robert Finch in speaking about a meeting of educators. "The group *cohesed,*" reported Finch. Presumably he meant "cohered."

cohort   Some years ago Gilbert Highet, writing in *Horizon* magazine, delivered his judgment on the use and misuse of *cohort* as a synonym for "companion," a judgment he has been kind enough to share with us. "Cohort," he wrote, "means a body of soldiers. A pure Latin word, it has been in English for hundreds of years. An excellent word, it got into everybody's mind from Byron's splendid poem 'The Destruction of Sennacherib,' which begins: 'The Assyrian came down like the wolf on the fold,/And his cohorts were gleaming in purple and gold.' From Byron's poem the word 'cohorts' probably passed through McGuffey's Readers. At some time within the last fifty years or so, a reporter remembered that fine poetic sentence and inserted a concealed quotation from it in a newspaper story, something like this: 'At today's parade in honor of St. Patrick, none stepped out more bravely than Police Captain XXX, followed by his cohorts.'

"Now you know what reporters are. They don't read books. They read newspapers. The word 'cohorts' stuck in the mind of another reporter who used it in the singular. He was the real murderer. . . . The mistake is a pure malapropism. It is still a complete mistake."

We felt he was a bit harsh on reporters, some of whom, to our positive knowledge, do read—and even write—books. However, the prob-

lem posed seemed worth the attention of our Usage Panel, with the results
and comments indicated below.

USAGE PANEL QUESTION

Cohort appears often in the press in the sense of "comrade" or "associate."
Would you approve "The gang leader and his *cohorts* held up the
bank"?
In writing   Yes: 43%. No: 57%.
In casual speech   Yes: 63%. No: 37%.

ISAAC ASIMOV: " 'Cohorts' gives the added flavor of a war band, which is
good."

SHERIDAN BAKER: "I would accept, with a sigh. I notice that my sociological
friends are now using 'cohort' impeccably to mean a group of young
contemporaries."

HEYWOOD HALE BROUN: "Not unless the gang leader is followed by a company of Roman soldiers."

ANTHONY BURGESS: "A cohort implies a considerable number of followers.
There is no word that quite carries its multitudinous flavour, and the
original meaning must be cherished."

WALTER CRONKITE: "Yes. You just forced me to look it up—a valuable
advantage to these exercises."

JOHN K. HUTCHENS: "Only an old Roman could object seriously to this."

ROBERT LIPSYTE: "Yes. The word seems to have only humorous connotations
in this instance."

WRIGHT MORRIS: "Usage seems to be winning this one—according to my
cohorts!"

STANTON PECKHAM: "Cohort suggests a military ally of some assumed respectability. A gang leader or a politician would more likely have cro-
nies."

ORVILLE PRESCOTT: "Yes, because it is used in the sense of force, appropriate
to its original military meaning."

PETER S. PRESCOTT: "For me the word has a slightly humorous, slightly
deprecating quality. I would use it only in joking."

VERMONT ROYSTER: "No. Might as well say, 'William Morris and his cohorts
on the Harper Dictionary.' "

DAVID SCHOENBRUN: "In casual speech, yes."

WALTER W. "RED" SMITH: "If it's good enough for Byron . . ."

DAVIDSON TAYLOR: "No. Unless he was an Assyrian."

BARBARA TUCHMAN: "No. It doesn't seem appropriate to a gang leader—
should be reserved for more important undertakings."

EARL UBELL: "A little fancy, but why not under the right conditions?"

coiffeur/coiffure Two borrowings from the French, both now standard English. *Coiffeur* (pronounced kwah-FER) is the hairdresser or "hair stylist," as he or she sometimes prefers to be called. *Coiffure* (pronounced kwah-FYOOR) is the style or manner in which the hair is arranged.

coinages, improper Pitfalls await the person who tries to invent new words. Two cases in point are "monokini" and "girlcott," both nonce creations that enjoyed some vogue during the 1960s. Though now forgotten, they may repay a brief examination, so that the errors committed in their creation may be avoided when similar inspiration strikes word coiners of the future. First, the inventor of "monokini" obviously thought that the "bi-" in "bikini" was the customary prefix meaning "two," so that replacing it with "mono-," the prefix meaning "one," would make the point that the monokini consisted of a single item of apparel, rather than two. Unfortunately for that theory, "bikini" actually took its name from the Bikini atoll of the Marshall Islands, where the U.S. did some early atom-bomb testing. Similarly the "boy" in "boycott" is not at all a youngster whose attention, incidentally, would be caught by the girl in the monokini. Far from it. This "boy" is merely the first syllable in the name of the infamous land agent in Ireland, Charles Cunningham Boycott, who treated the land tenants so badly that they ostracized him completely and thus created the first boycott. So "girlcott," obviously, is not only a nonce word but a nonsense word.

cole slaw/coleslaw/cold slaw Possibly because it is a salad which is served cold, this dish of shredded cabbage is often mistakenly termed *cold slaw.*

    Coleslaw, usually written as one word, is the correct term. It comes from the Latin "colis," meaning cabbage, and the Dutch "sla," meaning salad.

collaborator/collaborationist A *collaborator* is one who works with others for a common goal or to produce an artistic or literary piece of work. A *collaborationist* is one who cooperates or collaborates with an enemy occupying or trying to occupy his native land.

collectibles These are items from the not-too-far-distant past for which a fad born of nostalgia has developed. They include such things as baseball cards, comic books, political campaign buttons and posters, glass dishes given away at movie houses during the depression of the 1930s, and other such items. Some of them, especially comic books, bring good prices, depending on the age, condition, and rarity of the item but the value of most of them is to the collector in person or to another collector intent on increasing his or her own supply. They are a breed apart from antiques, whose values are determined by experts in the field.

collective *Collective* is an adjective whose use should be confined to phrases such as "*collective* judgment," "*collective* efforts," "*collective* strength," which indicate a number of individuals acting as a group. Phrases such as "turned their *collective* eyes," sometimes used to indicate simultaneous action, are preposterous.

collective nouns *Collective nouns* are nouns that are singular in form but that describe a group of people or things. Examples of *collective nouns* would include "family," "mob," "team," "couple," and "people." The problem—and it is one that has perplexed hosts of writers, judging by the frequency of its appearance in our reader mail—is whether the *collective noun* should be followed by a singular or plural verb. The rule is that you use the singular if the subject is regarded as a unit, the plural if it is regarded as a collection of individuals. Thus: "The couple was engaged" but "The couple featured in the picture were Fred Astaire and Ginger Rogers."

Despite the seeming simplicity of the rule, it does complicate life and one can't help envying the British, who generally follow all *collective nouns* with plural verbs. The result can be quite disconcerting to an American visitor to Britain. He hears on the BBC: "Today the Parliament have done so-and-so." His sports pages banner such headlines as AUSTRALIA TRIUMPH OVER SWANSEA and GLAMORGAN DEFEAT NEWCASTLE. The effect, as one American sportswriter commented, is of one vast howling typographical error. No doubt our press similarly horrifies visiting Britons at first reading. As one such might phrase it: "Your press horrify me."

collide/collision The original sense of *collide* was that of two persons, animals, or objects coming together with violent impact while both were in motion. However, when a fast-moving car strikes a tree or other stationary object, such an expression as "The car *collided* with the stone wall" has become entirely acceptable as standard English.

colloquial English As explained in the early pages of this book, we do not use the word *colloquial* as a usage label in this dictionary because it is so widely misunderstood by many literate users of the language. Even some of our distinguished Usage Panelists have made it clear from their comments on some of the questions put to them that they consider *colloquial* to be a classification for a sort of high-class slang, the kind of slang that might properly be used in writing without the necessity of enclosing it in quotation marks. Not so. *Colloquial* simply means "spoken" or "conversational" and is generally applied to expressions that are perfectly acceptable in ordinary speech or writing. Virtually all popular newspapers and magazines designed for the general public are now written in a style properly labeled *colloquial.* However, because of the widespread misconception about the word, we use "informal" as our label for that level of speech and writing in this dictionary. Incidentally, the late George Lyman Kittredge, who made great contributions to both the First and Second Editions of Webster's New International Dictionary (which used the label "colloq."), once commented: "I myself speak 'colloq.' and often write it." *See also* SLANG.

colonel   How did *colonel* come to be pronounced KER-nel? The explanation involves at least four centuries of British military history. In the sixteenth century the word was spelled "coronel" and pronounced with three syllables, pretty much as spelled. Then, thanks to the British tendency to streamline pronunciations, the word "coronel" acquired a two-syllable pronunciation, first KOR-nel, then KER-nel. The spelling was later altered to the one we use today—but the pronunciation remains the same.

column/columnist   Thanks in large part to the influence of the late Walter Winchell, who often spelled these words "kolyum" and "kolyumist," these mispronunciations at one time had a wide vogue and, according to readers of our column, still persist in some parts of the country. No matter. The correct pronunciation for *column* is KOL-um and for *columnist* KOL-um-nist. And note the "n" in the last syllable.

comforter   In British usage a *comforter* is the equivalent of the American baby pacifier or, as the *OED Supplement* puts it, "a dummy teat put into a baby's mouth to quieten it." In the U. S. a *comforter* is a quilt used as bedcovering.

comma, series or serial   There is a convention among careful text and reference-book copyeditors called the *series, or serial, comma.* These editors feel that the colors of our national flag are "red, white, and blue"— NOT "red, white and blue." If the distinction eludes you, rest assured that you have plenty of company. The comma before the "and" in such a series of adjective modifiers has long been abandoned by newspaper copyeditors, but is still retained by many editors of textbooks and reference books. That's why, when the Morrises are writing for newspaper publication, their column is called "Words, Wit and Wisdom"—without the comma before "and." But when they are writing for dictionaries or other reference books, they put it in.

comma, use with phrases in apposition   A Pittsburgh correspondent submits the following examples of comma misuse taken from a local newspaper: "Von Braun, has been living with rockets since he was twelve" and "Tim Stevens, said his brother walked out of the office." The only occasion in which commas may appear between a subject and its verb is when they set off a phrase in apposition to the subject—and then two commas, not one, must be used: "The champion, a fighter we knew well, soon found himself out of breath." When dealing with a word or phrase in apposition, a distinction is drawn between those restrictive or limiting in nature ("Mary Queen of Scots" or "Peter the newsboy") in which case no comma is used, and those which are nonrestrictive or merely descriptive, in which a comma is used ("Queen Elizabeth II, the ocean liner," or "Peter, the lad on our street").

commando   At the time of the Boer War of 1899–1902, the word *commando* meant "a small striking force, trained to make quick and devastating raids on enemy-held positions." Originally a *commando* was the troop unit. Now we tend to think of a *commando* as a single soldier and speak of the group as "*commando* forces" or "*commando* units."

commas, inverted   *Inverted commas* (also "ticks") is British for "quotation marks." It is wholly appropriate because the British use single quotes (') rather than double quotes (") for the primary punctuation of quoted material. In England the following sentence would be punctuated thus: He told Tommy, 'Sorry, lad, time's up,' while the American version would be: He told Tommy, "Sorry, lad, time's up."

commemorate/celebrate   A column reader noted a statement by a broadcaster that one of the events of the day was the admission of the first woman to practice on the floor of the stock exchange and that a ceremony was held to *commemorate* the occasion. How could one *commemorate* something that was just taking place? The answer, obviously, is that you can't honor the memory (which is what *commemorate* means) of an event at the time it is occurring. The correct verb would be *celebrate*.

commend/praise   *Praise* is, in a sense, a broader and more general word than *commend* in that it means "to express admiration for the total worth of a person or thing." *Commend* is usually used in connection with a particular quality or achievement which meets with approval, as in "The president commended him for his valor." Note the "for," which indicates the specific quality commended. It is not always necessary; it would also be proper to say, "The president commended his valor."

commentate

USAGE PANEL QUESTION

Commentate, a back-formation from "commentator," is well established in the intransitive sense of to give a commentary on an event. Today it is also heard often as a transitive verb: "Nancy will *commentate* the fashion show." Also heard are such formulations as "Nancy and Heidi will co-*commentate* the show."

Do you approve of *commentate* as a transitive verb in speech? No.
In writing? No.
Co-commentate? In speech? No. In writing? No.
(100% "No" on each question.)

DAVE ANDERSON: "It's a TV derivation. Enough said."

ISAAC ASIMOV: "The expression is 'comment on.' The trouble is 'commentator' itself is infelicitous. It should be 'commenter,' just as one who dissents is a 'dissenter' and not a 'dissentator'!"

BARRY BINGHAM, SR.: " 'Commentate' is an ugly and ungainly word and 'to co-commentate' is even less attractive."

ALEX FAULKNER: "What's wrong with 'comment'?"

FRANCES FRITCHMAN: "I won't even accept it as an intransitive verb. I hate it."

RAY GANDOLF: "A thousand times no. I would never orientate myself to such a corruption."

JOHN K. HUTCHENS: "An awful word, however used. Why not simply 'comment on'?"

DIANE JOHNSON: "I can't see the point or usefulness of this at all and it sounds stupid."

JAMES J. KILPATRICK: "As it happens, I am a TV commentator, but so help me, I do not 'commentate'; I 'comment,' or I do 'commentary' but that's it."

STANLEY KUNITZ: "Anyone with half an ear should know better."

DWIGHT MACDONALD: "Ye Gods! Never heard of this word. Let's forget the whole thing."

WADE MOSBY: "It's abrasive to the ears."

EDWIN NEWMAN: "I vote 'no' even though I am called a commentator."

MARGE PIERCY: "A commentator is one who comments. I do not understand how 'commentating' differs from 'commenting upon' or perhaps criticizing or interpreting."

ORVILLE PRESCOTT: "There is no such word and so obvious an outrage against the language must never become an accepted usage."

PETER S. PRESCOTT: "I won't even use the intransitive form."

LEO ROSTEN: "I would not even remarkate so adversely except that I resentate such unneededated neologisms."

HAROLD SCHONBERG: "To 'commentate' is just plain ugly and intellectually sloppy."

ELVIS STAHR, JR.: "I don't even approve of it in the intransitive sense."

EDWARD TRIPP: "Though this is no exception to the rule that back formations survive because they acquire different meanings from the original verb, it is a kind of jargon, like 'media' as a singular noun, that I detest."

common. *See* MUTUAL/COMMON

common cracker A *common cracker* is a plain, thick, unsalted cracker, easily split, and often served in New England with clam chowder and other soups. Apparently uncommon, despite the name, in other parts of the country, *common crackers* go unrecorded in most dictionaries, though Merriam-Webster's Third International does grant them a rather grudging cross-reference to "boston (usu. cap.) crackers."

commonwealth/state Four of the fifty states making up the United States of America officially label themselves *commonwealths,* rather than *states.* They are Massachusetts, Pennsylvania, Virginia, and Kentucky. Thus: *Commonwealth* of Massachusetts, not *State* of Massachusetts. Puerto Rico is also officially titled a *Commonwealth.*

communicate/communications. *See* VOGUE WORDS

company (its/their) *Company* is a collective noun which takes a singular personal pronoun, as in "The *company* had a policy of giving *its* employees at least one week's vacation regardless of length of employment." *Their* can be used only when speaking of more than one company. British usage runs directly counter to American usage in this instance and in the case of many other collective nouns. *See also* COLLECTIVE NOUNS.

comparative, lost Examples of a very common blunder in newspaper writing are: "Foley appears to have the largest budget of the two candidates" and "Lucy is the youngest of the two daughters." Both statements are in error. Of two budgets, one can be "larger," never "largest." Of two daughters, one may be "younger," never "youngest." *See also* ADJECTIVES, COMPARISON OF.

comparative, unfinished The *unfinished comparative* is a favorite device of advertising copywriters. Example: "Underarms sprayed with Zilch deodorant stayed drier longer." But they don't tell you what they stayed drier longer than. The listener is left wondering when that other shoe is going to drop.

compare/contrast *Compare* and *contrast* differ in that the former most often refers to comparison of like objects, often noting both similarities and dissimilarities, while *contrast* invariably cites differences between two objects: "The show judge *compared* the points of the competing poodles" but "The gloom of night *contrasts* sharply with the radiance of dawn."

The choice of a preposition to follow *compare* depends on the context. If the basis of comparison is an important aspect or quality common to both persons or objects, the proper preposition is "to." This is true when the intent is to emphasize similarity. When all aspects and qualities are examined for similarity or dissimilarity, the proper preposition is "with." This distinction should be observed in formal speech or writing but in informal speech or writing "to" and "with" are frequently used interchangeably.

The verb *contrast* is usually followed by "with." When using the noun form, we speak of the "*contrast* between" two persons, things, or events and of one being "in *contrast* to" the other.

comparison of adjectives. *See* ADJECTIVES, COMPARISON OF

compatriot   The essential meaning of *compatriot* is "fellow countryman," as is obvious from the elements of the word. It has acquired an extended meaning of "colleague" or "fellow member of a profession or academic faculty." This extended use is, however, informal.

compensate   What was once a psychologist's technical use of *compensate* has become common in the language of many laymen. The meaning is "to counterbalance an undesirable trait with stress on a trait which is more acceptable to society."

compere   *Compere* (pronounced kom-PAIR) is a British term, roughly equivalent to our "master of ceremonies." It is used both as a noun ("Vic Jones is *compere* of the variety bill at the Palladium") and as a verb ("Sally Hughes will *compere* the TV spectacular"). For the record, the British borrowed the word from the French, where it meant "godfather" —with no Mafia implications attached. The American show-business magazine *Variety* has used the term occasionally, so it may be making its way into American theatrical argot.

complacent/complaisant   The distinction between these two and between their noun forms, *complacency* and *complaisance,* is often ignored. A *complacent* person is one who is pleased with himself or herself, or contented with things as they are. A *complaisant* person is one who tries to please others and who complies with others' wishes, requests, or demands in a willing or cheerful manner.

compleat   Archaic spelling of "complete," now undergoing a revival of sorts. Its most notable appearance was in the title of *The Compleat Angler* by Isaak Walton, the classic book on fishing, which has rightly been called "one of the monuments of English literature." In Walton's time it had the meaning of "fully equipped or endowed, especially as regards some art or occupation." It is worth noting that the new *Supple-*

ment to the *Oxford English Dictionary* reports that *compleat* has been "recently revived in imitation of its 17th century use" and quotes from Mary McCarthy's 1963 novel, *The Group:* "She writes and sings and paints and dances and plays I don't know how many instruments. The *compleat* girl."

complected The expressions *dark-complected* and *light-complected* are commonly heard in regional dialect but must be regarded as substandard. Say rather: "dark-complexioned" and "light-complexioned." There is, incidentally, a verb *complect,* meaning to intertwine or weave together: "The strands of the hooked rug were tightly *complected.*"

complement/compliment These words, though similar in sound, are completely different in meaning. *Complement* means to fill out, to complete a whole: "The forty-degree angle *complements* the fifty-degree angle, making a full right angle." *Compliment* means to praise or congratulate, especially in a gracious manner: "He *complimented* the violinist on his impeccable performance."

complete Technically, *complete* is an adjective which is not subject to comparison through the use of limiting words such as "more," "most," or "less." In practice, however, it is acceptable in certain instances, such as areas in which it is hard to define when something is actually *complete.* Thus it is possible to say, "This is the most *complete* study to date of that period, but any or all of its conclusions may have to be changed if further research warrants."

completely/wholly There is a fine distinction between these two which should be observed in formal writing. *Wholly* is an antonym of "partly" and, just as "partly" means "in part," *wholly* means "as a whole." *Completely* is an antonym of "partially" and deals with the question of degree. So it would be proper to say, "He has a *wholly* erroneous concept of the situation," and "Continue spreading the frosting until the cake is *completely* covered."

complex The use of the noun *complex* to describe any unit made up of a number of related parts is very old. Recently it has been used to mean a group of related buildings, such as a "medical *complex.*"

composed of. *See* DIVIDED INTO/COMPOSED OF

compound words and phrases, plurals of. *See* PLURALS OF COMPOUND WORDS AND PHRASES

compulsory. *See* MANDATORY/COMPULSORY

computerese   With the advent of computers, there has evolved a sublanguage known as *computerese.* This bears no resemblance to the two languages, FORTRAN and COBOL, used by technicians in preparing programs for input to digital computers. Rather, *computerese* is the virtually incomprehensible jargon used by computer operators in communicating with each other. Here are two examples, the first from a data-processing guidance manual: "The application of this system requires the creation of a file of preformatted forms that can be accessed via an operator at a terminal. . . . The verifier can page through the specification forms manual and read what has been inputted." The second example is said to be an actual description of one of the computers —though you couldn't prove it by us. Anyhow, here goes: "This processor is a fourth-generation, hybrid, self-organizing, bionic, implicitly and heuristically programmed, pattern-recognizing, neural-dynamic, cybernetic, goal-seeking, problem-solving, self-replicating, evolutionary, micrologic, microprogrammed, multiaccess, redundant, cellular, adaptive, unsupervised, cluster-seeking, piecewise linear, hyperquadratic, self-teaching, time-shared, on line, real time, conversational mode, interactive, sketch-pad, nanosecond speed, non-parametric, feature-extracting, optimal, stochastic, artificially intelligent, recursive, list-processing, interruptable, robotological-computing automaton and symbol manipulator that works on a syntax-directed, cybercultural, systems approach with a mass, large-scale-integrated, microcircuit, thin film, associative, content-addressable, modular, hierarchical, virtual memory capable of graphic communications among any number and variety of man-machine interfaces."

To which we can only say that, as they say in *computerese,* it sounds like kludge to us—and kludge is what the hardware outputs when the input is not properly structured. That's also known as "gigo"—garbage in and garbage out.

In the years following the appearance of the words above in our first edition, no single area of activity has witnessed such astounding expansion as the use of computers in America's work and play. So it seems appropriate to add these comments from Christopher Earnest, a keen student of *computerese.*

This is my field, so I'm probably biased, but this particular jargon seems no worse than many others, and has some rather nice usages, in my opinion.

One such is the word "bug," meaning a logical error in a program, but without any connotation of guilt. As every programmer (two m's please!) quickly learns, some bugs creep in by themselves and are nobody's fault—a bit like an infection. Another example is the use of "virtual" in the phrase "virtual memory." Such a memory is not a real hardware component, but it can be used as such by a program. (The use of "memory" here *is* unfortunate; the British "store" is much better.) The mapping of virtual memory onto real memory is done by other hardware, which is "transparent" to the program—another nice usage. (If something is virtual, you can see it but it isn't there; if it's transparent, it's there but you can't see it.) Even the term "software," perhaps strange at first, grows on one, and is in any case indispensable.

English has adapted to computers much better than have some other languages. English computer terminology is often borrowed directly, leading to results verging on caricature. For example, "he updated the file" is in German usually "er hat die Datei upgedated," with the parts of "update" pronounced as in English. Translations of English terms can be just as odd. One of my favorites is a German term for "software": "immaterielle Ware," which connotes the incorporeal. ("Software" is also used.)

In any case, whatever you think of computer jargon, you should at least get it right. The jargon is not private to computer operators, but is used also by programmers, mathematicians, salesmen, managers, and even some secretaries. The past participle of "to input" is "input," not "inputted." The terms "associative" and "content-addressable" are synonymous. Most important of all, "kludge" (pronounced kloodj) means a program, hardware device, system, or organization that is the antithesis of elegance and simplicity. Rube Goldberg's devices were kludges, although some modern computer systems are far more inelegant. A kludge may actually perform a desired function, albeit clumsily. The adjective is "kludgey"; most bureaucracies are kludgey.

As this edition goes to press the most notable development in the evolution of computers for use by the lay person is the creation of devices that use ordinary English in programs. Quite possibly much of this *computerese* is already obsolescent. *See* ACRONYM.

conclave   *Conclave* is often mistakenly used to designate an open meeting or general assembly. It is not. It is a secret or confidential meeting.

concretize   Dictionaries do not even label this as slang but to us it is a linguistic horror akin to "finalize." It means to "make specific" or "give final form to" and is a favorite of business administrators, bureaucrats, and other semi-literates.

concur *Concur* has three different meanings, each of which requires a different preposition. In the sense of "agreeing" (with someone) the preposition is "with," as in "He *concurred with* the other Senators that such legislation was desirable." In the sense of "acting jointly and in agreement," it takes the preposition "in," as in "leaders of the House and Senate *concurred in* a plan to introduce identical bills in both houses." It is also used with an infinitive to indicate joint action, as in "They *concurred to* speed up passage of the bill."

condition In the sense of "ailment," *condition* (as in "heart condition") is hardly a precise term, but it is one that is understood by everyone and is acceptable in informal speech or writing, if not in formal speech or writing. "Ailment" or "disease" is preferable in such instances.

condominium The plural of *condominium* is *condominiums,* not *condominia.* This popular word, describing an apartment owned by an individual in contrast to one that is rented or part of a cooperatively owned building, is made up of Latin elements, but it's a word no ancient Roman ever saw. So it forms its plural according to the rules of English, not those of classical Latin.

confer/conference. *See* EDUCATIONESE

confrontation. *See* VOGUE WORDS

confute/refute *Confute* and *refute* both involve disproving an opponent's claim. *Refute* means merely presenting evidence contrary to the opposition position, while *confute* has the stronger sense of demolishing the other's position by proving error or falsity in his case. *See also* REBUT/REFUTE.

conglomerateur

USAGE PANEL QUESTION

Panelist JEAN STAFFORD notes: "I am down on a new word: conglomerateur." The Barnhart *Dictionary of New English* defines *conglomerateur* (and variants *conglomerator* and *conglomerateer*) as "the organizer or head of a conglomerate." Do you regard any or all of these coinages as useful additions to the language?

Yes: 17%. No: 83%.
If your answer is "yes," which do you prefer?
Conglomerateur: 4%. *Conglomerator*: 7%. *Conglomerateee*: 6%.

SHERIDAN BAKER: "No. For humor, where they may have originated, they would be fine."

JOHN BROOKS: "No. No problem. The word will soon be as dead as the phenomenon it describes."

HEYWOOD HALE BROUN: "No. Conglomerates aren't very useful either."

ROBERT CROMIE: "The coiner of this should be shot on sight."

ELIZABETH JANEWAY: "Yes. I prefer 'conglomerateee,' because it sounds as unpleasant as the activity it names. Echoes of 'buccaneer' and 'privateer' come through."

PHYLLIS MCGINLEY: "No. Those are *dreadful* words."

STANTON PECKHAM: "Monstrous!"

ORVILLE PRESCOTT: "Barbarous!"

PETER S. PRESCOTT: "Another ugly word to replace what might have been a graceful phrase. I don't doubt the word will catch on."

FRANCIS ROBINSON: "Since I deplore conglomerates, I try to avoid any reference to them and their kind."

LEO ROSTEN: "Yecch!"

VERMONT ROYSTER: "No. Would you call the head of a steel company a 'steeler,' or of a copper company a 'copper'?"

HARRISON SALISBURY: "I have never seen this word in print; hope I never do."

HAROLD SCHONBERG: "Coinage adds to the zest of a language. But this particular one has neither wit nor pungency nor necessity to recommend it."

DANIEL SCHORR: "Yes. 'Conglomerateur' has a nice French overtone."

congratulate/congratulation Pronounce these words kon-GRACH-oo-layt and kon-grach-oo-LAY-shun, not—as often heard on radio and television—kon-GRAD-yoo-layt and kon-grad-yoo-LAY-shun.

congregation. *See* AUDIENCE/SPECTATORS/CONGREGATION

conjunctions/conjunctive adverbs *Conjunctions* are the words that introduce or join clauses, phrases, other words, or sentences. In English the most common *conjunctions* include "and," "but," "although," "because," and "as." Similar functions are sometimes performed by adverbs (called *conjunctive adverbs*) such as "besides," "furthermore," "however," "moreover," and "nevertheless."

conscript   *Conscript* is pronounced KON-skript as a noun; kun-SKRIPT as a verb.

consensus

USAGE PANEL QUESTION

The phrases "general *consensus* of opinion" and "*consensus* of opinion" appear frequently in the press. According to some authorities *consensus* alone suffices.

Do you try to observe the distinction in your own speech and writing?
Yes: 91%. No: 9%.

ISAAC ASIMOV: "How about a 'general overall consensus of peoples' opinions'?"

S. I. HAYAKAWA: "I object to 'of opinion.' But there is a shade of difference between 'consensus' and 'general consensus.' "

JOHN K. HUTCHENS: "Yes, I observe the distinction—or, anyhow, I try to."

WALTER KERR: " 'General' is certainly superfluous—I'd accept the second."

ORVILLE PRESCOTT: "I would if I needed the usage, but I can't recall ever needing it."

BERTON ROUECHÉ: "This is a word I would hesitate to use any more—the politicians have ruined it."

LEONARD SANDERS: "The general consensus of opinion must be the one held by the general public."

WALTER W. "RED" SMITH: "I don't think this barbarism appears so often in the press."

WRIGHT MORRIS: "I doubt that I observe the distinction, but I may in the future."

CHARLOTTE ZOLOTOW: "Consensus *has* to be general."

See also VOGUE WORDS.

consequent/consequential   Both adjectives have the meaning of "following as a result," as in "The storm and the *consequent* lack of electric power disrupted the normal lives of hundreds of people." *Consequential* could properly be substituted for *consequent* here if you like.

There are differences of opinion, however, about the use of *consequential* to mean "important," as in "*Consequential* changes were made in the plans for urban renewal." There are those who argue that *conse-*

quential in relation to importance can be used only to mean "acting in a self-important or pompous manner," at the same time accepting *consequence* as meaning "importance," as in "an event of great *consequence*." Logically *consequential* should be the adjectival form for this meaning and we predict that it will in time be accepted.

consider   *Consider* is used by itself or with "to be" in the sense of "to judge": "I *consider* him (to be) an arrogant fool." When used with "as" *consider* means "to view or examine in a particular role," as in "If you *consider* him as a politician you will find him successful, but if you *consider* him as a father you will find him an utter failure."

considered judgment. *See* VOGUE WORDS

consist   *Consist* (pronounced kun-SIST) as an intransitive verb meaning "to be composed" ("the dressing *consisted* of oil and vinegar") is well known. Much less familiar is *consist* as a noun, with accent on the first syllable, KON-sist. It's an item from the language of railroading and refers to the tabulation of the makeup (types of car and so on) of a railroad train, whether freight or passenger.

consumerism/consumerist   *Consumerism* and *consumerist* are recently coined words which reflect a new and potent force in America's marketplace. The ultimate consumers of the products of farms and industries have found that, by banding together and finding articulate spokesmen, they can exert considerable pressure on the producers to improve their products. Many state and local governments have, as a result, set up Consumer Protection Bureaus. Massive recall of defective motor vehicles, unit pricing of foodstuffs on supermarket shelves, and the recall of defective or dangerous children's toys are only three examples of the powers of organized *consumerism*. A *consumerist* is one who participates or is a leader in *consumerism*.

consummate   *Consummate* has both verb and adjective forms. As an adjective it means "perfect, complete, absolute" and is pronounced kon-SUM-it. As a verb it means "to bring to completion or fulfillment" and is pronounced KON-sum-ate.

contact   When *contact* first appeared as a verb meaning "to get in touch with" or "to go see," connoisseurs of language were horrified by it. That most urbane of lecturers and writers, John Mason Brown, once remarked when told to *contact* someone, "Shall I 'office' him or 'sidewalk' him?"

Usage has outlived the scorn of purists and *contact* is deemed acceptable by several dictionaries as a colloquial verb. Remember, though, that "colloquial" means that it is acceptable for conversation and informal writing but not for formal papers and speeches.

For several decades *contact* as a verb meaning "to get in touch with" has been a commonplace of business jargon. Would you accept "Let's *contact* him at once"?

In writing   Yes: 35%. No: 65%.
In casual speech   Yes: 63%. No: 37%.

ISAAC ASIMOV: "Yes. Good word. Better than 'get in touch with.'"

SHERIDAN BAKER: "Yes . . . reluctantly."

STEWART BEACH: "This is a use that seems unnecessary. It is so much more expressive to say, 'Let's phone (or write) him.'"

JOSEPH A. BRANDT: "Reluctantly . . . in general use."

HEYWOOD HALE BROUN: "I do not use business jargon."

ANTHONY BURGESS: "Nothing wrong at all with it."

ABE BURROWS: "I don't like it but I suppose it's here forever."

JOHN CIARDI: "Yes . . . but I prefer 'get in touch with.'"

GEORGE CORNISH: "I would *not* say 'Let's contact him,' but I no longer quarrel with those who do. The battle has been lost."

ROBERT CRICHTON: "I don't like it, but with the era of the phone, that's just what you do."

RICHARD EDES HARRISON: "It seems right to me and I have accepted it from the start."

PAUL HORGAN: "No—administrative jargon."

JOHN K. HUTCHENS: "Yes—but I've been a long time getting around to this."

HELEN L. KAUFMANN: "Yes—because I've grown accustomed to its usage, which formerly affronted me."

WALT KELLY: "I suppose that, having admitted the camel's nose, we might as well admit the whole camel, but it makes for a messy tent."

WALTER KERR: "No . . . but it may be a lost cause."

CHARLES KURALT: "I don't like it, but I think 'contact' as a verb has entered the language. I knew that when I heard myself say it."

ROBERT LIPSYTE: "Yes—in business writing and speech."

RUSSELL LYNES: "I'm afraid this is a nearly lost cause, alas. 'Contact' as a verb is one of those 'sincere' business words. It is meant to sound efficient and active as opposed to 'get in touch with,' which is gentle and polite."

DWIGHT MACDONALD: "Yes—reluctantly. But it *is* neater; in another generation it will sound O.K."

EDWIN NEWMAN: "No. I did at one time but not since I learned better."

ORVILLE PRESCOTT: "Yes—reluctantly, but this cause is lost."

PETER S. PRESCOTT: "It's useful in speech, I'm sorry to say."

F. D. REEVE: "Only in special instances. Still, it is said all the time by EVERYONE."

BERTON ROUECHÉ: "Yes . . . I see no difference between 'contact' and 'touch.' "

VERMONT ROYSTER: "Yes—it is much better than the circumlocution 'get in touch with.' "

DAVIDSON TAYLOR: "No. Contact is physical, as in sports."

LIONEL TRILLING: "I 'accept' it from others but I don't use it myself."

EARL UBELL: "No. Sounds lubricious."

GEORGE WALD: "In speech—yes—with misgivings."

A.B.C. WHIPPLE: "No. As you say, it's jargon."

HERMAN WOUK: "In writing—yes—for characters who talk that way—not in narrative voice. 'Contact' is a lost battle, but I fight on."

containerize   *Containerize* is among the least objectionable of the "ize" coinages of recent years because it was a result of the development of a new method of shipping cargo and thus serves a real need. Late in the 1960s the shipping industry turned to the use of standardized containers, some of them huge, in which cargo could be prepacked, then quickly and efficiently loaded in and unloaded from ships. For example, the contents of an entire house could be prepacked in Australia, shipped to the United States, taken by truck to its destination and unpacked in the driveway by the removal of sections of siding.

Ships had to be built or rebuilt to accommodate the new containers and were said to be *containerized*. The prepackaged cargo is also said to be *containerized*. A ship so used is called a *containership* and the process is called either *containershipping* or *containerization*.

contemporary/contemporaneous   Both words mean "existing or occurring at the same period in time" but *contemporaneous* is usually applied to events in the past, while *contemporary* can refer to persons living in the same period either of the past or of the present. *Contemporary* as used in the title of this book means "present-day"—usage as accepted by literate *contemporaries* of yours.

contemptible/contemptuous   The choice between these two depends on the view of the person involved. *Contemptible* means "deserving contempt or strong disapproval"; *contemptuous* means "expressing or showing contempt." A *contemptuous* remark made by a child about his mother may be considered *contemptible* by those who hear it.

continual/continuous *Continuous* means absolutely without interruption, as one would say, "We had twenty-four hours of *continuous*
rain." *Continual,* by contrast, means frequently repeated with only
brief interruptions: "The day was marked by *continual* thunder-
showers."

contract *Contract,* as an item of Mafia language, means much the same
thing as the expression that was part of the language of the Old West:
"There's a price on his head." In other words, the criminal organization
will pay a specified amount for proof that an enemy has been eliminated
—permanently.

    The word is not new to underworld slang. For decades corrupt police
and politicians have referred to a bribe or "a fix" as a *contract.* The
specific application of the word to payment for murder can probably be
traced to the fact that the Mafia has a penchant for operating legitimate
businesses, either as fronts for its nefarious activities or as straightforward
moneymaking enterprises. So the language of legitimate business is well
known to underworld leaders today and it's the most natural thing in the
world for them to disguise the ultimate crime—murder—under the genteel euphemism, *contract.*

contractions *Contractions* ("didn't," "wasn't," "haven't," and the like) are
inappropriate in formal contexts, though perfectly acceptable in casual or
informal speech and writing.

contrast. *See* COMPARE/CONTRAST

controlled substance/substance abuse

USAGE PANEL QUESTION

Controlled substance is a euphemism, like "job action," which seems to say
precisely the opposite of its true meaning. If the *substances* involved—
narcotics, for the most part—were indeed *controlled,* there would be no
occasion for the multi-million-dollar "drug busts" that the press reports
regularly. In any event, the phrase has spawned another expression, *substance abuse,* which is currently much in vogue among leaders of youth.
Indeed there is reportedly a New York City Bureau of Substance Abuse.
If you were reporting on the very real problems of drug and alcohol abuse by
teen-agers, would you speak of the increase in *substance abuse* in a formal
report for the guidance of youth leaders? Yes: 3%. No: 97%.

In writing of an informal nature, as for a magazine? Yes: 2%. No: 98%.
In casual conversation? Yes: 2%. No: 98%.

DAVE ANDERSON: "A substance could be anything."

ISAAC ASIMOV: "I might as well speak of a disgusting illiteracy or an intolerable euphemism as 'sound abuse' (though, by God, it is)."

JOHN BROOKS: "A legalism. To use it outside a legal context, except as a joke, is outré in the extreme."

JOHN CIARDI: "They are, in a sense, 'controlled substances.' The controls have been circumvented."

WILLARD R. ESPY: "Not unless I happened to be suffering at the moment from 'substance abuse.' "

FRANCES FRITCHMAN: 'This is one of the worst in a long list of euphemisms currently popular among politicians. Its use should be punishable by a prison term."

RAY GANDOLF: "I would make a very poor bureaucrat."

JOHN K. HUTCHENS: "I would simply say 'drug abuse' or 'alcohol abuse,' etc. Why complicate it with 'substance'?"

WALTER KERR: "Why a euphemism at all?"

JAMES J. KILPATRICK: " 'Controlled substance' is one of those plastic products of bureaucratic extrusion. It means 'substance controlled by federal law.' It has value only to prosecutors drafting bills of indictment. I never heard of 'substance abuse,' and it would never occur to me to use the phrase in speaking or writing."

STANLEY KUNITZ: "A prissy and useless euphemism."

ROBERT LIPSYTE: "It's like reporting 'casualties' instead of people who were killed or maimed."

JULES LOH: "Let's leave the bureaucratic and academic jargon to the bureaucrats, academicians and other babblers, and try ourselves to write with simplicity and precision."

DWIGHT MACDONALD: "No, because nobody would know what I was talking about."

WILLIAM McGUIRE: " 'Substance abuse' appears to be an abbreviation or shorthand for the various kinds of 'substances' (grass, cocaine, alcohol, soft drugs, hard drugs) that are being abused. Let's hope for a better term."

MARGE PIERCY: " 'Don't abuse your substance' seems the advice of somebody in a Horatio Alger novel to a young spendthrift being contrasted with the stalwart and careful hero. 'Substance' in this case is another awkward euphemism."

LEO ROSTEN: "You may as well give the chemical formula. '$H_2 CO_2$ abuse' means banging away at the booze."

BERTRON ROUECHÉ: "What's wrong with 'drug abuse'?"

VERMONT ROYSTER: "What is being abused is the language!"

HAROLD SCHONBERG: "Ugly. Comes from police, with their peculiar English —'perpetrator,' etc."

JACK SMITH: "It's gobbledygook; a euphemism where straight talk is needed."

ELVIS STAHR, JR.: "Why add even a momentary oral hesitation or the slightest linguistic obfuscation to the very serious problems of dealing with alcohol or drug abuse?"

KARL V. TEETER: "Jargon. If I were in the field I might say this."

EDWARD TRIPP: "The rule in this situation should be to use the most specific term that is still broad enough to include all the substances (or whatever) normally implied by a phrase—in this case, drugs."

EARL UBELL: "However, not all substances that are abused—like airplane glue—are drugs."

JOSEPH VERGARA: "Dropping euphemisms is getting out of control—especially when a vague word like 'substance' replaces the specific 'drug.'"

JUDITH VIORST: "Never."

DOUGLAS WATT: "Just plain dumb, and at the same time self-consciously lofty, this lack of specificity."

A.B.C. WHIPPLE: "More of the pretentious euphemisms infecting our language."

WILLIAM ZINSSER: "A current example of Orwell's point about political language consisting of 'euphemism, question-begging, and sheer vagueness' to avoid harsh truth."

convenience food This is an overall phrase for food which takes little or no further preparation before eating. It includes canned, frozen, dehydrated, partially cooked, fully cooked—but in each instance packaged—food.

conversant *Conversant* is an adjective meaning "acquainted or familiar with": "He was thoroughly *conversant* with the intricacies of the Moog synthesizer." It should not be confused with "conversationalist" and we wouldn't have believed that it ever could be had we not seen the headlines NON-CONVERSANT HUSBAND THREATENS HIS MARRIAGE (meaning that he wouldn't talk things over with his wife) and BOTH CONVERSANTS ARE ARTICULATE (meaning "conversationalists").

convict *Convict* is pronounced KON-vikt as a noun; kun-VIKT as a verb.

convince/persuade Panelist Hal Borland wrote: "I keep hearing that one is 'convinced' to do such-and-such. 'Convince' is not a synonym for 'persuade.' One is convinced *of* something; one is persuaded *to do* something." A majority of the panelists (many with great reluctance) voted acceptance of "*convince* to (do something)" in view of its widespread use. At the same time, many expressed a preference for constructions involving *of* or *that*.

USAGE PANEL QUESTION

How about the use of *convince* for *persuade,* as in "I had to *convince* him to go with me"? Would you accept this in the speech of others?
Yes: 71%. No: 29%.

BENJAMIN APPEL: "I feel 'convince' and 'persuade' have become one in holy matrimony."

W. H. AUDEN: "No. I would say that one could say, 'I had to convince him that he should go with me.' "

ALVIN BEAM: "Yes, with regret. As an editor I would make the change to 'persuade.' "

JOSEPH A. BRANDT: "This is essentially a teleological question. The seriousness of the argument would determine my answer."

HEYWOOD HALE BROUN: "Yes. It is too universal to fight."

S. I. HAYAKAWA: "No. 'Convince' should not be followed by an infinitive. 'I convinced him of her guilt.' 'I convinced him that . . .' "

PAUL HORGAN: "Yes, but with invisible regret."

CHARLES KURALT: "Yes. That is, I had no reservation until you brought it up."

LAURENCE LAFORE: "No. I would not object if 'convince' were followed by 'that he should' instead of the infinitive."

JESSICA MITFORD: "Yes. In writing I should probably say 'persuade.' "

DANIEL PATRICK MOYNIHAN: "Do we mean 'convince' *or* 'persuade'—both are possible."

EDWIN NEWMAN: "No. It is a pointless, unnecessary use of 'convince.' "

LEO ROSTEN: "Yes. 'Convince' sounds stronger—not different."

VERMONT ROYSTER: "Yes (with a shudder). I am convinced we cannot persuade people to make the distinction."

LEONARD SANDERS: "Yes (with a shudder). The flaw lies in the infinitive 'to go,' and not in the choice of words. It is possible to persuade someone to act without convincing him of the necessity."

DAVIDSON TAYLOR: "No. Doubt it; 'convince' leads to conviction: a moral conclusion."

BARBARA TUCHMAN: "It seems that 'convince' ought to take an object of some sort—i.e., 'convince him of the need to go with me.' I don't know what rule applies here, if any. In my own writing I tend to go by what sounds right."

cook the books A phrase which has cropped up in news analysis on television, *cook the books* is a British expression meaning "falsify the accounts."

cool, to lose one's *Cool* as a noun (as in *to lose one's cool*) is slang but it is expressive and makes its point quickly and clearly. As an adjective applied to a poised person—*cool,* calm, and collected, as the saying used to go—*cool* has long been standard English. Now that it appears as a noun, some purists are affronted, but this is a path which many words have followed in years and centuries past.

coolth/warmth As an antonym for *warmth, coolth* has existed as an English word since 1547, according to the Oxford Dictionary. For some reason—perhaps because there is so much *coolth* in the British climate —it never caught on the way *warmth* did. Oxford says that in its present-day use it is chiefly "jocular and dialectal." The old Funk & Wagnalls Unabridged calls it "humorous and dialectal."

coon/real gone coon *Coon* is sometimes used as a derogatory term for a black and is considered highly offensive.
    Real gone coon, however, is not a racist term. Rather it is a hunter's term and the reference is to a raccoon which has been treed by hounds. In rural areas it is also used to mean a person in real trouble.

coop, to Investigation of police corruption in New York City in the early 1970s and the news stories of the hearings on it unearthed a number of interesting items in the argot of law officers. One of the abuses disclosed was the practice of *cooping,* which meant that officers assigned to patrol cars would park their cars somewhere off the street and proceed *to coop:* sleep through most of their "working" hours.

cop/officer/policeman Policemen in general object to the term *cop.* Perhaps this is partly the result of a campaign waged for many years by the late J. Edgar Hoover against the headline writers' favorite label for the FBI chief—"top *cop.*"
    Another reason why *cop* finds little favor with the men in blue is that over the centuries the word *cop* has been used by underworld characters in many different and usually unsavory senses. A thief doesn't steal a car; he "*cops*" it. When a person is assaulted from the rear, the perpetrator is said to have "*copped* a sneak." And, of course, the legal term "plea bargaining" is known in underworld slang as "*copping* a plea." When referring indirectly to an officer of the law, it is better to say *policeman* or *policewoman.* When addressing him or her directly, the best choice is "*Officer*" (which see).

copacetic   *Copacetic* was originally Negro slang and was popularized by the late, great dancer Bill "Bojangles" Robinson. It is now widely used to mean "fine, excellent" but is still slang.

cope

USAGE PANEL QUESTION

"Don't bother me; I can't *cope.*" "The man who gets the job must be able to *cope.*" Do you approve these examples of the use of the intransitive *cope* without any indication of what the subject is coping *with*?
In writing   Yes: 30%. No: 70%.
In casual conversation   Yes: 62%. No: 38%.

BARRY BINGHAM, SR.: "The usage is a colloquialism which I find inoffensive in speech, but not acceptable in writing."

HAL BORLAND: "No. However, this usage is becoming both widespread and accepted."

JOHN BROOKS: "Only in casual writing."

HEYWOOD HALE BROUN: "Conversationally it fulfills a need for the description of general disarray."

ABE BURROWS: "I like 'cope.' "

ALEX FAULKNER: "No, except humorously."

PAUL HORGAN: "Yes (in conversation) if comic."

ALEXANDER KENDRICK: "It's not the first intransitive and won't be the last."

CHARLES KURALT: "A valuable word in a frenetic age—who CAN cope?"

DWIGHT MACDONALD: "Slang once, but now sounds O.K. because it is necessary and pungent."

WRIGHT MORRIS: "God, how I hate it! (Can't cope with it!)"

ORVILLE PRESCOTT: "A good recent usage."

VERMONT ROYSTER: "This is the kind of Newspeak with which I cannot cope."

LEONARD SANDERS: "No. Yet, I have the feeling this usage may gain acceptance eventually; in time, the subject may not require explanation."

HAROLD SCHONBERG: "No, but it's omnipresent."

MARK SCHORER: "I would use many expressions such as this if I were trying to establish a very colloquial tone. I would not use them if I were speaking in my own voice. But writing is full of *many* voices."

HERMAN WOUK: "It's making the grade."

copyediting marks. *See* CORRECTIONS IN MANUSCRIPT OR IN PRINTER'S PROOFS

corporation. *See* FIRM/CORPORATION

corps *Corps* is pronounced KOR, not KORPS.

corrections in manuscript or in printer's proofs   Basically the marks for correcting manuscript and correcting proofs from the printer are the same. The difference is that copyediting marks are written within the text, since the person retyping the manuscript or the printer will be following the text word for word. In correcting printer's proofs for typographical or other errors, it is necessary to indicate corrections in the margins as well as in the body of the text.

The following are some commonly used proofreading marks:

Marginal Mark	Corresponding Mark in Proof	Meaning
the	Every man has in him possibility	insert
ℓ	Every man has in him the possibility	take out
⊃	Every man has in him the possibility	close up
l.c.	Every Man has in him the possibility	lower case letter
wf.	Every man has in him the possibility	wrong font letter
tr	Every man has in him possibility the	transpose
stet	Every man has in him the possibility	let stand
▢	Every man has in him the possibility	indent em quad
#	Every man has in him the possibility	space
V⋀	Every man has in him the possibility	even spacing
¶	purpose. Every man has in him the	make paragraph
⊏	⊏ Every man has in him the possibility	move over
(?)	Every man has in him the possibilities	query to author
x	Every man has in him the possibility	broken letter
⊙	Every man has in him the possibility	period
∨	Every mans possibility lies within him	apostrophe
∨ ∨	Every man has in him the possibility	quotation marks
-/	Some men sidetrack possibility	hyphen
caps	Every man has in him the possibility	capitals
sm.c.	Every man has in him the possibility	small capitals
rom.	Every man has in him the possibility	put in roman
ital	Every man has in him the possibility	put in italic
b.f.	Every man has in him the possibility	bold-face

corruption. *See* MENDACITY/DUPLICITY/CHICANERY/CORRUPTION

cosmetize   This is one of the uglier coinages created by reporters relaying news on corruption in government, as in "His chief concern was to conceal or *cosmetize* the facts." Unabridged dictionaries list a number of nouns, adjectives, and adverbs based on the word "cosmetic"—even "cosmetology"—but no verb. This word is part of a deplorable trend to add the prefix "-ize" to any word and create a verb, on the theory that, as long as people know what you mean, anything goes.

could care less Starting in 1960 and with increasing frequency in recent years readers of our column have posed questions on *could care less,* like this one from a young woman in Omaha: "Please discuss the current idiom, slang, or whatever regarding the two forms 'I couldn't care less' and 'I could care less.' I maintain the former is correct because one is trying to express a complete lack of any feeling whatsoever. Are the users corrupting the original expression or could it be that 'could care less' has become the acceptable form?" We replied that we had been dumbfounded by the increasing prevalence of "I *could care less*" when obviously what the speaker means is that he *could* NOT *care less.* It seemed to us an ignorant debasement of the language. Members of the Usage Panel overwhelmingly concur, though a modest percentage tolerate the idiom in casual speech perhaps, as panelist Peter S. Prescott notes, because "by its intonation in speech one cannot mistake its meaning, even if one has never heard the phrase before . . . and, of course, it means exactly the opposite of what it says." Here, then, the ballot question and comments from the members of the Usage Panel:

USAGE PANEL QUESTION

With increasing frequency the expression I *could care less* is heard in the speech of seemingly literate people who really mean to say "I *could* not *care less.*" Would you accept this expression?

In casual speech   Yes: 22%. No: 78%.
In writing   Yes: 7%. No: 93%.

ISAAC ASIMOV: "I don't know people stupid enough to say this."

SHERIDAN BAKER: "No. This is a real stupidity."

HAL BORLAND: "Not unless the speaker or writer means he could care less than he does. It's a stupid elision."

PAUL HORGAN: "No. It doesn't say what is meant."

ELIZABETH JANEWAY: "It makes me feel the way a piece of chalk that squeaks on the blackboard does. I wince at the pit of my stomach."

WALT KELLY: "No. The two expressions mean two different things."

ALEXANDER KENDRICK: "Yes. I'm not sure that is what they really mean to say, however."

WALTER KERR: "The expression doesn't mean what it means to mean."

PETER S. PRESCOTT: "Yes, in speech because (as I learned in the Army) the

tone of voice invariably conveys the meaning belied by the words. But No
to its use in writing."

HAROLD SCHONBERG: "I never came across *this* one."

ELVIS STAHR, JR.: "Yes in speech—if really casual. No in writing."

HAROLD TAYLOR: "I don't like the phrase at all but it's so common you can't
object to it. I just wouldn't use it."

JUDITH VIORST: "This drives me insane because it seems so mindless."

HERMAN WOUK: "It's a breezy vulgarism without tang."

could of. *See* SHOULD OF/COULD OF/WOULD OF

council/counsel/counselor/consul   Despite the fact that these words
are related to each other to a certain degree, each has a meaning peculiar to itself. A *council* is a representative body of people, such as a
town *council* or city *council,* whose role is to decide issues and establish rules and regulations. *Counsel* can mean a person (or persons) who
gives advice. In the case of "legal *counsel*" it is always singular
in form, even if it refers to a team of lawyers. (If it is used to refer to
only one lawyer the verb following is singular: *"Counsel is* ready"; if
used to refer to a team of lawyers, the verb is plural: *"Counsel are*
ready.") *Counsel* is also a verb meaning "to give advice." *Counselor,* as
in "guidance *counselor*" or "camp *counselor,*" is one who gives advice or
supervision. *Consul* is usually a government representative who is sta-
tioned in a foreign country.

counter-. *See* PREFIXES AND SUFFIXES, WITH AND WITHOUT HYPHEN

counterculture   The rejection by many young people in the 1960s and
1970s of the standards and values of the prevailing culture of the United
States resulted in the creation of a *counterculture* which, in many instances, involved communal living, a return to primitive living, the use
of hallucinogenic drugs, the publication of "underground" or "alternate"
newspapers, and, in general, a way of life completely different from that
of the established society.

A review of *The Making of a Counter Culture* by Theodore Roszak
defines a *counter culturist* as follows: "Ideally, the *counter culturist* seeks
to enter a world of real experiences, where plastic, computers, sonic
booms and acquisitive instincts do not scar the primeval beauty of the
human soul."

See also UNDERGROUND PRESS/ALTERNATE PRESS.

counterproductive/self-defeating   *Counterproductive* is a *vogue word*
(which see), an example of "sociological Choctaw," as William Zinsser
calls it, that some writers, especially bureaucrats, use to fancy up their

letters and speeches. *Counterproductive* says nothing that *self-defeating* doesn't say quite as well.

counterwords *Counterwords* is the technical term used by linguists to describe words like "cute," "grand," "darling," and "awful" that have been so much used and abused that their original and precise meanings are almost forgotten.

couple (is/are) *Couple,* when used collectively to refer to a man and a woman, is usually followed by a plural verb, especially if a personal pronoun is involved in the sentence. "The *couple are* saving their money for a down payment on a house" is logical, since it refers to two people.

couple of The "of" should never be omitted in phrases such as "a *couple of* chairs." A more formal phrasing would be "two chairs" or "several chairs."

court-martial The plural of *court-martial* is *courts-martial,* following the general rule for formation of *plurals of compound words and phrases* (which see). Its first meaning is the military court which tries those who violate military law, and the second meaning is the trial itself. *Webster's New World Dictionary* records that the plural of the second sense is "now often" *court-martials.* It may come to that but, if it does, logic would seem to dictate that the hyphen be removed and the word written solid.

couth. *See* ARCANE WORDS and LOST POSITIVES

c.q. The letters *c.q.* are used by writers and copyeditors after a word or name of unusual spelling to notify the typesetter that, despite the fact that it may seem erroneous, it is correct. Thus, if a woman's name is spelled "Lilyan" it should be followed by *c.q.* as a warning to the printer not to convert it to "Lillian." The symbols originally represented the sound (dah-dit-dah-dit-dah-dah-dit-dah) used by telegraphers at the start of transmission. *C.q.* is now defined by the dictionaries as the code signal used by radio operators, especially amateur ones, to invite all other operators to listen.

crackers British slang for addled, touched in the head, crazy, mad. *OED Supplement* traces this to service slang during the period following World War I. A person who is *crackers* or is *going crackers* would, in American slang, be said to be "going nuts,"

USAGE PANEL QUESTION

In a speech commemorating Law Day, President Reagan complimented the founding fathers on having "the wisdom to craft a system of government" that has survived for two centuries. *Craft,* as a transitive verb, appears in recent editions of American dictionaries but only in the sense of "to make by hand or as if by hand." Merriam cites as an example "scale models he has crafted."

Do you think Mr. Reagan's use of *craft* in the sense of "to create" a system is a useful extension of this word? Yes: 31%. No: 69%.

WHITNEY BALLIETT: "All these strike me as fabrications for perfectly sound and usable words."

BARRY BINGHAM, SR.: "A system of government cannot be made by hand, but rather by the brain. Some speech writer thought he was adding a touch of trendiness to the script by using 'craft.' "

HEYWOOD HALE BROUN: "I associate the word with inferior gift shop items."

JOAN SIMPSON BURNS: "It implies a careful, skillful way of putting together rather than simply 'to create.' "

ROBERT CROMIE: "Not useful—tortured."

WILLARD R. ESPY: " 'Statecraft' is well established and 'to craft a system of government' is as apt and honorable."

GERALD FRANK: "There must be some limit to how much wrenching of the language we can tolerate."

FRANCES FRITCHMAN: "Talk about trivialization à la Reagan!"

RAY GANDOLF: "If we can shape an idea or mold public opinion, we might as well be able to craft a system of government."

PETE HAMILL: "These bastards are nouning us to death!"

PAUL HORGAN: "Inoffensive."

JOHN K. HUTCHENS: "It seems to me that Mr. Reagan's extension of this word is entirely legitimate."

ELIZABETH JANEWAY: "No. In fact I don't even like it as used to mean 'made by hand.' It has a kind of meritricious medievalism."

WALTER KERR: "Pretty crafty, weren't they?"

JAMES J. KILPATRICK: "I see nothing wrong with 'to craft' in the sense in which Mr. Reagan employed the term. It is not synonymous with 'to create.' E.g., a presidential speech might well create a controversy, but it doesn't craft a controversy."

IRVING KOLODIN: "Misapplication."

STANLEY KUNITZ: "Too awkward."

JULES LOH: "Yes, in the sense of 'to make with care, as if by hand.' "

DWIGHT MACDONALD: "I don't admire the use of 'craft' as a verb in any context."

WILLIAM MCGUIRE: "Knitted potholder dept."

MARGE PIERCY: " 'Draft' may be what he meant; 'craft' can be applied to the arts by extension from hand labor, but beyond that is misused."

F. D. REEVE: "Politicians are mindless cheaters—why, soon they'll turn 'sun' into a transitive and take credit for 'sunshine.' Better they should 'craft' moonshine."

BERTON ROUECHÉ: "I don't approve of *anything* Reagan does."

DAVID SCHOENBRUN: "Nothing Reagan says makes sense."

HAROLD SCHONBERG: "I don't like—but it may be a legitimate extension of the verb."

JACK SMITH: "What's wrong with 'make'? And 'craft' should keep the idea of manual skill. The next thing you know someone may refer to 'the writer's craft.' "

ELVIS STAHR, JR.: "To my mild astonishment, I find myself admiring Mr. Reagan's creative use of the language, at least in this instance."

WALLACE STEGNER: "Not useful, but predictable."

KARL V. TEETER: "Advertising talk."

EDWARD TRIPP: "Since artisans often create as they 'craft,' I do not see this as necessarily an extension—especially since some of the materials of our system existed already. Though I would use neither, I object to neither."

JOSEPH VERGARA: "Seems a pleasant figurative use."

JUDITH VIORST: "But Reagan surely didn't invent this new usage."

DOUGLAS WATT: " 'Well-crafted' plays have been referred to often by theater critics, one in particular. But I would use it only in a pejorative sense."

A.B.C. WHIPPLE: "Seems to me a perfectly logical and painless extension."

HERMAN WOUK: "Not bad, actually."

crapshooter/craps-shooter A fellow newspaper columnist was quoted to us as having written, in a column about Las Vegas, the statement "Even the most fanatic *craps-shooter* shuts up quickly as soon as he throws a 7."

The only proper form is *crapshooter*. H. L. Mencken, in his *American Language*, records the appearance of "crap," meaning "money," in a 1698 collection of British criminal slang. He observed: "It is possible that the origin of 'crap,' the American dice game, may be found here. 'Crap' is always listed in the dictionaries as 'craps'—a curious pedantry, for it is called 'crap' by the players and appears in the singular in 'crap-shooter' and 'to shoot crap.' "

crash/crash pad   *Crash* is a slang word whose meaning has changed considerably over a period of thirty years. It once was used in the phrase *"crash* a party," which meant to walk in without being invited. In the 1960s it acquired a meaning of "to stay temporarily without cost" as in "You can *crash* here for as long as you like." A *crash pad* is the place where one stays for nothing. Both terms became popular among the young who traveled freely without much money but with names and telephone numbers for places where they could find a *crash pad.*

crazy   In slang, *crazy* is now used as a noun to designate a person of wild and erratic behavior, with no rational or even consistent attitudes toward life and other people: "He found himself at Woodstock surrounded by *crazies."*

credibility gap   The American public, made cynical about the truthfulness of statements by politicians and other public figures, has accepted *credibility gap* to describe the difference between what they hear and what they can believe. Its use should be limited to informal contexts.

credit crunch. *See* VOGUE WORDS

creepie-peepie   A bit of television jargon is the term *creepie-peepie.* This is a portable TV camera, used to get informal close-ups, often of moving subjects. Its name was coined by analogy to "walkie-talkie," a combination radio receiver and transmitter that can, like the *creepie-peepie,* be carried by one person.

crisis   The only plural for *crisis* is *crises.* It is pronounced CRY-seez.

criterion/criteria   *Criterion,* like "medium," is a word whose plural far too many people do not understand. *Criterion* is derived from Greek and means a standard for judgment. Its plural is *criteria* but, apparently because it ends in the letter "a" and has no "s" at its end, many persons, including one former President of the United States, think that *criteria* is the singular form. In a speech to the legislative assistants to Democratic Congressmen shortly after his announcement that he would not seek another term, Lyndon Johnson stated that his decision would enable him "to act independently and with complete liberty with only one criteria, the greatest good for the greatest number." There is no such thing as "one *criteria."* A sure way to avoid confusion is to use *criterions*, the alternate plural form.

critique

USAGE PANEL QUESTION

A recent issue of a journalism-school bulletin reported that an editor of *The New York Times* "sat in on several classes and critiqued the operation of the college paper." Would you approve this use of *critique* as a transitive verb?

In writing   Yes: 7%. No: 93%.
In casual speech   Yes: 13%. No: 87%.

BENJAMIN APPEL: "No. 'Critiqued' seems forced, affected to me."

ISAAC ASIMOV: "Yes. For a good reason. The correct term 'criticized' is now taken to mean 'found fault with,' and something is needed for the broader meaning of 'carefully analyzed the faults and virtues of.' "

JULES BERGMAN: "While we accept it generally, it is an aborted substitute for criticize, which is now used only as implying criticism or finding fault. In true definition, criticize means appraising merits AND faults. I submit 'critique' springs out of what I call compression synthesis—a journalistic disease characterized by lack of enough space to properly and accurately use words."

HAL BORLAND: "Since when was the word 'criticized' ripped out of this idiot's vocabulary?"

JOSEPH A. BRANDT: "The writer of this was a nonwriter."

HEYWOOD HALE BROUN: "It is ugly and unnecessary—'gave a critique' is better."

ANTHONY BURGESS: "No, no. A critique is like what Kant wrote about pure reason. There are plenty of honourable synonyms."

BEN LUCIEN BURMAN: "Ghastly! This sort of thing makes the world the mess it is today."

ABE BURROWS: "This one is just silly."

JOHN CIARDI: "There is no idiomatic reason for not turning many noun forms into verb forms. I just don't like people who critique. They always start out by 'quantifying' and then descend to 'finalizing.' "

ROBERT CRICHTON: "Yes. Since the real meaning of 'criticized' no longer means what it was meant to mean, 'critiqued' is more meaningful."

ROBERT CROMIE: "They should have finalized the guy who used this."

RICHARD EDES HARRISON: "You don't know whether the writer means reviewed or criticized."

PAUL HORGAN: "Pretentiousness wedded to illiteracy—always offensive."

JOHN K. HUTCHENS: "This is a real horror. What ever became of that fine old verb 'discuss'?"

ALEXANDER KENDRICK: "This should be no more appalling than 'to veto' but somehow it is."

WALTER LORD: "Why couldn't he *review* it?"

HERBERT MITGANG: "Why not criticized?"

STANTON PECKHAM: " 'Sat in on' only suggests the privy. If he also 'critiqued' he was in the right place."

PETER S. PRESCOTT: "Never! This use of a noun as a verb makes no sense because very good verbs exist which make the meaning clearer: criticize and evaluate."

HARRISON SALISBURY: "Never, never, never."

DAVID SCHOENBRUN: "New words should either fill a need or say better what is sought. 'Criticized' exists and is better than 'critiqued.' 'Reviewed,' 'evaluated,' 'analyzed,' all would serve well. Also, 'attended' is better than 'sat in on.' "

HAROLD SCHONBERG: "I don't even like 'critique' as a noun. I never write critiques—only criticisms."

crown stroller   British equivalent of the American "road hog," the driver who gets into the middle of the road, drives at a leisurely rate of speed, and refuses to budge.

crunch   If you are in a *crunch,* you are in an economic or financial bind. When you "come right down to the *crunch,*" you will have reached a decisive moment. *Crunch* is business jargon. *See also* VOGUE WORDS.

cud/quid   *Cud* is used when referring to animals and *quid* when referring to humans. A cow, in chewing regurgitated food, is chewing her *cud.* A man masticating a mouthful of tobacco is chewing on a *quid.* A point to bear in mind, though, is that the figurative expression "chewing his *cud,*" meaning to ruminate or deliberate over a problem, may be used in referring to humans.

culture shock   Technically, *culture shock* is the extreme discomfiture which a person may experience when plunged into a culture or way of life new and foreign to him.

cupfuls/cupsful   *Cupfuls* is correct; *cupsful* is incorrect. *Cupful* is a simple unit of measurement, like "quart" or "gallon," and forms its plural regularly by the addition of "s." If one wishes to say, "You will need three full cups to make the pie," you would, of course, also be correct.

cute. *See* COUNTERWORDS

cut the mustard   An expression that has had a considerable vogue, especially among politicians, in recent years, is *cut the mustard,* meaning to qualify in every respect. "Tom is one man who can really *cut the mustard.* I'm sure he'll make a fine governor." Despite its recent vogue, incidentally, it has a long history, having been used by O. Henry as long ago as 1904. It is informal.

cutting   British equivalent of the American "clipping"—as in "newspaper *cutting.*"

cycle. *See* HERTZ/CYCLE

cynic/skeptic   Both *cynic* and *skeptic* began as names of members of schools of Greek philosophy and each has an element of doubt in present-day meanings. There is a difference between the meanings of the two, however, which should be preserved. A *cynic* is one who criticizes society as a whole and persons as individuals on the basis that the motives for all actions are self-centered and material. A *skeptic* is one who questions and doubts assertions which others accept.

A *skeptic* may be difficult to convince. A *cynic* cannot be convinced. (*Skeptic* may also be spelled "sceptic" but most dictionaries label that spelling "chiefly British.")

cynosure of all eyes   This is a cliché which is also a redundancy. *Cynosure* by itself means the center of attention. The Greek word "kynosoura" (dog's tail) was used for the constellation of Ursa Minor, which includes the North Star. Navigators since the dawn of recorded history have used the North Star in plotting their courses, so *cynosure* became the point to which all eyes are drawn.

czar/tsar/tzar   Of these three spellings *czar* is the most common in the United States, although *tsar* is a closer transliteration of the spelling of the Russian word from which it came. *Tzar* is another variant spelling, again not commonly used. In the extended meaning of the word, to denote a person of great wealth or power, *czar* is the only spelling ever used: "Kenesaw Mountain Landis was the first *czar* of baseball."

D

dab/darb   *Dab* is British informal for an expert: "He's a *dab* at photography." In the plural *(dabs)* it is British underworld slang for "fingerprints." A variant, *darb,* with virtually the same meaning, is oddly labeled "Canadian slang" in the original *American Heritage Dictionary* and

defined as "Something considered especially excellent or outstanding."
We find the "Canadian" label odd because we have used the expression
since childhood. What is more, the *Dictionary of American Slang* lists it
with no such restrictive label, citing examples of its use from such resolutely American writers as Percy Marks and O. O. McIntyre.

dago A derogatory slang term for an Italian, Spaniard, or Portuguese. Like
all such terms, it is to be avoided. *See also* DEROGATORY TERMS.

dais/podium/lectern The three terms involve furniture in a meeting
hall, lecture hall, or concert hall, and are frequently confused and
misused.

A *dais* is a raised platform on which a speaker, along with officers
of the club or organization, sits or stands.

A *podium* is a special kind of dais in that it is intended to accommodate only one person, such as an orchestra conductor. The small stand
on which a speaker rests his notes is a *lectern,* not a *podium.* It would
be very unusual for a speaker to "grasp the *podium*" as one writer
reported. The only speaker likely to "grasp the *podium*" would be one
who had fallen flat on his face. The most common error, however, is in
pronunciation of *dais.* It is pronounced just as it is spelled: DAY-iss. An
astonishing number of otherwise educated people say DY-iss, which is
incorrect.

dame As used in the U.S. in reference to a woman, *dame* is a slightly
pejorative slang expression, carrying the implication that, in the Victorian
phrase, a *dame* is "no better than she should be." In British usage,
however, it is a title of great significance, the equivalent of that of a
knight.

dangling modifiers *Dangling modifiers* may be phrases, clauses, or adjectives, but they have one thing in common. They modify the wrong object.
Most common of these is the dangling participial phrase. Coming at the
beginning of the sentence, it should modify the subject of the main clause,
but what happens is that the main clause is so written that this is impossible. For example: "Coming out of the subway, the sun blinded me." It
wasn't the sun that came out of the subway. By reversing the main clause,
the problem is solved: "Coming out of the subway, I was blinded by the
sun."

Although dangling participles are the most common *dangling
modifiers,* note that infinitives may similarly be misused: "To get the best
result, the car should be tuned up." Revise to read: "To get the best result,
you should have the car tuned up." A simple rule: having written the
participial phrase (or other modifying phrase or clause) make the next
word the one which the modifier pertains to.

As specific examples of the problem, we submitted the following to the Usage Panel members:

USAGE PANEL QUESTION

Panelist A.B.C. WHIPPLE writes:

> Everywhere I keep seeing and hearing writers and speakers dangling their modifiers (maybe it's the new morality). Recently I've noticed some examples that are either (1) unforgivable or (2) exceptions to the rule that are not mentioned in any of my grammar books. I refer to some of the honorary degree citations at the last couple of commencements at Yale and Harvard.
>
> When a citation reads: "Distinguished alumna of Albertus Magnus College, Yale takes a great pride in conferring" etc., is this a form of greeting? (As in "William and Mary Morris, defenders of the true word, we salute you.") But what to make of the following: "Distinguished public servant, exemplar for the United States Foreign Service, tireless seeker of peace, your work in arduous posts around the globe has repeatedly demonstrated" etc.? Some greeting!

Do you regard the second specimen of Elegant English as violating the rules or standards governing misplaced or dangling modifiers? Yes: 64%. No: 36%.

Would you suggest that, given the august settings in which these sentiments were originally uttered, the perpetrators should be awarded a Scotch verdict ("guilt not proven")? Yes: 49%. No: 51%.

Returned to class for a semester of English A? Yes: 64%. No: 36%.

ISAAC ASIMOV: "It's just a harmless custom. As a recipient of a dozen honorary degrees, I'd miss it if literary English replaced this fulsome jargon."

BARRY BINGHAM, SR.: "A semester would hardly serve to correct such mistaken usage. A full year might possibly help."

HEYWOOD HALE BROUN: "Honorary degrees debase the aims of scholarship and so, usually, does the language used in awarding them."

ANTHONY BURGESS: "It's not at all wrong. It's a pure vocative like 'Almighty God.'"

BEN LUCIEN BURMAN: "To deny politicians and other orators and statesmen the right of dangling modifiers is unconstitutional and would be the end of American democracy."

ROBERT CROMIE: "I suggest that Yale and Harvard are sending out their citations to be written by some advertising agency."

WILLARD R. ESPY: "It is odd that the creators of such stuff fail to recognize that they are arousing risibilities rather than respect."

ELIZABETH JANEWAY: "I have a theory: I believe that this is the last, lingering touch of the use of Latin in the academy. A Latin citation would leave no doubt as to the case of the words used—they would be in the vocative —and word order, so necessary in English, would be irrelevant. Clearly this is a form of greeting, honorific and clumsy, as most honorific statements are."

DIANE JOHNSON: "I think this exhortation style is a bit silly, but surely not incorrect? But my grammar is merely instinctive."

JAMES J. KILPATRICK: "No (re Scotch verdict), because the perpetrator of that offensive sentence doesn't deserve to be let off."

STANLEY KUNITZ: "Panelist A.B.C. Whipple, your assault on academic telegraphese strikes me as supererogatory."

HERBERT MITGANG: "There is a 'you' implied in these quaint scrolls, with their imitation Oxonian script. So let them dangle their participles to make us feel superior to citationese language."

MARGE PIERCY: "This is bloated English, but it seems a form of direct address to me. The habit of addressing someone by a string of epithets feels archaic and falsely elegant but does not appear to me to be bad English by virtue of bad grammar but bad English by virtue of simple bad writing."

F. D. REEVE: "We're sinking under this crap."

VERMONT ROYSTER: "Who is this Yalie who graduated from Albertus Magnus College?"

ERICH SEGAL: "I insist that this is correct usage. The examples given are what I would call elegant Ciceronian vocatives."

DOLORES SIMON: "This is very florid writing, but does not seem a dangling modifier to me."

ELVIS STAHR, JR.: "As a greeting it would be grammatically acceptable although incredibly pompous, but I doubt that it was actually intended to be a greeting; thus, it is incredible grammar."

KARL V. TEETER: "On such occasions, rhetoric is superior to grammar."

BARBARA TUCHMAN: "There is a very great difference between the two examples. The first (Yale, etc.) is obviously unacceptable. The second, while not perfectly correct, is passable—because 'you' is obviously the person in question. Nevertheless, I agree with Prof. Whipple that the dangling modifier now appears more and more frequently."

EARL UBELL: "A colon would do wonders in the right place."

DOUGLAS WATT: "Have no objection to the first example as far as it goes, but the second one is inexcusably turgid."

HERMAN WOUK: "Fussiness."

dashes. *See* ELLIPSES/DASHES/LEADERS/AND OTHER DEVICES

dassn't/dare not *Dassn't* is one of several dialectal contractions of *dare not*. It began as a Yankee expression and traveled with Yankee peddlers all through the Eastern United States. It has been recorded as far west as Missouri and as far south as Alabama.

However, *dassn't* is not accepted as standard American speech. The dialect label means a form of language peculiar to a locality or group and thus differing from generally accepted standards of speech.

data/datum

USAGE PANEL QUESTION

Data as the plural of *datum* requires a plural verb in Latin. However, one frequently reads, especially in business, technical, and scientific writing, such expressions as "The *data is* inconclusive." Defenders of this usage point to "agenda," likewise technically a plural, but almost invariably regarded as a collective unit and hence taking a singular verb. Would you use "The *data* is . . ."?

In writing   Yes: 49%. No: 51%.
In casual speech   Yes: 65%. No: 35%.

ISAAC ASIMOV: "What's the use of saying, 'The data are' when to say it will cause everyone who hears it to consider you illiterate. 'Data' is plural in Latin, singular in English."

STEWART BEACH: "Despite its plural origin, I think it should be treated as a singular collective noun. That's what it is: a package of relevant facts on a single subject."

CHARLES BERLITZ: "Yes. In my opinion 'data' has evolved into a new word."

HAL BORLAND: "No, I wouldn't use these, but we purists are being snowed under by the casuals. Both these are so commonly used they have become accepted."

JOSEPH A. BRANDT: "In speech, the plural verb sounds as if you're overeducated."

HEYWOOD HALE BROUN: "No. Business, technical, and scientific writing are a problem in themselves. I would try to avoid 'data' as a subject."

ANTHONY BURGESS: "No. 'Agenda' has become singular because, being on a piece of paper, it *looks* singular. 'Data' are what they are."

ABE BURROWS: "This is one of those things. The plural verb is obviously correct. But its use jars the ear. So I've given up."

JOHN CIARDI: "I say yes to 'data' in casual speech. I really don't use it in this way, but I sense an inevitable change coming and I won't die resisting it."

RICHARD EDES HARRISON: "No . . . never."

JOHN K. HUTCHENS: "The comparison to 'agenda' is not legitimate. 'Data' are *not* a collective unit."

ALEXANDER KENDRICK: "No. If we yield on 'data,' we will soon be doing so on 'media,' 'criteria,' and 'phenomena.' "

CHARLES KURALT: "However much purists may object, the fact is, 'datum' ain't an English word. 'Data,' well, *is* . . ."

WALTER LORD: "This one has crossed over into respectability."

EDWIN NEWMAN: "No, but since I use 'agenda' as singular, this is inconsistent of me."

STANTON PECKHAM: " 'Data' refers to a series of individual items. 'Agenda' might justifiably take a singular verb in the sense that they constitute a list."

DAVID POLING: " 'Datum' is gone. . . ."

ORVILLE PRESCOTT: "This is now acceptable usage."

PETER S. PRESCOTT: "I probably do use it in speech, but I know I should not."

VERMONT ROYSTER: "The word 'data' is thoroughly Anglicized, and the use of Latin forms for English words is a bit pretentious."

DAVID SCHOENBRUN: "Casual speech is a useful testing laboratory, but writing is not a test procedure. It is a tested procedure."

HAROLD SCHONBERG: "Plural use may be grammatically correct, but somehow sounds affected. This one is a problem. I don't know. Myself, I avoid it."

DANIEL SCHORR: "In speech—yes—and thus risking my pedant credentials."

LIONEL TRILLING: "My impression is that 'Data are . . .' is gaining approval."

EARL UBELL: "A scientist I know makes a fetish out of making 'data' plural. It is now a lost cause along with 'agenda,' 'opera,' and others of that Latin ilk. Sometimes you will hear: 'Data are hard to get,' when the speaker or writer clearly has the plural in mind with many different classes of 'data.' "

WILLIAM C. VERGARA: " 'Datum,' which is widely used, appropriates the singular form of the verb. Anyhow, I always wince when I read, 'The data shows.' "

GEORGE WALD: "No. O, my God! I've been working on it for half a century, and my professor before that!"

CHARLES L. WHIPPLE: "No. A technical point, but how else can one be grammatical?"

daughter-in-law   The plural of *daughter-in-law* is *daughters-in-law*. See *also* PLURALS OF COMPOUND WORDS AND PHRASES.

davenport   In American use, a *davenport* is a sofa convertible into a bed. In British use a *davenport* is a small desk, especially one with many drawers.

daylight saving time   Among the much-abused words in the English language is *savings* (which see). It is a plural noun and can be properly used in such phrases as "savings account," "savings bank," or "savings bond."

In the phrase *daylight saving time, saving* is an adjective and should not be given a terminal "s." "Daylight savings time" is simply wrong.

dear *Dear* in the sense of "costly"—especially referring to the high price of a commodity normally low in cost—has been part of the language since the time of Shakespeare. Although it is heard infrequently these days, it is perfectly acceptable.

death. *See* CASUALTY/DEATH

debacle Both the meaning and the pronunciation of this word have changed somewhat since its introduction into English a century and a half ago. It came to us direct from the French and was originally a geologist's term for a sudden breaking-up of ice in a river. At the time of an early spring thaw, a sudden breaking of ice may cause a violent rush of water, bearing with it stones and debris, making a *debacle.* This technical term was later applied in a figurative sense to any catastrophic rout or stampede. Now its meaning has been extended still further to cover any great catastrophe.

Because the word has figured in our language for a relatively short time and because it is a rather uncommon word, it retains much of its original French accent, so to speak. The preferred pronunciation is deh-BAH-k'l; indeed, this is the only pronunciation accepted by the Oxford Dictionary. However, American usage in this instance differs from British, so most American dictionaries now list deh-BACK-ul as a second but acceptable pronunciation. You will also hear day-BAH-k'l from those who are trying to approximate as closely as possible the original French version.

debag *Debag* is British slang meaning, literally, to remove a person's trousers *(bags).* Since a man without trousers is a man without dignity—indeed, a traditional laughingstock—to *debag* a person is to deprive him of his poise.

debrief *Debrief* started as Pentagonese for what in World War II was called "post-flight interrogation." All pilots flying missions are subjected to intense *briefings* before they take off. The information given them at that time includes procedures to be followed, routes, weather conditions, destination, targets, probable enemy activity, and any other important data relating to the mission, including the best way to get back.

Then the Pentagon coined *debriefing* to mean, in wartime at least, the interrogation of pilots to obtain information of value to the intelligence arm of the service. It has come to be loosely used, by extension, to apply to any interrogation or examination, as in "The ambassador was *debriefed* after returning to Washington."

The federal government has gone even further. When a person leaves a government post in which he or she had access to classified or secret information, he or she is *debriefed:* instructed not to reveal any such information.

debut   *Debut* as a noun, meaning the first performance of an actor or of a concert artist, is well established. In recent years it has been used in the press as a verb, both as a transitive verb ("The Met *debuts* a new opera next month") and as an intransitive verb ("The new soprano *debuts* tonight"). These verb uses of *debut* have stirred sharp criticism. For the opinions of the Usage Panel see the entry *premiere/debut.*

decimate   In ancient times a favorite punishment inflicted by conquerors on defeated armies was to *decimate* them, that is to kill every tenth man chosen by lot. The same punishment was used in more recent times as a cautionary lesson to rebellious or mutinous troops. Strictly speaking, then, to *decimate* means to slaughter one in ten. It has long had the extended meaning of "to destroy or kill a large part of a group," as one might say that the drought *decimated* the herds of cattle. In recent years, however, *decimate* has appeared frequently in print in the simple meaning of "destroy." A newspaper story runs: "Katharine Dexter looked out the window of her apartment and watched the wrecker's ball *decimate* a brownstone apartment fifty feet away." Panelist Abe Burrows was moved to complain about this loose use of *decimate.* His comments were used as the basis of a Usage Panel Question, which, with the percentages of replies and a selection of panelists' comments, follows.

USAGE PANEL QUESTION

Panelist ABE BURROWS writes: "The word 'decimate' is being ruined. I am not saying that we have to stick to the original 'every tenth man' definition, but it still should only be used when it deals with the destruction of a great part of a group. On the good old television, I have even heard it used about the destruction of one person." Do you employ *decimate* in the strict or limited sense indicated in this quotation?
In speech   Yes: 84%. No: 16%.
In writing   Yes: 86%. No: 14%.

ISAAC ASIMOV: "The misuse of 'decimate' is part of the subliteracy of the 'educated.' "

STEWART BEACH: "Yes, in the limited sense, of course, of a large part of a group."

HEYWOOD HALE BROUN: "Yes. There are, unfortunately, enough commonly used words for 'massacre' without this incorrect one."

BEN LUCIEN BURMAN: "Good heavens, no. How fussy can you get?"

JOHN CIARDI: "Yes. Is a tenth a 'great part' of a group? It is a precise word and I use it precisely."

JOHN K. HUTCHENS: "No, if by this you mean 'every tenth man.' Yes, if you mean large-scale destruction."

WALT KELLY: "Yes. Many use 'decimate' to indicate complete destruction. I'm for sticking to the one-tenth idea."

RUSSELL LYNES: "Yes."

DWIGHT MACDONALD: "Yes, of course."

JESSICA MITFORD: "To me, decimate means widespread destruction—not one-tenth, certainly not *one.*"

EDWIN NEWMAN: "Yes. I learned the correct use of the word thanks to a friend who heard me misuse it."

HARRISON SALISBURY: "Yes, of course."

ELVIS STAHR, JR.: " 'Decimate' has nearly been ruined by non-Latin scholars. It didn't deserve it. It's more valuable than *defenestrate* [which see] by far."

DAVIDSON TAYLOR: "I would not use the word in writing. It is too imprecise now."

decriminalize   *Decriminalize,* a relatively recent coinage, is frequently used by persons seeking to abolish legal penalties for marijuana use, homosexual behavior, prostitution, or attempted suicide. It is their contention that none of these acts is criminal, even though there may be laws against them, and that they should be *decriminalized.* There is a nice distinction between this and "legalize." *Decriminalize* means merely to remove laws against an activity, while "legalize" means to enact legislation permitting but regulating. Gambling was "legalized" in Nevada—that is, laws were enacted regulating it. *See also* DEMYTHOLOGIZE.

deer in the balcony, shoot   Theatrical jargon for a half-empty house. It derives from the traditional show-business expression "Business was so bad you could *shoot deer in the balcony.*" This led one reviewer to write: "After her earlier performances, the concert of Maria Callas turned Carnegie Hall into a deer park."

de-escalate   "Escalate," of course, means to increase or intensify. Logically its antonym should be "descalate," just as the antonym for "accelerate" is "decelerate." The proper antonym is, however, *de-escalate.* To the best of our knowledge "descalate" appeared in print only once—in the late 1960s in an editorial in *The New York Times.* When we asked Ted

Bernstein, then the custodian of linguistic proprieties at the *Times*, whatever happened to "descalate," he replied, "I personally committed infanticide on that word."

defective/deficient   While dictionaries give *defective* as one of the synonyms for *deficient* there is a distinction between the two which should be observed. *Defective* means "imperfect" and defectiveness may be caused by a *deficiency,* which is a lack or insufficiency of an essential element. Something may also be *defective* because it was not made properly or because it has been broken and hence cannot function or be made to function. The words are not truly synonymous and *defective* should be used when quality is involved; *deficient* when quantity is involved.

defenestrate

USAGE PANEL QUESTION

Panelist STANTON PECKHAM writes: "Dictionaries enter the noun 'defenestration.' Oddly enough, they do not indicate a verb 'defenestrate.' A few years ago there was a case of defenestration from the John Hancock building in Chicago. Wasn't she defenestrated? Didn't somebody defenestrate her?" Leaving aside the matter of whether she did it herself or had it done to her, would you agree that we should recognize the verb "to *defenestrate*"?

Yes: 63%. No: 37%.

SHANA ALEXANDER: "No. It's a cutesy word. But would *you* accept 'cutesy'? Or, how about 'depontification' for jumping off bridges?"

ISAAC ASIMOV: "Yes. Good idea."

STEWART BEACH: "Yes. By all means. I always thought it *was* a verb, too."

HAL BORLAND: "No. The whole damn thing seems pretentious, like saying 'aliment' for 'feed.' "

JOSEPH A. BRANDT: "Yes, but they are affectations."

HEYWOOD HALE BROUN: "Yes. Why not?"

BEN LUCIEN BURMAN: "Yes, but why bother? Throwing out of a window is so much more vivid!"

ABE BURROWS: "No. Did she fall or was she pushed?"

JOHN CIARDI: "Yes. I accept old school ties around old school necks but I'd rather chuck her out the window."

PAUL HORGAN: "No. Historically, the noun is long accepted. But the verb would, I think, be pretentious or comical."

JOHN K. HUTCHENS: "Yes. Why not? It's an essentially comic word anyhow, if not a comic situation."

ELIZABETH JANEWAY: "No. She was thrown out the window. Or did she jump?"

WALT KELLY: "Yes. As a verb it is in use anyway."

WALTER KERR: "No. I don't like it even as a noun—fancy and evasive."

CHARLES KURALT: "Yes. Yes, but only William F. Buckley, Jr., would *use* the word. It is one of those show-off words, useful only for demonstration of one's erudition."

LAURENCE LAFORE: "Yes. Why not, unless we are to reject all neologisms? It breaks no rule and confuses no meaning."

RUSSELL LYNES: "Yes, if the occasion arises."

DWIGHT MACDONALD: "Yes. That's how a language grows. Also, it's logical."

EUGENE MCCARTHY: "No. What of 'incursion' as in Cambodia without a verb 'incurse'?"

WADE MOSBY: "I'd throw the whole word out of the window."

DANIEL PATRICK MOYNIHAN: "Yes. It means a form of political assassination."

PETER S. PRESCOTT: "To hell with it: the noun is a fancy word we don't need (but I enjoy it); let's allow it as an oddity, but when a verb is needed stick to 'push' or 'jump.' Orwell was good on this."

LEO ROSTEN: "Yes. Also for knocking out windows—with or without baseballs."

BERTON ROUECHÉ: "Yes—welcome it!"

VERMONT ROYSTER: "I would defenestrate a writer so pretentious."

MARK SCHORER: "Why would anyone want to use either of these stupidly heavy, Latinate inventions?"

ROBERT SHERRILL: "God, yes! We really need that!"

BARBARA TUCHMAN: "No, not necessarily. *Ça suffit.* Let's not add more Latin verbs to the language."

BILL VAUGHAN: "Yes. However, although it deals with a tragic subject, this word has comic overtones."

Defense Department/War Department. *See* EUPHEMISM

definite/definitive Contrary to the belief of many people, these two words are not interchangeable. Both mean "clear," "certain," and "precise," but *definitive* has an added meaning of not being subject to change or appeal. The error lies in trying to substitute *definitive* for *definite*. A plan may be *definite* because it is precise and worked out in detail but it is *definitive* only when it is final and no longer subject to amendment.

degreed A linguistic horror which is part of the jargon of the employment placement industry is the use of *degreed* as an adjective, as in "He is not *degreed* but he has good recommendations." We have even heard a college professor remark, "He is *degreed* in psych." Translation: "He has a degree in psychology."

déjà vu

USAGE PANEL QUESTION

Until World War II most American dictionaries defined "nostalgia" as an illness, specifically, in Webster's words, "a severe melancholia caused by protracted absence from home." Today this clinical meaning is virtually ignored by the lexicons and most define nostalgia as "a longing for things, persons or situations that are now remote . . . for something far away or long ago." Clearly this is an instance of changing popular usage.

Recently a *New York Times* headline referred to "Déjà vu in a cluttered bookshop." Technically, *déjà vu* means the illusion of having at some time in the past experienced something that is actually happening for the first time. Obviously the *Times* headline writer was using it in the broader sense of things known in the past and now rediscovered. This sense, in fact, is closer to the original French, which simply means "already seen."

Do you think this extension of meaning of *déjà vu* is valid?

Would you use it in writing? Yes: 36%. No: 64%.

In speech? Yes: 36%. No: 64%.

ISAAC ASIMOV: "I try not to use the term at all. If I want the sense, I would rather say 'false memory' or something like that."

WHITNEY BALLIETT: "The *Times* man misused it; such misuse would eventually destroy its ghostly overtones."

SAUL BELLOW: "It referred, once upon a time, to a delicate sort of experience. I don't like to see it 'broadened.' "

BARRY BINGHAM, SR.: "I still prefer the use of 'déjà vu' to describe a very particular sensation; a feeling that a current sight or incident is a repetition of an exactly similar sight or incident previously experienced, but not remembered. The extension of the phrase to cover remembered happenings now repeated, though admittedly closer to the literal meaning of the French words, offends me. It strikes me as yet another example of the current tendency to stretch words and phrases to cover wider and vaguer meaning, thus diluting precision of utterance."

ALTON BLAKESLEE: "And it is somewhat like confusing former sweethearts."

HEYWOOD HALE BROUN: "I am always disturbed by any loss of the mystic. What do you mean 'illusion'?"

JAMES MACGREGOR BURNS: "Fighting a losing battle with this one, I'm afraid. That subtle illusion is much more interesting than the idea of rediscovery."

JOHN CIARDI: "I accept this use of nostalgia. The real sense is 'longing (pain) to return.' Longing to return home (German *Heimweh*) was long asserted to be implicit, but the real as readily sanctions 'return to anything gone by.' "

ROBERT CROMIE: "This changed meaning removes the out-of-the-ordinary quality from the phrase, which is too useful to be given up."

WILLARD R. ESPY: "The established definition has a mystical preciseness. It would be a shame to superimpose another that could only blur the first, and isn't needed in any event."

ALEX FAULKNER: "Déjà vu in the traditional sense has such a clear meaning that it seems a pity to fuzz it up. Obviously (I hope) the *NYT* headline writer was indulging in a pun."

RAY GANDOLF: "To describe that universal, but infrequent, illusion 'déjà vu' is an accurate, terse phrase. To broaden that meaning, original French or no, to include "already seen" dilutes its meaning. I have experienced true déjà vu perhaps twenty times in my life. I would gladly forego the enjoyable snobbery of Frenchifying that feeling if the phrase were outlawed."

SID GOLDBERG: "When I first learned of the phrase 'déjà vu' I was thankful that such a concept existed to describe what I had thought was a totally private experience. Don't let them take it away. (But: How do the French express the more subtle thought? Are they stuck with the literal meaning of the phrase?)"

ROBERT GOTTLIEB: "I've never heard 'nostalgia' used any but the modern way. Obviously it was needed. However, the new use of 'déjà vu' is a dreadful change, since we need an expression for the phenomenon 'déjà vu' describes. The *Times* use should be rooted out!"

ELIZABETH HARDWICK: " 'Déjà vu' is difficult to use correctly with or without strain. The acceptable meaning represents a rare occurrence and yet I see no good reason for the extension of the kind you quoted. At best the sense is obscure and could be better said another way."

SYDNEY J. HARRIS: " 'Nostalgia's' change fills a need; 'déjà vu' is merely pretentious in its extension. It has become 'trendy.' "

JOHN K. HUTCHENS: "I strongly approve of today's definition of 'nostalgia.' To me it means tender remembrance—in any case a far cry from melancholia. I'll still take the technical definition of déjà vu—i.e., the illusion of having experienced in the past something now happening for the first time."

ELIZABETH JANEWAY: "Is [the changed use of 'nostalgia'] perhaps a familiar kind of weakening? Words do fade in intensity, through use. I find current usage OK—we need a word for this feeling, which is quite current in our lives today. [On the question of 'déjà vu'] I changed my mind, on the issue of value. We also need a phrase that connotes the special sensation of 'déjà vu' as it is properly used. As for the French: (1) My French isn't good enough to know whether the phrase carries any English-type connotation; (2) Does it matter? Lots of words that look the same in another language are traps—they don't mean the same."

WALTER KERR: "Whatever about its origins, we have been treating it as distinct from 'remembered'—and there is such a distinct experience. I'm in favor of our traditional usage."

JAMES J. KILPATRICK: "I wouldn't use 'déjà vu' in my newspaper column for the best of all reasons: few of my readers would understand what the hell I was talking about. They would think I was putting on airs: Ain't English good enough for him? But if an answer is required, yes, I believe 'déjà vu' is now understood in the high rent district to mean 'une recherche du temps perdu.' "

STANLEY KUNITZ: "The distinction is a fine one and should be preserved."

JULES LOH: "Some consider foreign expressions 'de rigueur'; I find them pretentious and avoid them. So I really don't care."

DWIGHT MACDONALD: "Seems a good example of the way the language changes with no loss. Would 'twere ever thus!"

WADE MOSBY: "I cringe a bit over the new usage of 'nostalgia' but I'm willing to accept it—but not to use it. ('Déjà vu') Fad words and fad phrases are often seen in public places."

EDWIN NEWMAN: "I remember hearing Arthur Koestler, perhaps thirty-five years ago, speak of 'nostalgia for the lost cause' as a characteristic of some people who seemed to want to be on the losing side. A useful expression, I thought. I think this usage has value. I think 'déjà vu' is taking on the meaning 'We've seen this all before and it is depressing or tiresome to see it again.' "

PETER S. PRESCOTT: "The term, of course, requires two accents. 'Rediscovery' is not quite its proper use: 'recognition of that which has been seen before' is more to the point. As a book critic, I coined the term 'déjà lu' for a book that borrows too heavily from previous models."

F. D. REEVE: " 'Déjà vu,' the professor said / On seeing Romeo and Juliet dead / 'O Bride of Corinth, would he were you! / Why did you fondle your déjà vu?' "

ANDY ROONEY: "I prefer the new usage for nostalgia: I don't equate it in any way with neuralgia. ('Déjà vu') Probably not but I don't mind writers who do use it as meaning already seen."

BERTON ROUECHÉ: "A la recherche du temps perdu is not an exercise in déjà vu."

VERMONT ROYSTER: "If we change the meaning, what do we then use to express the illusion of having seen before a place or thing actually seen for the first time?"

DAVID SCHOENBRUN: "You are correct in saying that 'déjà vu' means literally 'already seen.' But it is not used that way in France. It is used as you say . . . there is no other way to communicate this illusion so briefly and vividly. I do not want it to be made 'broader' for that would blur its true meaning and dull its imagery."

HAROLD SCHONBERG: "Déjà vu is something that happens *very* rarely in a person's lifetime, if ever. I have experienced it two or three times. Let's not adulterate the meaning."

JACK SMITH: "I would probably use 'déjà vu' in writing if I wanted to show off my French; but I would more likely write 'a feeling of having been here before.' "

HAROLD TAYLOR: "I don't like the words at all. I'd sooner say it some other way unless I was talking French."

KARL V. TEETER: " 'Valid' or not, it is preponderant current usage."

EDWARD TRIPP: "A common extension of déjà vu conjures up a somewhat weary sense of 'having seen it all before' when presented with an idea or situation purported to be new. Although it is quite unlike the technical psychological definition—which is, after all, seldom encountered—it is both close to the literal meaning of the phrase and an interesting idea in its own right. It fills a need for a simple term to describe a complex feeling, much as does the word 'paranoid' in common parlance. It does not trouble me that the psychologist or psychoanalyst may object. The use you quote, however, seems to rob the term of specificity without gaining much. It diffuses the meaning unduly to my mind."

EARL UBELL: "The illusion is so specific—in fact, it can be evoked by physically touching a part of the brain—that to lose the meaning would be a sorry loss of precision."

JOSEPH VERGARA: " 'Déjà vu' has a lovely air of mystery bordering on the supernatural. It would be a shame to lose this meaning."

GEORGE WALD: (Voting "yes") "The 'technical' usage is so rare that it should not be permitted to inhibit this otherwise widely useful expression."

DOUGLAS WATT: "Headlines impose special demands and allow for looser usage than actual writing. It's doubtful that the writer of the piece under the headline used 'déjà vu' in that manner."

HERMAN WOUK: "[The technical usage] is becoming recondite, though still precise usage. I don't know the *Times*' usage at all. To me it has come to mean, roughly, 'old hat.' I just glanced at my desk dictionary, Merriam-Webster's New Collegiate–8th. It concurs."

delible. *See* LOST POSITIVES

Delphic utterances A *Delphic utterance* is a statement somewhat obscure in its meaning and open to more than one interpretation. It is so called because a *Delphic utterance* (note the capital "D") was originally a prophecy given in ancient times by the oracle at the shrine to Apollo located at Delphi at the foot of Mount Parnassus. Those prophecies were usually worded ambiguously, so that two or more meanings could be read into them.

delusion. *See* ILLUSION/DELUSION

demean

USAGE PANEL QUESTION

HELEN L. KAUFMANN writes: "I would like the panel's opinion on whether to *demean* oneself necessarily means to debase or degrade oneself. Is the meaning 'to behave oneself, to observe a certain demeanor' now archaic?"

Yes: 69%. No: 31%.

ISAAC ASIMOV: "Yes. It would be misunderstood every time."

JOHN BROOKS: "No, but, because of usage change, one who uses it in the old sense must make the meaning clear through context."

STEPHEN H. FRITCHMAN: "Yes, definitely!"

ALEXANDER KENDRICK: "Yes, alas."

STANLEY KUNITZ: "If not, it is rapidly becoming so—alas!"

JULES LOH: "Not archaic literally, but certainly ambiguous in view of the adjective 'demeaning.'"

PHYLLIS MCGINLEY: "I'm afraid it is. I, as a purist, would like to keep the difference in the two words, but custom has erased them."

PETER S. PRESCOTT: "To demean oneself now means to debase, but demeanor still means behavior."

VERMONT ROYSTER: "Yes. The word has been too often demeaned for me to redeem it."

HARRISON SALISBURY: "Yes, it does imply 'lowering.'"

WALTER W. "RED" SMITH: "I think 'demean' now means only 'degrade.'"

BILL VAUGHAN: "Yes, except for being satirically fancy."

HERMAN WOUK: "Yes, again, in common usage."

demob British informal for discharge from the armed services. It is a shortened form of demobilization. It is often used attributively in expressions like *"demob* leave" and *"demob* suit" (clothing issued a serviceman on his departure from service). Pronunciation: dee-MOB.

Democrat/Democratic *"Democrat* party" is the idiotic creation of some of the least responsible members of the Republican party. It is correctly the *"Democratic* party." The only use for *Democrat* (with a capital "D") is as a noun to designate a member of the *Democratic* party.

demythologize The process of coining words by adding prefixes and suffixes is standard practice but the results are sometimes long and awkward words which can be found only in an unabridged dictionary. *Demythologize* is a case in point.

"Mythology" is defined in the dictionary as "A body of myths concerning some person, event or institution" and "mythologize" is a proper verb, although "mythicize" means much the same thing and is shorter. Now *demythologize* has been coined for use in such statements as "*demythologize* the controversy surrounding marijuana." "Disprove the myths" would be better.

depend *Depend* is followed by the prepositions *on* or *upon* in all senses except the now obsolescent "hang down," in which case it is followed by *from:* "The success of the argument *depends* on its logic," but "The ornate chandelier *depends from* the rococo ceiling." Omission of the preposition occurs occasionally in informal speech, notably in the expression "That *depends.*"

deprecate/depreciate The distinction between *deprecate* and *depreciate* is fast becoming blurred, if not obliterated, through usage by otherwise literate people. The most common example is the phrase "self-*deprecating,*" used to mean "self-belittling."

The true meaning of *deprecate* is "to plead or protest against" or "to express disapproval of."

Depreciate (which is actually an antonym for "appreciate") means "to make less or become less in value or price." Thus it is accurate to say, "A modest man, he *depreciated* the importance of his contribution to the work," or "He spoke of his work in a self-*depreciating* manner." This is not what you hear today, though. "Self-*deprecating*" has been substituted for "self-*depreciating.*" The reasons are obviously the similarity in appearance of the two words and lack of understanding of the difference in meaning.

depression/recession In terms of economics, a *depression* is a sharp decline in the economic health of a country, involving decreased business activity and widespread unemployment which last over a period of time. A *recession* is defined as a temporary slump in the economy during a period of generally prosperous business activity, especially during the recovery period after a *depression.*

Where the dividing line falls is debated by economists and laymen alike. One definition by a layman is: "If the man next door is out of work for two months, it's a *recession;* if I am out of work for two months and can't find any kind of a job, it's a *depression.*"

derision/derisive/derisory *Derision* is ridicule and *derisive* and *derisory* are directly related to *derision.* At one time *derisory* was solely synonymous with *derisive,* meaning "expressing ridicule," as in *"derisory* remarks about his appearance." *Derisory* has also acquired the meaning of "deserving or inviting ridicule," and thus may now be properly used to describe a person or thing that merits *derision* ("a *derisory* excuse for a racehorse").

derogatory terms   There are a number of slang terms in English which are used in derogation of a person because of his race or nationality. Some of them came into use as the result of wars, such as "Krauts" for Germans and "gooks" for Vietnamese. Others express the indiscriminate attribution of undesirable traits to a person because of his or her nationality, such as "Dutch" (which see), "welsher," "mick," "limey," and "frog." Thanks to a growing realization of the derogatory character of such terms, there has been a decline in use of them. They are always offensive and in very poor taste, except when used in fictional conversation to delineate a character capable of using such terms.

derriere/fanny   Derriere is an early euphemism not often heard today. Rather than speak of a person's hips or backside, it was once fashionable to use the French word *derriere* to avoid offense. It is pronounced deh-ree-AIR. More common today is the slang term *fanny.* Like *derriere,* it may be applied to persons of either sex. *See also* FANNY

descript. *See* LOST POSITIVES

desegregate/integrate   In current usage *desegregate* and *integrate* have become synonymous in the sense of abolishing separation by races in schools and communities.

desert/dessert   *Desert,* as a noun, comes from the Latin "desertum," meaning something abandoned or deserted, as the *Sahara* (which see) has been long abandoned by nearly all living things. It is pronounced DEZ-ert, but as a verb it is pronounced duh-ZERT.

   Dessert, on the other hand, comes from the French word "desservir" and merely means the last course before "unserving," that is, taking the dishes off the table. In the United States we think of a *dessert* as a sweet dish but in many countries, notably Great Britain, *dessert* is often a "savoury" (rather like our appetizers) served after the sweet. In China the *dessert* is often a thin soup or rice, while in France it is most often cheese served with fresh fruit. It is simply the last course of the meal, whatever that may be.

destroyed

USAGE PANEL QUESTION

"Completely *destroyed*" is a phrase commonly encountered, yet there are some who consider it redundant, that *destroyed* alone is sufficient. Do you agree?

Yes: 51%. No: 49%.

Would you use in your own speech and writing the phrase "partially *destroyed*"?

Yes: 72%. No: 28%.

ISAAC ASIMOV: "Completely' is an intensifier. As to 'partially destroyed,' why not? If a fire devastates part of a city, the city is 'partially destroyed.' "

SHERIDAN BAKER: "I find this expressive. I've seen some monasteries that Henry VIII's men did really 'partially destroy.' "

STEWART BEACH: "I think it quite acceptable to use 'completely' or 'partially' with 'destroyed.' They make the situation more descriptive."

SAUL BELLOW: "These days we must be precise about the destruction."

JOSEPH A. BRANDT: " 'Destroyed' means destroyed; 'damaged' is the alternative."

HEYWOOD HALE BROUN: "Yes to both parts. The two answers are inconsistent but you are concerned with usage not logic."

ABE BURROWS: "I might say 'almost destroyed.' "

PAUL HORGAN: "Natural tendency to emphasize justifies 'completely.' I would use 'partially'—journalistically."

ELIZABETH JANEWAY: "I don't much care, but surely one could use 'partially destroyed' of a city that had been bombed badly in some areas and not in others."

WALTER KERR (#1, #2, yes): " 'Destroyed' is certainly sufficient, but I would accept this. So where am I? Portions of a house can be truly destroyed, which means that the house is partially destroyed—it has some use and the meaning is clear."

CLARK KINNAIRD: "Rarely is *anything* destroyed completely; even some of Hiroshima survived. The extent of destruction being a matter of interest, it should be indicated more aptly than 'partially.' "

JOHN LEAR: "I might be able to rationalize 'partly destroyed,' but certainly not 'partially destroyed.' "

DWIGHT MACDONALD (#1, no; #2, yes): "Agree not logical—but see 'completely' as merely emphatic, atmospheric."

ORVILLE PRESCOTT: "A legitimate matter of degree. Complete destruction is rare. Many ancient cities were destroyed, but not completely."

PETER S. PRESCOTT (#1, yes; #2, yes): "There's inconsistency for you; I will reform and abstain from partial destruction."

LEO ROSTEN: " 'Really beautiful' or 'very expensive' adds *emphasis;* so does 'completely.' "

DAVID SCHOENBRUN: "There are degrees of destruction. 'Completely' is thus valid, as is 'partially.' "

MARK SCHORER: "I'd say 'almost' or 'nearly,' not 'partially.' "

ROBERT SHERRILL: "Some destruction needs or deserves this type of emphasis."

CHARLES E. SILBERMAN: "Depends on the circumstances: Hiroshima was not destroyed, it was *completely* destroyed!"

ELVIS STAHR, JR.: " 'Not quite destroyed' has real value in situations short of total physical destruction. Absentmindedly, I suspect I would use 'partially destroyed.' "

WILLIAM C. VERGARA: "I'd prefer 'partly destroyed' to indicate extent rather than degree."

détente. *See* VOGUE WORDS

deteriorate   The use of *deteriorate* as a transitive verb is uncommon but not wrong. A spokesman for Consolidated Edison, in explaining one of New York's "brownouts," stated: "There are all sort of factors, like the salt the city uses in the wintertime to melt ice. That gets to the cables and it will *deteriorate* the cables in time."

The Oxford Dictionary indicates that the transitive sense of *deteriorate* is even older than the intransitive sense, which is far more common today ("The situation continues to *deteriorate*"). The dictionary cites one example going back to the 1500s, so the Con Ed spokesman was speaking pre-Elizabethan English, even though not aware of it.

deterrent/deterrence/determent   The older and less frequently used *deterrence* and *determent* have the special sense of the act of deterring. The much more common *deterrent* signifies only the thing that serves to halt or confine an action. Thus, "as long as the major powers possess the nuclear bomb, knowledge of its power acts as a strong *deterrent* to its use."

diagnosis/prognosis   A *diagnosis* of an illness is the identifying of the nature of the disease through examination of the patient. It is the illness which is diagnosed, not the patient.

A *prognosis* follows *diagnosis.* It is the doctor's educated guess as to the course and outcome of the illness.

dialect, regional Perhaps the most colorful and interesting part of our American language is our folk speech—the pungent, homely, and ever-varying patterns of talk which word experts call *dialect.*

Dialect words are not necessarily slang; they are simply regional variations in everyday vocabulary. No matter what part of the country you come from, there are bound to be some words and phrases in your vocabulary which mark you as one reared in a particular region. The instances of such regional variations are so numerous that entire dictionaries of *dialect* have been compiled. The best of them is Harold Wentworth's *American Dialect Dictionary* (T. Y. Crowell, New York).

dialogue, meaningful. *See* MEANINGFUL and VOGUE WORDS

dicey *Dicey* is a recent borrowing from British slang. Obviously derived from the throwing of dice in various gambling games, it means "risky" or "chancy." Friends in the editorial department of the Tacoma *News Tribune* supplied a quote from Richard D. Altick's *To Be in England* that admirably shows how it is used there. Speaking of the relatively short distances between towns in England, Altick writes: "Some people prefer for this reason to take night as it comes, relishing not knowing where they will stay until they are there. But this is too chancy—the British would say 'dicey'—for me. Theoretically it is true, if one is disappointed at a certain place, there is usually another town a few miles away—but its inn may be full, also." Another correspondent reports that during World War II *dicey* was widely adopted by the Royal Air Force and used extensively to describe risky situations.

diction

USAGE PANEL QUESTION

Panelist PHYLLIS MCGINLEY writes: " 'Diction' means a choice of words, but all the world these days, except me, seems to employ it as if it meant 'enunciation.' " Do you agree that *diction* now has both meanings, equally acceptable?
Yes: 61%.
No: 39%.

SHANA ALEXANDER: "Again, I didn't know. . . . I think the distinction should be observed and will do so myself."
HEYWOOD HALE BROUN: "No. Not 'all the world'—there are at least two of us."

ABE BURROWS: "No, I usually just avoid it. This thing about 'diction' started back in radio when announcers used to get 'Diction Awards.' I suspect this was based on the fact that announcers wrote their own stuff or ad-libbed. The audience thought it meant their enunciation and it stuck forever."

STEPHEN H. FRITCHMAN: "Yes. It's a *long*-lost battle."

PAUL HORGAN: "Yes—the stage has made it so."

JOHN K. HUTCHENS: "Yes—probably, if it's understood that it means *clarity* of enunciation."

HELEN L. KAUFMANN: "In the singer's vocabulary, clear diction equals clear enunciation, and is accepted. So why not generally?"

LEONARD SANDERS: "Yes. Perhaps not 'equally acceptable,' but this seems to be another lost battle."

MARK SCHORER: "Yes. To different professions. It has an honorable history in the theater, and another in rhetoric. No one is going to be confused, and without becoming sloppily permissive, we can certainly allow multiple possibilities to language. Cf. James Joyce."

REX STOUT: "Webster II thinks so, but I don't."

LIONEL TRILLING: "Yes. I regret this, but so it is. In singing, diction has long meant enunciation."

dictionary entries, explanation of. *See* ENTRY, DICTIONARY

dictionary entries, order of definitions in There is a widespread misconception that the definition numbered "1" in a *dictionary entry* is (a) the most important or (b) the "most correct." This is seldom the case. Of the dictionaries commonly used in the U.S., both the Merriam-Webster series and the Oxford dictionaries endeavor to give the oldest meaning first and observe what they call a "historical" order of entry. As a result you will sometimes find an unfamiliar or obsolete meaning at the start of an entry. The first definition under "disease" in Oxford is "absence of ease, uneasiness, annoyance." Not until the second definition do you find the meaning most common today: "a condition of the body or of some part or organ of the body in which its functions are disturbed or deranged." Similarly, in Webster's Seventh Collegiate the first definition of the adjective "nude" reads simply "lacking an essential particular." What happened here is that the editors eliminated the label "Law" which had appeared in earlier editions and which would have alerted the reader to the fact that this is a highly specialized use of the word. Even with the label, though, the definition is so stripped—forgive the expression—that it doesn't really make sense. What is meant is that "nude" is used in law to indicate, as in "nude contract," that a contract has been made without consideration. Later in the entry, the editors do tell us that "nude" also means "devoid of clothing, naked, esp. unclothed."

Most other dictionaries follow the plan pioneered by Funk & Wagnalls of giving the "most common" or "most widely used" meaning first. But this is not always possible. Who can say, for example, which of the more than two hundred meanings of the common word "set" should be considered the most widely used?

Panelist Norman Hoss, managing editor of the original *American Heritage Dictionary,* reports that *AHD* follows neither the "historical" nor the "most common" order of entry method but that the first entry is chosen as "the central meaning about which the other senses may most logically be organized." Asked by one of the linguistic consultants on the staff of the dictionary if this didn't come down to a matter of subjective judgment on the part of the editors, he replied in the affirmative. Whereupon he was somewhat startled to be told that he had anticipated the newest trend in language research, "intuitional linguistics." In any event, the system works at least as well as any other.

die (of/from)   In the sense of "to cease living," *die* should be followed by the preposition "of " rather than "from." "He *died of* pneumonia," not "He *died from* pneumonia."

dieresis   A *dieresis* is a punctuation mark (or diacritical mark) consisting of two dots placed over the second of two adjacent vowels to indicate that the vowels are to be pronounced separately. Thus, what is now written "cooperate" used to be written "coöperate." More than fifty years ago the *dieresis* fell into disfavor (probably at the wish of printers) and was replaced by the hyphen, and the word became "co-operate." As the result of a growing tendency to eliminate hyphens, the word is now given solid in most dictionaries, with the earlier versions given as also acceptable. *See also* HYPHEN.

dietitian/dietician   Both spellings are in common use. The *dietitian* spelling is slightly more common.

different from/different than   The more common American idiom is *different from* but, as several leading grammarians have pointed out, the use of *different than* is becoming more popular among careful writers when the object of the preposition is a clause, as in "Please inform us if your address is *different than* it was in the past."

dig   *Dig,* as a slang word meaning "to understand, appreciate, or enjoy," did not come into general use until the 1960s, but it has been in the slang of jazz musicians since at least the 1930s. If a person was, as they say today, "into" jazz, he *dug* it.

dilemma

Dilemma in its traditional use refers to a situation in which one is faced with the necessity of choosing one of two equal alternatives. Frequently of late it appears in the more generalized sense of "acute problem" but not one necessarily offering two equal alternative solutions. Thus one reads: "Drug abuse is the major *dilemma* of our day." Do you accept this broader sense of *dilemma*?
Would you use it in your own speech?   Yes: 30%. No: 70%.
In writing   Yes: 29%. No: 71%.

STEWART BEACH: "No. I stick by the strict meaning of the word. In the quoted sentence 'problem' should be used."

HAL BORLAND: "No. The root meaning is 'a choice of two.' "

ABE BURROWS: "I don't like 'dilemma' as a synonyn for 'problem.' I think 'dilemma' should only be used when one is torn between alternatives. I don't mind the dilemma having more than two horns. But there still must be *horns.*"

ALEX FAULKNER: "Yes; e.g., *The Doctor's Dilemma.*"

STEPHEN H. FRITCHMAN: "No. Heaven forbid! Let's go for exactitude while we can."

JOHN K. HUTCHENS: "No. Why not just retain 'problem' and let 'dilemma' go about its business?"

ALEXANDER KENDRICK: "Not as long as 'problem,' 'challenge,' and 'crisis' are around."

WRIGHT MORRIS: "Yes. Contemporary 'dilemmas' obviously exceed 'alternative' solutions."

PETER S. PRESCOTT: "Yes, although I fear it is rather sloppy of me."

LEO ROSTEN: "No. It's not a 'dilemma' until you have analyzed the alternatives."

WALTER W. "RED" SMITH: "No. Let's hold the line for precise meanings."

dimensions. *See* PROPORTIONS/DIMENSIONS

dinner/supper/lunch   The interpretation of *dinner* and *supper* varies very considerably according to geographical region and to the generation involved. Until the early years of this century, when the United States was chiefly a rural culture, the main meal of the day was eaten at midday and it was called *dinner.* Farmhands came in from the fields and office workers walked to their homes for the noonday *dinner.* In the evening, a lighter meal called *supper* was served.

As the country became increasingly urbanized, this pattern changed in many parts of the country. The need for a heavy meal at midday diminished and so the lighter *lunch* became popular. The main meal of the day was then shifted to the evening and *dinner* became the evening meal, with the possible exception of Sunday *dinner*.

The older customs still obtain in some areas. A Nebraska correspondent wrote us: "In Nebraska in rural communities, *dinner* is still at noon, *supper* in the evening and *lunch* is the meal served after a ball game or an evening of bridge."

diphtheria   This word should be pronounced just as it is spelled: DIF-theer-ee-uh with the "ph" given the sound of "f." However, with the exception of doctors and nurses, it is doubtful that one in ten Americans pronounces this word any way other than DIP-theer-ee-uh. The recent editions of several standard dictionaries have recognized this fact and have entered the DIP-theer-ee-uh pronunciation as well as the technically accurate one used by the medical profession.

diphthong   Like *diphtheria, diphthong* is commonly pronounced in disregard of its actual spelling. Technically, it should be pronounced DIF-thong but countless Americans ignore the fact that "ph" should be sounded as "f" and pronounce it as DIP-thong. Dictionaries now give this as an alternate pronunciation.

direct/directly   As an adverb, *direct* is usually interchangeable with *directly* except in a few idioms in which one or the other is called for. Two senses in which they are not interchangeable are that of "immediately; at once" ("Once I get your phone call, I will be there *directly*") and that of "exactly" or "precisely" ("The dart landed *directly* in the bull's-eye").

In other instances, either may be used: "He went *direct (directly)* from his office to the railroad station."

Direct is, of course, also an adjective.

director/managing director   In the U.S. the term *director* is most commonly met in films, the theater, and as title of a member of a board of *directors* of a business. In England, the *director* and more especially the *managing director* are figures of great importance in many areas of business. In publishing, for instance, a firm's *managing director* would be very much the same as the president and publisher of an American firm, the person with ultimate decision-making authority, subject only to the will of his board of *directors* or, ultimately, the stockholders or shareholders.

disc/disk   A *disc* is a phonograph record; a *disk* is any thin, flat, circular object. Dictionaries state that each is a variant spelling of the other but the distinction is a useful one.

discombobulate   This is a dialect term which has been in use since the latter part of the nineteenth century. Meaning "to throw into a state of confusion or disorder," it is sometimes heard as "discombooberate" or "discomboobulate."

discomfit   Once strictly held to mean "to cause utter frustration or defeat," *discomfit* has now come to be practically synonymous with "discomfort."

discotheque/disco   Pronounced dis-koh-TEK, this is a word borrowed from the French as a term for a nightclub where dance music is supplied chiefly by phonograph records (discs). The French coined the word by analogy to "bibliothèque," which means "library." The first such establishments were in Paris but by the 1960s had sprung up in many parts of the United States. The term is no longer confined to clubs with only recorded music. During the 1970s a form of dance music called *disco* enjoyed a brief vogue.

discrete/discreet   *Discrete* may look like a misspelling of *discreet* but it isn't. Both are standard English words which stem from the Latin "discretus," which means "separate." *Discrete* has retained the Latin meaning of "distinct, unattached, and unrelated" while *discreet* has an extended meaning of "careful" or "showing good judgment."

disincentive   The Board of Managers of the Harvard Club of New York, in reviewing its rules for admission to the club, wrote the membership that they wished "to assure that these processes and procedures do not unintentionally provide *disincentives* for alumni who might be interested in joining." At first blush the word may seem an awkward coinage but it can be found in the pages of an unabridged dictionary though not, amusingly enough, in the pages of the so-called college dictionaries. *Disincentive* is defined as "something which stands in the way." It would have been much simpler, though, to write "do not discourage."

disinterested/uninterested

USAGE PANEL QUESTION

Disinterested and *uninterested* are often used interchangeably, though there is a distinction to be made between them. An *uninterested* person is one not concerned with an issue, while a *disinterested* person may be very deeply concerned but completely impartial. Thus a judge may—indeed, should —be *disinterested* but assuredly not *uninterested* in the merits of cases brought before him. Do you observe this distinction?

In writing   Yes: 91%. No: 9%.
In casual speech   Yes: 90%. No: 10%.

MICHAEL J. ARLEN: "Here, again, is an instance of precision vs. ineptness—with no gain from being inept."

ISAAC ASIMOV: "I'm very proud of knowing the distinction and insist on it, correcting others freely."

W. H. AUDEN: "Impossible!"

SHERIDAN BAKER: "I hold the line on this one, and insist on 'indifferent'—if that's what they mean."

STEWART BEACH: "The distinction is important and should not be blurred by using the words incorrectly."

HAL BORLAND: "A simple test of these two prefixes: 'The gun was uncharged. . . . The gun was discharged.' "

HEYWOOD HALE BROUN: "The loss of any shade of meaning is to be deplored."

ANTHONY BURGESS: "This is one of the worst of all American solecisms and it makes me boil. The very notion of 'disinterestedness' may leave American life if the word itself loses its true meaning. This diminution of meanings is what Orwell's Newspeak is about."

BEN LUCIEN BURMAN: "If a judge was uninterested, he should be impeached!"

ABE BURROWS: "I think this is an important distinction."

JOHN CIARDI: "This one I will fight for."

GEORGE CORNISH: "Why rob the language?"

ROBERT CRICHTON: "Put a man on trial and see if he doesn't learn the crucial difference pretty damn fast."

THOMAS FLEMING: "A very important distinction these days."

PAUL HORGAN: "Completely different meanings; not to be confused."

ELIZABETH JANEWAY: "This is the kind of confusion of words that seems very unfortunate because it results in the loss of a useful distinction."

HELEN L. KAUFMANN: "Indeed, yes."

ALEXANDER KENDRICK: "Yes. Anyway, I try."

STANLEY KUNITZ: "A fine distinction—why spoil it?"

CHARLES KURALT: " 'Disinterested' is used wrongly only by those uninterested in the language."

PHYLLIS McGINLEY: "I feel very strongly about this. The language grows far poorer when we lose such a distinction."

JESSICA MITFORD: "My husband received a letter from a Southern lawyer: 'Please have your client sign this paper in the presence of two uninterested witnesses.' Which conjured up in his mind two witnesses looking out of the window, saying, 'Ho-hum' as they signed."

HERBERT MITGANG: "Two different words."

WRIGHT MORRIS: "A crucial word—if we lose this refinement, we ARE losing all distinctions worth a damn."

EDWIN NEWMAN: "Yes . . . but the distinction is not widely understood and is disappearing."

STANTON PECKHAM: "Having grown disenchanted with living in New York, you may be unenchanted by the most spectacular view of the city."

ORVILLE PRESCOTT: "Yes. Essential."

PETER S. PRESCOTT: "Absolutely: again, a very important word—'disinterested'—is now virtually useless because (it seems to me) it is misused most of the time. I see no hope for its recovery and I am sad and angry about it."

BERTON ROUECHÉ: "Please, let's not give in to this barbarity!"

VERMONT ROYSTER: "I am trying to be a 'disinterested' panelist, but hardly an 'uninterested' one."

LEONARD SANDERS: "Only uninterested writers would fail to observe the distinction."

ERICH SEGAL (voting "yes"): "My Midwood H.S. English teachers have had a lasting impact!"

CHARLES E. SILBERMAN: "I try to. I don't always succeed!"

WALTER W. "RED" SMITH: "This one always makes me squirm."

ELVIS STAHR, JR.: "Assuredly. Doesn't everyone?"

MIMS THOMASON: "No. But I am wrong."

LIONEL TRILLING: "I fear that this is a lost cause. I take it very hard—without the word, we can't have the thing."

EARL UBELL: "Absolutely."

BILL VAUGHAN: "A losing battle, however."

JUDITH VIORST: "I'm very fond of this distinction and would like to see it preserved."

CHARLES L. WHIPPLE: "Every Goddam time!"

HERMAN WOUK: "Absolutely."

USAGE PANEL QUESTION—SECOND EDITION

When questioned about whether *disinterested* and *uninterested* could be used interchangeably, panelists for the first edition responded with a resounding "no." More than 90% insisted that an *uninterested* person is one not concerned with an issue, while a *disinterested* person may be deeply concerned but completely impartial. Anthony Burgess called disregard of this distinction "one of the worst of all American solecisms." Still, the new edition of a "college" dictionary, while noting the "traditional rule," lists the two meanings as equally valid and cites C. L. Sulzberger, late of *The New York Times*, as author of a quotation illustrating the use of *disinterested* as synonymous with *uninterested:* "supremely *disinterested* in all efforts to find a peaceful solution."

Do you observe the distinction between *disinterested* and *uninterested* in speech? Yes: 100%.

In writing? Yes: 100%.

ISAAC ASIMOV: "C. L. Sulzberger is *wrong.*"

BARRY BINGHAM, SR.: "The tendency to blur the sharp outlines of words by careless and sloppy usage is an abomination of our time. The willful confusion of 'disinterested' with 'uninterested' is a prime example."

HEYWOOD HALE BROUN: "I try to avoid contact with those who don't observe the distinction, usually people who wear ready-tied evening ties and use 'graduate' as a transitive verb."

ALISTAIR COOKE: "Sulzberger was illiterate in this instance."

FRANCES FRITCHMAN: "Up with Burgess; down with Sulzberger. The two words *don't mean the same.*"

SYDNEY J. HARRIS: "If we lose 'disinterested,' there is no good single word to take its place."

JOHN K. HUTCHENS: "It still gives me a jolt to see them used synonymously."

ELIZABETH JANEWAY: "I do hope this is not a lost cause, in a profoundly interested way."

DIANE JOHNSON: "I think it is vital to preserve this very valuable distinction."

JAMES J. KILPATRICK: "The distinction between 'disinterested' and 'uninterested' ought to be preserved, Sulzberger to the contrary notwithstanding."

JULES LOH: "Any writer who uses 'disinterested' when he means 'uninterested' is simply wrong. I wasn't aware that this clear distinction was even threatened and see no reason ever to yield. What word would substitute for 'disinterested'?"

DWIGHT MACDONALD: "Thought we'd won this battle."

EDWIN NEWMAN: "Sulzberger was wrong."

MARGE PIERCY: "Here is an annoying loss of precision. We need a way of distinguishing between boredom and impartiality."

JACK SMITH: "Even though this distinction seems to be fading, I refuse to abandon it."

EDWARD TRIPP: " 'Disinterest' in its original sense is too valuable—and rare —to be lost through ignorant misuse of the term."

dissect Used by the general public mainly to mean "to examine" or "to analyze," *dissect* has been subjected by radio and TV announcers to several pronunciations other than the traditional dis-SECT. The most frequent variation is DIE-sect, probably because of a mistaken idea that *dissect* is analogous to "bisect." The trouble with that theory is that the prefix in "bisect" is "bi-," meaning "two," and hence "bisect" means to cut into two equal parts. The prefix in *dissect* is "dis-," which means "apart," and hence *dissect* means to cut apart. While the newer dictionaries enter DIE-sect as a third pronunciation (after dis-SECT and die-SECT), the preferred pronunciation remains dis-SECT.

dissipate In the two sentences "He had a *dissipated* look" and "The fog *dissipated* around noon," there might seem to be two different meanings and uses of the word *dissipate.* They are in fact merely slightly different senses. A man who is or appears *dissipated* is one who has wasted or squandered his talents and health, especially through carousing or the intemperate pursuit of pleasure. The basic sense of wasting, scattering, or dispersing remains in "The fog *dissipated* around noon." The word came into English from the Latin "dissipare," meaning to disperse or squander.

distress In the furniture and antique trades, *distress* has acquired a meaning that has little to do with the sense of "to cause anguish and mental pain." When a furniture expert *distresses* a piece of wood or furniture, he gouges out fake wormholes and mars it with phony scars of pipe and cigar burns. The result is frequently passed off as an antique, if the buyer is not knowledgeable.

dive (noun) *Dive* has long been current in the United States as a slang term for a low, disreputable bar or saloon. In England, notably in London, we observed its use as a designation of a perfectly proper pub whose entrance was down a flight of stairs. So in British use *dive* may be considered merely informal, not slang.

dived/dove *Dove* instead of *dived* as the past tense of *dive* is another instance of changing speech. While there are those who would restrict its use to informal speech or writing, there is a growing tendency to consider it acceptable on any level of speech and writing.

diversion A *diversion* sign on a British road is the equivalent of "detour," not at all a laughing matter.

divided into/composed of Generally speaking, *divided into* applies to a thing once whole which has been made into separate parts, while *composed of* applies to a whole created from several or many parts.

divisive The preferred pronunciation of *divisive* is with the middle vowel given the sound of the long "i," as in "divide." Also acceptable is the pronunciation of the middle "i" with a short sound: dih-VIS-iv, although this is more common in England than it is in the United States.

divorce (granted/obtained) Instead of saying "She got a *divorce*" it is better to say "She was *granted a divorce*" or "She *obtained a divorce,*" as long as she was the plaintiff. To say that she "was divorced" might carry the implication that she was the defendant, although the trend to "no-fault" divorces may well eliminate even that implication.

divorcee. *See* BACHELOR

do (dishes/homework/hair) *Do* in the sense of "to treat or deal with" has been well established for centuries. It is entirely correct to *do the dishes, do your homework,* or *do your hair.*

dock/pier/wharf The way in which extended meanings of words become accepted is illustrated by the words *dock* and *pier* or *wharf.* At one time it was necessary to observe a fine distinction between *dock* and *pier.* This is exemplified by a statement from a nineteenth-century book about words and their use: "Dock is used by many persons to mean a wharf or pier. Thus 'he fell off the dock and was drowned.' . . . A man might fall into a dock but to say that he fell off a dock is no better than to say he fell off a hole."

The original meaning of *dock* as the waterway between two *piers* or *wharves* remains the first definition given in current dictionaries but the word is also defined as a *pier* or *wharf.* When that latter definition first appeared, it was labeled "colloquial." Now the three words can be used interchangeably in all but the most technical writing.

doctor Many physicians would like to limit the title *doctor* to those in the medical profession, but there are today probably many more nonmedical men and women entitled to the title than there are within the medical profession.

Actually it was not until the Middle Ages that the title acquired a specifically medical connotation. The first *doctors* were teachers, for the word comes directly from Latin and is the noun formed from the verb "docere," meaning "to teach." Originally it was applied to any learned man. Indeed, in many parts of the world today, *doctor* is simply an honorific for any wise man, whether or not he has graduate degrees. In the United States it is properly applied to any person who has a doctoral degree in any branch of learning, whether it be academically earned or honorary.

dodgy British slang for difficult, tricky, or chancy. *Dodgy* is very similar in meaning and use to "dicey." Thus a character in Harold Pinter's *The Room* says: "It'd be a bit *dodgy* driving tonight."

dog A slang expression may often have two completely different meanings, often two contradictory meanings. Such is the case with *dog.* In service slang, a man who is *dogging* it is one who is "goofing off" or shirking his duty. *Dog* also has the sense of "to pester someone; to follow another, as to collect a debt, get information, or the like; to hound."

dog control officer   Bureaucratic euphemism for "dog catcher."

dominion/republic   A *dominion* is a territory or country ruled by a sovereign power or under a particular government or control. In centuries past, a ruler was often referred to as ruler of his land "and his *dominions,*" meaning the foreign lands which were part of his domain. Nowadays, the *Dominions* (note the capital "D") are the self-governing members of the Commonwealth of Nations, such as New Zealand, Australia, and Canada. It can certainly be argued that the name today is a misnomer, since the real authority in the *Dominions* now resides in the electorate of each individual commonwealth, rather than with the crown or mother country.

A *republic,* on the other hand, is any state or country in which the supreme power is vested in the electorate (those of its inhabitants qualified to vote) and exercised by representatives who are responsible to the electorate.

don   British term for a teacher in a college or university. Although originally a university slang contraction of "Domine" (from the Latin "domine," vocative case of "dominus," Lord), it is now standard English. The derivative adjective *donnish,* meaning "pedantic," is often seen in phrases like *"donnish* humor," which is the kind often found in books like this.

donnybrook   An informal expression, common in both Britain and the U.S., for a free-for-all brawl, a knock-down-and-drag-out fight. It comes from the town of Donnybrook (now part of Dublin), where fairs were held from the Middle Ages until midway through the nineteenth century, when they were discontinued because the mayhem finally became too much for even the Irish.

don't   Because such expressions as "he *don't* know any better" are obviously ungrammatical, many persons have cast *don't* into outer darkness. In reality it is a perfectly good word of impeccable grammatical standing when used with the first or second person as a contraction of "do not." When a person says, "I *don't*" or "you *don't,*" he speaks informally perhaps but with complete correctness. When it comes to the imperative, *don't* is far superior to "do not." Think how much weaker would be the slogans "Do not give up the ship" or "Do not tread on me."

do our own thing

USAGE PANEL QUESTION

Increasingly we are exhorted to *do our own thing*. Apologists for the phrase claim to have found its antecedents in Emerson and even Shakespeare. Do you feel that this phrase has implications and connotations that will make it a lasting part of the language?
Yes: 41%. No: 59%.

SHANA ALEXANDER: "Yes. Well, I just rather like it. . . ."
BENJAMIN APPEL: "Yes—if American society continues open-minded."
ISAAC ASIMOV: "I prefer 'do as you will,' which was good enough for Rabelais (in French equivalent, of course)."
CHARLES BERLITZ: "No!"
HAL BORLAND: "No. You can find antecedents for anything in Shakespeare, but not all of them deserve to live."
HEYWOOD HALE BROUN: "No. It will be as ephemeral as all chic vagaries."
ROBERT CROMIE: "No more so than twenty-three skidoo."
THOMAS FLEMING: "No, it has been cheapened by the media."
A. B. GUTHRIE, JR.: "Perhaps, but I am doubtful."
PAUL HORGAN: "No. Fugitive."
JOHN K. HUTCHENS: "No. Not as of now, anyway."
WALT KELLY: "Yes. The lame use of the crutch 'thing' is very old—it saves time and thought, but it's a bad thing."
ALEXANDER KENDRICK: "No. Believe it is already expiring from overexposure."
WALTER KERR: "No. Not graphic enough."
STANLEY KUNITZ: "No. Already a tiresome cliché."
CHARLES KURALT: "God, I hope not."
JULES LOH: "No. At least I hope not."
RUSSELL LYNES: "No. 'How do I feel? Swell!' Passing slang."
PHYLLIS MCGINLEY: "I don't know the answer. Some fads pass and who am I to say this will not soon be too dated to use?"
HERBERT MITGANG: "Yes. But it has become a cliché."
WRIGHT MORRIS: "Yes. On the evidence—however regrettable."
WADE MOSBY: "No. Transitory!"
PETER S. PRESCOTT: "No. A fad phrase, surely. 'Thing' is never a strong word. (A better poet than Shakespeare would have written: '. . . the play's the net/Wherein I'll catch the bloody bastard yet.')"
LEO ROSTEN: "No. It is lazy, ambiguous and blurred."
HARRISON SALISBURY: "Yes . . . but I'm sorry."
WALTER W. "RED" SMITH: " 'He bugs me,' 'doing his thing,' and 'the intellec-

tual bit' are all accepted and readily understood in current colloquial usage. Chances are they'll go out of fashion but meanwhile they're not objectionable in speech, periodicals, and sermons."

EARL UBELL: "I am only expressing a hope because I hate the phrase and the idea behind it since it extols a philosophy in which artistic standards take the hindmost. I'm afraid that if writers 'did their own thing' with the language, projects like this one would have no meaning."

HERMAN WOUK: "No. A tiresome banality already. The young who briefly took it up now despise the dodderers who use it."

dope *Dope* in the sense of narcotics is now fully accepted as standard English even though as late as 1959 the Second Edition of the Merriam-Webster unabridged dictionary labeled its use for narcotics intended for any other than purely medicinal purposes "slang."

After all, it comes from a respectable Dutch word "doop," which means a sauce or other thick liquid. It was first used in America too as a medical term for the thick liquid that results when opium is melted, and eventually meant any narcotic—especially the kind used to *dope* horses.

It is also a legitimate term for the varnishlike preparation used to strengthen and toughen the cloth surfaces of model-airplane wings.

Dope in phrases like "inside *dope*," for secret information, and "an utter *dope*," for a stupid person, remains slang.

Doppelgänger *Doppelgänger* is a word which we have found fascinates lecture audiences in all parts of the country. The theory of Doppelgängers is a psychic one of dubious merits but it holds that each of us has a ghostly double who looks and acts exactly like oneself and is often visible only to oneself. It is a German term, meaning "double-goer." By extension, *doppelgänger* (small "d") has come to mean someone who could be a person's identical twin. Those who believe in *doppelgängers* believe that somewhere in the world is an exact duplicate of oneself, one who walks, talks, and acts in precisely the same way. In view of some rather dramatic cases of mistaken identity, there may be some truth in this theory.

dotty Informal for "eccentric" or "daft." More commonly heard in Britain than in the U.S. The *OED Supplement* gives this amusing example: "Quite wrapped up in herself—with something pretty rum staring out of her eyes. A bit dotty, perhaps."

double entendre/double entente The English borrowed the phrase *double entente* (double meaning) from the French and somehow scrambled it in the process so that it became *double entendre*. It has been so used since 1670, long enough for it to acquire status as standard English. It is most often used when the second meaning of a phrase is improper, bordering on the salacious.

double negative. *See* NEGATIVE, DOUBLE

double possessive. *See* POSSESSIVE, DOUBLE

doublespeak. *See* EUPHEMISM

doubt if/doubt that/doubt whether Each of these has restricted functions, depending on the sense and intent of the sentence in which it is used. Here are the conventional style-book "rules" in this matter. *If* is incorrectly used in "I *doubt if* there are many members of this Congress who live more than a few blocks from here who would dare leave their cars in the Capitol garage and walk home alone tonight." Since this expresses an absence of doubt, the proper wording would be *doubt that. That* is also used in an interrogative sense, as in: "Do you *doubt that* I believe you?"

When there is real doubt, *whether* is the appropriate word, at least in formal writing, but *if* is accepted as informal.

A question bearing on this matter was put to the Usage Panel. Here is the question, together with the percentages of their replies and comments from the panelists.

USAGE PANEL QUESTION

This sentence appeared in a State of the Union address: "I *doubt if* there are many members of this Congress . . . who would dare leave their cars in the Capitol garage and walk home alone tonight." Some grammarians hold that when there is no real doubt—as in this case—the proper idiom is *doubt that,* not *doubt if.* Would you accept the statement as made?
Yes: 54%. No: 46%.
Would you prefer "doubt that there are . . ."?
Yes: 79%. No: 21%.

ISAAC ASIMOV: "I would even accept 'doubt whether.' "
JOHN O. BARBOUR: "I doubt that any of them walk very often anywhere."
JULES BERGMAN: " 'If' and 'that' in this usage are virtually interchangeable."
HAL BORLAND: "Wordy. I would change the sentence to read: 'I doubt that many members of Congress would dare . . . .' "
ANTHONY BURGESS: "This is British usage."
BEN LUCIEN BURMAN: "I'm easygoing. I'd accept it, but I much prefer 'that.' "
SYDNEY J. HARRIS: "Yes. The distinction seems prissy."
RICHARD EDES HARRISON: " 'Doubt if' will most likely win because it rolls off the tongue more easily and does not appear a serious grammatical slip."

JOHN K. HUTCHENS: "No preference at all."

ELIZABETH JANEWAY: "I would accept the sentence as written out of laziness. On the other hand, I wish some members of Congress WOULD leave their cars in the Capitol garage and walk home tonight."

ALEXANDER KENDRICK: "It's hard to distinguish between real and rhetorical doubt, especially in presidential speech. No preference."

WALTER KERR: " 'If' doubles the doubt, which is exactly what you don't want."

RUSSELL LYNES: "I would automatically say 'that.' "

FRANCIS T. P. PLIMPTON: "Why not 'doubt whether'?"

ORVILLE PRESCOTT: "Reluctantly, but it is not very objectionable."

PETER S. PRESCOTT: "Because it is clear, I would accept it in speech, not in writing. I find that because the demands of the publications I write for make me conscious of economy, I tend to drop 'that' altogether. I sometimes write: 'I doubt there are many . . .' etc."

VERMONT ROYSTER: "You have to be a mindreader to judge the extent of the speaker's doubt. Personally, though, I prefer 'whether.' "

HERMAN WOUK: "This sloppiness is gaining, like smog."

dove. *See* DIVED/DOVE

down. *See* PREFIXES AND SUFFIXES, WITH AND WITHOUT HYPHEN

down East   *Down East* is a curious, seemingly contradictory idiom heard in the New England states when reference is made to traveling from Boston to Maine. A variant of it is "down to Maine," which seems even more illogical, since Maine is the northernmost state on the Eastern Seaboard and well north of Boston.

   The expression *down East* is older than our nation. It goes back to Colonial times, when Maine was, at least technically, part of the Massachusetts Bay Colony. In those years, long before railroads, most of the traffic between Boston and Maine was by sailing ship. Since a ship plying that route in the northerly direction would be sailing "downwind," the expression "going down to Maine" or *down East* became commonly used.

   There is another theory as to why the phrase became common in New England. This is that the early Colonists were influenced by British speech patterns, as indeed they were. To this day an Englishman will speak of going "up" to London, no matter what direction is involved. When he leaves London he goes "down" to whatever town is his destination. At that time, Boston occupied a position in the Colonies just as important as London's in Britain. In fact, Boston was called, only half jokingly, "the hub of the universe." It is little wonder that anyone leaving Boston for the provincial areas of Maine would be said to be going *down East.*

downers/uppers A slang term connected with the illegal use of narcotic drugs, *downers* are barbiturates. These are defined in a "Glossary of Narcotic Terms" received from Senator Lowell P. Weicker as "sedatives, called 'downs' or 'goofballs.' They relax the nervous system, slow the heart beat, lower blood pressure and slow down breathing. Effects can resemble drunkenness and users sometimes become irritable and angry. Physically addictive, like heroin, barbiturates are a leading cause of accidental deaths in the country."

Uppers, slang for which the medical term is "amphetamines," have the opposite effect. They are described as "stimulants used to combat fatigue. Taken in pill form, although some stronger forms are dissolved in a liquid and injected with a needle, they speed action of the heart and metabolism. Called 'bennies,' 'pep pills,' 'diet pills' and, in strong doses, 'speed.' Not addictive physically but psychological dependence is common. Larger doses are required for the same effect after a while."

Downs, the Confusing to American visitors is the fact that *the Downs* in England are ranges of hills—going up, not down, of course—in southern England. The puzzlement disappears when one knows the etymology of this particular *down*. It's from the Old English "dun," meaning hill—and clearly analogous to our "dune," a windblown hill of sand.

down the drain/down the pipe/down the tube Informal expressions meaning "gone for good." "Think of all the money that has gone *down the drain.*"

down the pike Informal for "along." "The meanest man that ever came *down the pike.*" One notable malaprop was the statement by a federal judge that "I used to think the FBI was one of the greatest bureaus that ever came 'down the pipe.' But I think it has deteriorated."

doyen This is a currently voguish borrowing from France via Britain. It means simply "senior member" or "dean." "Congressman So-and-so is currently *doyen* of the House Ways and Means Committee."

dozen/dozens When a specific number of *dozens* is stated, the idiom is "two *dozen* eggs," not "two *dozens* eggs" or "two *dozens* of eggs." When the number is unspecified, as in *"dozens* of compliments on my dress," the plural form is used.

drastic There is no element of lowness in the word *drastic,* as seemed to be the belief of a school principal who stated that "attendance had fallen to drastic levels." *Drastic* means "violently effective or especially severe." A *drastic* change in attendance could result in either a higher or lower level. Which it was would have to be specified, as "extremely low level."

draw   In seafarers' parlance, *draw* can mean the money disbursed by the captain or purser to the sailors in local currency in port, not at sea.

drawing room   The *drawing room* is well-nigh obsolete in the United States but the term is still standard in England for the room Americans now call the "living room." The *drawing room* was originally the "withdrawing room," the room to which Victorian ladies withdrew at the close of dinner, so that the menfolk could sit around the dining-room table, enjoying brandy, cigars, and off-color stories. Thanks to the Women's Liberation Movement, the chances of a return of the *drawing room* to the American scene seem dim indeed.

dreck. *See* YIDDISHISMS

dribble/drivel   In the sense of an infant's drooling, these two words are synonymous, but, when it comes to asinine speech or writing, the word to use is *drivel*.

drive/ride   *Drive*, in the sense of transporting a person by automobile, is an acceptable idiom in our language. A variation involving *ride* ("I'll *ride* you to work") is heard in some parts of the country but is considered informal.

drive up the wall   This current slang expression, popular among youth, seems to have originated in England. In any event it's equivalent to the earlier slang expression "drive (someone) nuts": "That steady diet of country-and-western twang is *driving me* right *up the wall*."

dropout   *Dropout* is a person who leaves school before completing all the requirements for graduation. It came into widespread use during the 1960s with student unrest and dissatisfaction at many colleges and universities.

drought/drouth   A long dry spell, especially one which occurs during the season for growing crops, can be identified by either of these words, although *drought* is more often seen in formal writing. The first is pronounced DROWT and the second DROWTH, but even the pronunciations are used interchangeably.

drowned/was drowned   If a person suffocates in water or other fluid, the proper statement is that he or she *drowned*. To say that he or she *was drowned* is to imply that another person caused the death by holding the victim's head under water.
   Drown should be pronounced DROUN (with "ou" as in "out"), not DROUND. Similarly, *drowned* (past tense) is pronounced DROUND, not DROUN-ded.

drugs   While the word *drug* retains its basic meaning as a medicine used in the treatment of illness, the plural form *drugs* is now usually interpreted to mean addictive narcotic drugs used illegally.

drunk/drunken   Which of these two adjectives you should use depends on its position in the sentence. If the adjective comes before the noun, the word is *drunken,* as in *drunken* driver. When the adjective falls in the predicate, it should be *drunk,* as in "The driver was *drunk.*"

duel   A newspaper photo showed eight horses and the cutline stated that they would *duel* for the trophy. This was an inaccurate use of the word, since a *duel* is a contest of two individuals. The only exception is when two powerful forces or peoples meet in contest, as one might have said that the RAF and the German Luftwaffe *dueled* for air supremacy over the English Channel during World War II.

due to/because of/owing to   The debate about *due to* as a substitute for *because of* has been raging for many decades, if a discreet interchange of opinions among scholars can be said to "rage." British linguist H. W. Fowler reported in *Modern English Usage* (1926) that " 'due to' is often used by the illiterate."

A leading American scholar, John S. Kenyon, wrote in 1930: "Strong as is my own prejudice against the prepositional use of 'due to,' I greatly fear that it has staked its claim and squatted in our midst alongside and in exact imitation of 'owing to,' its aristocratic neighbor and respected fellow citizen." By 1940 the distinguished, if conservative, scholars of the Modern Language Association were voting two to one against including *due to* among the approved usages, but other groups of equally notable linguists were voting by a considerable majority in its favor. One savant summed it up thus: " 'Due to' is particularly annoying to me but it is rapidly gaining headway."

Then, in the revised edition of Fowler's *Modern English Usage* (1965), the editor, Sir Ernest Gowers, ruefully noted that "the offending usage has indeed become literally part of the Queen's English" and quotes a speech by Elizabeth II on the opening of the Canadian Parliament in 1957: "Due to inability to market their grain, prairie farmers have been faced for some time with a shortage of sums to meet their immediate needs."

There are still some purists and careful writers who would not accept the Queen's English as their own in this instance but they are in the minority, at least as far as informal use is concerned.

duffer   *Duffer* is informal for a slow or dull-witted person, especially one who is maladroit at sports and games: "He's an absolute *duffer* on the golf course." It is also British slang for a person who deals in cheap merchandise, especially, in the words of the *OED*, "one who sells trashy articles as valuable, upon false pretences." Note, here, the difference in prepositional idiom and in spelling between British and American usage. The American version would be "under (not upon) false pretenses (not pretences)." It might be worth further note that the very expression "false pretenses" is redundant, since "pretense" means "a false appearance intended to deceive." However, the idiom "false pretenses" is well established and perhaps deserves rank in that group of illogical and redundant expressions that H. W. Fowler labels the "sturdy indefensibles."

dumb The substitution of *dumb* for *stupid* is unfortunate even in informal speech and should never be made in formal writing. The primary meaning of *dumb* is "speechless, either because of inability to speak or unwillingness to speak."

dummy This is a British term for a baby pacifier. It is short for "dummy teat."

duplicity. *See* MENDACITY/DUPLICITY/CHICANERY/CORRUPTION

duplicity/duplication/multiplicity A letter announcing the winners of a contest involving suggestions for the use of a design principle stated: "What really surprised us was the great number of people who had similar ideas or suggestions. The *duplicity* of these made it most difficult to isolate the winners."
  Duplicity means "deceit," "treachery," or "double-dealing" and is not what was meant in this instance. It can be assumed that the writer was trying to avoid *duplication* on the ground that there were more than two versions of each idea. *Multiplicity* might have served his purpose.

dustbin/dustcart/dustman These are the British equivalents of the American "trash can," "garbage wagon," and "trashman."

dust-up British informal for argument, quarrel, and, sometimes, a brawl amounting to a small-scale *donnybrook* (which see).

Dutch *Derogatory terms* (which see) include the word *Dutch,* which is rooted in what the *Oxford English Dictionary* calls "the contempt and derision which the British once held for the *Dutch* people." During the seventeenth and eighteenth centuries the Dutch and the English were great rivals both on the battlefields and in conquest of international commerce on the high seas.
  Among the expressions which have survived are "*Dutch* courage," the kind that comes out of a bottle; "*Dutch* treat" or "*Dutch* luncheon," the kind in which the host, instead of picking up the tab, expects each

guest to pay for himself; "*Dutch* reckoning," guesswork; "*Dutch* defense," retreat or surrender; and "His *Dutch* is up," meaning "He's pigheaded." Perhaps the ultimate in these anti-Dutch expressions, though, is "do the *Dutch*," meaning to commit suicide.

While both editors of this book are of English-Welsh-Irish ancestry, it pains us to record these terms, especially since William is President Emeritus of the Dutch Treat Club, a New York luncheon club which has been famous since 1905 as a consortium of outstanding writers, artists, and theatrical luminaries. (The irony here, in passing, is that while each member must pay for himself, no guest is ever allowed to do so.) "*Dutch* treat" no longer seems so pejorative, especially since we have all heard "go *Dutch*" since childhood, but the other terms should all be avoided. *See also* NO HOST.

dying/dyeing   *Dying* is ceasing to live; *dyeing* is changing the color of something by applying a solution or material. Hairdressers avoid the term and use euphemisms such as "frosting," "tinting," "streaking," "highlighting," or "naturalizing."

dynamic. *See* VOGUE WORDS

dynamo   British motoring term equivalent to the American "generator."

dysphemism/euphemism   *Dysphemism* is still buried in the pages of unabridged dictionaries but it is a useful, if quite recent, coinage. It means the exact opposite of *euphemism*. A *euphemism* is, of course, the substitution of a pleasant term for an unpleasant one. Thus, "toilets" become "powder rooms."

Dysphemism is the substitution of an unpleasant term for a pleasant one. An example is the use of "axle grease" for "butter."

Dysphemism comes from a term in psychology, "dysphemia," which means "neurotic disturbance of speech" or "stammering."

each. *See* EITHER/EACH

each other/one another   In formal usage, *each other* is restricted to situations involving only two persons, while *one another* applies to more than two persons. In general usage, however, such restrictions are not observed, as in "Members of the committee had reached the point where they were not talking to *each other.*" Conversely, many a newlywed couple has received the admonition "Be kind to *one another.*"

eager. *See* ANXIOUS/EAGER

early on *Early on* is a borrowing from the British. It may be argued that it says nothing that "early" alone doesn't say. However, there is nothing wrong with the formulation and it is rather charming, especially in casual speech.

earth and other planets The word *earth* has other meanings besides its use as the name of our planet. Because of the frequency of its appearance in these other uses, it is generally spelled with a small "e." Note, though, that the *Style Manual* of the Government Printing Office calls for it to be written with a capital "E" (Earth) when used with the names of the other planets. The other planets are always capped because they were originally names of classical gods and goddesses: Mars, Venus, Mercury, Saturn, and so forth.

easy/easily There are certain idioms in which *easy* functions as an adverb, such as "*easy* come, *easy* go," "take it *easy,*" and "go *easy* on." Aside from these, *easily* is the proper adverbial form.

eatery *Eatery* is a word which should be regarded as slang or at best informal English. "Lunchroom" or "diner" is not only more specific but preferable.

ecology/environment With increasing frequency, *ecology* is mistakenly used as a synonym for *environment. Environment* is the totality of conditions surrounding an organism or organisms, including human beings. *Ecology* is the science or study of the relationship between an organism and its environment. The Barnhart *Dictionary of New English Since 1963* ascribes to *ecology* the meaning of "any balanced or harmonious system," which it labels "extended sense of the technical term for the balanced relationship between organisms and their environment." Standard dictionaries, however, do not accept this extended meaning and the Associated Press Writing and Editing Committee states flatly: "They are not synonymous." The committee cites as an example of misusage: "Even as simple an undertaking as maintaining a lawn affects the *ecology.*" *Environment,* it says, is right. We agree.

economics/economical The initial "e" in these words may be sounded either long or short. Say either ek-uh-NOM-ix or ee-kuh-NOM-ix and either ek-uh-NOM-ih-kul or ee-kuh-NOM-ih-kul.

ecumenical   When Pope John XXIII of the Roman Catholic Church called the Second Vatican Council for the Furtherance of Christian Unity, in 1962, the word *ecumenical* suddenly became part of everyday language. *Ecumenical* councils had been held a number of times in the centuries-old history of the Church but none had been called for nearly one hundred years previously.

   Ecumenical, in the language of the Church, means "universal," with special reference to the unity of the entire Christian church. It comes from the Greek "oikoumenikos," meaning "of or from the whole world."

editor   *Editor* as a transitive verb is a horror rivaling if not surpassing "author" ("he authored three books"). Nonetheless, it has appeared in print and in connection with no less distinguished a publication than the *Encyclopaedia Britannica.* According to *American Speech,* the following appeared in print in 1961: "The Britannica is now *editored* by Walter Yust." There is no record of any further appearances of *editor* as a verb but this one instance qualifies it for membership in our Gallery of Linguistic Horrors.

educationese   Something strange happens to the language when it falls into the hands of professional educators or "educationists," as some of them like to be called. The simple word is never adequate. Polysyllabic monstrosities and tortured rhetoric are the order of the day when educators ("educationalists" is still another name favored by some) set about drafting speeches, memoranda, or even something as seemingly simple as a summons to a PTA meeting.

   Here is a fine example of schoolmaster syntax or *educationese* over the signature of the principal of an Arlington, Virginia, junior high school. "Since we believe, from much conferencing experience, that it is helpful for a teacher and parent to mutually discuss the pupil's progress, we are inviting you to come to school for a conference with the child and his conferencing teacher."

   Leaving aside the use of the royal "we" by the principal, and even ignoring the redundancy of "to mutually discuss" (how can a discussion be other than "mutual"?), the transmutation of the noun "conference" into the verbal adjective "conferencing" is enough to appall anyone— save, perhaps, a school administrator.

   One of the parents who received this verbal horror wrote plaintively: "Can you tell us if the use of the word 'conferencing' here is correct? I find it annoying and would use the word 'conferring.' Perhaps I am behind the times."

   We assured her that she was not behind the times and that the person responsible for the letter was the guilty one. The temptation was great to make the punishment fit the crime by suggesting that he go to the blackboard to write "conferring *not* conferencing" a few hundred times. It would also be helpful if he and his kind were to strike the word "experience," as used in the jargon of *educationese,* from his vocabulary. It's bad enough to hear such redundancies as "learning experience," "reading experience," and even "enrichment experience." But when it comes to such utter illiteracies as "conferencing experience," someone must call a halt—and that we now do.

-ee, suffix Until relatively recently, American dictionaries recorded *-ee* as a suffix as, in the words of the Merriam-Webster Collegiate (1936), "used to indicate the object of an action, the one to *whom* an act is *done* or *on whom* a right *is conferred,* as in assign*ee,* grant*ee.*" But the past few decades have seen a very considerable widening in the use of this suffix. For instance, *Webster's New World Dictionary* (1970) gives the earlier sense and adds "a person in a specified condition, as absent*ee,* employ*ee.*" Merriam-Webster Third International (1961) adds: "A person that performs a specified action: escap*ee,* stand*ee.*" With this as background, we cited examples of the newer use in the question that follows. Panelists emphatically favored their acceptance in speech and were about evenly split on the question of their use in writing. Here are the question, the percentages of voting, and typical comments from panel members.

USAGE PANEL QUESTION

The suffix *-ee* is chiefly used to indicate the receiver of an action: "draftee," "trainee," and so on. Panelist HAL BORLAND notes that broadcasters in particular now use the term "escapee" for "fugitive." Similarly one hears of "standees" at a hit play. Would you use these words?

In speech   Yes: 66%. No: 34%.
In writing   Yes: 47%. No: 53%.
Would you use "escaper" in preference to "escapee"? Yes: 24%. No: 76%.

ALTON BLAKESLEE: "Standee, yes; escapee, no."

JOHN BROOKS: "Yes (to 'standee'), but not 'escapee.' "

HEYWOOD HALE BROUN: "I'll take 'standee' because there doesn't seem another good word. 'Escapee' seems silly, hard to say."

ANTHONY BURGESS: "The 'ee' is only admissible after a transitive verb."

BEN LUCIEN BURMAN: " 'Standee,' yes, 'escapee,' no."

ABE BURROWS: "I'm ambivalent about this one. If a show of mine has 'standees' I enjoy the bad grammar. 'Standers' would be correct but I can't picture that in *Variety.*"

JOHN CIARDI: "I prefer 'fugitive' to 'escapee.' What do I use in place of 'standees'?—standers-uppers?"

RICHARD EDES HARRISON: "O.K. where *giver* of action exists, i.e., *trainer.*

'Escapee' not good; however 'standee' has been in common usage nearly fifty years."

PAUL HORGAN: "No, except comically."

ALEXANDER KENDRICK: "Only under duress. Anything wrong with 'fugitive' (or 'flee-ee')?"

CLARK KINNAIRD: "Yes, as long as 'nominee,' 'fiancee,' 'devotee' are acceptable."

LAURENCE LAFORE: "I'd use some other word. 'Escaper' sounds odd."

ROBERT LIPSYTE: "How about 'flee-ee'?"

DWIGHT MACDONALD: "No to 'escapee' since 'fugitive' is OK."

JESSICA MITFORD: "The word to use should clearly be 'escaper.' Surely the guard is the 'escapee.' "

ORVILLE PRESCOTT: " 'Standee' now accepted; no, to 'escapee.' "

FRANCIS ROBINSON: "I'll certainly use 'standee' every chance I get!"

WALTER W. "RED" SMITH: " 'Standee' is the one stood upon."

BARBARA TUCHMAN: "I dislike this usage in general and would not use it—*except* for 'standees,' which has become standard."

effect. *See* AFFECT/EFFECT

effects/affects Confusion between *effect* and *affect* as verbs is quite common, although each has a meaning quite distinct from the other (see *affect/effect*). When it comes to the noun, especially in the plural form, the confusion is not so common but still exists. "Personal *effects*" or "household *effects*" are belongings or property. *Affect* as a noun is a term confined to psychology and literary criticism, where it means an "emotion or feeling" or "that which evokes an emotion or idea." "Personal *affects*" is simply an error.

effete Millions of Americans got a wrong impression as to the meaning of this word when the phrase *"effete* Eastern snobs" was coined by former Vice President Spiro Agnew's speechwriter. But even back in the 1940s Frank Colby characterized it as "the most frequently misused word of all." He stated further: *"Effete* does not mean exclusive, sophisticated, above average in culture and social position." Originally it meant "exhausted from child-bearing or unable to produce further children." Its meaning has been extended to "worn-out, spent, self-indulgent, and decadent."

e.g. *See* I.E./E.G.

egger Among Americans of German descent the expression "Don't *egger* me so" is frequently used in reprimanding children. When the query as to its meaning and origin was put to readers of our newspaper column, the response from readers was unanimous that it means "Don't annoy me" or "Don't make me mad." The original German version of the phrase is "Ärger mich nicht!"

egoist/egotist   While dictionaries state that *egoist* and *egotist* can be used interchangeably to refer to a very vain and conceited person, there is a distinction which is worth preserving. An *egoist* is a person who is concerned only with himself or herself and thinks only in terms of personal interest or advancement. An *egotist* is a person with an exaggerated opinion of his own worth and importance and one who never hesitates to proclaim his "virtues." One might define an *egotist* as "an *egoist* with chutzpah."

eighty-six (86)   This is a term in bartender's slang. To *86* a person is to indicate—usually to a bouncer—that that person will not be served anything more and may have to be evicted from the premises. Most often the reason is that the customer has already had more than is good for him and is likely to become drunk and disorderly.

either   *Either,* like *neither* (which see), is used in speaking of two things or persons and requires a singular verb. This is obvious when the two are named separately, as in "Either Mary or Joe accompanies her when she sings." But when a plural noun or pronoun is used, as in "Either of the pianists is acceptable to her," a plural verb is sometimes mistakenly used.

EE-ther is the preferred American pronunciation, although EYE-ther is very widely heard, especially in New England and along the Eastern Seacoast reflecting the influence of England, where EYE-ther is heard almost exclusively. Interestingly enough, although England and Wales say EYE-ther, Scotland and Ireland make it AY-ther.

either/each   Although the Associated Press Writing and Editing Committee says of *either* as a pronoun that "it means one or the other, not both," there is much support for the use of *either* in the sense of "one and the other" or *each.* Most standard dictionaries given *each* as a synonym for *either.* H. W. Fowler's *Modern English Usage* states: "The sense of each of the two, as in *the room has a fireplace at either end,* though more naturally expressed by *each,* cannot be considered unidiomatic." *See also* IDIOM.

elder/eldest; older/oldest; younger/youngest   "The *eldest* daughter" is a common mistake made when referring to the older of two daughters. When only two persons are involved, the reference should be to the *elder* rather than the *eldest* (or *older* rather than *oldest*). The same applies to *younger* and *youngest.* We can speak of our *youngest* son and our *youngest* daughter because we have three of each. If there were only two of each, this would not be possible.

electronic surveillance. *See* EUPHEMISM

Elegant English A Pittsburgh reader reports: "Not long ago I received a letter which ended: 'It is incumbent on we who serve. . . .' Later I attended a wedding ceremony in which the minister said, 'Bless he who gives this ring. . . .' And now I find in your column: 'Let he who will dispute it with me.' What I want to know is whether I am losing my mind or is this somehow a typographical error?"

We assured him that he was not losing his mind but that each of the examples he cited is a shocking instance of *Elegant*—and erroneous—*English.* In each case some misguided soul used the nominative case where the objective case was called for. The correct forms of the first two are: "It is incumbent on us who serve . . ." and "Bless him who gives this ring. . . ."

But the error in our own column surely calls for a fuller explanation. To start at the beginning, the phrase—illustrating the origin of "lion's share"—was from a fable of Aesop about the lion who demanded all the spoils of a hunt: one quarter due him as King of Beasts, one quarter because of his superior bravery, a third quarter to feed his dam and cubs, and, "as for the fourth, let who will dispute it with me."

The language, you will note, is fairly archaic—"Let who will dispute it with me"—but it is a direct quotation from the standard English version of the fables and is quite acceptable grammatically. The clause "who will" is subject of the infinitive "dispute," so the construction is sound enough. But somewhere along the way between typewriter and print an overzealous editor decided that the quotation needed a personal pronoun to fill it out. Instead of inserting "him"—the objective case necessary as the subject of the infinitive—the editor dropped in the more elegant-sounding but hopelessly incorrect "he." It's the sort of thing that shouldn't happen—but all too often does.

element. *See* FACTOR/ELEMENT/PART

elephant tablets One might assume that *elephant tablets* referred to medication almost too large to swallow, but the term is the product of a process known as *folk etymology* (which see). *Elephant tablets* is a popular and mistaken name for "alophen tablets," a laxative. Ironically, alophen tablets are anything but elephantlike in size, being tinier than a coffee bean.

elevate As a verb, *elevate* normally means to "raise up," but in the jargon of those who manufacture and install elevators in buildings it has a different meaning. An employee of one of the largest such companies startled us when he spoke of "the year we *elevated* the Empire State Building."

elevenses/elevens   *Elevenses* (sometimes also called simply *elevens*) are the British equivalent of the American "coffee break," but they represent a much older tradition. While the fairly formalized "coffee break" didn't make its way into American offices until after World War II, *elevenses,* representing a halt in work or other activity at about 11 A.M. for coffee and a snack, are recorded by the *OED Supplement* as far back as 1849, along with "fourses," presumably a similar break taken at 4 P.M. Civilized chaps, the British! All the terms mentioned, including "coffee break," should be considered informal.

Eleventh Commandment   The meaning of the phrase *Eleventh Commandment* in religious circles was explained to us by the Rev. Dan B. Bravin of Pittsburgh. It is from the Gospel of John: "A new commandment I give unto you, That ye love one another; as I have loved you, that ye also love one another." This became known unofficially and unauthoritatively as the *Eleventh Commandment.*

Other column readers reported that they had heard it as "Mind your own business" or "Don't get caught," but we prefer the Rev. Mr. Bravin's version.

elite   The American pronunciation of this French word is ay-LEET or sometimes ee-LEET. A collective noun meaning "select members within a group or society," it requires a plural verb. In England the standard pronunciation is ee-LIGHT.

ellipses/dashes/leaders/and other devices   During the 1930s and 1940s by all odds the most widely read popular newspaper columnist was Walter Winchell, who contributed some flashy neologisms ("infanticipate," "Reno-vate," and many more) and left as one of his heritages the still-used device of separating gossip-column items with *ellipses* (three dots) like this: . . . Other columnists happily seized on the em-dash in place of commas—and other marks of punctuation—like that. A third group, mostly society and movie columnists, is still devoted to exclamation points, capital letters, and, on occasion, a combination of all these elements.

Obviously this can be trying to an editor, especially one reared in the sensible school of copyediting where simple words and minimum punctuation are the order of the day. At one point one of our syndicate editors, Elmer Roessner, who had handled far more junk copy than any of us would like to think about, began to crack under the strain. "Just think" he wrote, "what Lord Byron could have done with a bucketful of dots, dashes and bangs!" And he proceeded to demonstrate:

> She walks in "beauty" . . . like the night . . .
> Of cloudless climes and starry skies!!
> And all that's best of dark—and bright—
> Meet in her ASPECT and her EYES!!
> Thus mellow'd . . . and to that tender light
> Which heaven . . . to "gaudy" days . . . DENIES!!

The moral is obvious but Roessner phrased it well: "Writers should avoid overuse of dashes, leaders, capitals and other devices to stress points. Better rely on word craftmanship."

As a very minor footnote, we know copyeditors so punctilious that they insist on adding a period to an ellipsis when it comes at the end of a sentence, making four dots—carefully counted—in place of the customary . . .

elliptical illiteracies Over a span of two decades we have received many letters from readers newly moved into communities with large representations of people of German descent, commenting on what may best be called *elliptical illiteracies.* From Milwaukee we repeatedly hear of the expression "My hair needs washed" and "The dog wants out." A Pittsburgh reader quoted two newspaper headlines: RADIOLOGISTS WANT PAID DIRECT and 100 HOMES THAT NEED PAINTED, as well as a comment in a homemaking article: "On some synthetics perspiration and perfume will show up as spots only after dry cleaned."

The tendency toward ellipsis (omission of a word or phrase that can be understood from the context) seems to be most prevalent, as noted above, among people of German descent and quite possibly mirrors a usage that is perfectly acceptable in the German tongue. But it is not good English and we can hope that—at least on metropolitan newspapers—copyeditors will be more vigilant about inserting the missing phrases—"to be," "to go," and "being" in the instances cited—that add grace to the language.

embarrass. *See* SPELLINGS, TRICKY

emigrate. *See* IMMIGRATE/EMIGRATE

eminently. *See* IMMINENTLY/EMINENTLY

emote *Emote* is a back-formation from "emotion," formed, as one dictionary puts it, by analogy to "devote." At best, it is informal and should not be used in writing of a serious nature. Panelist John K. Hutchens is so opposed to it that he states: "I would hand out a twenty-year sentence to anyone saying 'emote.' "

empathy   This is a vogue word now being used by many people instead of "sympathy." It has two special meanings of its own, however. One is "the intellectual and emotional understanding of and identification with another person." The other meaning is "the projection of emotions and responses onto an object." The latter meaning is the same as "pathetic fallacy," a literary device of attributing human feelings and characteristics to inanimate objects, as in "This stupid pen won't write." *See* PATHETIC FALLACY.

employe/employee   While some corporations and publications have adopted the spelling *employe* as standard usage in preference to the spelling *employee,* the latter form continues to dominate.

From one point of view the spelling *employe* could be considered preferable. It is, after all, the spelling of the French word for "one who is employed." French, as might be expected of a well-organized language ruled over by a scrupulous French Academy, also has a word for a female worker: *employee.* So there is a nice distinction there, observed by the French but ignored by the English and Americans. Indeed, the English took the feminine form and applied it to all workers, and Americans followed suit. Apparently in an effort to right this wrong, some firms, as noted above, have tried to standardize on the more logical *employe* spelling. However, in America (unlike France), it is simply not possible to legislate language. Despite all well-intentioned efforts, *employee* is still the first choice of dictionaries and is the only spelling sanctioned by the U.S. Government Printing Office *Style Manual.*

empty-nest syndrome   This is a voguish phrase made popular by the sociologists to describe the mental and emotional state of a mother who, after devoting years of her life to raising children, feels desolate and abandoned when her children grow up and leave home.

-en, verbs ending in   The letters *-en* when added to a verb indicate a gradual change in condition. There are only a few such words remaining in the English language, among them "wors*en,*" "dark*en,*" "deep*en,*" "length*en,*" and "light*en.*"

enact into law   Since *enact* means "to make into law," *enact into law* is redundant. A statement such as "The Senate passed and sent to the House a bill, that, if *enacted into law,* would spell trouble" should have the phrase "into law" struck from it.

enclave, pronunciation of. *See* ENVELOPE/ENCLAVE/ENVOY

endorse/indorse While *indorse* is just as good English as *endorse,* the latter form is more commonly used in this country. Most dictionaries enter *indorse* with the simple definition "to endorse." This indicates that, in the opinion of the editors, *endorse* is more frequently seen.

-endous This suffix is so uncommon that there are only four words in the English language that have it as an ending: "tremendous," "stupendous," "horrendous," and "pudendous."

"Pudendous" is defined by the Merriam-Webster Second International Dictionary (1934) as "shameful" and labeled "rare." In fact, the editors of that unabridged dictionary considered it so rare that it was not entered in the Third Edition.

We discovered it only by reference to an eight-volume set of books called *The Normal and Reverse English Word List,* which was compiled by a team of linguists at the University of Pennsylvania operating under a grant from the Air Force Office of Scientific Research. The entry list of the Merriam Unabridged (Second Edition) and similar lists from special dictionaries of medicine and other sciences were fed into a computer in such a way that it would print out all the words in two ways—first in the normal spelling and second spelled backward.

What is particularly charming about the word list is this comment in the preface: "342,252 entries were fed into Univac. For reasons best known to the computer there are two entries more than this in the reverse list." In other words the computer created two words which have not been identified as yet.

end result A *redundancy* (which see). *End* should be deleted.

engaged/engaged tone *Engaged* and *engaged tone* are the standard British equivalents of the American "busy" and "busy signal." As the *OED Supplement* rather elegantly puts it, *engaged* indicates that the "line is in use and therefore unavailable to a second caller."

enormity/enormousness

USAGE PANEL QUESTION

Enormity and *enormousness* have different meanings according to most lexicons, *enormity* being defined as something monstrously evil, an outrage and utter violation of all decency, and *enormousness* meaning vastness or immensity. Yet many writers consider them synonymous. Reporting a recent ecologically inspired drive to collect bottles and newsprint for recycling, one caption writer added this cutline to a newspaper picture of the event: "Some of those who brought their goods joined in [to help] when they saw the enormity of the task." Would you accept *enormity* in this context?

Yes: 31%. No: 69%.

ISAAC ASIMOV: " 'Enormity' is a good word that shouldn't be misused."

SHERIDAN BAKER: "No. 'The enormity of our wastefulness' would make sense."

HAL BORLAND: "God no! This is even worse than barbarous usage!"

HEYWOOD HALE BROUN: "No. Every nuance lost is like a sandblast on a bas-relief."

STEPHEN H. FRITCHMAN: "No. It would be a disaster to lose a useful word like 'enormity' to such trivial use."

PAUL HORGAN: "No. I am glad to see this included for a vote—I proposed it—I hope the results will be conclusive."

JOHN K. HUTCHENS: "No—because 'enormity' still, for me, suggests wickedness."

ALEXANDER KENDRICK: "In spite of the moral implications of pollution I don't think 'enormity' quite makes it here."

ORVILLE PRESCOTT: "Vile, ignorant usage."

LEO ROSTEN: " 'Enormity' suggests a negative moral judgment; 'enormousness' is descriptive only."

DAVID SCHOENBRUN: "I would accept it, but not use it."

MARK SCHORER: "No—blurs distinctions that etymologically proved useful —quality and quantity differentiation."

HERMAN WOUK: "No. I reached for my dictionary (Webster's Seventh New Collegiate) to confirm my instinct on this one."

enquiries   *Enquiries* is the British equivalent of what used to be called in the U.S. "Information," now "Directory Assistance."

· **ensure/insure**

USAGE PANEL QUESTION

H. W. Fowler, reflecting primarily British usage, of course, wrote that the spelling *ensure* was to be preferred to *insure* in all contexts save "the financial sense, in which the form 'ensure' is wholly obsolete." Some American copyeditors follow this precept, with results like this: "The 7:30 curtain will *ensure* that commuters can get home by midnight." Do you observe a distinction between *ensure* (to make sure or certain) and *insure* (to guarantee against financial loss)?

Yes: 62%. No: 38%.
Would you use *insure* in both senses? Yes: 38%. No: 62%.

STEWART BEACH: "I know the British cling to 'en' but I am an 'in'-man for all seasons. I don't feel there is any difference and don't forget that the British, while they may 'insure,' usually speak of insurance as 'assurance.'"

RICHARD EDES HARRISON: "I like to keep 'insure' distinct because it so rarely ensures anything."

ALEXANDER KENDRICK: "Beneficiary's choice."

STANLEY KUNITZ: "A nice distinction that ought to be preserved, though I doubt that it will be."

WALTER LORD: "Why not assure?"

BERTON ROUECHÉ: "I see no sense in this traditional distinction."

VERMONT ROYSTER: "I thought I settled this long ago. To the victim the distinction is trivial."

LEONARD SANDERS: "The distinction is worth preserving."

BILL VAUGHAN: "A blurred and useless distinction."

enthuse

USAGE PANEL QUESTION

Enthuse is a back-formation from *enthusiasm* and has not met with favor from some students of language. Would you approve of a statement like "The critics *enthused* over the new play"?

In writing   Yes: 14%. No: 86%.
In casual speech   Yes: 24%. No: 76%.

BENJAMIN APPEL: "Part of the language pattern now."

ISAAC ASIMOV: "No . . . schoolgirlish."

JOHN O. BARBOUR: "It sounds and reads as a forced word."

STEWART BEACH: "This is a word that should never have been coined as a verb."

HAL BORLAND: "I would fire the critics for poverty of vocabulary."

JOSEPH A. BRANDT: "Give this back-formation the back of your hand."

JOHN BROOKS: "Nor would I approve any piece of writing in which this ghastly word appeared."

HEYWOOD HALE BROUN: "No . . . but I would like to be in the cast of the play."

ANTHONY BURGESS: "It's piquant. It suggests its opposite because of the oo (booooo!) in it. It's a joke really."

BEN LUCIEN BURMAN: "Fifty-fifty. A little cheap, like dime store decorations."

ABE BURROWS: "The critics 'enthuse' so rarely that I should welcome the word. But I don't like it."

GEORGE CORNISH: "I hate to see or hear 'enthuse'—but I can think of no reason why I do except early conditioning."

WALTER CRONKITE: "No. Only because I had an editor once who was death on this one."

PAUL HORGAN: "This seems to me to be fading out, and deservedly so."

JOHN K. HUTCHENS: "No. But, then, I'd hand out a twenty-year sentence to anyone saying 'emote.' "

CHARLES KURALT: ". . . but the audience 'apathied' over it? Lord, no. A terrible word."

HERBERT MITGANG: "Hold the fort."

WRIGHT MORRIS: "HELP!"

EDWIN NEWMAN: "I fail to see the advantage over 'were enthusiastic.' "

ORVILLE PRESCOTT: "With reluctance. I would not use 'enthuse' myself."

PETER S. PRESCOTT: "The worst kind of jargon."

FRANCIS ROBINSON: "As Sir Thomas Beecham said, 'We are drifting back to barbarism.' "

VERMONT ROYSTER: "I am unenthused by this. . . ."

WALTER W. "RED" SMITH: "And no, and no."

BARBARA TUCHMAN: "I don't *approve* but wouldn't outlaw it as incorrect."

EARL UBELL: "The best example of 'enthuse' was Herblock's cartoon done during the Oppenheimer hearings in which a scientist's lab was depicted showing a THINK sign replaced with ENTHUSE. Except in a humorous sense in casual speech, I vote no."

HERMAN WOUK: "This one is making it, I believe."

entomologist/etymologist An *entomologist* is a person who studies insects and their habits. An *etymologist* is a student of words and their origins. More than thirty years ago, the then editor of the Merriam dictionaries, John F. Bethel, told us his favorite definition of the latter term: "An *etymologist* is a person who knows the difference between an *entomologist* and an *etymologist.*"

entry, dictionary Of all the claims made by dictionary publishers in advertising their wares, none is more proudly trumpeted than the claim that Dictionary A contains "X thousand more *entries*" than Dictionary B. To the layman this seems to mean that Dictionary A contains X thousand more words fully defined than Dictionary B.

It means nothing of the sort. According to standards laid down during New Deal days by the government's Procurement Division (now called the Federal Supply Service), an *entry* is not only the major word heading up a series of related definitions, but every variant form—defined or undefined—that appears. Principal parts of verbs count as separate *entries*. Comparative and superlative forms of adjectives and undefined adverbial forms of adjectives also count as *entries*. So do variant spellings, archaic forms, and the like.

For example, here's a typical short *entry:*

en • **twist** (en-TWIST) *v. tr.* • **twisted,** • **twisting, twists.** Also **in** • **twist.** To twist together or make into a twist.

To the non-lexicographical eye, that looks like a single *entry*. To the professional, it's not one but FIVE entries. Each of the variants indicated in boldface type counts as an *entry*. In years past, dictionary makers often resorted to inclusion of long lists of obsolete and archaic forms (like the famous "under-the-line" entries in the Merriam-Webster Second Edition). Set in tiny type, these served no very useful purpose—as witness their elimination from the Merriam Third—but they certainly served to run up the entry count.

It should be emphasized that there is absolutely nothing illegal about this method of counting *entries*. Indeed, as noted earlier, the practice began as a result of a governmental ruling based upon the need to establish a quantitative basis for assigning dictionaries to uniform categories for bidding on government purchase contracts. It is, or should be, obvious that quantitative evaluation of dictionaries is ridiculous because it ignores the qualitative merits of the definitions, as well as the more practical considerations of typography and timeliness. However, the latter really are matters for subjective judgment, which could only lead to endless argument, and, if there's one thing bureaucrats don't want, it's argument.

So a bureaucratic decision made decades ago established the basis on which today's dictionary publishers base their competitive claims. Just for the record, we might note that a series of *entry* counts of the various dictionaries now in print indicates that the *entries* claimed are approximately twice the number of major bold-faced *entry* headings. In other words, if a dictionary claims 160,000 *entries*, you may safely assume that it will have about 80,000 fully defined *entries* in the layman's sense of that much-abused word. *See also* ABRIDGED/UNABRIDGED.

envelope/enclave/envoy   All three are borrowings from French and all three are victims of people using what they take to be an approximation of the French accent by pronouncing the first syllable as ON. The results are ON-vel-ope, ON-voy, and ON-clave, fair examples of what someone once called "bargain basement French."

In the case of the first, EN-velope is unquestionably the more logical pronunciation. Probably we'd be sensible if we all adopted it. Equally unquestionably there is no sense to the pseudo-French pronunciation of ON-vel-ope, but so many well-educated people use it that all American dictionaries enter it as an alternate and entirely acceptable pronunciation.

Not so with *enclave* and *envoy*. The mispronunciation of these is sanctioned by only one lexicon, the Merriam-Webster Third International. Some of the worst offenders are newscasters, who seem to think it adds a touch of elegance to their pear-shaped tones to say ON-clave and ON-voy. If they would take the time to check an authority like *Webster's New World Dictionary,* they would find that EN-clave and EN-voy are the clearly preferred pronunciations.

environment. *See* ECOLOGY/ENVIRONMENT

envoy, pronunciation of. *See* ENVELOPE/ENCLAVE/ENVOY

epicure Many a gift box of assorted food oddities, ranging from dried grasshoppers to thumbnail-sized packages of tasteless imported cheese, are advertised as "designed for the epicure."

An *epicure* today is a person noted for his discriminating taste in food and wines. The meaning of this word has changed slightly over the years since Epicurus, a Greek philosopher of about 340 B.C., took the view that life need not be as grim as his rivals, the Stoics, seemed to think. As a result of his stress on happiness as an important element of living, he came to be thought of as advocating luxury and sensual pleasure. This was not exactly what Epicurus had in mind, but, like many wrong ideas, it took hold, and *epicure* came to mean "a person excessively fond of luxury and sensual pleasure." That definition is labeled "archaic" in the most recent dictionaries, leaving the essential meaning that of "discriminating."

Episcopal/Episcopalian While *Episcopalian* may appear to be an adjective, it is the noun form and is applied *solely* to persons not otherwise identified: "He is an *Episcopalian*"; or "She is an *Episcopalian.*" At the same time, it is correct to say "He (or she) is an *Episcopal* priest," since *Episcopal* is the adjective form. Thus you refer to "an *Episcopal* service," "*Episcopal* theology," "*Episcopal* church," etc.

This is the official position of the church itself, although one of its officials admitted that *Episcopalian* is used as an adjective in "sloppy writing" even by some members of the faith.

epithet Strictly speaking, an *epithet* is any descriptive word or phrase and is not necessarily derogatory. Common usage, however, has given it a derogatory element, and a person who is said to have "shouted *epithets*" is understood to have spoken in an abusive manner.

epitome. *See* ACME/EPITOME

ept. *See* ARCANE WORDS

equal, more   In a literal sense, *equal* is an uncomparable adjective. Yet we hear people speak of a "*more equal* distribution of wealth." What is really meant is "more equitable."

The most memorable use of *more equal* is George Orwell's comment in *Animal Farm:* "All animals are equal, but some animals are *more equal* than others."

equally as   There is little, if any, need to use these words together to express comparison. "She plays *equally as* well as her sister" does not need the *equally*. When the two things or persons being compared are named in the same sentence, the word to use is *as*. When only one is named within the sentence, the word to use is *equally:* "Her sister plays *equally* well."

equitable. *See* EQUAL, MORE

-er/-or   Agent nouns (which is what linguists call the words for persons or things performing an act) are formed by the addition of either *-er* or *-or* at the end of the verb form. In general, those verbs which come from Latin or French become agent nouns by the addition of *-or,* while those which are English in origin do so by adding *-er*.

There are many exceptions to this, however, and some such nouns can be spelled with either ending. Some agent nouns even end in "-ar," as "liar." The only solution is to consult a dictionary.

If the verb ends in a "y," it is changed to "i" before adding *-er* unless the "y" is preceded by a vowel, as in "play."

err   With the exception of the original *American Heritage Dictionary* and possibly the Merriam-Webster Third International, American dictionaries give URR as the only acceptable pronunciation, although all of us have often heard AIR. (We say possibly Merriam-Webster Third International because, although more than three lines are devoted to the pronunciation of this simple word, the explanation is couched in such impenetrable dictionary shorthand that it is impossible to understand it.) The original *American Heritage Dictionary* gives both URR and AIR as acceptable.

Some years ago the late Frank Colby wrote "It must be that dictionary editors are under oath not to listen to people talk. Why else would the dictionaries refuse to recognize the Standard American pronunciation of 'air' for 'err'? They insist on 'urr' to rhyme with 'burr.' The truth is that 'err' is so closely associated with 'error' (both are from the Latin 'errare') that 'air' and 'air-or' are the natural and logical pronunciations." We agree.

errata   This is the plural of "erratum," which is an error in printing or writing. *Errata* is used as a term for a list of corrections of such errors, usually inserted in a book after it has been printed.

Even though it is used in a collective sense, *errata* still takes a plural verb.

erstwhile An adjective meaning "former," *erstwhile* is seldom used except in formal writing and even then is often misunderstood. The adverbial use of the word is now considered archaic.

erudite At least one sports announcer is not *erudite,* as reported by a reader who complained that he pronounced the word er-OO-ih-dite and AREA-dite. The correct pronunciation is ER-oo-dite, with ER-yoo-dite as a somewhat more polished alternative.

escalate/escalating/de-escalate *Escalate* is derived from "escalator," which was the trade name for a moving staircase. The picture it conveys is of a steady, almost inexorable rise.

The term, which began in the jargon of economists, may well have made its first move into the general language in the form of "escalator clauses" in union contracts. These provide that each rise in the government's cost-of-living index figures be matched by proportional rises in pay for workers. The wide use of *escalating* and *escalation* began in the 1960s, when government officials and media commentators began to use it in reference to the increasing scope of our involvement in Southeast Asia. Then *"escalating* war" and *"escalating* cost of war" became catch phrases. The word *de-escalate* has been coined as an antonym, but it is seldom seen. *See also* VOGUE WORDS.

escape When used in the sense of physically breaking out or getting out of, *escape* must be followed by "from," as in *"escape from* prison" (not *"escape* prison"). When used in the figurative sense of "to successfully avoid," "from" is not necessary, as in "He hoped to *escape* criticism."

escapee. *See* -EE, SUFFIX

especial/especially/special/specially The adjective forms *especial* and *special* are in most instances interchangeable, with *special* being much more commonly used than *especial.* For those who do wish to make a distinction, *special* has a broad meaning of "not general" and *especial* that of "pre-eminent."

The adverbs *specially* and *especially* still have separate roles to play. *Specially* indicates that an action is taken for a defined reason as in *"specially* trained" or *"specially* chosen for his knowledge of architecture." *Especially* is preferred to mean "particularly" or "to a marked degree," as in "He knew he must hurry, *especially* in view of the impending storm" or "She is an *especially* talented young woman." "More *especially*" is a *redundancy* (which see); the "more" is unnecessary.

Esperanto. *See* INTERNATIONAL LANGUAGE

Esq. *Esq.* is the abbreviation of "Esquire," a label with a long history and one which has been used exclusively for men. We were sent, on one occasion, a conference program in which every speaker was listed as "So-and-so, *Esq.*" One of the stars was none other than "Dr. Beatrice E. Willard, Esq.," making two errors in one listing. In the first place, *Esq.* should not be used with another title, be it "Dr." or even "Mr." In the second place, "Esquire" has referred only to members of the male sex since the Middle Ages. The first esquires were candidates for knighthood, attendants and shield bearers for knights. The word came into English at the time of the Norman Conquest and was borrowed from the French "esquier," which, in turn, came from the Latin word for "shield bearer." During later centuries *Esq.* was used to indicate persons (always male) of social position above that of tradespeople. The latter were simply "Mr." In America, *Esq.* is usually used only in addressing letters to lawyers. We question whether women lawyers have any desire to be labeled *Esq.* They may prefer the title *Ms.* (which see).

essential, more/most *Essential* is, strictly speaking, an *uncomparable adjective* (see *adjectives, uncomparable*) and cannot be limited by *"more,"* since something is either *essential* or it isn't. The phrase *most essential* is a common idiom which is used only for emphasis and not for comparison. "It is *most essential* that the city enforce the law against autoists passing stopped school buses" does not mean that it is more important to enforce that law than to enforce any other law but simply that it is very important in itself.

establishment, the This term acquired an extended meaning during the 1960s, when it was used by young people to denote the sum total of all established social institutions of the country and especially the people who ran them. Previously it has been used (with a capital "E") to refer to the Church of England or the Presbyterian Church in Scotland or any powerful group which controlled a government or group of people. In its broader extended sense it was used by young people, especially students, who sought to change "the system."

estate agent This is the standard British equivalent of the U.S. "real-estate agent" or "real-estate broker."

esthetic. *See* AESTHETIC/ESTHETIC

estimated at about A *redundancy* (which see). Delete *about.*

et cetera Since *et cetera* is translated from the Latin as "and other (things)," it is redundant to say or write "and *et cetera.*" The same holds true for the abbreviation "etc.," of course.

eternal *Eternal* is by virtue of its meaning one of the *uncomparable adjectives* (which see). Since it means "everlasting," it cannot be limited by "more" or "less."

eternity. *See* INFINITY/ETERNITY

ethnic *Ethnic* has become a vogue word and is used both as an adjective (which it has always been) and as a noun. As an adjective it means "having racial, religious, cultural, or national characteristics," as in *"ethnic* group" or *"ethnic* background." With the increase in attention paid to the needs and desires of *ethnic* groups, especially by politicians, *ethnic* has come to be used as a noun, in the singular and plural, to designate persons of *ethnic* groups and in the plural to refer to all such groups.

   Panelist Jean Stafford reports an even more extended use of *ethnic* which is unacceptable to her and to us: "How would you like," she wrote, "to be invited, as I once was, to an 'ethnic dinner party,' at which the guests were to be common garden variety Wasps? The menu, you see, was to consist of some raw fish done in a Japanese way, moussaka with braised Belgian endive, cucumber salad prepared according to a Pakistani recipe and Nesselrode pudding. I didn't accept." *See also* VOGUE WORDS.

etymologist. *See* ENTOMOLOGIST/ETYMOLOGIST

euphemism According to the dictionaries, *euphemisms* are words substituted for more plainly explicit words which might prove offensive to some readers or listeners. *Euphemism,* which we borrowed directly from a Greek word meaning "to speak with good words," has spawned such related words as *euphemize, euphemist,* and *euphemistic* and, for many centuries, the simple dictionary definitions seemed adequate. However, during the period since the days of the New Deal in the U.S., the tendency on the part of political figures to resort to *euphemisms*—always a part of their makeup—has been extended to nearly ludicrous extremes. Similar use and abuse of *euphemisms* have become characteristic of much advertising and promotion language. And, particularly in the 1960s and the 1970s, the U.S. government indulged in such extended use of *euphemisms* in its reports to press and public that some scholars have redefined *euphemism* as the "language of deceit."

   In the field of government, attention first became focused on the overuse of *euphemisms* when Maury Maverick, then in charge of a World War II agency, lashed out at what he called "gobbledegook language" and said that anyone using words like "activation" and "implementation" in place of their simple equivalents "will be shot." His warning, it need not be said, was not heeded and decades later matters in Washington, linguistically speaking, were incomparably worse. The list of such abuses of the mother tongue could, quite literally, be endless. Here are a few chosen at random from a twenty-year collection.

A sewer commission is now a pollution-control agency. An employee is not "fired"; he is "selected out" or "riffed," an acronym from "reduced in force." A "janitor," of course, has long since been raised to the status of "custodian," just as the old-fashioned "garbage man" is now a "sanitation engineer." A "trash barrel" is now an "ecological receptacle," while at least one enterprising trash collector has restyled himself "garbologist" and adopted the slogan: "Satisfaction guaranteed or your garbage refunded." A second-hand car is never called that today. It's "reconditioned," "rebuilt," or, simply, "previously owned."

An entire chapter could be devoted to the *euphemisms* exposed during the Watergate hearings and in the presidential tape transcripts released thereafter. Illegal entry into a psychiatrist's office was referred to as an "intelligence-gathering operation," which was part of a "game plan." Money channeled through Mexican banks to hide the identity of its donors was "laundered." Flattery became "stroking" or "puffing." Wiretapping or bugging was "electronic surveillance," and breaking and entering became "surreptitious entry."

Our involvement in the Indochina conflict resulted in creation by Pentagon spokesmen of countless *euphemistic* expressions. When it became embarrassing for the military to report destruction of native junks and sampans, they were converted overnight to "wiblics," a failed acronym for Water Borne Logistical Craft. What were initially labeled "search and destroy" missions became "search and clear." Mention of a U.S. Army pullout was explicitly forbidden. Instead it was referred to as "light and scattered action." Mass bombing raids were "protective retaliation." On one occasion when our troops accidentally shelled another U.S. position, the report called it "accidental delivery of ordnance equipment." Perhaps all this should not surprise us, since we have long since accepted the change from the blunt and accurate "War Department" to the *euphemistic* "Defense Department."

It may be argued that the faddish use of *euphemisms* by participants in the Watergate affair was not unrelated to the fact that so many of them had worked for advertising agencies before going to the White House. Certainly the advertising fraternity has led the way in promoting *euphemistic* labels for many of its products. Nothing is ever "large" or "cheap"; it's "king-sized" or "economy-priced." One doesn't have a "smell" but an "aroma" or "scent." Fat boys are not fitted with fat-boy suits but with "chubby" sizes and their fathers are never fat but "portly." Similarly the mother is directed to dresses for "mature" (not fat) women.

Naturally this widespread use of *euphemisms* to cloak meaning could not entirely escape the notice of the academic world. A committee of the National Council of Teachers of English—the Committee on Public Doublespeak—has issued a notably comprehensive study, *Language and the Public Policy,* edited by Hugh Rank and available from the council (1111 Kenyon Road, Urbana, Illinois 61801). We commend it to anyone wishing to explore the subject further.

But, before leaving this generally depressing topic of calculated abuse of the language, we should like to share with you two less melancholy fruits of our researches. The first is a confession from a poor young woman. "I used to think I was poor," she wrote. "Then they told me I wasn't poor; I was needy. Then they said it was self-defeating to think of myself as needy, that I was culturally deprived. Then they told me deprived was a bad image, that I was underprivileged. Then they told me that underprivileged was overused, that I was disadvantaged. I still don't have a dime—but I have a great vocabulary!"

And the second item is reported here to prove that at least one public servant, Harry S Truman, subscribed to the preachings of the Honorable Maury Maverick. At a meeting of her garden club, Mrs. Truman was approached by a fellow member who asked her if she couldn't use her influence with Mr. Truman to persuade him to stop talking so much about "manure." "Heavens no," replied Mrs. Truman. "You have no idea how long I had to work on him to get him to say 'manure'!"

A delightfully informative, comprehensive and readable study of *euphemisms* past and present is *Kind Words* by Judith S. Neaman and Carole G. Silver, published by Facts on File Publications, New York, N.Y. *See also* DYSPHEMISM/EUPHEMISM and WATERGATE LANGUAGE.

ever so often/every so often   If you try to analyze these two idioms, you will find no logic in either, but each serves a purpose of its own. *Ever so often* means "frequently and repeatedly," as in *"Ever so often* she drops in for a cup of coffee and stays for lunch." *Every so often* means "once in a while" or "occasionally," as in *"Every so often* I find a bargain in fabrics but I never know when to expect it."

every   "I want *every* supervisor and employee to continually ask themselves these questions" is an example of a common error in choice of personal pronoun. In this sentence, *every* means each person individually and separately, hence the pronoun should be "himself or herself" not "themselves." If the sentence were to be changed to read "all supervisors and all employees" the use of "themselves" would be proper.

The sentence could also be improved by moving "continually" out of its present infinitive-splitting position and putting it at the end of the sentence—not because we are against split infinitives but because it has greater impact there.

every day/everyday   A full-page advertisement for pantyhose which was carried in the magazine section of the Sunday *New York Times* stated in large boldface type: "I've worn one pair *everyday* since purchasing them, which is seven weeks ago. Other hose never lasted over one week." Obviously the meaning intended was "each day in succession, without interruption," and the proper wording is *"every day." Everyday,* written solid, is an adjective which means "common" or "not unusual," as in "the *everyday* problems of the average housewife." There are two other things in the wording of the advertisement which could be improved: the phrase "which is" is ungrammatical and unnecessary and "more than" is preferable to "over" in this context.

everyone/everybody   *Everyone* may seem to be a plural, since it is all-inclusive, but it requires a singular verb and a singular pronoun. *"Every-one* should stay in *their* seats" is inaccurate; it should be *"Everyone* should stay in *his* seat," or "All persons should stay in their seats." It would be unthinkable to use a plural verb with *everyone,* as in *"everyone* are," so the plural pronoun should also be avoided. The same holds true of *everybody.*

evoke/invoke   The distinction between *evoke* and *invoke* is based on their prefixes. *E-* means "out" and *in-* means "in" or "into"; *voke* comes from the Latin "vocare," meaning "to call." Thus *evoke* means "to call or draw out" or "to elicit," as in "The reports of his accident *evoked* immediate offers of help from his neighbors." *Invoke* means "to call on" or "to call for" or "to put into use," as in *"invoke* God's mercy" or *"invoke* a long-forgotten law."

ex-. *See* PREFIXES, AND SUFFIXES, WITH AND WITHOUT HYPHEN

exacerbate   *Exacerbate* can mean either "to increase the severity or intensity of" or "to irritate" but the most common usage today is in such sentences as "The difficulties were *exacerbated*" or "Such statements only tend to *exacerbate* the existing difficulties."

exact same   A *redundancy* (which see). Delete *exact.*

example. *See* SAMPLE/EXAMPLE

excellent   A reader raises the question whether "very excellent" is acceptable—since *excellent* in itself seems to be a superlative. There are in English a number of words like *unique* (which see), "absolute," and "supreme" which linguists regard as not subject to comparison. *Excellent,* however, does not quite fall into this category. There are varying degrees of excellence. To take a pedestrian example, it is still customary in many

exotic

schools and colleges to consider any grade above 90 percent worthy of an "A"—the mark of excellence in studies. Yet obviously the student scoring 98 percent is more *excellent* than the one with 92 percent.

except   When used as a preposition meaning "but," *except,* followed by a personal pronoun, takes the objective case: "No one *except me* can open this door," NOT "No one *except I* can open this door." *Except* as a verb meaning "exclude" or "excuse" is a formal word and is seldom heard in everyday speech. It is proper in sentences such as "The names of all persons under the age of sixteen will be *excepted* from the list of those required to return later."

exceptional   When used as an adjective to describe retarded children, *exceptional* is welcomed by the parents of such children but questioned by some who think it can mean only "better than average; superior." If we go back to the Latin origin of *exceptional* we find that it describes something "taken out" or "singled out" of the ordinary run of persons or things. It is true that we usually think of an *exceptional* child as being one who differs from the rest by being superior. But it is technically accurate to use *exceptional* to describe a retarded child, since the child differs from most of his or her fellows. Granted that this use of *exceptional* probably started with the sociologists, it is one phrase from the frequently frustrating jargon of that science that we admire.

excuse. *See* PARDON/EXCUSE

execute/kill/murder   *Execute* is not synonymous with either *kill* or *murder* because *execute* has the basic meaning "to carry out" or "to put into effect." Thus to *execute* a person is to kill him in compliance with a military order or judicial decision. To *murder* is to kill unlawfully but purposely.

executive   *Executive* is properly pronounced eg-ZEK-yoo-tiv, not ex-EK-uh-tiv.

exit   There are two equally acceptable pronunciations for this: EGGS-it and EX-it. As a verb it is intransitive (having no object). To say, "He *exited* the window" is illiterate. It should be "He *exited* through the window."

exotic   *Exotic* once meant only "introduced from a foreign country," which is the way it is defined in Webster's Second International Dictionary. Nowhere in that volume is it defined as "singularly beautiful" or "strange and different in a way that is striking or fascinating," which is the definition given it by *Webster's New World Dictionary* today.

As recently as 1944 Frank Colby in his *Practical Handbook of Better*

215

English wrote, "*Exotic* does not mean glamorous, alluring and mysterious. It simply means 'from a foreign country' as any good dictionary will attest." The dictionaries did so attest in 1944 but the extended meaning is now accepted, with the original meaning also still given.

expecting/expectant with/pregnant Pregnancy is among the topics which people once felt should be disguised by the use of euphemisms such as *expecting* or *expectant with*. There is nothing really wrong with them, but the simple word *pregnant* is no longer viewed with alarm in "polite circles."

The use of another euphemistic phrase—"in a family way"—is apt to expose the speaker to hoots of derision, though.

expediate/expedite/expedient "An envelope is enclosed to *expediate* your reply" is illiterate. There is no such word as *expediate*. The proper word is *expedite*. *Expedient* is the noun and adjective.

expert A problem which many people encounter with the word *expert* is one of pronunciation. Traditional usage is that the noun *expert* is pronounced with the stress on the first syllable. As an adjective the stress is on the second syllable. Dictionaries now recognize the pronunciation EX-pert for both the noun and adjective, with the ex-PERT pronunciation reserved for the adjective alone.

expertise This is a fairly recent borrowing from the French and it refers to the qualities of expert knowledge of a subject or a skill in a particular procedure. It is a vogue word and one that may well fall into disuse. It says nothing that "expertness" does not.

(expletive deleted) An *expletive* is, of course, any sudden exclamation or oath, especially one profane in nature. Thanks to the frequent appearance of *(expletive deleted)* in the transcripts of Richard Nixon's taped White House conversations with staff members, the expression became popular slang for "obscenity" or "profanity."

explosion. *See* IMPLOSION/EXPLOSION

express/expressed *Express* is the form usually found in phrases such as "*express* purpose," meaning a "definite, particular, and sometimes exclusive purpose." *Expressed* means "having been stated or made clear," as in "his *expressed* intention" or "her *expressed* wish." There is a special and subtle sense of *expressed,* meaning "not necessarily true," as in "The *expressed* purpose of the school board meeting might be to pass on nominations for the new year but the actual purpose was to criticize certain textbooks."

exquisite   The preferred pronunciation is EKS-kwiz-it. Indeed it is the only one given by the original *American Heritage Dictionary*. Other dictionaries do list eks-KWIZ-it also. If you care to puzzle them out, Webster's Third International (Unabridged) gives half a dozen variations, after listing the preferred pronunciation first.

extemporaneous   Teachers of speech in grade schools make an arbitrary distinction between *extemporaneous* and "impromptu" when referring to classroom performances. An "impromptu" talk is one that, as actors say, is completely ad lib, made with no advance preparation and without notes of any sort. An *extemporaneous* talk, in the lingo of speech teachers, is one that has been written or at least outlined in advance and has been carefully rehearsed before the performance takes place.

   For those who are not teachers of speech, however, *extemporaneous* will continue to mean "spoken with little or no advance preparation."

F

face up to   Critics of the phrase *face up to* contend that the words *up to* are superfluous. *Face up to* is defensible in that the phrase means a bit more than the sum of its parts and decidedly more than simply "to face." One can "face facts" and, terrified by what one sees, back away or even turn and flee. However, when you *"face up to* the facts," you have resolved to face a situation with courage and resolution. Also, there is an element of analysis involved. A man who has decided to *"face up to* a situation" has already given it some thought and has decided to meet it head on. For these reasons, the idiom can be considered acceptable in speech and writing.

factor/element/part   *Factor* is essentially a mathematical or business term but it has been used so widely as a substitute for *element* or *part* as to become hackneyed. It is easy to recognize why it acquired the figurative meaning of "being an important and contributive part of a process or situation" but it is wise to avoid its overuse.

fair dinkum   This is an Australian informal phrase which has enjoyed some popularity in the U.S. It was apparently brought back by men who served in the forces in Australia or in combat alongside Australian troops. It means "fair and square," according to the *OED*, but, as an exclamation of approval, it means much more—"Excellent!" or "Top quality!"

Katherine Adamson, of Columbus, Ohio, draws on her Australian heritage for this comment on the preceding paragraph:

You didn't get your information on *fair dinkum* from *dinkum* Aussies. I must admit to never having heard it from Americans, who may have changed the meaning, but the few Australians who still use the term mean "true," "honest," or "real" by it. If I said, "He's *fair dinkum*," it should be translated as "He's for real," not "He's great." Or I could say, "He almost ran me down! Fair dinkum!" where an American child would add "Cross my heart!" for the emphasis. By the way, Americans need to be told that "Aussie" is pronounced with a Z, not an S.

fall guy Slang, meaning a chronic loser. Also a person who assumes the responsibility for the failure or misconduct of another. The first *fall guys* were professional wrestlers. Until the 1920s wrestling was a reputable sport and its champions were as highly esteemed as the champions in boxing and other professional sports. But rigging or fixing of matches became so widespread that various state courts decreed that the wrestling shows could no longer be called "contests" or "matches" but must be labeled "exhibitions." The *fall guy,* of course, was the wrestler who took the prearranged fall in order to make the "champion" look good.

fall off of A *redundancy* (which see). Delete *of.*

fallout Originally coined to describe the minute particles of radioactive material coming down through the atmosphere after the detonation of a nuclear bomb, *fallout* has acquired two extended meanings. It is used to denote the reactions of people and the news media to important statements or actions, as in "the *fallout* resulting from the scandal of Watergate." And, according to the Barnhart *Dictionary of New English,* it also means "a by-product of something, usually unexpected." The 1970 *Compton Yearbook* states under the heading "Valuable By-Products of Space Research": "From the research that produced the rocket motors . . . liquid propellants, space suits and other necessities of space flight there emerged . . . unexpected applications—in medicine, industry and the home—for materials, equipment and the services that had been created for use in space. Such by-products are called 'spin-off' or 'fallout.' "

false pretenses. *See* DUFFER

famed/famous Although *fame* as a verb meaning to "make *famous*" is now archaic, the adjective *famed* has come to be synonymous with *famous*. The trend was started by *Time* magazine, which, in its early days, was committed to a "curt, clear and concise" style. *Famed,* although only one letter shorter than *famous,* seemed better suited to "*Time*style," as the editors called it. Some writers find it more acceptable when used in the predicate, as in "The state was *famed* for its beaches," rather than placed before the noun, as in "the *famed* beaches of the state," but most authorities admit it as standard in all contexts.

famously   The expression "get along *famously*" has proved a puzzler for at least one of our readers. "To me *famous* means 'known to just about everyone,' " she writes, "as you might say 'George Washington was a very *famous* man.' But that doesn't make sense in such a sentence as 'Tom and Bill get along *famously.*' " The solution to the problem lies in the fact that *famous* also has an informal sense of "excellent or first rate." So, if the adverb "excellently" is substituted for *famously,* the meaning is quite clear.

fan   *Fan,* in the sense of "an enthusiast," was once labeled slang in American dictionaries but it is now considered to be informal or colloquial. As such, it may properly be used in casual speech or writing but should be avoided in situations calling for formal language.

fanny   *Fanny* in the U.S. is low slang for the buttocks. *Fanny* in the United Kingdom is far more vulgar, referring to a female's most private parts. Transplanted Americans are well advised to drop *fanny* from their vocabularies, no matter how informal, when talking to Britons.

fantastic   *Fantastic* is a word which has almost lost its true meaning through overuse as an exclamation of approval *("Fantastic!")* or an adjective of gushing praise ("I met this *fantastic* boy"). Strictly speaking it means "imaginary" or "incredible." It also has a less common sense of "strange, especially in appearance."

far out   A slang phrase, used as an exclamation *("Far out!")* in much the same way as "Fantastic!" and with much the same intent. Used as an adjective (and with a hyphen: *far-out*), it means "extraordinary," "marvelous," or simply "very unconventional."

farther/further

USAGE PANEL QUESTION

Farther, according to traditional grammarians, is used in reference to measurable physical distance and *further* is confined to figurative senses, especially of degree or quantity. Recently linguists have reported a tendency to use *further* in all instances. Do you make a distinction between the two?

Yes: 80%. No: 20%.

Would you say or write: "Nothing could be *farther* (20%) or *further* (80%) from my mind"?

How about "Washington is *farther* (90%) or *further* (10%) from New York than Baltimore"?

STEWART BEACH: "I agree with the distinction, though I think it's true that there is a growing tendency to use 'further' in both senses."

ROBERT CRICHTON: "Yes, but I slip. I still like the difference between the two."

THOMAS FLEMING: "No. But I know there is a difference between the two and strive to do so."

S. I. HAYAKAWA: "Yes. I find that I never use 'further' except as a verb, 'furthering a project.' "

PAUL HORGAN: "I try to, but in sound they are so close that I often interchange them as in example 'a.' "

JOHN K. HUTCHENS: "Yes. Anyhow, I *hope* I would."

ELIZABETH JANEWAY: "Yes. Or at least I try to, but don't always manage."

CHARLES KURALT: "Yes. Now that you mention it, I *do* make a distinction; I wasn't even aware of it!"

PETER S. PRESCOTT: "I certainly do when the distance itself is what is important."

F. D. REEVE: "Yes, but copyeditors give me grief (as they say)."

LEO ROSTEN: "No. 'Further' is an aspect of reasoning; 'farther' is an aspect of space."

RICHARD H. ROVERE: "When I remember to."

VERMONT ROYSTER: "Yes. The concept of 'distance from the mind' is figurative only."

DAVID SCHOENBRUN: "Yes. Would anyone say 'farthermore'?"

HAROLD SCHONBERG: "I seem to use both interchangeably. Never could figure out the difference."

MARK SCHORER: "Yes, I try to. Recently I made a copyeditor keep both spellings in one sentence to show the difference."

REX STOUT: "I like neither the sound nor the looks of 'further' and never use it. 'Farther' does for me."

EARL UBELL: "Yes, when I remember."

fascia   British automotive equivalent of the American "dashboard."

fatal/fateful   Despite the fact that dictionaries indicate that *fatal* and *fateful* may sometimes be synonymous, it is well to preserve a distinction because each has implications which do not hold for the other. Originally *fatal,* according to the *Oxford English Dictionary* as well as others, meant "allotted or decreed by fate; destined; fated" but, as *OED* records, it acquired a "weakened sense" of "disastrous." Now the original *American Heritage Dictionary* gives as its primary meaning "Causing or capable of causing death; mortal." *Fateful* has its own special meanings of "having important consequences which may affect one's destiny" or "decisive." It is true that most of the definitions given to each word are also assigned to the other in some dictionaries, but we would argue that *fatal* is much more ominous than *fateful,* which can apply to something beneficial as well as something disastrous.

father/mother In general, the words *mother* and *father* are not capitalized. The most common exception is when referring to one's own parents, as *"Mother* and *Father* will be here today." If, however, you were to write "my *mother"* or "my *father"* there should be no capitalization. In a letter, of course, one would write "Dear *Mother"* or "Dear *Father."*

Capitals are also used in referring to members of the Catholic clergy: *Father* Walsh, *Mother* Cabrini.

father-in-law The plural of *father-in-law* is *fathers-in-law. See also* PLU-RALS OF COMPOUND WORDS AND PHRASES.

fault When used as a transitive verb, *fault* has become a vogue word and as such is greatly overused as a substitute for "blame" or "criticize," either of which is preferable. It is Elegant English to say, "I can't *fault* him for that," rather than "I can't criticize him for that."

faze/phase When this word is used in the sense of "disconcert" or "embarrass," the spelling is *faze.* When used to designate an aspect or a stage, the spelling is *phase.*

February The pronunciation FEB-roo-er-ee is preferable to FEB-yoo-er-ee, though the latter is heard with increasing frequency among otherwise literate speakers, especially among radio and television commentators.

fed An investigative or enforcement agent of a federal governmental agency, such as the Federal Bureau of Investigation or the Federal Bureau of Narcotics, as distinguished from local or state officials. Slang. *See also* FUZZ.

feel. *See* GOOD/WELL and LINKING VERBS

feet. *See* FOOT/FEET

feisty This is a dialect term which has appeared in many spellings but most commonly as *feisty.* Other spellings include "ficety," "fisty," "feesty," and "fausty." Originally it came from "fice," meaning "a small, snapping dog." One authority gives these synonyms for *feisty:* angry, peevish, snippy, quarrelsome, and stubborn. *Feisty* may also mean spirited in a positive sense.

fell. *See* SWOOP, ONE FELL

feminist   A *feminist* is not necessarily a woman, although that is usually the case. Feminism is merely the doctrine that women should be granted the same rights as men in political, legal, and economic matters. Anyone, male or female, who subscribes to this doctrine is a *feminist. See also* FEM LIB/FEMLIB; SEXISM; SEXISM IN LANGUAGE.

Fem Lib/Femlib   Women's Liberation Movement is an overall term for the activities of many women's groups which evolved during the 1960s and 1970s in an effort to organize women to demand and receive recognition, status, and pay equal to men. It is also called "the feminist movement" and, by some of the most dedicated members, "the Women's Movement." It met with some ridicule, as well as opposition, on the part of both some men and some women and resulted in the creation of some mocking nicknames for the proponents of the movement as well as the movement itself. "Women's Lib," "Women's Libbers," "Fem Lib," "Femlib," and "Fem Libbers" were among them.

With the growth of support for the Equal Rights Amendment to the Constitution and the increasing acceptance by both government and industry of a single standard for competence, there has been a decrease in the use of such nicknames. In the interest of accuracy, as well as fairness, even those who disagree with the aims of the movement tend to (and should) use the proper terminology for the movement and its participants. *See also* FEMINIST; SEXISM; SEXISM IN LANGUAGE.

fender   On American automobiles the *fender* is the metal guard over each wheel. In Great Britain that part of the car is called a "wing" and *fender* is the name for the U.S. "bumper."

fetish/penchant   *Fetish* has acquired a meaning broader than its original one but it still does not have the meaning indicated in the store window sign which read: "If you have a *fetish* for the finest sports shirts, come in and view our superb selection."

Among primitive peoples, a *fetish* is an object believed to have magical powers. It has acquired a slightly broader meaning in today's culture —any object of irrational reverence or devotion. It does not mean a *penchant,* yen, or liking.

fiancé/fiancée   These are borrowed from French and should have acute accents over one of the terminal "e's," indicating that they are to be pronounced as separate syllables. They are both pronounced FEE-ahnss-say or fee-AHN-say. Because they often appear in print without the acute accents, and because many people are not familiar with French rules of pronunciation, the masculine form *(fiancé)* is often pronounced FEE-ahnss or fee-AHNS, which is incorrect.

fiddle   *Fiddle* originated as British underworld argot midway through the nineteenth century. In the sense of "to swindle" it is still considered slang. Generally speaking, a person who has been *fiddled* has been taken for a small amount—the sort of minor cheating that would lead an American to complain that he had been "diddled."

fiddle-faddle. *See* RICOCHET WORDS

fiddlesticks!   This is an informal and essentially meaningless exclamation or interjection, usually uttered in a spirit of mild annoyance or vexation. The original *fiddlestick* was the horsehair-strung bow used in playing a fiddle, but just why it, in the plural, should have become an expression of annoyance passes understanding, unless one takes into account the fact that the sounds committed by beginning fiddlers could certainly be a source of great irritation.

Fifth Estate. *See* FOURTH ESTATE

figuratively. *See* LITERALLY/FIGURATIVELY

figure   *Figure* should be pronounced FIG-yer, not FIG-ger, though the latter is widely heard in England and in some American regional dialects.

filet/fillet   In the sense of "a boneless cut of meat or fish," this word can be spelled with either one or two "l's." The final consonant is not doubled for the past tense *(fileted* or *filleted)* and the pronunciation does not follow the spelling. It is usually pronounced fil-LAYD, following the French pronunciation of *filet* rather than the British (FIL-it).

finalize

USAGE PANEL QUESTION

Finalize made its first appearance in print in Australia in 1922. In the United States in the years since World War II, it figured prominently in the vocabularies of at least two Presidents—Eisenhower and Kennedy. Would you approve "The committee met to *finalize* plans for the dinner"?

In writing   Yes: 14%. No: 86%.
In casual speech   Yes: 26%. No: 74%.

MICHAEL J. ARLEN: "No. It's inept."

ISAAC ASIMOV: "I associate the phrase with administrative gobbledegook, for which I have a hatred. I am far more tolerant of the mistakes of honest ignorance than of those of false gentility—and I firmly believe God is, too."

SHERIDAN BAKER: "Only humorously."

JOHN O. BARBOUR: "Not unless we can tentativize a date for tomorrow."

STEWART BEACH: "I have always thought this a dreadful and entirely unnecessary verb."

HAL BORLAND: "Gobbledegook. They never say they are going to 'initialize' plans, do they?"

JOHN BROOKS: "Only jocularly. Eisenhower destroyed this theoretically legitimate usage for at least a generation."

HEYWOOD HALE BROUN: "We have not, for a long time, looked to Presidents for literary leadership."

ANTHONY BURGESS: "It has its points. It suggests a very American efficiency. I wouldn't use it in a novel about Europeans."

ABE BURROWS: "It's obviously a part of American speech and I accept it but I don't approve. Words like 'finalize' have a curious effect on me. When it's used, the sentence and speaker immediately become boring."

WALTER CRONKITE: "A valuable new form."

RICHARD EDES HARRISON: "I like 'complete' myself. 'Finalize' is the perfect example of 'jargonese' in the making."

PAUL HORGAN: "One of the worst of governmental usages."

JOHN K. HUTCHENS: "Not until the cookie crumbles completely and nobody looks to see if the flag is being saluted or the fenders dented. It's still Madison Avenue, and the hell with it."

ELIZABETH JANEWAY: "I don't like it, but I have a feeling it's needed. What would you say instead that is as brief?"

CHARLES KURALT: "It's a Washington word. The Washington example has very often served to bastardize (to use a non-Washington word) the language these last twenty years, with the connivance, alas, of reporters in Washington, who should know better."

LAURENCE LAFORE: "Acceptance as standard usage is, I judge, a matter of time. To use words like 'finalize' is merely to be inelegant and to uglify the language."

JESSICA MITFORD: "Actually, we've been using this for twenty years."

EDWIN NEWMAN: "I fail to see the advantage over 'make final plans.' "

ORVILLE PRESCOTT: "No . . . still evidence of an education that did not take."

PETER S. PRESCOTT: "It is hard to say how, in a language like English, some words are uglier than others, but 'finalize' is an ugly word—as well as a grotesque one."

FRANCIS ROBINSON: "Another reason the country is going to hell."

BERTON ROUECHÉ: "What's wrong with 'complete'?"

VERMONT ROYSTER: "Let us not accept Presidents as final authorities on good usage."

HARRISON SALISBURY: "People who use 'finalize' should themselves be . . ."

HAROLD SCHONBERG: "Ted Bernstein scared this out of *Times* writers years ago."

ROBERT SHERRILL: "No . . . except that it is a useful word for mocking."

CHARLES E. SILBERMAN: "This grates as much as the use of '. . . wise.' "

WALTER W. "RED" SMITH: "It may be bipartisan, but it's still vile."

HOWARD TAUBMAN: "Eisenhower? No surprise. But Kennedy? What was his high-level stable of speech and document writers doing at the time?"

EARL UBELL: "The 'izes' are often wonderful. Standardize, vaporize, etc. Even in fun: elocutionize, eroticize, etc. But 'finalize' sticks in my throat. Maybe because it is used as a lazy or jargon substitute for complete. Anyhow, no."

WILLIAM C. VERGARA: "Even worse is 'finalization.' "

JUDITH VIORST: "Absolutely, no."

fink   A word recently popular with young people is *fink,* especially in such combinations as "rat-*fink.*" They use it to designate any undesirable person, especially one who is not trustworthy. This is a somewhat extended meaning of the word, which, in the days when unions were being organized, was one of the strongest terms in the lexicon of labor. To say that a man was a *fink* was to say that he was a strikebreaker, an informer, or worse. The dictionary definition at that time was "A man paid by his employer to disrupt union activities." Now it has become a general term of abuse or disrespect but it remains slang.

fired/riffed. *See* EUPHEMISM

firemen/firefighters   Members of various trades or occupations have often tried to change the names used for those trades or occupations, usually in an effort to lend more dignity to their work. The results are sometimes ridiculous, like "custodian" for janitor. The case of *firemen* who would prefer to be called *firefighters* does make sense. Men who stoke furnaces are properly called *firemen* and they encourage and coddle fires. The men and women who defend our homes and businesses against fire are *firefighters* and deserve the distinction in terminology.

firestorm   Originally a military term, *firestorm* came into widespread use on two occasions during the so-called Watergate affair. First was the use of *firestorm* by presidential assistant Alexander Haig to describe the barrage of letters and telegrams that hit the White House after the "Saturday Night Massacre" of Messrs. Cox, Richardson, and Ruckelshaus. The second was the similar barrage when Mr. Nixon's admission of his part in the "cover-up" was made public, shortly before his resignation from the Presidency.

A third *firestorm* was the torrent of critical telegrams, mail, and phone calls that reached the White House after President Ford granted a general pardon to Richard Nixon, and his press secretary, Jerald ter-Horst, resigned as part of what some called "the Sunday Morning Massacre."

Firestorm, in its technical military application, referred to the results of mass bombing raids like those on London and the nuclear holocaust at Hiroshima in World War II. The Department of Defense Dictionary defines *firestorm* as follows: "A stationary mass fire, generally in built-up urban areas, generating strong, inrushing winds from all sides; the winds keep the fire from spreading, while adding fresh oxygen to increase their intensity." *Firestorm* in the extended sense indicated in the previous paragraph may now be considered standard.

firm/corporation   A *firm* may be a partnership of two or more persons, usually unincorporated, although the term is loosely used for both incorporated and unincorporated business concerns. A *corporation,* on the other hand, has to be chartered under the laws of incorporation and, once formed, has the standing of a legal entity with its own rights and liabilities.

first annual   An example of "instant tradition," *first annual* is a contradiction in itself. The only possible excuse for its use would be in a situation where an event was certain to be repeated each year in the foreseeable future. A truly preposterous use of the term appeared in the announcement of a school's *"First Annual* Traditional Christmas Play." That announcement, needless to say, had not been cleared with the English Department.

first blush, at   The informal expression *at first blush* may be the source of some confusion because "blush" in the current meaning of a gradual reddening of the features, usually from embarrassment, has nothing to do with the meaning of the phrase. In medieval times, when the expression originated, a "blush" was merely a glance. So *at first blush* means "at first glance."

first floor   In England the *first floor* is what Americans call the "second floor." The American *first floor* or "street floor" is the British "ground floor."

First Lady   The custom of using the title *First Lady* for the wife of a United States President is no longer as prevalent as it was at one time. *The Boston Globe Stylebook* has long taken a position against it, stating flatly: "The President's wife is not called the First Lady in *The Globe.*"

As a matter of fact, newspaper, radio, and television writers and commentators are as likely to call the President's wife by her first and last names as to call her "Mrs. So-and-so."

firstly/thusly   A minister given to Elegant English is quoted as saying, *"Firstly,* we must concede to the doctrine of Original Sin and *thusly* we are led inevitably to believe. . . ." The "-ly" in each case is unnecessary. "First" and "thus" are perfectly adequate adverbs as they stand. *Thusly* is not even entered in most dictionaries and, when it is, it is marked "obsolete." *Firstly* has not reached that point yet but we hope that it will soon.

first two/two first

USAGE PANEL QUESTION

In much speech and writing today one finds the term "the *first two*" in such expressions as "The *first two* runners to finish." Not many years ago grammarians insisted that the phrase should be "The *two first* . . ." Do you draw a distinction?

Do you prefer "The *two first*": 19%. "The *first two*": 81%.

BENJAMIN APPEL: "Equal."

ISAAC ASIMOV: "You can't have two first runners unless it's a tie. Stupid grammarians!"

W. H. AUDEN: "Don't care."

SHERIDAN BAKER: "There can't be 'two first'—it's illogical! Should be 'the first pair,' if you really mean 'the two first.' "

HAL BORLAND: "Both are illogical, but 'the two first' is absurd. 'The first two' is idiomatic."

JOHN BROOKS: "Neither. Different meanings. 'The two first' implies a tie."

HEYWOOD HALE BROUN: "['The first two'] for no good reason. The other usage has the awkward ring of a split infinitive."

ANTHONY BURGESS: "No distinction. Use them indifferently."

ABE BURROWS: " 'Two first' sounds like a dead heat."

ROBERT CRICHTON: "Either way does it and one isn't any better or worse than the other."

ELIZABETH JANEWAY: "This is just a reaction by ear. 'First two' sounds better."

ALEXANDER KENDRICK: "The 'two first' means a dead heat."

WALTER KERR: " 'Two first' suggests a tie; the other leaves it open."

RUSSELL LYNES: "I'll accept (and use) either."

PHYLLIS McGINLEY: "There cannot be two firsts."

EDWIN NEWMAN: "No preference."

ORVILLE PRESCOTT: "Prefer ['the first two'] but only slightly. Might easily use the first myself."

FRANCIS ROBINSON: "['The two first'] . . . even though I don't bother to say it that way."

LEO ROSTEN: " 'First two' means 1 and 2; 'two first' means a tie."

WALTER W. "RED" SMITH: "I incline to use 'the two first' but don't quarrel with the other. I would urge eliminating 'two' where possible, e.g., 'The first to finish were Smith and Jones' but of course you'd need a number if you wrote, 'The first to finish had broken legs.' "

HOWARD TAUBMAN: "Wouldn't the 'two first' sound like a dead heat?"

fiscal year A *fiscal year* is a twelve-month period, usually not corresponding to the calendar year, on which the financial account of a firm or organization is based. The U.S. government's fiscal year runs from July 1 to June 30. Most large businesses find it helps their bookkeeping to make some similar arrangement.

fish/fishes Both forms *fish* and *fishes* are accepted plurals for *fish*. There are lots of good *fish* in the sea and there are lots of good *fishes* in the sea. The distinction is nicely set forth by Usage Panelist Stewart Beach in this comment: "The normal plural, of course, is *fish*. *Fishes* is used only where various species of *fish* are being considered. For example, you might read an article called 'Game *Fishes* of the Gulf Stream off Florida.' But, if you went out trolling for them on a good day, you would simply say when you got back, 'The Stream was boiling with *fish*.' "

fix *Fix*, in the senses of "prepare," "arrange," and "mend," is accepted usage, but in formal speech or writing it is certainly preferable to use the precise word, such as "cook dinner" or "prepare dinner," rather than "*fix* dinner."

flagrant. *See* BLATANT/FLAGRANT

flail/flay Sometimes confused by people who are unsure of their meanings, *flay* and *flail* have one thing in common: whipping or threshing motion. If you wave your arms wildly in an effort to hit someone you are *flailing* your arms. The term comes from an old farm instrument consisting of a long stick with a shorter free-swinging stick at the end which was used for threshing grain. Just as the stick at the end of the *flail* swings about, so do arms that are *flailed*.

Flaying involves a different form of attack. Literally it means to strip off the skin by whipping. Figuratively it means to tongue-lash a person.

flak/flack   *Flak* means "bursting shells fired from antiaircraft guns." It also has a slang meaning of "criticism" or "argument," as in "He gave me a lot of *flak* when I told him what I planned to do." *Flack* is theatrical slang for "press agent."

flake   This is an item of police jargon which came to public notice during hearings into police corruption in New York City in the early 1970s. A *flake* is an arrest made on the basis of planted evidence. It is also a slang equivalent of "oddball."

flammable/inflammable   These two words are identical in meaning. Each means "easily set on fire" or "combustible." However, fire-insurance underwriters have been operating on the theory that foreigners, unfamiliar with the inconsistencies of English spelling, may think that "in-" in *inflammable* means "not." So they have succeeded in having tank cars and, indeed, all containers for combustible fluids labeled *flammable*. The scientific community has taken up the crusade, and scientists go straight down the line for *flammable*. This does not change the fact that both terms are acceptable and are synonymous.

As the results of the poll of Usage Panelists shown below indicate, a substantial majority still prefers *inflammable*, both in speech and writing.

USAGE PANEL QUESTION

Inflammable, in the sense of "combustible," has been largely replaced in the literature of science and technology by *flammable*. One argument put forward in favor of the change is that non-native speakers of English may misconstrue the "in-" prefix as meaning "not." Do you use *flammable*?
In your speech   Yes: 27%. No: 73%.
In writing   Yes: 28%. No: 72%.

ISAAC ASIMOV: "No, but the argument is right and 'flammable' should be used."
SHERIDAN BAKER: "No. It seems appropriate only on gasoline trucks, etc."
STEWART BEACH: "I have said 'inflammable' for so long that I would find it hard to change, though I agree with the comment about non-native speakers."
ALVIN BEAM: "I use 'inflammable' only out of habit. I like the drift toward 'flammable.'"

HEYWOOD HALE BROUN: "No. The other may be confusing but it is familiar and doesn't confuse *me.*"

BEN LUCIEN BURMAN: " 'Flammable' is probably better and clearer, but I'm an unreconstructed Kentucky classicist, suh."

ROBERT CRICHTON: "No, but I think I will. It's better."

STEPHEN H. FRITCHMAN: "I like to see 'flammable' on trucks because it is a clearer warning (to a non-Latin-oriented people) than 'inflammable.' One up for a neologism."

S. I. HAYAKAWA: "No, but I believe 'flammable' is O.K. as a sign on gasoline trucks and such. It could not be used in metaphorical sense, as in 'Russo-Chinese relations are dangerously inflammable.' "

PAUL HORGAN: "No, but commerce uses it widely and it will prevail."

JOHN K. HUTCHENS: "Yes, although it takes a slight effort to get over '*in*-flammable.' "

ELIZABETH JANEWAY: "No, but I might very well use it if I were writing labels for children's clothes."

DWIGHT MACDONALD: "No, but I think 'flammable' should be used on public signs, for the practical reasons given."

EUGENE MCCARTHY: "No, but I agree with the reason given for using it."

PETER S. PRESCOTT: "No, but just from habit. 'Flammable' makes more sense."

BERTON ROUECHÉ: "No, but I think maybe I shall."

MARK SCHORER: "No, just habit, probably."

WALTER W. "RED" SMITH: "No—maybe we all should."

LIONEL TRILLING: "No, but I see the point of the objection to 'inflammable.' "

BARBARA TUCHMAN: "Never had occasion to use 'flammable'—but probably would."

JUDITH VIORST: "No, but I should! 'Inflammable' is a very confusing word."

flap/flappable In international political jargon, "unflappable" was first applied to the former Prime Minister of Great Britain, the imperturbable Harold Macmillan. The label first appeared in the American press at the time of the Profumo-Keeler-Ward episode, during which the Prime Minister remained resolutely "unflappable" and probably saved his government by his composure.

In Washington, during the 1950s and '60s, the term *flap* was used to describe the tension and turmoil which characterizes a government agency under investigation by a Congressional committee. For reasons obvious to anyone who has ever served there, one local nickname for the Pentagon is the "Five-Sided *Flap* House."

Flap was originally army slang and referred to an alarm, especially one leading to panic. It soon became standard slang in all the services and broadened in meaning until it came to mean any argument or controversy, especially one big enough to threaten the job tenure of important officials. *See also* VOGUE WORDS.

flare/flair

USAGE PANEL QUESTION

Panelist DWIGHT MACDONALD draws our attention to this from a *New York Times Book Review* article by a Barnard College .teacher of English: "... and the American *flare* for commercial organization and marketing. ..." Some dictionaries indicate that the spellings *flair* and *flare* are interchangeable in certain senses, as "the *flare* (or *flair*) of an urn or fireplace." Would you use *flare* in a context like the one cited?
Yes: 9%. No: 91%.

JOHN O. BARBOUR: "All's 'flair' that doesn't burn; all's 'flare' that does."

STEWART BEACH: " 'Flair' and 'flare' have separate meanings which should be preserved."

JULES BERGMAN: " 'Flare,' correctly used, is an emergency illuminating device."

HAL BORLAND: "Would you write, 'His temper flaired up'? or 'I watched the flair of Northern Lights'? *I* wouldn't!"

ERNEST K. GANN: " 'Flare' is something you shoot—usually in distress."

CLARK KINNAIRD: "How does one know it was *not* a typo? The *Times* is riddled with them!"

EUGENE MCCARTHY: "Not interchangeable."

HAROLD SCHONBERG: " 'Flare' is just damn wrong."

DANIEL SCHORR: "I accept the enrichment of language through change in the meaning of words through usage. But I do not accept simple confusion between words. 'Flair,' as a bent or talent in some direction, sounds like, but is not the same as 'flare,' which is a matter of combustion."

WALTER W. "RED" SMITH: "I sware, this usage curls my hare."

DAVIDSON TAYLOR: " 'Flair' for a conspicuous talent; 'flare' for flame and temper."

A.B.C. WHIPPLE: "Again, it's just wrong. A fireplace can have both 'flair' and 'flare.' "

flat   *Flat* was once standard American for a suite of rooms on a single floor of a residential building. Now it has been pretty much supplanted by "apartment." However, it is still standard British, and a "block of *flats*" in England is what Americans would call an "apartment house."

flaunt/flout   There are few pairs of words more frequently misused, each for the other, than *flaunt* and *flout*. Our files abound in examples sent in by readers, editors, and even publishers. In our own immediate experience we were chilled to hear a now happily departed Superintendent of Public Schools in New York City, speaking of a threatened school boycott, say, "I hope no parents, by their example, will teach their children to flaunt the law." This from a Ph.D. who later went on to the presidency of one of the city colleges! The distinction is really very simple. *Flaunt* means to "show something off proudly or boastfully": "The drum corps proudly *flaunts* its colors." *Flout* means to "show scorn or contempt for a person or thing": "The speeding driver *flouts* the law." Herewith the Usage Panel Question with samples of the panelists' comments.

USAGE PANEL QUESTION

In recent years one Supreme Court Justice used *flaunt* in a written opinion when he meant *flout* and, on the same day, another justice used *flout* when he meant *flaunt*. (NOTE: Neither Justice, of course, was panelist William O. Douglas.) In your judgment is there a distinction between these two words worth preserving?

In writing   Yes: 97%. No: 3%.
In casual speech   Yes: 96%. No: 4%.

SHANA ALEXANDER: "These words are similar *only* in sound, not in meaning."

MICHAEL J. ARLEN: "I should damn well hope so."

ISAAC ASIMOV: "Yes, when you have a good distinction, flaunt it; otherwise, flout it."

STEWART BEACH: "There is a distinction that *must* be preserved. Otherwise, readers or listeners won't know which meaning is intended."

HAL BORLAND: " 'Flout' means to scoff, and 'flaunt' means to brandish. How can you wipe out the distinction?"

JOHN BROOKS: "I am glad to have this opportunity to reverse the Supreme Court."

HEYWOOD HALE BROUN: "Their only resemblance is phonetic."

ANTHONY BURGESS: "Of course. The meanings are totally distinct. It's only a prosodic accident that makes for confusion."

BEN LUCIEN BURMAN: "No wonder Roosevelt wanted to fire the Supreme Court!"

JAMES McGREGOR BURNS: " 'Flaunt' is usually the wrongly used word—let's stop flaunting it.'

JOHN CIARDI: "General usage is, I think, confusing these two words into one, but they are valuably different."

ROBERT CRICHTON: "Because they are fools should we lose two fine feisty words?"

ROBERT CROMIE: "I hate to surrender *any* words."

THOMAS FLEMING: "I'm shocked at the Supreme Court."

RICHARD EDES HARRISON: " 'Flount' will appear in print any day; you just watch!"

PAUL HORGAN: "Emphatically. Perhaps a literacy test should be administered to Supreme Court nominees."

ALEXANDER KENDRICK: "Yes . . . Members of the Mixed Flouters and Flaunters Society to the contrary."

STANLEY KUNITZ: "I flout those who flaunt their ignorance."

WRIGHT MORRIS: "How otherwise? They are totally different words. This is Abusage not Usage . . . or where's Justice?"

EDWIN NEWMAN: "So there is between 'tout' and 'taunt.' "

ORVILLE PRESCOTT: "Of course! Are our Supreme Court Justices only semi-literate?"

PETER S. PRESCOTT: "Of course. The words have nothing to do with each other and each is necessary."

BERTON ROUECHÉ: "My God—they'll have us talking pidgin English yet."

VERMONT ROYSTER: "Let Justices flaunt their opinions but not flout the Constitution."

HAROLD SCHONBERG: "Two absolutely different words, and they should *never* be confused."

ROBERT SHERRILL: "I had heard that the court was badly split."

WALTER W. "RED" SMITH: "He who flouts grammar flaunts his ignorance. Clout the lout with a knout!"

HOWARD TAUBMAN: "Considering the hair-splitting some of the Justices resort to, I think it's not too much to ask them and us to preserve what is really not too fine a distinction."

DAVIDSON TAYLOR: "One flaunts his ignorance if he flouts the distinction."

BILL VAUGHAN: "If this distinction were to disappear, thousands of editors would be unemployed as changing 'flout' to 'flaunt' and vice versa is their sole function."

JUDITH VIORST: "Absolutely yes."

GEORGE WALD: "Don't you flaunt proudly and flout in disparagement?"

CHARLES L. WHIPPLE: "Who uses 'flaunt' when he means 'flout' will always score a lasting 'out.' "

T. HARRY WILLIAMS: "I would guess 'flout' and 'flaunt' are among the most misused words."

flavor Usage Panelist Clark Kinnaird sends a headline indicative of what he calls "an extension of usage" of *flavor*. It reads: FARMHOUSE RETAINS ITS ORIGINAL FLAVOR. At the risk of seeming to differ with one of our distinguished advisers, we should note that this sense of *flavor* (a distinctive, characteristic quality) is pretty well established as standard usage. *Webster's New World Dictionary* puts it this way (as the fourth definition of *flavor*): "the characteristic quality of something; distinctive nature: the *flavor* of the city."

flay. *See* FLAIL/FLAY

Fleet Street   At one time most of the major London newspapers had their headquarters in or close by Fleet Street, so the name of the street became an informal label for the press itself, almost synonymous with *Fourth Estate* (which see). Though some papers have moved their headquarters, *Fleet Street* remains widely used as a term for the daily press and, last time we looked, still was the location of a very pleasant newsmen's club.

flex   The verb *to flex* is derived from the Latin flectere, "to bend." Presumably for this reason, such dictionaries as the old Funk & Wagnalls Unabridged (1913) and even the Merriam-Webster Second Edition (1934) limited the definition of *flex* to "to bend." As a result we had a missive from a reader stating, in criticism of our using the phrase "flexing their muscles," that he was "always annoyed by writers who speak of *flexing* muscles, since *flex* means to bend and muscles are not bent, they are tightened." He went on to suggest that we "stay after school and write 'muscles don't *flex*' 1,000 times." Obviously we have not followed his advice, for the very good reason that more modern dictionaries have fully recognized the idiom and enter as a second meaning of *flex* "to contract (a muscle)." What's more, the *OED* cites, "A single muscle *flexes* the thigh"—and the date of that quotation is 1845. So our self-styled "purist" was actually misguided and *flexing* muscles is a well-established idiom suitable in any context.

flier/flyer   In general *flier* and *flyer* are considered synonymous by the dictionaries, but *flier* is given as a full entry in most cases with *flyer* simply labeled "Variant of *flier*" or "Same as *flier.*" The Boston *Globe,* however, takes no such tolerant view. Its style book says: "*Flier* is an aviator; *flyer* is a train." The latter strikes us as a bit of amusing obsolete jargon, perhaps still cherished in Boston but now unknown in the rest of the nation. For the record, either spelling may be used as the informal designation of a leaflet or broadside intended for wide distribution.

flim-flam   This is *ricochet word* (which see) or reduplication based on the word "flam," which as a noun means "lying" and as a verb means "to deceive." Both "flam" and *flim-flam* are informal.

flotsam and jetsam   The word *flotsam* is used in maritime law to describe goods swept from a vessel and found floating in the sea. *Jetsam* refers to cargo deliberately thrown overboard (or jettisoned) when a ship is in imminent danger of wreck, especially goods which sink and remain under water. *Flotsam and jetsam* is often loosely used to refer to wreckage either floating or washed up on shore. By further extension, it now means chronically unemployed people, vagrants, and drifters, who are regarded as the *flotsam and jetsam* of the social order. *See also* JETSAM/ JETTISON.

flounder. *See* FOUNDER/FLOUNDER

flunky/flunkeys/flunkies *Flunky,* meaning originally a "manservant" and, by extension, "any person (usually male) who is obsequiously servile toward a presumed superior," is usually *flunkies* in the plural, both in Canada and the U.S. However, the British plural is most often *flunkeys.*

flute A term in police jargon used in connection with the practice of drinking on duty which was discovered during an investigation of corruption in the New York City Police Department during the early 1970s. A *flute* is a Coke bottle with liquor in it.

flyer. *See* FLIER/FLYER

flyover British term for what Americans call an "overpass."

F.O.B./f.o.b. *F.O.B.* or *f.o.b.* is often mistakenly thought to be an abbreviation for "freight on board." Actually it means "free on board." It indicates that the price quoted *F.O.B.* includes costs and charges at the point of manufacture or shipment but does not include transportation charges, which must be borne by the consignee.

fogged in While it may sound like slang, this phrase is perfectly acceptable English. Used in the airline industry to describe airport conditions when it is too foggy to allow planes to land or depart, it may also be used to apply to situations when any kind of travel is made impossible by dense fog.

folk etymology *Etymology* is the study of the true or earliest meanings of words and of their subsequent evolution. *Folk etymology* is something else again. It is much more often the popular and incorrect notion of the origin of a word, usually based on a faulty analogy to a better-known word. In folk speech one can find many examples: "Johnnyquit" for "jonquil," "high-bred" for "hybrid," "cowcumber" for "cucumber," and "sparrow-grass" for "asparagus."

A variation, which might more properly be called "popular etymology," would include such widely believed but false theories as the one about "marmalade" being derived from "Marie malade." (See *Morris Dictionary of Word and Phrase Origins,* Harper & Row.)

foolscap   *Foolscap* designates stationery measuring from 12 × 15 inches up to 13½ × 17 inches. The most common size is 13 × 16, which is often folded to make pages of 8 × 13 inches. Originally it was a printing paper and got its name from the ancient watermark of a fool's head and cap used to identify the paper. The earliest specimens of such watermarked paper go back to before the time of Shakespeare.

foot/feet   If English were always logical, a pole measuring three *feet* would be described as a "three-*feet* pole." The accepted idiom, however, is "three-*foot* pole." It is difficult to make a rule on this, but if the modifier comes before the noun it is singular and plural if it comes after: "a pole six *feet* long."

Such an expression as "He's a six-footer" is acceptable as a shortened form of "He's a six-*foot* man." "She's five *foot* two," despite the popular song of the twenties, is an error. The correct form is "She's five *feet,* two inches."

for. *See* BECAUSE/FOR/SINCE/AS

forbid   *Forbid* should be followed only by an infinitive or a gerund and never with "from" or "for." It is proper to say, "I will *forbid* you to leave" or "I will *forbid* your leaving" but not "I will *forbid* you from leaving" or "I will *forbid* for you to leave." *See also* GERUND.

forcible/forceful/forced   There are fine distinctions to be observed in the choice of the word which is proper under a given set of circumstances. *Forcible* applies to that which is accomplished by the use of brute force, as in "*forcible* entry" or "*forcible* ejection." *Forceful* should be used to mean "possessing or showing the potential of force," as in a "*forceful* speaker" or "*forceful* personality." Another definition of *forceful* is "effective." *Forced* may be used for *forcible* as in "*forced* entry," but generally it is used to describe persons or things which are the objects of outside influence, as in "*forced* landing" and "*forced* labor."

forcible rape/statutory rape   At first glance *forcible rape* seems redundant since, by definition, *rape* involves force. However, the distinction in legal terms is that *forcible rape* is rape by the use of force upon a person above the age of legal consent, while the crime of *statutory rape,* not necessarily involving the use of force, refers to sexual intercourse with a person under the legal age of consent.

foremost

USAGE PANEL QUESTION

Foremost, being a superlative, is said by some purists to be in the same category as "unique" and should refer to only one person or thing: "Brooks Robinson is the *foremost* third baseman of his time." Yet one often sees statements like "Yehudi Menuhin ranks among the *foremost* violinists of this century." Is this broader concept of *foremost* to be heard in your own speech?
Yes: 72%. No: 28%.
Do you use it in writing? Yes: 59%. No: 41%.

STEWART BEACH: "I would never think of 'foremost' as having the same arbitrary uniqueness as the word 'unique.' "

ALVIN BEAM: "Yes, just as I would say, 'among the best.' If, that is, I use 'foremost' at all."

HAL BORLAND: "We say 'among the best,' don't we? Yet 'best' also is the superlative."

HEYWOOD HALE BROUN: "No. Only one horse is foremost in the Kentucky Derby."

ABE BURROWS: "I like the broader concept of 'foremost.' The word would be fairly useless if it referred to only one person. Saying that a fellow is 'among the foremost third basemen' or 'among the foremost violinists' or even 'among the foremost idiots' saves an awful lot of arguments. 'Foremost' is a pretty subjective term."

THOMAS FLEMING: "Yes, but I realize now it is incorrect and will stop."

STEPHEN H. FRITCHMAN: "No, I very seldom use it in any case."

JOHN K. HUTCHENS: "Why must it be one or the other? Both samples seem acceptable—Robinson is simply the foremost of the foremost."

WALTER KERR: "I don't remember so using it—but I think it acceptable."

STANLEY KUNITZ: "Yes. I visualize the foremost as a phalanx, not as a unique specimen."

PETER S. PRESCOTT: "I don't think you have to be a purist here; superlatives used as comparatives denote illiteracy."

VERMONT ROYSTER: "I think the objectives here are pedantic—in any marching crowd, several can be 'foremost' together, but I would nonetheless here prefer 'outstanding.' "

HOWARD TAUBMAN: "Yes. It is easy to show that there have been several violinists in this century who have a right to be considered among a group that could be called foremost. Kreisler and Heifetz, to name two, but not, incidentally, Menuhin."

HAROLD TAYLOR: "I usually just say 'best.' 'Foremost' sounds as if you're writing a speech."

LIONEL TRILLING: "It isn't a word I use at all—if I did, I wouldn't give it the force of 'unique.' There can be a quality of eminence: Picasso and Matisse are the foremost painters, etc."

forensic medicine/forensic gemology *Forensic medicine* is well established as standard English. It refers to the use of medical reports as part of legal, especially courtroom, proceedings. The term comes from the Latin "forensis," having to do with the Forum, where such matters were argued in the days of the Caesars. A more recent expression, *forensic gemology,* refers to the critical evaluation of gems so that an authoritative statement of their value can be submitted in a court of law. The term is, needless to say, standard English.

for free/for real The phrases *for free* and *for real* are slang and are used only facetiously by careful writers.

fork it over The resemblance of the human hand to a fork is the basis for the slang expression *fork it over,* meaning "hand it over." It has been in common use since 1840.

former, the *The former* can be used for reference only when just two persons or things are mentioned and you wish to refer to the one first named. When three or more are involved, it becomes necessary to say either "the first" or "the first-named" or to repeat the name itself.

formidable *Formidable* should be pronounced FOR-mid-uh-b'l, not for-MID-ih-b'l.

forte *Forte* (derived from the French word "fort"), meaning "one's strong point," is sometimes pronounced for-TAY. This is wrong. The final "e" is a false feminine ending, acquired by analogy to words such as "morale" and "locale."

Those who say for-TAY do so on the false assumption that all French words ending in "e" have the final syllable pronounced AY. This is true only of words ending in "é" with an acute accent. Actually the final feminine "e" in French is always silent.

FORTRAN This is a computer programming language for problems that can be expressed in algebraic terms. It is an acronym of FOR(mula) plus TRAN(slation).

fortunate/fortuitous The distinction between *fortunate* and *fortuitous* is becoming blurred, even among educated people. Something which is *fortunate* is "lucky" or "favorable," but it does not necessarily involve any element of chance or accident, as does *fortuitous*. "I was *fortunate* to have enough money in the bank to pay the damages" does not mean that suddenly and unexpectedly the bank balance increased, as it would if you were to say, "It was *fortuitous* that I had enough money. . . ." While some dictionaries do give *fortunate* as one of the meanings of *fortuitous* (*Webster's New World* among them), the fact remains that something which is *fortuitous* can also be *fortunate*, but unless it happened by chance or accident, the proper word to use is *fortunate*.

fortunately. *See* THANKFULLY/FORTUNATELY

Fort Worthers/Fort Worthians   Natives of Fort Worth, Texas, prefer to be called *Fort Worthians*, though *Fort Worthers* has been seen in print.

founder/flounder   These two verbs are often confused and consequently misused. *Flounder* means to "thrash about," as would an animal mired in mud. *Founder* means to "fail completely, collapse, or sink." In the case of a ship it means to "fill with water and sink"; hence it is redundant to say that the ship "*foundered* and sank."

four-letter words. *See* CANT WORDS

Fourth Estate   *Fourth Estate* is a well-established metaphor for the press, dating back to the time of Edmund Burke, when, according to legend, he noted in a speech before Parliament the three estates of the realm: the Lords Spiritual, the Lords Temporal, and the Commons. "And yonder," he is supposed to have added, "sits the Fourth Estate [waving at the press gallery], more important than them all." In recent years there have been a few fitful, and thus far unsuccessful, attempts to dub the electronic media—TV and radio—the "Fifth Estate."

foyer   *Foyer*, the lobby or entrance hall of a theater, may be pronounced FOY-er or FOY-ay. The latter is in imitation of the original French FWAH-yay. In French, incidentally, *foyer* means hearthside. It was originally borrowed into the British theater to designate the greenroom, the place where actors retired for informal and private chitchat. Gradually it moved farther offstage, so to speak, and became the name for the theater lobby.

Franglais/Frenglish/Hinglish   During the De Gaulle regime, leading French linguists mounted a somewhat strident campaign to discourage the importation into French of English and American terms, the results of which they labeled *Franglais*. Singled out for special scorn were the likes of "le drugstore" and "le hamburger." The British, rising to the challenge, mounted a tongue-in-cheek attack on borrowings into English from the French—a procedure that has been standard linguistic practice ever since the Norman Conquest. They also took the characteristically British position that French would be improved by further borrowings from English and suggested that a better label for the new acquisitions would be *Frenglish,* rather than *Franglais.*

In 1983 France's High Committee for the French Language renewed its attack on the use of English expressions by Frenchmen. This time the regulations against *Franglais* were strengthened by the threat of fines of as much as fifty francs ($7) for each taboo word, multiplied by the number of times it was used. Among the forbidden expressions were "drive-in theater" ("ciné-parc" is mandated), "pay-TV" ("télévision à péage"), "jet plane" ("l'avion à réaction"), and "jingle" ("sonal").

Nothing, of course, was accomplished by either faction, for the processes of linguistic change are not often much affected by the actions of committees, no matter how earnest they are or how pure their motives. One side effect, though, was the discovery of *Hinglish,* resulting from the liberal borrowing of English words by native speakers of Hindi in India. Here is a sample: "Thairo. Military Checkpost Ko Report Karo." Translated, this means: "Wait. Make a Report to the Military Checkpost." According to Reuters, this is a perfect sample of *Hinglish*—three words of Hindi and three of English.

Frankenstein (monster)　A common error is reflected in a statement such as "He created a *Frankenstein*" when what is meant is that he created a monster which eventually destroyed him.

Frankenstein was a doctor (the protagonist of a book of the same name) who created a monster who got out of control and, in the motion-picture version, destroyed the doctor. *Frankenstein* was NOT the monster. The phrase that should have been used was "a *Frankenstein monster*" or "a *Frankenstein's monster.*" It applies to anything which becomes dangerous to its creator.

freak out. *See* VOGUE WORDS

free gift　A *redundancy* (which see). Delete *free.* A *gift* by any definition, including that of the Federal Trade Commission, must be *free.*

freeway.　*See*　TURNPIKE/THRUWAY/PARKWAY/HIGHWAY/FREE-WAY/SUPERHIGHWAY

French fries　Though the menu boards of American fast-food restaurants usually lower-case the "French" in *French fries,* it should always be capped in print. The "French" in the expression refers to the method of preparing the potatoes by cutting them in long strips before cooking. It's the same "French" that appears in "French-cut green beans."

fresco. *See* MURAL/FRESCO

frieze   The correct pronunciation of *frieze* is simply FREEZ, not, as is sometimes heard, free-ZAY. A *frieze* is an ornamental decorative band, usually around the upper part of the wall in a room. The phony French free-ZAY is especially laughable, inasmuch as the actual French word for this ornamentation is "frise," pronounced exactly the same as the English word.

from ... to/ ... through/ ... to and including   Such an expression as "He was paid for work *from* October 1 *to* October 15" properly indicates pay for a fourteen-day period. Correspondents report its use by some business firms as indicating a fifteen-day period, including the second date. This is incorrect. If the intention is to include the second date, either of two phrasings should be followed: "*from ... through ...*" or "*from ... to and including. ...*"

from whence

USAGE PANEL QUESTION

"Take back your mink to *from whence* it came," wrote Frank Loesser in *Guys and Dolls,* using *from whence* for humorous effect. Many writers regard *from whence* as a redundancy, while some defend it, citing Psalm 121:1: "I will lift up mine eyes unto the hills, *from whence* cometh my help." Would you use *from whence* in writing, other than in dialogue to establish character?
Yes: 12%. No: 88%.
In casual speech, again without seeking humorous effect   Yes: 7%. No: 93%.

W. H. AUDEN: "No. Old-fashioned."
BARRY BINGHAM, SR.: "The one instance cited from the King James version, though a noble example, does not seem to me to justify a usage which is essentially redundant."
HAL BORLAND: "You can find many strange constructions in the Bible to illustrate almost any thesis."
JOSEPH A. BRANDT: "Sounds nice in writing, affected in speech."
JOHN BROOKS: "No. Maybe the distinction is a bit pedantic."
HEYWOOD HALE BROUN: "No. But then I don't write as well as the Psalmist."
BEN LUCIEN BURMAN: "No. If I were David writing the Psalms in the King James version, yes."
ABE BURROWS: "Believe it or not, Frank Loesser and I thought 'from whence'

was very funny. So did the audience. I still think it should only be used for laughs. As far as the Psalms are concerned, some of King James's translators were pretty comical themselves."

ERNEST K. GANN: "Are you taking a survey of gals and guys? The Bible, originating in Hebrew, is victim of *horrible* translations!"

S. I. HAYAKAWA: "No. However, Sir Walter Scott wrote: 'Down to the vile dust from whence he sprung, unwept, unhonored, and unsung.' "

PAUL HORGAN: "I would rarely use 'whence' itself."

WALTER KERR: "No. O.K. but no longer common coin."

WRIGHT MORRIS ("yes" in writing): "It has this echo, and on occasion has its place."

PETER S. PRESCOTT: "It's difficult for me to imagine myself using 'whence' in conversation!"

VERMONT ROYSTER: "Whence cometh thou defenders and whither shall we send them?"

DAVID SCHOENBRUN: "The citation from the Psalms is, after all, a translation, not a style example."

ERICH SEGAL: "No. Aha, I do not always vote *for* vulgarisms."

WALTER W. "RED" SMITH: "No. Would you use 'to hence'?"

DAVIDSON TAYLOR: "Whence comprises the meaning, 'from where.' "

HAROLD TAYLOR: "It just sounds too fancy even when correct."

HERMAN WOUK: "Total archaism, for deliberately cute use only, if ever."

NOTE: After publication of the first edition of this Dictionary of Usage, James Anderson of Cape Canaveral, Florida, had these comments:

"The punctuation of Psalm 121:1 in the King James version has caused problems for centuries. All modern translations render the second part of the verse as a question: "I lift up my eyes to the hills. From whence does my help come? My help comes from the Lord . . ." (RSV)

" 'From whence' is not an invention of the King James translators, as some of your panelists seem to think. 'Whence' is as old as the language. 'From whence' first appeared in the twelfth century, according to the OED, and seems to have gained immediate acceptance. It was probably a product of the linguistic confusion which followed the Norman conquest.

"By the early seventeenth century, 'from whence' was already somewhat archaic, yet both 'whence' and 'from whence' are used throughout the King James translation. The explanation is that much of the language of this Bible is based on earlier translations, going back to the fourteenth-century Wycliffe or Lollard Bible. . . . One version of the Wycliffe Bible has: 'I rered myn eyen in to the mounteynes, from whannus shal come helpe to me.'

"Both 'whence' and 'from whence' must now be considered obsolete, except when used humorously or as a deliberate archaism."

We thank Mr. Anderson for his scholarly exegesis and rejoice that he arrived at precisely the same conclusion as our rather less reverent panelists.

frontier   The tendency to convert nouns into verbs is a part of the growth of language but there are times when it is carried to appalling lengths. A television reporter, in describing a building under consideration for "landmark" designation, said that "the buildings *frontier* on 86th Street." *Frontier* is still only a noun and an adjective and it is a little difficult to consider 86th Street in New York City as "a boundary" or "an undeveloped area." The word he should have used is "front," which has long been a verb as well as a noun.

front runner   The term *front runner* is currently used to designate the candidate who seems most likely to win a nomination or election. This is a change from its original meaning. In racing parlance a *front runner* was a horse that looked fine as long as it was out in front and setting the pace but which would quickly fall back when challenged.

fry pan/frying pan   The use of the phrase *fry pan* in place of *frying pan* is one more instance of subliterate advertising jargon.

-ful, plurals of words ending in   Plurals of words ending in *-ful* are usually formed by the addition of the letter "s" at the end of the word, as in "cupfuls" and "teaspoonfuls." There was a time when the "s" was inserted before *-ful* in such words ("teaspoonsful" and "cupsful") but it is now standard to place the "s" at the end of the word. *See also* PLURALS OF COMPOUND WORDS AND PHRASES.

full/fuller/fullest   One school of thought holds that *full* should be included among the "uncomparable" adjectives, like "unique," on the ground that when a glass is *full* it cannot be made *fuller* or *more full.* That's true enough, as far as it goes, but down the years *full* has acquired a number of related meanings, such as "well-supplied or stocked," as "the woods are *full* of game." Obviously, in such a case, one forest could be *more full* or *fuller* than another. Also, if a glass is only "partly *full,*" another may be *fuller,* and a third *fullest.*

fulsome   One of the most commonly misused words in the language is *fulsome.* Again and again well-intentioned people use it in phrases like "*fulsome* oratory" or "*fulsome* praise" under the mistaken impression that they are using terms of commendation. Actually *fulsome* (pronounced either FOOL-sum or FULL-sum) means offensive to good taste, especially because of insincerity or base motivation. One of our readers, George Johnson of Wausau, Wisconsin, wrote to former Secretary of State Dean Acheson, expressing amazement that he would use the expression *"fulsome* praise" on the cover of his autobiography, *Present at the Creation.* Acheson replied that he was using the word in the sense given in the first definition of *fulsome* in the Merriam-Webster Second International (1934): "full, copious and abundant." But what the distinguished diplomat had failed to do was to read the entry carefully. That meaning was labeled "archaic," meaning that it might have passed muster in Shakespeare's day but certainly not in ours. Today the Shorter Oxford Dictionary defines *fulsome* as "Offensive to good taste, especially from excess. . . . Now chiefly of flattery, overdemonstrative affection and so forth." Herewith the question put to members of the Usage Panel with their comments:

USAGE PANEL QUESTION

Panelist WRIGHT MORRIS notes that *"fulsome* is currently and chronically assumed to mean flattering—a fulsome talent is one that is ripe or flowering." Would you accept *fulsome* in this sense?
Yes: 16%. No: 84%.
Would you restrict it to its more generally accepted meaning of disgusting or offensive to good taste?
Yes: 69%. No: 31%.

ISAAC ASIMOV: "One of my favorite criteria of illiteracy."
STEWART BEACH: "Or overblown praise (as a definition). Let's not fiddle with the meaning of 'fulsome.' "
HAL BORLAND: "This is an obsolete meaning and probably should be restored."
PAUL HORGAN: "No. 'Fulsome praise' has about 'made it' though."
HELEN L. KAUFMANN: " 'Fulsome' to me means exaggerated, overdone—e.g., 'fulsome flattery,' 'fulsome praise,' but never 'fulsome blame.' "
CHARLES KURALT: "Happened to me once—as a young writer for Douglas Edwards, I had him wish the viewing millions a 'fulsome Christmas.' Thousands of the millions were scandalized, and wrote tons to say so. The word, to me, means 'nauseating' *and nothing else.* "
LAURENCE LAFORE: "Perhaps not quite *disgusting*—more *excessive.* "
ROBERT LIPSYTE: "I take a center position—the word has a slightly ironic connotation—'fulsome praise' as being overripe, somewhat excessive."
DWIGHT MACDONALD: " 'Fulsome' always used with 'praise' now—so here is a simple example of displacement."
EDWIN NEWMAN: "I take it mainly to mean excessive."
ORVILLE PRESCOTT: "Vile."
LEO ROSTEN: "You can't win them all. The usage is so common it has ceased to be offensive—to most."

VERMONT ROYSTER: "Those who thus use it have a fulsome talent indeed."

DAVID SCHOENBRUN: " 'Fulsome' is a frightful word. I never use it."

ROBERT SHERRILL: "Sorry, I guess I use it wrong in a different way. I use it to mean excessive, but not necessarily in a bad sense."

WALTER W. "RED" SMITH: "Let's cling to old established meanings. This 'new' meaning is the fruit of ignorance."

functional illiterate   Bureaucratic euphemism for "an uneducated person."

fund/finance

USAGE PANEL QUESTION

In 1934 the Merriam-Webster Second International Dictionary entered the verb "to *fund*" and defined it (in part) as "to finance, as to *fund* an enterprise." This definition it then labeled "obsolete." Yet newspapers today carry many stories about measures to "*fund* the space program" and the like. Do you feel that *fund* is again entirely acceptable in speech and writing?

Yes: 61%. No: 39%.

Do you feel that it is merely enjoying a voguish revival and says nothing that "finance" does not say quite as well?

Yes: 51%. No: 49%.

BENJAMIN APPEL: "A contradiction seemingly—but Wall Streeters I know use both 'fund' and 'finance'—say one 'fund' to ten 'finances.' "

W. H. AUDEN: " 'Fund' sounds better because it is shorter."

ISAAC ASIMOV: "One syllable is better than two, and 'fund' sounds good."

SHERIDAN BAKER: " 'Fund' is not entirely acceptable, but almost!"

CHARLES BERLITZ: "No. Simply a euphemism for obtaining money from some organization or individual."

SIMON MICHAEL BESSIE: "It says nothing that 'finance' does not say."

HEYWOOD HALE BROUN: "I never thought it other than a noun, but then words of that sort are rarely used among gentlefolk."

ABE BURROWS: "I find 'fund' useful. These days it means (to me) to arrange for something to be financed, whereas I think finance means to turn over money to someone or something."

ROBERT CRICHTON: "It really is a foundation kind of word. People in business *finance;* government organizations *fund.*"

THOMAS FLEMING: "Frequent usage is our chief criterion, it seems. 'Finance' suggests a constant flow of cash—'fund' is more for government spending, e.g., to 'fund' the Public Broadcasting System."

PAUL HORGAN: "Yes, because of popular pressure."

JOHN K. HUTCHENS: "Why not? It's a *good* synonym for 'finance.'"

ELIZABETH JANEWAY: "Times have changed economics-wise. (Ha!) A pension plan that is 'funded' will pay fully all that is guaranteed. One that is merely 'financed' may not. In this special sense the word is needed."

ALEXANDER KENDRICK: "It has a governmental-bureaucratic connotation beyond that of 'finance.'"

LAURENCE LAFORE: "I do think it acceptable, if silly."

WRIGHT MORRIS: "Yes. A matter of taste."

EDWIN NEWMAN: "I hope it is a voguish revival."

HARRIET PILPEL: "Yes. It is in very widespread use."

VERMONT ROYSTER: "They are two separate words with different meanings, and the distinction is worth preserving. *To finance* is the general term referring to the gathering of money by whatever means, borrowing, taxing, or whatever. *To fund* describes the accumulation of money over a period of time either to finance something at a later date or to repay a previous financing. Example: You may *finance a project* by borrowing money and then *fund the loan* by periodically setting aside money to repay the loan when due. Or you may *fund* a project by the accumulation of savings to *finance* it later. Among bankers, accountants, etc., the distinction is quite well understood. The confusion is caused (mainly) by ignorant journalists. Even as editor of the *Wall Street Journal,* I never completely succeeded in avoiding the confusion in that otherwise estimable journal!"

MARK SCHORER: "No. It offends my ear. I didn't know that it was obsolete. I had assumed that it was Newspeak."

HOWARD TAUBMAN: "It is probably a voguish revival, but isn't fashion a factor in the constant changes in so much usage?"

LIONEL TRILLING: "I *like* it better than 'finance.'"

BILL VAUGHAN: "Relax and enjoy it."

funds solicitation. *See* NOUN PLURALS, USED ATTRIBUTIVELY

funeral service Technically, *funeral service* can be considered redundant since the basic meaning of *funeral* is "the ceremony conducted in connection with the burial or cremation of the dead." It is so regarded by the Associated Press Writing and Editing Committee. However, a secondary meaning of *funeral* is "the procession which accompanies the body to the place of burial or cremation," so there may be occasions when it is more precise to refer to a *funeral service* and a *funeral procession.*

funny/odd *Funny* in the sense of "odd" or "peculiar" is very often heard in informal conversation, as: "He had a *funny* habit." However, in formal contexts *funny* should be used only in the sense of "comic" or "humorous."

funny as a crutch This popular simile has never seemed to us to make much sense, for we cannot imagine any person crippled enough to need the help of crutches regarding them as the least bit amusing.

NOTE: A number of readers of the first edition were kind enough to write us that, in their experience, *funny as a crutch* was always used as sarcasm, to indicate that whatever was said or done was totally unfunny. Peter Haraty of Burlington, Vermont, put it this way: "To describe an oafish practical joker as 'funny as a rubber crutch,' with the proper intonation and emphasis, makes the sarcasm clear."

fun thing *Fun* as an adjective in phrases like "*fun* fur," "*fun* people," and "*fun thing*" enjoyed a considerable vogue, especially among the *fun* people, during the early 1970s. It can be defined as "affording fun; amusing" and should be considered informal. These expressions and the people who used them were a source of irritation to many. Comments Usage Panelist John K. Hutchens: "I propose that it be made a federal offense to use *fun* as an adjective. Twenty years for the first offense; life sentence for second offenders."

fuzz *Fuzz* as a slang term for "policeman" can be traced to the narcotics users and dealers from the 1920s onward. Federal narcotics agents—now known by the slang term "narcs"—were then simply called "feds." The theory is that the whispered "Feds!" as warning of an impending raid could easily be corrupted into *fuzz*. The *OED Supplement* tends to support this theory, giving 1929 as the first appearance of *fuzz* in print and labeling it "originally U.S." However, Usage Panelist Stewart Beach reports finding *fuzz* used as a term for British policemen in a novel written by Edgar Wallace in 1915. So it is possible that our criminal elements simply borrowed the expression from the British underworld. In any event, slang it is.

G

gainly. *See* LOST POSITIVES

gall In the United States *gall* means, in addition to its medical senses, nerve, brash effrontery, and *chutzpah* (which see). In the United Kingdom it has the very different sense of virulence or rancor, and the author of a particularly bitter review may be said to have "dipped his pen in *gall.*"

galore (postpositive adjective) In English adjectives usually precede the nouns which they modify, although there are many instances (notably predicate adjectives) where they follow. Some adjectives are regularly placed "postpositively," as the grammarians say, for example, the "martial" in "court martial." These follow the French pattern, in which the adjective follows the noun it modifies. *Galore,* although it comes from the Gaelic, also is used postpositively, as in "He makes mistakes *galore*" or "There was candy *galore* left after the party."

gambit

USAGE BALLOT QUESTION

Gambit in chess involves an opening move in which one or more pawns are sacrificed to gain a more favorable position. Today *gambit* is often used in the extended sense of any opening move, whether or not concessions are involved.

Would you approve "The owners' opening *gambit* was to stonewall any discussion of players' grievances." Yes: 59%. No: 41%.

Would you approve "The owners' opening *gambit* was to present a complete program, including minor concessions on salaries." Yes: 63%. No: 37%.

ISAAC ASIMOV: "Hell, 'move' has one syllable less."

BARRY BINGHAM, SR.: "The chess usage is precise and simple and should be preserved in its original form."

ALTON BLAKESLEE: "How many people understand chess?"

HEYWOOD HALE BROUN: "It's a useful word and the inaccuracy is harmless."

ANTHONY BURGESS: " 'Gambit' has to involve a loss."

BEN LUCIEN BURMAN: "It is very useful and just the way language should grow. I like it as much as I hate 'stonewall.' "

WILLARD R. ESPY: "I accept 'gambit' as an opening move in a confrontation, whether or not it involves a tactical sacrifice. Such metaphorical modifications are inevitable, and to be welcomed."

ROBERT GOTTLIEB: "Useful."

SYDNEY J. HARRIS: "A good metaphorical word—need not be literal."

JOHN K. HUTCHENS: "A good, terse word that should not be limited to a game."

ELIZABETH JANEWAY: "I don't like either phrase—'gambit' sounds pretentious."

WALTER KERR: "First not a 'gambit' in any way; second might be."

JAMES J. KILPATRICK: "I would keep trying to preserve the precise meaning of 'gambit' but I expect it's a lost cause."

STANLEY KUNITZ: "When used correctly, with the allusion to chess in mind, the word has a beautifully precise meaning."

JULES LOH: "An opening move that involves a ploy, but not necessarily a sacrifice."

HERBERT MITGANG: "No—mixed metaphor with 'stonewall.' "

EDWIN NEWMAN: "Stonewalling is not a gambit, which implies some move."

BERTON ROUECHÉ: "I would simply use 'move' and save two letters."

HAROLD SCHONBERG: "It's prevalent but *wrong.*"

ERICH SEGAL: "It is the triumph of usage over tradition."

WALLACE STEGNER: " 'Gambit,' si; 'stonewall,' no."

BARBARA TUCHMAN: "I would use 'opening move' in both cases. 'Gambit' connotes for me something a bit tricky; a game plan."

DOUGLAS WATT: "But kill 'stonewall' and 'opening.' "

gamesmanship. *See* BRINKMANSHIP

gamut   *Gamut* is sometimes confused with "gantlet," probably because each of them is preceded by the words "run the," as in "run the *gamut*" and "run the *gantlet.*" A West Englewood, New Jersey, reader reported the following sentence in a report on prison riots: "Prisoners were forced to run a *gamut* formed by club-swinging guards and police while being returned to their cells." What was meant was *gantlet* (which see).

A *gamut* refers to a range or extent of anything, such as a complete *gamut* of colors. A notable, indeed unforgettable, use of the word was in Dorothy Parker's review of a play, *The Lake,* in which Katharine Hepburn made her Broadway debut. "Miss Hepburn," wrote Mrs. Parker, "ran the *gamut* of emotions from A to B."

gangway/aisle   *Gangway* in the U.S. is reserved almost exclusively for the portable passageway used for passengers entering a ship, though it is also sometimes used as a peremptory challenge meaning "Clear the way! We're coming through." In the United Kingdom, *gangway* has the very different meaning of *aisle,* as in a theater.

In the U.K. *aisle* is used chiefly in reference to the area between ranks of pews in a church. The *Supplement* to the *OED* reports that the U.S. meaning of *aisle* is sometimes heard and seen in England today but labels it "originally northern dialect and U.S."

gantlet/gauntlet   Reporting a prison riot, *The New York Times* stated that, after the rebellion had been put down, the prisoners had to run the *gantlet* of guards holding oaken clubs. Thus the *Times* observed a distinction between *gantlet* and *gauntlet* that many lexicographers feel is fast disappearing. *Gauntlet* originally had a single meaning—"glove." The phrase "throw down the *gauntlet,*" meaning "to challenge," goes back to the days of dueling, when casting down a glove was a sign of a desire to settle an argument with swords. "Picking up the *gauntlet,*" of course, meant accepting the challenge to duel.

Gantlet, on the other hand, meant an ordeal or punishment, usually one in which the person being punished was required to run between two lines of tormentors armed with clubs, as in the situation reported by the *Times.* Popular usage, however, has made the two words virtually interchangeable in this sense of ordeal. However, in the sense of a challenge to a duel, *gauntlet* is distinctly preferable.

Care should be exercised to avoid the common error of confusing "run the *gauntlet/gantlet*" with "run the *gamut*" (which see).

gaol British spelling of "jail." This was the standard American spelling during the Colonial period for the very good reason that the colonies were simply that—colonies of the mother country. However, with the Revolution, many patriots felt that there should be a drastic break with England in the matter of language. There were even suggestions that we should abandon English entirely in order to demonstrate a complete break of all ties to England. Cooler heads prevailed, but some leaders—Noah Webster among them—saw this as an opportune time to simplify our spellings. By the date of publication of his *American Dictionary of the English Language* (1828) Webster had already published many pamphlets urging this course of action. One of them, *Dissertations on the English Language,* was called by H. L. Mencken "Webster's Linguistic Declaration of Independence."

Webster's treatment of *gaol* in his *American Dictionary* is a good example of his work in this direction. He notes that *gaol* was often pronounced "gole" and "as the pronunciation 'gole' accords with that of 'goal,' a different word, it would be convenient to write and pronounce the word uniformly 'jail.' " At the entry "jail," he takes a much stronger position. The word, he writes, is "sometimes written very improperly *gaol,* and as improperly pronounced 'gole.' " History shows that he won his point—in the U.S. anyway.

gasify Here is a term which was brought from the language of science into newspaper reports of efforts to solve the energy crisis when it first really affected the United States. Seeing no need for explanation of the term, *The New York Times* quoted Senator Lloyd M. Bentsen as saying, "We can now *gasify* coal at $1.46 per MCF (million cubic feet), which is economically sound." Despite the *Times*'s complacency, we suspect that some readers would like to be told that *gasify* is standard English, not slang, and means simply "to convert (a substance) into gas."

gat This is underworld slang. It is a contraction of "Gatling gun," the name of the first machine gun, invented by R. J. Gatling. The first *gats* probably were Thompson submachine guns (also called Tommy guns) of the type used by the Al Capone gangster mob in the infamous St. Valentine's Day massacre. Eventually, *gat* came to be slang for any kind of handgun.

gauntlet. *See* GANTLET/GAUNTLET

gay

USAGE PANEL QUESTION

Panelist PETER S. PRESCOTT writes: "The most important usage you must confront this time around is the use of 'gay.' I am pleased that the more distinguished homosexual writers—Patrick White, Gore Vidal—refuse to use it." The *OED Supplement* cites its earliest record of "gay" in the sense of a homosexual male as appearing in a collection of underworld and prison slang in 1935. By 1969 it had appeared, labeled *slang,* in the first edition of the *American Heritage Dictionary.*

Do you think that *gay* in this sense should now be accepted as standard English? Yes: 36%. No: 64%.

Do you think that, like *gay* used by Victorians in referring to prostitutes, this sense of *gay* may prove short-lived? Yes: 38%. No: 62%.

ISAAC ASIMOV: "This use of 'gay' has killed a wonderful word and I will never forgive the perpetrators."

BARRY BINGHAM, SR.: " 'Gay' is an inexact label, especially when stretched to include the 'Well of Loneliness' type of Lesbian. It is so pat and convenient, however, that it seems destined to become a permanent part of common language."

JOHN BROOKS: "As to the question of being short-lived, I fervently hope so. 'Gay' in the proper sense is a lovely word."

HEYWOOD HALE BROUN: "It may be deplorable in that it steals a meaning but it is too widespread to ignore. Since it is defensive, it will probably be dropped when we're all a little less tense."

ANTHONY BURGESS: "Give it the Cockney pronunciation it had when it was a prison term: 'guy.' That is what I do."

ALISTAIR COOKE: "It's awful but it's here."

ROBERT CROMIE: "A case of linguistic shoplifting and a deplorable one."

FRANCES FRITCHMAN: "This is a real problem. Nobody can really like it. But it has become necessary. Someday a short but non-pejorative term may emerge. Meanwhile the old rule obtains: call people—individuals and groups—what they prefer. 'Homosexual' or 'homophile' sounds foreign, pretentious, sinister to too many people—pace Gore Vidal, a brilliant snob."

RAY GANDOLF: "Homosexuals may call themselves anything they want, and clearly they want to be 'gay.' I mourn only for the loss of the word's original meaning."

PAUL HORGAN: "Journalism may cement it in popular usage."

JOHN K. HUTCHENS: "No, because I hate to see a fine, old poetic word debased. I'm afraid it's here to stay but I hope as no more than slang."

ELIZABETH JANEWAY: 'I really see no choice. The word is very widely used, pace White and Vidal."

DIANE JOHNSON: "Wait and see. I don't think that Gore Vidal would consider himself a 'homosexual writer.' "

WALTER KERR: "Euphemisms keep changing."

STANLEY KUNITZ: "Most homosexuals, and certainly most homosexual organizations, seem to prefer the designation 'gay.' It would be presumptuous to reject their preferences."

ROBERT LIPSYTE: "I have no problem with the use of 'gay.' People should certainly be allowed to name themselves, especially in the case of groups who are discriminated against by, among other things, the establishment language. This includes women, Hispanics, peoples of color, etc."

JULES LOH: "Rarely does language devise a word that looks and sounds like what it means so perfectly as that lovely adjective 'gay.' I resent its theft, especially by a group which has absolutely no right to it."

HERBERT MITGANG: "Homosexuals—like other groups—ought to have freedom of choice on sensitive self-descriptions. A black who wishes to be so called, not 'Negro,' should have that option. So, too, with the word 'gay' which is a word that many, if not most, homosexuals prefer for organizations of their own as well as themselves."

EDWIN NEWMAN: "It won't be short-lived because society now tends to accept terms particular groups prefer to apply to themselves."

MARGE PIERCY: "The word is valuable because it indicates an attitude; you don't say 'Let's go out and beat up some gay men in Provincetown tonight.' When the need to indicate tolerance has passed, the need for a word indicating tolerance will pass."

ORVILLE PRESCOTT: "Homosexuals will keep 'gay' alive because they prefer it as a label for themselves. But it can't be standard because most educated people refuse to use it."

PETER S. PRESCOTT: "Here's an example of a usage severely damaging the language; it must be resisted. We need 'gay' in its old sense; it is an indispensable word now rendered virtually unusable."

F. D. REEVE: "Another middle-class euphemism."

BERTON ROUECHÉ: "The trouble with 'gay' is not only the irony of its application but also its obliteration of a valuable word."

ERICH SEGAL: "It robs our language of a lovely adjective and caused a perfectly legitimate phrase like 'young and gay' to draw sniggers."

EDWARD TRIPP: " 'Gay,' like black for Negro, may be a change without improvement."

BARBARA TUCHMAN: "My negative is because the word used in this sense is meaningless and also because this usage spoiled a perfectly good word."

EARL UBELL: "If gays want to be called 'gay,' as indicated by their organization names—gay alliances, etc.—then they are 'gay,' just as blacks became blacks in the 1960s."

JOSEPH VERGARA: " 'Short-lived or not, the sad fact is that we have lost a fine, useful word. 'Our Hearts Were Young and Gay' just doesn't sing."

GEORGE WALD: "Using 'gay' that way we lose it. I await its return."

DOUGLES WATT: "But capitalizing the 'g' might clear things up."

WILLIAM ZINSSER: "Probably should be 'colloquial' rather than 'slang.' It's most surely here to stay."

gear box   British automotive equivalent for the American "transmission."

gender   *Gender* is a grammatical term whose application is much more common in other languages, such as French, than in English. The *gender* of a noun, pronoun, or accompanying modifier may be feminine, masculine, or neuter and, as such, governs the form of spelling of the word in question. In French, for example, the feminine *gender* of the word for "an engaged person" is "fiancée"; the masculine *gender* is "fiancé." There are only a few words in the English language which are characterized by *gender,* such as the pronouns "he," "she," and "it" and the nouns "man," "woman," "boy," and "girl."

The use of *gender* to mean "sex" in senses other than grammatical is considered "colloquial" by some dictionaries but is frowned upon by careful users of the language. However, it is worth noting that some supporters of the Equal Rights Amendment argue that it would have passed if it had used the word *gender* rather than "sex." That's a semantically interesting point.

generation gap   The *generation gap* is the result of a lack of understanding and communication between parents and children reflecting differences in thought and attitudes. It is a phrase probably invented by sociologists but now in common use. It should be limited to informal contexts. *See also* VOGUE WORDS.

generic words   Many words start in life as trademarks and achieve such popularity that they become *generic* terms. Two of the best examples of this "debasement" of a word—making common property of what was once the private possession of a single firm—are the words "cellophane" and "nylon."

Each was originally a trademark owned by a single company and used exclusively to describe the product of that firm. In each instance the particular product became so popular that the public soon began to use the trademark name to describe not only the original product but many similar or imitative ones. Thus the words became *generic:* descriptive of a kind, class, or group, as opposed to a specific product.

Must a manufacturer lose the exclusive right to a name? Not at all, providing that he zealously protects his trademark by warning all who use it improperly that they will be prosecuted if they continue.

How, then, can an ordinary person distinguish between a trademark and a *generic* term? Usually a trademark word is entered in the dictionary with the first letter capitalized. Thus you will see "Coke," a trademark for Coca-Cola, spelled with a capital "C," while "coke," the fuel, is spelled with a small "c."

The holders of valuable trademarks (Coca-Cola, for instance) are forever on guard to protect those trademarks from conversion to *generic* terms. The word "Xerox" is a case in point. If the Xerox Corporation finds its trademark printed with a small "x" in a newspaper, book, or magazine, you may be certain that the publisher will receive a letter of admonition within a week and, if he doesn't stop the practice, a legal suit may follow.

The classic case of a trademark slipping to *generic* status is "nylon," as noted above, originally a trademark of the DuPont Company. When DuPont failed to prosecute—or, at least, to threaten to prosecute—persons who printed the word with a small "n," it lost the right to exclusive use of the word it had invented.

Interestingly enough, though the Xerox Corporation uses its own machines as extensively as any other giant corporation, its employees do not speak of "Xeroxing" material. They "zero" it and thus avoid any faint chance of contributing to the debasement of their trademark.

genius   From the mouths of politicians and public figures we hear some of the worst abuses of the English language. In voicing support for an officeholder seeking re-election, one such politician spoke of the *"genius* job" which he had done. *Genius* is a noun and should not be used as an adjective. "Extraordinary," "outstanding," and "exceptional" are adjectives which might have been used but not *genius*.

Gentlemen: Before the evolution of the Women's Liberation Movement, the salutation *Gentlemen:* at the beginning of a business letter was accepted without any thought as to its appropriateness. Then "Ms." was proposed as a salutation or title for women regardless of their marital status. In writing to companies and organizations, though, it is frequently impossible to know the sex of the person who will receive the letter and *"Gentlepersons"* has been suggested as a unisex solution to the problem. One alternative would be to eliminate any salutation. Another would be to follow the example of Morris père, an attorney, who sometimes started letters with "To whom it may concern." *See also* MS.

genuine   *Genuine* should be pronounced JEN-yoo-in, not JEN-yoo-wine.

gerrymander The pronunciation JEHR-ee-man-der is today unquestionably preferred by the majority of Americans. Yet, until the 1930s, the hard-"g" version (GEHR-ee-man-der) was given first place in all major dictionaries and most did not even include the soft-"g" version. Elbridge Gerry, the Massachusetts Governor who presided in the first *gerrymandering,* did indeed pronounce his name with a hard "g." How do we know? Well, in our youth, we used to skinny-dip at a sheltered inlet in Cambridge's Charles River known as Gerry's Landing, named for the Governor's family. *See also* BLEND WORDS/BRUNCH WORDS/PORTMANTEAU WORDS.

gerund *Gerund* is the name given a verb form ending in "-ing" when it is used as a noun. Both *gerunds* (as in "Sewing is my hobby") and *gerund phrases* ("Weeding the garden is one of his chores") can be used in any way in which a noun is used: as the subject of a verb, the object of a verb, the object of a preposition, or as a predicate nominative.

get/got/gotten While *get* and *got* are generally regarded as two of the most overused words in the English language, there are instances where their use makes an expression more meaningful than it would be without one of them. If you say, "I didn't *get* to go," it means more than "I didn't go" because it implies that you were prevented from going or didn't have a chance to go.

The use of *got* as a linking verb, meaning the same as "become," is acceptable in informal English. You will find it so entered in modern dictionaries. However, many people feel that the rather ugly monosyllable *got* is inappropriate in such phrases as "*got* engaged" or "*got* married."

Got in the sense of "must," as in "I've *got* to go to the store" should be avoided in favor of "I must," especially in formal speech or writing. "I have" is also preferable at any time to "I've *got.*"

Gotten as the past participle is common in America, although *got* is prevalent in England. "We had *gotten* as far as Cleveland when the car broke down."

Gotten is also used in the idiom "ill-*gotten* gains."

get high. *See* HIGH, GET

get the sack. *See* SACK/GET THE SACK

get the wind up *Get the wind up* is a British informal expression, meaning to be uneasy, jumpy, or nervous about something: "Basil has really *got the wind up* about the coming cricket match."

get up. *See* RISE/ARISE/GET UP

geyser   *Geyser* (pronounced GEE-zer) is the British name for a small hot-water heater, usually located in the kitchen or bathroom.

ghetto/slum   *Ghetto* is a widely used euphemism for the poverty-ridden slums where people, usually blacks, are forced to live because of social or economic pressures—or both. It is really a misnomer, since some of the early European *ghettos* were populated by wealthy Jews who lived there by choice, but its use as a synonym for *slum* has been accepted as standard by the dictionaries.

ghost word   A *ghost word,* as the name implies, is a word that never actually existed, one that was created by typographical error or mis-reading of manuscript and that, through error or calculation, was per-petuated. Our favorite was "dord." The early printings of the Merriam-Webster Second Edition (1934) carried this entry: "dord *n.* Density." What had happened was that, through a really incredible series of mis-chances, an entry ("D. or d. Density") intended for the section on com-mon abbreviations lost its way, wound up in the citation slips for the main body of the dictionary, was restyled and labeled "*n.*" for noun. The editors soon discovered what had happened, but, pretty much for their own amusement and out of curiosity about just how many readers would query "dord," they allowed the *ghost word* to stand through several printings. Finally, more sober-sided editors prevailed and it was dropped.

Another common *ghost word* is "Ye" in names like "Ye Olde Curiosity Shoppe." This results from a misreading of the runic letter "thorn," which simply stood for "th." So "Ye" really was "The" all the time.

gibe/jibe   *Gibe* and *jibe* are pronounced the same but have basically differ-ent meanings.

Gibe means "to taunt or to heckle," as a verb; as a noun, it is an expression of scorn.

Jibe is a nautical term meaning "to shift a fore-and-aft sail from one side of the boat to the other." It also has an informal meaning of "to agree or harmonize" ("His account of the accident did not *jibe* with those of the other witnesses").

Some dictionaries list *jibe* as a variant spelling of *gibe* but it is best to ignore that and preserve the distinction.

gift

USAGE PANEL QUESTION

We usually think of *gift* as a noun, though it has been long recorded in the lexicons as a verb. Oxford records *gift* in the sense of "make a present of " as early as 1619, though noting that it is "chiefly Scottish." In recent years this sense has enjoyed something of a vogue, starting with gossip columnists ("So-and-so *gifted* her with a twenty-carat diamond") and has appeared widely in advertising ("*Gift* Mother well at Christmas time"). Do you find this use of *gift* acceptable?

Yes: 5%. No: 95%.

BENJAMIN APPEL: "It's not 1619; 'gift' is a noun."

ISAAC ASIMOV: "I think we should brick the gossip columnists."

STEWART BEACH: "I think it is dreadful. I wince whenever I see it."

BARRY BINGHAM, SR.: "Vulgar advertising jargon. NO, NO, NO."

ALTON BLAKESLEE: "Between nouns and verbs, vive la différence!"

HEYWOOD HALE BROUN: "The marriage between Oxford and Broadway seems an odd one. I wouldn't use 'gift' as a verb even though I'm Scottish."

ANTHONY BURGESS: "It's time-saving."

ELIZABETH JANEWAY: "There's a kind of anti-charisma about such usages. Were anyone to 'gift me' with anything, even a twenty-carat diamond, I would feel in my heart it was fake."

WALTER KERR: "Whatever the early sanctions, it sounds like one of those noun-verb substitutions."

ALEXANDER KENDRICK: "Even in Scottish the 'giftie' *gies* a gift."

CHARLES KURALT: "No. Neither can we host a party to gift Mother with her Christmas present."

LAURENCE LAFORE: "Loathsome."

JULES LOH: "Horrors! This is like the sportscasters who 'defense' people."

ORVILLE PRESCOTT: "Highly objectionable."

PETER S. PRESCOTT: "Incredible. I had no idea literate people would consider 'gift' a verb."

VERMONT ROYSTER: "Pretentious! 'Gave her' is so much shorter and more expressive than 'gifted her with.' . . . UGH!"

HARRISON SALISBURY: "This is one of the most despicable column-isms. Probably a Winchellism."

HAROLD SCHONBERG: "Barbarous. Like the noun 'debut,' which is so often used as a verb in musical circles: 'He debuted in Carnegie Hall.' "

WALTER W. "RED" SMITH: "I will accept 'gift' as a verb when I am allowed to write that he donationed generously and contributioned unselfishly."

BARBARA TUCHMAN: "Horrible."

HERMAN WOUK: "It disgusts me, and I'm sorry there's an accidental justification in *OED*."

gigo. *See* COMPUTERESE

girl friend/boy friend   There is little logic in the treatment given these phrases by current dictionaries, except in the case of *Webster's New World Dictionary*, which lists them both as single words: *girlfriend* and *boyfriend*. *American Heritage Dictionary* enters *boy friend* (as two words) but ignores *girl friend* entirely. Webster's Third International (Unabridged) and *Random House Dictionary* both give *boyfriend* as one word but leave *girl friend* as a phrase. *New York Times* reporters and copyeditors are told to make each phrase into a single word but Boston *Globe* men and women are told to "make these labels two words." It seems to be a matter of choice but we recommend that, whichever forms are used, they be consistent.

give (something) a miss   This is a British informal expression roughly equivalent to the American "pass it up." Where an American would say that he's going to pass up a particular movie, his British counterpart would be *giving* the cinema (or flick) *a miss*.

give eyeteeth for, would   This is an informal expression which means "prepared to make a great sacrifice (to get something)." The logic behind it is that the eyeteeth (more accurately called "canine teeth") are those which lie directly below the eyes and they are also among the most important teeth in the mouth.

glamour/glamorous   The British spell it "labour," Americans use "labor." Similarly "honour" and "honor," so why not "glamor" instead of *glamour*? We can thank Noah Webster for the simplified spelling of "labor" and "honor." Among the many changes from established British spellings which he proposed in his earliest dictionary, this one—dropping the silent and meaningless "u" from "-our" words—was one of the most logical. It was quickly adopted and only *glamour* retains its "our." This is largely because *glamour* is a word not much in vogue until the last three or four decades.

Already the "u" has dropped completely from the spelling of the adjective *glamorous* and today the spelling *glamor* is recognized by dictionaries as acceptable. In time it may take precedence over *glamour*.

Glaswegian   A *Glaswegian* (pronounced glas-WEE-jun) is a person native to or resident in Glasgow.

glimpse/glance   The difference between *glimpse* and *glance* as nouns is, in a sense, the difference between active and passive roles. You give a *glance* at something or someone but you receive or get a *glimpse* of something or someone.

As transitive verbs, they have entirely different meanings, with *glimpse* meaning "to see briefly and incompletely" and *glance* meaning "to strike or cause to strike at such an angle as to bounce off." *Glance* as an intransitive verb followed by "at" is very familiar in the sense of "to take a brief look at" but it will probably be a surprise to most people to learn that dictionaries also give *glimpse* the same sense and the same function. Despite this, it is rare to hear or read statements such as "She *glimpsed* at the stranger as he passed her."

glisten   *Glisten* is pronounced GLISS-en, not GLIST-en.

glitch   A borrowing from the language of electronic engineering, *glitch* is rather loosely used in newspapers to mean a space-age gremlin, some minor malfunction of an intricate electronic apparatus. By extension, it has come to mean any snag in a procedure.

It is employed in the trade (electronic engineering) to mean simply a notch, spike, or other minor perturbation in the trace appearing on the screen of an oscilloscope. Because the trace is a graphic representation of the electrical signal being fed into the oscilloscope, *glitch* by extension also describes the signal disturbance responsible for the visible effect.

go ape. *See* APE, GO

gobbledegook. *See* EUPHEMISM

goes without saying   On the face of it, this is a foolish formulation, but it is not intended to be taken seriously. When a speaker uses it, he is aiming to please his audience. The implication is along these lines: "You and I are sufficiently knowledgeable that we needn't be told this. For us, it *goes without saying,* but there are others—not so well informed as thee and me—and for them we will say it."

Another consideration, well known to those who have to make speeches but not known to those who meekly listen, is that any good speaker has to use such phrases as transition devices to get from one thought to the next. The human mind can grasp only so many ideas in any given time, especially when its only avenue of approach is via the ear.

So it is that effective speakers usually plan to make any point three times. "Tell them what you are going to say. Then say it. Then tell them what you have said" remains an excellent rule for speech making. The "it *goes without saying*" lead is a very useful one for this purpose.

Goethe   The simplest approximation of the pronunciation of the name of the German poet is GER-tuh. It is not entirely satisfactory, though, since there isn't actually any "r" in Goethe. Frank Colby, in his *American Pronouncing Dictionary,* suggested this: "Purse the lips as if to say 'oo' as in 'foot,' and then, without moving the lips, say 'eh.' "

go for a burton   *Go (or gone) for a burton* is a British slang expression meaning to be killed, especially in a wartime airplane crash. It is similar to the American service slang expression of the same meaning, "He bought the farm." Like its American counterpart, the origin of *go for a burton* is not known and the *OED Supplement One* notes: "None of the several colourful explanations of the origin of the expression is authenticated by contemporary printed evidence."

goggle-box   British slang for a television set ("telly"), equivalent of the American "boob tube."

go him one better   There is a seeming inconsistency here. If you can't "go" a person, how can you *go him one better*? The answer is that English is a highly idiomatic language and the phrase *"go (a person) one better"* is entirely acceptable informal usage. It should not be used in formal writing but it is often heard in the daily speech of educated persons and found in newspapers and other popular writing.

gonfalon   Here is a word which is seldom seen except on the sports pages of newspapers. *Gonfalon* is sportswriters' Elegant English for "pennant." It usually makes its first appearance about mid-August, especially in major-league cities whose baseball clubs have a fighting chance for league leadership.

gong   British slang for "medal," especially one awarded for military service. Quoting the *OED Supplement*: "Wilf, G——, and First Sgt. F—— had all been awarded *gongs* after Dunkirk."

good/well   Of the two phrases "I feel *good*" and "I feel *well,*" the first is the correct one if you are speaking your state of health (physical or mental). "Feel" here is a "linking verb" and is followed by a predicate adjective. So if you mean that your health is good, your spirits are high, and your outlook is optimistic, say "I *feel good.*"

On the other hand, if you use *"feel"* in its literal sense of touching something, like feeling for a light switch in the dark, say, "I feel *well.*" *See also* BAD/BADLY.

good-by/good-bye   There are actually four forms of this word: with or without the hyphen and with or without the final "e." Most dictionaries give one of the hyphenated forms first but there is no real consensus on the subject. The one most commonly seen in writing seems to be *good-by.*

Good show!   British informal expression of enthusiastic approval or commendation.

gook   A derogatory term for a person of another race or nationality. It is most commonly applied to Orientals and is thought to have originated as a Korean word *(gook)* meaning "person," without any pejorative connotations. Though heard most frequently in connection with the Korean and Vietnam conflicts, we have received evidence that *gook* was used as a derogatory label for Filipinos during the 1920s. *See also* DEROGATORY TERMS.

gopher   Originally theatrical jargon for the person holding the lowest, most menial post in the producer's staff. The name *gopher* derives from the fact that he or she is forever being ordered to "Go for cigarettes," "Go for coffee," and the like. Now *gopher* is not restricted to the theater. It is used in many offices.

got/gotten. *See* GET/GOT/GOTTEN

got to. *See* MUST/HAVE TO/GOT TO

gourmet/gourmand   The distinction between *gourmet* and *gourmand* is a nice one and one worth observing. A *gourmet* is a person who is an authority on the selection and preparation of fine foods; almost invariably he or she is also a qualified judge of vintage wines. A *gourmet* is not necessarily a heavy eater. Indeed, he is likely, by reason of the discrimination he brings to his choice of viands, to eat sparingly. A *gourmand,* on the other hand, while he often shares the *gourmet's* liking for rare and unusual delicacies, is primarily one who loves good eating and, usually, plenty of it. The word *gourmand* (pronounced goor-MAHND) was originally a French adjective meaning "gluttonous" and some slight vestige of the earlier meaning carries over into our language.

  Both words came from the French word *gourmet,* which originally meant groom or stableboy. Gradually *gourmet* came to mean any manservant, and eventually the term was reserved for the winetaster or steward. Since the prime requisite of a wine steward is the ability to discriminate among the choicest vintages, the word *gourmet* came to have the meaning of "epicure," a person with refined and cultivated taste in both eating and drinking—and that is the sense in which it is used most accurately today. The correct pronunciation is goor-MAY, with the accent on the second syllable. *See also* EPICURE.

government   *Government* should be pronounced without slurring or omitting the "r": GUV-ern-ment, not GUV-uh-ment or GUV-ment.

The British speak of the Wilson *government* or the Churchill *government* in quite the same way as Americans refer to the Roosevelt "administration."

Government is one of the collective nouns treated differently by the English and the Americans. In the United States *government* is followed by a singular verb: "The *government* is . . . ," while in Britain it is "The *government* are. . . ."

grab   The slang expression "How does that *grab* you?" has become a very tiresome way of saying, "What do you think of that?"

graduated

USAGE PANEL QUESTION

Purists formerly insisted on the formulation *was graduated* in sentences like "She *was graduated* from Vassar." Today the simpler "She *graduated* from . . ." is considered entirely acceptable. However, the formulation "She *graduated* college" is frequently heard. Do you consider this acceptable?

In speech   Yes: 15%. No: 85%.
In writing of an informal nature   Yes: 10%. No: 90%.

STEWART BEACH: "Anyone who would seriously say or write 'she graduated college' will never pass freshman English—I hope."

BARRY BINGHAM, SR.: "An ugly and incorrect contraction."

HEYWOOD HALE BROUN: " 'She graduated from' is not acceptable to me (Swarthmore, '40). Years ago, Herbert Bayard Swope, one-time editor of the *World,* asked me when I had left college. 'Sir,' I replied, beginning as most people did in addressing Swope, 'I was graduated in 1940.' Although he was elderly and heavy, he dragged himself up from an easy chair and lumbered across the room with outstretched hand. 'I haven't heard it correctly used in years,' he rumbled in a voice agrowl with emotion. It was, for me, a ribbon on my diploma."

ANTHONY BURGESS: "I'm doubtful. The British don't even know this usage exists."

STEPHEN H. FRITCHMAN: "I don't even accept 'graduated from Vassar.' She did not do it—the trustees did it."

JOHN K. HUTCHENS: "No college should graduate a girl who says this."

ALEXANDER KENDRICK: "All you can really graduate is a thermometer."

CLARK KINNAIRD: "I still prefer 'was graduated.' "

CHARLES KURALT: "A New-Yorkism, I believe, used by the same people who call it the 'Port of Authority.' "

ELVIS STAHR, JR.: " 'She graduated from' is quite far enough to go."

HAROLD TAYLOR: "Sounds as if you've done something to the college—you've graduated it forcibly."

graffiti/graffito Wall writings have been part of our popular culture since ancient times. Scholars have made collections of them and have made learned analyses of what they reveal of the manners and mores of the period when they were written. Many, if not most, such wall writings were of a scatological nature and were most frequently encountered in the form of scrawls on the walls of public toilets. In recent years, however, writings of a political and personal nature have made their appearance on walls of buildings and on the sides of subway cars. They are generally referred to as *graffiti* and the word is usually treated in the press as a singular noun, though it is actually the plural form of the Italian word *graffito*. A poll of the Usage Panelists shows them about equally divided on the question of whether *graffiti* may properly be considered a singular noun in English. The ballot question, with percentages of the replies and comments of the panelists, follows.

USAGE PANEL QUESTION

A number of words (for example, "spaghetti") have been taken into English as singular, though plural in the original Italian. In recent years the word *graffiti* (whose singular form in Italian is *graffito*) has appeared often in print and in speech with a singular verb. Would you accept "The *graffiti* was held not to be obscene"?

In speech   Yes: 57%. No: 43%.

In writing   Yes: 51%. No: 49%.

ISAAC ASIMOV: "Yes. In fact, it is inevitable that we are going to get 'graffitis' as plural. Who speaks of 'banditti'?"

JOHN O. BARBOUR: "Yes, for the same reason I couldn't say, 'The spaghetti were hot.' "

STEWART BEACH: "I would always go for 'graffito' as the singular and in recent works I see it more and more."

SIMON MICHAEL BESSIE: "Yes, if it referred to a single item."

HAL BORLAND: "If we accept 'data' as singular, how can we stickle over 'graffiti'?"

ABE BURROWS: "If there are several examples of 'graffiti,' I'd use the plural verb. If there is just one dirty sentence, I'll accept the singular . . . grudgingly."

ROBERT CROMIE: "No. Only if stated as this bit of 'graffiti'—or example of. . . ."

A. B. GUTHRIE, JR.: "Yes, as collective."

RICHARD EDES HARRISON: "No. From its nature, 'spaghetti' is used as a collective; not so 'graffiti.' "

JOHN K. HUTCHENS: "I'd *accept* it, but would prefer it as a plural noun with a plural verb."

WALT KELLY: "A borrowed word is understood by its usage, not by its actual meaning or *correct* usage. Very few know the singular and to the borrower it makes no difference."

WALTER KERR: "I think plural in this case."

STANLEY KUNITZ: "No, but the corrupt usage is too prevalent to be denied."

RUSSELL LYNES: " 'Graffito' would seem frightfully pretentious."

FRANCIS T. P. PLIMPTON: "Never."

PETER S. PRESCOTT: "Spaghetti is usually thought of as an undifferentiated mass; not so graffiti, which are often strikingly individual. The problem is that graffito is an awkward word."

VERMONT ROYSTER: "I am so ignorant I do not even know the singular of spaghetti." (NOTE: It's "spaghetto.")

ERICH SEGAL: "Spaghetti is more easily swallowed than are graffiti."

DAVIDSON TAYLOR: "The singular 'graffito' has not lost its usage."

HAROLD TAYLOR: "The trouble is, who would ever say 'graffitos'?"

LIONEL TRILLING: "No. But I would not say, 'The spaghetti are ready; come and eat them.' "

BILL VAUGHAN: " 'Graffito' seems prissy, like 'insigne' for one insignia."

grand. *See* COUNTERWORDS

Grand Prix prize   A *redundancy* (which see). *Prix* is the French word for "prize."

grass widow   *Grass widow* is a term which has fallen into disuse in America with the changing mores of our times. When divorce was more uncommon than today, a divorced woman was called a *grass widow*. The term was also applied to a woman whose husband was absent for a considerable length of time. Her male counterpart was a *grass widower*. In Denmark, a reader reports, the Danish equivalent is used to designate a woman whose husband is off fishing or hunting for a few days. Its earliest use was in England, where it referred to an unwed mother.

gratified/grateful   There are many instances in which *gratified* and *grateful* can be used interchangeably, in the general sense of "pleased." (Both come from the Latin "gratus" meaning "pleasing.") Each, however, has a distinct shade of meaning not found in the other. In the strict sense, *gratified* means "satisfied," indicating fulfillment of a desire or expectation, as in "I was *gratified* that he recognized my right to a share of the profits." *Grateful* may be used to mean "thankful," whether the things which happen or are received were expected or not.

graze/browse. *See* BROWSE/GRAZE

gridlock

USAGE PANEL QUESTION

A recent coinage is *gridlock* to describe the condition in a major city (specifically, New York City) when avenues and cross streets are jammed, so that all vehicular traffic is at a standstill. (During the Christmas season pedestrian traffic was so heavy that even it came to a dead halt at some intersections. This condition was referred to as "pedlock.")

Do you regard *gridlock* as a vogue word, soon to be forgotten? Yes: 24%. No: 76%.

If your answer is "no," would you use it in speech? Yes: 90%. No: 10%. In writing? Yes: 86%. No: 14%.

MICHAEL J. ARLEN: "It's a happy new concept: concrete, brief, and evocative."

ISAAC ASIMOV: "Colorful and useful. I'm a New Yorker, of course."

WHITNEY BALLIETT: (Soon to be forgotten) "Yes, but it's a nice bit of onomatopoeia."

SAUL BELLOW: "There's something grimly attractive about it. It makes one think of prisons."

BARRY BINGHAM, SR.: "I find this a useful and logical new word. It describes a situation frequently met in modern life. New occasions call for new expressions. Also the word has the virtue of being onomatopoetic."

ALTON BLAKESLEE: "Just enforce traffic rules and it couldn't happen."

DAVID H. BRADLEY: "This is a precise phenomenon. It requires a new, unique form. Fortunately 'gridlock' is both phenomenologically and symbolically accurate."

HEYWOOD HALE BROUN: "It will not disappear while New York City is run by realtors."

ANTHONY BURGESS: "My first meeting with the word. It sounds fine. It can't last because it isn't securely locked to its referent."

BEN LUCIEN BURMAN: "It's a new word to describe a new condition, therefore a worthy addition to the language."

JAMES MACGREGOR BURNS: "I dislike the thought of the city as a grid, but this is no doubt an idiosyncracy on my part." (As to being forgotten) "In this context perhaps, but I like it as a word and think it may find some sort of place for itself."

JOHN CIARDI: "I'd rather be left with jam on my face."

ROBERT CROMIE: "This sounds like a headline writer's way of describing a tie football game: ARMY AND NAVY IN GRIDLOCK."

WILLARD R. ESPY: "I welcome this word: a happy invention, and metaphorically sound. It may be a nonce term but from the look of New York traffic the nonce will be around a long, long time."

ALEX FAULKNER: "Take pity on people all over the world who read books written in English. How can they be expected to know what a gridlock is? Gridlock has a long way to go before it acquires the universally understood meaning of Zebra Crossing, if Zebra Crossing has."

GERALD FRANK: "A useful and highly appropriate (because it is visual and graphic) word."

RAY GANDOLF: " 'Gridlock' is a bright new coin, pungent and descriptive. 'Pedlock' is awful and proves that when you open the door to an attractive newcomer, you have to slam it shut before her brother-in-law gets inside."

ROBERT GOTTLIEB: "This seems to me a useful word to describe a new situation. My hunch is the word will last as long as the condition exists."

ELIZABETH HARDWICK: "I admire 'gridlock' as an inventive, interesting and delightfully descriptive coinage."

PAUL HORGAN: "Vivid, and also increasingly applicable."

JOHN K. HUTCHENS: "I might sometime get around to 'gridlock,' though I prefer 'congestion' perhaps with an adjective denoting intensity. 'Pedlock'? Never!"

ELIZABETH JANEWAY: "This is a real dandy. It not only describes, it expresses."

WALTER KERR: " 'Gridlock' is clear and useful."

ROBERT LIPSYTE: "It has a real meaning. I see it as a useful technical word."

JULES LOH: "This is one of those rare coinages that describes precisely, in a vivid word that even looks and sounds right. It deserves a long life. (I put on the brakes at 'pedlock,' though. Sounds like chain gang hardware.)"

BILL MAULDIN: "I don't like 'gridlock' but it makes sense and my objection is probably conservatism."

WILLIAM McGUIRE: "It seems to fill a need."

EDWIN NEWMAN: "I expect 'gridlock' to be with us as long as the automobile."

ORVILLE PRESCOTT: "A useful word to describe a new development in urban decline."

PETER S. PRESCOTT: "It's a vogue word, all right, soon to be more in vogue, and not soon to be forgotten. I'm afraid we need it."

F. D. REEVE: "Depends on how long the paint on the pavement lasts. 'Don't lock the box'—direct from London."

ANDY ROONEY: "Absolutely the best kind of permanent addition to our language. It expresses an idea we all understand and there's no other good word that does."

LEO ROSTEN: "An exact word for a condition unknown to the Greeks and Romans."

BERTON ROUECHÉ: "A truly new word for a new phenomenon."

DAVID SCHOENBRUN: "This is a new coinage, a technical word that is valid to describe a new condition. It is not ugly. It does not offend and it serves a useful purpose in speech. It is not elegant enough for proper writing."

HAROLD SCHONBERG: "It seems to be all over the place and is a nice descriptive new word. Didn't it originally turn up in a science-fiction story?"

ROBERT SHERRILL: "It's useful because it's as awful as the thing it describes."

KARL V. TEETER: "It names a state which is becoming more and more widely familiar. Good word, terse and understandable."

EDWARD TRIPP: " 'Gridlock,' like 'mirandize,' may well be useful as professional jargon . . . I would hope that the vogue use would fade away."

EARL UBELL: "Hooray for new words that express meanings that are difficult to describe in any other way."

JOSEPH VERGARA: "Might be a useful word for traffic specialists."

JUDITH VIORST: "I like the power of 'gridlock.' The word works. I don't expect either the condition or the word to go out of style."

HERMAN WOUK: "This is felicitous coinage. . . . It may catch on, unless we run out of oil and traffic jams."

A.B.C. WHIPPLE: "A good example of how the language can add colorful and useful words and phrases—as, for example, 'laid back' or 'flat out.' "

grieved   The conversion of nouns into verbs is a legitimate process in the evolution of the language but there are some instances of this which can only be described as "linguistic horrors." A newspaper story about a strike of telephone workers over the suspension of one of their number reported: "A company spokesman said the workers returned to their jobs about noon. 'The suspension is being *grieved,*' the spokesman said." *Grieved* are we at this unforgivable back-formation from the noun "grievance."

grievious/grievous   The words *grievious* and *grieviously* simply do not exist, although they turn up all too often in popular speech when *grievous* or *grievously* is meant. Some people apparently associate the words with the more common "previous" and put in an extra syllable.

grifter. *See* BINDLE STIFF/GRIFTER/HOBO

grimace   *Grimace* may be pronounced either grih-MAYSS or GRIM-iss.

grinder/hero/hoagie/submarine   These four words are all slang terms for a popular sandwich made with a small loaf of crusty bread split lengthwise and stuffed with lettuce, several varieties of meat and cheese, and assorted condiments. Each of the terms is heard more frequently in one area of the country than in others but the food it designates is the same everywhere in America.

gringo   In English there are a number of derogatory slang terms based on the land of a person's origin. [*Gringo,* a Latin American's or Spanish American's term for a white foreigner, especially an Englishman or American, is not slang but a proper term used contemptuously.]

The word *gringo* first appeared in a Madrid publication in 1787 and meant any person with a peculiar accent that prevented him from achieving the true Castilian accent. Today, it is used in Latin America to refer derogatorily to any American or Englishman.

groom/bridegroom

USAGE PANEL QUESTION

Some writers feel that *groom* should be reserved for men who handle horses and that reports of weddings should refer to the man chiefly involved as the *bridegroom.* Do you observe this distinction?
In speech   Yes: 31%. No: 69%.
In writing   Yes: 42%. No: 58%.

JOHN BROOKS: "I wouldn't dream of using either."

HEYWOOD HALE BROUN: "The language of weddings is, in any case, a weed patch of vulgarities."

ANTHONY BURGESS: "Yes, but only if the bride is mentioned in the same phrase."

PAUL HORGAN: "No. The horse has receded in general society and the military."

HELEN L. KAUFMANN: "Yes, except when bride and groom are mentioned together and the meaning is clear."

ALEXANDER KENDRICK: "Of course the bridegroom could also be of the horsey set."

CLARK KINNAIRD: "Yes, but there should be a more appropriate term than 'bridegroom.'"

HENRY W. MALONE: "Yes, this is horse country!"

PETER S. PRESCOTT: "No. The bridegroom is clearly one who strokes and calms the bride."

BERTON ROUECHÉ: "Yes. The horse is coming back."

WALTER W. "RED" SMITH: "Any time the subject is a wedding, call him 'groom' and be damned. It's O.K."

BILL VAUGHAN: "Yes, because it's in our style book."

A.B.C. WHIPPLE: "No. There aren't that many stable grooms any more."

groovy *Groovy* is slang for "very pleasing" or "wonderful."

ground floor. *See* FIRST FLOOR

ground-nut *Ground-nut* is the British equivalent of the American "peanut."

ground zero

USAGE PANEL QUESTION

Ground zero is defined as the place at or directly above the detonation of a nuclear blast. Obviously *ground zero* is a scene of indescribable devastation. Yet, increasingly often, we hear it used as a synonym for "square one." On a major television panel show, Hugh Sidey of *Time* magazine said (July 1982), "That starts us back on ground zero." This is far from an isolated instance.

Would you accept "It is time to go back to ground zero and rethink the entire plan?"

In speech? Yes: 6%. No: 94%.

In writing? Yes: 4%. No: 96%.

THOMAS S. BARBER: "On finding myself at ground zero, I'd want to run like hell."

BARRY BINGHAM, SR.: " 'Ground zero' in its true sense would be a hell of a poor place to rethink anything."

JOHN CIARDI: "Go directly to jail. Do not pass Go. Do not collect $200."

ROBERT CROMIE: "If you wish, for a lark,/To glow in the dark/Or be known as a hero/Go back to Ground zero . . . But only a quare one/Would use it for square one."

WILLARD R. ESPY: "Not in speech. Not in writing. Not in rethinking. Hugh Sidey, generally an examplar of good usage, was simply trying to prove that he could say something worse than had ever been said before."

FRANCES FRITCHMAN: "Blasphemous."

WALTER KERR: "Are they trying to render 'ground zero' harmless?"

JAMES J. KILPATRICK: "I'm sorry to hear that my colleague Hugh Sidey used 'ground zero' so inaptly. The precise meaning ought to be preserved."

WILLIAM MCGUIRE: "Aside from being—as you say—incorrect, it's drearily stylish, like 'square one' was. (It was also, originally, British-snob.)"

EDWIN NEWMAN: " 'Ground zero' is an excellent term. It should be preserved in its correct meaning. There is still time."

MARGE PIERCY: "It takes a phrase with a powerful and specific meaning (for which we have no easy synonyms) and sloppily confuses it with another idiom: square one."

VERMONT ROYSTER: "But I have used the phrase 'point zero' to indicate a return to the original starting point."

HAROLD SCHONBERG: "Modish but sloppy usage."

JACK SMITH: "To confuse 'ground zero' with 'square one' is ludicrous, unless it's meant as a sardonic joke."

EDWARD TRIPP: "Why disseminate ignorance?"

BARBARA TUCHMAN: "It's a new phrase—and its meaning is not yet generally understood."

JOSEPH VERGARA: " 'Square one' isn't elegant but it does the job."

GEORGE WALD: "The technical meaning is esoteric. 'Ground zero' is useful as a center, an origin, from which something radiates *concentrically,* i.e. in all directions, not lineally."

grow. *See* LINKING VERBS

Grubstreet *Grubstreet* is used to describe writing which is third rate or produced by literary hacks. Samuel Johnson once referred to dictionary editors as "harmless drudges" and "Grubstreet hacks." In his famous dictionary, he defined Grubstreet as "originally the name of a street in Moorsfield in London, much inhabited by writers of small histories, dictionaries and temporary poems; whence any mean production was called grubstreet." It is used in sentences such as "It is one of the most extraordinary, crooked, malignant *Grubstreet* epistles that ever appeared on paper."

gruntled. *See* ARCANE WORDS and LOST POSITIVES

guarantee/guaranty Either form is proper as a noun meaning an agreement or arrangement to insure quality of a product or completion of a promised action. As a verb, however, the spelling *guarantee* is more common.

guess/suppose In the sense of *suppose,* the verb *guess* has been accepted as proper usage since the time of Shakespeare. In *Henry VI* we find "Not all together. Better far, I guess,/That we do make our entrance several ways." Hence "I guess so" is just as proper as "I suppose so." *Guess,* used precisely, means to make an estimate of the value of a thing or an estimate of the probability of the outcome of a proceeding still in progress without sufficient data to make a proper prediction. *Guess* also has the informal meaning of "expect": "Will he win? I *guess* so."

guesstimate. *See* BLEND WORDS/BRUNCH WORDS/PORTMANTEAU WORDS

guidelines. *See* VOGUE WORDS

guillotine The Anglicized pronunciation of this word is GIL-oh-teen but some Americans pronounce it GEE-uh-teen, a fair approximation of the original French pronunciation. Most dictionaries give the Anglicized pronunciation; a few give both.

gunny sack This may sound like a colloquial expression but it is standard English. *Gunny* comes from the Hindu word "goni" and refers to the coarse hemp fabric, like burlap, from which the sacks are made.

gust *Gust* as a noun meaning "a sudden brief rush of wind" is apparently one of those nouns which has achieved acceptance as a verb, partly at least because of its use by weather forecasters.

The original meaning of the verb *gust* was "to taste; to relish" but over the years that meaning has been lost, for the most part, and today "winds *gust* to forty miles an hour."

gut reaction/gut feeling/gut issue *Gut reaction* is a rather inelegant slang phrase used instead of "instinctive reaction" in an effort to indicate honesty and forcefulness. A *gut feeling* is a deep feeling, based on emotion rather than logic. *Gut issues* are basic issues. Some politicians and businessmen consider these phrases suitable for emphasis but we do not. The euphemistic "intestinal fortitude" for *guts* (courage) is a sadly overworked cliché and should be avoided.

guy As a synonym for "man," *guy* is labeled slang by some dictionaries, informal by others. It has a long, if not entirely honorable, history in England, where they celebrate Guy Fawkes Day, the anniversary of the attempt by Fawkes to blow up the British House of Lords on November 5, 1605. The day is marked with parades and noisy demonstrations, accompanied by much burning of effigies of Fawkes. After this had been going on for a century or two the word *guy,* originally used only for the effigies, became a casual term for any male person. In recent years *guys* has often been used informally as a form of what might be called "unisex" greeting. Young people will often greet a group that includes both male and females as "Hi, you guys!"

gynecology Even those who specialize in the field do not all agree as to the pronunciation of this but the one preferred is gy-nuh-KOL-uh-jee (with a hard "g" and long "i" sound for "y"). Jy-nuh-KOL-uh-jee and jin-uh-KOL-uh-jee are considered acceptable also.

"h," words beginning with. *See* A/AN

hail/hale   The difference is nicely put by the *Boston Globe Stylebook:* "You may hail (signal, salute) Columbia but you're haled (hauled by force) into court."

hair   *Hair,* referring to the covering of the human scalp, is regularly regarded as a singular collective noun in English: "My *hair* was cut last Tuesday." However, in some areas of the country, where many residents are of German descent, *hair* is construed as a plural: "I must shampoo my *hair.* They are so dirty" and "My *hair* need cutting." The reason seems to be that the influence of the original German usage, calling for a plural verb, is still dominant. For example, "Die Haare standen ihm zu Berge" translates as "His *hairs* stood on end."

hairy   *Hairy* is a slang word that is understood and used more by young people than by adults. A *hairy* situation is one which can be characterized as difficult, extremely uncomfortable, dangerous, or potentially explosive.

half-mast/half-staff   Although *half-mast* is the more common term for the position in which a flag is flown as a symbol of mourning, at least one major newspaper insists that *half-staff* be used in its place. Dictionaries generally give a full definition to *half-mast,* with *half-staff* given as a synonym. Either is correct.

half-quart   A *half-quart* is, of course, a pint. However, *half-quart* has been widely used by advertising copywriters apparently convinced that the public will consider a *half-quart* something more than simply a pint. There have even been advertising claims of "great big half-quarts," as though one *half-quart* could somehow be larger than another.

Halifax. *See* SAM HILL

USAGE PANEL QUESTION

Donald Freuhling, interviewed by *The New York Times* shortly after his appointment as president of the McGraw-Hill Book Company, was quoted as saying: "I'm basically a hands-on manager. . . . I'm sure I'm going to be pretty darn busy in the next few months." Do you regard this use of *hands-on* as valid?

Would you use it in writing? Yes: 18%. No: 72%.
In speech? Yes: 18%. No: 72%.

ISAAC ASIMOV: "I'm a hands-on person but I refer to women when I do."

WHITNEY BALLIETT: "Rather frightening to junior female employees."

JOHN BROOKS: "Worst kind of professional jargon; no real contribution . . ."

HEYWOOD HALE BROUN: "Doesn't good old busybody mean the same thing?"

JAMES MACGREGOR BURNS/JOAN SIMPSON BURNS: "Ugh!"

ROBERT CROMIE: "Valid, perhaps, but keep your hands off female employees."

WILLARD R. ESPY: "If 'hands-off' is accepted colloquial usage, as it seems to be, I don't object to 'hands-on.' In fact, I like it."

THOMAS FLEMING: "It's a technical management consultant term."

FRANCES FRITCHMAN: "And this guy publishes textbooks?"

RAY GANDOLF: "I wish Mr. Freuhling well in his new venture, but I suspect that he would feel more at home writing speeches for Alexander Haig."

PETE HAMILL: "Sounds like a phrase invented by the Boston Strangler."

JOHN K. HUTCHENS: "A phony term!"

ELIZABETH JANEWAY: "To this I can only reply: 'Unhand me, sir! And my fellow authors, too! Get thee out of the publishing business.'"

DIANE JOHNSON: "Yes, for a certain effect where 'hands-off' would be expected."

WALTER KERR: "In writing: no. In speech: yes, around the office."

CHARLES KURALT: "'Hands-on' seems a vivid and useful expression—though I'd never use it to describe any book company executive I've known."

WILLIAM MCGUIRE: "Not as offensive as the 'incentivize' sort of neologism, though."

EDWIN NEWMAN: "It's valid, yes, but excessively used."

MARGE PIERCY: "He should watch out for a sexual harassment suit. In my secretarial days, I had a hands-on boss once."

PETER S. PRESCOTT: "Another barbarism."

F. D. REEVE: "You're really socking the jargon and the bombast to us."

LEO ROSTEN: "Is 'hands-on' the antonym for 'hands-off'? Or is it a version of 'brains on, brains-off'?"

HAROLD SCHONBERG: "The only 'hands-on' manager I know was Jesus."

ROBERT SHERRILL: "What's it supposed to mean? Sounds silly."

JACK SMITH: "No. No. It belongs to revival meetings."

ELVIS STAHR, JR.: "I don't like it and I'll bet that feminists abhor it."

WALLACE STEGNER: "Possibly (in speech). Metaphor is as hard to legislate against as alcohol, but it ought to be treated with care."

KARL V. TEETER: "Already established."

BARBARA TUCHMAN: "Maybe there's something significant for our culture about a book company acquiring an illiterate president."

JOSEPH VERGARA: "Okay as used as facetious opposite of 'hands-off.' "

hand up an indictment. *See* INDICTMENT, HAND UP AN

hanged/hung

USAGE PANEL QUESTION

The legal terminology remains "*hanged* until dead" but some authorities accept the alternate past participle *hung* in this sense. Would you accept: "Vigilante law saw many men *hung* without trial"?
Yes: 45%. No: 55%.

SHANA ALEXANDER: "Yes—reluctantly."

STEWART BEACH: "As for the Old West, I would think 'hung' was the most probable form. But I prefer 'hanged,' though not for myself."

CHARLES BERLITZ: "Yes—alternate is archaic."

ALTON BLAKESLEE: "No. Only because I wouldn't admire being hung—or for that matter, hanged."

JOHN CIARDI: "No. Unless the point is to reproduce dialect."

GEROLD FRANK: " 'Hanged' is not only correct, it is far more powerful."

ALEXANDER KENDRICK: "No. If only to distinguish between people and pictures or laundry."

CLARK KINNAIRD: " 'Hung' is the accomplished fact."

RUSSELL LYNES: "When you're 'hanged,' you've had it. Juries (not murderers) are 'hung.' "

PETER S. PRESCOTT: "I do accept 'hung' with reluctance. 'Hanged' means by the neck and is therefore a useful distinction. Jesus was hung, not hanged, from a cross."

WALTER W. "RED" SMITH: "Yes. Though I still use 'hanged.' "

hanging matter, not a "That's *not a hanging matter*" is a British informal expression, meaning "That's not something to take too seriously."

hang out The phrase *hang out* has been in use for a long time, both in informal and slang contexts. When a young doctor opens his first office, he *hangs out* his shingle. Young men with nothing else to do have long *hung out* at drugstores or other public places. "*Hanging out* dirty linen" has long meant "exposing a scandal."

The Barnhart *Dictionary of New English* gives "let it all *hang out*" as Afro-American slang meaning "to be carefree and uninhibited; let one's hair down."

A further use of the phrase was well publicized during the investigation of the Watergate scandal of the 1970s when aides of former President Richard M. Nixon discussed among themselves whether the facts of the scandal should be covered up or whether they should "take the *hang out* road" and reveal what they knew to the public. While "the *hang out* road" may be merely an extension of earlier slang, it has an association with deceit and corruption that may well prevent it from becoming a very popular phrase.

hang-up *Hang-up* is slang which has been in use for some time but so overused as to be irritating. A *hang-up* is a problem, usually an emotional one, or a sense of irritation or annoyance. It can also mean a fixation, obsession, or phobia. The implication is that, whatever the problem may be, it does not lend itself to easy solution. *See also* VOGUE WORDS.

hanky-panky *Hanky-panky,* meaning "trickery," "deceit," "double-dealing," and the like, is sometimes labeled slang but, in our view, should now be classed as informal. It has been part of the language since 1841, according to the *OED*, and seems to us to have meliorated. Incidentally, like "hocus-pocus," *hanky-panky* originated as an item in the jargon of carnivals and sideshows.

happenstance. *See* BLEND WORDS/BRUNCH WORDS/PORTMANTEAU WORDS

hara-kiri There are various pronunciations indicated for this term for the Japanese ritual suicide, but the one most widely accepted is hah-rah-KEAR-ee. Incidentally, the Japanese do not themselves use this term when referring to the ceremony resorted to by high-ranking Japanese to avoid disgrace. They speak of "seppuku."

harass/harassment *Harass* and *harassment,* meaning "annoy" and "annoyance" respectively, should—according to many authorities including the *NBC Handbook of Pronunciation*—be pronounced with the stress on the first syllable: HAR-us and HAR-us-ment. However, many respected announcers and commentators, to say nothing of average literate users of the language, have been paying little attention to the "authorities." As a result huh-RASS and huh-RASS-ment are widely heard in the speech of educated people and both pronunciations must now be deemed acceptable.

harbor. *See* PORT/HARBOR

hard-boiled/hard-cooked   The average person, when referring to an egg cooked in its shell until both the white and the yolk are solid, uses the term *hard-boiled,* since the cooking is done in water that has come to a boil.

Cookbook authors and editors have in recent years come to insist on the term *hard-cooked* on the ground that the water should be kept just below the boiling point for the eggs to be done properly. What they overlook is that frying and other cooking methods can also result in *hard-cooked* eggs if overdone. So, in the interests of both tradition and accuracy, we favor *hard-boiled.* Needless to say, *hard-boiled* will remain popular in its slang sense of callous, tough, and ornery.

hard hat   This term, originally referring simply to the reinforced plastic or metal hats worn by construction workers, became a faintly pejorative label for construction workers themselves after the Wall Street confrontation of spring, 1970, when anti–Vietnam War protesters were attacked by bands of workers wearing such hats.

That the term may also be used in a favorable sense is indicated by the fact that the former Secretary of Transportation John Volpe, deploring outbreaks of violence on the part of some workers, addressed them as "one hard hat speaking to other hard hats." The reference was to the fact that Volpe had been a construction worker in his youth.

hardly   There are two ways in which *hardly* is commonly misused. One is in a double negative formulation. *Hardly* itself is negative and should never be used with "without," as in "Without *hardly* a murmur of protest the children allowed the nurse to give them polio inoculations" or "The pancake batter should be almost smooth without *hardly* any lumps in it."

The other common error is made when *hardly* is used in the sense of "no sooner." "No sooner" is correctly followed by "than," as in "No sooner had I opened the door than all three cats dashed in," but *hardly* should be followed by "when," as in "I had *hardly* opened the door when all three cats dashed in."

hardly ever. *See* ALMOST NEVER

hard-nosed   Originally *hard-nosed* meant little more than "stubborn" or "persistent." Recently it seems to have had a new popularity with politicians who take a "hard line" so that the "thrust" of their policies will reach their targets with plenty of "clout." So it appears that *hard-nosed* now connotes a rather pugnacious determination to see a project to successful completion, with delicacy and finesse cast to the winds. *Hard-nosed* is acceptable in all informal contexts.

   Interestingly enough, though *hard-nosed* in these current senses did not appear in dictionaries until about 1970, the old Funk & Wagnalls (1913) listed it but applied it solely to dogs "lacking a sense of smell."

hardy/hearty   From the world of advertising copywriters, we sometimes get *hardy* as a substitute for *hearty,* as in *"hardy* breakfast food." This is illiteracy. *Hardy* means "strong or robust" and *hearty* means, among other things, "giving abundant nourishment."

harum-scarum. *See* RICOCHET WORDS

hassle

USAGE PANEL QUESTION

Hassle, originally a slang term for argument or fight, has lately appeared more and more often in the public prints. Examples: ASSEMBLY ANXIOUS TO AVOID HASSLE and "GM's speedup *hassle* results in Model-T pace on assembly line." Do you use *hassle* in speech?
Yes: 69%. No: 31%.
Would you approve its use in journalistic contexts, as in the examples cited?
Yes: 72%. No: 28%.
Would you approve its use in formal contexts of speech or writing?
Yes: 35%. No: 65%.

ISAAC ASIMOV: "Yes—a colorful word."
STEWART BEACH: "Never. It's still slang to me."
CHARLES BERLITZ: "The choice may no longer be ours."
HAL BORLAND: "This is a newspaper headline writer's usage. Taken over, I grant, by sports writers, but not generally."
JOHN BROOKS: "A perfectly respectable and quite useful slang word."
HEYWOOD HALE BROUN: "It is ugly and, worse, imprecise."
JAMES MACGREGOR BURNS: "Yes. Not all informal writing is journalistic."
JOHN CIARDI: "Yes. In fact, I like it."
JOHN K. HUTCHENS: "I'm all for this one—a good, short, blunt word with only one meaning, at least as of now."

HELEN L. KAUFMANN: "Hassle is onomatopoetic and has a place in journalese, though not, I believe, in formal writing."

ALEXANDER KENDRICK: "Yes. It's no more informal than 'ruckus.'"

PETER S. PRESCOTT: "It's a useful neologism, vivid and instantly understood."

VERMONT ROYSTER: "Yes. I once had quite a hassle over this with a headline writer and lost the argument!"

HAROLD SCHONBERG: "Accepted usage."

ERICH SEGAL: "Yes. Reluctantly, but recognizing its inevitability."

WALTER W. "RED" SMITH: "O.K. in informal use."

DAVIDSON TAYLOR: "Yes . . . only as humor."

BILL VAUGHAN: "The main problem is that it has become tiresome. Why not 'tsimmis'?"

DOUGLAS WATT: "'Hassle,' for me, applies only to a fairly disorderly dispute involving three or more persons. Thus, the first cited example would qualify."

have to. *See* MUST/HAVE TO/GOT TO

he Usage is divided about the capitalization of pronouns when referring to the deity. We prefer the capital: *He.* For feminists who aver that God is a woman, the correct form would obviously be *She.*

he/him In a sentence such as "I knew it would be *him,*" strict grammatical rules would require the use of *he* in place of *him,* since the verb "to be" never has an object. However, the idiom is so well entrenched that, except in formal speech or writing, "would be *him*" is acceptable. *See also* ELEGANT ENGLISH.

he/she/him/his/her With the increasing consciousness of how the language reflects the male orientation of society, we have seen the coinage of "chairperson" as a substitute for both "chairman" and "chairwoman." There have been rising protests, too, against the continuation of the traditional use of "*him*" and "*his*" when the person referred to is unidentified as to sex, as in "Anyone who crosses that road on foot takes *his* life into *his* hands." Aside from recasting the sentence to avoid the problem, the only solution to date has been to use "*his* or *her*" or "*he* or *she.*" Even feminists themselves have failed to come up with a single word which could mean either sex. "One" is a possible substitute, but it becomes very awkward to say, "takes one's life into one's hands," so the problem remains unsolved.

head/head up *Head* as a transitive verb meaning "to be in charge of" is completely acceptable, as in "She *heads* the speakers' bureau." It is slightly more formal to say, "She is *head* of the speakers' bureau." But the use of *head up,* as in "She *heads up* the speakers' bureau" is unacceptable to careful speakers and writers.

headquarter/headquarters The use of *headquarter* as a verb, though accepted by some dictionaries as standard and labeled informal by others, can still cause careful users of the language to shudder. "The firm, which is *headquartered* in Chicago" is better described as "The firm, which has its *headquarters* in Chicago." Even more distasteful to such purists is its application to a person, as in "He will be *headquartered* in St. Louis."

As a noun, *headquarters* can be followed by either a singular or a plural verb, the choice seeming to be influenced by the content. It sounds natural to say, "The firm's *headquarters* is in Chicago" since "firm" is singular, but "Their *headquarters* are . . ." since "their" is plural, even though it is only one *headquarters.*

head shrinker. *See* SHRINK

healthy/healthful While television commercials urge us to come to Florida because of its *healthy* climate, the proper word in this instance is *healthful,* which means giving or promoting health. *Healthy* should be reserved for those possessing good health, except when used to indicate "a considerable quantity" as in "a *healthy* serving of potatoes."

heart-rending/heart-rendering An unwitting malapropism appeared in a motion-picture review calling a film "funny, *heart-rendering,* brilliantly witty." *Heart-rending* literally means heart-breaking, but it's generally taken to mean deeply moving, poignant, or arousing feelings of sympathy. *Heart-rendering,* on the other hand, would mean literally heart-melting, since *render* means to melt down fat, like whale blubber.

hearty. *See* HARDY/HEARTY

heck. *See* SAM HILL

hectic

USAGE PANEL QUESTION

Hectic originally meant "flushed" or "feverish" and was used chiefly with medical connotations. Now it is often found in nonmedical speech and writing in the sense of "characterized by excitement, wild activity, confusion or haste," in expressions like "a *hectic* ride to the airport" or "a *hectic* party after the opening." Do you use *hectic* in these latter senses?

In speech   Yes: 84%. No: 16%.
In writing   Yes: 78%. No: 22%.

ISAAC ASIMOV: "Sure!"

STEWART BEACH: "While I know the original medical sense of this word, any non-doctor would be a fool to use it that way today. I wonder if even a doctor would. The second usage has taken over so completely that the medical beginning was lost years ago. You would certainly confuse anyone if you went into a room where a patient was lying with an obviously high fever and said, 'He looks quite hectic, doesn't he?' "

BARRY BINGHAM, SR.: " 'Hectic' is a good, strong, specific word to describe a feverish condition or appearance. It is wrong to stretch it to cover quite different connotations, a besetting sin of modern usage."

HAL BORLAND: "I don't use it, but many do and I find it not too objectionable. I prefer the adjective 'frantic.' But *not* 'frenetic,' even though it does have Greek precedent."

HEYWOOD HALE BROUN: "I would use it for a febrile atmosphere at a party, not for a ride to the airport."

ABE BURROWS: "I think the last person to use 'hectic' in the medical sense was an M.D. named Hippocrates."

JOHN K. HUTCHENS: "No. But only because it is such a tiresome cliché."

ELIZABETH JANEWAY: "It seems a legitimate extension of the original use."

ALEXANDER KENDRICK: "No. It has joined the clichés."

CHARLES KURALT: "Glad to be able to say 'yes.' I wasn't even aware of the medical connotations. Words *do* change in meaning, and enrich the language thereby. It's the *hectic,* poorly considered changes to which I object so frequently."

PHYLLIS McGINLEY: "I have no doubt lapsed from my puritanical standards often; but not very often because the word so used is such a cliché."

LEO ROSTEN: "Who doesn't since 1780?"

VERMONT ROYSTER: "I have had a N.Y.C. taxi ride that left me flushed and feverish!"

HAROLD SCHONBERG: "Yes, and so does everybody else."

WALTER W. "RED" SMITH: "This question reminds me of a fact of life. In usage, I accept what I have come to accept and reject what I don't accept. It is that subjective. In my lifetime, 'hectic' has come to have the newer meanings and this seems perfectly reasonable to me. But to make a verb of a noun like 'gift' or 'host' offends me to the soul. Why? Probably because these usages are newer than, say, 'hectic,' and because I'm older. In short, I rule from prejudice."

EARL UBELL: "No. But I've given up explaining the difference."

height   This word is commonly mispronounced as if it ended in "th." In fact there are some people who think that a word spelled "heighth" does exist.

One correspondent argued: "The *height* of the building is 36 feet" and "The building is 36 feet in heighth." These mistaken ideas probably developed through association with such words as "length" and "breadth." The fact is that there is no such word as "heighth," either written or spoken, except as substandard or dialect.

It is true that the Old English form of the word ended in "h" but then it was spelled "highth."

heinous As an adjective meaning "monstrous," "wicked," or "atrocious," the word *heinous* has a singular attraction for people who have never bothered to learn to pronounce it. Most often heard in the phrase "*heinous* crime," it is frequently mispronounced as HI-nus and even as HEE-nee-us.

The proper pronunciation is HAY-nus. A simple way to remember is to recall the lines from *Kiss Me, Kate,* based on Shakespeare's *Taming of the Shrew,* which go: "If she says your behavior is *heinous,* kick her right in the Coriolanus." Nonsensical, of course, since Coriolanus was just a Roman noble about whom Shakespeare wrote another play, but effective.

helicoptered The conversion of nouns into verbs has been a phenomenon of English throughout its history. However, today's broadcasters and advertisers seem bent on accelerating what had been a gradual process of evolution to something approaching the speed of light. One broadcaster spoke of the President being *helicoptered* to an engagement and then going on to Camp David "where he is overnighting."

Neither the First Edition of the *American Heritage Dictionary* nor the Second Edition of the Merriam-Webster Unabridged recognizes the use of the word *helicopter* as a verb, although the Random House and the Third Edition of Merriam define it as "to transport by helicopter." It could be argued that there is an analogy with "to plane," as "He planed in from the coast today," but it still seems that *helicoptered* is a singularly graceless use of the language. As for "overnighting" instead of "spending the night," it seems wholly unwarranted. The preferred pronunciation is HEL-ih-kop-ter, with HEEL-ih-kop-ter also acceptable. But not HEE-lee-uh-kop-ter.

Herculean *Herculean* may be pronounced either her-KYOO-lee-un or her-kyoo-LEE-un.

here *Here,* when placed before the noun in such phrases as "this *here* tree," creates an illiteracy. It is not much better to say "this tree *here*" when "this tree" is perfectly adequate.

hero. *See* GRINDER/HERO/HOAGIE/SUBMARINE

hertz/cycle *Hertz,* a unit of frequency equal to one cycle per second, has been adopted by the scientific community to replace *cycle.* Thus one no longer speaks of "kilocycles" but of "kilohertz," abbreviated kHz. Note that "kilohertz" is the same form for both singular and plural. The *hertz* was named for one Heinrich Hertz, a nineteenth-century German physicist. We hope he's happy with his belated recognition.

he's All American dictionaries now accept *he's* as an abbreviation for both "he is" and "he has." There was a time when grammarians restricted it to "he is" but today *"He's* (he has) been here twice" is acceptable.

he (she) is a man (woman) who ... Persons introducing speakers or guests of honor seem to have a compulsive need to use the phrase *He (she) is a man (woman) who ...* before listing the sterling qualities or magnificent accomplishments ascribed to their victims. Such a statement is not only boring, it is clearly redundant. *See also* REDUNDANCY.

hex *Hex,* meaning to cast a spell on someone or to bring bad luck to a person through occult methods, is a borrowing from the German "Hexe," meaning witch. It is most commonly encountered in the so-called Pennsylvania Dutch country. "Dutch" in this expression is simply a transliteration of "Deutsch" and should properly be rendered as "German," not "Dutch."

high, get As with *stoned* (which see), the phrase *get high* used to be connected solely with excessive consumption of alcohol. Now this slang phrase also applies to the effect of use of marijuana and other drugs. *See also* DOWNERS/UPPERS.

highfalutin/hifalutin/highfaluting *Highfalutin,* with its variations as noted above, was first recorded in print about 1850 as an item of frontier slang. It was originally used to disparage high-flown, bombastic oratory. In fact, there is reason to believe that *highfalutin* was originally simply another form of "high-flown"—to refer to the puffed-up phrases used by old-time Fourth of July orators. Originally slang, *highfalutin* is now classified informal. Our favorite literate ad man, David Ogilvy, once used *highfalutin* this way: "It is a mistake," he wrote, "to use highfalutin language when you advertise to uneducated people. I once used the word 'obsolete' in a headline, only to discover that 43% of housewives had no idea what it meant. In another headline, I used the word 'ineffable,' only to discover that I didn't know what it meant myself."

high noon. *See* NOON, HIGH

highway. *See* TURNPIKE/THRUWAY/PARKWAY/HIGHWAY/FREEWAY/SUPERHIGHWAY

hillbilly   *Hillbilly* is an obvious blend of *hill* plus *billy,* since the first *hillbillies* came from hill country, most particularly the Appalachians and the Ozarks. It is regarded by mountain folk themselves as a derogatory or disparaging term. It is classified as informal, rather than slang.

hippie. *See* BEATNIK/HIPPIE

hisself/theirselves   Since there is such a word as "herself," logic would dictate that there be parallel forms such as *hisself* and *theirselves.* In fact, not too many centuries ago, *hisself* was commonly used by good speakers, especially in Great Britain. Over a period of many years, people who have the most influence in setting standards for our language—teachers, writers, editors, and clergymen among others—have shown a preference for "himself" over *hisself* and "themselves" over *theirselves.* As a result, you now hear *hisself* and *theirselves* only in the speech of people who have not been educated to the more proper forms.

historic/historical   There is a fine distinction between *historic* and *historical* which is not always observed. *Historic* means important in the framework of history, as a *"historic* occasion," a *"historic* building," or a *"historic* landmark." A *historic* building is usually one in which important events took place or one whose architecture is such a prime example of a particular era as to be worth preserving.

   A *historical* novel is one based on a particular period in history and a *historical* fact concerns the truth about something which happened in the past.

historical/hysterical   The one thing these two words have in common is the fact that far too many people insist on using the article "an" before them rather than "a," which should be used. Both words begin with a consonant sound, in this case an articulated "h." As a result, the article "a" is called for. In the case of "honest" and other words in which the "h" is silent, the article "an" is proper. *See also* A/AN

hit   As a slang term, *hit* means "burglarized" or "held up." The expression originated in underworld slang, probably among tramps and hobos, in the sense of accosting a person for money or a handout.

   In today's cities, especially with the high rate of burglary in some sections, it has become fairly commonplace to hear a person say, "My apartment was *hit* while I was at work today."

hit on/over the head   While the phrase *hit over the head* is common, it is more precise to say that a person is *hit on the head.*

hoagie. *See* GRINDER/HERO/HOAGIE/SUBMARINE

hoarding   British term for "billboard." "Mark the obscene graffiti on that *hoarding!*"

hobnob   Far from being slang, *hobnob* is a word of impeccable ancestry. In its present form it has been in the language since Shakespeare's day and can be found in at least one of his plays. In Chaucer's time, it appeared as "habnab," which literally meant "to have and have not." The reference here is to the social custom, practiced then as now, of alternating in the buying of drinks: one chap buys a round, then his companion buys the next. Thus each has, then has not, the honor of treating. In time, *hobnobbing* came to mean any form of social contact on easy, familiar, and informal terms. It is in this sense that it is commonly used today.

hobo. *See* BINDLE STIFF/GRIFTER/HOBO

hocus-pocus   *Hocus-pocus* is an example of a method of word formation known to linguists as "reduplication." It is quite common in slang, especially rhyming slang, and has given us words such as "chitchat," "helter-skelter," "hanky-panky," and "hoity-toity."
    Many people believe that *hocus-pocus* is derived from "hoc est corpus" (this is my body), a phrase used in the Roman Catholic Latin mass. More likely, the phrase is what the Oxford Dictionary calls a "sham Latin" phrase invented by a magician to distract the audience while he works his tricks. *Hocus-pocus* is now standard English. *See also* RICOCHET WORDS.

hodgepodge. *See* RICOCHET WORDS

hoi polloi   *Hoi polloi* means "the many" and is generally used to refer to the great mass of humanity, the common people. Purists shudder at the sight of "the *hoi polloi*" in print, pointing out that it is equivalent to "the the many." However, theirs is probably a futile struggle. Even such conscientious writers as John Dryden refer to "the *hoi polloi*" and in British university slang that is the common designation for students who graduate without honors.

hoity-toity. *See* RICOCHET WORDS

hold/holt   *Holt* as a pronunciation for *hold* is still often heard in many parts of the country. It is especially common in backwoods New England and in the area ranging from West Virginia south through Tennessee, the Carolinas, and on to Florida. It is considered a "dialect variant" of the generally accepted pronunciation. As part of the genuine speech pattern of natives of these regions, it can hardly be objected to in the informal context of conversation, though it would certainly be considered sub-standard in writing.

hold a candle to, not   The expression "he couldn't *hold a candle to* (someone else)" meaning "he's not nearly as good as (someone else)" is standard English. Indeed, it has been part of the language since Shake-speare's time. In those days a person returning from a night at the theater or a round of evening pub crawling would be accompanied by a link boy, who carried a torch or candle. These link boys were considered very low on the social scale, so to say that Tom couldn't *hold a candle to* Harry meant that Tom was much inferior to Harry.

hole in one   The plural form of *hole in one* is *holes in one. See also* PLURALS OF COMPOUND WORDS AND PHRASES.

hollow tube   A *redundancy* (which see). All *tubes* by definition are *hollow*.

holocaust

USAGE PANEL QUESTION

Holocaust originally meant simply a burnt offering but soon acquired its most widely used sense of "great destruction by fire." More recently its use has been extended to apply to any widespread destruction, whether or not accompanied by fire. Would you use *holocaust* in this more general sense?

In speech   Yes: 44%. No: 56%.
In writing   Yes: 37%. No: 63%.

ISAAC ASIMOV: "Yes. Primarily because of the use of 'holocaust' for the Nazi slaughter of Jews."
STEWART BEACH: "Never. It always will mean 'fire' to me and a bad one."
ALVIN BEAM: "No. I suppose I'd use it now probably with a capital letter, only to speak of the destruction of the Jews in Poland and Germany in Hitler's time."
HAL BORLAND: "No. It *still* means g.d.b.f. Let this stand and we will next be calling minor accidents disasters."
JOHN BROOKS: "Yes. It is memorably used in the general sense in *The Great Gatsby* (1926)."
HEYWOOD HALE BROUN: "No. I also refer to a 'libation' only when I pour it on the ground."
JOHN CIARDI: "No. As with 'shambles.' Save that root sense!"

WILLARD R. ESPY: "I was using 'holocaust' to mean 'widespread destruction' for years before I learned it started out as a burnt offering."

STEPHEN H. FRITCHMAN: "No. There are other words!"

JOHN K. HUTCHENS: "Yes—although I guess I would think fire was involved, unless and until I knew otherwise."

ALEXANDER KENDRICK: "No. I prefer the precise to the metaphorical."

ROBERT LIPSYTE: "Yes—in speech. No—in writing—except, perhaps, in the specific evocation of the 6,000,000 Jewish deaths, where the word has been used to a great extent in the original sense."

PETER S. PRESCOTT: "The word has acquired a precise secondary meaning. 'Holocaust literature' pertains specifically to the murder of Jews by any means during World War II."

VERMONT ROYSTER: "No. An earthquake is a disaster, but it might well cause a holocaust."

HARRISON SALISBURY: "Never heard it used in general terms until the Jews began using it for Hitler's wartime destruction. I like its use in that connection—but in no other."

HAROLD SCHONBERG: "Yes. By now it seems to be accepted usage."

CHARLES E. SILBERMAN: "Not to *any* widespread destruction. 'Holocaust' has taken on a new meaning as a result of Auschwitz and Dachau!"

home/house   The word *home* has been overused, especially by real-estate agents, when *house,* dwelling, or residence would be more appropriate. An unoccupied house can hardly be considered a *home* although it may have been and will be again. Presumably the word *home* in real-estate advertisements is motivated by the semantic overtones of warmth, security, and happiness.

In a sentence such as "I will be *home* all afternoon," the preposition "at" before *home* is preferred in formal writing or speech but its omission is accepted informal usage.

Home, Lord   More than a few people have been perplexed by the fact that a Prime Minister of England, Lord Home, insisted that his name be pronounced, not as spelled, but HYOOM. One of his ancestors was a leader of the Scottish forces in the battle of Flodden Field, which saw the defeat of the army of James IV in 1513. According to legend, at a particularly critical point in the battle, Home sought to rally his battered troops and instill new bravery in them. Resorting to the magic of his name to inspire them, he cried, "Home, Home, Home!"—using the conventional pronunciation. Taking him at his word, the troops headed for the road toward home. The next day the third Lord Home, for so he was, decreed that henceforth his name would be pronounced HYOOM.

home economics   The changes which take place in the meanings of words are well illustrated by the term *home economics.* The word *economics* (from the Greek "oikos," "house," and "nemein," "to manage") originally meant "household management," just about the same thing as *home economics* today.

However, the term was soon extended to mean the management of the affairs of a community or a nation as a whole and, in time, came to mean the science of production, distribution, and consumption of wealth.

The original meaning is many centuries (and two languages, Greek and Latin) behind us in the evolution of language. So today we must use the phrase *home economics* when we refer to the science or skills of homemaking, not *economics* alone.

homely   Malcolm Muggeridge, British writer and one-time editor of the humor magazine *Punch,* once wrote that Queen Elizabeth is "a nice, homely woman doing her best to fill a ludicrous role." Many Americans interpreted this as meaning "lacking in physical beauty." However, British usage is closer to the original meaning of "belonging to the home." Thus, Muggeridge meant to use *homely* as synonymous with "simple" or "plain."

home-officed/home-ported   A newspaper story referred to the number of business firms *home-officed* in New York City. At a guess we'd say that *home-officed* was probably invented by a former Navy man. For many decades Navy men have been using the expression *home-ported* in expressions like "The carrier is *home-ported* in Newport News, Virginia." As for us, we feel this bit of Navy jargon could well stay where it started and not crop up in business jargon in the form of *home-officed.* Let's label *home-officed* a barbarism.

homicide   While this word is sometimes given the pronunciation of HOME-ih-side, the preferred pronunciation is HOM-ih-side, with the first syllable rhyming with "Tom."

homogenize   As recently as 1936 the Merriam-Webster Collegiate recorded the pronunciation of *homogenize* as HOH-moj-en-ize. But then *homogenized* milk made its appearance in every American household and the precisely scientific pronunciation went by the boards, directly paralleling the experience of penicillin, which was originally peh-NISS-ih-lin but soon became pen-ih-SIL-in. In any event, the standard American pronunciation of *homogenize* today has the accent on the second, rather than the first, syllable: huh-MOJ-eh-nize.

homographs/homonyms/homophones   Dictionaries differ in their definitions of these three closely related terms, some of them giving *homonym* and *homophone* as synonymous. To us this seems a needless source of confusion, especially since the distinctions can be clearly analyzed from the derivations of the respective words. First, *homographs* (from the Greek "homos," "the same," and "graphein," "to write") are words that are spelled alike but pronounced differently. Examples would be "tear," as in "crying tears" and "tear," as in "tearing cloth." Second, *homonyms* (from "homos" plus "onuma," "name") are words that are spelled alike and sound alike but, because they have different origins, have different meanings. "Bear," the animal, and "bear," to carry, are *homonyms*. *Homophones* ("homos" plus "phone," "sound") are words which are not spelled alike but have the same sound. "Peace" and "piece" are *homophones*. Incidentally, we still recall with affection a nursery rhyme once very popular in our house which is a good example of *homophones* gone berserk. It went: "Fuzzy Wuzzy was a bear./ Fuzzy Wuzzy had no hair./ Fuzzy Wuzzy wasn't fuzzy, was he?/ No, he was a bare bear!" For maximum effect, the last line was usually shouted.

honky/honkie The term *honky* (or *honkie*) is used exclusively as a term of abuse directed toward whites by blacks.

There are two theories of the origin of this term, first popularized by H. Rap Brown. One is that *honky* is a corruption of the term "hunky," used derogatorily in reference to Hungarian or other people of Eastern European ancestry, such as the Slavs, Poles, and Lithuanians.

If this theory is correct, it would constitute an ironic sidelight on the use of derogatory racial labels, since it would mean that some elements among the black population are applying the same label to all whites that some elements of the white community used years ago when referring to minority groups among themselves.

The other theory is that *honky* may be the first element of "honky-tonk" or "honky-tonky," long the name for a low resort patronized chiefly by blacks and "poor white trash," as the saying goes. Little is known of the origin of "honky-tonk," save that it seems to be of African origin and, obviously, was never applied to anything but disreputable dives.

honor/honour *Honour* is British spelling and is seldom seen in the United States except in the phrase "request the *honour* of your presence" in formal invitations, such as to weddings. *Honour* is insisted on by those busy ladies who make a rather parasitical living by arranging weddings, debutante cotillions, and the like. The very essence of their approach to the work is an insistence on frills, fuss, and elegance. In their view, elegance connotes starchy formality, and formality in turn evokes the spirit of Edwardian England.

hooch/hootch In Prohibition days, bootleg whisky was known by the slang term *hooch* or *hootch.*

During our involvement in the Vietnam War, *hooch*—still slang— was used to refer to the small native huts found in many Vietnamese villages. The Vietnamese *hooch* is probably a variation of "hutch," a small makeshift structure similar to a coop made for the confinement of small animals.

The Prohibition *hooch* got its name from a tribe of Alaskan Indians, the Hoochinoos, who distilled a notably potent brand of firewater.

hooter   British term for a loud whistle or siren formerly used for a "works" (factory) signal at 6 A.M., noon, and closing-down time. *Hooter* is also sometimes used as the equivalent of the American automobile "horn."

hopeful. *See* OPTIMISTIC/HOPEFUL

hopefully   *Hopefully* in the sense of "in a hopeful manner" (as "The mayor aspires *hopefully* for higher office") has been a part of the language for centuries. The *OED* gives examples of its appearance in print as far back as 1639. However, in recent years *hopefully* has been very widely used in the sense of "we hope" or "it is to be hoped" (as "*Hopefully* the Dodgers will win the doubleheader"). Panelist PAUL HORGAN, commenting on this latter use, writes: "We've had 'hopefully' as a hanging adverb for a while now. Imagine my dismay to see 'thankfully' in a *New York Times* movie review used in similar construction. Are we to put up with 'Thankfully, son of Hopefully'?"

The prevailing opinion of the panelists would indicate that they reject *hopefully* in the second sense (and, by implication, "thankfully") in writing, though they are somewhat more tolerant of it in speech. One panelist who takes an intransigent stand in the matter is JEAN STAFFORD, who writes: "On the back door of my house there is a sign which I had made by a gifted calligrapher. It reads: THE WORD 'HOPEFULLY' MUST NOT BE MISUSED ON THESE PREMISES. VIOLATORS WILL BE HUMILIATED."

The question put to the panelists, with the percentages of replies, follows, together with typical comments, many of them just as emphatic as Miss Stafford's.

USAGE PANEL QUESTION

The adverb *hopefully* is often heard in the sense of "we hope" in such sentences as "*Hopefully,* the war will soon be ended." Would you accept this formulation?

In speech   Yes: 42%. No: 58%.
In writing   Yes: 24%. No: 76%.

SHANA ALEXANDER: "No. Slack-jawed, common, sleazy."
ISAAC ASIMOV: "This particular usage grates on me."

HAL BORLAND: "I have fought this for some years, will fight it till I die. It is barbaric, illiterate, offensive, damnable, and inexcusable."

JOHN BROOKS: "No. Although to my shame I once wrote it before I learned to hate it. And there may be a lesson in that."

BEN LUCIEN BURMAN: "I can't see any reason why not."

ROBERT CRICHTON: "Yes. It depersonalizes the expression and that is good. No one cares if *I* hope the war is over and *we* has to be defined—the adverb makes a kind of general unspecific yearning that suits many occasions."

THOMAS FLEMING: "Mea culpa—I can see myself writing it—but it's wrong."

A. B. GUTHRIE, JR.: "I have sworn eternal war on this bastard adverb."

RICHARD EDES HARRISON: "Strike me dead if you ever hear me using it in this way."

PAUL HORGAN: "This 'suspended' adverb must be done away with."

JOHN K. HUTCHENS: "Yes, but chiefly because there's really nothing to be done about it."

ELIZABETH JANEWAY: "Sloppy but useful."

WALT KELLY: "Again, we should know better. It is a sloppy elegantism."

ALEXANDER KENDRICK: "No, if only because it is so overused."

WALTER KERR: "We're losing."

STANLEY KUNITZ: " 'Hopefully' we can scotch this vulgarism."

CHARLES KURALT: "Chalk squeaking on a blackboard is to be preferred to this usage. I don't accept it, but I fear we are all stuck with it."

LAURENCE LAFORE: "No, no, no, no."

JULES LOH: "Please tell me I'm not alone in rejecting this."

PHYLLIS McGINLEY: " 'Hopefully' so used is an abomination and its adherents should be lynched."

ORVILLE PRESCOTT: "Popular jargon at its most illiterate level."

PETER S. PRESCOTT: "It is ungrammatical, and therefore not in my writing (though I once wrote it, to my shame)."

F. D. REEVE: "No. *Very* hopefully."

FRANCIS ROBINSON: "You ask if I would accept it and I say No but I have to. It is awful!"

LEO ROSTEN: "This is simply barbarism. What does 'hopefully' modify? Does a war 'hope'?"

WALTER W. "RED" SMITH: "I deplore it, I curse it and I'm losing the war."

HAROLD TAYLOR: "This is one that makes me physically ill."

EARL UBELL: "Hopefully has become a shorthand for 'I hope,' and it eliminates the pronoun in third-person writing."

JUDITH VIORST: "I want to correct everyone who makes this mistake."

T. HARRY WILLIAMS: "The most horrible usage of our time."

HERMAN WOUK: "I don't like chalk squeaking on blackboards either."

In view of the continued controversy over the use of *hopefully,* we re-submitted the question to the panel and found that resistance to its use had grown, rather than lessened, within less than a decade.

USAGE PANEL QUESTION—SECOND EDITION

In balloting for the first edition of this book *hopefully,* used in the sense of "we hope" ("*Hopefully* the Dodgers will win the pennant"), was voted acceptable in speech by nearly one-half of the panelists, though 76% found it unacceptable in writing. Feelings ran high among those opposed, many agreeing with Jean Stafford, who mentioned a sign posted on the back door of her house: "The word *'hopefully'* must not be misused on these premises. Violators will be humiliated."

Do you think that this use of *hopefully* is now so frequently heard in the speech of literate Americans that it should be considered acceptable in conversational speech? Yes: 30%. No: 70%.

In writing? Yes: 17%. No: 83%.

MICHAEL J. ARLEN: "There is no reason for someone who knows better to use 'hopefully.' Besides, in most instances it is unnecessary—a clumsy bit of padding."

ISAAC ASIMOV: "It may come in, but never with my approval."

WHITNEY BALLIETT: "Yes, hopefully."

SAUL BELLOW: "I'm with Jean Stafford."

BARRY BINGHAM, SR.: "I can see no legitimate excuse for this misuse of a respectable word. It is sloppy and lazy."

ALTON BLAKESLEE: "I am whelmed by its common acceptance."

DAVID H. BRADLEY: "No, just because a majority of jerks use language unprecisely . . ."

HEYWOOD HALE BROUN: "I quarrel with the unsupported conclusion that this use of 'hopefully' is found in the speech of literate Americans. Those who misuse it are not literate."

JAMES MACGREGOR BURNS: "People should speak as they write. But heaven forbid vice versa!"

JOHN CIARDI: "I shall continue to drink hopefully."

ROBERT CROMIE: "Hopefully not."

WILLARD R. ESPY: "A lexicographer may have to record that 'hopefully' in the sense of 'we hope' is accepted, but I do not have to accept that it is acceptable. It's not."

ALEX FAULKNER: "If I cleaned up at Las Vegas I would cheerfully give all my winnings to anyone who promised never to use 'hopefully' again."

RAY GANDOLF: " 'Hopefully' was the defending champion until 'as far as . . .' came along and knocked it out of first place."

SID GOLDBERG: "The perpetrators have, I believe, won this battle."

ROBERT GOTTLIEB: "No. It's still ungrammatical and unsettling."

ELIZABETH HARDWICK: "I deplore the ubiquitous 'hopefully' and find that often it is used out of a wish to be decorative and refined rather than merely clear. In teaching I have asked students if they would say, 'fearfully it will rain for the picnic,' but they often appear so pleased with the possibility I begin to fear 'fearfully' is coming next. There is no reason to be optimistic about stemming the tide and I suppose it will soon be prudent to surrender."

SYDNEY J. HARRIS: "Hopefully it will dwindle and disappear but I don't have much hope."

JOHN K. HUTCHENS: "No, in the sense that I myself do not use it, but I reluctantly realize that it is probably here to stay."

ELIZABETH JANEWAY: " 'Hopefully' is useful or it would not be used so universally. There is no easy replacement. We do know what it means when it's used, so it's not a muddle-producer. . . . I'd try to avoid it in writing, I guess, but I expect it would take forethought, and I don't blame anyone who falls into it."

DIANE JOHNSON: "This battle is lost."

E. J. KAHN, JR.: "Anybody using 'hopefully' in the non-fiction course I teach gets one hundred lashes."

WALTER KERR: "We'll have to keep saying 'no' on all levels to save the word."

JAMES J. KILPATRICK: "I positively refuse to give a home to the orphan 'hopefully.' Bill Safire, the quitter, has surrendered on this one. I haven't."

STANLEY KUNITZ: "Never!"

JULES LOH: "Maybe the battle is hopeless. Maybe 'literate' Americans are abandoning ship. But why? Why diffuse a word's meaning for the convenience of illiterates? No, on this one I will go down lashed to the mast."

DWIGHT MACDONALD: "NO, both ways. Adds zero to the language; just mucks it up."

WILLIAM MCGUIRE: "Hold the line as long as possible!"

EDWIN NEWMAN: " 'Hopefully' misused is dreary, jarring and evasive. Who's doing the hoping? Why not say so?"

ORVILLE PRESCOTT: "Still inexcusable."

PETER S. PRESCOTT: "Hope it never will be."

LEO ROSTEN: " 'Hopefully' is absurd, no matter who uses it or approves of it. 'Hopefully, the gnats won't bite' attributes both self-consciousness and virtue to insects."

BERTON ROUECHÉ: "I don't use it."

VERMONT ROYSTER: "Hopefully, I will hear no more hereafter of this issue."

DAVID SCHOENBRUN: "I have fought the good fight against the misuse of 'hopefully.' But the fight is lost, in speech. I will fight to the end against the misuse in writing."

HAROLD SCHONBERG: "I hate it. But it is omnipresent. Hopefully, I hope that it will disappear but I see little hope that will happen."

JACK SMITH: "I don't use it myself, even in speech. I don't object to it strictly on grammatical grounds; it has become such a commonplace that everyone sticks it in where hope isn't even involved."

ELVIS STAHR, JR.: "This is one on which we should hold out until the bitter end."

HAROLD TAYLOR: "It is one of the worst things anyone could possibly say."

KARL V. TEETER: "It is, in fact, a cliché, which should be considered in using it in writing."

BARBARA TUCHMAN: "In spite of all the disapproval of my learned colleages, I think 'hopefully' is here to stay and rightfully, for one very good reason: that it is *needed* and when a word is truly and really needed and there is no substitute ('It is to be hoped' is unusable) it *should* enter the language, no matter if technically ungrammatical."

JUDITH VIORST: "I can no longer answer this question. I used to find 'hopefully' acceptable, but some of the people I most love and admire scorn it. As a result I have become a pessimist."

DOUGLAS WATT: "Much to its discredit is the fact that it's become worn to death in such usage."

A.B.C. WHIPPLE: "It still is an abomination."

HERMAN WOUK: "A lost cause in conversation. An infelicitous usage which caught on. In serious writing as an adverb it remains unthinkable."

CHARLOTTE ZOLOTOW: "Spoken or written, it's a misuse—another that destroys the *quality* of language."

hornswoggle   *Hornswoggle,* meaning "to cheat, swindle, or deceive with larcenous intent," has been around in American speech for more than a century and a half. Despite its longevity, *hornswoggle* is still recorded as regional dialect or slang. According to Mencken, an Australian student of language once remarked that *hornswoggle* is "the only American coinage which has left us breathless with admiration."

Experts agree that it is an American coinage that can be traced to the early days of the nineteenth century. It is still used in daily speech in some rural areas of the country.

hors d'oeuvres   This French phrase has been Americanized both as to meaning and as to formation of the plural. In French, more than one *hors d'oeuvre* are still *hors d'oeuvre,* because the phrase means "outside the meal." When Americans adopted the term to apply to small appetizers served before a meal, they simply added an "s" to indicate more than one such appetizer. Thus *hors d'oeuvres* as the plural form became standard usage in the United States.

host/co-host

USAGE PANEL QUESTION

Host as a transitive verb is relatively new—the creation, perhaps, of radio and
TV. However, it has moved into general use in news dispatches, such as
"Miami may, after all, *host* the Republican Convention." Do you approve
of this use of *host*?
In speech   Yes: 30%. No: 70%.
In writing   Yes: 29%. No: 71%.
What about *co-host,* as in "Henry Fonda and Peter Ustinov will *co-host* the
Tony Awards"?
Yes: 35%. No: 65%.

ISAAC ASIMOV: "Yes. Useful new use, inoffensive to my ear. ['Co-host'] How
else would you say it in two syllables?"
HEYWOOD HALE BROUN: "No. 'Host' like 'gift' is one of those gritty usages
born of three-dot writing."
ABE BURROWS: "I don't approve but I think we're stuck with 'host' as a verb
for good."
ROBERT CRICHTON: "I don't like the use or the word much, but it does get
itself understood, and quickly."
S. I. HAYAKAWA: "No. But I guess it can't be helped on TV."
PAUL HORGAN: "No . . . though 'show-biz' really lives on relaxed usages,
preferably 'clever.' "
JOHN K. HUTCHENS: "Yes, because it does save a little time without being
unduly offensive."
CLARK KINNAIRD: "No. Neither is a host, entertaining guests at his own
expense."
LAURENCE LAFORE: "No. An odious usage."
PHYLLIS MCGINLEY: "These are all distasteful to me but I am on the losing
side."
ORVILLE PRESCOTT: "Vile jargon! ['Co-host'] Worse!!"
PETER S. PRESCOTT: "No! It is no more a verb than 'gift' and 'author.' This
business of making all succinct nouns into verbs must be discouraged."
HARRISON SALISBURY: "God, NO!"
HAROLD SCHONBERG: "Yes. Even though I don't like it. It's now part of the
language."
CHARLES E. SILBERMAN: "No. It is a TV term, and seems to fit that context."
ELVIS STAHR, JR.: "I'm resigned to it."
DAVIDSON TAYLOR: "It's a part of usage whether I approve or not."
BARBARA TUCHMAN: "Almost as bad as 'gift' as a verb—let's not be vulgar-
ized by TV-radio usages."

EARL UBELL: "No . . . and I'm in TV!!!"
A.B.C. WHIPPLE: "Yes. If you accept one, you have to accept the other."
HERMAN WOUK: "Journalism, yes; belles-lettres, no."

hot pants   *Hot pants* is a slang term that has been a part of American speech at least since the 1920s. At that time it was used to describe the state of arousal of members of either sex who were more than ordinarily excited by the presence of a member or members of the opposite sex. As one dictionary, labeling the expression "vulgar slang," rather primly put it: "*Hot pants* means anxious sexual desire." During the 1960s clothing manufacturers put out lines of extremely abbreviated shorts for women and gave them the hitherto taboo label *hot pants.* According to a 1974 fashion report in *The New York Times,* the *hot pants* designation was already obsolescent and they are now simply "short shorts," a term long ago used by the defunct *Liberty* magazine to designate short short stories. The more things change . . .

hot shot. *See* RICOCHET WORDS

hot walker   A *hot walker* is slang for a person who walks "hots." And a "hot" is a horse heated up after long practice runs. The *hot walker* takes the horse for a slow walk, so that it can gradually cool off. The *hot walker* is the lowest rung on the ladder to racing stardom. Virtually every jockey has served an apprenticeship as a *hot walker.* He or she is just about the equal in rank of the theatrical *gopher* (which see).

house. *See* HOME/HOUSE

house, dress the   Theatrical jargon for the technique whereby box-office managers (often called "treasurers") assign seats to ticket purchasers with an eye toward making the house look well filled, even if it is not.

house, paper the   Theatrical jargon for the technique of issuing lots of free passes ("paper" in theatrical slang) so as to guarantee a capacity audience.

housen/housens   *Housen* and *housens* are now archaic plurals of *house,* still sometimes heard among old people on Cape Cod, among the so-called Jackson whites of the Ramapo Mountains in northern New Jersey, and, though rarely, from Virginia as far west as Missouri. At one time English had plurals ending in "-en" but now there are very few left, with "oxen," "children," and "brethren" being the most notable.

housewife/househusband/houseperson   With some of the changes that are evolving in marriage relationships and in the roles of men and women in the home, much has been said and written about the choice of words which will reflect such changes. *Housewife* has long been a term for a woman who did not work outside the home and who devoted her time to the functions necessary to maintain a home. When a few married couples decided that it was more to their liking for the wife to be employed outside the home while the husband stayed home and did the cooking and cleaning and other chores, *househusband* was coined. *Houseperson* was then proposed as a means of eliminating any hints of *sexism* (which see). Neither *househusband* nor *houseperson* has made its way into the standard dictionaries, and they are not likely to be widely used until and unless the reversal of roles becomes more common.

In the late 1960s we asked the women readers of our column, many of whom reported being offended by the phrase "just a *housewife,*" what term they would find acceptable as a description of their role. "Homemaker" was the choice of the large majority of the hundreds of women who responded, although there were many other suggestions, some of them highly imaginative. Not one *househusband* was reported at that time.

hover The Louisville *Courier-Journal* has an in-house publication which calls attention to some of the errors which make their way into print. One of these was a reference to "the roof that *hovers* over the stadium." "Sounds unsafe, at the least" was the comment following the quotation.

how come? This formulation, as in *"How come* you always eat standing up, Mother?"* is an informal abbreviation of "How does it come about that . . . ?" and as such is acceptable as informal idiom. It is not acceptable in formal speech or writing.

how ever When used to begin a question, the phrase *how ever* may express wonder or admiration as well as curiosity. The *ever* in such instances serves as an intensive and can be placed either following *how* or later in the sentence, as in *"How ever* did you manage to drive home without headlights?"* or *"How* did you *ever* manage to drive home without headlights?"*

however/nevertheless Purists, including Panelist WILLIAM O. DOUGLAS, contend that *however* in the sense of *nevertheless* should not be used at the beginning of a sentence. *However* (with a bow to Justice Douglas), it has become standard practice to do so with the understanding that the comma which follows *however* in such cases indicates that its meaning is *nevertheless.* When it is used in the sense of "no matter how," as in *"However* short of funds he might be, he always paid his pledge to the church," there is also no question as to the propriety of using it at the beginning of a sentence. *See also* CONJUNCTIONS/CONJUNCTIVE ADVERBS.

hubris   *Hubris* (pronounced HYOO-bris) is not a new word; indeed, we took it directly from the Greek, where it means insolence or outrage. However, it has been very voguish in recent years in the sense of arrogance, over-bearing pride, and presumption. You might call it the Park Avenue equivalent of *chutzpah* (which see).

hugger-mugger. *See* RICOCHET WORDS

human/human being

USAGE PANEL QUESTION

Panelist WILLIAM C. VERGARA writes: " 'Human beings' seems to me redundant, though long established in literature. Why can't we settle for simply 'humans'?" Would you use *human* in this sense?

In your own speech   Yes: 46%. No: 54%.

In your writing   Yes: 43%. No: 57%.

BENJAMIN APPEL: " 'Humans' strikes me as stiff—it is the 'beings' with associations of mind, soul, culture, etc. that I find important."

ISAAC ASIMOV: "I *do* use 'humans' constantly. All science fiction writers do."

CHARLES BERLITZ: " 'Human' was an adjective when last I looked."

HAL BORLAND: "True, 'canine' and 'equine' are used as nouns, but to me they are barbarisms."

JOHN BROOKS: " 'Human' is terrible!"

BEN LUCIEN BURMAN: "Only satirically, as 'He's a queer human.' "

ABE BURROWS: "It's a tossup. Curiously enough, 'humans' seems stronger than 'human beings.' I'd use it to make a literary point."

JOHN CIARDI: "The fact is I tend to 'human beings' but often let 'humans' stand."

STEPHEN H. FRITCHMAN: "No. This may be another lost cause but I feel strongly about rescuing it."

PAUL HORGAN: "No. Custom—depends on context."

LAURENCE LAFORE: "I should not use either—'humanity' or 'people.' "

DWIGHT MACDONALD: "No. I agree—it is redundant. But 'human' strikes my ear as sentimental, in fact all too human."

WRIGHT MORRIS: "This is a matter of style and taste—on occasion, one is preferable, then the other."

EDWIN NEWMAN: "No. My wife rescued me from this one many years ago."

ORVILLE PRESCOTT: "The matter is one of taste and an ear for language."

PETER S. PRESCOTT: "No. Obviously, 'human' is an adjective."

RICHARD H. ROVERE: "Yes, but with no strong feeling."

MARK SCHORER: "See Rollo May, who suggests that we think of 'being' as a participle—*a living person.*"

WALTER W. "RED" SMITH: "Yes, though I prefer 'immortal souls.' "

LIONEL TRILLING: " 'Human beings' seems to me sanctified by long usage."

BARBARA TUCHMAN: "My agent thinks 'human beings' is cause for desertion, but it has never bothered me."

BILL VAUGHAN: "Yes, but I don't object to 'human being.' "

humbug   This amusing word for "hoax" or "fraud" first appeared during the eighteenth century as a bit of popular slang and quite possibly came out of the jargon of the underworld. It first was recorded by the Earl of Orrery, who termed it a "new-coined expression which is only to be found in the nonsensical vocabulary and sounds disagreeable and absurd." Then Charles Dickens used it in *A Christmas Carol,* in which Ebenezer Scrooge, the master miser, retorted, "Bah, humbug," to the Spirit of Christmas.

It has lost the label of slang and is now a perfectly acceptable word, meaning either a hoax or the perpetrator of a hoax. It also means "nonsense."

hundred/hundreds   When a specific number is stated, the word is used in its singular form, as in "three *hundred* dollars." When the number is not specified, it becomes plural: "*hundreds* of dollars."

-hurst   In Anglo-Saxon, the suffix *hurst* meant "wooded hill" and it appears in many English place names, Sandhurst, where the Royal Military College is located, being one. In the U.S. it has been widely used in place names, like Pinehurst, chiefly to give a feeling of exclusivity.

Hush my mouth! *See* SHUT (HUSH) MY MOUTH!

hustings   *Hustings* in American speech usually refers figuratively to a place where political activities are held. *Hustings* is plural in form but singular in construction. The most common American use is in expressions such as "He's mounting the *hustings*" or "He'll be on the *hustings* in a month or so," meaning that he will start his political campaigning at that time. In England the *hustings* was literally the raised platform on which candidates for Parliament used to stand when addressing their constituents.

hyphen   Over the past half-century, largely through the influence of lexicographers and of copyeditors and printers who slavishly follow the dictates of lexicographers, there has been a marked tendency to write and print compound words solid and to eliminate such marks as the *hyphen* and the *dieresis* (which see). A case in point is "cooperate," which formerly might be written "co-operate" or "coöperate," but now is almost invariably written solid. Many writers, especially newspapermen, deplore this tendency because the resulting solid compounds often mislead and confuse the reader.

Some years ago a reader of our column commented on a distinction drawn by the late Dr. Sigmund Spaeth between "singing-teacher" and "singing teacher." It was, simply, that a "singing-teacher" is one who teaches singing, while a "singing teacher" can be a teacher of anything who just happened to raise his voice in song. So far as we know, nobody has yet proposed to write the expression solid—singingteacher—but that too may come.

The whole matter of hyphenation is fraught with peril. Some years ago a distinguished reference-book publisher commissioned a whole book on the subject to be written by a woman who was chief arbiter on commas and hyphens for the U.S. State Department. They could not, thought the publisher, find a better-qualified authority.

The book was finally printed, at very substantial expense, and the publisher made the belated discovery that almost no one in the business of editing and printing books, newspapers, or magazines agreed with their author. It seems that she had been conducting a one-woman feud with all other agencies of the government. In hundreds of cases she used hyphens when all others wrote the words solid and vice-versa.

So the one thing that can be said with certainty about *hyphens* was well said by John Benbow in the style book of the Oxford University Press: "If you take hyphens seriously, you will surely go mad."

For an example of the confusion that can be caused by injudicious omission of *hyphens,* see the Usage Panel Question and comments that follow.

USAGE PANEL QUESTION

On Ballot Six one question (concerning *flammable/inflammable*) referred to *non-native speakers.* Several panelists questioned the omission of a *hyphen* in "nonnative." The "rule" promulgated by the Government Printing Office style book and various other style guides is, briefly, that all compounds should be written solid unless a mandatory capital is involved (for example, "trans-Canadian") or an awkward series of three consonants occurs ("bell-like"). Many writers are vexed by the appearance of words that result in some instances. In the particular case cited, BARBARA TUCHMAN comments: "For God's sake, restore the hyphen! No advantage is gained by its elimination and the results, as in this case, frequently come out as unreadable and ridiculous. It took some time before it dawned on me what 'nonnative' (which I read as 'nonna-tive') meant."

Would you advocate a relaxing of the style manual "rule" on *hyphens,* to encourage their use wherever ambiguity results from their omission? Yes: 100%.

ISAAC ASIMOV: "Yes. In fact, I think 'nonnative' is as stupid as 'unionized,' which, to a chemist, is pronounced 'un-ionized.' "

SHERIDAN BAKER: "Yes. I read it ['nonnative'] with exactly the same puzzlement."

STEWART BEACH: "I have just had a similar experience to Barbara Tuchman's. I came across a word I thought was a series of typos for 'collaborators.' Reading it again I realized the word was 'colaborers.' But a hyphen would have avoided the confusion."

SIMON MICHAEL BESSIE: "Clarity is lost without the hyphen."

BARRY BINGHAM SR.: "I agree entirely with Mrs. Tuchman. The word 'nonnative' left me utterly baffled. Why eliminate a modest hyphen when it can serve a useful purpose?"

HAL BORLAND: "The whole purpose of punctuation, as I see it, is to help clarify meaning. As a writer, I will break any rule in the book to make my meaning not only understandable, but clearly *not misunderstandable.* And this elimination of the hyphen is both arbitrary and stupid."

JOSEPH A. BRANDT: "Yes. Absolutely!"

HEYWOOD HALE BROUN: "I didn't know what it meant either."

BEN LUCIEN BURMAN: "Should we use hyphens again? I never knew we'd stopped!"

THOMAS FLEMING: "I agree with Mrs. T."

STEPHEN H. FRITCHMAN: "God bless Barbara!"

RICHARD EDES HARRISON: "I consider it good practice to keep the hyphen to separate two vowels; e.g., 'co-operate,' 'semi-insular,' 'intra-uterine.' The grammarians look bad on this one."

PAUL HORGAN: "Yes. By all means."

JOHN K. HUTCHENS: "Mrs. T. is entirely right. Why risk confusion just to save a hyphen?"

ELIZABETH JANEWAY: "Surely the point of having rules at all is to achieve clarity. I too misread 'nonnative.' "

WALTER KERR: "I agree with Miss Tuchman."

HELEN L. KAUFMANN: "Decidedly, the hyphen clarifies meaning when judiciously used. I'm *for* it."

ALEXANDER KENDRICK: "If life-styles change, why can't hyphen-styles?"

LAURENCE LAFORE: "Yes—emphatically; I agree with Barbara Tuchman."

JULES LOH: "Bring back the hyphen as a rule, and allow it to disappear of its own accord, in words that shed it naturally. (I too found 'nonnative' to be non-sense.)"

RUSSELL LYNES: "Bravo to Barbara! . . . or should I say Brava?"

DWIGHT MACDONALD: "How could one vote 'NO'? I agree with Miss Tuchman—except that I never deciphered the word. Assumed it was a new school of philosophy."

HENRY W. MALONE: "I agree with Barbara Tuchman on the use of the hyphen because I, too, misread 'nonnative.' "

JESSICA MITFORD: "I've never heard of the Government Printing Office style book—but judging by the style of spokesmen for this government, it can't be very good."

WADE MOSBY: "When I was a cub reporter-editor, I followed the style book out the window. One night I wrote a headline with the word 'antinoise' in it, making it solid because the style book said 'anti' as a prefix is solid unless it doubles the vowel. The editor came roaring out, saying, 'What the hell is this "anTIN-oh-ese"?' My indignant explanations went for naught. Put a hyphen in it, the man said. And the *Journal* (Milwaukee, that is) thenceforth hyphenated when it made better sense."

DANIEL PATRICK MOYNIHAN: "Yes. But—'nonnative' is a non-word."

GEORGE PLIMPTON: "Hooray for the hyphen! Or, rather, Hoo-ray!"

PETER S. PRESCOTT: "Barbara T. is absolutely correct. I couldn't understand the word, thought it had to do with the number nine. The function of punctuation, as I understand it, is to promote clarity, to break up the written sentence into measures approximately corresponding to speech. Without the hyphen, I tried to pronounce the word as if it were náh-nahtive."

LEO ROSTEN: "If we rob the hyphen of its proper, useful, swiftly communicating role, why not drop all periods? The 'mandatory capital' will tell us a new sentence is there—like hell! Please crusade for the return of the hyphen. The idiotic consequences are exasperating, at best, and confusing as hell."

BERTON ROUECHÉ: "I feel as strongly as Mrs. T. about this."

VERMONT ROYSTER: "Why should we let the government dictate to us on style?"

LEONARD SANDERS: "I emphatically agree with Miss Tuchman's view. Newspaper and wire-service style books encourage some atrocious combinations. I know a reader who has assembled his own definitions: 'A costar is what you put under a drink,' etc."

ROBERT SHERRILL: "Yes. I read it this way, too."

WALTER W. "RED" SMITH: "Yes, yes, yes. I never know what to hyphenate, but let's relax, suspend, or eliminate any 'rule' that makes it difficult for the reader."

ELVIS STAHR, JR.: "Definitely. I can't abide people who insist on substituting rules for brains."

BILL VAUGHAN: " 'Style' should never get in the way of clarity."

JUDITH VIORST: " 'Nonnative' without a hyphen is gibberish!"

A.B.C. WHIPPLE: "Of course. Aren't we trying to communicate?"

NOTE: Merriam-Webster did just as Leo Rosten suggests—eliminated all periods in Webster's Third International Dictionary. The results were, to us at least, puzzling.

hysterical. *See* HISTORICAL/HYSTERICAL

I

I English is one of the few languages in which the pronoun for the first person singular is capitalized. For example, the French "je" and the Spanish "yo" are not capitalized unless they are at the beginning of a sentence.

This has nothing to do with egotism on the part of English-speaking people. Printing and handwriting have everything to do with it. In Middle English the first person singular was "ich" with a lower-case "i." When this was shortened to "i," manuscript writers and printers found that it often became lost or attached to an adjacent word. So the reason for the capital *I* is simply to avoid confusion and error.

I, personally This is perfectly good grammar if used when appropriate to intensify the force of a statement or in stating an opinion opposite to those which have just been quoted. But far too many people start every other sentence with "*I, personally*" and in such cases are guilty of redundancy as well as an irritating egotism.

"i" before "e" The question whether a word should be spelled with "ie" or "ei" can usually be solved by the rule "i before e except after c, or when sounded as 'a' as in 'neighbor' or 'weigh.' "

There are some exceptions to this, as is illustrated by the sentence which one reader reported that he had to learn in school: "Neither of the scientists seized upon that weird species of leisure." He commented: "I never learned what this unusual form of recreation might have been but I have had no trouble spelling words with 'ie' or 'ei' ever since."

-ible/-able The only completely workable rule for correct spelling of words ending in *-ible* or *-able* is this: look them up in the dictionary. There is really little apparent rhyme or reason to these variations in spelling. Most students of language agree that life would have been pleasanter if these words, almost all of them of Latin origin, had come into our language with the *-able* ending. Though there are far more *-able* words than *-ible* ones, there are enough of the latter to give even experienced writers a lot of trouble.

To complicate matters even further, a few words may be spelled either way, such as "diffusible"/"diffusable," "connectible"/"connectable," "permissible"/"permissable," and "collapsible"/"collapsable."

There are available long lists of words spelled with one or the other of these suffixes, but to try to commit them to memory would be madness.

ice-lolly   This is roughly the British equivalent for the confection we know in America by the trademark Popsicle.

iconoclast/radical   Possibly because of its classical origin (it comes from medieval Greek and Latin words meaning "image breaker"), *iconoclast* is now not often used in its extended sense of "someone who attacks and seeks to overthrow traditional and established institutions or ideas." The more common word is *radical.* Originally, an *iconoclast* was one who opposed the use of sacred images in the church, sometimes to the extent of actually destroying them.

identical with (to)   When a preposition is needed to follow *identical,* either *with* or *to* is acceptable, as in "The cigarette case that I found at the church bazaar was *identical with (to)* the one that I bought in Alexandria during World War II."

Possibly by analogy to the phrase *identify with, with* has become the more popular choice, but either is acceptable.

identify with   A news dispatch from Taiwan contained this statement: "Officials here are most concerned about indications that a growing number of young people have been identifying with Communist China since Peking began to take a more active part in world affairs." Normal grammatical construction would call for the use of a reflexive pronoun: *"identify* themselves *with* Communist China." That is, one would expect to find the word *identify* followed by an object. While the use of *identify* without the direct object is becoming more common, it is still frowned upon by many careful users of the language.

identity crisis   This is a psychological term which became a vogue phrase in the 1960s, especially among adolescents and young adults. It was supposed to mean a self-conscious uncertainty as to what sort of person one wanted to be or would become, what values to hold, and what course to pursue. Many *dropouts* (which see) associated their actions with *identity crises.* The phrase was also common during the evolution of the *Women's Liberation Movement* (which see). Technically it means a serious self-examination and self-determination.

idiom   In the broad sense, *idiom* simply means the usual way in which words of a particular language are put together to convey ideas or information. *Idiom* may encompass grammar, but it may also violate grammar. If an expression or phrase is used widely enough and accepted long enough it becomes idiomatic, regardless of whether or not it conforms to strict rules of grammar. In certain situations, one word may be preferred to another simply because it is the *idiom.* This can be seen especially in translations from one language to another, when a literal translation violates the *idiom* of the second language.

In a sense, then, this entire book is concerned with *idioms,* most of them grammatical, others not.

Idiom is a term also applied to the word usage peculiar to a particular region, profession, or field of activity, where a word may have a meaning that is different or more specific than that in general use.

idle *Idle* is long established as an adjective and intransitive verb, but the use of the word as a transitive verb meaning "to cause to be unemployed" is sometimes questioned. There should be no question as to its acceptability, however. The *Oxford English Dictionary* has long given the verb definition "to induce to be idle." A pink slip can be a powerful inducement.

i.e./e.g. Both of these are abbreviations for Latin phrases, and because the meaning of the phrases is not always understood, the abbreviations are sometimes confused: *i.e.* is a shortened form of "id est" which means "that is (to say)"; *e.g.* is the shortened form of "exempli gratia" and means "for instance." Use *i.e.* only when rephrasing a statement to make it more understandable; *e.g.* only when giving an example to illustrate a point. It is preferable to avoid the use of either by simply spelling out "that is to say" or "for example." One of the major style innovations in our original *American Heritage Dictionary* was the elimination of such abbreviations, an action taken on the ground that such "dictionary shorthand" made the definitions less, rather than more, comprehensible.

if/that. *See* DOUBT IF/DOUBT THAT/DOUBT WHETHER

if/whether/though *If* is too often used when *whether* or *though* would be more precise. *Whether* is preferable to *if* when alternatives are involved, as in "I didn't know *whether* (not *if*) I should laugh or cry." When *if* is substituted for *though* it sometimes causes confusion as to the exact meaning intended, as in "Turquoise jewelry, *if* increasingly rare and expensive, is an ideal gift for a woman." The implication is that only when it is rare and expensive is it an ideal gift. What is meant is *though* or, at least, "even if."

if and when The use of both *if* and *when* usually represents an effort to express extreme doubt that something will happen, but in most instances one or the other word alone will do. To express possible consequences, *if* is sufficient, as in "*If* it rains much more, the basement will be flooded."

If consequences are certain, *when* is sufficient, as in *"When* the storm is over we will be able to collect the broken branches." *See also* UNLESS AND UNTIL and WHEN, AS, AND IF.

if I were. *See* SUBJUNCTIVE MOOD

ill. *See* SICK/ILL

illegal/illicit/illegitimate   All three of these words are used to describe acts which are in some way or to some degree outside the law. *Illegal* means strictly and specifically forbidden by law, as in "In most states it is *illegal* to sell beer on Sunday." *Illicit* acts are ones for which legal permission has not been sought or obtained, or acts which constitute an evasion of the law. A hunter who has not obtained a hunting license before going out with his rifle is guilty of *illicit* behavior. *Illegitimate* acts are not only *illegal* and in violation of the written law of the land but are also in violation of the rules of propriety and even of reason and logic.

illegitimate   An Australian who calls himself an *illegitimate* does so with pride because the word has a very special meaning in that country. The early settlers of Australia were convicts who were sent Down Under in lieu of being sent to British gaols (jails). Those who migrated of their own free will distinguished themselves from the convicts by the term *illegitimate:* "not (il-) because of the law (lex, legis)." So in Australia an *illegitimate* is not a person born out of wedlock but a prideful descendant of honorable forebears.

illeism/illeist   The practice of referring to oneself in the third person is called *illeism* and one who does so is an *illeist.* An example from Dickens comes to mind: "Barkis is willing." Pronounced IL-ee-ism and IL-ee-ist, these words record perhaps the consummate egotism. We're told that General Douglas MacArthur ranked high among practicing *illeists,* but even he, on the occasion of his most famous public pronouncement, was modest enough to use the first personal pronoun: "I shall return."

illiterate

USAGE PANEL QUESTION

Strictly speaking, *illiterate* describes a person who can neither read nor write. However, it is widely used as a synonym for "ignorant" or "stupid." Not long ago a noted university administrator said: "It is common knowledge

that our professional students and candidates for the Ph.D. are *illiterate*."
Granted that he was indulging in hyperbole, would you accept *illiterate* in this extended sense?

In speech   Yes: 51%. No: 49%.
In writing   Yes: 32%. No: 68%.

ISAAC ASIMOV: "I have used it myself in this sense."

STEWART BEACH: "The university administrator should have a writer who knows the language as he obviously does not."

BARRY BINGHAM, SR.: "We hear 'illiterate' frequently used in conversation as a synonym for 'ignorant,' but I can't agree with its use in written English. As in so many other cases, a precise and fully descriptive word is being stretched out of all shape. Why couldn't the college administrator describe his Ph.D. candidates as 'ignorant,' a statement which would no doubt be beyond challenge, instead of overstating a strong case, by saying that they are unable to read and write?"

HEYWOOD HALE BROUN: "If we do, what word do we use for those who can't read? What word also do we use for the educational deficiencies of university administrators?"

BEN LUCIEN BURMAN: "Exaggerated, but useful."

ABE BURROWS: "I don't think he was 'indulging in hyperbole' at all."

JOHN CIARDI: "No. But with a little modification, yes; e.g., 'They are technically competent but lack the vocabulary of the humanities to the point of being illiterate.' "

LEON EDEL: "Yes . . . so used by me."

WILLARD R. ESPY: "The university administrator was not being hyperbolic; many professional students and candidates for the Ph.D. *are* illiterate."

STEPHEN H. FRITCHMAN: "Very useful as a hyperbolic put-down—but not in serious factual writing."

S. I. HAYAKAWA: "Yes, so long as hyperbole is intended and understood."

PAUL HORGAN: "No. He should know better."

ALEXANDER KENDRICK: " 'Illiterate' shouldn't be taken too literally."

LAURENCE LAFORE: "No. Like 'mindless' it was once acceptable as a figure of speech. It has now become a menace to clarity."

JOHN LEAR: "I think it's important to maintain distinctions between those attributes that circumstances impose and those for which the individual is clearly responsible."

WALTER LORD: "Yes, but *only* when indulging in hyperbole."

WRIGHT MORRIS: "It's an honorable word—let's hold the line."

VERMONT ROYSTER: "No. But in this case it is quite possible he is not engaging in hyperbole!"

LEONARD SANDERS: "Yes. His point apparently was that they were functional illiterates in their areas of expertise."

DAVID SCHOENBRUN: "The extension of meaning to include the characterization 'not literate enough' fills a need, a gap in our vocabulary."

MARK SCHORER: "Yes. I think he *meant* 'can't read or write.' They can't!"

WALTER W. "RED" SMITH: "Yes. So many illiterates win critical acclaim today."

JEAN STAFFORD: "Yes, as hyperbole, of course."

HAROLD TAYLOR: "Yes. He really means they write badly and too much."

EARL UBELL: "I'm beginning to hear the terms 'scientific illiteracy' and 'a scientific illiterate.' Perhaps these are cooler than 'scientific ignoramus' or 'scientific idiot,' etc. The 'illiteracy' implies that one can neither speak nor write the 'scientific language' without being generally stupid, just as one can be an illiterate in French, Swahili, or whatever without admitting to a lack of intelligence or knowledge in other areas. A useful extension—if not overused."

GEORGE WALD: "I think he meant that they couldn't write good and correct English—which is right!"

illusion/allusion. *See* ALLUSION/ILLUSION

illusion/delusion One way to remember the distinction between *illusion* and *delusion* is to associate each with another word which begins with the same letter. *Delusion* is a form of deceit, even though it be self-deceit. *Illusion* is imaginary in that it is unreal or nonexistent. If you are suffering under a *delusion,* you have the wrong idea or you don't know the facts. *Delusions* of grandeur, which are difficult to eradicate, come from self-deceit, if not mental imbalance, and lead to the adage "He will ride to the poorhouse in a limousine." A *delusion* can be a firmly fixed but false belief. An *illusion* is more fragile and temporary. It is a false impression or perception (mental or visual) or even just wishful thinking. Magicians create *illusions,* as do three-dimensional pictures. As Fowler's *Modern English Usage* so succinctly puts it: "Delusive hopes result in misguided action; illusive hopes merely in disappointments."

image

USAGE PANEL QUESTION

Panelist PETER S. PRESCOTT writes: "Particularly at this time in political history, the word 'image' has come into great vogue with politicians, their speech writers and publicity agents." Recently a journalism publication proposed a change in name of the journalism sorority to create "an image to reflect professionalism." Would you use *image* in this sense?

In your speech   Yes: 35%. No: 65%.
In your own writing   Yes: 28%. No: 72%.

ISAAC ASIMOV: "I think 'image' is a colorful term if not overused."

JOHN O. BARBOUR: "Yes. I prefer 'to reflect a professional image.' "

STEWART BEACH: "Yes. Though I usually avoid vogue words. This one says something definite for which, as far as I know, there is no synonym."

CHARLES BERLITZ: "Yes—lightly and with quotes."

JOSEPH A. BRANDT: "The mirror shows that it is here and now, but I don't like it."

HEYWOOD HALE BROUN: " 'Image' should be put in a bag with 'viable,' 'option,' 'relating,' and a hundred other half-hip words and burned."

JOHN CIARDI: "Yes, but always as a semi-satirical borrowing thrown back at those who use it earnestly. I have even ventured 'primage' as a portmanteau of PR for 'public relations' + 'image.' "

PAUL HORGAN: "No. Connotes a cheapness of values."

JOHN K. HUTCHENS: "No, because this word has become a nuisance, like 'charisma.' "

ELIZABETH JANEWAY: "No. But I find it *technically* useful in some more or less sociological contexts."

ALEXANDER KENDRICK: "Not as reflection, but as that which is reflected."

WALTER KERR: "An image should not be a front."

CHARLES KURALT: "This is one of the worst usages of our times. Its popularity may be remembered when historians turn to the shallow and artificial nature of so many people's lives in the mid-twentieth century."

LAURENCE LAFORE: "What is usually meant is 'reputation.' But sometimes 'image' *is* handy."

JULES LOH: "No. Fad word."

WALTER LORD: "I only object because it's overdone."

RUSSELL LYNES: "No. Madison Avenue highfalutin slang."

DWIGHT MACDONALD: "Yes, but with tip of tongue in cheek."

HERBERT MITGANG: " 'Image' has been made a phony, ridiculous word by the 'image makers' of television."

ORVILLE PRESCOTT: "A jargon word best avoided at any cost."

PETER S. PRESCOTT: "The usage of 'image' as a reflection is dying. We need help. It is now a synonym for something that is projected. I use the corruption in speech because I am a weak mortal, but not in writing!"

VERMONT ROYSTER: "A mirror reflects an image; not vice versa."

LEONARD SANDERS: "Although the fad may (and should) wane, this usage obviously fills a void in the language, and undoubtedly will be retained."

HAROLD SCHONBERG: "This has entered the language and it would be pedantic to oppose it."

WALTER W. "RED" SMITH: "Evelyn Waugh used it way back in *Vile Bodies*."

ELVIS STAHR, JR.: "Yes . . . alas . . . and woe is me . . . I guess I would and
   do."
DAVIDSON TAYLOR: "An 'image' is a reflection or a portrait. It may or may
   not be a lie."
BILL VAUGHAN: "No. Only in desperation."
GEORGE WALD: " 'Images' sure don't *reflect*! They *are* reflected or projected.
   'Image' used that way is O.K."
HERMAN WOUK: "A dreary counterword that has turned into shorthand."

immigrate/emigrate   Sometimes confusion arises as to which of these
words to use in a given situation, as in "His grandparents *(immigrated,
emigrated)* from Norway." In this instance, since the country to which
they moved is not named, *emigrated* is the proper word. *Emigrate* means
to leave one country to go to live in another. *Immigrate* means to come
into the new country. The Latin prepositions involved ("ex," "out of";
"in," "into") give the clue.

imminently/eminently   Because of similarity in sound, these two are
sometimes confused, but they are far apart in meaning. *Imminent* means
"on the verge of happening"; *eminent* means "outstanding." So a candidate may be said to be *"eminently* qualified," but not *"imminently* qualified," as one Wisconsin paper reported.

immoral. *See* AMORAL/IMMORAL

impact (as a verb)

USAGE PANEL QUESTION

Impact as a verb, meaning to pack firmly together, has long been part of the
   language. It is often heard today in the sense of "to have an impact on."
   Donald Freuhling, president of the McGraw-Hill Book Company, was
   quoted in *The New York Times* as saying that elementary and high school
   publishing "is a tough market and is being impacted by declining enroll-
   ments. . . ."
Would you use *impact* in this fashion in writing? Yes: 5%. No: 95%.
In casual speech? Yes: 8%. No: 92%.

HEYWOOD HALE BROUN: "One hopes his writers meet a higher standard."
ROBERT CROMIE: " 'Impact' is a bat meeting a ball—not a market meeting
   a weakened enrollment."
WILLARD R. ESPY: "Impacted bones, impacted molars, very well; but, please,
   not 'an impacted publishing industry.' It hurts too much."

GEROLD FRANK: "More muddying of words."

PETE HAMILL: "This is the single most infuriating use of a word in contemporary life. Politicians who hang out with businessmen use it all the time, and it is a vile, stupid alteration of the language!!"

JOHN K. HUTCHENS: "It seems to me that it should be only a noun, despite the first sentence in the ballot."

ELIZABETH JANEWAY: "This use is really due to sheer laziness. Why not say, as you do here, 'to have an impact on' if that's what you mean?"

JAMES J. KILPATRICK: "This is bureaucratese and ought to be rejected."

IRVING KOLODIN: "I do not approve making nouns into verbs."

STANLEY KUNITZ: "Definitely 'no.'"

JULES LOH: "Affect and effect are perfectly good words."

WILLIAM MCGUIRE: "Association: a wisdom tooth."

MARGE PIERCY: "'Affected' is what Freuhling means."

PETER S. PRESCOTT: "Another barbarism."

LEO ROSTEN: "What's wrong with 'effect, influence,' etc.?"

VERMONT ROYSTER: "I would think declining enrollment would make students less impacted in the classroom."

HAROLD SCHONBERG: "Again, an ugly verb from a noun."

ERICH SEGAL: "I know my protest is futile; this beastly verb has impacted itself on too many."

JACK SMITH: "No. No. When you see or hear 'impact' there is almost always a better word."

ELVIS STAHR, JR.: "One's wisdom teeth may be impacted and one's disposition thereby also be impacted, but thank goodness you didn't suggest using 'impact' as a transitive verb. Some do, I fear."

WALLACE STEGNER: "'Affected' is good enough without any jargon taint."

HAROLD TAYLOR: "Never. All these examples are instances of making verbs out of nouns and I hate the whole thing."

KARL V. TEETER: "Source is bureaucratic jargon, specifically government."

EDWARD TRIPP: "The verb causes a sharp ache in my one remaining wisdom tooth."

BARBARA TUCHMAN: "This is one of the new fads I *most* dislike."

JOSEPH VERGARA: "Awkward and unnecessary."

DOUGLAS WATT: "Freuhling obviously belongs in television or the auto industry."

HERMAN WOUK: "This is a very ugly and boring instance of slovenly use."

WILLIAM ZINSSER: "Bad."

impeachment   A common misconception is that *impeachment* refers to the trial, conviction, and removal from public office of an official.

While *impeachment* could lead to such a result, in itself it is only the bringing of charges. The language of our Constitution is quite clear on this point. "The President, Vice President and all civil Officers of the United States, shall be removed from office on Impeachment for, and Conviction of, Treason, Bribery, or other high Crimes and Misdemeanors." Note that *impeachment*—or accusation—is not enough. Conviction, by a two-thirds vote of the Senate, must follow if the accused is to be found guilty. If fewer than two-thirds of the Senators vote for conviction, the accused is cleared of charges and remains in office, as was the case with Andrew Johnson.

implementation. *See* EUPHEMISM

implosion/explosion *Implosion* has long been in the technical vocabulary of speech experts but, with the development of the atomic bomb, it moved into the field of nuclear phraseology. As a speech term it was used to describe the sudden cutting-off of breath when pronouncing such consonants as "p," "t," and "k." In dictionary language, *implosion* is a bursting inward, especially an explosion guided inward. Since the atomic bomb does have an effect opposite to that produced by the ordinary explosion of bombs, *implosion* is the logical term to use.

imply/infer Two words very commonly confused, each with the other, are *imply* and *infer*. The difference between the two is really quite simple. To *imply* is "to suggest," "to insinuate," "to hint." *Infer* means "to deduce or draw a conclusion from evidence at hand."

Still the confusion persists. The late Alvin F. Harlow put it this way in a letter to us a few years ago: "Two words which speakers and even writers don't seem to be able to keep in their proper places are *imply* and *infer*. In fact, I think there are many who write and talk in public who don't know that the word *imply* exists. It seems in danger of being crowded out of the lexicons by *infer*. We hear by the radio that a certain eminent person has *inferred* that he is not a candidate for President and that a congressman, investigating a TV quiz program, has *inferred* that it was rigged. So many people nowadays are taking what bits of culture they get from the radio or the TV screen that *infer* is getting an unfair advantage and *imply* may presently be confined only to the most erudite scholars."

As the following Usage Panel Question and the comments of panelists indicate, even the "most erudite scholars" can sometimes be confused.

USAGE PANEL QUESTION

A brochure of the Magazine Publishers Association recently quoted Dr. Samuel Johnson as having written: "Advertisements are now so numerous that they are very negligently perused." Making its point, the copy continued: "Sam then went on to infer that reach and frequency were really of no importance unless there was perception of the advertising as well."

Dictionaries define *infer* as "to deduce from evidence," while *imply* is defined as "to express indirectly, to suggest." Which do you think Johnson did?

Imply: 72%. Infer: 28%.

SHERIDAN BAKER: "Imply. I hold the line on this one too."

HAL BORLAND: "Imply. I see no need to approve or even condone Madison Avenue illiteracy, even when it is only a pose, as it is now and then."

JOSEPH A. BRANDT: "Imply. Sam was being logical rather than deductive."

HEYWOOD HALE BROUN: "Imply. I suspect that the magisterial doctor implied, but a brochure which calls him 'Sam' might never make it clear."

BEN LUCIEN BURMAN: "Depends on whose ox is being gored. If the old boy's mother-in-law ran an advertising agency, he meant 'infer.' Incidentally Johnson made a howler here himself. How can you peruse (read thoroughly) negligently?"

JAMES MACGREGOR BURNS: "Imply. Let's keep 'infer' for its proper usage!"

ABE BURROWS: "Imply. As an old brochure watcher, I would never infer that this brochure meant that Dr. Johnson was inferring. Sam was implying."

JOHN CIARDI: "Imply. Why give away to the illiterate a precision the literate must value?"

JOHN K. HUTCHENS: "Imply. The doctor knew perfectly well what he had inferred. He was now implying."

WALT KELLY: "Imply. Knowing what I do of Doctor Johnson, I'd say he implied. He probably did no research after lunch."

ALEXANDER KENDRICK: "Imply. The ad copy, as usual, could be taken either way, but it seems to me he was merely implying."

WALTER KERR: "Probably imply but can be read either way."

CLARK KINNAIRD: "Infer. By the way, 'very' is usually superfluous. When I worked on the copy-desk of the Louisville *Courier-Journal* in the last days of Henry Watterson, it was barred from usage in the paper. Watterson had ruled, 'If anything is very good, it is damned good; say so!' Did Johnson ever *suggest*? No!"

DWIGHT MACDONALD: "Infer. Good question."

PHYLLIS MCGINLEY: "Imply. Of course, Sam *might* have inferred if he was merely speculating but it does not sound likely."

EDWIN NEWMAN: "It is not possible to say. It could have been either."

PETER S. PRESCOTT: "In the first case, Johnson inferred that ads were negligently perused from the fact there were so many. The magazine should have said he implied the rest unless he actually did say it; typical of the magazine's vulgarity is the way it calls him 'Sam.' Good God!"

LEO ROSTEN: "He *inferred* carelessly (how did he know magazines are negligently perused?) and *implied* an unproved connection between quantity and consumption."

VERMONT ROYSTER: "Imply. Dr. Johnson implied, while I infer that the copywriter was ignorant. . . ."

LEONARD SANDERS: "Johnson implied; Boswell inferred."

HAROLD SCHONBERG: "Infer. Sam was using a premise to arrive at a stated conclusion. Hence, *infer.*"

MARK SCHORER: "There is nothing to 'infer' *from,* unless it is Johnson's own statement, in which the implications are already clear."

ROBERT SHERRILL: "Imply. Of course, he had to 'infer' *before* he implied; but writing it was the second step."

EARL UBELL: "Imply. Two more disaster words. Actually the copywriter is restating Johnson's statement . . . so I do not know what 'went on' means here."

GEORGE WALD: 'Infer' is increasingly misused when 'imply' is meant."

important/importantly

USAGE PANEL QUESTION

"The truth is evident; more *important,* it will prevail." Some writers would prefer "more *importantly*" in such a construction, though the adjective seems called for if the second part of the sentence is interpreted as an elliptical version of "what is more important. . . ." In such a sentence would you write *important*?

Yes: 75%. No: 25%.

Importantly   Yes: 25%. No: 75%.

STEWART BEACH: "This construction puzzles me grammatically, but there is a difference to my ear in the two uses. I wouldn't object to either, but prefer 'important.' "

ALTON BLAKESLEE: "Let's conserve *some* adverbs."

HEYWOOD HALE BROUN: "Oddly in the cited case, it doesn't scan, as does 'from whence.' "

JOHN CIARDI: "I once had a dentist who never failed to say 'open widely.' "

RICHARD EDES HARRISON: "This clearly calls for the adverb."

ELIZABETH JANEWAY: "Right or wrong, I never use 'importantly.' "

JULES LOH: " 'Importantly' sounds affected."

RUSSELL LYNES: " 'Important' seems more emphatic than 'importantly.' "

VERMONT ROYSTER: "No one would write: 'Truth will prevail importantly.' The adverb has the wrong connotation."

DAVID SCHOENBRUN: "Probably better to write it all out: 'What is more important. . . .' "

BARBARA TUCHMAN: "Yes—but I could never tell the logical rationale. 'Importantly' just sounds pretentious."

impotent   *Impotent* should be pronounced IM-puh-tent, not im-POH-tent.

in. *See* AMONG/IN and AMID/AMIDST

in-. *See* PREFIXES AND SUFFIXES, WITH AND WITHOUT HYPHEN

inalienable/unalienable. *See* UNALIENABLE/INALIENABLE

incentivize

USAGE PANEL QUESTION

The *Wall Street Journal* now supplies copy for a daily radio program about financial matters. A recent broadcast reported on methods to "*incentivize* employees" to improve production.
Would you approve the use of *incentivize* in speech? Yes: 2%. No: 98%.
In writing? No: 100%.

ISAAC ASIMOV: "I think we need a punishing committee for the *WSJ.*"
WHITNEY BALLIETT: "Strikes me as a fabrication for perfectly sound and usable words."
BARRY BINGHAM, SR.: "I would deincentivize the urge of an employee to use such a silly, ugly word."
ALTON BLAKESLEE: "Migawd, are all nouns to become switch hitters?"
HEYWOOD HALE BROUN: "No wonder the Japanese out-produce us."
BEN LUCIEN BURMAN: "NO, a thousand times no!"
ROBERT CROMIE: "Not outside a Woody Allen movie."
GEROLD FRANK: "This sounds simply awful to me."
RAY GANDOLF: "If I were the *WSJ* I would incentivize that broadcaster to seek employment elsewhere."
PETE HAMILL: "Horrible!"
PAUL HORGAN: "Hideous!"
JOHN K. HUTCHENS: "No! It's both false-sounding and obscure."
ELIZABETH JANEWAY: "Good God! What's wrong with 'motivate'?"
E. J. KAHN, JR.: "All words ending in 'ize' should be outlawed except 'exor-cize.'"
JAMES J. KILPATRICK: "'Incentivize' is an abomination, in a class with 'prior-itize'; and shame on the *Wall Street Journal.*"
STANLEY KUNITZ: "Dreadful!"
JULES LOH: "Jargon."
WILLIAM McGUIRE: "An especially offensive locution."
ORVILLE PRESCOTT: "Abominable!"

LEO ROSTEN: "Barbaric, which is pretty awful for even a barbarism. That is how I opinion this usage."

VERMONT ROYSTER: "I decline to answer on the grounds of conflict of interest and wish to conceal my disgust."

DAVID SCHOENBRUN: "*Wall Street Journal*ese is as dreadful as its thinking."

HAROLD SCHONBERG: "Ugly. You can't go around willfully or arbitrarily making verbs of nouns. Maybe e.e. cummings could get away with it."

ROBERT SHERRILL: "Crap!"

JACK SMITH: "If our speech is to remain civilized, we've got to stop 'izing' everything."

ELVIS STAHR, JR.: "Horrors!"

HAROLD TAYLOR: "Never."

EDWARD TRIPP: "As the victims of comic book heroes are wont to say, "Aarrgh!' "

BARBARA TUCHMAN: "Whoever used it and whatever editor allowed it should be exiled *forever* to some house organ for plastic cups or what not, and never allowed back."

JOSEPH VERGARA: "Ugly, barbarous and self-defeating. Sounds like insensitize."

DOUGLAS WATT: "He who identifies/ways to 'incentivize'/our hate intensifies/till in cement he lies."

A.B.C. WHIPPLE: "More jargon. Businessmen are especially bad at this."

HERMAN WOUK: "Squeaky chalk on a blackboard."

WILLIAM ZINSSER: "As bad as prioritize. The worst is deincentivize."

incident

A report of an airplane crash includes this sentence: "The incident took the lives of nine persons." Definitions of *incident* include "An event, happening or occurrence" and "a minor or trivial occurrence." Would you regard "minor" as a controlling factor in the use of *incident* and would you therefore find it inappropriate in the sentence quoted?

Yes: 66%. No: 34%.

ISAAC ASIMOV: "Yes. The writer probably meant 'accident,' the jackass."

STEWART BEACH: "Yes. If nine persons were killed, it is no longer an 'incident.' 'Tragedy' would be a more appropriate word."

JULES BERGMAN: "Yes. 'Accident,' not 'incident.' 'Incident' implies, even if not literally, a happening or occurrence where physical damage does not take place. 'Accident' *means* damage occurred, as in a crash."

CHARLES BERLITZ: "Yes. Curious to note that 'incident' means 'accident' in the language closest to Latin (Italian)."

HAL BORLAND: "Yes. No fatal accident can be an incident."

HEYWOOD HALE BROUN: "Yes. It has the same heavily inappropriate quality which describes a war as 'the late unpleasantness.' "

BEN LUCIEN BURMAN: "If nine people dead is only an incident, not a tragedy, it's a shocking commentary on what Vietnam has done to the U.S.A."

JOHN K. HUTCHENS: "Yes, for the same reason one of the victims would, if he could file an answer here."

ALEXANDER KENDRICK: "Yes. Not only 'minor,' but preferably nonlethal."

WALTER KERR: "No. I happen to work in the theater where a dramatic incident may be major."

STANLEY KUNITZ: "Used in this way, 'incident' takes on a somewhat ironic connotation—e.g., the incident at My Lai."

WALTER LORD: "I was in London during The War and 'incident' was used as the standard, official way to describe any individual bomb landing—whatever the casualties and damage. Perhaps this has led to the far wider implications today."

PETER S. PRESCOTT: "No. Although I like the irony of implied triviality: *Incident at Owl Creek Bridge,* and *The Ox Bow Incident.*"

BERTON ROUECHÉ: "Yes. Excellent as a deliberate understatement."

VERMONT ROYSTER: "Yes—especially if I were one of the victims."

DAVID SCHOENBRUN: "Yes. 'Accident' is the proper word to use. Or crash, etc."

DANIEL SCHORR: "Yes. Except in diplomacy, where an 'incident' can be a major occurrence, such as the Agadir Incident."

ERICH SEGAL: "No. Etymologically, there *is* a sense of 'accident' in the term 'incident.' "

WALTER W. "RED" SMITH: "Yes, and Nixon called Kent State an incident!"

ELVIS STAHR, JR.: "Yes. Even if not *controlling,* it's a subtle part of the meaning."

HAROLD TAYLOR: "I wouldn't say it that way. The 'incident' didn't take the lives. I would say nine people were killed."

BILL VAUGHAN: "Yes. Rather like a fatal tiff."

HERMAN WOUK: " 'Accident' would be so much better."

inclement   The consistent inconsistency of the English language is reflected in the pronunciation of *inclement:* in-CLEM-n't. This is so despite the fact that both "increment" and "implement" are pronounced with the accent on the first syllable.

including (I/me)   A New Jersey reader sent us a clipping from a newspaper column which stated: "Many Americans, including I, have received a slick mailing piece with 16 kopeks in striking Russian stamps offering a subscription to Soviet Life Magazine." Here is another example of the compulsion to avoid the use of "me." *Including* is the present participle of "include" and the pronoun following must be in the objective case. The correct usage is *including me.*

incomparable adjectives. *See* UNCOMPARABLE and ADJECTIVES, UN-COMPARABLE

incumbent. *See* PRESENT INCUMBENT

incursion   Pentagonese euphemism for "invasion." Used to describe the military invasions of Cambodia and Laos, apparently for the reason that, since the word was relatively unfamiliar, the American people would regard an *incursion* as somehow less serious than an invasion. *See also* EUPHEMISM.

in depth. *See* VOGUE WORDS

Indian summer/Indian giver   *Indian summer* is a completely accept-able term with no racial overtones. The brief period in the fall when we have a return to summer's warm weather was so called by the colonists because it resembled something with which they were familiar but was not quite the same. Gradually the adjective "Indian" came to be applied to many things that seemed to the new settlers bogus or phony. The term *Indian giver* was applied to a person who made a gift only in expectation of getting it back. In fairness to the Indians, who have been mistreated enough since the white man came to North America, *Indian giver* is a term best forgotten, since it is considered derogatory by Indians.

indictment, hand up an   An *indictment* is voted by a grand jury whose members feel that there is sufficient evidence of criminal action to justify a trial of the suspect. An indictment is *handed up* to a judge who will conduct the trial. When the trial is over, the judge will, if the suspect is found guilty, *hand down* the decision.

indorse. *See* ENDORSE/INDORSE

infamous   *Infamous* is pronounced IN-fuh-mus, not in-FAYM-us.

infinitive, split   An infinitive is split when other words, usually adverbs, are inserted between the "to" and the verb.
   Perhaps it would be well to quote a classic case of *split* vs. *unsplit infinitive.* It came about when Adlai Stevenson was the somewhat reluc-tant candidate for his party's nomination to the presidential race. In a filmed interview he said he would be happy to run if his party "sees fit

to so honor me." Reading the statement later for the press, he carefully *unsplit the infinitive,* making the sentence read: "sees fit so to honor me." Each was perfectly good English, with the carefully unsplit one perhaps a bit stuffier.

The definitive statement on *splitting infinitives* is to be found in *Dictionary of Modern English Usage* by H. W. Fowler: "The English-speaking world may be divided into (1) those who neither know nor care what a split infinitive is; (2) those who do not know, but care very much; (3) those who know and condemn; (4) those who know and approve; (5) those who know and distinguish. . . . Those who neither know nor care are the vast majority, and are a happy folk, to be envied by most of the minority classes."

The *split infinitive,* in actuality, is another pedantic bogey, carried over from the Latinate prescriptions of the nineteenth century. There was no such thing as a *split infinitive* in Latin for the simple reason that each Latin infinitive was a single word. Our "to hold" is expressed in Latin simply as "tenere." So such a construction as "to fully hold the water" was literally impossible in Latin. Therefore, the pedants reasoned that both elements of an English infinitive should be considered as fused into one—unsplittable and sacrosanct. Only that's not the way English works.

Still, there remain no hard-and-fast rules as to when one may and when one may not *split an infinitive.* The consensus is that *split infinitives* should be unsplit when too many adverbial elements intrude and cause perplexity by their very number. Such a sentence as "The chief undertook to forcefully, fully, firmly, and systematically advise the laymen of their rights" leaves even the attentive reader or listener baffled. The remedy in this case is simply to *unsplit the infinitive* and move all those adverbs to the end of the sentence: "The chief undertook to advise the laymen of their rights—forcefully, fully, firmly, and systematically." That sentence still will not receive any prizes for simple, effective rhetoric—but it's much more comprehensible than the first version.

However, if the intrusion of one or at most two adverbs between the elements of an infinitive sounds right to your ear and if it aids in clarity, feel free to *split the infinitive.* "He wanted to really help his mother" sounds less stilted than "he wanted really to help his mother," and an alternative *unsplitting of the infinitive*—"he wanted to help his mother really"—is practically meaningless.

So the advice on *split infinitives* is: proceed with caution, but not in fear.

infinitive, subject of the   The confusion about the use of "I" and "me" is reflected in such statements as "The first thing for somebody like you or I to do. . . ." The *subject of the infinitive* "to do" must be in the accusative or objective case. Since the objective case of the first personal pronoun is "me," the statement should be "The first thing for somebody like you or me to do. . . ."

infinity/eternity *Eternity* refers only to time: specifically, time without beginning or end and especially the limitless extent of time into the endless future. *Infinity* is a broader term and can be applied to limitless space or time or quantity. So one can speak of "constellations reaching to *infinity*" or "an *infinity* of centuries stretching before us" or "an *infinity* of space in the upper reaches of the sky."

infix Just as a prefix is an element put at the front of a word and a suffix is an element attached at the end of a word, an *infix* is an element thrust into the middle of a word. There are few *infixes* in American speech but they are great favorites with Australians, especially the "bloody" *infix* which turns up many times in slangy popular speech. An example is the description of a character in a book as being so drunk that he could be "swinging from the chander-bloody-lier."

One American example of an *infix* is Joseph Pulitzer's description of Frank Cobb, editor of the New York *World,* as his most "indegoddam-pendent editor."

inform. *See* ADVISE/INFORM/WRITE

infra-. *See* PREFIXES AND SUFFIXES, WITH AND WITHOUT HYPHEN

infrastructure

USAGE PANEL QUESTION

During a recent campaign a number of candidates called for a new "jobs program" to ease the unemployment problem. Many suggested that the unemployed be put to work repairing the *infrastructure* of America's cities: its bridges, subways, tunnels, and roads. *Infrastructure* is not a new word. Its first appearance in print in the late 1920s involved the tunnels and culverts that were to become France's supposedly impregnable Magi-not Line. Later it was used metaphorically, as when Winston Churchill in 1950 spoke of the "usual jargon about the *infrastructure* of a super-national authority." Today *infrastructure* seems to be coming back to its earlier meaning. Indeed, a recent *New Yorker* cartoon showed a city manhole open with, on one of the surrounding guard rails, the sign "Infrastructuralists at Work."

Do you regard *infrastructure* as a word suitable for use in describing a program designed to put laborers back on the job? Yes: 43%. No: 57%.

Would you use *infrastructure* in your writing? Yes: 37%. No: 63%.
In speech? Yes: 40%. No: 60%.

DAVE ANDERSON: "Not enough people know what it means."

ISAAC ASIMOV: "We must allow new words when they have meanings the old ones can't easily supply."

CHARLES BERLITZ: "Yes, if writing about a lower structure as in the original meaning."

ALTON BLAKESLEE: ("No" to all questions) "I have my own (biological) infrastructure—heart, lungs, kidneys, etc."

DAVID H. BRADLEY: "Only if the jobs produce an infrastructure."

HEYWOOD HALE BROUN: "Like the Maginot Line, the word is ponderous and useless, but if its bureaucratic ring will help with a job program, let's keep it."

ANTHONY BURGESS: (Would use) ". . . but only as a Marxist and highly technical term."

BEN LUCIEN BURMAN: "Choctaw would be easier to understand."

FRANCES FRITCHMAN: ("Yes," in writing) "In its original meaning."

PAUL HORGAN: "Fugitive jargon in this sense."

JOHN K. HUTCHENS: "Suitable but why not the simpler 'jobs program'?"

JAMES J. KILPATRICK: "It's a useful word, properly understood. It strikes me as captious to fuss about it."

STANLEY KUNITZ: ("Yes" in writing) ". . . but cautiously and only in fitting circumstances. Too fancy for my taste."

JULES LOH: "Vogue usage; it will pass."

EDWIN NEWMAN: "With regard to the 'yes,' I'd rather say 'roads and bridges.' "

ORVILLE PRESCOTT: "Clumsy jargon and unnecessary. Just say, 'repair roads,' etc."

VERMONT ROYSTER: " 'Infrastructure' is a useful word in economics but its relation to a 'jobs program' is a misuse of it."

HAROLD SCHONBERG: "Why not merely 'put to work repairing cities'?"

ELVIS STAHR, JR.: "It's probably suitable but not very palatable."

WALLACE STEGNER: "Like other jargon, it has nine in ten chances of falling into disuse."

HAROLD TAYLOR: "I've found that 'infrastructure' is used for a whole array of things these days, not just for the physical systems for cities—e.g. educators who say 'the infrastructure of the curriculum or of the society.' "

KARL V. TEETER: "Pretentious word—but, if bridges have a superstructure, why not an infrastructure?"

JUDITH VIORST: "We don't need this awful word."

DOUGLAS WATT: "If I used it at all, I would limit it to its structural sense."

HERMAN WOUK: ("Yes") ". . . in writing, as journalistic cant."

WILLIAM ZINSSER: "Though I wouldn't use it. It's o.k. in the specific sense of pipes, tunnels, etc."

ingroup. *See* VOGUE WORDS

in line. *See* LINE, IN/LINE, ON

innovate   While *innovate* is most commonly used as a transitive verb, its use as an intransitive verb (meaning "to be creative") has an honorable history. The great British statesman Edmund Burke once said, "To innovate is not to reform."

innovation   An *innovation* is, by its very nature, "new." There are no "old *innovations,*" and to speak of a "new *innovation*" is a *redundancy* (which see).

innumerable/many   There are occasions when *innumerable* is inappropriate, even when referring to a vast number. Such is the case in this statement about the wife of Jonas Salk: "She was the subject of innumerable Picasso paintings and drawings." Such paintings and drawings may be "uncounted" but surely there must be a definite number of pictures involved.

inquire/enquire. *See* BRITISH-AMERICAN SPELLING VARIATIONS

in re. *See* RE/IN RE

inside (of). *See* outside (of)/inside (of)

insignia

USAGE PANEL QUESTION

Insignia is the plural form of *insigne,* although it often appears construed as singular: "He proudly wore the *insignia* denoting his rank." Occasionally another plural form, *insignias,* is seen: "The book showed the *insignias* of various army groups."
Do you regard *insignia* as a singular form? Yes: 68%. No: 32%. *Insignias* as a plural? Yes: 58%. No: 42%.
Would you use the "correct" singular *insigne* in speech? Yes: 17%. No: 83%. In writing? Yes: 22%. No: 78%.

ISAAC ASIMOV: "I refuse to make memorandas concerning datas even when temptations are at maximas. Why then should I use insignias?"

BARRY BINGHAM, SR.: " 'Insigne' is so uncommon in usage as to seem highly mannered in prose and even more so in speech."

ALTON BLAKESLEE: "No, but not worth a punch in the nose."

HEYWOOD HALE BROUN: "Practically all military insignia are in pairs, a practical way of solving the problem. The singular is hard to say."

WILLARD R. ESPY: "I use the form 'insignia' as both singular and plural—though, inconsistently, I would never permit such liberty with 'data.' "

ROBERT GOTTLIEB: " 'Insigne' would be hideously pretentious today."

SYDNEY J. HARRIS: "A pedantic distinction."

JOHN K. HUTCHENS: "Just as I regard 'agenda' as a singular noun, or anyhow use it as such."

ELIZABETH JANEWAY: "I think of it as a collective noun and would use 'insignia' at all times."

DIANE JOHNSON: "I didn't know this and would probably not change."

WALTER KERR: "Practically speaking it's lost (and we should get rid of 'practically speaking,' shouldn't we?)."

JAMES J. KILPATRICK: "I can't recall ever having met one insigne. The military brass of my acquaintance have lots of 'insignia.' "

STANLEY KUNITZ: "To insist on 'insigne' is pedantic. I wince at 'insignias' for the plural form, but doubt the possibility of stopping its acceptance."

EDWIN NEWMAN: "This was decided by usage long ago. There is no going back."

ORVILLE PRESCOTT: " 'Insigne' is now obsolete past all recovery."

VERMONT ROYSTER: "Five years in the Navy keep me from being a purist on this one."

HAROLD SCHONBERG: "I've never seen it in the plural, with 's.' Ugly."

ELVIS STAHR, JR. "As a former Secretary of the Army, I feel constrained to be faithful to the tenet that 'insignia' itself (themselves?) is (are) both singular and plural."

WALLACE STEGNER: "Along with datum, stratum, medium, et al.? I would fight for them all."

BARBARA TUCHMAN: "As both singular and plural, i.e. 'he wore the insignia of his rank' or 'the insignia of various groups.' I would regard both as correct."

JOSEPH VERGARA: " 'Insigne' is joining 'datum' in the obsolete bin."

GEORGE WALD: "Yes (insignia as a singular form). But *a* data—*a* bacteria—never!

DOUGLAS WATT: "Singular and plural."

A.B.C. WHIPPLE: " 'Insigne' is accurate but it does sound archaic now."

HERMAN WOUK: " 'Insignia' has firmly established itself as singular."

instant/second. *See* MOMENT/MINUTE/INSTANT/SECOND

insurance/assurance In addition to the possible intent to give the impression that one can assure a little more time on earth by paying life-

insurance premiums, there is a certain logic behind the practice of some life-insurance companies of calling themselves *"assurance* companies." The reasoning seems to be that an *"assurance* company" writes only *insurance* for that which you can be assured will happen—death. Actuaries for such companies have only to estimate what percentage of people will die at a given age.

A company offering compensation in case of fire, theft, or illness may designate itself as an *insurance* or "casualty" company, since it is all a matter of chance that any of these situations will occur.

insure. *See* ENSURE/INSURE

integrate. *See* DESEGREGATE/INTEGRATE

intelligence-gathering operation/illegal entry. *See* EUPHEMISM

intelligentsia   This word was coined in Russia as "intelligentsiya" to mean intellectuals as a class, and the Russian "g" is hard as in "go" or "get." When it was first introduced in this country (without the "y"), purists insisted that it be pronounced with a hard "g." However, words like "intelligent" and "intelligence" came into English from Latin by way of French at the time of the Norman Conquest and thus acquired the French soft "g." With these pronunciations well established before *intelligentsia* entered the English language in the twentieth century, the Russian word has become completely Americanized and the soft "g" prevails.

inter-. *See* PREFIXES AND SUFFIXES, WITH AND WITHOUT HYPHEN

interface

USAGE PANEL QUESTION

Interface originally meant the place at which two different systems, persons, or even thoughts meet and act upon each other. In the words of one authority, "The equipment that makes the computer's work visible to the user is often called the *interface* and the word is used highly metaphorically as in 'the *interface* between scientist and society.'" Recently the word has been used as a verb meaning little more than "communicate," as "President Reagan will continue to *interface* with members of Congress."

Would you use the broader meaning of *interface* in speech? No: 100%.

In writing? No: 100%.
Would you favor limiting *interface* to its original technical meaning? Yes: 88%. No: 12%.

ISAAC ASIMOV: "What's wrong with 'interact'? When I interface with a girl, I'm *kissing* her, by God."

BARRY BINGHAM, SR: "This is another fancy vogue word, for which we have no use."

DAVID H. BRADLEY: " 'Technical' meanings have social implications. This term has a useful and precise meaning."

HEYWOOD HALE BROUN: "I guess that's what the President does with Congress, although it hardly sounds like communication."

RAY GANDOLF: "I never knew until now that this dreadful word had an original meaning. Are you sure that it's not something E. T. brought with him?"

DIANE JOHNSON: "This, in its true sense, has a valuable use, designates something very particular; it should be preserved."

WALTER KERR: "Computer, O.K.; makes sense. Reagan usage, no."

JAMES J. KILPATRICK: "Both parameter and interface have become turkey words, used by pompous folks who want to wiggle their wattles and strut their stuff. I would restrict both words to technical use."

JULES LOH: "Bureaucrats and other showoffs should return this awful word to the technocrats, but they won't."

HERBERT MITGANG: "Interface is for jargonites."

MARGE PIERCY: "I like the original meaning of the word, emphasizing the point of tangency between different, almost alien intellectual or physical systems. The metaphor must exploit that sense. It cannot mean simply speaking or meeting with, except by sloppy usage that abrades its original intention."

PETER S. PRESCOTT: "Technical words should be allowed into the broader language only when adequate general words don't exist."

LEO ROSTEN: "Loathsome word and totally unnecessary to replace a dozen exact synonyms."

HAROLD SCHONBERG: "As home computers become more and more common, it will become entrenched in a multiplicity of meanings."

ELVIS STAHR, JR.: "This is just one more example of how people with limited vocabularies will bend out of shape words they don't know but that sound important."

BARBARA TUCHMAN: "As a verb, no—beyond the pale."

JUDITH VIORST: "I would favor eliminating it from the language altogether."

DOUGLAS WATT: "Aren't 'interact' and 'face-to-face' still in the language?"

Interlingua. *See* INTERNATIONAL LANGUAGE

---

international language In spite of centuries of effort, man seems little closer to a common language than he was when God, according to the Bible, condemned the builders of the tower of Babel to speak many languages instead of one. There have been at least three major efforts to create a language which would serve as a common medium of communication for all peoples. Esperanto, invented in 1887, utilizes roots common to several European languages. Despite zealous efforts by converts, it was never widely used. The name "esperanto" means literally "one who hopes" but there is little hope for the acceptance of Esperanto.

Interlingua was a somewhat more recent creation, aggressively promoted by an organization called the International Auxiliary Language Association. Efforts to secure worldwide use of Interlingua seem still far from success.

Much energy has gone into the promotion of *Basic English* (which see), a simplified English vocabulary devised by the distinguished scholars C. K. Ogden and I. A. Richards. Actually some variant of Basic English is very likely to become—if it has not already become—the world's "second language." Almost without exception delegates to the United Nations and leaders in world trade have some English at their command. Many of them speak it better than some native Americans. To some degree, then, our native tongue is the closest thing to a common language that the human race has had since God smote the builders of Babel.

International Phonetic Alphabet (IPA). *See* SCHWA

internecine

USAGE PANEL QUESTION

Internecine traditionally means either "mutually destructive, deadly to both sides" or "characterized by great bloodshed and carnage." More recently it has been widely used to describe struggle within a group or a nation: "The *internecine* nature of the factional struggle in the United Mine Workers."
Would you use *internecine* in this newer sense in speech? Yes: 60%. No: 40%. In writing? Yes: 64%. No: 36%.

ISAAC ASIMOV: "My God! The new wrong meaning is the only one I knew."
DAVID H. BRADLEY: "Intramural is a nice, precise word."
JOSEPH A. BRANDT: "This battle is lost."
JOHN BROOKS: "No. At least I hope I wouldn't."
WILLARD R. ESPY: "There is no excuse for stretching the meaning of 'interne-

cine' to include 'a furious struggle within a group,' but there does seem to be a need for a word with some such meaning. Why not 'intranecine'?"

FRANCES FRITCHMAN: "In the second sentence 'internecine' is tautological."

ROBERT GOTTLIEB: "We need this meaning of the word."

ELIZABETH JANEWAY: "The shorter *OED* gives your first use as 'originally' but adds the second as 'modern.' I feel modern today."

DIANE JOHNSON: "In your example both senses could apply."

JAMES J. KILPATRICK: "I think 'internal' would usually suffice—or maybe 'fratricide.' "

EDWIN NEWMAN: "My 'No' is caused not by the sense that the use would be incorrect but rather the fact that it seems a pompous word for the writing I do."

MARGE PIERCY: "The newer use of the word supplies a useful adjective; I suspect by now it is the commoner use in both speech and writing."

ORVILLE PRESCOTT: "Acceptable now."

VERMONT ROYSTER: "A very useful word."

HAROLD SCHONBERG: "By now the original meaning seems to have been forgotten."

ERICH SEGAL: "I really don't see the problem. What's wrong with metaphors?"

ELVIS STAHR, JR.: "It is not a newer sense. It still means destructive to both (or all) factions."

WALLACE STEGNER: "This meaning has made it into campground."

HAROLD TAYLOR: "I wouldn't use the word in the old or new sense . . . can't explain why. It sounds fancy."

KARL V. TEETER: "I don't understand that it is a 'newer' sense. The struggle in question has certainly been 'deadly to both sides.' "

JOSEPH VERGARA: "Sounds right somehow—by association with internal?"

GEORGE WALD: "We scientists use it all the time. Intra-species conflict is internecine."

WILLIAM ZINSSER: "In fact, this is the only sense in which I know the word."

intra-. *See* PREFIXES AND SUFFIXES, WITH AND WITHOUT HYPHEN

intransitive. *See* TRANSITIVE/INTRANSITIVE

invoke. *See* EVOKE/INVOKE

Irish, bog-trotting/lace-curtain/shanty With a large number of persons in this country having ancestors who emigrated from Ireland, various terms have been coined as racial labels. Most of these labels are derogatory. This was once the case with the term *bog-trotting Irish,* which used to mean laborers or peasants in Ireland's bogs. Later the name gained dignity when accounts appeared of British soldiers pursuing rebellious Irishmen across bogs where the fugitives sought concealment but all too often were discovered and bayonetted until "the bogs ran red with Irish blood."

Shanty Irish, the most derogatory of the terms, has an origin in history which also casts shame on the British rather than the Irish. The Irish people were so oppressed by the English overlords that any improvements on their "cottages" meant an increase in taxes. Naturally this policy destroyed ambition and led to a slackness in caring for their homes or shanties.

In contrast, the term *lace-curtain Irish* reflects a determination to better their lot, as evidenced by the display of lace curtains at their windows. The immigrants to whom that label was applied sacrificed and endured and worked to achieve that small status in a British-oriented, American Protestant society which believed at that time that Irishmen and dogs should not be allowed in public places.

Today most American-born Irishmen banter these terms casually among themselves but, heard from the lips of Americans not of Irish ancestry, they remain pejorative expressions.

ironic/ironical Either is correct as the adjectival form of "irony." Both mean "characterized by or constituting irony" or "the opposite of what was to be expected." We prefer the shorter form, simply because we are against unnecessary syllables. Many people, knowing that the adverbial form is "ironically," insist on using *ironical* as the adjective, but this, though not wrong, sounds a trifle stuffy and pretentious.

irregardless

USAGE PANEL QUESTION

The head of a major law firm recently reported that junior members of his firm, law school graduates all, sprinkled briefs with the word *irregardless.* College teachers report that *irregardless* appears frequently in student writing. Do you feel that the time has come to accept this widespread usage?

In speech   Yes: 14%. No: 86%.
In writing of a serious nature   Yes: 5%. No: 95%.

STEWART BEACH: "No. It sounds dreadful."
BARRY BINGHAM, SR.: " 'Irregardless' of how many people use this barbarous and utterly useless word, I must still regard it as less than the lowest standard of English."

HAL BORLAND: "Only as an amusing illiteracy."

HEYWOOD HALE BROUN: "It is useful only as a means of displaying playful vulgarity."

ANTHONY BURGESS: "No excuse for doubling negative."

ROBERT CRICHTON: "We must never let this one get ahead of us."

ROBERT CROMIE: "No. I am irrelentless in my opposition."

HERBERT MITGANG: "There are usually two categories—speech and writing —but there is a third: the accepted usage by writers of dialogue in fiction or quotes in nonfiction to indicate character, education, regional talk, etc. Thus, if a student uses 'irregardless' it would be wrong for a professional writer to correct his English in quoted material. On the other hand, if, in the example, a law school graduate used it in a brief, I would wonder seriously about his education and ability, and recommend him for a job as a Nixon speechwriter or some similar place where ignorance counts."

ORVILLE PRESCOTT: "Abominable!"

DAVID SCHOENBRUN: "Must the ignorant triumph any more?"

ERICH SEGAL: "NEVER!"

CHARLES E. SILBERMAN: "No, except in a joking way."

WALTER W. "RED" SMITH: "Irregardless of consequence, I reject this as utterly unsenseless."

ELVIS STAHR, JR.: "Emphatically NO. 'Irregardless' is not only a non-word but, unlike much slang, it is wasteful of breath. It's ignorant and somehow pompous to use it."

EARL UBELL: "I use it ironically in speech and I'm surprised nobody picks up the irony."

DOUGLAS WATT: "Ignorant; contrary to good usage."

irreparable. *See* REPARABLE/REPAIRABLE/IRREPARABLE

Italian   *Italian* should be pronounced ih-TAL-yun, not eye-TAL-yun.

iterate/reiterate   Both of these mean to "utter again, to repeat." It would seem that English could get along without one or the other. However, there is a slight shade of difference in that *reiterate* implies more forceful and more numerous repetitions.

it's   *It's* is often thought to be the possessive case of "it" rather than the contracted form of "it is" or "it has." This confusion is understandable because the apostrophe is most commonly used as the mark of the possessive case. However, this is one case where " 's" does not indicate possession. The other possessive pronouns which end in "s"—his, hers, theirs, ours, yours—do not involve the apostrophe, either.

it's me   Many people—most of us, in fact—were taught in school that "The verb 'to be' takes the same case after it as before." This is widely interpreted to mean that, since the subject of a verb is nominative, the predicate noun or pronoun must also be nominative. Generally speaking this is true. Purists and perfectionists in language carefully say, "It is I" and "It is he." These forms, however, strike many ears today as needlessly stilted and affected. The accepted colloquial idiom favors *it's me*.

Here is a case where the preponderance of educated, intelligent people (the two aren't always the same) favors the less formal version. Even such eminent users of the English language as Queen Elizabeth and Winston Churchill have been known to say "It's me." The situation is well expressed in a short poem offered by one of our readers: "If you hear someone cry,/'It is I, it is I',/Look around and you will see/It's not me, it's not me." *See also* ME/I/MYSELF.

J

janitor/superintendent. *See* EUPHEMISM

Jap/Japanese *Jap,* which the Oxford Dictionary gives as "a colloquial abbreviation of Japanese" dating back to 1880, has acquired a derogatory connotation as the result of World War II and hence should not be used even in casual speech. *See also* DEROGATORY TERMS.

jawbone The meaning of *jawbone* has come a long way since Samson slew one thousand Philistines with the *jawbone* of an ass. In the physical sense, *jawbone* still has the same meaning, but in political jargon it is now used as a verb meaning "to persuade by verbal pressure." It has also been defined as "the use of moral suasion, arm-twisting or official coercion." It is, of course, slang.

Between Biblical times and the end of the nineteenth century, *jawbone* picked up the meaning of "talk without action." Then it acquired still another meaning within a few years' time. It became common slang among American soldiers for the word "credit," a meaning still listed in current dictionaries.

jazz *Jazz* was originally a term of Creole (New Orleans) patois and referred to the graphically sexual motions involved in certain dances of African origin. As such, *jazz* originally would have been entered in the lexicons with the label "vulgar slang"—if it had been entered at all. In time the term was applied to the music devised for these and other dances, a music at first played extemporaneously by black musicians but later adapted— some would say refined, others debased—by white influences. With the passage of many decades *jazz* meliorated, as linguists say, and it is now admissible in any context. It is also often used as a general label for almost all American popular music.

Jazz retains the slang label only in extended senses, such as "Don't *jazz* (or *jive*) me," meaning "Don't lie to me," and "*Jazz* it up," meaning to enliven or make more interesting.

jealous There are three different ways in which *jealous* can be used. The most common is in phrases such as "a *jealous* husband," where the meaning is "fearful of losing affection."

Another broad sense is "possessive" or "protective," as in "*jealous* of his prerogatives as president of the club" or "a *jealous* watch over her children."

A third usage is in the sense of "envious," as of another person because of his or her belongings, abilities, or achievements.

jet lag Informal for the phenomenon resulting from disruption of the human "body clock" or *circadian rhythm* (which see).

jetsam/jettison *Jettison* originally had the meaning of deliberately discarding cargo by throwing it overboard as a desperate effort to save a ship in danger of wreck. The cargo thus discarded came to be called *jetsam*. In recent years *jettison* has acquired the extended meaning of any kind of discarding or abandonment of objects, persons, or ideas: "Plans for a new playground were *jettisoned* by the council's refusal to appropriate needed funds." *See also* FLOTSAM AND JETSAM.

jet set An unorganized international social group made up of persons who frequently travel by jetliners to attend social events. This social classification was formerly termed "café society."

jew down To use *jew down* to mean "bargain for the purpose of reducing price" is to be offensive not only to Jews but to anyone of good taste. *See also* DEROGATORY TERMS.

jibe. *See* GIBE/JIBE

jitney A *jitney* is a private automobile or bus which carries paying passengers. It is still found in parts of the country, especially resort areas. Such vehicles, although usually unlicensed, follow regular routes and help fill the gaps in mass transportation within a city or town. In the early twentieth century, *jitney* was slang for the five-cent piece—and that was all it cost to ride such a car or bus in those days.

job action

In recent years in our major metropolitan areas there has been a considerable use in broadcasts and in the press of the phrase *job action,* to designate a strike, slowdown, or planned program of absenteeism from work—especially on the part of our so-called public servants. Granting the need for brevity in headline writing and on the air, do you regard this as a valuable addition to the language?

Yes: 37%. No: 63%.

ISAAC ASIMOV: "No, but I would accept 'job inaction.' "

STEWART BEACH: "I hate the phrase, but I'm sure we'll have to live with it."

HEYWOOD HALE BROUN (voting "yes"): "It's useful to describe tactics other than a strike."

ABE BURROWS: " 'Job action' is a euphemism for an illegal strike. Perhaps a better expression would be 'two-week lunch hour.' . . . The euphemistic thinking that creates 'job action' has been very common. Businessmen have become 'industrialists.' Bankers are 'financiers.' One of the oldest was the change from 'undertaker' to 'mortician.' But before that, in about 1870, people who stole very large sums of money from banks had their titles changed from 'thieves' to 'embezzlers'—a mark of respect. I expect that one of these days our local dogcatcher will be called 'Master of the Hounds.' "

STEPHEN H. FRITCHMAN: "Call me a snob, but I'm not going to corrupt the language to accommodate headline writers."

JOHN K. HUTCHENS: "No, because in this sense *where* is the action?"

ALEXANDER KENDRICK: " 'Job action' is an obfuscation of language, a semantic cop-out."

STANLEY KUNITZ (voting "yes"): "This locution is not elegant, but it serves as a useful catchall for various tactical alternatives to a strike."

PETER S. PRESCOTT: "Yes, but reluctantly; it's jargon. I wouldn't use it. But it has become clear."

LEO ROSTEN: " 'Job action' is a fake."

DAVID SCHOENBRUN: "I would use 'job action' only in quotes or preceded verbally by 'so-called.' "

WALTER W. "RED" SMITH: " 'Job action' is jargon with no clear meaning; a fad phrase."

ELVIS STAHR, JR.: "It's so euphemistic as to be nearly dishonest."

jock   Slang for "athlete," originally a college athlete. Now, with the evolution of women's professional tennis and golf competition, applied to athletes of either sex.

jocose/jocular   Among the many words relating to humor, *jocose* and *jocular* have a precise meaning of their own: "given to or characterized by joking; meant to amuse." They are not truly synonymous with any of the other words dealing with humor, as "funny," "facetious," "merry," or "jolly."

john   *John* is a slang term for toilet and should be avoided in formal contexts. *John* is also slang for a prostitute's client. *See also* LOO.

John Doe/Richard Roe   These are fictitious names used in legal documents when the names of the parties are unknown or when it is felt that it is necessary to conceal the actual names of the parties concerned. *John Doe* is usually the plaintiff and *Richard Roe* the defendant.

   The use of these names goes back to the Magna Charta (1215), which required that two witnesses be produced in every legal action. Prosecutors soon fell into the habit of using these fictitious names when they couldn't find two bona fide witnesses or when they wished to protect the names of actual witnesses.

   For many centuries thereafter women had few rights in courts of law, especially in civil courts, so the companion name "Jane Doe" did not come along until until much later. When it did become needed, the "Jane Doe" form was so obvious as to suggest itself.

juberous   *Juberous* is a word you'll not find in many dictionaries, yet it exists and is still widely heard in many parts of rural America. It is, in essence, a dialect pronunciation of "dubious" and figured prominently in the humorous writing of the early and mid-nineteenth century. In that time, when Bill Nye was the ranking American humorist, mispronunciations and misspellings were among the chief characteristics of American humor.

   Juberous, according to Harold Wentworth's *American Dialect Dictionary,* is still heard in a variety of forms in various parts of the country. He reports that it is also spelled "jubous," "duberous," or "jubious." Sometimes, instead of being used adjectively to describe a state of mind ("I'm *juberous* about our chances"), it is applied to the object of the anxiety ("That car looks mighty *juberous*"—meaning in poor shape for the trip ahead). All of these variations on "dubious," of course, are classed as regional dialect and, while admissible in conversation among back countrymen and in fiction to establish character or locale, should be avoided in conventional contexts of speech or writing.

Judas Priest One of the many euphemisms invented to avoid swearing when angry is *Judas Priest*. Judas was, of course, a priest in the sense that he was one of the apostles, the one who betrayed Jesus. The expression is merely one of several used by people when they want to express strong feelings without using profanity.

judge. *See* JURIST/JUDGE

judgment/judgement While the spelling *judgement* is more common in England than in the United States, both it and *judgment* are acceptable American usage.

judicial/judicious *Judicial* applies to matters of law, specifically having to do with judges and the courts, as in "*judicial* process" or "*judicial* review."

Judicious is a much broader term and means "based on careful judgment; wise."

juncture "At this *juncture*" is often loosely used to mean simply "at this time," but it should be reserved for times of importance or of crisis, such as a time of special development in a momentous chain of events.

junior/sophomore/freshman/senior A reader asks just what the rationale is behind the names assigned to the various grades in most American secondary schools and colleges. "*Senior,*" she notes, "is obvious—the highest or oldest class. But how about *junior*? I should expect that to be the name of the very first or youngest class." We noted that it is indeed the name for the lowest grade in certain preparatory schools which rank pupils by "forms" rather than grades: *junior,* lower middle, upper middle, and *senior.* We noted also that *junior* has the meaning of simply "lower in rank," and that the *junior* class is indeed next lower in rank to the *senior* class. *Freshman,* we further noted, is also fairly obvious, merely being made up of "fresh," in the sense of new and inexperienced, and "man." *Sophomore* is a more interesting label, being a blend of two Greek words "sophos," "wise," and "moros," "foolish." So the *sophomore* is literally the wise fool and that is why the adjective "sophomoric" has long had the meanings of "pretentious, immature, and superficial."

junket While *junket* can be used to mean either a custardlike dessert or a social event (as a party or picnic), its most common use is to designate an extensive and lavish excursion made at the taxpayers' expense. Although such tours are ostensibly taken in the public interest by officials such as Congressmen, the true motivation is often suspect.

junkie In the sense of "a drug addict, especially one who uses heroin," *junkie* is a fairly recent addition to the language. It is still considered slang but it is used constantly in newspaper stories, especially those which originate in large cities.

Junkie was once used as a slang term for "junkman," one who collects and resells things discarded as broken, wornout, or otherwise considered of no further use to their owners. Dictionaries now give "junky" as an alternate spelling but the "-ie" spelling is much more common.

junta *Junta* is a word of Spanish origin which has been anglicized for more than three centuries and, in the process, has acquired new pronunciation and meaning. In Spanish it is pronounced HOON-tah but the English version is JUN-tah. Its original and now secondary meaning is an assembly or legislative body which is a permanent division of a Spanish or Latin-American government. Most recent *juntas,* though, have been factions, usually opposed to the powers-that-be, that undertake to seize control of a city or country. Technically such groups or cabals should be called "juntos" but the *junta* form is much more common in the American press.

jurist/judge A *judge* is, or should be, a *jurist* but a *jurist* is not necessarily a *judge.* While newspapers tend, especially in headlines, to label a *judge* as a *jurist,* the word has a broader meaning in that it applies to any scholar or skilled practitioner of the law. This includes lawyers and professors as well as judges.

just As an adjective relating to justice or fairness, *just* has been well established in both Britain and the United States for a very long time. Its use as an adverb in indirect questions, as in "*Just* how many chairs will be needed has not been determined," is labeled an Americanism by Fowler's *Modern English Usage* but one which has "now a firm footing with us [the British], colloquially at least."

Such use of *just* is not considered colloquial in America. Its other adverbial usages, meaning "barely," "exactly," or "a moment ago," are considered standard. "Just exactly," however, is redundant.

just growed A reader wondered aloud just why Alistair Cooke should have written "The unions didn't have to move. They just growed wherever the manufacturer moved his tent." The query: Shouldn't Cooke have written "grew," not "growed"? Technically and grammatically, the answer, of course, is "yes." But the author was attempting an allusion to the famous phrase used by Topsy in *Uncle Tom's Cabin:* "I 'spect I growed. Don't think nobody never made me." The expression that this line inspired—"Like Topsy, it just growed"—has been a staple American idiom for more than a century.

juvenile   *Juvenile,* referring to an adolescent, has acquired unpleasant connotations because of its use in the phrase *"juvenile* delinquent." The term "teen-ager" seems to many to be a preferable substitute.

In the worlds of the theater and book publishing *juvenile* is accepted without reservation. In the first instance it means a role of a young person, either male or female, and in the second it means a book for children.

kaput   *Kaput* is informal, meaning "spoiled, done for, or broken down." It comes straight from the German, probably picked up by American soldiers during World War II. It is pronounced kuh-POOT and is usually used with a form of the verb "to go," as in "The motor on my boat has gone *kaput.*"

kempt. *See* ARCANE WORDS and LOST POSITIVES

ken   In a figurative sense, *ken* means understanding or comprehension, as in "Matters of nuclear science are beyond my *ken.*" It also has a literal sense, "view" or "sight," so that "beyond my *ken*" in that sense would be "out of my sight." The first sense, however, is more common than the second.

ketchup/catsup   There really is no difference between *catsup* and *ketchup* beyond a difference of opinion as to which spelling is preferable. Both words are the English equivalents of the Chinese word "ke-tsiap" which came to us by way of the Malay word "kechap." Originally these words meant "taste" and, of course, our *catsup, ketchup,* and even *catchup* all refer to a tomato-based, spicy sauce which we use to add taste and flavor to our food. Probably because it is used on food after it is cooked rather than in the cooking process, it is ignored by many cookbooks. Both *Joy of Cooking* (Bobbs-Merrill) and *The Fannie Farmer Cookbook* (Little, Brown) show preference for *catsup,* with the former ignoring *ketchup* entirely and the latter giving it as a cross-reference to *catsup.* On the other hand, the bottle on our pantry shelf is labeled *ketchup* and the original *American Heritage Dictionary* gives *ketchup* as the entry with *catsup* listed as a variant spelling. It's all a matter of taste.

kibosh To put the *kibosh* on something is to put an end to it. It is a phrase that has been used informally in America for more than a century. It is pronounced KY-bosh.

Some authorities label it "probably Yiddish in origin" and indicate that it comes from a Middle High German word "keibe" meaning "carrion." On the other hand, the famous Irish poet Padraic Colum has advanced the theory that it comes from the Gaelic "cie bais," meaning "cap of death."

kickback While it is labeled slang by the current dictionaries, *kickback* is a word which often appears in news stories involving corruption in government or business. It occurs when a person in a position to award a contract for goods or services makes that award to a particular individual or firm with the understanding that part of the payment for such goods or services will be "kicked back" to him. This is by secret arrangement because the practice is unethical and usually illegal.

kid The use of the slang term *kid* as applied to young children is viewed with distaste by many (including some young people) but, despite this, the word is now almost universally accepted in informal speech and writing. Originally *kid* had only one meaning: a young goat. However, the use of it to designate a child has been well established since the time of Shakespeare. Some language students believe that the wide use of this term for human children may be due in part to its resemblance to the German words "Kind" and "Kinder" for "child" and "children."

kidnaped/kidnapped There has been a long-term trend on the part of printers and writers to simplify spelling by eliminating double consonants in the past tense of words like "kidnap" and "travel." The result has been *kidnaped,* which, as one correspondent writes, "sounds as though someone had done away with the fancy table linen or 'napery.' "

The double "p" spelling is still standard in England and Australia and is given as an alternate spelling in American dictionaries. *Kidnapped* may be a somewhat special case because of the sustained popularity of the novel of that name by Robert Louis Stevenson.

kike A pejorative slang word for Jew. Like all such words, it is to be avoided. *See also* DEROGATORY TERMS.

kill. *See* EXECUTE/KILL/MURDER

kilohertz/kilocycle. *See* HERTZ/CYCLE

kilt The pleated skirt worn by men of the Scottish Highlands is a *kilt.* It is singular and takes a singular verb: "He wore a *kilt,*" not "He wore *kilts.*"

The same name is given to a similar skirt worn by schoolgirls in the United States.

kin/kith and kin *Kin* is a collective noun and refers to all of one's relatives or family. As such it takes a plural verb. It is not used to refer to a single relative ("a *kin* of John Doe), but the statement "He is no *kin* of mine" is an accepted idiom.

Kith in Anglo-Saxon was "cyth" and simply meant "known." So *kith and kin* means "friends and relatives."

kind/kindly There is a widespread misconception that all words ending in "ly" are adverbs and only adverbs. This view resulted in a correspondent's objection to the following text on an acknowledgment card: "Your Spiritual Bouquet and *kindly* expression of sympathy will always be held in grateful remembrance." In this instance *kindly* is entirely appropriate and just as proper an adjective as *kind*. Similarly it is used as an adjective in such phrases as "*kindly* old man" and "the *kindly*, gracious host."

kindly, thank you. *See* THANK YOU MUCH

kind of/rather/somewhat The use of phrases such as "It's *kind of* cold today" and "I was *kind of* startled by the sound" is commonplace in American speech but substandard or, at best, informal. "*Rather* cold" and "*somewhat* startled" are acceptable forms.

kind of a/sort of a One often hears "that *kind of a* book" or "that *sort of a* thing." The intrusion of "a" or "an" is wholly unnecessary and should be avoided in formal writing or speaking. Some authorities allow it in informal speech and writing but it is wiser to avoid it entirely.

kind of things are, these

USAGE PANEL QUESTION

"Kind" is a singular noun and normally would be followed by a singular verb. Yet the formulation "*These kind of things are . . .*" occurs often, even in the writing of standard authors. Thomas Henry Huxley wrote: ". . . these kind of marks have not been left by any other animal than man." One writer on usage notes: "Only the vigilance of editorial copy readers keeps the construction from being as common in writing as in speech." Would you write, *These kind of things are . . .* ?
Yes: 13%. No: 87%.

Would you use the expression in the context of casual speech?
Yes: 26%. No: 74%.

Clearly the overwhelming majority of panelists disapprove this locution both in speech and in writing, though the percentages indicate a markedly greater acceptance of it in the context of casual speech. Comments from panelists making this distinction between speech and writing or favoring acceptance of the illogical combination of a singular subject and a plural verb follow.

WALTER CRONKITE: "Yes, I use it in speech—but accidentally!"
A. B. GUTHRIE, JR.: "Regretfully, in both cases, yes."
ROBERT SHERRILL: "I do [use this expression] unless I catch myself. I would like to see it accepted."
HERMAN WOUK (indicating acceptance in speech but not in writing): "One just does."

Typical comments of the majority who oppose the formulation both in speech and writing follow.

SHERIDAN BAKER: "It sounds odd and eighteenth-centuryish."
ALTON BLAKESLEE: "I prefer to be specific—'this kind' or 'these kinds.' "
HAL BORLAND: "If this is true, which I doubt, God bless the copy readers. In my own editorial years I found that most writers very soon learned to write good English, once their common errors were pointed out."
JOSEPH A. BRANDT: "I agree with the copy readers."
HEYWOOD HALE BROUN: "I would never use this expression—unless I were very tired."
ROBERT CROMIE: "No. No. PLEASE. No."
JEAN STAFFORD: "Certainly not. The very idea!"
ELVIS STAHR, JR.: "Vive la vigilance!"

kit and caboodle "The whole *kit and caboodle*" is used informally to mean "everything," especially everything in a collection of items.

Kit comes from the kit bag of a soldier in which he had to carry all his belongings. There are two possibilities as to the derivation of *boodle*. Some authorities attribute it to "buddle," meaning "bunch" or "bundle." Others think it came from the Dutch "boedel," meaning "property." In this sense it has been long used by New England longshoremen. It is thought that *caboodle* is a corruption of *kit and caboodle* and that, after this happened, someone tacked another *kit and* in front of *caboodle*, making it truly an all-inclusive phrase.

kith and kin. *See* KIN/KITH AND KIN

kitsch. *See* YIDDISHISMS and VOGUE WORDS

kitty-cornered/cater-cornered   *Kitty-cornered* is a variation of *cater-cornered,* meaning "diagonal." *Cater-cornered* comes from the French "quatre" (four) and "cornered." It has a long history, appearing in print as early as 1519, so it was probably well established in the popular tongue not long after the Norman Conquest.

   The long history of the word is one reason it has so many dialect variations. In various parts of the United States you may hear "catty-corner," "kitterin" and "kittering," "kittercorner," and—our own favorite—"catawampus" or "cattywampus." There are also a couple of similar, though not directly related, expressions popular in folk language to express the same idea of "diagonal" or "diagonally." They are "slaunch-ways" and "skewgee." None of these variations is recommended, of course, for any but the most informal speaking or writing. It is interesting, though, to see just how much variety and color one finds in that part of the language which seldom finds its way into formal reference books and dictionaries. *See also* CATER-CORNER/CATER-CORNERED/CATAWAMPUS.

kludge   This term from electronics is finding its way into common use. If it really catches on, it could be the latter-day replacement for "snafu" and "fubar" rolled into one. *Kludge* can be defined as "an ill-assorted collection of poorly matched parts, forming a distressing whole." It seems a handy word in some situations, as in "The political situation surely is a *kludge.*" It is pronounced KLOOJ. *See also* COMPUTERESE.

klutz. *See* YIDDISHISMS

kneeled/knelt   *Kneel* is one of a small handful of words for which you have the choice of "-ed" or "-t" in formation of the past tense and past participle. Others, such as "feel," which could once be handled either way have since been consigned by usage to one form or the other. It is still acceptable to use either *kneeled* or *knelt* as you prefer, though there are indications that *knelt* may in time become the only acceptable form.

knock up   In Britain this is an informal expression meaning "to rouse by knocking on the door." In America it is vulgar slang meaning "to make pregnant." American travelers in England should be aware of the difference, since it is not uncommon to be asked, "What time do you wish to be *knocked up* in the morning?" We first heard the expression several decades ago and found it still in use in Britain today.

knot   Since *knot* is a unit of speed and not of distance, it is incorrect and redundant to say *"knots* per hour." A boat traveling six *knots* is traveling six nautical miles an hour. A nautical mile is the equivalent of 1.15 miles.

know-how   Meaning "technical skill," *know-how* is still regarded as informal in the United States, where the expression originated. The British, however, have accorded it "unassailable status" (Fowler's *Modern English Usage*) and report that it "evidently fills a need, and its plebeian appearance ought not to count against it."

knowledgeable   This is a perfectly good word meaning "having or showing knowledge or intelligence" but some writers object to it as a "fad word." Undoubtedly it has been overused in recent years, but it remains a convenient description for someone well-informed in general or in a particular field. *See also* VOGUE WORDS.

kosher   An adjective, *kosher* refers to food which has been prepared and handled in accordance with Jewish dietary laws. As slang, it has acquired the extended sense of "proper" or "legitimate," as in "There is something not quite *kosher* about this operation."

kowtow   *Kowtow,* as a verb meaning "to show submissive respect for (a person)," is not slang. It is not even designated as informal by American dictionaries. This is probably because of its original meaning in China of the Mandarins, where to *kowtow* was to show respect for a superior by kneeling before him and touching the forehead to the ground. In Chinese the word was "k'o-t'ou" but it has been completely Americanized into *kowtow.*

kraut/krauthead   *Kraut* and *krauthead* are among the derogatory words which came into English as the result of animosity between nations in past years. The word *kraut* has, since World War I, been used derogatorily in reference to Germans and people of German descent. In fact, toward the end of World War II, the Army newspaper *Stars and Stripes* announced that it would use *kraut* in its stories of enemy action because it "gives less dignity to the enemy."

The epithet *krauthead* was also fairly common among U.S. servicemen of World War II and was always used unflatteringly in referring to German soldiers. Later it came to mean "stupid" or "thick-headed." In any event, these *derogatory terms* (which see) are offensive to persons of German nationality or descent and should be avoided.

kudos   There is no such thing as a "kudo." The word is *kudos* and it is singular. It means praise or credit for an outstanding achievement and is pronounced either KYOO-doss or KOO-doss.

The word comes from the Greek "kydos," meaning "glory," and

owes its popularity to the influence of the Luce magazines. In its early days, *Time* strove for a unique style, highlighted by curious inversions of phrasing, terse, staccato sentences, and the use of a fairly bizarre vocabulary.

These idiosyncrasies have long and happily been abandoned, but among the legacies of the experiment is a scattering of words like *kudos* and "tycoon" which early *Time* editors dug out of the unabridged dictionaries and restored to the popular tongue.

Somewhere along the way, the lively and sometimes verbally eccentric show-business magazine *Variety* started using *kudos* as though it were a plural form of "kudo," which doesn't exist. Although some dictionaries contend that the form should be *kudos* for both singular and plural, this seems to violate normal rules for making plurals. So, if it is more than one high honor you are talking about, make it *kudoses*.

labor/labour. *See* BRITISH-AMERICAN SPELLING VARIATIONS

laboratory *Laboratory* should be pronounced LAB-ruh-tor-ee, not LAB-ruh-tree. The pronunciation luh-BOR-uh-tor-ee is British.

lace-curtain Irish. *See* IRISH, BOG-TROTTING/LACE-CURTAIN/-SHANTY

lack (in/for) The simpler and more direct use of the verb *lack* is as a transitive verb, without any preposition following it, as in "*lack* sufficient funds to make the trip." The use of the verb with "in," as in "What he *lacks in* brilliance is outweighed by his dependability" is acceptable. A construction such as "I do not *lack for* money" is not widely used.

lacquer In England one doesn't use hair spray to curb unruly locks; it's hair *lacquer*, or simply *lacquer*.

ladder/hose In England women don't get runs in their stockings, they get *ladders* in their *hose*. Nylons are sometimes advertised as *ladder-proof*.

lady/woman The changing economic and social status of women has almost completely eliminated the notion that the term *woman* is somewhat disparaging as compared to the term *lady*. In the past, the term *lady* had two curiously contrasting connotations. The most prevalent one was that a *lady* was a female person of breeding and refinement. In some circles, *ladies* were what were euphemistically known as "*ladies* of the evening." We still have "*ladies'* auxiliaries," but organizations such as the "Greenwich *Women's* Club" have been joined by the "League of *Women* Voters," and, more recently, by "*Women's* Liberation" and the "National Organization of *Women.*"

Obviously, women are taking more pride in the term *women* and it is standard usage. "*Ladies* and gentlemen" is perhaps the last remnant of general usage of the term *lady,* except as part of a noble title (*Lady* Astor).

ladybug/ladybird   The tiny reddish beetle with black spots known to generations of children by the rhyme "*Ladybug, ladybug,* fly away home" is known in England as the *ladybird.* Incidentally, according to Iona and Peter Opie, whose *Lore and Language of School Children* (Oxford University Press) is a classic in the field, English children regard finding a *ladybird* on their way to school an omen of good luck for the day. American children also regard finding a ladybug (not only on the way to school, though) as the omen of a good day.

laid/lain. *See* LAY/LIE

laissez faire   This phrase borrowed from the French and meaning "leave well enough alone—don't interfere in the affairs of others" is pronounced less-ay FAIR.

laity. *See* LAYMEN/LAITY

lame duck   In America a *lame duck* is an officeholder who fails of re-election but still has some time left in his term until the successful candidate takes office. In England, by contrast, a *lame duck* is any person who seems to be a perpetual hard-luck fellow, the type who, in the slang phrase, can't win for losing. A *lame duck* in British financial jargon is a person who defaults on his financial responsibilities.

lands acquisition. *See* NOUN PLURALS, USED ATTRIBUTIVELY

larder   A *larder* in England is loosely equivalent to the American pantry, though it is often restricted in use to describing a room in which meat and other foods are kept.

large/largely   The usual adverbial form of *large* is *largely* but there are two instances where *large* is the proper form to use: after the verbs "loom" and "bulk." The proper idioms are "loom *large*" and "bulk *large,*" not "loom *largely*" or "bulk *largely.*"

lashings British slang equivalent of the American "lots," "loads," or "scads."

last/latest *Last* is labeled as an alternative superlative of *late* in the dictionaries but to purists there is a distinction: *last* has a connotation of finality, while *latest* can mean only "most recent."

last name as form of address During the 1930s and earlier it was the practice of the more snobbish male students at private schools and colleges to address their peers by last names only. Even in recent years, we have had letters from readers who argue that it represents a form of salutation suitable to all classes of society. The practice was irritating then and is today, for implicit in it is a snobbery which does not belong in our democratic society. There are occasions, however, when something between the formality of "Dear Mr. Doe" and "Dear John" is called for. When one has met a person briefly but does not know him well, a form of address employing both given name and surname is sometimes useful: "Dear John Doe."

late The use of *late* in referring to a person recently deceased has been standard since before Columbus made his first trip to the New World. There is no precise time element involved in determining how long a person must be dead before he is no longer considered *late*. As a general rule, *late* is used in reference to persons whose death has occurred within the twenty or thirty years just past. On the other hand, it is proper for an elderly person to refer to a contemporary who has preceded him in death as "the *late*."

late, widow of the The basic meaning of the word "widow" makes the phrase "*widow of the late* Senator Joseph Jones" redundant. She would not be his widow if he were not deceased.

latest. *See* LAST/LATEST

Latin-American. *See* AMERICAN

latter

USAGE PANEL QUESTION

Latter is defined as "the second of two things mentioned." A recent news story went: "The president, vice president and press attaché appeared and the *latter* remained to answer questions after the meeting adjourned."

Would you accept this use of "latter" in this context? Yes: 24%. No: 76%.

BARRY BINGHAM, SR.: "A horrible solecism."

HEYWOOD HALE BROUN: "I feel as strongly about this as about the limitation of alternatives to two."

ROBERT CROMIE: "I would have left with the president and vice-president."

WILLARD R. ESPY: "The sentence cited raises a simple question of clarity. At first reading, I thought both the vice-president and the press attaché had remained to answer questions. Any change in language which creates needless uncertainties of meaning must be blackballed."

PAUL HORGAN: "No. But usage is swaying toward it."

JOHN K. HUTCHENS: "Yes—though aware that I really should use 'last named.'"

JAMES J. KILPATRICK: "'. . . and the attaché remained,' etc."

STANLEY KUNITZ: "What's wrong with 'last'?"

HERBERT MITGANG: "Except in legal documents and such, the trick is to avoid 'former' or 'latter' in a well-done sentence."

ORVILLE PRESCOTT: "Prefer period after 'appeared.' 'The attaché,' etc."

F. D. REEVE: "Slang and obscenity are alive; this is bureaucratic garbage."

BERTON ROUECHÉ: "No, but only out of habit. I don't think it matters much."

HAROLD SCHONBERG: "'Last-named' is how we get around it."

ERICH SEGAL: "Let's keep *some* standards."

ELVIS STAHR, JR.: "Yes, just barely. 'The last named' is awkward."

HAROLD TAYLOR: "Yes, can't think of another short way of saying it."

EARL UBELL: "Last."

A.B.C. WHIPPLE: "It seems to have become accepted."

laudable/laudatory Often confused because both words are related to praise, *laudable* and *laudatory* are not synonymous. *Laudable* means "worthy of praise" or "commendable," while *laudatory* means "expressing praise." A *"laudable"* effort" or *"laudable"* project" may receive *"laudatory* comments." In effect one is the cause of the other.

law/lawyer *Law* should be pronounced as written, to rhyme with *awe*. The mispronunciations LOR and LOR-yer are especially prevalent in the New England states.

lawman *Lawman* is not even entered in standard desk dictionaries. Webster's Third International (Unabridged) does list it as meaning a hereditary official of medieval England or a present-day law-enforcement officer, such as a sheriff or policeman. It has a "wild West" connotation, though. As the Associated Press style book states: "There are policemen, detectives, deputies, investigators, etc., but not 'lawmen.' "

lax   Most people are well aware of *lax* as an adjective with the senses of "loose," "not strict," and "not conscientious." One reader raised the question of whether *lax* is also a verb, a "lost positive" form of the verb "relax."

There is such a verb as *lax,* from which the forms "laxed" and "laxing" come. It is so little used, however, that it is not even entered in most American dictionaries. Here is the definition as given in the Oxford Dictionary: "to make lax; to unloosen, relax; to purge." In this verb form *lax* has been part of the language since before 1685. *See also* LOST POSITIVES.

lay/lie   As a general rule, the distinction between *lie* and *lay* is that *lie* is an intransitive verb (having no object) and *lay* is a transitive verb (requiring an object). The basic meaning of *lie* is to be in a lying position. *Lay* means to put something (or someone) down. Confusion, especially in spoken English, exists (for many people) as to which are the proper forms for the past tense and the past participle. For *lie,* the past tense is "lay"; the past participle is "lain." For *lay,* the past tense is "laid"; the past participle is also "laid." Many persons do not seem to be aware of the existence of "lain" and substitute "laid" in sentences such as "I have lain here for an hour." Such substitution is, of course, incorrect.

Further confusion results from the fact that the correct verb may differ as the situation changes. After you *lay* a book on a table it *lies* there until you or someone else moves it. Here again the difference is between transitive and intransitive verbs.

A Milwaukee reader told us of a method used by her English teacher to remind pupils of the correct use of *lie* and *lay.* To a statement such as "There is a lot of fog laying in this area," ask the question "Laying what? Eggs?"

Frank Colby once quoted a rhyme which might help some to bear in mind that *lay* means to place and *lie* means to recline: "In 'place' the sound of 'lay' occurs,/As if 'twere spelled with a 'y';/And always in the word 'recline'/We hear the sound of 'lie.' "

lay an egg, to   In America the phrase is *to lay an egg;* in Britain it originated as "to lay a duck's egg." Meaning to fail in an enterprise, it was based on the resemblance between a duck's egg and the figure zero: "O." It was a popular expression in the jargon of variety entertainers in England and was soon taken up by American show folk, who popularized the shorter form here. It is, of course, slang.

lay-by A *lay-by* in the British Isles is an area by the side of the road where motorists can pull off for a brief rest or even a picnic lunch. It is rather similar to the roadside "rest areas" found in many parts of the U.S.

laymen/laity *Laymen* were originally all persons not belonging to the clergy; *laity* was a collective noun covering all such persons. By extension, the words have come to apply to all persons outside any given profession, even though they may have professions of their own. A journalist is a *layman* as far as the medical profession is concerned. A lawyer is also.

laze/lazy. *See* BACK-FORMATIONS

lb./lbs. The formation of *lbs.* as the plural of *lb.* (pound) is an example of a foreign abbreviation which has become so commonly used that it is completely integrated into the English language and thus is subject to ordinary rules. *Lb.* is an abbreviated form of the Latin "libra," the plural of which is "librae." Obviously, there is no "s" in the Latin form and there are those who argue that *lb.* should be used for both singular and plural forms in English. However, *lb.* is very much a part of the English language by now and is subject to our rules for forming plurals, not the rules of Latin.

leader A *leader* in British journalistic jargon is the chief editorial, often representing a forceful statement of the position taken by the paper on an important issue of the day.

leaders. *See* ELLIPSES/DASHES/LEADERS/AND OTHER DEVICES

leak *Leak,* both as a noun and as a verb, has acquired acceptance as having to do with the disclosure of confidential or previously secret information, usually to the news media. In this figurative sense, *leak* may sound like slang but the Oxford Dictionary records the use in 1840 of *"leak* out" as meaning "to become known despite efforts at concealment," and American dictionaries accept it as standard.

learn/teach The use of *learn* as a substitute for *teach* (to instruct or give knowledge) is nonstandard English and as such is never acceptable, except when used in dialogue to represent semi-literate speech.

leastways/leastwise Neither word is suitable for formal speech or writing. Both mean "at least." *Leastwise* is considered by dictionary editors to be acceptable in informal speech; *leastways* to be a dialect term.

leave/let   Aside from *leave me alone* and *let me alone* (which see), these are not interchangeable. When it is not used in this sense of "not disturbing," *leave* has two basic meanings: "to go away from" or "to cause to remain." It should not be substituted for *let*, especially in such gaucheries as "*Leave* us go to the movies." In the proper phrasing, "*Let* us go to the movies," *let* functions as an auxiliary verb, which *leave* never can. Neither should *leave* be substituted for *let* in the sense of "allow" or "permit."

leave me alone/let me alone   *Leave me alone* in the sense of "Do not bother me" is regarded as informal, meaning that it is widely heard in popular speech but is not accepted in more formal speech or writing. *Let* is preferred in this construction.

lectern. *See* DAIS/PODIUM/LECTERN

leery   *Leery*, meaning "wary" or "distrustful," is regarded by some as slang but it is more accurately classified as informal, that is, acceptable in all but formal writing or speech.

legend/legendary   The totality of fact and fiction that is the legacy of our great folk heroes is properly called *legend* and their fame *legendary*, despite the view of some purists that *legend* should be confined to mythical stories. The objection so raised—that the adjective *legendary* and the noun *legend* should not be used in reference to actual historical personages—is simply not valid. Indeed, the labels may rightly be applied to anyone whose accomplishments were so great that they have been recorded in history books. In current usage we often speak of a person as being "a *legend* in his own time." And we cannot forbear reporting on one prominent entertainer notable as much for his conceit as for his talent. According to one of his sizable staff of ghost writers, he is a "*legend* in his own mind."

legitimatist   This is a word whose meaning has not changed over the centuries but whose application has changed with the changing political scene.

    Legitimatist means "one who supports legitimate or legally constituted authority." Its origin dates back to feudal times. Indeed we borrowed it from the French "légitimiste." Then it meant one who supported a monarchy based on rights of heredity. During U.S. intervention in the Dominican Republic in the middle of this century, a newspaper columnist wrote, "There would have been no further elections and the legitimist party—that of the Constitutionalists—would have been barred from coming back into power through the democratic process." His point was that there had been a duly constituted and elected party and its only chance of escaping obliteration lay (or seemed to President Johnson to lie) in our invading and preventing a Communist coup.

legpull   The expression "You're pulling my leg," meaning "You're playing a joke on me," is fairly common in America. However, the British have created a noun from the phrase, so that a *legpull* is roughly synonymous with "gag," "prank," or "jest." Slang.

leisurely   A reader questioned the correctness of a radio commercial for a restaurant boasting that "meals are served leisurely." While *leisurely* as an adjective ("in a *leisurely* fashion") is more common and perhaps more graceful, there is nothing wrong with the use of *leisurely* as an adverb, the way it is used in the example. Since every second counts in a brief spot commercial, perhaps the advertiser couldn't afford the *leisurely* approach of using four words ("In a *leisurely* fashion") where one would do.

lemon. *See* CLUNKER

lend/loan   There have been efforts made by purists to effect a distinction between *lend* and *loan,* keeping *loan* only as a noun form and *lend* only as a verb. The American public, which has never shown any great sympathy for authoritarian dictates, blandly ignores the proscription of the purists. As a result, prevailing opinion holds that *loan* is perfectly acceptable as a verb.

length   *Length* should be pronounced LENGKTH, not LENTH.

lengthy/long   *Lengthy* is characterized in Fowler's *Modern English Usage* as "an Americanism long established in Britain, sometimes used as a jocular or stylish synonym for *long* but more commonly and more usefully as implying tediousness as well as length." A further distinction might be made, in that *lengthy,* in the U.S. where it originated, is used to refer to the element of time, as in "a *lengthy* discussion," and does not necessarily imply tediousness.

less/fewer

USAGE PANEL QUESTION

A doctor promoting a diet book on TV repeatedly spoke of consuming *"less calories a day."* Many careful users of language draw a distinction between *less* and *fewer,* restricting *less* to quantities that can be measured (*"less* flour in the batter") and *fewer* to things that can be counted (*"fewer* people in the audience"). If this distinction had been observed by the doctor—or even, perhaps, known to him—he would have been talking about *fewer* (not *less*) calories. Do you observe this distinction?

In speech   Yes: 76%. No: 24%.
In writing   Yes: 85%. No: 15%.

Clearly a substantial majority of panel members advocates retaining this distinction between *less* and *fewer,* with rather *fewer* members observing it in speech than in writing. Here are comments of some of the members who favor retaining the distinction in both contexts.

HAL BORLAND: "There is a clear and definite difference that should be observed."

HEYWOOD HALE BROUN: "The distinction between greater or lesser mass, greater or fewer numbers seems essential in a society which tends to think of us as mass."

STEPHEN H. FRITCHMAN: "Let's be as exact as we're allowed to be."

JOHN K. HUTCHENS: "Anyhow I try to observe the distinction, though it's probably a hopeless battle, like trying to preserve 'data' as a plural noun." (NOTE: See entry *data/datum.*)

ELIZABETH JANEWAY: "I'm so glad you brought this up! For some reason this misuse drives me batty."

JULES LOH: "A nice distinction that it would be useful to keep."

PETER S. PRESCOTT: "Absolutely. This falling-off is one of the principal illiteracies of our time and must be resisted to the end."

VERMONT ROYSTER: "However, fewer and fewer writers observe it, so the distinction is becoming less and less."

HERMAN WOUK: "More or less instinctively. I never thought about it. That [diet book] doctor sounds like a Winston ad."

And here are comments from panelists who, for a variety of reasons, do not observe the distinction:

ISAAC ASIMOV: "I do not observe the distinction but I should, now that it has been explained to me."

ABE BURROWS: *"Fewer* doesn't sound like enough to help you lose weight."

JUDITH VIORST: "I try to."

let/leave *See* LEAVE/LET

level In addition to its literal meanings, *level* as a verb has acquired a special meaning in informal speech. Used with "with" it means to be frank or to give the facts, as in "If you will *level* with me, we can solve this problem."

lever British pronunciation of this word has always used the long "e." Indeed the famous soap-making concern Lever Brothers, originally a British firm, still calls itself LEE-ver Brothers. American pronunciation has long favored the short "e" and today all American dictionaries indicate that LEV-er is more widely used than LEE-ver. However, though LEE-ver may sound affected, it is still acceptable.

lewd *Lewd,* which today means lascivious or prurient, intended to incite lust, has strayed far from its original meaning. In Shakespeare's time it meant simply uncultured, ignorant, or unlettered.

lexicographer/philologist *Lexicographer* is the precise term for a person who writes or edits dictionaries, as we do.

Philologist indicates a broader interest in words and literature than is implied in the technically more specialized profession of dictionary making.

liable. *See* APT/LIKELY/LIABLE

libel/slander One of the basic precepts taught in schools of journalism is to avoid *libel* since it can be the basis for both civil and criminal charges.

Libel is technically the defamation of a person by holding him up to public ridicule or damaging his reputation by means of written statements or by pictorial expression. The only defenses against charges of *libel* are (1) that the statements can be proven to be true, and (2) that they were published in the public interest and without malicious intent.

Slander means similar statements made orally. H. W. Fowler, commenting on British usage, states: "In popular usage they [*libel* and *slander*] are synonymous, meaning a deliberate, untrue, derogatory statement, usually about a person, whether made in writing or orally." This may be true in Britain but American writers would do well to observe the distinction between the two, even in general usage.

liberationist   *Liberationist* is a word which is currently used in the phrase "*liberationist* army" to designate a group which opposes the established government of a country, but the word has been in the language for more than a century and a half. The original *liberationists* were those who favored the disestablishment of the English churches and the ending of all ties between the Church and the state. The term as used by radicals of today implies opposition to all established forms of society, including corporations, governments, and their agents.

library/librarian   The initial "r" should not be slurred or omitted in pronouncing these words. Say LY-brer-ee, not LY-ber-ee, and ly-BRAIR-ee-un, not ly-BAIR-ee-un.

lido   The original Lido is the fashionable seaside resort in Venice on the Adriatic. In England a *lido* is simply a municipal swimming pool, open to the public. Today *lido* is also used as the name of swimming pools on the open decks of cruise ships of all registries, including American.

lie. *See* LAY/LIE

lie doggo   *Lie doggo* is a British slang term roughly equivalent to "play possum" or "play dead." It also has the figurative meaning of "lie low until the trouble passes."

lief/leave   *Lief,* which means "willingly" or "gladly," is heard nowadays only in informal speech, but it dates back to the Old English "leof," meaning "beloved." Example: "I would as *lief* go for a walk as watch television."

Although there is no connection between *lief* and *leave,* in some regions a statement such as "I would as *lief* go to the movies as watch television" has been corrupted to "I would as *leave* go," which is patently incorrect.

lifemanship. *See* BRINKMANSHIP

life-style   This compound word, which has come into general use in recent years to mean the overall pattern of one's attitudes and conduct, is seen written solid, as two words, or hyphenated. When it is written solid, the meaning is not so readily recognizable. Writing it as two words somehow seems to destroy the "oneness" of its meaning. *The New York Times* prefers the hyphenated form and so do we.

lift   *Lift* is the British equivalent of the American elevator.

lighted/lit *Lighted* and *lit* are completely synonymous and in equally good use both as the past tense and past participle of the verb "to light." *Lighted* is probably more common as the adjective and past participle. "The cigarette was *lighted*" and "She had *lighted* the candles." However, *lit* appears to be a trifle more common as the past tense. "Despite the high wind, he *lit* her cigarette."

lightning/lightening *Lightning* is a noun meaning the flash of light which appears in the sky. *Lightening* is the present participle of the verb "to lighten," meaning to make less, as "to lighten a burden."

like/as Probably no single question of usage has created greater controversy in recent years than the use of *like* as a conjunction, as exemplified in the widely heard advertising slogan about the cigarette that "tastes good *like* a cigarette should." This grated on the ears of many readers and writers reared on the dictum of the Merriam-Webster Second Edition (1934) that: "*Like* introducing a complete clause, or an incomplete clause in which the predicate, and sometimes the subject, is to be supplied from the context, is freely used only in illiterate speech and is now regarded as incorrect."

Thanks in large part to the influence of radio, TV, and print advertising, the use of *like* as a conjunction has become widely prevalent, so the question of its acceptance by literate users of the language was put to the panel.

USAGE PANEL QUESTION

Like as a preposition ("He writes *like* Hemingway") is well established in both written and spoken English. *Like* as a conjunction ("He writes *like* a good writer should") is increasingly heard, even in the speech of literate people. Do you approve of *like* as a conjunction in writing?
Yes: 12%. No: 88%.
In casual speech   Yes: 28%. No: 72%.

Obviously members of the panel were somewhat more inclined to accept *like* as a conjunction within the more informal context of speech than in writing. Indeed, the overwhelming percentage of votes against the acceptance of *like* as a conjunction in writing would indicate that most of the panelists still subscribe to the dictum of the Second International, noted above.

Here are some comments of panelists who favor acceptance of *like* in both contexts:

W. H. AUDEN: "This seems to be standard American—but not English."

ALVIN BEAM: "I 'approve' it in others and occasionally now use it myself in casual speech. Only cowardice keeps me from letting others use it on the book page I edit. There is really much to be said for it."

ANTHONY BURGESS: "I wouldn't use it myself, but I'm not affronted by Americans' use of it."

LAURENCE LAFORE (approving its use in casual speech): "If quotation marks and jocular intent are clearly understood."

HARRISON SALISBURY: "Strong and earthy."

Here are comments of panelists who disapprove the use of *like* as a conjunction in both speech and writing:

MICHAEL J. ARLEN: "Some grammatical distinctions seem fussy and encumber good strong speech. This one doesn't."

ISAAC ASIMOV: "I'm against tobacco and anyone who misuses 'like' would smoke a Winston."

SHERIDAN BAKER: "I've always thought that if Winston's adman had put a comma after 'good' and added *'as* a cigarette should,' everyone would have thought it natural—and he might have saved a useful distinction from erosion."

HAL BORLAND: "Even Madison Avenue now says it's bad grammar—and capitalizes on it."

JOHN BROOKS: "It was bad already. Now it has been used as a symbol of belligerent illiteracy by cigarette ads."

GEORGE CORNISH: "In a day when the young use either 'like' or 'you know' as meaningless punctuation in almost every sentence, what hope is there of blocking 'like a good writer should'?"

SYDNEY J. HARRIS: "This monster is omnipresent and will win."

PAUL HORGAN: "Illiteracy imposed by commercial persuaders ought not to be accepted."

CHARLES KURALT: "NO! And the ad writer who dreamed up the Winston commercial should be jailed."

DWIGHT MACDONALD: "There is no gain in concision—and it still grates badly on my ear."

BILL MAULDIN: "I don't approve, but I am guilty sometimes."

DAVID MCCORD: "This is the hole in the dike that needs a round-the-clock finger."

DAVID SCHOENBRUN: "It is not a popular evolution out of common speech, but a deliberate vulgarism by hucksters to whom I will not surrender easily."

EARL UBELL: "Let's form a wall against advertising corruption of the language."

CHARLES L. WHIPPLE: "Sen. Birch Bayh, in Boston *and knowing it,* has said he would 'tell it *as* it is.' A progress note."

HERMAN WOUK: "I think we can win this one if we fight on. This is pure vulgate."

In the hope that Herman Wouk is right, we re-submitted the question to the Usage Panel in preparation for the Second Edition of this book. The percentage of the panelists willing to accept like as a conjunction in either speech or writing has dropped during the past decade.

USAGE PANEL QUESTION—SECOND EDITION

When queried for the First Edition of this book, panelists reacted very strongly in opposition to *like* as a conjunction. At the time, discussion of the slogan *"like* a cigarette should" was much in the news and the Merriam Third was soberly recording as an example of accepted usage Art Linkletter's "they ask questions much *like* I do on the air." More recently, the newly named "Teacher of the Year," in his speech accepting the honor, said *"like* I tell my students."

Do you think that this use of *like* is now so common in the speech of presumably literate Americans that it should be considered acceptable in conversational speech? Yes: 21%. No: 79%.

In writing? Yes: 6%. No: 94%.

ISAAC ASIMOV: "Not until we have a showing of Shakespeare's 'Like You Like It.'"

WHITNEY BALLIETT: "The battle should continue."

DAVID H. BRADLEY: "'Like' requires a comparator and comparative—'x is like y.'"

JOSEPH A. BRANDT: "Like Hell!"

HEYWOOD HALE BROUN: "Majority rule is for politics, not for purity of language."

BEN LUCIEN BURMAN: "My Catfish Bend animals talk that way and so do I but I wouldn't use it in writing."

JOHN CIARDI: "Common, yes. Will it become standard?—Probably. Will I accept it?—No."

ROBERT CROMIE: "Again, to quote the splendid Harry Hansen, 'The Merriam Webster Third reads good, like a dictionary should.'"

WILLARD R. ESPY: "Some expressions will always be as offensive as attending a funeral unshaven. 'Like' as a conjunction is one."

GEROLD FRANK: "It still jars."

RAY GANDOLF: "If the 'like-as-a-conjunction people' can't trot out anybody more formidable than Art Linkletter and the 'Teacher of the Year,' the battle is still worth waging."

PAUL HORGAN: "Remains ugly."

JOHN K. HUTCHENS: "It may go back to my early training but the use of 'like' as a conjunction jars me under any circumstances."

DIANE JOHNSON: "A lost cause."

JAMES J. KILPATRICK: "The use of 'like,' as in 'like I told you,' may have become as common as the common cold, but it gives me an Excedrin headache. No!"

IRVING KOLODIN: "Usage does not always confer acceptability."

STANLEY KUNITZ: "A losing battle, but let's not give up!"

JULES LOH: "I hope (not hopefully) others will stand their ground on this, too."

DWIGHT MACDONALD: "As Fowler said: 'One must decide which meanings have become so common they are part of the language. But one shouldn't surrender too early.' I think this still can be combatted. ('Hopefully,' I fear, is a lost cause.)"

WILLIAM McGUIRE: "But a losing battle on this one."

ORVILLE PRESCOTT: "It still is vile."

PETER S. PRESCOTT: "King Lear had a word for it: 'Never,' repeated five times."

F. D. REEVE: "Between you and I, students love it, like you figured they would: 'One size fits all.' "

ANDY ROONEY: "I am the only person on the panel who lived across the street from the man who invented 'like a cigarette should. 'As a cigarette should' now sounds to me as though the writer was trying too hard."

BERTON ROUECHÉ: "Some teacher!"

VERMONT ROYSTER: "I still don't *like* it!"

DAVID SCHOENBRUN: "Who says they are literate? What a presumption!"

HAROLD SCHONBERG: "Certain things must be fought."

ROBERT SHERRILL: "No, but not a major sin, even in writing."

JACK SMITH: "Yes. Yes. The question has already been decided. It is pervasive, not only in speech, but in writing by generally careful writers. It's better, anyway, than the ungrammatical *as* used by many writers, especially journalists, who have been frightened into thinking that *like* is always wrong. ('It flew as an arrow.') Of course *as,* in its proper place ('as a cigarette should') sounds much better than like and I'm not giving it up."

WALLACE STEGNER: "No, nor should the literacy of those who use it be presumed."

HAROLD TAYLOR: "It marks the people who are deaf to the sound of proper usage from those who pay attention to sound and content."

KARL V. TEETER: "Not a matter of opinion anymore (though I avoid it)."

BARBARA TUCHMAN: "It grates on the ear (which I think 'hopefully'—a similar case—does not)."

A.B.C. WHIPPLE: "While it has been metastasized through the language, I still think that professional writers—and teachers—should hold the line."

likely

likely. *See* APT/LIKELY/LIABLE

likely (as an adverb)

USAGE PANEL QUESTION

Likely, used adverbially, is practically synonymous with "probably." Some authorities contend that *likely* should be preceded by "quite," "very," or "most" (quite *likely,* very *likely,* most *likely*). Today one often hears "He will *likely* come on Tuesday" or "The new management will *likely* accept suggestions."

Would you accept this use of *likely* in speech? Yes: 37%. No: 63%.
In writing? Yes: 28%. No: 72%.

ISAAC ASIMOV: "I hate it much."

DAVID H. BRADLEY: "Less elliptical construction, using the word in question as a predicate adjective ('is likely to') would be preferable."

HEYWOOD HALE BROUN: "It sounds like something folksy from Petroleum V. Nasby."

ANTHONY BURGESS: " 'Likely' is only an adjective."

BEN LUCIEN BURMAN: "No wonder they say kids ain't got no education today."

ROBERT CROMIE: "Not bloody likely."

WILLARD R. ESPY: " 'Likely,' used adverbially, needs no preceding modifier, any more than 'much' needs the preceding 'very' in 'Thank you very much.' I suspect I would not be a minority of one in those two opinions if Mark Twain were still alive."

GEROLD FRANK: "Simply sounds awkward to me."

FRANCES FRITCHMAN: "It's probably grammatically possible. It just doesn't *sound* right. I'll take 'probably' every time."

JOHN K. HUTCHENS: "Perhaps it's just an old habit, but 'probably' is my choice."

WALTER KERR: "I keep hearing the 'very' and think it's implied but in writing it looks regional."

JAMES J. KILPATRICK: "I am reminded of Marshall's disquisition on 'necessary.' An act of Congress doesn't have to be *absolutely* necessary."

EDWIN NEWMAN: "I prefer 'is likely to.' "

ORVILLE PRESCOTT: "Prefer 'it is likely he will come.' "

F. D. REEVE: "It's regional."

BERTON ROUECHÉ: "Why should 'likely' need a modifier and 'probably' not?"

VERMONT ROYSTER: "Yes, but I prefer 'probably.' "

HAROLD SCHONBERG: "He will likely come on Tuesday, hopefully."

ELVIS STAHR, JR.: "An abuse of an often useful word."

BARBARA TUCHMAN: "No, but I don't think 'likely' needs a qualifier—if it is followed by 'to'—'He is likely to succeed' or 'a program likely to appeal.'"

DOUGLAS WATT: "Yes, but often with the more emphatic 'quite,' 'very,' or 'most.'"

WILLIAM ZINSSER: "This seems to me one of the prevalent barbarisms. I would never use it."

like to have   *Like to have,* in the sense of almost or nearly, is common on the level of folk or dialect speech, as in the statement "He *like to have* slipped when he stepped onto the icy sidewalk." It may be amusing in folk speech but it is to be avoided as substandard.

likewise   The notion that *likewise* is a colloquialism probably sprang from the use of the phrase *"Likewise,* I'm sure," by radio and television comedians in answer to such salutations as "Glad to see you." In such use, the line is usually delivered with a nasally Bronxish accent so that it sounds slangy. However, it is not only not a colloquialism, it has been well established (according to the Oxford Dictionary) at least since 1449. It was originally a contraction of "in like wise," meaning "in the same way," which is still its basic meaning.

The use of *likewise* as a conjunction is improper. A sentence which read, "Lack of time, *likewise* lack of money, prevented his going," should be changed to "Lack of time and lack of money prevented his going."

limerick   This is a five-line verse form (rhyme scheme AABBA) which has enjoyed great popularity in all ranks of society since its introduction by Edward Lear in his first *Book of Nonsense* (1846). Curiously enough, though there are several examples of the form in that volume, the verse seems not to have received the name *limerick* until 1898, when a song "We'll All Come Up, Come Up to Limerick" was widely popular as a drinking song. Most *limericks,* including many by the famous "children's poet" Eugene Field and others from the pen of the illustrious Norman Douglas, are in a category that, until recent years, was classified "unprintable." One of the earliest *limericks,* this one by Lear himself, betrays just a faint hint of the impropriety that marks most limericks. It runs:

> There was a young lady of Wilts,
> Who walked up to Scotland on stilts;
> When they said it was shocking
> To show so much stocking,
> She answered, "Then what about kilts?"

limey/frog   Both *limey* (Englishman) and *frog* (Frenchman) are derogatory racial labels, and no native of England or France is very happy to hear them used.

Limey originated as a derogatory nickname for British sailors. For many centuries scurvy was the disease known as the "calamity of sailors" and thousands of seafaring men are known to have died from it. Today we know that it results from the absence of Vitamin C in the diet but, in those days, vitamins were unknown. Finally a Scottish doctor, James Lind, reported that the consumption of limes and oranges greatly reduced the number of scurvy cases on His Britannic Majesty's ships. So lime juice was made part of the regular food issue.

At first only British sailors were called *limeys* but American servicemen in two world wars picked up the term, and now it is widely heard as a pejorative term for a person of British birth.

The term *frog,* which is equally distasteful to the person to whom it is applied, was originally used only when referring to natives of Paris, but it has been extended to all Frenchmen over the years. There are several theories about the origin of the term. Perhaps the simplest is that frogs' legs are regarded as very special items in the haute cuisine of France, while they are seldom eaten in other parts of the world. A more likely source of the nickname is that the emblem of the ancient kings of France, the "fleur de lis," was often referred to as "the three frogs." *See also* DEROGATORY TERMS.

limpid   This is often misused to mean "lifeless" or "unexciting," but its true meaning is "clear, transparent" or "calm, serene."

linage/lineage   While dictionaries say that the spelling *lineage* can be used for all meanings of both of these words, it is best to restrict that spelling to meanings having to do with heritage. *Linage* should be the spelling for the number of lines of written or printed material or the payment for such lines of writing. The pronunciation should be LINE-ij.

Lineage (pronounced LIN-ee-ij) means direct descent from a particular ancestor or one's ancestry in general.

line   *Line,* as denoting a trade or occupation, is listed in dictionaries as standard, as in *"line* of work." It can also mean the products in which a person deals, as in "his *line* is wallpaper." Despite its acceptance by the dictionaries, this second usage still has a slangy sound, and we recommend that it be avoided in writing.

line, in/line, on   No one questions the propriety of the expression "wait *in line.*" However, many newcomers to New York express themselves as startled by the local idiom, which is "wait *on line.*" Some readers have written to complain about "wait *on line,*" calling it "dreadful" and "not sensible." Perhaps because our ears are attuned to it after many years of living in the New York area, we find it unobjectionable, especially in the speech of native New Yorkers.

lingerie The pronunciation of *lingerie* as lahn-jer-RAY is a good example of what the late Frank Colby used to call "bargain-basement French." In truth, it's not French, English, or American, despite the use of it in detergent and soap commercials on TV. The correct French pronunciation closely approximates lan-zh'-REE. Note that there is no "ay" sound in the last syllable. Best American pronunciation is, or should be, lahn-zhuh-REE.

linking verbs A *linking verb* is a verb which, in some instances, has little meaning of its own and which serves chiefly to link the subject and its predicate modifier or noun. While it is estimated that there are approximately sixty such verbs in the English language, the most common ones are those dealing with the senses: "taste," "smell," and "feel." Other common ones are "be," "become," "seem," "grow," "appear," "look," "remain," "stay," and "sound."

Usually a *linking verb* is followed by an adjective. Possibly because many people are not fully aware that some verbs can function either as a *linking verb* or as an action verb, they have a tendency to use an adverb when an adjective is proper after the verb. Such people may say, "She looks badly," when they mean that "she looks bad" (doesn't look well).

One simple test as to whether a verb is being used as a *linking verb* or as an action verb is to substitute a form of the verb "be." If the result makes sense and does not greatly change the meaning of the sentence, the original verb is a *linking verb.*

lint *Lint* in Great Britain means a medical dressing, not, as in the U.S., the flecks of dust or fabric that must be brushed off an article of apparel.

liquidity A reader reported that a newspaper headline reading BANK LIQUIDITY HELD CLUE TO MONEY POLICY drove her to commit the following verse:

> A word I'd not seen is "liquidity."
> Could this be a personal quiddity?
> Or really a sign
> Of an elfin design
> Not merely a headline's stupidity?

Her dictionary defined *liquidity* only as "the state or quality of being liquid."

As used by financiers, *liquidity* means having funds readily available in the form of liquid assets, rather than tied up in long-term loans, mortgages, and bond issues.

lit. *See* LIGHTED/LIT

literally/figuratively *Literal* and *literally* are too often used to intensify a statement which is actually a figure of speech. If you say, "He *literally* hit the ceiling" when you describe a very angry man, you are saying that he struck the plaster overhead. What is meant is that he *figuratively* hit the ceiling.

live. *See* RESIDE/LIVE

lived, long-/short- Two of the most common mispronunciations heard on the air and in the speech of average and otherwise literate Americans are *long-lived* and *short-lived* pronounced with the short "i" of the verb "live." Both words should be pronounced with a long "i," as heard in the noun "life." Why? Simply because the adjectives are formed from the noun "life," not from the verb "live."

liverish A Briticism meaning "bad-tempered, irritable, having a disagreeable nature."

Liverpudlian A *Liverpudlian* (pronounced liv-er-PUD-lee-un) is a person native to or resident in Liverpool.

livid *Livid* does not mean "red." It means "pallid" or "ashen," so if a person's face is *livid* it is not flushed. *Livid* also means furiously angry. It is also used to describe a discoloration of the skin resulting from a bruise.

loan. *See* LEND/LOAN

loath/loathe/loathing There is a curious difference of degree of feeling between the adjective *loath* and the verb and noun forms of this word. If a person is *loath* to do something, he is hesitant, reluctant, or unwilling. A stronger element of intense dislike or hatred is found in the verb *loathe* and the noun *loathing*.

The ancestry common to all three involves words meaning "hatred," but somewhere along the way the meaning of the adjective *loath* was moderated. (Dictionaries note that it is sometimes spelled "loth.")

Loathsome retains the original meaning, however, and is synonymous with "repulsive," "disgusting," or "hateful."

local Americans usually think of British bars as "pubs" and it's quite true that this abbreviation of "public house" is widely heard in England, especially when a Briton is talking to an American. However, at least equally common is *local,* especially when talking with a fellow townsman ("Let's go down to the *local* for a drop or two of bitter").

logomania/logorrhea. *See* TALK THE HIND LEG OFF A DONKEY and MANIA

lonely/lonesome Usually *lonely* and *lonesome* can be used interchangeably. Both describe a place not frequented by human beings or a person without company. *Lonesome,* however, has a connotation of emotion which is not attached to *lonely.* A *lonely* man can be one who lives by himself by choice, simply because he is antisocial. A *lonesome* person is one who is desolate, or at least very sad, because of lack of company. In usage, this is even carried to the point of *lonesomeness* for one particular person.

long. *See* LENGTHY/LONG

long last, at/at last Characterized by Porter Perrin as "a recently revived archaic idiom," *at long last* was originally *"at the long last."* Its revival has been a highly successful one, possibly because it gives a little more emphasis than *at last.* The Oxford Dictionary defines *at long last* as "at the end of all; finally; ultimately."

long-lived. *See* LIVED, LONG-/SHORT-

long-sighted *Long-sighted* is the British equivalent of the American "far-sighted."

long-time/longtime Some dictionaries give this adjective in hyphenated form, others as solid. Consequently either has to be considered acceptable, but those who deplore the tendency toward elimination of hyphens will continue to write it *long-time.*

longuette. *See* VOGUE WORDS

long way/long ways A fairly common usage in rural dialect is the pluralization of "way" as in "a *long ways* home" or "a *long ways* to go." Such expressions are used mostly by people of little education. "A *long way*" is the accurate form and the one used by literate, educated persons.

loo This is British slang for toilet, roughly equivalent to the American "john" (which see). A few years ago there was a bit of a teapot tempest in the British press when Princess Margaret was quoted as admiring the *loo* in a bachelor friend's apartment (called "flat," of course). Many Britons would have been shocked to hear her make any reference at all to what is generally referred to by the euphemism "water closet" or "w.c." But to learn that a member of the royal family had used the slang expression *loo* was a bit much. Incidentally, *loo* is thought to be a shortened form of "gardy loo," a call familiar since the Middle Ages, when a jar of slops (another euphemism) was being tossed out of an upper-story window. "Gardy loo," in turn, is a corruption of "gardez l'eau," French for "Watch out for the water."

look. *See* LINKING VERBS

loom. *See* LARGE/LARGELY

loosen/unloosen While the prefix "un-," when added to a word, usually expresses the opposite of the original word, this is not true in the case of *loosen* and *unloosen*. The two words mean precisely the same thing, just as "unravel" means the same as "ravel." There is neither logic nor need for this sort of duplication but that's how things often are with the English language.

lorry A *lorry* in the United Kingdom is what Americans call a "truck."

lost positives *Lost positives* are words like "couth," "sheveled," and "kempt," which some people think formerly existed as positives of "uncouth," "disheveled," and "unkempt." They are simply common words stripped of their usual prefixes.

Uncovering *lost positives* is harmless and amusing word play, an exercise we commend to one and all, old and young. There is nothing new about it, however. In the middle of this century, columnist John Crosby represented a group labeled "The Society for the Restoration of Lost Positives," and Bernice Fitz-Gibbon, the top advertising copywriter of her time, once handed in an ad for teen-age clothing with an admonition to girls to be "Couth, Kempt, and Sheveled."

One of our column readers suggested "ane" (inane), "descript" (nondescript), "gruntled" (disgruntled), and "digent" (indigent). It was the late James Thurber who first devised "gruntled." Asked to comment on fellow staff members on the Paris *Herald Tribune* during the halcyon days following World War I, Thurber called them "the most gruntled group I ever knew."

The form "ane" cropped up in the early 1960s on the bulletin board in the Phillips Exeter Academy bookstore in the following lines:

> I know a little man both ept and ert.
> An Intro? Extro? No, he's just a vert.
> Sheveled and couth and kempt, pecunious, ane:
> His image trudes on the ceptive brain.

Clive Barnes, the drama critic for the *New York Post,* once commented on a performer who failed to impress him: "Few have left so colorless and delible a memory in this role."

Evidence that the game is also played by Australians appeared in a letter to a national American news magazine: "The Society for the Preservation of Titheses commends your ebriated and scrutable use of delible and defatigable, which are gainly, sipid and couth. We are gruntled and consolate that you have the ertia and eptitude to choose such putably pensible titheses, which we parage." "Titheses" is a shortened form of "antitheses," chosen on the theory that the scuttling of part of the prefix makes a word the antithesis of its original meaning.

There should be some law, however, against words like the Australian's "eptitude," wherein he raised the ghost of a word which never left the language at all. You'll find it in the dictionary, spelled "aptitude."

lot/lots In the senses of "very much" and "a great amount," *lot* and *lots* are accepted as standard by the latest dictionaries. However, they are still considered informal by many, and a different choice of words is advisable in writing.

loud hailer The British term for a hand-held electrically powered megaphone, the kind Americans generally call "bullhorn."

lounge suit This is not, as you might surmise, a suit designed for casual wear or lounging. Quite the contrary, it's the British term for what Americans call a "business suit."

lousy While *lousy* may be a convenient word to describe something disgusting or inferior, it has only one meaning accepted as standard: "infected with lice." All others are slang.

love/luv These are terms of very modest endearment as used by British shopgirls, barmaids, and the like. When you hear "A pint of bitters, *love*? Coming right up!" be assured that there is no special sentiment involved. The *love* has no more romantic implications than "friend" used in similar circumstances in many parts of the American South and West. The spelling *luv* is British informal.

LSD Lysergic acid diethylamide. Popularly known as "acid." Both the popular name and the three-letter abbreviation for the drug *(LSD)* became widely known in the United States during the 1960s. Classified as a hallucinogen (producing hallucinations), it causes sharp changes in perception. Experiences while under the influence of the drug are called *trips* (which see).

lucked out

USAGE PANEL QUESTION

During World War II it was commonly said that "So-and-so *lucked out,*" meaning that he was a casualty in a military action. Similarly a loser in a poker game was said to have *lucked out.* In recent years, however, the expression has been used to mean that a person has had a run of good luck. Merriam-Webster cites such an example: "He *lucked out* on the exam."

In your opinion, has this new meaning of *luck out* replaced the earlier meaning? Yes: 74%. No: 26%.

ISAAC ASIMOV: "Either way the expression is insupportable."

WHITNEY BALLIETT: "Yes, but better to abolish both meanings. An ugly term."

BARRY BINGHAM, SR.: "I prefer the newer usage. A person sounds fortunate when he 'lucks out' on an exam. It sounds odd to me to refer to a battle casualty as having 'lucked out,' meaning his luck has run out."

HEYWOOD HALE BROUN: "I accept neither meaning and am learning not to call 'luck' a lady."

ANTHONY BURGESS: " 'Lucked out' is too close to 'out of luck' to mean its opposite."

BEN LUCIEN BURMAN: "I think both are horrible."

JAMES MACGREGOR BURNS: "Not yet but it may. Peculiar, isn't it?"

ALEX FAULKNER: "Yes, with the proviso that obviously it is slang."

RAY GANDOLF: "I was around in World War II and lucked out. I was too young to be drafted. But I never heard of the earlier meaning and I hope never to hear of it again."

ELIZABETH HARDWICK: "I have never been sure whether 'lucked out' meant good fortune or bad fortune. If the current meaning of good fortune is established I think it is the best usage. Of course, it isn't grammatically sound but I think there is a certain vitality to it."

JOHN K. HUTCHENS: "I certainly prefer the new one. 'Luck' to me means *good* luck unless otherwise designated."

JAMES J. KILPATRICK: "I never heard 'lucked out' in the sense of bad luck. . . . As a verb form, 'to luck out' now has no other meaning but to get lucky in a particular endeavor."

EDWIN NEWMAN: "In the original sense 'lucked out' meant 'ran out of luck.' The new use is better, especially because 'ran out of luck' is still available."

ORVILLE PRESCOTT: "But it's still deplorable."

F. D. REEVE: "Depends when you were born. It's a good way to determine a birth year."

ANDY ROONEY: "I wrote my way through World War II as a reporter and never used or read 'lucked out' in the sense that meant 'he bought it.' To me it has always meant a run of good luck."

LEO ROSTEN: "The phrase should be deathed out."

VERMONT ROYSTER: "I use it only in what you call the 'newer meaning.' "

DAVID SCHOENBRUN: "It has not replaced the earlier meaning, it has extended it. Both meanings of 'lucked out' are currently used and not confused."

HAROLD SCHONBERG: "I don't even know the older meaning—and I'm a World War II vet."

JACK SMITH: "I have more trouble trying to remember whether 'to bomb' is to succeed or to fail."

KARL V. TEETER: "To be truthful (and I do go back to World War II), I thought what was meant was that he was lucky that he wasn't killed and the other usage is strange to me."

EDWARD TRIPP: "I have never heard the original meaning, which sounds analagous to 'struck out' and fairly good slang. I wouldn't use either."

lumme!   This is a British expression registering surprise and amazement, roughly equivalent to the American "Good God!" or "For heaven's sake." It's a corruption of "love me" and is sometimes heard in extended form as "Lor' *lumme,* love a duck!'"

lunch/luncheon   Technically, a light midday meal can be called either a *lunch* or a *luncheon,* whether it is enjoyed by one person or by a number of people.

    Lunch, however, is more informal than *luncheon* and implies eating alone or with someone else simply for the sake of nutrition. *Luncheon* is usually reserved for an organized social event involving a number of people and taking place in a fairly formal setting. It also may involve speakers or be related to a group activity. Participation in a *luncheon* may also depend on invitation or subscription. *See also* DINNER/SUPPER/-LUNCH.

luxuriant/luxurious   The confusion between these two stems from the fact that they both derive from the verb "luxuriate," which has two different meanings. From the meaning of "to grow vigorously and abundantly" comes the word *luxuriant.* The other meaning, "to enjoy luxury," is reflected in *luxurious.* Thus a man may have a *luxuriant* beard or a *luxuriant* garden. He may also live in a *luxurious* home, complete with servants and swimming pool.

luxury/luxurious   The preferred pronunciation for *luxury* is LUK-shuh-ree. The preferred pronunciation for *luxurious* is lug-ZYOOR-ee-us. The seeming inconsistency results from the shift in stress from the first to the second syllable. At least that's the doctrine according to the phoneticians. As for us, we prefer the "luk" pronunciation for the first syllable in both words.

-ly Many people subscribe to the theory that an adverb has to end in the letters -*ly*. As a result, they hold that "slow" can be only an adjective and that the adverb form must be "slowly." (*See also* SLOW/SLOWLY.) In the same vein, it is insisted that one must say "Slice the bread thinly" and that "slice thin" will not do. Nor will "cut it close," in their view.

However, "slice it thin" and "cut it close" are perfectly acceptable colloquial idioms. That is, these phrases are more commonly found in the day-to-day speech and writing of educated people than similar phrases with the -*ly* attached to the adverb: "slice it thinly," "cut it closely." The latter form may be preferable in strictly formal writing.

M. *See* A.M./P.M./N./M.

machismo Borrowed from the Spanish word meaning "masculinity," *machismo* is a vogue word for an excessive display of actions and attitudes which are supposed to demonstrate masculinity and virility, such as boldness, aggressiveness, physical courage, and domination over women.

macho Long common as both noun and adjective in Spanish English, *macho,* meaning a robust, virile male in its noun usage, and bold and manly as an adjective, has enjoyed considerable vogue in recent years. It's especially favored by advertising copywriters who are given to lines like "Tequila, the *macho* drink of Mexico." Unlike most vogue words, *macho* may well endure in informal usage because of its Spanish pedigree.

mad at/mad with In both these expressions the sense of "mad" is the informal one of "angry." While such expressions as "I am *mad with* you" are sometimes heard in Middle America, *mad at* is the more commonly heard idiom.

maddening/madding A very common error is the misquotation "*maddening* crowd" for "*madding* crowd," both in citation of the title of Thomas Hardy's novel *Far from the Madding Crowd* and the lines from Gray's "Elegy Written in a Country Churchyard": "Far from the *madding* crowd's ignoble strife,/Their sober wishes never learn'd to stray."

The adjective *madding,* now obsolete, meant "acting as if mad, raving, wild." *Maddening,* of course, means "making mad, driving insane" or, on a less formal level, "irritating in the extreme, exasperating." The two should not be confused. Indeed, save for its appearance in the quotation and title cited above, *madding* should be allowed to linger in the limbo of lost words.

made your way(s)   The idiom is *make your way,* whether one person or a large group is involved, as long as it is a single operation. Thus, in a report on a mountain-climbing trip, it would be correct to say, "We *made our way* to the peak." The only exception would be if members of the party followed different trails to the top. Then the correct expression would be "We *made our* separate *ways* to the peak."

Madison Avenue and other misnomers   Quite often we hear the expression *Madison Avenue* used as a term to describe the advertising world in general. Some of its denizens use "Mad Avenue" as a generic term for the advertising industry. The term originated from the fact that, during the 1930s and 1940s, many of the nation's leading agencies had their offices on Madison Avenue, New York City.

In the 1960s, however, some of the larger agencies moved to Fifth and Park avenues or to Third and Sixth avenues, perhaps in a conscious effort to evade the opprobrium which now attaches to *Madison Avenue* in the public's mind. Thus the label has become a misnomer as agencies show a marked inclination to locate their offices anywhere but on Madison Avenue.

New York City has many such misnomers. Madison Square Garden is more than ten blocks removed from Madison Square. Times Square is no longer the location of *The New York Times,* whose editorial offices are a block away and whose main printing plant is many blocks distant. Park Avenue, once synonymous with swank society living, is now the location of many large office buildings. Broadway, legendary home of the theater, no longer can boast many legitimate playhouses.

mafia   *Mafia* is usually associated with organized crime and is used to designate an alleged international criminal organization operating in Italy and the United States. It was not always thus. *Mafia* was an Arabic word "mahyah" and meant "boastful" or "bragging." By the time it reached Italy—or Sicily, to be precise—it meant boldness and lawlessness. It was first used as the name of a secret antigovernment terrorist society in nineteenth-century Sicily. Later the scope of its activities was expanded into organized crime and, under such names as Black Hand and Cosa Nostra, it expanded its territory to include the United States.

During the administration of John F. Kennedy, the phrase "Irish *Mafia*" was coined, but *mafia* in this instance was used merely to connote a tightly knit and very powerful organization—not necessarily evil in intent.

maitre d'/maitre d'hotel.   The Style Book of *The New York Times* insists that this highfalutin synonym for "headwaiter" be spelled out in full, never shortened to *maitre d'*. No *maitre d'* in our fairly extensive travels has ever objected to being called simply that—providing the tip was adequate, and we think we have eaten in restaurants quite as elegant as those frequented by *New York Times* executives. So we suggest you choose whichever suits your fancy or, preferably, use standard American "headwaiter."

majority/plurality   *Majority* may be followed by either a singular or plural verb depending on the sense of the subject. If *majority* refers to a precise number, it is followed by a singular verb: "The mayor's *majority* was 356 votes." When *majority* refers to members of a group as individuals, it takes a plural verb.

NOTE: *Majority* and *plurality* should not be used interchangeably. A *majority* of votes in an election means more than 50 percent. If 10,000 votes are cast, any number from and including 5,001 upward is a *majority*. If the vote is divided three ways, 4,500, 3,000, and 2,500, the highest figure denotes the winner with a *plurality* of 1,500 votes.

majority of one   This is a phrase used facetiously in situations like that of the publisher who discussed a new project with his staff, asked for a vote from them, received unanimous "No's," and proceeded to publish the book. Asked his justification for overriding the unanimous opinions of his advisers, he said, "I am a *majority of one.*" There's a prestigious literary antecedent for this expression. In his "Essay on Civil Disobedience," Thoreau wrote: "Any man more right than his neighbors constitutes a majority of one already."

malaprop/malapropism   *Malaprop* and *malapropism* both mean misuse, through ignorance, of a word or phrase for a similar one of quite different meaning. Both words come from the character Mrs. Malaprop in Sheridan's *The Rivals. Malapropisms* are usually humorous in effect, if not in intent. The mayor of one important Midwest city committed a brace of notable *malapropisms* in a single speech when he said that he "resented the insinuendos" of his opponents and was speaking "for the enlightenment, edification and hallucination of the aldermen." We have also heard and cherished "cockeyed bull story," "stereotripe," "colliloquy," "implifications," "lascivicious," and "exterminating circumstances." Occasionally *malapropisms* can be invented for a specific purpose, as was the case when an overly ambitious upward-striving young executive was warned to stop undercutting his superiors or else he would be in for a "shrewd awakening." The penchant of politicians for *malapropisms* and mixed metaphors continues unabated. Since publication of the earlier edition of this dictionary a few notable examples have surfaced. Former President Gerald Ford, commenting on a Republican defeat in the early stages of his campaign for the presidency, said: "We must turn the tide and stop this stampede." Earlier a Republican member of the House Judiciary Committee, asked what would be the effect of a Nixon refusal to honor a subpoena during the Watergate hearings, replied: "The Democratic majority will run slipshod over the Republican majority." Still another political figure was testing the reactions of his constituents on a particularly sensitive issue. "We'll just put out as many feelers as possible," he said, "and see if one will bite." *See also* MIXED METAPHORS.

malversation   *Malversation* is a prime example of what is called "government gobbledegook," but until the New York State Constitutional Convention of 1967 it was part of Article 13 of that state's constitution.

Malversation, which means corruption in office, was labeled "The Word Nobody Understands" by a New York State representative named Theodore Black, who mounted a one-man campaign to prevent it from being carried into the new constitution. The result was that the entire Article 13 was dropped.

As Mr. Black pointed out at the time: "After providing for the removal of all malverers (malversaters? malversationists?), it proceeded to exempt (1) the judiciary, (2) the legislators, (3) all local officials and (4) all appointed state officials. That left the Governor, Lt. Governor, the Attorney-General and the State Comptroller as its only subjects."

manage. *See* RUN/MANAGE/OPERATE

managing director. *See* DIRECTOR/MANAGING DIRECTOR

man and wife   Since the earliest days of spoken English, certainly since the Norman Conquest, the phrase used in the marriage ceremony has been *man and wife.* The word "man" then meant, among other things, "husband"—a meaning which the Oxford Dictionary says it still has in Scotland, although it is obsolete elsewhere. The word "husband," in turn, was used to mean a man who tilled the soil or one who managed matters well, a sense we still have in "he husbanded his resources." Interestingly, in today's marriages the phrase used is often "husband and wife."

man/person. *See* CHAIRMAN/CHAIRPERSON

mandatory/compulsory   There is a fine distinction between these two words which can be illustrated by the automobile insurance situations in various states. In some states, a minimum of auto insurance is *mandatory:*

the law states that each driver must have a certain amount of insurance. This mandate is enforced only if a driver is involved in an accident and it is discovered that he or she is uninsured. He or she then faces a fine and possibly a jail sentence, as well as the revocation of both driver's license and car registration. In states where automobile insurance is *compulsory* it is impossible for a driver to obtain a car registration without proving that he or she has a minimum of insurance in force.

mania   "Phobia" is often used mistakenly by people who want to indicate that a particular interest or hobby has become something of an obsession. Such remarks as "Sailing has become a regular 'phobia' with me" are not uncommonly heard. The word these misguided folks are looking for is, of course, *mania.* Some *manias* are indeed obsessive in a destructive sense, like *monomania,* the pathological obsession with one idea; *megalomania,* the psychopathological delusion of greatness and omnipotence; or *pharmacomania,* the morbid fondness for taking drugs. But most *manias* are of a more pleasurable and harmless kind. For example, *bibliomania,* passionate love for books; *logomania* and *verbomania,* love of words; *orchidomania,* what might be termed the Nero Wolfe syndrome (from the name of panelist Rex Stout's fictional detective, Nero Wolfe, who was a passionate cultivator of orchids); *timbromania,* love of stamps and philately; and *zoomania,* love of animals. *See also* PHOBIA/MANIA.

maniacal   The correct pronunciation of *maniacal* (meaning "insane"), is muh-NY-uh-kul, despite the fact that one of our correspondents reported hearing it as MAY-nee-ak-ul on a TV news broadcast. Years ago, when radio was the number-one electronic medium, the networks paid close heed to training their announcers. NBC had James Bender to oversee the diction and pronunciation of its staff members and CBS had a distinguished professor, Cabell Greet, performing the same function. Perhaps because in TV the emphasis is on the picture rather than the spoken word, all networks seem now to be tolerating slovenly diction.

manner born, to the   There is considerable confusion in the public mind between the expressions *to the manner born* and "to the manor born." The solution to the dilemma is simple: the first is right, the second is wrong.

At first glance, it does seem that there is some logic to "to the manor born," if the meaning were merely "born to high estate or riches," as symbolized by a manor house. However, the meaning of the expression is "fitted by endowment or birth for a certain position in life." The source of the popularity of this phrase and an example of its correct use may be found in *Hamlet* (Act 1, Scene 4). Horatio asks Hamlet whether the carousing of the court under the new king is customary. Hamlet answers: "Ay, marry, is't;/But to my mind, though I am native here/And to the manner born, it is a custom more honour'd in the breach than the observance."

mantel/mantle   Although some dictionaries indicate that *mantle* can be used as a variant spelling for *mantel* (and even that the two words are interchangeable), it is wise to preserve each spelling for its own meaning.

Mantel means the facing around a fireplace, including the shelf or ledge above the fireplace.

Mantle has a basic meaning of cloak and is sometimes used figuratively as in "a mantle of darkness." There is no record of "mantelpiece" being respelled "mantlepiece."

many. *See* INNUMERABLE/MANY

margarine   *Margarine* is an example of changed pronunciation over a period of years. If you check the dictionaries of the 1920 era, you will find that all of them insist that the word should be pronounced with a hard "g": MAR-guh-rin or MAR-guh-reen. Even as late as 1950 Frank Colby was able to report that, in a tabulation of eleven dictionaries, only one listed MAR-juh-rin as its first choice of pronunciation. Despite this, the overwhelming preference of the American people was for the soft "g" and MAR-juh-rin is now standard throughout the U.S.

margin/score   When a sports reporter states that "such and such a team won the game by a six-to-three *margin,*" he means *score.* The *margin* of victory was three, not six to three.

marketing. *See* MERCHANDISING/MARKETING

marrow   Readers of British stories, especially those by Agatha Christie, are often puzzled by the mention of a vegetable called *marrow.* This is simply the British name for "squash." In the words of the *American Heritage Dictionary* it is the variety of squash that has "a large, elongated greenish fruit," rather like a very large zucchini.

marshal/Marshall   In the United States, this word ends with a double "l" only when it serves as the proper name of a person or place. In other instances, it is *marshal,* whether it be "field *marshal*" or "to *marshal* one's forces."

Mary Jane   A slang term for marijuana. Also called "pot" or "grass."

marzipan/marchpane   Until fairly recently, the term *marzipan* (small almond-flavored confections shaped like fruit or animals) was not entered in American dictionaries. If you looked under *marchpane,* the British term, you would find a full explanation. Both words are now entered and are considered interchangeable.

mashed potato/potatoes   The concern of the average citizen with correct word forms has been reflected by the number of queries we have received as to whether the correct form is *mashed potato* or *mashed potatoes* once the food is ready for serving. Those who argue for the singular form contend that, after the mashing, it is a homogenous mass.

The fact remains that, until the time when someone creates a single giant potato that, mashed, will feed a family, the proper term is *mashed potatoes.*

massive/monster   Both *massive* and *monster* are perfectly acceptable adjectives, though both have been overused and much abused by advertising copywriters. There's probably nothing much that can be done about *massive,* since it usually appears in institutional ads about such things as the "*massive* campaign against littering" or the "*massive* impact of our foreign trade on domestic markets." But *monster* may well have outworn its usefulness, if indeed it ever had any. Among young fry we know, claims of a "*monster* sale" led to demands that parents purchase a *monster*— something, obviously, that no well-run American family can do without.

masterful/masterly

USAGE PANEL QUESTION

Masterful is usually defined as "domineering, imperious, vigorous, powerful." *Masterly* means "possessing the knowledge or skill of a master." Some reference books indicate that the two words may now be used interchangeably. Do you agree?
Yes: 33%. No: 67%.

Some of the comments of those panelists who do not agree that the words are synonymous were very forthright.

NORMAN HOSS: "No—but 'masterly' is a dying word."
PETER S. PRESCOTT: "More needless destruction of the language by those who are too lazy to perceive needed differences."
F. D. REEVE: "Blurred because seldom used in common speech and the teachers don't know the difference."
BERTON ROUECHÉ: "This is exactly the sort of shoddiness that erodes a language."

VERMONT ROYSTER: "Each is a useful word and the meaning of neither should be lost."

HAROLD SCHONBERG: "No. And yet I find myself doing it. 'Horowitz gave a masterful recital.' I should say 'masterly.' "

Among those voting "yes," these comments:

SHERIDAN BAKER: "Masterful, yes. Masterly only in the second sense as you give it."

JOHN O. BARBOUR: "Sparingly."

BILL VAUGHAN: "A lost distinction."

master's In describing the extent (but not the type) of formal education which a person has had, it is acceptable to say "He has his *master's.*" The word "degree" is understood.

masthead The name of a newspaper as printed in large type across the top of its front page is not the paper's *masthead,* as many believe. The true *masthead,* which usually appears on the editorial page of a paper, gives basic information about the publication: its title, names of the proprietor and top officials, and whatever other data the publisher decides to include.

The top of the front page, where the name of the paper is printed, is known simply as the "name plate" or "the flag."

material/matériel *Material* is a very general term which can be used for any matter or substance from which something is made. *Matériel* refers to apparatus or equipment, especially military supplies.

maverick Two men from Texas, both named Maverick, have contributed to the present-day meanings of *maverick,* which are related but not identical. The first *mavericks* were unbranded calves running loose on the open range in Texas. They were so named because an enterprising rancher, Sam Maverick, deliberately left his own cattle unbranded so that, at roundup time, he could claim that all unbranded strays were his. The definition of *maverick* as "an unbranded stray calf or colt" is still the primary one in most dictionaries.

In the 1930s another Maverick, Maury Maverick, became known as a lively and contentious U.S. Congressman, leading the fight for such then-radical measures as TVA and slum clearance. His claim to a place in American letters was assured when, in 1943 as a top official of the War Production Board, he expressed his distaste for governmental gobbledegook in these words: "Be short and say what you are talking about. Stop 'pointing up' programs, 'finalizing' contracts that 'stem from' the district, regional or Washington levels. No more 'effectuating' or 'dynamics.' Anyone using the words 'activation' or 'implementation' will be shot." So *maverick* in the sense of "one who roams independently" is today applied to both cattle and human beings, especially those active in politics.

mavin/maven *Mavin* is one of a considerable number of Yiddishisms that have been borrowed and are still being borrowed into English. According to Leo Rosten's *The Joys of Yiddish,* a *mavin* is "an expert, a really knowledgeable person, a good judge of quality, a connoisseur." *Mavin* was given considerable publicity by a series of newspaper advertisements for herring tidbits: "The herring *mavin* strikes again," proclaimed the caption. The picture showed an empty jar. *Maven* is an alternate spelling.

may. *See* CAN/MAY

may/might Between the two statements "I *may* go to the theater tonight" and "I *might* go to the theater tonight" there is a small but distinct difference in meaning. The difference between *may* and *might* in these sentences is that *might* connotes somewhat greater doubt, an implication that there is less likelihood of your going to the theater than if you had said *may.*

Might was originally the past tense of *may,* but it does not have any implication of past time in the sentence given. Here it is used, in the grammarian's phrase, as a modal auxiliary.

mayonnaise People who pronounce this word as if it were spelled MYonnaise are misguidedly striving for Elegant English. This pronunciation has absolutely no sanction in American or British speech.

mayoral/mayoralty The lure of extra syllables has led many politicians and news commentators to speak of a *"mayoralty* campaign." *Mayoralty* is a noun meaning "the office of mayor" or the term of an incumbent mayor. *Mayoral* is the adjectival form, just as "gubernatorial" and "presidential" are the adjectival forms of "governor" and "President." Those who use *mayoralty* as an adjective also usually mispronounce it as mayyor-RAL-ih-ty, thus adding even one more syllable.

M.C./emcee *M.C.,* as capitalized initials, can stand for either "Master of Ceremonies" (when used as a title) or "Member of Congress." In informal language, the abbreviation has been transformed into a verb which means "to serve as a master of ceremonies." This poses a problem as to how it should be written. You will find it in two forms: "John Jones M.C.'d the dinner" and "John Jones emceed the dinner." Simpler and more formal is "John Jones was master of ceremonies."

me/I/myself Because countless schoolteachers have campaigned against the expression *It's me* (which see), many Americans have developed a fear of grammatical error in the choice of *I* or *me*. The result has been that they have come to believe that any expression with *me* in it is wrong or, as "Red" Smith so succinctly puts it, that "me" is a dirty word.

One area in which this is all too obvious is in prepositional phrases. Three examples of misuse were reported in one evening's conversation with two college seniors and a college dean: "With Tony and *I* splitting everything right down the middle," "The idea of him and *I* sharing a steak is like old times," and "Remember that this must be kept a secret between you and *I*." We can only hope against long odds to convince such people that "between you and *I*" is wrong and that "between you and *me*" is right.

This fear of the objective case, coupled with a fondness for spurious elegance, has led to the use of *myself* when *me* is called for, as in "He wants to entertain you and *myself*" or "It was a pleasure for Mrs. Grant and *myself*." While there may be nothing grammatically wrong with such usage, the results are awkward and pretentious. *See also* IT'S ME.

USAGE PANEL QUESTION

Myself as a reflexive or intensive pronoun is completely established in such expressions as "I hurt *myself*" or "I'll do it *myself*." Other often-heard uses of *myself* include such sentences as "The chairlady and *myself* were the chief speakers" and "The captain invited my roommate and *myself* to dinner." Do you approve of these uses of *myself*?

In speech   Yes: 16%. No: 84%.
In writing   Yes: 12%. No: 88%.

Of the small minority which approved the use of *myself* in the examples given, no one really tried to defend it. A panelist wrote (voting "no"): "Once in a while you have to use it when 'me' seems too egocentric." Those who refused to accept *myself* as a substitute for *me* or *I* were more vehement.

SHANA ALEXANDER: "No! No reason—A change in grammar that does not strengthen, weakens."

HAL BORLAND: "All such attempts at 'flossy' talk should be damned. 'I' and 'me' are still in the language and should be used."

HEYWOOD HALE BROUN: "Its principal value would seem to be as a shorer-up of weak identities."

ROBERT CRICHTON: "Whenever you use 'myself' when 'I' or 'me' will do, you are getting delicate and getting delicate is dangerous business."

GEROLD FRANK: "Sounds grotesquely formal."

ELIZABETH JANEWAY: "The only ameliorating circumstance is that it's better than calling yourself 'Aquarius.' "

WALT KELLY: "I don't even like 'chairlady.' "

STANLEY KUNITZ: "Let's not intensify everything."

RUSSELL LYNES: "Only for those people who don't know when to use me or I."

DWIGHT MACDONALD: "Is this *really* in doubt?"

PHYLLIS MCGINLEY: "Surely only the ignorant indulge in so crass an example of bad grammar."

PETER S. PRESCOTT: "This usage is a clear sign of illiteracy; fear of the blunt directness of 'me' or perhaps fear that 'me' is not elegant enough for 'myself.' "

WALTER W. "RED" SMITH: " 'Myself' is the foxhole of ignorance where cowards take refuge because they were taught that 'me' was vulgar and think 'I' egotistical."

DAVIDSON TAYLOR: "There are distinctions between me, myself, and I."

meal. *See* REPAST/MEAL

mean for   *Mean,* in the sense of "to have in mind or intend," is sometimes heard in such sentences as "I did not *mean for* you to wait so long." This is nonstandard usage. The proper form is "I did not *mean* that you should wait so long."

meaningful

USAGE PANEL QUESTION

A word much in vogue recently is *meaningful,* in such expressions as "a *meaningful* relationship" and a "*meaningful* dialogue." Do you use *meaningful* in speech?

Yes: 37%. No: 63%.

In writing   Yes: 30%. No: 70%.

HAL BORLAND: "Sheer cant wrapped in pretensions."

JOHN CIARDI (voting "yes" on speech): "The damn thing slips in." (Voting "no" on writing): "If I catch it."

GEROLD FRANK: "It has become a parody of itself."

ERNEST K. GANN: "It is the very worst offense to the language since the phrase 'would you believe' and belongs in the same category."

ELIZABETH JANEWAY (voting "yes" on both): "Sorry about that. I try to use something more precise but can't always find a better word."

HELEN L. KAUFMANN: "Why not?"

CLARK KINNAIRD (voting "no"): "*Anything* uttered or written is *meaningful.*"

HERBERT MITGANG: "Social worker and kid jargon."

F. D. REEVE (voting "no"): "It is one of the giggles around our house; the children invent splendid absurdities with it."

LEO ROSTEN: "This is student cant of the 1960s. Baloney."

DANIEL SCHORR: "No, because it has become so outworn a cliché as to have a humorous overtone."

BARBARA TUCHMAN: "Not often—but see nothing wrong with it."

See also VOGUE WORDS.

means *Means,* when used to refer to money or property, always takes a plural verb. In phrases like *"means* to an end," it is treated as either a singular or plural noun, depending on the context. If you say "a *means*" or "one *means*" the verb will obviously be singular. If you say "all *means*" or "several *means*" the verb will obviously be plural. There is no such thing as "one mean."

meantime/meanwhile Technically, these are both nouns and adverbs and have the same meanings. In actual usage, however, *meantime* functions as a noun ("in the *meantime*") and *meanwhile* is used when an adverb is needed, as in the sentence "I had to wait an hour for the bus; *meanwhile,* I read two newspapers."

mecca The original Mecca is a town in Saudi Arabia which is the Holy City of the Muslims and the goal of many pilgrimages. In general use, *mecca* (not capitalized) is a place that many people visit or desire to visit or, by extension, a goal which many greatly desire or try to achieve. Because of its origin, the term in its extended sense should never be used when speaking or writing of a religious group other than Muslims.

Medal of Honor Despite the fact that this medal is awarded by Congress, it is not the "Congressional Medal of Honor" but simply *Medal of Honor.* It is the highest U.S. military decoration, awarded for gallantry and risk of life above and beyond the call of duty.

media

USAGE PANEL QUESTION

Some Latin plurals, notably "agenda," are routinely followed in English by a singular verb. Similar treatment of other such borrowings has not met with general approval. A case in point is *media*. Would you accept "The news *media* is to be commended"?

In speech   Yes: 30%. No: 70%.

In writing   Yes: 30%. No: 70%.

How about "The White House requested the cooperation of all the *medias*"?

In speech   Yes: 5%. No: 95%.

In writing   Yes: 3%. No: 97%.

Despite the pessimism of two of the panelists, more than two-thirds of the panel members refused to approve the use of *media* with a singular verb in either speech or writing. JOHN K. HUTCHENS (voting "no" on all questions on the topic): "I don't expect to be on the winning side but I'm still a hold-out on this." PAUL HORGAN (voting "no"); "Not yet but I am losing."

From others who disapproved of *media* as singular came these comments:

ISAAC ASIMOV: "I'm sick and tired of 'media' anyway. Let's put out a few memorandas on the subject after collecting the necessary datas."

HAL BORLAND: "Eventually it will win but I resent it." (Regarding the second question): "And here is a gross example of why."

JOSEPH A. BRANDT: "Latin is too integrated in the language to be violated easily."

HEYWOOD HALE BROUN: "Although I would not be surprised by a White House use of the sentence."

WALTER CRONKITE: "Mr. Agnew probably would say: 'The media is all graffiti and they're all obscene'—but I wouldn't."

ALEX FAULKNER: "I dislike the use of 'media' for newspapers, magazines, radio and TV so much that I would never use it in this sense in any circumstances."

GEOFFREY HELLMAN: "Don't like the word."

HELEN L. KAUFMANN: "Just plain wrong."

FRANCIS T. P. PLIMPTON: "Awful!"

ERICH SEGAL: "The use of 'media' as a singular infuriates me!"

JEAN STAFFORD: "Good God!"

ELVIS STAHR, JR.: "I detest it and I will not give in on this one."

EARL UBELL: "I also hate the word used alone without the 'news.' It lumps together newspapers, magazines, television, radio, usually for pejorative purposes."

GEORGE WALD: "The trouble is that this word is now used out of context. It means 'mass communication media.' With these qualifiers attached, one could use 'medium' as singular. Without those qualifiers, 'medium' is out. My solution: if it's singular, name it: press, radio, TV. If it's plural, accept 'media' but then treat it as plural."

Comments from those willing to accept *media* as singular.

ABE BURROWS: "People seem to think that 'media' is a much prettier word than 'medium.' I'm afraid it is here to stay in the singular." (But on the second half of the question): "This one I hate. 'Medias' is a plural plural. Never never!"

A. B. GUTHRIE, JR.: "Yes, as collective. But 'no' on "medias.""

WALT KELLY: "Using it as 'news group,' why not?" (On "medias"): "No. Except I would expect such use coming from the White House."

VERMONT ROYSTER: "I hate 'media' in this sense but if it must be used it is a collective noun." (On "medias"): "Good God!"

HAROLD SCHONBERG: "Why not call 'media' a collective noun? Using it in plural sounds stuffy and pedantic." (Voted "no" on "medias," as did most of those accepting "media" as singular.)

mediate. *See* ARBITRATE/MEDIATE/ADJUDICATE

medieval   *Medieval* may be pronounced either MEE-dee-ee-vul or MED-ee-ee-vul, but not MED-ee-vul or MEED-ee-vul.

meeching/meaching/miching   *Meeching,* which can also be spelled *meaching* or *miching,* is a vogue word taken from the pages of the unabridged dictionaries by the literary "in" set, including book reviewers and literary critics. It is a dialect word which means "skulking, cringing, or whining."

meet/meet with   The addition of the word *with* to the verb *meet* gives a new dimension to the verb. By itself *meet* has a number of meanings involving contact, acquaintanceship, or assembly. If, however, the mayor *meets with* union officials in an attempt to avert a strike, the phrase implies a lengthy discussion of the issues involved. The phrase *meet with* is also the appropriate idiom when one is referring to experiences undergone: "*meet with* misfortune" or "*meet with* an accident" or "*meet with* opposition."

mega-   *Mega* in classical Greek means simply "big" or "great" but in the long centuries since ancient Greece, it has acquired new and important functions. It is now used as a prefix and, besides its original meaning in such medical terms as "megadont" (having large teeth) and "megaprosopous" (having a large face), it has also proven very useful in other areas of science in its newer meaning of "one million."

In physics, for example, "megacycle" is one million cycles. In electricity a resistance of one million ohms is known as a "megohm." It is only natural that nuclear physicists, seeking a simple term to measure the most awesome force that man has ever conceived, would reckon the strength of atomic blasts in tons, then kilotons (one thousand tons), and finally (we trust) in megatons. The label "fifty-megaton" describes a nuclear device which has the destructive power of fifty million tons of old-fashioned TNT.

As a further extension of the use of *mega-* in the lingo of today's scientists, we have the deplorable "megabuck" ($1,000,000) to represent the cost of those fearsome bombs and the unspeakable "megadeath" to record the havoc they could wreak. *Mega*-has also passed into popular usage. *Megabucks* can mean simply lots of money: "Corporate lawyers earn *megabucks*."

megalomania. *See* MANIA

melioration/pejoration   *Melioration* is the process by which a word "improves" by becoming more elevated or positive in meaning with the passage of years. For example, the word "pretty" meant tricky, wily, and crafty in Old English but, with the passing of several centuries, it came to mean what we know today as very attractive. The opposite of *melioration* is *pejoration,* the process by which a word changes for the worse. For example, "egregious" (from Latin "ex", out, and "grex," herd or flock) originally meant outstanding and distinguished. Today it still means outstanding—but outstandingly bad or blatant.

memento   A common error is the substitution of a manufactured word, "momento," for the word *memento,* which means a souvenir or a keepsake or any other reminder of past occasions. There is such a word as "momentum," meaning "force in motion," but it has nothing to do with keepsakes. A simple way to remember how to spell this word for "keepsake" is to remember that it has to do with memories, and that "memories" and *memento* have the same first syllable.

memorandum/memoranda/memorandums   *Memorandum* is of Latin origin and the formation of its plural according to rules of Latin has led to many errors in speech and writing. *Memorandum* is singular.

Memoranda is the plural as formed by Latin rules. There is no such thing as "one *memoranda*" or "several *memorandas.*"

Memorandums is the plural as formed by the rules of English and, since *memorandum* has been so completely accepted into the English language, *memorandums* is an acceptable plural. The most common error is the use of *memoranda* with a singular verb: "The *memorandum* (not *memoranda*) is incomplete." *See also* DATA/DATUM and MEDIA.

memories of the past   A *redundancy* (which see).

mendacity/duplicity/chicanery/corruption   Historian Henry Steele Commager is a very precise man, both in his concern for facts and in his use of language, so when he uses these four words in one sentence it is worthwhile to note the distinctions among them. His sentence was: "Never has there been an administration so versed in *mendacity, duplicity, chicanery* and *corruption.*"

Mendacity (pronounced men-DASS-ih-tee) means "habitual lying" or "untruthfulness." *Duplicity* means "deception" or "double dealing." *Chicanery* means "deception" or "trickery," especially, as *World Webster Dictionary* reminds us, "the use of clever but tricky talk or action to deceive or evade, as in legal actions." *Corruption,* unfortunately, needs no definition. Taken together, the four words cover a great deal of human misconduct.

mental telepathy. *See* REDUNDANCY

mercenary/soldier of fortune   These terms are almost but not quite interchangeable. A *mercenary* is simply any trained soldier who is willing to serve under a flag other than his own as long as he is paid, and usually well paid, for the effort.

A *soldier of fortune* may be equally lacking in scruples or political conviction but he is usually as much in search of adventure as of money.

merchandising/marketing   These are very close in meaning and are often used interchangeably. However, *merchandising* has more of the implications of the "hard sell." If you are *merchandising* a product, you are using every possible means of advertising, display, and promotion to find every possible customer. When you *market* an item, you see to it that it gets into the proper outlets for distribution and sale but you don't necessarily promote it as forcefully as the merchandiser does.

metaphors. *See* MIXED METAPHORS

metathesis. *See* SPOONERISMS

meticulous   There are still a few linguists who insist that *meticulous* retains the meaning of its Latin ancestor: "fearful." They are, however, greatly outnumbered by those who accept its present-day meaning of "extremely careful" or "painstaking." It can be used to mean "excessively or overly careful," thus retaining a slight trace of the element of fear, but that trace is fast disappearing.

met up with   This expression, though often considered redundant, may be defended when it refers to meeting by chance or inadvertence. One cannot *meet up with* a person by appointment. *See also* MEET/MEET WITH.

Mexican-American. *See* AMERICAN and CHICANO

mezzanine, in the/on the   Because a *mezzanine* can mean either a half story of a building (one between the ground floor and the second floor) or the first few rows of a theater balcony, the query arises whether it is proper to say *in the mezzanine* or *on the mezzanine*. In terms of a theater *in the mezzanine* is preferable, by analogy to "in the orchestra" or "in the balcony." However, if a floor of a building is meant you should say *on the mezzanine*.

mick   Irishmen are sometimes called *micks*—a term they resent—because the name Michael is so common among them. That is because the archangel and saint of that name is such a popular figure among the devout Catholics of Ireland. *Mick,* however, is a *derogatory term* (which see) and should be avoided.

mickey finn   The first Mickey Finn was probably a bartender and the potion to which he gave his name is justly famous and, at the same time, greatly misunderstood. In the public mind a *mickey finn* is a drink containing some sort of nonlethal drug, sufficient to render the drinker unconscious. This is untrue. Actually the function of a *mickey finn* is to induce diarrhea, promptly and efficiently. A moment's reflection will prove the point. No bartender wants an unconscious person on his hands. He does want to render an objectionable patron so uncomfortable that he will depart from the premises abruptly and, he hopes, permanently. The expression is slang.

midnight   The correct designation for *midnight* is 12 P.M.—twelve hours post meridiem (past midday). *See also* NOON.

might. *See* MAY/MIGHT

mighty/very   *Mighty,* in the sense of *very,* is heard in such phrases as a "*mighty* fine horse" and is an informal expression accepted in speech but to be avoided in writing, except where used to indicate character.

migrate/emigrate/immigrate To *migrate* is simply to travel from one place to another. Birds *migrate* from the North to the South; farm workers *migrate* from one job location to another, then reverse their routes. *See also* IMMIGRATE/EMIGRATE.

militate/mitigate This pair, obviously because of similarity of sound and spelling, are sometimes confused, though their meanings are very different indeed.

Mitigate, which is ultimately derived from the Latin "mitis" (kind or gentle) means "to soothe, soften, or alleviate." It is most often met in the phrase *"mitigate* the punishment."

Militate, by contrast, means almost the exact opposite—"to fight against" or "to war against." It too comes ultimately from the Latin ("miles" meaning "soldier"): "The stubbornness of the striking workers *militated* against an early settlement of the issues."

million/millions The plural form of *million* can be either *million* or *millions.* Determination of which plural to use is simple: *millions* is never used with a specific number; "two *million*" is the correct form. On the other hand, it is correct to say, "There seemed to be *millions* of birds in the sky."

mimsy. *See* BLEND WORDS/BRUNCH WORDS/PORTMANTEAU WORDS

mineral British equivalent of the U.S. "soft drink" or "pop."

mingy "Within the *mingy* limits of their political ideas" is a quote which was called to our attention by a reader who failed to find *mingy* in his dictionary. It is a fairly rare dialect term which means "niggardly," "mean," or "stingy." In fact, there has been speculation that it is merely a combination of "mean" and "stingy."

minimal/minimum While *minimal* ("smallest in amount or degree") is used as a noun in the field of mathematics, it is an adjective in all other instances. A *"minimal* amount" is the *minimum. Minimum* may also be used as an adjective, as in "the *minimum* number needed."

minimize If you bear in mind that *minimize* and "minimum" come from the same Latin word ("minimus" meaning "least"), the basic meaning of *minimize* is clear: "to reduce to the least possible amount or extent." Since the sense of the word is absolute, it is impossible to qualify it by the use of adverbs such as "greatly" or "considerably." If you need a verb which can be qualified, use "reduce."

minion   *Minion* is a word whose meaning has changed considerably since its entry into English. In French, as "mignon," it meant "darling" and was derived from "mignot," meaning "dainty" or "wanton." In English it originally carried much the same idea, the meaning of a "servile, obsequious, fawning person," dependent, as courtiers always are, on the favor of a king or ranking noble. Nowadays the sense has broadened to mean any subordinate, especially one with official or quasi-official status, such as a deputy or agent of a state or federal agency. The term is perhaps most commonly met in the phrase *"minion* of the law," a journalistic cliché for "policeman."

minuscule, sometimes misspelled "miniscule." *See* VOGUE WORDS

minute. *See* MOMENT/MINUTE/INSTANT/SECOND

mirabile dictu/visu   *Mirabile dictu* (pronounced mih-RAH-bih-leh DIK-too) is an elegant version of "Believe it or not!" It is a Latin phrase, common in the epic poetry of Virgil, and literally means "wonderful to tell." There is a parallel term *mirabile visu* (mih-RAH-bih-leh WEE-soo) meaning "wonderful to behold."

mirandize

USAGE PANEL QUESTION

A recent addition to the language of law-enforcers is *mirandize* (from *Miranda* vs. *Arizona* decision of the U.S. Supreme Court, 1966), meaning to read or recite to a prisoner his or her rights before interrogation. Example: "He'll go free because the officer neglected to *mirandize* him." Do you regard *mirandize* as a useful addition to the language? Yes: 23%. No: 77%.

ISAAC ASIMOV: "A colorful word that will give etymologists of the future healthful exercise. How many will trace it back to Miranda's 'Oh, brave new world!'?"

WHITNEY BALLIETT (voting "no"): "Is 'simonize' useful?"

BARRY BINGHAM, SR.: "My teeth are set on edge by the tendency to attach the syllable 'ize' or 'wise' to perfectly adequate words, thus creating slovenly new expressions not needed in the language. I make an exception of 'mirandize,' however. It is a compact and exact word, describing a point which would otherwise require several words to explain. It is a legitimate addition to the language, born of an event of modern life—a landmark Supreme Court decision."

ALTON BLAKESLEE: "It means nothing to people innocent of police or legal jargon. By the way, does anyone other than policemen ever say 'perpetrator'?"

JOSEPH A. BRANDT: "Okeh for lawyers and Supreme Court justices!"

HEYWOOD HALE BROUN: "If this is allowed we will sink into Deweyizing, Darrowizing, and Brandeisery."

BEN LUCIEN BURMAN: "I would like to unmirandize any person that uses the word and put him behind bars for life."

JAMES MACGREGOR BURNS: " 'Useful' is the key here. Vulgar and awful, but useful."

JOHN CIARDI (voting "no"): "Unless, of course, I violated."

ROBERT CROMIE: "Too many people are unfamiliar with the event for the phrase to be valid."

WILLARD R. ESPY: "You ask the way/we two may play/and never soul the wiser?/Be you for me/mirandizee—/I'll be your mirandizer."

RAY GANDOLF: "There are some perfectly good '-ize' verbs—one can quite properly patronize someone who must simonize his car himself. But, of course, it has become farcical. A pleasant carafe of modest Burgundy has become a bathtub full of Thunderbird, and we're drowning in it."

SID GOLDBERG: "No, because the precedent is bad. Supreme Court decisions are interpreted, amended, reversed, and the word would lose its precise meaning. It's kind of a lazy man's use of language. Why not Lincolnize ('freeing slaves during wartime') or Carterize ('winning someone's belief through eye contact')? Look at the problems the use of a building's name (Watergate) as a synonym for scandal led us to: Koreagate and the other 'gates.' "

ROBERT GOTTLIEB: "Just laziness. This can be said properly."

ELIZABETH HARDWICK: "A barbarism indeed. I daresay the *Miranda* decision itself is not widely known and for the occasions requiring this knowledge or practice I believe concreteness is particularly to the point. In any case, we must stand against as many 'izes' as possible."

SYDNEY J. HARRIS: "Serves a purpose, sacrificing grace to brevity."

JOHN K. HUTCHENS: "A less than useful and, I think, fleeting word, probably unfamiliar already to many readers, especially younger ones."

ELIZABETH JANEWAY: "Anything that persuades the legal profession to quit thinking and speaking in medieval Latin is fine with me. This is an ugly word but I suppose it's useful, it's clear and we can hope, for many reasons, that it will soon become obsolete."

E. J. KAHN, JR.: "Horrible."

WALTER KERR: "Perelman could have done something with it."

JAMES J. KILPATRICK: "No! Have our public schools been *Browned*? A prayerless classroom *Engelized*? A pornographer *Millerized*? A white worker *Weberized*?"

ANTHONY LEWIS: "If I heard such a thing, I would have to be physically restrained from responding too strongly."

ROBERT LIPSYTE: "NO! This is an example of the worst kind of cop-TV jargonizing in which police and police shows reinforce language useful for the professional only, but used on TV to give a patina of reality. It should be Martinized out of civilian language."

JULES LOH: "Police jargon. All other users should be lynchized."

DWIGHT MACDONALD: "Too special—am sure only law officers know what the term means."

WILLIAM MCGUIRE: "The word may come into acceptance as jargon and then extend to general use. It seems to fill a place. But I'd wish for a different neologism—'mirandize' has other connotations. . . . If it wins its way, though, that's the way language behaves."

WADE MOSBY: "Yes, but 'read him his rights' is more readily understood."

ORVILLE PRESCOTT: "It's occupational jargon, totally mystifying to all but a few professionals."

PETER S. PRESCOTT: "Of course, it's a barbarism, but a useful one, it seems to me (once I recovered from my shock), for it invigorates, rather than depletes, the language of the police station, where language, by tradition, takes peculiar turns."

F. D. REEVE: " 'Real' slang is great—adds imaginative vigor—but bureaucratic shortcuts—Bah!"

LEO ROSTEN: " 'Mirandize' is as barbaric as 'Brownize' would be."

ROBERT SHERRILL: "A wax polish job?"

JACK SMITH: "Sooner or later, the court will alter *Miranda* beyond recognition. Let us hope they also get that verb."

ELVIS STAHR, JR.: "There are other cases bearing on the rights of suspects. And 'mirandize' not only could confuse the matter but it is an inelegant word at best."

WALLACE STEGNER: "God, no."

HAROLD TAYLOR: "I hate, in general, all nouns as verbs."

CALVIN TRILLIN: "Useful for policemen, perhaps. If lawyers can say 'Shepardize,' why can't cops say 'Mirandize'? Also, it beats 'apprised the suspected perpetrator of his rights.' "

EDWARD TRIPP: "This kind of verbal shorthand in the cant of a particular profession probably saves a lot of unnecessary words. To me it seems quite legitimate—if it doesn't spread to others who use it only to prove their familiarity with law or the police."

EARL UBELL: "It is an amusing bit of jargon that fits only in writing about cops and robbers."

JUDITH VIORST: "Mirandize, prioritize—both are sore sights for the eyes."

DOUGLAS WATT: "Too awkward and, anyway, subject to change as new words come into being."

A.B.C. WHIPPLE: "Another lazy example of turning nouns into verbs."
HERMAN WOUK: "Jargon of a trade that has not come out of its milieu. Not usable."
CHARLOTTE ZOLOTOW: "I hate it! We don't need unintelligible shorthand for simple sentences."

mischievous *Mischievous* should be pronounced MISS-chiv-us, not miss-CHEEV-ee-us.

mishap *Mishap,* as the style manual of the Boston *Globe* states, should be restricted to "relatively minor incidents or accidents. If someone dies in a car crash, it is not a *mishap.*" *See also* INCIDENT.

mishmash/mishmosh A *mishmash* is a mixed-up situation or any mixture of odd things. Groucho Marx was quoted as pronouncing it *mishmosh* but he is less than 100 percent right in this verdict. When Groucho said *mishmosh* he was using a dialect variation common in the Yiddish-speaking area of New York City where he was raised. *Mishmash,* pronounced exactly the way it is spelled, has been part of English since 1450, nearly five centuries before Groucho ever heard the word.

mitigate. *See* MILITATE/MITIGATE

mixed metaphors A *metaphor* is a way of writing or speaking figuratively and of describing something in terms of something else. Difficulty arises when two comparisons are mixed into one.

Politicians are often guilty of the use of *mixed metaphors.* Winston Churchill once wrote, "How infinite is the debt owed to metaphors by politicians who want to speak strongly but are not sure what they are going to say."

One politician who recognized a *mixed metaphor* when he saw one was W. Willard Wirtz, who served as Secretary of Labor under Lyndon Johnson. He collected a banner crop of them from the utterances of businessmen and labor leaders with whom he had conferred. We quote a few choice ones here to underline the need to watch your metaphors:

"You know, I have been keeping my ear to the grindstone lately and I tell you that we have to do something to get a toehold in the public eye."
"We'll all go down the drain in a steamroller."
"If we try this, we're likely to grab a bear by the horns."
"Let's not go off the deep end of the reservation."
"It's just a matter of whose ox is being goosed."
"We've got to be careful about getting too many cooks in this soup or somebody is going to think that there is dirty work behind the crossroads."

Then Lyndon Johnson, after announcing that he would not seek another term, was quoted by the *Nation* magazine as saying, "I hope that my decision will remove me from the nose cone of a volcano, so that I can act independently and with complete liberty." Space vehicles have nose cones; volcanoes have plain cones.

The New York Times, quoted in *The New Yorker,* once reported: " 'Without this money,' Mr. Diamond observed, 'three out of five of the important projects we have on the drawing board would have been left at the starting gate.' " *The New Yorker* commented: "Tugging at their tracings?"

And *The New Yorker* reprinted—without comment—from the Indianapolis *Times:* "Donald Nixon said of Watergate that 'it's unfortunate that what happened, happened, but people are using this as a political football to bury my brother.' "

mob   *Mob,* descriptive of a large and usually disorderly crowd of people, is now accepted as standard by all lexicons. Indeed, it has long been a favorite with newspaper copyreaders who know how useful such a marvelously compact, expressive word is when headlines have to be written.

It is almost amusing, in light of this, to note that *mob* had a long, hard struggle before it was accepted. Originally it was a part of the Latin phrase "mobile vulgus," which meant an excited or fickle crowd. Shortened to "mobile" in the sixteenth century and to *mob* in the seventeenth, it brought howls of protest from self-appointed guardians of linguistic purity. Richard Steele wrote in *The Tatler:* "I have done my utmost for some years to stop the progress of 'mob' and 'banter,' but I have been plainly borne down by numbers, and betrayed by those who promised to assist me."

mobile/movable   The distinction between the meanings of these two adjectives rests on the ease and frequency of movement.

To say that an object or thing is *movable* means simply that it can be moved if one so desires.

Mobile means "designed to be easily and frequently moved," as in a "*mobile* television camera." As an adjective, *mobile* is frequently seen and heard in the phrase "*mobile* home," which is ironic in view of the number of "*mobile* homes" with permanent installations.

The noun *mobile* is applied to an art object whose various parts may be moved by a breeze or wind. *See also* MOVABLE/MOVEABLE.

moment/minute/instant/second   For a decade or two, radio and TV announcers were accustomed to interrupting programs for commercials with the statement: "We'll be back in just a *minute* with more of such and such." The *minute* was usually two, three, or even more actual sixty-second minutes. As more and more listeners registered irritation, a change was made to "And now a word from our sponsor." That, too, went by the board as listeners complained that the honor of being the Longest Word in English went hands down to that Word from the Sponsor.

Of late the tendency seems to be to say, "We'll be back in just a *moment.*" But that, too, raises the hackles of some listeners, who complain that a *moment,* properly speaking, is simply an *instant,* a very brief interval. Challenged, the broadcasters retort that *moment* may also relate to a fairly prolonged interval, as in "Great *Moments* in History."

Broadcasting aside, however, there are useful comparisons to be made between these two words and the related words *instant* and *second.* "Just a *second*" implies very speedy action. *Instant* and its related adjective "instantaneous" similarly denote action after an interval so trifling as to be almost imperceptible. *Minute,* as we have noted, technically means the duration of sixty seconds but, in casual use, has about the same meaning as *moment,* an indeterminate but very brief interval of time.

In sum, then, *minute* may well be reserved for use to designate that precise interval of time. *Moment* serves well to designate a short interval of indeterminate length. *Instant* and *second* are virtually interchangeable as denoting a very short period, with *instant* having the implication of extreme urgency in certain contexts: "Come here this very *instant!*"

momentarily

USAGE PANEL QUESTION

Momentarily is frequently heard in the sense of "in a moment, instantly," as "The plane will arrive *momentarily.*" Its earlier meaning was "for a moment," as "The actor paused *momentarily* before finishing his speech." The Oxford Dictionary records *momentarily* in the sense of "instantly" as having appeared in print back in 1654 but indicates that it is now "archaic." Would you agree that this very old meaning is now showing new life and should be accepted as standard usage? Yes: 60%. No: 40%.

ISAAC ASIMOV: " 'In a moment'—four syllables. 'Momentarily'—five syllables. Why add a syllable?"

WHITNEY BALLIETT: "But is an instant faster than a 'moment' and even if the old meaning returned, 'momentarily' will now—at least to me—mean the same as 'instantly.' A moment, perhaps, is a full second, while an instant is less than a second."

SAUL BELLOW: "I am unwilling to stop at 1654. The real 'momentarily' must be of greater antiquity."

BARRY BINGHAM, SR.: "Let's put it back with the archaisms of 1654."

ALTON BLAKESLEE: "I like the word. In either usage, the 'in' or 'for' is implied if not spoken or written."

JOHN BROOKS: "Can't fight provenance like that (O.E.D. 1654)."

HEYWOOD HALE BROUN: "The misuse of 'momentarily' like the constant misuse of 'presently' is confusing, unnecessary, and presents the dilemma of whether one wants to be correct or endure."

BEN LUCIEN BURMAN: "The announcements on loudspeakers at airlines terminals are confusing enough without making them worse."

ROBERT CROMIE: "If this died three centuries ago it seems best to let it rest undisturbed."

WILLARD R. ESPY: "It is certainly showing new life, and it is not intrinsically revolting in the sense that 'hopefully' is. But no, it is not yet standard usage."

ALEX FAULKNER: "I am sorry to hear that 'momentarily' is heard frequently in the sense of 'in a moment,' and feel that no effort should be spared to stop this ghastly practice in its tracks. Like the plane that arrived momentarily it should take off immediately it touches down and fly straight to the nether regions reserved for all linguistic mongolisms."

RAY GANDOLF: "This strikes me as one of those words which can shuffle comfortably back and forth from one meaning to another without performing a disservice to either one."

ROBERT GOTTLIEB: "I don't really like it, but it seems to me it's gaining on us. Nor does it seem to me the worst of crimes. . . ."

ELIZABETH HARDWICK: "If my ear is correct, the current use of 'momentarily' is a fancy way of saying 'soon.' I think the word is inferior to 'soon' and 'in a moment' and I would not myself use it in speech or writing. . . . In answer to your question, there is no doubt about the new life of 'momentarily,' but I do not think it is good usage in the sense of 'in a moment' and 'instantly' and actually that it is not precisely what is meant when the word is uttered."

JOHN K. HUTCHENS: "I'll hedge a bit on this one. I use it in both senses, though usually as 'instantly' or 'very soon.' "

ELIZABETH JANEWAY: "I disapprove, as a result of the loss of the earlier meaning, which we need. 'In a moment' will usually do for the current use."

JAMES J. KILPATRICK: "I dunno. I checked 'yes,' but now I'm not sure. Trouble is, 'in a moment' and 'instantly' are not synonymous. I see no objection to the phrase 'The plane will arrive momentarily' if the meaning is some time within the next five or ten minutes, but that is not at all the same thing as "The plane will arrive instantly."

JULES LOH: "Not yet. Give it another moment in history."

DWIGHT MACDONALD: "Why not?"

BILL MAULDIN: "It is showing new life but should be hit on the head with a shovel."

WILLIAM McGUIRE: "No. Try to discourage it!"

EDWIN NEWMAN: "It is showing new life. It should not be accepted."

PETER S. PRESCOTT: "Why not use this word in both senses, depending on its placement in the sentence? I can't imagine anyone being confused."

F. D. REEVE: "But I hear it only from people who puff up their verbs; others say simply, 'The plane will arrive soon.' "

VERMONT ROYSTER: "The plane won't arrive 'momentarily' unless it's a touch-and-go landing. (In real life it wouldn't even arrive 'in a few minutes'—no matter what the announcer says.)"

HAROLD SCHONBERG: "I don't like it, but it's with us, like 'hopefully.' At least there's some rationale for 'momentarily,' while there isn't for 'hopefully' as it is currently misused."

KARL V. TEETER: "It's showing new life but need not be accepted."

EDWARD TRIPP: "In general it is a bad thing to let a single word have two meanings so closely related as to cause confusion. In this case, however, the two seem unlikely to be used in the same sense, so it will probably cause no such problem."

BARBARA TUCHMAN: "Both meanings seem acceptable."

JOSEPH VERGARA: "Its new life should be snuffed out."

DOUGLAS WATT: "Yes, along with, of course, its essential earlier meaning."

A.B.C. WHIPPLE: "Why be sloppy when there are any number of ways to say that the plane will arrive in a moment—soon—shortly—etc."

HERMAN WOUK: "New life, yes. Acceptance, not yet. Halfway there, as 'hopefully' was ten years ago, but still confined to ignoramuses. Ten years hence it may be English again."

momentous/monumental   The misuse of *momentous* is illustrated by such sentences as this from a small Midwestern newspaper: "Neighbors are helping farmers whose clean-up problems are *momentous.* "

Momentous should be used only in the sense of "having the greatest significance" or "having very grave consequences," as in the phrases *"momentous* issue" or *"momentous* decision." The problems of the farmers may be serious or even *monumental* but they are scarcely *momentous.* An example of the correct use of *momentous* may be found in this note from Herman Kahn, the man who boasted that his mission was "to think the unthinkable": "The decision to initiate thermonuclear war is a *momentous* one."

Monday (or Tuesday, etc.) week   There is a British expression that has attained a certain popularity in America, *Monday week,* meaning "a week from next Monday" or "the next Monday but one." It's a very handy expression, especially if the person you're talking to understands it. And that's not quite as simple as it seems, for the British also use *Monday week* to indicate the Monday in the week preceding the previous Monday. However, confusing though that may sound, bear in mind that—in actual conversation—the tense of the verb used will keep matters clear. For instance, "The lady returned from Boston *Monday week*" (a week ago last Monday) or "She will go to Boston *Monday week*" (a week from next Monday).

monger   *Monger* is the British equivalent of the American "dealer." Thus a *fishmonger* is a fish dealer; an *ironmonger,* a hardware dealer; and a *cheesemonger,* one who deals in cheeses.

monkey wrench. *See* STILLSON WRENCH

monomania. *See* MANIA

monster. *See* MASSIVE/MONSTER

month of Sundays   This is a figurative expression meaning "practically never." As to what it means literally, the intent is thirty Sundays, rather than just four.

monumental. *See* MOMENTOUS/MONUMENTAL

moot   *Moot* came into general use from the language of law and the result has been some confusion as to its meaning and use. As popularly used today, it means "open for discussion or debate." However, in law schools a "*moot* question" is a hypothetical one used as the basis for a mock trial which provides legal exercise and experience for the students. This has given *moot* a connotation of "insignificant," "unimportant," and "academic."

mopery   *Mopery* is what a person does when he mopes or broods or sulks or simply dawdles along. The fact that Merriam-Webster's Third International gives a cross-reference to "vagrancy" indicates that it may be used in legal documents in that sense.

moral/morale   The final "e" in *morale* helps to distinguish between these two words whose meanings have some resemblance but which are not synonymous.
      Moral, as either a noun or adjective, has to do with right and wrong. *Morale,* a noun, means "mental or emotional condition as reflected in confidence, enthusiasm, discipline, and willingness to cooperate with others or obey orders."

more. *See* ANOTHER/ADDITIONAL/MORE

more perfect   There are some purists who contend that *perfect* is an adjective which cannot be qualified, that nothing can be "almost *perfect*" or *more perfect.* These purists claim that *perfect* is in the same class of uncomparable adjectives as "unique," "inevitable," "eternal," and "universal."

Two classic examples of *more perfect* are part of our country's history. The lesser known is the epitaph on Ben Franklin's tombstone: "The body of B. Franklin/Like the cover of an old book/Its contents torn and tattered/And stripped of its lettering and gilding/Lies here food for worms./But the work will not be lost/For it will, as he believed,/Go on in a new and more perfect edition/Corrected and amended by the Author."

The more widely known instance is the preamble to the Constitution, which begins: "We, the people of the United States, in order to form a more perfect union . . ."

When our country's language was younger, even those most skilled in its use sometimes formulated phrases that we would look askance at today. Obviously, however, the union that existed under the Articles of Confederation was anything but "perfect." It was, indeed, a confederation very loosely held together, which is why the founding fathers believed that the new Constitution was necessary. *More perfect* had a high-sounding ring to it and, logic or no, it was the phrase they used. It seems to us entirely possible that the Franklin epitaph deliberately borrowed the phrase from the Constitution.

They were giants who founded our nation and we trust that their sometimes cavalier handling of our language will not be taken by today's advertising copywriters as justification for such horrors as "more unique" and "most unique," which we see and hear today. *See also* UNIQUE.

more than one   Despite logic and grammar, the established idiom is that *more than one* is followed by a singular verb: "*More than one* factor was involved in the decision."

moron   *Moron* has long been accepted in the popular tongue as synonymous with "fool" or one who is not very bright. There are still those who object to this use on the ground that *moron* was coined and is still used as a precise scientific term. In 1910 Dr. Henry H. Goddard proposed the word to a meeting of the American Association for the Feeble-Minded and it was adopted as the official designation for a person whose mental age is between eight and twelve years and whose Intelligence Quotient is below 75. *Moron,* the highest rating in mental deficiency, is above "imbecile" and "idiot."

When coining the word, however, Goddard went back to Greek, where he chose the neuter form of "moros," meaning "foolish," so the popular or colloquial meaning is actually very close to the original Greek.

mortician *Mortician* is an outgrowth of a general movement by members of various trades to dignify their occupations by changing their names. Thus undertakers became *morticians,* trash and garbage collectors became "sanitation men," and other such euphemisms were born. Real-estate agents became "realtors," despite the fact that some of them persist in calling themselves "real-a-tors."

While *mortician* was regarded as pretentious when it was first used, it is now accepted as standard American usage.

Moscow Pronunciation of this place name has been a source of some perplexity to many Americans who have heard the statement: "There is no cow in *Moscow.*" That's true if you are referring to *Moscow,* Idaho. That's pronounced MOSS-koh. The vastly better-known capital of Russia does indeed "have a cow in it." The preferred pronunciation is MOSS-kow, though MOSS-koh is also accepted.

Moslem/Muslim This is clearly an instance of changing usage. Until 1950 the spelling *Moslem* was standard in all newspapers, periodicals, and books, including most dictionaries, published in the United States. By 1960, however, thanks in large part to the propaganda activities of the Nation of Islam, an organization of American blacks who follow the religious practices of Islam, the spelling *Muslim* was seen with increasing frequency. The newspaper and magazine stories devoted to the activities of the black followers of Mohammed, nicknamed the Black *Muslims,* had a marked influence on the change in spelling. In addition, most scholars prefer *Muslim* and such basic reference books as the *Encyclopedia International,* as early as 1964, adopted this spelling throughout. So, while the *Moslem* spelling certainly must still be deemed acceptable, the trend is very definitely in favor of *Muslim.*

most. *See* ALMOST/MOST

most all/almost all The phrase *most all* is self-contradictory. What people mean when they use this phrase is *almost all.* The tendency to omit the first syllable is very marked, especially in the speech of Southerners and Midwesterners. This is so generally true that it has become almost the prevailing pattern of speech in some parts of the country, even among well-educated people. So, in ordinary conversation, *most all* must be deemed acceptable. "Most everybody" is also commonly heard.

However, there is no excuse whatever for it in print because it can readily lead to confusion and error.

most certainly/most carefully We were asked if a businessman who habitually uses these phrases in correspondence were not being "a bit corny," and if the adverbs weren't strong enough without *most.*

Corny, perhaps, but not wrong. The person using these superlatives is trying to impress his readers with his great sincerity and that might prove to be an asset, depending on what business he is in. In general use, however, the addition of *most* is unnecessary and pretentious.

most unique Substandard usage. *See* UNIQUE and UNCOMPARABLE ADJECTIVES.

mother-in-law The plural of *mother-in-law* is *mothers-in-law*. *See also* PLURALS OF COMPOUND WORDS AND PHRASES.

movable/moveable The more common American spelling *movable* results from dropping the "e" before adding the suffix. *Moveable* is, however, listed in American dictionaries as an alternate spelling and is also the preferred spelling in Great Britain.

This question arose in connection with the spelling in the title of Ernest Hemingway's *A Moveable Feast.* We suspect that Hemingway, like nearly every writer of the past three centuries in England and America, was profoundly influenced by the King James Bible and the Anglican Book of Common Prayer. After all, the title of Hemingway's most famous book, *For Whom the Bell Tolls,* was taken from a poem by John Donne, an Anglican clergyman at the time the King James version was created. Then, too, you will find a "Table of Moveable Feasts" in the Book of Common Prayer. *See also* MOBILE/MOVABLE.

move. *See* RELOCATE/MOVE

moving violation There is nothing affecting the emotions about this item from policemen's jargon. A *moving violation* is simply one in which the offending vehicle was in motion at the time the offense was perpetrated (another favorite item from lexicon of police officers).

moxie In its slang sense *moxie* means "courage, pluck, or grit, especially in the face of difficulty."

When capitalized it is the trademarked name of a soft drink found chiefly in New England. The original Moxie had a bitter taste, which some of its non-admirers claimed would petrify your taste buds. We always were convinced that the slang sense of *moxie* derived from the fact that you had to have plenty of *moxie* to drink it. Since the days of our youth, the trademark Moxie has been sold to another company and the present-day Moxie is not at all like the original. Now it is a sweetish, cherry-flavored soft drink.

Ms. A prime example of the introduction of a new word into the language of Americans and the degree of its acceptance is the case of *Ms.,* which was coined during the early days of the Women's Movement. We submitted it to the members of the Usage Panel for their consideration and the results, with their comments, are given below. A decade later, with the preparation for the second edition of the *Harper Dictionary of Contemporary Usage,* we re-submitted the question of *Ms.* to our panel, with some very interesting results. Here is the first ballot of a decade ago:

USAGE PANEL QUESTION

A new form of address has recently caused considerable discussion. It is *Ms.* One lexicon calls it a "title of courtesy used before a woman's name . . . without regard to her marital status." Panelist JEAN STAFFORD reports that when she receives an envelope addressed to her as *Ms.* she marks it, "Not acceptable to addressee. Return to sender"—after first checking to see if there is a check inside. Her opinion, strongly voiced in a *New York Times* article, is that she should be addressed as "Miss" Stafford, if the subject at hand has to do with her and her business, or as "Mrs." Liebling, if inquiries are being made about her late husband.

1. Do you share her preference for the established forms of address for women?
Yes: 70%. No: 30%.
2. Do you use *Ms.* in correspondence?
Yes: 56%. No: 44%.
3. Solely to women whose marital status is unknown to you?
Yes: 45%. No: 55%.
4. To women regardless of marital status?
Yes: 21%. No: 79%.
5. Do you ever use *Ms.* (pronounced "Mizz") as a spoken form of address?
Yes: 19%. No: 81%.

SHANA ALEXANDER: "Yes. I do this to emphasize the legal deprivations women suffer when forced to declare their marital status . . . married or single . . . by using Mrs. or Miss. Men are not so obliged. Personally, I would favor dropping Mr. too and just using people's names."

STEWART BEACH: "The brouhaha over 'Ms.' strikes me as an argument over something that is quite unnatural. I would never use it. One thing that may confuse the Women Liberators is that when they meet a somewhat rural person they may be addressed as 'Mizz Jones,' or whatever the name is. But the speaker is not referring to 'Ms.' He is taking a short cut to pronouncing 'Mrs.' "

ALVIN BEAM: "I always use it when the woman addressed is likely to prefer it or seems likely to. It certainly is useful when marital status is unknown."

JULES BERGMAN: "In jocular reference only."

CHARLES BERLITZ: "MIZZ—as a *slurred* Mrs.—is of antique vintage and therefore has been in use for generations."

HAL BORLAND: "Blather and blither, or whatever is the female form of blather. Jean is right. Why use any of them? I seldom do, much preferring simply to use first names: Jean Stafford, Mary Morris, etc."

JOHN BROOKS (#2): "Only in cases when I learn the recipient wants to be addressed that way. In writing to women I know, I customarily write her name with no form of address."

HEYWOOD HALE BROUN: "As the child of a feminist leader, I am here a welter of old fears and loyalties! In general, I think people should be addressed as they wish to be addressed."

JAMES MACGREGOR BURNS: "No, or only when I believe the recipient will be gratified."

WILLARD R. ESPY: "I suspect Ms. is here to stay. But I don't know how much longer I can stand the jokes about it."

ALEX FAULKNER: "Awfully useful when you don't know whether the lady is married or not."

STEPHEN H. FRITCHMAN: "To the hot question of the hour—'Ms.'—the distaff side of the Fritchman team responds as follows: I do *not* resent being addressed as *Ms.*—on the contrary; I just don't understand the violent reaction of Miss Jean Stafford. But I agree that it is an awkward solution of a real problem. So I have adopted the solution of the Society of Friends and of the People's Republic of China, where I recently visited: no titles at all. Just the given name and surname of the addressee(s). If I don't know the given name(s), what am I writing to him/her/them for? Think about it."

S. I. HAYAKAWA: "Good for Miss Stafford!"

PAUL HORGAN: "I use it only when it is explicitly preferred by the person addressed."

NORMAN HOSS: "I try to do what I think the recipient would prefer."

JOHN K. HUTCHENS: "Why not ask around and find out what her status is?"

ELIZABETH JANEWAY: "I address people (to the best of my ability) as they seem to wish to be addressed. It is my practice, when in doubt, simply to use NO title. But I certainly do not share Jean Stafford's reaction. *Ms.*, when spoken, is indeed rather a noisome noise, but my life leads me into circumstances where I am both called this and obligated to use it. Jean Stafford's (to me excessive) reaction to being addressed in this fashion indicates that 'Ms.' is perceived as being symbolic of some chosen or assigned status. It is important to some women to be addressed in this fashion, just as it is important to Miss Stafford not to be. I do not, therefore, believe that it is possible to settle this usage as a matter of usage. The usage stands for something. I am wholeheartedly on the side of what it stands for; therefore, support it for those to whom it is—ha-ha!—meaningful.

"In general, I think its use is now widespread enough so that it should be included on forms as a possible desired usage. At any rate, when I recently received an invitation to attend an awards ceremony to acclaim various 'Women of the Year,' which offered only a *Miss* or *Mrs.* alternative, my consciousness rose to full tide (or staff, or something) and I wrote back that 'Ms. Elizabeth Janeway regrets etc. etc.' Ordinarily, I would simply have replied that Elizabeth J. (no title) regretted.

"In correspondence, I tend to address people as John Doe, Jane Doe, etc. A neologism, yes. Complain if you want, no one has much; or ever, I guess.

"Of course, when I address the academic establishment, I call everyone Dr. Why not? It can only make people happy, while ignoring their possible Doctor-hood (that's a pun, son) might distress them.

"I'm a doctor now myself (Hon. Litt. D. I don't take them [Hons.] seriously) so you might think that would solve any problems. Well, I did once say, in full merry spate, 'Call me Doctor and you won't have to worry,' and MY GOD they did!!!"

HELEN L. KAUFMANN: "I am old-fashioned. If I marry, I expect to take my husband's name and the honorable status of *Mrs.* Even in my professional life, I cling to this evidence of the married state as something to be proud of, not lost in the swamp of Women's Lib."

ALEXANDER KENDRICK: "I am unregenerate and regard all such revisions as misnomers. I use "MS" only with reference to manuscripts."

WALTER KERR: "Sorry, means manuscript to me."

LAURENCE LAFORE: "I am required to by university regulations. Not in my own correspondence."

ROBERT LIPSYTE: "I would like to see Mr., Mrs., Miss dropped—all people referred to by name only."

WALTER LORD: "I might. On this one, I only want to do what they want me to do."

RUSSELL LYNES (#3): "I have, but I blush when I do."

HENRY W. MALONE: "Yes . . . we have been hassled so much on the campus."

EUGENE MCCARTHY: " 'Ms.' is very useful in correspondence—if marital status is unknown—and if known—as a proper address for those you know or believe prefer it."

PHYLLIS MCGINLEY: "Occasionally, when marital status is unknown."

JESSICA MITFORD: "Yes—in correspondence to women whose marital status is unknown—to me, that is its *only* usefulness."

HERBERT MITGANG: "I believe anyone has a right to be called Ms., if desired."

DANIEL PATRICK MOYNIHAN: "I believe that Congresswomen are now designated 'Ms.' in the *Record.*"

EDWIN NEWMAN: "I am often obliged to on television."

STANTON PECKHAM: "Hope to see it die out."

HARRIET PILPEL: "I think 'Ms.' is an essential addition to the language. There is no more reason to signify a woman's marital status when communicating with her than there is in connection with a man's. A man is 'Mr.' whether he is married, widowed, divorced, or single and a woman should similarly be 'Ms.' whether married, widowed, divorced, or single."

PETER S. PRESCOTT: "Only to women who feel strongly about it, as a courtesy; never in published writing."

F. D. REEVE: "Only when requested to do so by the woman addressed."

FRANCIS ROBINSON: "No, and I never will."

LEO ROSTEN: "Every woman is entitled to her preferred name. Chacun etc. I don't give a damn one way or the other—if women insist on Ms., I Ms. them; if not, I don't."

VERMONT ROYSTER: "I would prefer that ladies properly identify themselves in correspondence, but since they don't, Ms. saves a lot of frustration. But I use it only in times of uncertainty."

HARRISON SALISBURY: "It's a convenience word, and like convenience foods, to be abhorred."

HAROLD SCHONBERG: "No, unless, of course, the writer has expressed a desire for Ms."

ROBERT SHERRILL: "I use it when I don't know status *and* when I suspect the woman to whom I'm writing would prefer it. When I review a book by a woman writer, I don't use any title at all. I just write 'Stafford.' "

WALTER W. "RED" SMITH: "I just don't give a damn."

HOWARD TAUBMAN: "I use the old forms but have no objection to changes, especially if they make some persons feel better."

HAROLD TAYLOR: "I use it most of the time because it indicates a kind of respect for the singularity of the named."

EARL UBELL: "If a person prefers 'Ms.,' I use it; if a person signs Miss or Mrs., I use same."

WILLIAM C. VERGARA: "It's not possible to answer your first question. Mrs. Liebling's preference does *not* reflect established forms of address. The established procedure for a married woman is to drop the 'Miss' and assume the 'Mrs.' I have no objection to changing this procedure, but 'Ms.' is a particularly ugly alternative."

DOUGLAS WATT: "No. Articulated, it has sound of old-fashioned 'darky' address to white female."

Now we have submitted the question in a slightly different form, the main questions now being to what degree it has been accepted and how and when it is used. There is a curious contradiction in that a greater percentage of the panel regard it as valuable for use in business correspondence than consider it "a candidate for oblivion," which may be explained by comments of "I hope" to the first question. Also, the form of "Miss" as a title, which many years ago was sometimes used to address a woman whose marital status was unknown, seems now to be used only for women whose marital status is known and who have not expressed a preference for *Ms.* A number of the panelists reported that they omit all titles for both men and women, using names only.

In instances where panelists have not changed their positions on the basic questions, we have not duplicated their comments. However, their votes have all been included in the tally on each question. Here, then, is the second ballot:

USAGE PANEL QUESTION—SECOND EDITION

At the time of our earlier balloting the use of *Ms.* as a title of courtesy before a woman's name without regard to her marital status was being rather hotly debated. Most respondents (70%) preferred to use the established forms of address: "Miss" or "Mrs." A slight majority (56%) reported they used *Ms.* in correspondence when the marital status of the woman addressed was unknown to them. Several women panelists expressed a preference for being addressed simply by given name and surname— "Jane Doe," not *"Ms.* Jane Doe." Yet, this does not solve the problem of salutations in letters.

Do you regard *Ms.* as what *Vanity Fair* used to call "a candidate for oblivion"? Yes: 48%. No: 52%.

Do you feel that it has become established as valuable for use in business correspondence? Yes: 58%. No: 42%.

In social correspondence? Yes: 29%. No: 71%.

What form of address do you use when writing to a woman whose marital status is unknown to you? Please check your preference: Dear Ms. Doe: 42%. Dear Miss Doe: 16%. Dear Jane Doe: 42%. Or do you have some other solution to the salutation problem?

DAVE ANDERSON: "There is no solution."

ISAAC ASIMOV: "I would like to start my letters 'Hello.' Calling everyone 'dear' indiscriminately strikes me as an invitation to pansexual activity."

SAUL BELLOW (re solution): "Yes. Abate false sensitivities."

DAVID H. BRADLEY: "Ms. is and should be applied to all women, regardless of marital status, known or unknown, in professional correspondence unless other form of address (Rev., Dr.) is appropriate. Sex (and/or) marriage is professionally irrelevant."

JOSEPH A. BRANDT: "It's awkward and I hate it but it is useful now and then."

HEYWOOD HALE BROUN: "Being M rather than F I try to use what the F I am addressing prefers."

BEN LUCIEN BURMAN: "I always call them 'Miss' and if they're a 'Mrs.' they're flattered. It makes them feel younger."

JOHN CIARDI: "I sometimes register a protest by using 'Dear Citizen Doe.' "

WILLARD R. ESPY: "It will probably last longer in junk mail than anywhere else."

ALEX FAULKNER: "I still think it is handy in business correspondence if you don't know what your correspondent's marital status is. Pity someone can't think of a feminine equivalent of Esq."

GEROLD FRANK: "Ambivalent."

RAY GANDOLF: "Yes, in [business] correspondence, never in social discourse. I find it more respectful to use 'Ms.' when a woman's marital status is unknown than to use any of the other awkward solutions."

SID GOLDBERG: "I vehemently resisted 'Ms.' when it was first introduced, but the trend has prevailed. It most likely is more prevalent in the media—where feminism is more active—than in any other areas of business and society."

ROBERT GOTTLIEB: "I use these interchangeably depending on circumstances and my mood. Basically I deplore 'Ms' as eliminating a distinction but use it as a courtesy to women who might prefer it."

ELIZABETH HARDWICK: "This is a difficulty, since more and more mail is addressed 'Ms.,' even in preference to a known 'Mrs.' or 'Miss.' I do not think the nude 'Jane Doe' is very inspiring as a substitute or resolution. I still use 'Miss' and 'Mrs.' when addressing someone whose marital status I am sure about. However, I do not think that the oblivion of 'Ms.' is a cause I would rally about. There is every reason to see it as useful and it is in the tradition of 'Mr.' and 'Mrs.' as an abbreviation. But what is it an abbreviation of? Only 'Mister' and 'Miss' are words in current use, since 'Mistress (Mrs.)' has an unfortunate, or fortunate in some cases, current meaning."

SYDNEY J. HARRIS: "Married women should use 'Mrs.' when it will be helpful. Its absence should indicate that 'Miss' is appropriate."

PAUL HORGAN: 'Miss Jane Doe' and 'Dear Miss Doe' unless specified as 'Mrs.' by correspondent."

JOHN K. HUTCHENS: "In business and social correspondence, I think one should ask the correspondent how she is to be addressed."

ELIZABETH JANEWAY: " 'Ms.' is a much needed form of address. It ain't pretty nor easy to pronounce, but maybe that's because we try to do it as spelled. Pronounce 'Mrs.' for me, please. Most people who don't like it are not grumbling at the word, I suspect, but at the concept. Quit it, kids. 'Ms.' is here to stay. My own chosen form of address is just plain name. Call me Ishmael, or Elizabeth if you want to be accurate. And I'll do the same for you, unless you tell me you're a Ph.D."

DIANE JOHNSON: "Drop 'Miss,' 'Mrs.,' 'Mr.,' and 'Ms.'—all of them."

WALTER KERR: "I examine signature, letterhead, and return address for a clue. If no clue, then 'Miss.' If she doesn't like it she'll begin *giving* clues."

JAMES J. KILPATRICK: "I go reluctantly with 'Ms.' but I don't like it."

ROBERT LIPSYTE: "I use 'Ms.' reluctantly because I would like to see all such dumb, divisive, unnecessary salutations deleted. Until then, I would use a person's preference—or 'Ms.'—or nothing."

JULES LOH: "I resisted 'Ms.' for as long as I dared. When the Postal Service changed the abbreviation for Mississippi from Miss. to MS, I determined it was time to throw in the towel."

DWIGHT MACDONALD: "I use it even when I know she's married because all we men hide behind 'Mr.' "

BILL MAULDIN: "I *wish* it were a candidate for oblivion, but am afraid it will stick. It is established but not very valuable. My objection to 'Ms.' is that it seems to diminish the wearer. It's the sound and look of it—purely a gut reaction."

EDWIN NEWMAN: " 'Ms.' seems to have taken hold. There are people who expect it to be used. What is the alternative?"

PETER S. PRESCOTT (re oblivion): "Would that it were."

ANDY ROONEY: "We desperately need help. I don't like and don't use 'Ms.' but I don't know how to address a woman who writes me and simply signs her name. I don't call her by her first name nor by her last name alone. Help!"

VERMONT ROYSTER: "I follow the lady's wishes if stated, otherwise I take a cowardly retreat to 'Ms.'—but I've noticed that those who are 'Mrs.' usually so note—and that those preferring 'Ms.' are usually really 'Miss.' "

HAROLD SCHONBERG: "The *New York Times* has proscribed 'Ms.' I see it less and less and I do think it is slipping out of general usage."

JACK SMITH: "I use 'Ms.' in speech and writing when I know that the woman addressed or referred to prefers it. Otherwise, no, except for some special effect—satire, for example. But that's risky."

ELVIS STAHR, JR.: "I'm still a bit uncomfortable with it."

HAROLD TAYLOR: "I think the 'Ms.' salutation is useful for everyone, the person addressed as well as the one who addresses."

CALVIN TRILLIN: "I try to guess from the letter I'm answering how the woman would prefer being addressed. I'm usually wrong."

EDWARD TRIPP: "I still go to a lot of trouble to guess whether one will or won't—just as I used to do over a woman's marital status. My wife detests 'Ms.' on the perhaps unusual grounds that a woman's salutation is prettier with three characters! She uses 'M/s,' to be considered an equivalent of 'M . . . s.' "

JOSEPH VERGARA: "Really would prefer to take the Fifth on this—but usually I omit 'Ms.' and 'Miss' if I know the woman and use 'Ms.' if I don't."

GEORGE WALD: "Increasingly I use just the name for both sexes."

A.B.C. WHIPPLE: "It may be an imperfect solution but 'Ms.' is the best I've seen so far."

HERMAN WOUK: "It disgusts me but secretaries tend to use it when the woman doesn't indicate status. I called my cat 'Ms.', pronounced Miz, a great cat, so now I am used to it—as a name for a cat."

much/muchly An expression reported as being in use in many parts of the country is "Thank you *muchly*." More recently, the formation "Thank you *much*" has been heard. Both of these expressions fall strangely on the ears, the first because there is no such word as *muchly* and the second because it seems less gracious than the traditional "Thank you very much."

Apparently there are many well-intentioned people who feel that they add elegance to their speech by the use of such non-words as *muchly*. It is a wholly misguided effort at sophistication, for it fails completely. Knowledgeable people whom they are trying to impress recognize the effort for what it is: an indication of ignorance. *See also* THANK YOU MUCH.

mud guard/mud wing   British automotive equivalents of the American "fender."

mulligrubs   *Mulligrubs* means bad temper or sulkiness, so a person with a case of the *mulligrubs* would be a "sourpuss." It is a dialect term heard chiefly in the area running from Tennessee north to Indiana and Pennsylvania.

multi-. *See* PREFIXES AND SUFFIXES, WITH AND WITHOUT HYPHEN

multiplicity. *See* DUPLICITY/DUPLICATION/MULTIPLICITY

mural/fresco   A *mural* is a large painting on a wall or ceiling. It can also be a large photograph attached to a wall. In either case, it is redundant to say "the *mural* on the wall." A *fresco* is a special type of *mural*, in that it is done with earth colors dissolved in water on fresh plaster.

murder. *See* EXECUTE/KILL/MURDER

murderer. *See* ASSASSIN/MURDERER

Muslim. *See* MOSLEM/MUSLIM

must   *Must* as a noun meaning "that which is absolutely necessary" has long been accepted. Many years ago, when the influence of the advertising department on the editorial department of a newspaper was more overt than it is today, a "business office *must*" took precedence over all other news. *Must* is now also accepted as an adjective meaning "essential," as in "*must* legislation."

must/have to/got to   In expressing compulsion or requirement, some preference is occasionally indicated for *must* rather than *have to* ("he *must* go to the city" instead of "he *has to* go to the city") on the ground that the latter is somehow more informal. This judgment is without foundation. One is quite as good as the other and *have to* has an added advantage in that it can be conjugated in past and future tenses, while *must* is restricted to the present tense. So you can say, "We *had to* go to the city," a concept beyond the capacity of *must* to express.

Similarly the much-overused *got* frequently appears in such expressions as "We have *got to* go." This is not incorrect but merely trite and redundant. It says nothing that "We *have to* go" or "We *must* go" does not say and say more simply. Still another formulation, "We *got to* go," though commonly heard, is simply illiterate.

mutual/common   *Mutual* is usually used when only two persons are involved and the noun which it modifies names a feeling or emotion, as in "*mutual* respect." The exceptions to this are "*mutual* friend" and "*mutual* acquaintance," two phrases firmly established in American idiom.

Common is used to refer to something shared by two or more persons, as in "a *common* interest" or "a *common* goal," and reflects the relationship only as it concerns one particular thing. A class of high school seniors may have the *common* goal of graduating but that may be the only thing they all have in *common*.

myriad   Myriad originally meant 10,000 but this specific figure is long since obsolete. Today *myriad* is used as an adjective ("*myriad* tongues are spoken") or as a noun ("A *myriad* of stars blazed in the skies") meaning any very large number.

myself. *See* ME/I/MYSELF

N. *See* A.M./P.M./N./M.

naïve/naïveté   The French, from whom we borrowed the adjective *naïve,* have both a masculine form and a feminine form: *naïf* and *naïve* respectively. Since English makes no such distinction with adjectives, *naïve* (with or without the dieresis over the "i") applies to both men and women.

The noun, *naïveté,* is sometimes written with the dieresis and sometimes without but it always carries an acute accent over the final "e." There is an Anglicized form, *naivety,* but it is seldom seen.

naked/nude   *Naked* and *nude* are, in most uses, synonymous, though *nude* has the edge in gentility and is more likely to appear in polite publications than *naked*. *Nude* has a further special meaning in law: lacking in some essential detail, as in a *nude* contract.

namby-pamby. *See* RICHOCHET WORDS

namely   An editor of long experience writes, "I am confused by the increasing use of the word 'namely' in the sense of 'for instance.' My feeling is that 'namely' should mean 'by name' and should not be used except in sentences that include a proper name, such as 'He referred to England's greatest playwright, namely Will Shakespeare.' Yet I see in print examples of its use without any reference to a person or place. For example: 'They finally got around to the most important part of the discussion, namely the nomination of a new president.' "

Our comment is that this limitation of *namely* to the introduction of proper names sounds like an edict of one of the newspaper editors of yesteryear, given to flat pronouncements (see *raise/rear*) often without any basis but their own whims. In any event, there is no supporting evidence for this particular dictum. The Oxford Dictionary reports that *namely* has been used as synonymous with "to wit" or "that is to say" since shortly after the time of Chaucer. Even the starchy Funk & Wagnalls Unabridged (1913) makes no mention at all of restricting *namely* to the introduction of a specific name. But the advice from here is to eliminate *namely* wherever possible. It belongs with such expressions as "i.e.," "c.f.," and "viz.," which may have a place in scholarly, footnoted prose but can best be avoided in writing for the general reader. In our opinion, both of the sentences cited by our editor friend would benefit by the deletion of *namely*.

naphtha   The accurate pronunciation of this word is NAF-thuh, with the "ph" being sounded as "f." The task of enunciating "ph" and "th" in quick succession seems to be too difficult for most Americans, so they settle for NAP-thuh.

Long ago the makers of Fels Naptha soap decided that there wasn't any point in trying to educate their customers into the pronunciation NAF-thuh so they simply dropped the first "h" out of the name of their product. *See also* DIPHTHERIA and DIPHTHONG.

narc/narco   Narc is slang for a member of the Federal Bureau of Narcotics assigned to find sellers and buyers of illegal narcotic drugs. *Narco* is a variant form.

nation   Since Alaska and Hawaii became states it is no longer possible to refer to the "highest" (or "lowest") anything in the *nation* unless statistics from those states are included. The Weather Bureau has devised a phrase to cover highest and lowest temperatures when Alaska and Hawaii are not included: "in the forty-eight contiguous states."

"nattering nabobs of negativism." *See* ALLITERATION

nature "A storm of violent *nature*" says nothing that "a violent storm" does not say. *Nature* is too often used unnecessarily and often results in an awkward sentence. Try eliminating it and see if the result is not improvement.

nauseated/nauseous The use of the expression "I feel *nauseous*" instead of "I am *nauseated*" is increasingly widespread. At first we regarded it as an item of local dialect. Readers in all parts of the country have commented on it, however, and at least two members of our panel suggested that the question be put to the board. In answer to these suggestions—from Isaac Asimov and W. H. Auden—we did poll the panel, asking, "How about 'I feel *nauseous*' for 'I am *nauseated*'? Would you accept this in the speech of others? Would you employ this usage in your own speech?" Seventy-six percent of the panel indicated that they would not themselves say or write, "I am *nauseous.*" Of the balance who approved this usage five (Alton Blakeslee, Jules Loh, Shana Alexander, Bill Mauldin, and Daniel Lang) write primarily for newspaper and periodical publication. It seems reasonable to infer that we may be here considering an instance of gradually changing usage, though the overwhelming majority of panelists would echo Dwight Macdonald's comment: "To accept it [*nauseous*] is to lose a word—and a needed distinction."

USAGE PANEL QUESTION

How about "I feel *nauseous*" for "I feel *nauseated*"? Would you accept this in the speech of others?
Yes, without reservation: 24%.
Yes, but with a shudder: 9%.
Would you employ this usage in your own speech?
Yes: 24%. No: 76%.

BENJAMIN APPEL: "The feeling is what counts."
W. H. AUDEN: "Never! Never!"
HAL BORLAND: "I have heard speakers who were nauseous. Anyone who said that would be nauseous to me."
JOSEPH A. BRANDT: "Difficult to anwer. Just how loathsome it is? A matter of degree."

ABE BURROWS: "These two are different to me. 'I feel nauseous' seems to call for an Alka-Seltzer. But 'I am nauseated' is a phrase I would use in attacking something."

STEPHEN H. FRITCHMAN: "Hurray for striking a blow at this nauseating practice, too long neglected."

HELEN L. KAUFMANN: "I am nauseated when the two words are used interchangeably."

WALT KELLY: "The two expressions mean two different things."

ALEXANDER KENDRICK: "It's like feeling obnoxious."

PHYLLIS McGINLEY: "A very bad and vulgar usage."

WADE MOSBY: "The last guy I 'corrected' became my boss. He can feel nauseous any time he wants to."

VERMONT ROYSTER: "I never feel nauseous, but others may think differently of me!"

JEAN STAFFORD: "Really! Is this a leg-pull?"

ELVIS STAHR, JR.: "If someone says 'I feel nauseous' I'll reply 'You sound it.' "

REX STOUT: "It would nauseate me."

DAVIDSON TAYLOR: "Nauseous is to be nauseating to others. This is a repulsive misuse."

WILLIAM C. VERGARA: "There are, of course, people for whom the expression is appropriate."

HERMAN WOUK: "The Collegiate gives these as synonymous."

nearest. *See* NEXT/NEAREST

near miss   The term *near miss* has come into widespread use as a synonym for what an earlier and less sophisticated generation called "a close shave" —that is, an accident, usually a collision, that didn't quite happen. We read often of aircraft in the same flight pattern escaping disaster by a *near miss.*

Several readers have written us to comment on the inaccuracy of this term. What is described, they say, is a "near hit," not a *near miss.* However, one meaning of "near" is "close in degree," as in "a near escape," so this quibble can be ignored. However, as a Washington reader points out, "the expression 'near miss' developed in World War II when it was applied to an aerial bomb aimed so as to miss a ship but to fall so close to it that an underwater detonation near the hull of the ship would cause even more damage than a direct hit from above."

So it seems clear that the current use of *near miss* is inaccurate, if judged by its military antecedents. What is equally true, however, is that *near miss* is by now solidly entrenched in the American vocabulary, and, so long as headline writers count characters, the expression will remain *near miss,* not "near collision."

near-perfect

USAGE PANEL QUESTION

SHERIDAN BAKER reports an upsurge in the use of *near-perfect* for "nearly perfect" or "almost perfect." Would you accept: "The program included a *near-perfect* performance of a seldom-heard fugue"?
Yes: 52%. No: 48%.

Comments with "yes" votes:

BENJAMIN APPEL: "All these 'nears' have made it to my ear."
ISAAC ASIMOV: "Sounds right."
STEWART BEACH: "Yes—but, music critics being what they are, I would want to find out what kept the performance from being perfect."
WILLARD R. ESPY: "I like the crispness of these formations ["near-perfect" and "near-panic"]; where you find them I will be near-by."
ORVILLE PRESCOTT: "A reasonable change in usage."
VERMONT ROYSTER: "But would prefer 'almost.' "
WALTER W. "RED" SMITH: "I accept it without enthusiasm."
ELVIS STAHR, JR.: "It isn't elegant but I *have* heard myself say it."
BILL VAUGHAN: "But I'd rather not."

Comments with "no" votes:

HAL BORLAND: "Sloppy journalese. Note that I qualify. Some journalese is good."
HEYWOOD HALE BROUN: " 'Nearly' or 'close to' seem less offensively laconic."
LEON EDEL: "Used but careless journalese."
CLARK KINNAIRD: "As impermissible as 'nearly unique' but critical language has to have its vague compliments. How close is 'near'?"
ROBERT LIPSYTE: "It's an almost unique sentence."
HERBERT MITGANG: "Also objected to 'seldom-heard' in sentence."
BERTON ROUECHÉ: "What's wrong with 'almost'?"
HAROLD TAYLOR: "I just don't like the hyphenated form. *How* near to perfect?"

See also PERFECT/PERFECTLY.

near-sighted. *See* SHORT-SIGHTED

nebby This is a term occasionally found in regional dialects, notably in Pennsylvania, West Virginia, and the western parts of the Carolinas. Originally a Scottish term, it means "meddlesome" or "nosy." A "neb" may be anything pointed, like the beak or bill of a bird. *Nebby* is inappropriate for use in formal contexts.

necessity/need *Necessity* can be followed by either "of" or "for," as in "There is no *necessity for* (or *of*) alarming him at this time." An infinitive is never used after *necessity;* rather, *need* is used with an infinitive, as in "There is no *need to* alarm him at this time." Since *necessity* and *need* are synonymous, there is little logic to this. It is simply a matter of idiom.

née Spelled with or without an acute accent on the first "e," *née* (pronounced NAY) comes from French and means "born." It is used to identify the maiden name of a married woman, as in "Mary Morris, *née* Davis." "Mary Morris, *née* Mary Davis" is illogical and redundant, since she had only a family name when she was born and marriage did not change her first name. "Baptized Mary Elizabeth Davis" is the way to say it if you wish to further identify Mrs. William Morris.

need. *See* NECESSITY/NEED

negative, double Perhaps by analogy to the adage that "two wrongs don't make a right," there is general agreement that two negatives do not make a positive and that, while a certain emphasis is gained by use of the *double negative* in sentences like "We don't go there no more," the total effect is one of illiteracy, whether calculated or unwitting. In other languages —French, for example—the *double negative* is standard ("ne . . . pas"). Perhaps through the influence of Norman French, the *double negative* construction ("Be not too tame neither") was not uncommon well into the Elizabethan era. For the past few centuries, however, standard English has demanded one negative—and only one.
　　Warning: There are a few adverbs of negative connotation—such as "scarcely" and "hardly"—that may lead a writer into an accidental *double negative.* Such a sentence as "You don't hardly care for me any more" is, at best, redundant. "You hardly care for me any more" is much to be preferred.

negotiate In the sense of "bargaining to reach agreement," *negotiate* is completely acceptable in all contexts. In the sense of "crossing" or "achieving a goal," as in "*negotiate* the rapids" or "*negotiate* a sharp turn," it is considered inappropriate in formal speech or writing.
　　Negotiation is properly pronounced nih-goh-shee-AY-shun, not nih-goh-see-AY-shun, as often heard on the air. *Negotiate* is properly pronounced nih-GOH-shee-ayt, not nih-GOH-see-ayt.

Negro. *See* BLACK/NEGRO

neighborhood of, in the   There is nothing wrong in saying *"in the neighborhood of two thousand gallons"* but it is often better and simpler to use "about" or "approximately."

neither   *Neither* is a word used when speaking or writing of two items or subjects and is followed by a singular verb. In our sentence *"Neither* of the two current unabridged dictionaries lists the word" the verb was changed by a copyeditor to "list," apparently because it followed the plural "dictionaries." The change was wrong.

When a *"neither* . . . nor" construction is used, the same is true. The verb is singular: *"Neither* John nor William is willing to take the assignment."

nephew   The standard American pronunciation for *nephew* follows the spelling: NEF-yoo. However, the pronunciation NEV-yoo is occasionally heard, especially among persons of British descent. Indeed, NEV-yoo is still the standard British pronunciation and has been since the word was borrowed from the Norman French "neveu." *See also* NEPOTISM.

nepotism   Today *nepotism* means favoritism on the part of anyone in a high position toward his relatives and close friends, usually shown by appointment to well-paid or desirable jobs. It comes from the Italian "nepotismo," which means "favoring of nephews," the "nephews" in this case being the sons of supposedly celibate medieval churchmen, who started the practice of *nepotism. See also* NEPHEW.

never-never/hire purchase   *Never-never* is British informal and *hire-purchase* is British formal for what Americans call the "installment plan" of deferred payment for purchased goods. *See also* BRITISH ENGLISH/AMERICAN ENGLISH.

nevertheless. *See* HOWEVER/NEVERTHELESS

news   Plural in form, *news* takes a singular verb: "The *news* today is good." According to hoary journalistic legend one mannered and strongly Anglophile editor insisted on regarding *news* as plural. "How are the news today?" was his customary greeting to members of his staff. One day he varied the formula slightly, calling out "Are there good news today?" To which his chief copyeditor replied: "No, not a single new."

Incidentally, *news* is not, as many believe, an acronym of North, East, West, and South. It is simply a translation of the Old French "nouvelles," which in turn comes from the Latin "nova," things that are new.

next/nearest   *Next* and *nearest* are often, though not always, synonymous. *Next,* as in "You're *next* in line," usually implies a succession of people or things in a series. *Nearest* merely means in closest proximity, as in "The number-one post position is *nearest* to the rail."

nice   *Nice* is one of the most overworked words in the English language but this is probably so because it is so all-encompassing in its application. It can be applied to anything which is pleasing or which is designed to please: "a *nice* dress," "*nice* weather," "a *nice* thing to do," "a *nice* person." Only in a few instances does it retain its original meaning of "exact or precise," as in "a *nice* distinction."

-nik   The suffix *-nik* is common in the various Slavic languages to designate a person who is an enthusiast or ardent practitioner of a hobby or trade. It has been commonly used in the speech of Yiddish-Americans for many decades and burst into the general public consciousness with the flight of the first Soviet satellite, the "Sputnik." The avant-garde Bohemian writers and artists who had hitherto styled themselves members of the Beat Generation were quickly relabeled "beatniks," a term which was extended in use during the 1960s to cover all youthful rebels, especially those who failed to conform to traditional modes of dress or decorum on college campuses. Since these "traditional modes" no longer are traditional on most campuses, the term has fallen into well-merited disuse. However, such lively Yiddishisms as "real-estatenik," for a sharp real-estate dealer, and "noshnik," for a person who is forever nibbling at food, continue to be heard.

nimrod   This is one of the words that turn up, predictably, in the sports pages of newspapers when hunting season comes around. Captions of pictures of hunters returning with their kill often refer to them as *nimrods.* The reference is to the original Nimrod, great-grandson of Noah (Genesis 10:8–10), who was called "a mighty hunter before the Lord." This is one of the many hoary newspaper clichés that have long since earned one-way tickets to oblivion.

nitty-gritty   This is a slang term, borrowed into the general language from the argot of black America. It means the basic facts of a situation, the harsh truth, the hard core of the matter. During the mid-1960s *nitty-gritty* enjoyed a sudden vogue, and public figures were forever pledging to "get down to the *nitty-gritty*" of whatever problems faced the nation. Like many other quickly voguish slang expressions, this seems already to have passed the peak of its popularity and probably should be avoided in writing, unless a deliberately dated effect is sought.

no. This abbreviation for "number" has caused confusion for some because it appears to have no relation to the word "number." Actually it is the contraction of "numero," the ablative form of the Latin word "numerus," number.

no bed of roses This is a particularly meaningless cliché as well as one so worn out from overuse as to be best avoided. As another cliché has it, "There's no rose without a thorn," and it has always seemed to us senseless to regard a thorny *bed of roses* as synonymous with ease and pleasure.

nocuous. *See* ARCANE WORDS

no host In many parts of the not-so-wild West today, what many Easterners call a "Dutch treat" lunch or dinner is called a *no host* affair. The expression is different but the meaning is the same. Each person pays for his own meal and there is *no host* to pick up the tab.

noisome/noisy *Noisome,* though often confused with "noisy," is in no way related to it in meaning. *Noisome,* meaning foul-smelling, fetid, disgusting, comes from a Middle English word "noyesum" which is related to "annoy"—and a noisome odor is indeed annoying to most of us. Example: "The stagnant pond gives off a *noisome* stench." But not, "The hometown crowd gave the team a *noisome* reception at the airport."

nominal A low price, even a very low price, is not necessarily a *nominal* price. A *nominal* price is so low as to bear no relation to the real cost or value and, as a result, is only a token price. The "dollar-a-year" men of Franklin Roosevelt's administrations received *nominal* salaries. A *nominal* amount is involved in such situations as the transfer of ownership of property from one member of a family to another, where the law provides that "in consideration of the payment of $1.00" a legal transfer can be achieved. Otherwise the property has to be considered a gift.

non-. *See* PREFIXES AND SUFFIXES, WITH AND WITHOUT HYPHEN

nonce words A *nonce word* is, strictly speaking, a word coined for use on a single occasion. For instance, some years ago citizens of a small Midwestern town, Lincoln, Illinois, decided, on the occasion of the hundredth anniversary of the town's founding, to circulate a special wooden coin worth 7½ cents. Since the value was midway between that of a dime and a nickel, they coined the blend word "dickel." The coin was, of course, valueless—except perhaps to collectors—as soon as the festivities concluded, making dickel truly a *nonce word.* Somewhat more recently, a linguistic researcher named Sarah Gudschinsky devised a theory, involving a great deal of advanced mathematics including far-out logarithmic theory, whereby she claimed to be able to date the origin of words, just as Dr. Willard Libby's Carbon-14 technique succeeded in establishing the age of ancient artifacts. To describe her method she invented two interchangeable *nonce words,* "glottochronology" and "lexicostatistics." At least we trust they are *nonce words.* They are much too ugly to survive.

none   A widely held misconception is that, since *none* is a contraction of "no one" (though its etymology is a good deal more complicated than that), it should be followed by a singular verb: "*None* is happy at the result." One reader put it this way: "Since I have always believed the word 'none' to be, in meaning, 'no one,' I have always practiced the use of the singular form of the related verb. Am I in error, am I being pedantic, or am I guilty of 'elegant' usage?" The answer is simply that, while it is usually correct to use a singular verb, there is nothing at all wrong with using a plural verb, especially when sense is better served thereby. Indeed, both H. W. Fowler in *Modern English Usage* and Porter Perrin in his *Writers' Guide and Index to English* state that the plural verb is now more common. So, if you use a plural verb after *none* ("*None* of the people are unhappy with the results"), you're traveling in excellent company.

nonetheless   *Nonetheless* means "notwithstanding," "nevertheless," or "in spite of that." It's a word everyone has seen many times yet, curiously, it did not appear in dictionaries until fairly recently. For example, the Funk & Wagnalls Unabridged Dictionary (1913) did not enter the word, though we're sure every editor of that work had used the expression on many occasions. Why was *nonetheless* not included? Simply because at that time the common practice was to use the expression in the form of three separate words, *none the less.* As a result of the steady trend to write such expressions "solid," as printers say, the copyeditors of America actually created a new word where three had existed before. Incidentally, *Webster's New World Dictionary,* Second Edition, enters the three-word version as an acceptable alternative spelling, though neither American Heritage nor Merriam-Webster Third Edition records it. So the verdict is overwhelmingly in favor of the one-word version: *nonetheless.*

non sequitur   The English translation of this Latin phrase is "it does not follow" and the two forms of *non sequiturs* fit this definition. Within a sentence, a *non sequitur* is a fact or statement which has absolutely no connection with the main sense of the sentence. It is usually a forced effort to include a bit of irrelevant information, as "Born in Ohio, she loved cats."

Another kind of *non sequitur* is a comment or answer to a query which bears no relation to the query to which it is supposed to be a response. This is sometimes done deliberately to evade the question or to create confusion.

noon The correct designation for midday is 12 M. The "M." is an abbreviation of "meridies," the Latin word for midday. *See also* MIDNIGHT.

noon, high In a strict sense, noon and *high noon* are synonymous, but in actual practice if one says, "I'll meet you at noon," the meaning can be precisely at noon or in the general area of noontime—give or take ten or fifteen minutes. *High noon,* by contrast, means precisely at 12 M., not a minute before or a minute after.

normalcy Used to indicate a state or condition of normality, this word has, as H. L. Mencken says, "been much derided by American intellectuals, though of respectable ancestry."

When President Warren G. Harding called for a "return to *normalcy*" after World War I, he started a controversy about the propriety of his word choice. However, *normalcy* has been in the language since the mid-nineteenth century, according to the Oxford Dictionary, and is perfectly normally derived from the Latin "normalis," which means made according to the carpenter's rule, hence of standard or normal design.

normal routine procedure A *redundancy* (which see).

nosh *Nosh* is a slang contribution from Yiddish and does double duty as a noun and a verb. As a noun it means a snack or tidbit, especially one consumed between meals. A person who *noshes* is one who is forever nibbling between meals. It's from the Old High German "nascon," to gnaw or nibble. *See also* NOSHNIK under -NIK.

nostalgia Here is a prime example of a word that has changed its meaning quite completely—rather, added a whole new dimension of meaning—within the past few decades. The 1934 Merriam-Webster Second Edition defined *nostalgia* as "a severe melancholia caused by protracted absence from home . . . a brooding or poignant, enervating homesickness." The Oxford Dictionary put it this way: "a form of melancholia caused by prolonged absence from one's country or home." But language constantly is changing and, even as the editors were writing these definitions, more and more people were beginning to use *nostalgia* in a much looser sense. The current meaning of "a longing to return to times long past and places and persons almost forgotten" is very different, for it isn't focused, as homesickness is, on a specific place existing at the present time. Instead, in its currently popular use, *nostalgia* is a recollection of places and events that, more often than not, no longer exist. Perhaps the most signal recognition of how rapidly the general public's use of this word has changed its meaning over the short span of thirty years is the fact that the Merriam-Webster Third Edition includes the same definition as the 1934 edition—but labels it "archaic."

notable. *See* NOTORIOUS/NOTABLE

not about to. *See* ABOUT TO/NOT ABOUT TO

not all that. *See* NOT THAT MUCH

notate   This is a back-formation from "notation." Not yet entered in most general-purpose dictionaries, it's a word primarily used in the fields of musical composition and dance. Example: "The arranger was *notating* the score prior to rehearsal." Many such back-formations (for example, "enthuse" from "enthusiasm") are frowned on by purists. Because of its special application and usefulness, however, *notate* must be considered standard American.

nothing   *Nothing* requires a singular verb in all cases, even when it is followed by a phrase containing a plural noun, as in *"Nothing* but a few coins was in the box." If this seems awkward to you, change the sentence to "Only a few coins were in the box."

not nearly. *See* NOWHERE NEAR/NOT NEARLY

not only . . . but also   There are instances in which *not only* calls for more precise placement than does *only* (which see). In sentences which have only one main verb, *not only* should immediately precede the word or phrase which it modifies so that it will form a construction parallel to the *but also* phrase which necessarily follows. "He *not only* broke his right leg *but also* his right arm" would be better as "He broke *not only* his right leg *but also* his right arm."

Where there are two main verbs in one sentence, however, *not only* falls in front of the first verb and *but also* in front of the second verb, as in "He *not only* broke his arm *but also* knocked out two front teeth."

notorious/notable   Both of these are applied to persons who are well known but well known for different reasons. *Notorious* has a connotation of unsavoriness, as in "He's a *notorious* liar."

A person is *notable* when he or she has achieved a position or accomplished something which is worthy of notice. A *"notable* scientist" is one who has earned respect and fame through his or her achievements. *See also* FAMED/FAMOUS.

not that much

USAGE PANEL QUESTION

The younger set has adopted *not that much* and *not all that much*. Example: "Do you like carrots? *Not that much.*" Would you use this idiom?
In speech   Yes: 44%. No: 56%.
In writing   Yes: 29%. No: 71%.

As the percentages show, a number of panelists said they would use the idiom in speech but not in writing. Of those who said they would use it in writing, several limited that use to dialogue.

JOHN BROOKS ("no" on both): "But I rather like it when *they* use it."
ALEXANDER KENDRICK (split vote): "Why limit it to the younger set? I see no harm."
DWIGHT MACDONALD ("no" on both): "Like the evasive and redundant 'too': 'I didn't enjoy the carrot too much.'"
PETER S. PRESCOTT ("yes" on speech): "I blush to admit." (He voted "no" re writing.)
ELVIS STAHR, JR. ("no" on both): "But I don't object to others' innocent slang—and have often adopted other terms with (I hope) tongue in cheek."

not too good/not too bright

USAGE PANEL QUESTION

Phrases like *not too good* and *not too bright* have been criticized by purists as illogical. How can anything be *too* good, they ask? Yet this locution has appeared in the utterances of such careful phrasemakers as Winston Churchill and Adlai Stevenson. Would you approve "He's *not too bright*"?
In speech   Yes: 94%. No: 6%.
In writing   Yes: 72%. No: 28%.

ISAAC ASIMOV: "It's a way of softening an insult or derogation. If not overused it is all right."

HAL BORLAND: "The comparison is implied, but there is a sense of comparison."

JOHN BROOKS: "An example of technical misuse that adds a new and vivid meaning. Slang at its best."

ANTHONY BURGESS: " 'Too' is used here as an intensifier and as such is long established."

BEN LUCIEN BURMAN: "Yes. They're both vivid. Why not?"

ABE BURROWS: "This is a useful way of making a point crisply—but only in speech."

ALEXANDER KENDRICK: "Usage, vigor, and color must in this case prevail over logic."

WADE MOSBY: "Seems to me that 'too' and 'very' are becoming synonymous among the young."

FRANCIS T. P. PLIMPTON: "Useful as polite understatement."

PETER S. PRESCOTT: "Though the objection is technically correct, it seems pedantic to me now. These uses have a nice value as humor, too. The usage here is more rhetorical than grammatical."

BERTON ROUECHÉ (approving for speech but not for writing): "What happened to 'very'?"

HARRISON SALISBURY: "Yes—and frequently."

LEONARD SANDERS: "Though not appropriate for formal writing, this is an expression of singular color and clarity."

DAVID SCHOENBRUN: "The phrase can be used, alas, almost universally."

DANIEL SCHORR: " 'Too' has simply become a synonym for 'very.' "

WALTER W. "RED" SMITH (one of the few who rejected its use in either speech or writing): "Sportscasters hired by baseball teams use this locution: 'He's not hitting for too big an average' because they are afraid to say, 'The bum can't hit.' "

JEAN STAFFORD: "I would approve of the use of 'too' in both speech and writing if the intention is colloquial."

ELVIS STAHR, JR.: "Yes. I like understatements. Provided, of course, the user knows what he is doing."

BILL VAUGHAN (approving for speech but not for writing): "Not in scholarly writing, of course, but there is a precise, though idiomatic, meaning here."

HERMAN WOUK: "They've entered the language but some of these things are unbearable solecisms still: 'even more impossible,' 'very excellent.' It depends on the absoluteness of the adjective."

See also TOO/VERY.

not to worry

USAGE PANEL QUESTION

Panelists for the first edition were asked to comment on "Thank you much," an expression then enjoying something of a vogue. More than three fourths of the respondents vetoed its use in speech and nine out of ten voted against its use in writing. The feelings of the majority were neatly put by panelist WADE MOSBY, who noted: "This irks me much." Today one often reads and hears *Not to worry,* as in this news report: "Parsnips, according to FDA researchers, may present some toxicological risk to man. . . . *Not to worry.* They said 'may.' "

Do you regard *not to worry* as a useful alternative to "don't worry"?

Would you use *not to worry* in speech? Yes: 38%. No: 62%.

In writing? Yes: 13%. No: 87%.

ISAAC ASIMOV: "Not to use it! Not *ever* to use it!"

CHARLES BERLITZ: "Translated from Yiddish. Use should be left to individual in speech only."

BARRY BINGHAM, SR.: "This is another expression borrowed, without acknowledgment, from our English cousins."

DAVID H. BRADLEY: "Don't be so uptight."

JOSEPH A. BRANDT: "Cf. 'no problem,' which seems addictive."

JOHN BROOKS: "Harmless and surely transient."

HEYWOOD HALE BROUN: "Why, when it is longer than 'Don't worry'?"

WILLARD R. ESPY: "My impression is that 'not to worry' is an import from Britain, perhaps an elision of 'you are not to worry.' It's a silly little affectation, but harmless and even, to me, diverting."

GEROLD FRANK: "Yes—but only if I wanted to be cute."

FRANCES FRITCHMAN: "I have a weakness for this phrase. It's not the equivalent of 'Don't worry.' It's more impersonal—shorthand for 'It's nothing to worry about.' "

RAY GANDOLF: "I have jumped from the rearguard to the van. I'm too busy remembering to say 'no problem' to worry about 'not to.' "

SYDNEY J. HARRIS: "A notorious Briticism. We borrow from them and they from us. Why not?"

JOHN K. HUTCHENS: "As A. Woollcott once said in another connection, a case of fallen archness."

DIANE JOHNSON: "No—but presumably it's a part of a legitimate imperative: 'You are not to worry.' "

WALTER KERR: "I wouldn't object to it in casual speech."

JULES LOH: "Overuse will soon put this vogue expression out of business, so, not to worry."

HERBERT MITGANG: "It's a neat Briticism often used as a cheerer-upper in London."

EDWIN NEWMAN: "I think that it can be used by people who are able to say it without embarrassment. It is an import from England and so attractive to many."

MARGE PIERCY: "There are vogue phrases that have an air of the media about them; this is one. They generally come and go with speed."

JACK SMITH: "Cute fake Yiddish but too much a cliché."

ELVIS STAHR, JR.: "This is an English but *not* an American expression. It *may* catch on, however, as a rather pleasant bit of slang."

WILLIAM C. VERGARA: "Although I can't prove it, I have the impression that 'not to worry' is a rather old expression. I use it to inject a bit of humor —and only in an informal context."

JUDITH VIORST: "I find 'not to worry' extremely affected. If someone spills a drink on Queen Elizabeth *she* could say 'not to worry.' "

DOUGLAS WATT: "A transitory cliché."

noun modifiers The use of nouns to modify other nouns is so firmly established in English as seemingly to need no comment. Yet we frequently have queries whether, for example, the title "education director" should not more properly be "educational director." The answer in this instance is that either version is acceptable. However, there are many instances where the *noun modifier* is distinctly correct and essential to express the meaning desired. For instance, a "book salesman" is not necessarily a "bookish salesman"; a "nerve doctor" is not, one hopes, a "nervous doctor"; nor a "seed merchant" a "seedy merchant." One of our favorite instances in which the *noun modifier* was correct and the adjective if not incorrect at least misleading had to do with a newspaper editor of our acquaintance. He violently objected to being labeled the "religious editor," demanding that his title be changed to "religion editor" because, as it happened, he was an agnostic.

noun plurals, used attributively A correspondent in the District of Columbia noted that he has contended, "mostly in vain, that English has only two plural adjectives ('these' and 'those') and that the growing use of pluralized adjectives is ungrammatical, non-euphonious, and obnoxious. A local paper carried a story on 'funds solicitation,' another on phonograph 'records sales.' I have seen in print 'resources conservation,' 'fisheries management,' 'regulations development,' and 'lands acquisition.' " We noted in reply that the examples cited were not adjectives used as plural modifiers and that English, being a non-inflected language, has never required agreement between an adjective and the noun it modifies. These actually are *nouns used attributively.*

A grievous example of this mismating of plural nouns and singular nouns is found in the widely advertised slogan about "colds misery." This, we suspect, is a deliberate device of an advertising copywriter schooled in the irritation technique of the "hard sell." Like the authors of "like a cigarette should," the copywriter knew perfectly well that he was violating the decencies of the mother tongue—and he chose to do so in order to engrave his message indelibly in the minds of his readers and listeners. He gambled that, for every listener who was revolted and refused to buy his product, at least ten would remember the name the next time they saw it on a drug counter. As to the mismatched plurals and singulars from the language of Washington bureaucrats cited by our correspondent, we might quote Henry L. Mencken's comment that "public jobholders, taking one with the other, are anything but masters of prose; their writing, indeed, is pretentious and shabby." Mencken wrote that forty years or more ago. Sadly, it remains quite true today.

nouns, plurals of compound. *See* PLURALS OF COMPOUND WORDS AND PHRASES

nouns into verbs The pattern of conversion of nouns into verbs is well established in English. However, perhaps under the influence of advertising copywriters employing shock tactics to gain the reader's or listener's attention, the ignorant misuse of nouns for verbs has become all too common in recent years.

One reader quoted a mailing from her college president: "Certain property has been bequested to this institution." This forced conversion of "bequest" from noun to verb is as unnecessary as it is ridiculous. Two verbs, "bequeath" and, even more simply, "will," stand ready to serve. We suspect that this particular example resulted from sheer ignorance on the part of the letter writer.

More serious, it would appear, are the deliberate abuses reflected in expressions like "He thefted the necklace," "She guested on the TV show," and "X and Y co-hosted the dinner." But the unnecessary conversion of nouns to verbs is not confined to the worlds of advertising, radio, and television. Some time ago the expression "efforting to get into Czechoslovakia" appeared in *Time* magazine. This moved an anonymous *Time* staff member to complain in the magazine's house organ, *F.Y.I.*: "If 'efforting to get into Czechoslovakia' is acceptable Timese, then I, too, should effort my luck at writing. Further, I should success in it without too much try." *See also* AUTHOR (AS A VERB); IMPACT (AS A VERB).

nouveau riche. *See* PARVENU/NOUVEAU RICHE

no way! *No way!*, an abbreviated form of response to a request or suggestion, became popular in the early 1970s and even crept into the speech patterns of educated people, who found it more succinct than the traditional "I am sorry but there is no way that it can be done." It is a vogue phrase and, like all such, it will pass.

nowhere near/not nearly   *Nowhere near* is a very informal way of saying *not nearly.* Adding an "s" to "nowhere" to make it "nowheres near" renders the phrase substandard.

now pending   *Now pending* is in the same category as "present incumbent." If you are speaking or writing in the present tense (as the *now* would indicate) the *now* is redundant. The matter is *pending;* it is not decided or concluded.

nuclear

USAGE PANEL QUESTION

Early in the Eisenhower Presidency, the press commented several times on Mr. Eisenhower's pronunciation of *nuclear*—noo-kyoo-ler. Perhaps reacting to these comments, the President changed to noo-klee-er later in his administration. In 1961 Merriam-Webster's Third Edition reported noo-kyoo-ler as appearing "chiefly in substandard speech." In 1969 *The American Heritage Dictionary* recorded noo-klee-er and nyoo-klee-er as the only accepted pronunciations. Still, transcripts of speeches at the 1982 "*nuclear* freeze" rallies in New York City and San Francisco show the presumably literate spokespersons for the movement almost equally divided between noo-klee-er and noo-kyoo-ler. More recently still, an Air Force Lieut. General, appearing on the "Today" show to speak in favor of reviving the B-1 bomber, spoke of its "noo-kyoo-ler potential."
Should the pronunciation of *nuclear* as noo-kyoo-ler be accepted as an alternative? Yes: 1%. No: 99%.

NOTE: The nearly unanimous vote on this question is rivaled only by the vote on *hyphens.* The lone dissenter, Professor KARL V. TEETER, makes an interesting point—as do the panelists who consider the pronunciation noo-kyoo-ler unacceptable.

ISAAC ASIMOV: "Since when is an Air Force Lieut. General representative of anything beyond the third grade?"
BARRY BINGHAM, SR.: "I cannot accept the direct distortion of a word from its phonetic form, no matter how many sloppy and careless people use it."
JOHN CIARDI: "U.S.A.F. standards are hardly the measure of speech."

ROBERT CROMIE: "I never saw a nookyooler./I never hope to see one;/But I can tell you, anyhow,/I'd rather see than B-1."

FRANCES FRITCHMAN: "This is my favorite *bête noire.* The noo-kyoo-ler version is easier to say. People generally find it hard to pronounce two consonants together—but this is no excuse."

RAY GANDOLF: "I won't accept noo-klee-er until they start calling Uncle Walter Cronkite a-vunk-lee-er."

PAUL HORGAN: "The spelling is clear enough. Why confirm illiteracy?"

WALTER KERR: "Tell the illiterates to look to the spelling."

JAMES J. KILPATRICK: "Damned if I see how you rationally could get a pronunciation of noo-kyoo-ler out of *nuclear.* I'd stick to noo-(or nyoo)-klee-er."

PETER S. PRESCOTT: "Officers of general rank are rarely literate in the panelists' use of the word. What we have here is a word many Americans find difficult to pronounce but are determined to use anyway."

JACK SMITH: "Anybody who has nuclear power over us ought to be able to pronounce it."

ELVIS STAHR, JR: "My God! Is decent diction itself to be consigned to rubble even before the next nuclear bomb is dropped? (As a former Secretary of the Army, I am not too surprised about the Air Force general.)"

KARL V. TEETER: "Jimmy Carter says it. A whole region of the country says it. It is a normal variant."

WILLIAM C. VERGARA: "If we accept noo-kyoo-ler, we open up a vast can of worms that includes noo-kyoo-li, noo-kyoo-lon-iks, and noo-kyoo-lus. Lord save us from weak minds and lazy tongues."

nude. *See* NAKED/NUDE

number. *See* AMOUNT/NUMBER

number, the/a   When *number* is preceded by "the" a singular verb is required, as in "The *number* of accidents on the states roads has decreased during the past month." If *number* is preceded by "a" the verb is plural, as in "A *number* of students are signing up for the new course in ecology."

number/routine/bit

USAGE PANEL QUESTION

ERICH SEGAL cites the increasingly frequent use of *number* in the sense of *routine,* as in "He did the whole 'concerned liberal' *number.*" Would you use *number* in this sense?

In writing   Yes: 19%. No: 81%.
In casual speech   Yes: 50%. No: 50%.

SHERIDAN BAKER: "With humor, as a specific allusion to show biz."

ALVIN BEAM ("yes" on speech; "no" on writing): "But I would use 'bit.' "

BARRY BINGHAM, SR.: "It strikes me as a legitimate act of borrowing from theatrical usage."

JOHN BROOKS (voting two "no's"): "Nothing but successor to 'the bit.' "

ABE BURROWS: "Good God! 'Number' is old hat. 'Bit' is in. For true elegance one should say 'The concerned liberal bit.' "

PAUL HORGAN ("no" on both): "The 'whole bit' is ominously gaining currency."

ALEXANDER KENDRICK: "Not when I can use 'thing.' "

ROBERT LIPSYTE: "Of course, in this case 'number' is merely the new showbiz slang for 'routine,' old showbiz slang—and 'bit' which also had its 'turn.' "

JULES LOH (voting "no" on writing but "yes" on speech): "A fad usage."

RUSSELL LYNES (voting "yes" on speech but "no" on writing, says re writing): "Or 'bit' or 'routine'—slang from the theater."

STANTON PECKHAM: " 'Act' or 'bit' would somehow seem more acceptable here, probably only because they are monosyllables."

MARK SCHORER (voting "yes" on both, says re writing): "In certain kinds of writing, for particular tones."

WALTER W. "RED" SMITH ("no" on writing; "yes" on speech): "It's slangy."

BILL VAUGHAN (voting "no"): "Or 'bit' or 'shtick.' "

A.B.C. WHIPPLE: "It sounds like mere mod jargon."

HERMAN WOUK: "He means 'bit,' doesn't he? In hip talk, why not?"

number plate   *Number plate* is the British motoring equivalent of the U.S. "license plate."

numbers (in printing style)   Most newspapers spell out *numbers* ten and below and use Arabic numerals for eleven and above. Thus: "The car carried five passengers and was traveling over 60 miles an hour." Most book publishers follow the precepts of the style manual of the University of Chicago Press, which says to spell out in ordinary text matter every number of less than three digits, and any whole numbers up to 100 followed by *hundred*, *thousand*, *million*, etc.

numerous   *Numerous* is an adjective only, never a pronoun. Thus, "*numerous* volunteers were ready to serve," but not "*numerous* of the volunteers . . ." Say rather: "Many of the volunteers . . ."

O

O/oh *O* has become almost obsolete, except in poetry and religious writing. It is always capitalized, regardless of its position in a sentence, as in "To Thee, *O* Lord." It is never followed directly by punctuation.

The more common form, *oh,* is used as an interjection and is capitalized only when it stands at the beginning of a sentence or stands alone. It is usually followed by a comma or an exclamation point, depending on the strength of the statement.

objective case. *See* ACCUSATIVE CASE/OBJECTIVE CASE

obliged/obligated, to be In the sense of being required or necessary, *obliged* and *obligated* are sometimes interchangeable and sometimes not. If the compulsion or commitment is strong and unavoidable, either *obliged* or *obligated* may be used: "I am *obliged* (or *obligated*) to spend one day each week working in my father's store."

If the necessity exists only in the mind of the person involved, *obliged* is the proper choice: "I felt *obliged* to send them a Christmas gift because of their many kindnesses."

oblivious/unaware *Oblivious* originally meant "forgetful of something known in the past" or "no longer aware," and some purists still restrict it to that meaning. Through usage, however, *oblivious* has acquired a much broader meaning, one of "completely *unaware* or unnoticing" of something in the present.

The preposition "of" is preferred with *oblivious* but either "of" or "to" is acceptable, except in the original meaning, which requires "of."

observance/observation Several centuries ago, *observance* and *observation* were synonymous, but over the years each acquired its own distinct meaning, *observation* becoming confined to "the act of seeing or noticing" and *observance* to "the act of complying to a rule or custom." *Observation* thus relates to a spectator and *observance* to a participant. This is a useful distinction and one worth observing.

obtain/prevail A reader protested the use of *obtain* in the sense of *prevail* with the comment, "I always thought you *obtain* a job or a cat or a wife or a tax refund." He recognizes *obtain* only as a transitive verb, but it is also an intransitive verb meaning "to be in force or general usage." The statement to which he objected was written by a newspaper reporter concerning reading inability among students: "The same picture *obtains* in New York." There is nothing wrong with such usage except that it is a bit stilted. A simpler formulation would be "The picture (or the situation) is the same in New York."

oculist/ophthalmologist/optician/optometrist   One man or woman may be an *oculist,* an *ophthalmologist,* and an *optometrist,* yet only two of these occupations are identical. An *oculist* and an *ophthalmologist* have the same training and do the same work: diagnosis and treatment of abnormalities and diseases of the eye. The term *ophthalmologist* is preferred in the profession as being more distinctive and less apt to be confused with *optician* or *optometrist.*

An *optometrist* is one trained to test eyes and prescribe corrective lenses, which most *ophthalmologists* also do.

An *optician*'s work is confined to the making or selling of optical goods.

odd   *Odd,* when used with a round number to indicate a few more than that number, should be preceded by a hyphen to avoid an *odd* (strange) effect, as in "forty *odd* children," which might better be written "forty-*odd* children." *See also* FUNNY/ODD.

odd shaped/odd-shaped/oddly shaped   John Ciardi reports that a sign in the checked baggage section of O'Hare Airport reads: "Kennels, skis and odd shaped luggage is hand carried to the claim area."

"Leaving 'is' out of the discussion as obviously ungrammatical, does anyone," he asks, "want to argue for 'oddly shaped' or 'odd-shaped' or 'luggage of odd shape'?"

Any of the three he suggests would be preferable to the one chosen by the sign writer for the airport. The first two make it clear that *odd* (or *oddly*) applies to the shape of the luggage. The third is also more explicit but would not be acceptable to a sign maker who was fitting letters into a limited space.

odor. *See* STINK

of/for; we/us

USAGE PANEL QUESTION

Panelist VERMONT ROYSTER poses this problem: "Sample sentence: 'It is presumptuous of (for) we (us) journalists to offer our opinions on everything.'"

Which preposition would you use?
Of: 68%.
For: 32%.
Which pronoun?
We: 10%.
Us: 90%.

ISAAC ASIMOV: " 'Of we' sounds queer."

STEWART BEACH: "Either 'of' or 'for' is correct."

HAL BORLAND: "Either preposition will do, with the proper pronoun."

JOHN BROOKS: " 'We—us'—a trap. I'd duck using this construction."

HEYWOOD HALE BROUN: " 'Of—us' . . . not because I think it's all that grammatical. It seems the most unobtrusive way out of an awkward sentence."

JOHN CIARDI: " 'Of—us' . . . but I don't like this usage and always rephrase around it. I prefer, for example, 'It is presumptuous of us as journalists . . .' "

ALEX FAULKNER: " 'For' . . . neither 'we' nor 'us.' "

ALEXANDER KENDRICK: "Will toss you for 'of' or 'for'—but 'we'? Never!"

REX STOUT: "Either 'of' or 'for' [with 'us']."

DAVIDSON TAYLOR: " 'For' . . . but neither 'we' nor 'us.' "

ROSS MCLAURY TAYLOR: " 'For,' 'us' . . . Idiomatic use has played hob with this one!"

JUDITH VIORST: "I refuse to answer on the grounds that it might incriminate me."

of (as in "should of" and "could of" and "would of") Not long ago a reader of our column sent in a letter from a woman who strongly opposed an editorial favoring legalized abortion. The text read, in part, "If my mother had of killed me, I wouldn't of been able to know this world that God gave to us to live in. But most of all, I wouldn't of had a chance for eternal life. . . . I wouldn't of had three children." We were duly appreciative of the clipping because it underscored the prevalence of the expressions *would of, should of,* and *could of.*

Over the years we have often bewailed this increasingly common debasement of language, and every time we do we get scores of letters from well-meaning people who tell us that we're simply not listening carefully, that people we think say *should of* and *could of* are actually saying *should have* and *could have.* But it so happens that we have spent our entire adult lives writing about and listening to our language—and we know very well what we hear and don't hear. So we'd like an end to apologies for slovenly speech—and an end to *should of* and *could of* and *would of* in speech as well as in print.

of (introducing prepositional phrases) From a major newspaper: "Mrs. Bartlett is a natural for anything to do with a Williamsburg theme in that collecting antiques is a great interest *of* both she and her husband." This is an all-too-common error, a part of the mistakenly Elegant English often found on society pages. The correct version, of course, is ". . . a great interest *of* both her and her husband," since the objective case is required after the preposition *of.*

of (omission of) A Milwaukee reader of our column writes to comment on expressions like "You can't overload this type motor" or "What kind carpet are you buying?" "The omission of 'of' after 'type' or 'kind' seems to be growing and it bothers me. Is this omission laziness or does it stem from literal translation from some foreign language?" asks A. B. Beverstock. It seems to us significant that this query comes from Milwaukee, a city with a large proportion of citizens of German ancestry. We ourselves have heard this omission of "of" chiefly in the speech of New Yorkers influenced by Yiddish tradition. "Six bagels, a half-pound cream cheese, and a quarter-pound lox" is a standard order in New York delicatessens. Since Yiddish is, in large part, a dialect of German, the origin of this omission of "of" seems clear. Nevertheless, though its ancestry is apparent, it should be avoided by careful speakers and never used in writing except to portray character or atmosphere.

officer One writer on usage has objected to the term *officer* being applied to a patrolman, on the ground that he has no rank. Granted that he may not be a sergeant or captain, but a patrolman is an *"officer* of the law" and, as such, is entitled to be addressed as *"Officer."*

officiate (at) A reader reports that she often reads in the society page of her paper expressions like "he *officiated* the wedding." This is clearly an error, since *officiate* is an intransitive verb and so does not take a direct object. One *"officiates at* a wedding" or, alternatively, "So-and-so *officiated."* One can no more *officiate* a wedding than one can graduate school. *See also* GRADUATED.

off of A very common redundancy, especially in speech, is the phrase *off of* in such expressions as "Take your hat *off of* the bed" or "Take your feet *off of* that stool." The *of* is simply unnecessary. Careful speakers and writers avoid this duplication of prepositions and simply use *off.*

often *Often* should be pronounced OFF-un, not OFF-tun, though the latter pronunciation is often affected, especially by singers.

oh. *See* O/OH

O.K./OK/okay/okeh This term, which Henry L. Mencken once called "the most successful of all Americanisms," came into the language during the 1830s as a slang term, most particularly as an item of political slang. In the years since, it has, as the linguists say, meliorated somewhat and now is acceptable for use in all forms of informal speech and writing. It still seems out of place in formal documents and should surely not be used in a legislative document, a white paper, a real-estate deed, or the like. It is especially appropriate for business use, since its meaning is unmistakable and its conciseness admirable. *O.K.* is a very versatile word, functioning as a noun ("He gave the project his *O.K.*"), as a verb ("He will *O.K.* the plan"), as an adjective ("an *O.K.* idea"), and an adverb ("the car runs *O.K.* now").

NOTE: The history of *O.K.*, with comments on various theories of its origin, is detailed in articles appearing in our *Morris Dictionary of Word and Phrase Origins* (Harper & Row).

old adage A *redundancy* (which see).

older/elder While both are used to mean "having existed for a greater number of years," *elder* applies only to persons while *older* can apply to either a person or a thing. *Elder* and *eldest* are usually reserved for persons within a family or group of similar persons, as "an *elder* sister" or "*elder* statesman."

ombudsman An *ombudsman* (om-BOODZ-man) is a watchman for the interests of the ordinary citizen. His function is to cut through layers of bureaucratic red tape, acting on complaints from the citizenry to see that justice is done. His role is not anti-government or even anti-bureaucracy. If he finds that a complaint is unjustified or that all possible action has already been taken, he so reports to the complainant and the matter is closed. Common for years in Sweden and New Zealand, the *ombudsman* is relatively new to America. The word is now standard English.

on account of (because) This phrase is heard in speech in two different patterns, one an acceptable speech idiom and the other not. When used as a prepositional idiom, it is acceptable in speech: "He failed the entrance exam *on account of* his poor spelling." When used as a conjunction instead of *because,* it is a regionalism and is considered substandard: "He failed the entrance exam *on account of* he couldn't spell." We have even heard *on account of because* used in calculated jest.

one another. *See* EACH OTHER/ONE ANOTHER

one . . . he

USAGE PANEL QUESTION

Panelist ALEX FAULKNER writes: "I wonder whether other panelists shudder with me when they encounter the tandem 'one . . . he.' Examples: "In the five-minute aerial view of the West Coast that *one* gets as *his* aircraft cruises" and "*One* finds little to detain *him.*" Continues Faulkner: "It had always seemed to me that, if one starts with 'one,' one should go on with it. . . . Apart from anything else, isn't there a touch of male chauvinism in the assumption that 'one' is 'he,' never 'she'?"

Do you share his shudder?

Yes: 45%. No: 55%.

Would you favor the "one . . . one" construction primarily as a matter of writing style?

Yes: 54%. No: 46%.

Primarily to avoid the implication of male chauvinism implicit in the "*one . . . he*" formulation?

Yes: 9%. No: 91%.

BENJAMIN APPEL: "Yes, because read out loud it sounds 'wrong,' awkward, but male chauvinism is far-fetched nonsense."

SHERIDAN BAKER: "No. [The 'one . . . one' usage is] too prissy."

JOHN O. BARBOUR: "One may be one, but one may also be he or she."

STEWART BEACH: "Of course Alex is correct technically, but if he has ever composed, say, a ten-line paragraph using only 'one' he will know it is gibberish, and tiresome. The answer is to recast the paragraph. While I think the male chauvinism label is always silly (someday the girls may learn what the word means), the only alternative is to use 'he or she' instead of 'he' alone. And how tiresome that would become, repeated a dozen times. I stand by my suggestion that the paragraph should be recast."

ALVIN BEAM: "No. But I would say 'one . . . one' (I rarely shudder but, as an editor of copy, may change a usage to conform to a prejudice of my own)."

JULES BERGMAN: "One should remain one."

HAL BORLAND: "It's only a mild shudder."

JOHN BROOKS: "The rule should be: 1. Don't use 'one'; 2. If you must use it, be careful not to follow it with a possessive pronoun."

HEYWOOD HALE BROUN: "Once one starts it, however, one thinks one will throw up before one gets out of it. Not because of male chauvinism but because of inaccuracy."

JAMES MACGREGOR BURNS: "I think the use of 'one' should be avoided in general."

WILLARD R. ESPY: " 'One . . . he' is a loathsome construction, but 'one . . . one' sounds affected to American ears. In writing, fine. I feel no shame that I often say 'you . . . you' in the place of 'one . . . one.' Perhaps I am incapable of feeling shame."

THOMAS FLEMING: "Yes, but not for the same reason. It just sounds bad. 'One . . . one' is worse."

STEPHEN H. FRITCHMAN ("one . . . one"): "Wooden and pedantic. There are better ways to fight male chauvinism."

ERNEST K. GANN: "No. But, oh how dull a writer who employs 'one' in *any* sense. While it may have served English travel writers in the 1800s it's the immediate signal of pomposity today. Banish the usage *totally* and never mind the male-female bit."

PAUL HORGAN (#1, #2, "yes") (#3): "Certainly not. The Women's Lib movement would require restructuring the whole system of English pronouns."

NORMAN HOSS: "As a feminist, I can sorrow that the male pronoun represents both sexes in English, but language doesn't legislate, it merely reflects culture, and 'his' is more idiomatic than 'one's.' "

JOHN K. HUTCHENS: "The trouble is, if one starts with 'one,' and goes on for three hundred words or so, the effect is merely comic as in a parody of an English comedy. By the way, speaking of chauvinism, why are ships called 'she'?" [See *"she" as pronoun for ships.*]

ELIZABETH JANEWAY: "I have worse things to shudder about."

ALEXANDER KENDRICK: "No shudders here. In fact, it is 'one . . . one . . . ones' which causes them. Nor is there any chauvinism. 'He' is here generic, as 'mankind' is."

ROBERT LIPSYTE: "*One* feels *its* hair prickle at the archness of the whole construction."

JULES LOH: "When I start with 'one,' I end with 'one' . . . but I also favor the masculine when both genders are meant, for clarity. Male chauvinism has nothing to do with it. I'm loath to leave a tried and useful usage."

PHYLLIS MCGINLEY: "A continuation of 'ones' is boring and pedantic."

JESSICA MITFORD: " 'One' is a bit of a bore in any event."

HERBERT MITGANG: "No . . . the 'one' usage has become concealment usage for true, personal feelings . . . better to use first or second person."

STANTON PECKHAM: " 'One' is pretty ghastly to begin with. To hell with 'one'!"

ORVILLE PRESCOTT: "When in doubt don't use 'one' at all. But I still distrust use of 'one' as always self-conscious and usually clumsy. There is no implication of male chauvinism. 'He' stands for any human when sex of the antecedent is not specified!"

PETER S. PRESCOTT: "Because one must continue with the singular construc-

one of those things

tion once one has begun it, a good writer will use it sparingly. I often recast a sentence to avoid it."

VERMONT ROYSTER: "One gets the feeling that one is re-reading Rebecca of Sunnybrook Farm which one read in one's youth and one has difficulty in restraining oneself."

HARRISON SALISBURY: "I would avoid the 'one . . . one' and make it 'he . . . his,' 'you . . . yours,' 'they' . . . their.' "

HAROLD SCHONBERG: "I wouldn't favor it ('one . . . one'). One finds it a bit awkward and pretentious. Just as bad as the editorial 'we.' But there's nothing grammatically wrong with it."

ROBERT SHERRILL: "No. Does he also shudder at 'a person . . . he'? Too many ones add up to a 1932 Hollywood butler."

CHARLES E. SILBERMAN: "We need an English counterpart to the French 'on.' There are times when 'one' is unavoidable, but it is an awkward term."

WALTER W. "RED" SMITH: "Usually I find 'one' self-conscious, studied, cutey-cute, but if one uses it, let one be consistent. Nuts to that chauvinism nonsense."

HAROLD TAYLOR: "I would shudder more with all that 'one' business. As Thurber said, it begins to sound like a trombone solo."

EARL UBELL: "Yes. But then I don't like 'one' at all—too stiff. I prefer 'you.' "

BILL VAUGHAN: "The big mistake is getting involved in that 'one' prissiness in the first place."

WILLIAM C. VERGARA: "I prefer the masculine pronoun when referring to such words as 'one, anybody, everyone, nobody, someone, person.' Instead of 'One must do one's duty as one sees it,' I prefer the less affected, 'One must do his duty as he sees it.' If I'm accused of male chauvinism, so be it!"

HERMAN WOUK: " 'One . . . one' is more formally correct, but starts out awkward and quickly gets intolerable; best avoided."

one of the, if not the   Fear of repetition of words sometimes leads to the destruction of proper grammatical construction, as in *"one of the, if not the* greatest hazards" when the proper formulation should be *"one of the* greatest hazards, *if not the* greatest." A simple solution is to leave it as *"one of the* greatest hazards."

one of those things

USAGE PANEL QUESTION

JOHN K. HUTCHENS cites two statements: (1) "It is *one of those things* that happen" and (2) "It is *one of those things* that happens."
He asks, "Are they interchangeable?"

431

Yes: 26%. No: 74%.
If your answer is "no," which version do you consider correct?
#1: 78%. #2: 22%.

ISAAC ASIMOV: "No. I'm a hypocrite. I probably use either."

STEWART BEACH: "I don't know which is *correct* but #2 is out of cadence and silly."

ALVIN BEAM: "Clearly, #1."

ALEX FAULKNER: "#2 better grammar, I suppose, but the ear seems to pick up the plural 'things.'"

PAUL HORGAN: "No. Ear calls for #1."

NORMAN HOSS: "No. #1 clause modifies 'things.'"

ELIZABETH JANEWAY: "This is a strictly by ear answer. #1 sounds better to me."

ALEXANDER KENDRICK: "They have become interchangeable, to all intents and purposes, but #1 would seem more precise, grammatically."

JULES LOH: "No. 'None but the brave deser*ves* the fair.' Nothing wrong with subject and verb agreeing [#2]."

PETER S. PRESCOTT: "No. 'Things that happen' is the unit from which one has been selected. Seems self-evident to me."

BERTON ROUECHÉ: "I prefer #1 because it's easier to say."

VERMONT ROYSTER: "No. This is a familiar case of the lost subject."

HAROLD SCHONBERG: "No. 'One' is the subject, demonstrably."

HOWARD TAUBMAN: "They are not interchangeable, but, depending on the precision of your use of the language and your meaning, either could be correct."

DAVIDSON TAYLOR: "No. 'That happen' agrees with 'things' in number."

WILLIAM C. VERGARA: "The 'one of those things that' construction logically requires a plural verb because *that* refers to *things*. The singular verb is merely a grammatical 'mistake.'"

one-up-manship. *See* BRINKMANSHIP

one . . . who One sure way to unleash a barrage of critical mail from self-styled purists is to use a sentence like the following in our column: "Here is *one* of the best football players *who* ever were chosen for the Hall of Fame." "Not so," cry the critics, including a shocking number of schoolteachers. "The antecedent of 'who' is 'one,'" they say. "Therefore, the verb in the clause should be singular and it should read: '. . . *who* ever WAS chosen.'" This strikes us as nonsense. The antecedent is "players," a plural noun, so the verb must be plural also—"were." As proof, let's reverse the order of elements in the sentence. "Of the best football players *who* was/were ever chosen for the Hall of Fame, he was *one*." Can there be any questions as to the form of the verb called for? As H. W. Fowler noted in this connection, "With *one* and *men* to attach the relative to, writers will hark back to *one* in spite of the nonsense it gives." Hear, hear!

For the Usage Panel's reactions to a question about a directly parallel construction, see the panel on ONE OF THOSE THINGS.

ongoing. *See* VOGUE WORDS

on line. *See* LINE, IN/LINE, ON

only The placement of *only* in a sentence is a matter of great concern to a few self-styled purists, but happily not for most speakers and writers. In theory, of course, *only* should be placed next to the element it modifies: "I want *only* orange juice," not "I *only* want orange juice." Unfortunately, though, that's not the way our language is actually spoken—even by highly literate, well-educated people. Indeed, if one were to say "I want *only* orange juice," he might be considered to be fussily overprecise in his speech. The simple fact is that the "rule" about placing *only* next to the element modified is honored now more in the breach than in the observance. Especially in speech, the normal placement of *only* is before the verb and this must be considered to be a perfectly acceptable part of the American idiom.

on the part of. *See* PART OF, ON THE

on the spot This is a phrase whose meaning has been greatly modified over the years. In current usage, it is used figuratively to mean "in danger of being embarrassed."

In old-time gangster movies, a person *on the spot* was destined to be "rubbed out." Earlier usage, in the days of pirates, came from the ace of spades playing card which bears only one printed black spot. This was shown to a suspected traitor or informer as notice that he was *on the spot* and was to be executed.

on to/onto The function of the words determines whether they are written as one or two words. When *on* serves as an adverb and *to* as a preposition, they are written separately: "We stayed at the hotel while the others went *on to* the convention hall."

If the two words together serve as a preposition, they are written solid: "Two grand pianos were brought *onto* the stage before the concert."

onward/onwards Both forms are acceptable as adverbs but only *onward* is used as an adjective: "traveled *onward* (or *onwards*)" and "*onward* motion."

opaque/translucent It would appear that there could be no possible confusion between these two words. A dictionary definition of *opaque* is quite specific: "Not able to be penetrated by light; neither transparent nor translucent." *Translucent*, by contrast, is defined as "permitting the transmission of light but so diffusely as not to permit perception of distinct images." Nonetheless, one reader of our newspaper column sent us a sample of *translucent* sealing tape clearly labeled *opaque.* Obviously, then, some people do confuse the two words.

The confusion may result from the fact that in the printing trades various stocks of paper are judged by their relative opacity—that is, on how much the type on the underside of a sheet shows through. Obviously a sheet that is insufficiently *opaque* is one that is letting some light through and is, hence, somewhat *translucent.* Leaving this one special instance aside, however, the distinction between *opaque* and *translucent* should be carefully observed.

operate When *operate* is used in the medical sense, the idiom is *operate on* or *upon.* A Frankfurt, Kentucky, reader reported that she often heard "She was *operated* this morning." But this is sheer illiteracy. It belongs in the same class—forgive the expression—as "She graduated high school." The idiom in the first case is, of course, "She was *operated on* (or *upon*)." In the second, "She was graduated from . . ." or "She graduated from high school."

operate. *See* RUN/MANAGE/OPERATE

operating theatre British equivalent for the U.S. "operating room." It is staffed in large part by "theatre sisters," who are the nurses in attendance.

ophthalmologist. *See* OCULIST/OPHTHALMOLOGIST/OPTICIAN/OPTOMETRIST

opt The *Oxford English Dictionary* gives *opt* as a verb meaning "to make a choice between alternatives" and dates its origin to 1877, proof that it is not a recent coinage, as some people think. Possibly because of overuse it has been the target of protest such as that voiced by Professor John W. Chaiken of Long Island University in *The New York Times:* "Is it not regrettable so to whittle down our 'choices' and 'alternatives'? 'Select' I say! Forget not your freedom of 'choice.' Elect not to forever 'opt'!"

optician. *See* OCULIST/OPHTHALMOLOGIST/OPTICIAN/OPTOMETRIST

optimistic/hopeful Optimism is an attitude of believing that the best will happen at all times and, as such, is thought by some careful writers to be too broad a concept to be applied to a situation or problem of limited scope. These people do not accept *optimistic* as a synonym for *hopeful,* but the preponderance of good usage indicates otherwise.

optimize   The tendency of politicians and bureaucrats to use long or unusual words to cloud the real meaning of what they are saying has resulted in a suspiciousness on the part of the American public as to whether some of these words actually exist.

A spokesman for the Defense Department, when questioned about the 1974 air raids on Cambodia, was quoted as saying: "When the weather opens up and you can see your target, it makes sense to optimize that advantage." Questioning the word *optimize,* a member of our Usage Panel asked: "Isn't this a new horror in the Pentagonese vocabulary or have I been living too sheltered a life of late?"

Optimize is indeed in the dictionaries, where it is defined as "to make the most efficient use of." It is hardly an everyday word, though, and is at very least pompous. *See also* VOGUE WORDS.

optimum   This is a noun first used in biology to describe the conditions under which the greatest growth is possible. It has come into general use as an adjective meaning the most favorable degree, amount, or condition. In the strictest sense it means more than "best" (as compared to other degrees, amounts, or conditions); its meaning is closer to "best that can possibly be achieved" or "most favorable."

optometrist. *See* OCULIST/OPHTHALMOLOGIST/OPTICIAN/OPTOME-TRIST

oral/verbal   There is a nice distinction between these two words—a distinction that should be observed. Briefly, *oral* refers solely to words spoken, while *verbal* may refer to words either spoken or written. Some precisionists prefer to limit *oral* to words spoken and *verbal* to words written but current usage does not support the latter part of this distinction.

orchestrate

USAGE PANEL QUESTION

The press and other media frequently referred to the "carefully *orchestrated* Nixon campaign" or the "carefully *orchestrated* Republican convention." Though the frequency of appearance of such phrases lately might make it seem a new voguish expression, panelists PAUL HORGAN and JEAN STAFFORD have been collecting citations for several years past. Here are examples: "It was well-orchestrated politics and the Lindsay camp was pleased" *(Time).* "President Kennedy and his advisers orchestrated the force that brought down . . . Diem" (*New York Times,* letter from Senator John Tower). "Senator Byrd had orchestrated his 'Southern strategy' " (Philadelphia *Bulletin*). Would you use *orchestrate* in this sense of "organize" or "arrange"?

In speech   Yes: 43%. No: 57%.

In writing of an informal nature   Yes: 50%. No: 50%.

In writing of a formal nature   Yes: 30%. No: 70%.

Many of those who oppose any nonmusical use of the term were vehement in their comments:

SHANA ALEXANDER: "Not wrong; just cliché, especially news-magazines—the worst kind."

BENJAMIN APPEL: "It makes me hear horns."

STEWART BEACH: "This is just self-conscious writing, reaching for an effect that makes no real sense."

JOSEPH A. BRANDT: "An incredible abomination of the English language. Nothing in the history of 'orchestrate' or derivatives justifies this affectation."

ERNEST K. GANN: "It has become a constant editorial cliché."

RICHARD EDES HARRISON: "What they mean is 'manipulate'—a far better word. If the intent is to show that the 'orchestration' is by one person I would accept it as having more emphasis than 'organization' or 'arrangement.' "

S. I. HAYAKAWA: "Horrors!"

WALTER KERR (voting "no" on speech and formal writing but putting "?" on informal writing): "I do use it in reference to the theater, yet find this political usage offensive. Should it be confined to the arts? I don't know."

EUGENE MCCARTHY: "It is impossible."

PETER S. PRESCOTT: "I think it is an awkward verb but suitable in writing about music."

WALTER W. "RED" SMITH: "I would have used this anywhere if I had thought of it first. Now it's threadbare as well as cute."

DAVIDSON TAYLOR: "It is a specific term of music: the assignment of instruments to the parts of a composition already written or being scored as written."

HAROLD TAYLOR: "I hate the constant use of any metaphor to cover every kind of situation."

Comments from those approving its use in informal writing but not necessarily in speech or formal writing:

ABE BURROWS: "I answered 'yes,' although I feel an interesting word is being worn out by the media men."

GEROLD FRANK: "A vivid word in casual writing."

ELIZABETH JANEWAY: "I find it a proper and useful metaphor."

CLARK KINNAIRD: "Gilles Perrault wrote one of the greatest espionage books, *The Red Orchestra,* likening operatives to instrumentalists under the baton of a master conductor."

JULES LOH: "To 'orchestrate' in a non-musical sense doesn't mean to 'organize' or 'arrange.' I take it to indicate organizing and arranging to a degree that seems overly precise, unnecessary or excessive. I applaud the writer who first chose to use the word in this sense; I would hate to see it diluted by overuse and misuse."

VERMONT ROYSTER: "I am one of those who called it 'the well-orchestrated Republican convention.' "

LEONARD SANDERS: "The search for clarity shapes the language. Perhaps this word will survive as an example—if not killed by excess usage."

HOWARD TAUBMAN: "Why not? Anyone who knows how cannily a composer has to orchestrate his effects must approve the usage."

Four panelists who accepted its use in speech and writing urged care in its application:

SHERIDAN BAKER: "But only with metaphorical awareness."

ALVIN BEAM: "The danger lies in overdoing it. Of the examples here, I would accept only 'the carefully orchestrated Nixon campaign.' The last two are dreadful."

BARRY BINGHAM, SR.: "Yes, but only when referring to the careful blending of various elements, as with orchestra instruments. I'd never use such a phrase as "orchestrated the force.' "

DOUGLAS WATT: "Only when the analogy is clear-cut."

orchidomania. *See* MANIA

ordinance/ordnance   These two words are close in spelling but far apart in meaning. An *ordinance* is a law, decree, or rule, usually of a city; *ordnance* is armament.

oreo   This is a bit of slang from the black community, a derogatory reference to blacks who are regarded by their fellows as insufficiently militant. The word, spelled with a capital "O," is a registered trademark of the National Biscuit Company, the name of a biscuit made of two cookies held together by a white filling. The more popular version of this cookie has chocolate-flavored cookies. So the disparaging use of *oreo* by blacks indicates their belief that some of their leaders are "black outside but white inside."

Another term used in the same sense is "Eskimo Pie." *See also* HONKY/-HONKIE.

organization/organisation. *See* BRITISH-AMERICAN SPELLING VARIATIONS

"-or" syllables, pronunciation of Words such as Florida, authority, and orange are usually pronounced with the *-or syllable* said just the way we say the word "or." One correspondent, however, complained that TV announcers pronounce it with the *-or syllable* rhyming with "are."

The "or" sound is the preferred pronunciation but dictionaries also record a second pronunciation in which that syllable is sounded with the "o" as in "pot."

Orwellian An *Orwellian* occurrence or situation is one that might have been imagined and described by George Orwell, an English writer whose real name was Eric Arthur Blair and who left two satiric masterpieces on totalitarianism: *Animal Farm* and *1984*.

1984 was a look into the future, when society would be completely controlled by propaganda and when the language would be something called Newspeak, in which words would mean just what the government said they should mean. In Orwell's view the totalitarian conquest would be complete by 1984, hence the title. With the 1970s exposure of corruption in high places some commentators remarked that "1984 nearly came early."

other than The question as to when it is acceptable to use the phrase *other than* can be tricky and it is best to avoid the phrase when another will serve. There is no question of its validity when speaking or writing of "fuels *other than* coal" or "sports *other than* football." "Apart from" and "aside from" are preferable to *other than* in such statements as "*Other than* a brief reference to them in his introduction, he ignored the hecklers."

ought *Ought* is normally followed by an infinitive but there is one case when the "to" may be omitted: when the statement is in the negative, as in "We *ought* not try to cross the street against the light." The entire infinitive can be omitted if it is understood from the context: "He doesn't think we should go but I think we *ought.*" "Had (or hadn't) *ought*" and "should (or shouldn't) *ought*" are substandard usages.

"-ough" words Foreign-born speakers of English invariably have trouble learning the various pronunciations of the *-ough* syllable in English. A simple sentence like "She had enough doughnuts to last through the meal" can trap almost any newcomer to English, with three different phonetic equivalents for *-ough* in a single sentence. In the correspondence columns of the London *Daily Telegraph* there appeared a few years ago a long interchange of letters from similarly baffled native-born Britons, all trying to find the largest possible number of variant pronunciations.

The winning sentence went like this: "A red-coated dough-faced ploughman thoughtfully strode coughing and hiccoughing through the streets of Scarborough." That accounts for seven varying pronunciations. Another reader, a Mr. Hougham (pronounced HUFF-am) reported that he works in his firm's Madrid office and "You can perhaps imagine the Spaniards' comments on the English language when I was joined by another Englishman, Mr. Hough (HOW)." There is, alas, no easy solution to this riddle of the *-ough* variations. Each must be learned individually and that can be a tough (TUFF) assignment.

out-. *See* PREFIXES AND SUFFIXES, WITH AND WITHOUT HYPHEN

outgroup. *See* VOGUE WORDS

out of/off of   The *of* is superfluous most of the time when *out* or *off* is being used in the sense of motion. There is one exception: when *out of* is used to mean "away from," as in "He ran *out of* the park." But "He jumped *off* (not *off of*) the roof," "The book fell *off* (not *off of*) the table" and "The cat jumped *out* (not *out of*) the window."

out of date/out of town   When phrases such as *out of date* and *out of town* precede and modify a noun, they are usually hyphenated: "*out-of-date* magazine" and "*out-of-town* engagement." When they stand alone in the predicate, there are no hyphens: "My father is *out of town*" and "My science textbook is *out of date.*"

out of sight   This is a slang phrase meaning "wonderful beyond description." It sometimes is written "outtasight."

output. *See* VOGUE WORDS

outside (of)/inside (of)   *Outside of* as used in place of "except for" ("*Outside of* Tim, we had a good time") is informal and should be avoided in writing.

Whenever *outside* is used as a preposition, the *of* is unnecessary and awkward. "*Outside* the house" and "*outside* the scope of the investigation" are better. The same is true of *inside.*

outtake   This is an item from the jargon of the radio, motion picture, and television industries. It refers to material filmed or taped that is edited out of the version finally shown or played. It is common practice to tape far more film or television material than can possibly be used, to enable the editors to have plenty of material to choose from. The material winding up on the cutting-room floor, so to speak, represents the *outtakes*.

over/more than

USAGE PANEL QUESTION

Many style books used to decree that *over* should not be used in the sense of "more than" but was to be restricted to use as an indication of physical position ("a sign *over* the door" but not "priced at *over* ten dollars"). Do you make this distinction?

In writing Yes: 63%. No: 37%.
In speech Yes: 39%. No: 61%.

The editors were surprised and pleased at the number of panelists who still make the distinction in writing at least. PAUL HORGAN, in saying that he does not make the distinction, commented: "Pressure of usage has won"; and JULES LOH, who still makes the distinction in both speech and writing, was also pessimistic: "But I no longer have the energy to fight it since I became over forty." Others voted to preserve the distinction at all times.

STEWART BEACH: "Pretty much, I think, though the use of 'over' is so well established that I see no harm in it."

ERNEST K. GANN: "We must have some dignity in the English word."

LEONARD SANDERS: "I have edited copy to conform to the style books cited. My response may be Pavlovian."

WALTER W. "RED" SMITH: "I do. It is evidence of a misguided youth."

A.B.C. WHIPPLE: "This is one still worth preserving."

Among those who voted for the distinction in writing (but not in speech):

ALVIN BEAM: "But I always feel bullied."

HAL BORLAND: "This use of 'over' is now common and accepted but I am a stickler."

ROBERT SHERRILL: "And because I worked for so many years out of that old style book."

over-/overly In most instances, the prefix *over-* serves as well as or better than the adverb *overly:* "*over*anxious," "*over*cautious," "*over*excited," for example. There are occasions, however, when *overly* may be preferred. "*Overly* friendly" is somehow easier to say than "*over*friendly," and "*overly* cautious" has a connotation of greater concern than "*over*cautious."

When the prefix "*over-*" is used it is usually not followed by a hyphen. When *overly* plus an adjective is followed by a noun, a hyphen may be used, as in "an *overly-*friendly dog" but, when used with a predicate adjective, there is no hyphen: "I felt he was overly anxious."

over/under At first glance it would seem that no other two words are such obvious antonyms as *over* and *under.* Yet the various media of communication are everlastingly assaulting our ears and our intelligence with claims that such-and-such an automobile is a better buy than the competitor's product by hundreds of dollars *over* the rival's price. A leading ice-cream maker, advertising a cut-rate special, says that the customer will save ten cents *over* the regular retail price.

It seems to us that this is calculated abuse of the language inspired by the advertising fraternity. The message from Madison Avenue, apparently, is that the gluttonous beast that is the American public, in the advertiser's view, can always be counted on to want more, not less, and *over* sounds like more, though the advertised price is actually less and so actually *under.* Thus the sense of the language is once again defiled and a word is made to mean what ad writers, like Humpty Dumpty in *Through the Looking-Glass,* "choose it to mean—neither more nor less." But what is funny in Lewis Carroll's fantasy is less than amusing as a slick contrivance of advertising hucksters.

overexaggerated This is an illiteracy that probably would not bear recording had it not been used by a ranking press adviser to an American President. A statement by Herbert Klein in late 1968 read: "Any idea of a major plot is *overexaggerated.*" The word is clearly redundant, since "exaggerate" alone says all that need be said. *See also* BUREAUCRATIC BARBARISMS.

overlay/overlie *Overlay* and *overlie* may result in the same condition or state but *overlay* refers to the act of placing or spreading a substance over another. *Overlie* is what that substance does once it is placed or spread.

overlooked The British use the verb *overlook* in a sense not common in the United States, as in "He was not aware that he was *overlooked* by the postman." The meaning is "that he had been seen," especially when going somewhere or doing something, and it is analogous to "overheard," which is more common in the United States.

overview. *See* VOGUE WORDS

owing to. *See* DUE TO/BECAUSE OF/OWING TO

Pablum/pabulum   *Pablum* (capital "P") is the trade name of a finely ground precooked cereal for infants, which can be mixed with either milk or water.

Used in a figurative sense and without the capital "P," *pabulum* means unexciting, tasteless ideas, either written or spoken, which are fed to people.

package/package deal   In the sense of a proposition or plan which has to be accepted or rejected in its entirety, *package* has become accepted in informal speech and writing. If the proposition is accepted, it becomes a *package deal.*

As a verb meaning to bring all necessary elements together, package is not yet as widely accepted as it is as a noun. It retains, of course, its original meaning of putting something (or some things) in a container or wrapping and then sealing it.

package store   In the early days after repeal of the Prohibition Act, several state legislatures piously voted that the "saloon" must never return, so the saloons reopened as "taverns" or "lounges." (One such establishment when ordered to take down its "Saloon" sign simply changed the first letter and became a "Baloon.")

The expression "liquor store" was similarly taboo in many districts. So the euphemism "package goods store" became widely used and later was cut down to simply *package store.* In some communities, the statutes stay on the books and the liquor stores remain *package stores.*

pad   *Pad* is a slang word which gained popularity in the 1960s as a synonym for a "place where a person lives or sleeps." It can mean anything from just a bed to an expensive apartment.

It is also slang for the graft shared by policemen for ignoring illegal activities within their precinct.

Paddy/Patrick   *Paddy* is the symbolic Irishman, just as John Bull symbolizes the Englishman. Irishmen accept the phrase "as Irish as *Paddy*'s pig" in all good humor, with the thought that the "pig" is there simply for alliteration.

However, when news commentators and others refer to March 17 as "Saint *Paddy*'s Day," true Irish blood boils. For one thing, *Paddy* is a variation of the Gaelic forms "Padraic" or "Padraig."

Patrick, on the other hand, is the English form, and St. *Patrick* came by it honestly because he was originally named "Patricius," during the Roman occupation of Britain.

Pago Pago   The pronunciation of *Pago Pago,* a seaport which is the capital of American Samoa, reflects the fact that the name of the seaport was formerly Pango Pango. The proper spelling today is *Pago Pago* but the pronunciation PAHN-go PAHN-go is preferred.

pair   Expressions like "three *pair* of stockings," like "six foot tall," should be classed as substandard. When you are speaking of more than one *pair,* the plural form of the noun is required: "three *pairs* (not *pair*) of stockings."

The verb form to be used with *pair* depends on whether the elements that make up the *pair* are considered as mates or as individual items. So it is correct to say, "This *pair* of gloves is wearing out" and "The *pair* of boys are lazy."

pair of   The problem whether "pants," "slacks," and "scissors" are followed by singular or plural verbs can be clarified by the addition of the phrase *pair of,* which, when used with each of them, is followed by a singular verb. Without it, the plural verb is proper. "The *pair of* pants is at the cleaner's" but "My pants are baggy."

When speaking of two individuals, even when they are acting jointly, the verb is plural, as in "The *pair of* them are going to Toronto in the morning."

palate/palette/pallet   Your *palate* is the roof of your mouth and, by extension, your sense of taste: "The cook has a sensitive *palate.*"

A *palette* is a board, with a hole for the thumb, on which an artist lays out and mixes pigments.

A *pallet* can be a sleeping mat, a part of a clock, or an instrument used in pottery making.

Obviously it is wise to choose the correct spelling.

pale, beyond the   This has become a figure of speech meaning "unthinkable" or "completely unacceptable in conventional society." Originally, the *pale* had to do with a fence erected for the protection of the inhabitants of a town. Then, during the Tudor Era, the term "the English Pale" came to mean those Irish counties in and around the city of Dublin over which England had control. Any person or thing *outside the pale* was considered beyond the jurisdiction of the English law and custom.

palm/Palmer   Until fairly recently the pronunciations of these two words left the "l" silent: PAHM and PAHM-er. However, there has been a marked tendency among TV and radio announcers to insert the "l," giving us the pronunciations PAHLM and PAHL-mer. To these ears this seems an affectation, but if persons bearing the name of *Palmer* choose to pronounce it in that fashion, it is indeed their privilege. We still opt for PAHM (not PAHLM) Beach, though.

palm off/pawn off   As an example of misusage, Elizabeth Janeway sent us this quote from a *New Yorker* advertisement: "We tell you this not because we are trying to pawn Countess Isserlyn [a cosmetic] off as a bargain." "Apparently the copywriter," she adds, "believes that there is an expression 'to pawn off,' which means something like 'to pass off' or 'to palm off.' "

If he or she does so believe, he or she is in error. To *pawn* something is to give it up temporarily for a loan of money. What is meant here is to *palm off,* to pass off by deception.

palpable   *Palpable* originally meant "touchable" or "able to be felt." By extension, it came to mean "easily perceived by any of the senses." The most common meaning today is "obvious," as in such phrases as "*palpable* nonsense" or "*palpable* lies."

panacea   *Panacea* means "an all-powerful remedy for all ills, diseases, and evils" and should not be used to designate a cure-all for a single one of those ills, diseases, or evils.

pank   *Pank* has been in use among skiers in Michigan for many years and may spread to other skiing communities. It means to flatten snow or to pack it down tightly when going uphill on skis. It is not in dictionaries as yet, but Michael Johnson, a humanities instructor at Michigan Tech, gave this explanation:

"The origin of 'pank' is as interesting as the country which adopted it. During the period 1850–1900, Michigan's northernmost counties, Houghton and Keweenaw (popularly called 'Copper Country'), were in need of bodies to mine the copper recently discovered there. Not just any bodies, though. Finns, French and Italians were fine for the menial labor involved but where to get the mining engineers?

"It happened that the Welsh at this time were among the world's most experienced miners and it was here that the Eastern mining interests turned for their engineers. For a while Copper Country was a linguistic nightmare as the various ethnic groups settled down and tried to work with each other. As with most second languages, curse words and occupational jargon were the first learned.

"And it's here that we see 'pank' being used and abused. 'Pank' is a corruption of a Cornish mining term, meaning to tamp, as in tamping dynamite. Since tamping is the same as packing, it is easy to see how 'pank' was picked up by the immigrant miners learning English from their bosses who were also learning English. So now we 'pank snow' here in Copper Country."

pantyhose. *See* TIGHTS

par   *Par* has a basic meaning of "a state of equality" and is used in this sense in the phrase "on a *par* with." In the phrase "up to *par*" it has a meaning of "normal standard," as in "His work is not up to *par* this week" or "I am not feeling up to *par* today."

paraffin   British equivalent of the American "kerosine" or "kerosene." What Americans call *paraffin* is "white wax" in the United Kingdom.

parameter

USAGE PANEL QUESTION

Parameter is a term from science meaning "a variable or arbitrary constant appearing in a mathematical expression. . . ." In recent years it has become very popular with bureaucrats and others who seem to think it is merely a more elegant form of "perimeter." Do you approve this extension of the meaning of *parameter* to include the sense of "boundary," as "Congress must learn to live within the *parameters* of a mandated budget." Would you use *parameter* in this extended sense in writing? Yes: 5%. No: 95%.
In speech? Yes: 5%. No: 95%.

ISAAC ASIMOV: "Because a bureaucrat speaks some vague and illiterate language should not force real people to do the same."
CHARLES BERLITZ: "Nevertheless, the word may force its own acceptance."
BARRY BINGHAM, SR.: " 'Parameter' as currently used is an example of fancy language to replace plain and completely adequate words."
DAVID H. BRADLEY: "A perimeter is a special case of a parameter. The meaning of parameter is a multi-dimensional boundary. In re budget, for

example, it includes economic, political, social factors. Perimeter is two-dimensional only. Parameter, used properly, is useful."

JOHN BROOKS: " 'Parameter' in this sense is simply a classy-sounding mistake. The word being groped for is 'perimeter.' "

HEYWOOD HALE BROUN: "Bureaucrats have a natural fondness for the inexact."

BEN LUCIEN BURMAN: "Chalk up another crime against Washington."

ROBERT CROMIE: "Would you say 'Iran and Iraq are having a parameter dispute'? Of course not. The word has no impact and should be forgotten except in its proper place."

GEROLD FRANK: "Its very use and reuse make it ostentatious to me."

RAY GANDOLF: "The word is certainly overworked but it seems to have become standard usage. I try not to use it but feel no shame when I slip."

SYDNEY HARRIS: "Sheer ignorance and pretentiousness."

STANLEY KUNITZ: "But I'm afraid this is a lost battle."

ROBERT LIPSYTE: "I never understood it before. Now I certainly won't use it at all."

JULES LOH: "What Mencken called bow-wow language."

DWIGHT MACDONALD: "Would mean losing a word—also confusing two widely different words."

EDWIN NEWMAN: "Perimeter does the job. So do boundary and limit. No need to use parameter for the purpose."

LEO ROSTEN: "Parameter means a variable constant; to use it as boundary or alternative is inexact."

HAROLD SCHONBERG: "It's a chic word. I hate it. But, God help me, it sometimes creeps into my speech."

ERICH SEGAL: "The battle on this one is lost."

HAROLD TAYLOR: "But I think it is now generally used as if it were perimeter and I'm not sure there's any way we can stop it."

NOTE: Among the very few who voted to accept *parameter* was DAVID H. BRADLEY, whose general comment was: "I am distressed by a hint of humanistic bias against technical (scientific) terms. The problem with terms such as 'interface,' 'parameter,' etc. is not their origin but their adoption and usage by people who do not understand them—which is the problem with *all* words. Ronald Reagan's stupidity is not a reason to restrict usage—rather to more precisely define it." In essence, proper usage and precision are the goals of the entire panel.

paramount This adjective represents an absolute which cannot be qualified. It means "chief" or "supreme," as in "of *paramount* importance." There is no possibility of degree; it is incorrect to say "most *paramount*" or "more *paramount*." *See also* ADJECTIVES, UNCOMPARABLE.

pardon/excuse A generation or two ago children were taught that "*pardon* me" was the correct form of apology for some slight breach of etiquette, and "*excuse* me" was to be used only when asking permission to leave the presence of others. Today such difference as may have existed between *pardon* and *excuse* in their use as apologies exists only in the minds of linguistic snobs.

  Pardon is still thought to be somehow more formal than *excuse,* perhaps because of its association with the more elegant French "pardonnez-moi."

parenting

USAGE PANEL QUESTION

To "father" and to "mother" have been part of the language since before the time of Shakespeare. Of much more recent vintage is the use of "parent" as a verb. It is enjoying a certain vogue, being used to mean "to care for, look after, or raise a child," whether this caring for or raising is done by the father or the mother.

Do you think that *parenting* says anything that "fathering" and "mothering" do not and is, therefore, a useful and welcome addition? Yes: 39%. No: 61%.

ISAAC ASIMOV: "Since the accent now is on much more equal time-sharing, 'parenting' gets across the joint-labors involved."

JOHN BROOKS: "No, and I oppose 'mothering' and 'fathering' except when used metaphorically."

HEYWOOD HALE BROUN: "It seems a way of avoiding responsibility, a means of concealing the identity of the inadequate."

BEN LUCIEN BURMAN: "Unspeakable!"

ROBERT CROMIE: "Where will it stop? Would you eventually 'brother' and 'sister' and 'cousin' someone?"

ALEX FAULKNER: "I suspect 'to parent' is yet another manifestation of the Women's Lib assault on the language."

FRANCES FRITCHMAN: " 'Useful,' yes, perhaps indispensable; 'welcome,' no —stylistically speaking."

RAY GANDOLF: "To father=to beget. To mother=to nurture. To parent=0. 'Parenting,' however, covers a multitude of duties beyond fathering and mothering, including those of single parents and surrogates."

PETE HAMILL: "Yes, but only if it refers to someone other than a real father or mother; otherwise it's an ugly word. Use it with precision."

PAUL HORGAN: "Yes, since it allows either gender."

JOHN K. HUTCHENS: "Why use such a general word as 'parenting' when the others are more specific?"

ELIZABETH JANEWAY: "It's a needed term, expressing a relationship which is not covered by 'fathering.' The latter appears to mean simply the physical contribution of the male in mating. Both parents are now more often engaged in active, day-to-day childraising. Consequently some ambiguous word is called for to take account of papa's contribution. A more subtle shade of expression is conveyed by the non-sex nature of the term, the fact that gender roles within the family are broader and more similar then they used to be."

DIANE JOHNSON: "It might be useful but I don't think I would use it."

JAMES J. KILPATRICK: "The need for 'to parent' is not at all apparent to me. In these genderless times, maybe the verb will be adopted by the chicspeak set, but I'd never use it."

IRVING KOLODIN: "Essentially faddish."

STANLEY KUNITZ: "Too awkward."

CHARLES KURALT: "My parents 'brought me up.' 'Parenting' would have been too intense an activity for them. Sounds like something you have to learn in school."

ROBERT LIPSYTE: "Useful, welcome, and *important*. It strips away the sexist implications of mothering and fathering in those instances where traditional use merely suggests the stereotypical notion that fathers' and mothers' roles are always distinct and circumscribed. Aren't William and Mary 'parenting' the *Harper Dictionary of Contemporary Usage*? I guess I'm no language purist. It's too easy to fragment or ridicule or discriminate using words. As much as "biz speech" and "computalk" make my tongue itch, the holding to old words sometimes means holding to old ways. I really like 'parenting' with its sense of sharing and freedom and fair play."

JULES LOH: "I don't think I would ever use it, but it's all right."

WILLIAM MCGUIRE: "It has acquired a technical meaning—to take care of children, as at a nursery school, etc. There are courses in parenting in the high schools."

WADE MOSBY: "Seems to me it is quite explicit, whereas 'fathering' and 'mothering' can mean a number of things besides devoting attention to an offspring."

MARGE PIERCY: "The notion of fathering and mothering under patriarchy is quite distinct from the negating of sex roles reflected in 'parenting,' which can also refer to the work of a nurturing adult not related as mother or father."

F. D. REEVE: "Seems to me like putting labels outside the clothes."

ANDY ROONEY: " 'Mothering' has a special meaning. 'Fathering' does, too, but they aren't parallel meanings. 'Raising' or 'rearing' would be better examples. . . . Do you think 'parenting' says anything that 'raising' or 'rearing' do not?"

LEO ROSTEN: " 'Fathered' does not mean 'cared for.' Anyway, I do not approve of 'parented,' unless we are prepared to accept 'He brothered his sister but refused to uncle his niece. So his sister aunted the wretch!' "

VERMONT ROYSTER: "I don't like unisex haircuts, unisex clothes, or unisex language."

DAVID SCHOENBRUN: "Fathers father; mothers mother, parents worry and have intercourse to become parents."

RUTH PAGE SCHORER: "Yes, since fathers take care of children in a way that is new. To father a child means to beget a child."

ERICH SEGAL: " 'To parent' has a distinct and useful meaning. Even if you father a child, you do not ipso facto 'parent' it unless you get up at 3 A.M. when it cries."

JACK SMITH: "Yes. Yes. With today's public discussions of what used to be strictly a mother's and father's business, the word seems useful."

ELVIS STAHR, JR.: "Yes, both 'fathering' and 'mothering' have differing meanings of their own which are different from 'parenting'—i.e., 'mothering' a stray dog or 'fathering' an illegitimate child but abandoning it to the mother."

HAROLD TAYLOR: "It has a certain virtue in giving a transitive element to being a father, 'caring for,' etc. but I'm not ready for turning any noun into any verb."

KARL V. TEETER: "We need good unisex terms in many areas and this is a good one and clear."

EDWARD TRIPP: "Without it one would have to say 'fathering' and 'mothering,' which is clumsy. Unfortunately the word smacks of social work cant, so I would not use it."

BARBARA TUCHMAN: "I think it does say something that fathering and mothering do not, simply because it includes both genders. That is useful—though I don't like the word myself and can't imagine using it."

JOSEPH VERGARA: "I don't like the word but reluctantly agree that perhaps there's a need for it. How else would you describe what an 'unwed father' does? To father means simply to beget, no?"

parkway. *See* TURNPIKE/THRUWAY/PARKWAY/HIGHWAY/ FREEWAY/SUPERHIGHWAY

parrhesian There is a marked tendency on the part of some columnists and editorial writers to attract attention and interest by the use of unusual words. The following excerpt from an editorial is an example: "The first lie an office-seeker tells is to announce that he is not yet a candidate, but only testing the waters. From that lie the politicians move easily into greater deceptions, manipulating the media, faking 'spontaneous' crowds and even 'homemade' signs, finding nonexistent missile gaps and pretending dovish intentions when plans for war escalations are being made. Reporters are stopped from editorializing or simply making *parrhesian* statements calling politicians liars, even if true."

Parrhesian can be found only in the unabridged dictionary and even there it is labeled "rare." It is taken from Greek and means "boldness or freedom of speech." Though use of such uncommon words in newspapers is not to be generally encouraged, the use of *parrhesian* in this editorial context seems acceptable.

parricide/patricide   *Parricide* is the murder of either parent or of a close relative. *Patricide* is restricted to the murder of one's father.

parson's nose/pope's nose   The *parson's nose* is the British equivalent of the American slang "the pope's nose," that part of the fowl that goes over the fence last.

part. *See* FACTOR/ELEMENT/PART

partake   There are two uses for *partake,* both rather old-fashioned and formal. *Partake of* means "to have a meal," especially in company with others. *Partake in* means "to participate," as to *partake in* a sailing race. In this sense "take part" or "participate" is preferable.

partially/partly

USAGE PANEL QUESTION

Panelist LAURENCE LAFORE writes: "I would like to have you ask the panel about 'partially.' It seems to me inelegant jargon. 'Partly' means the same thing and sounds better. 'Partially' is an example of a foolish impulse to add superfluous syllables in the manner of 'administrate' and 'orientate.' " Would you make these distinctions?

In speech   Yes: 62%. No: 38%.
In writing   Yes: 71%. No: 29%.

Comments with "yes" votes:

ABE BURROWS: "I answered 'yes' but my mind has been 'partially blocked' by the football announcers."
RICHARD EDES HARRISON: " 'Partially' is considered obsolete but it has elegant antecedents."
RUSSELL LYNES: "I would no more use 'partially' in that sense than use 'impartly' for 'impartially.' "
BARBARA TUCHMAN: "I agree with Lafore."

Other comments:

JOHN BROOKS: "Maybe the distinction is a bit pedantic."

WALTER LORD: "The kick was 'partly' blocked? He never saw a football game."

PETER S. PRESCOTT: "Maybe we should restrict 'partially' to use as the adverbial form of 'partial,' as in 'I'm for Nixon,' he said, 'partially.' "

participatory democracy/participatory theater During the 1960s and 1970s, these phrases became popular in the United States, particularly among young people.

Participatory democracy, with everyone having some say in decisions of policy, is applied to communal living and to running the government.

Participatory theater is a form of drama which calls for members of the audience to become members of the cast rather than remaining purely spectators. It also, in some instances, involves the regular cast members going among the audience, taking the action from the stage to the floor of the theater.

participial phrases, dangling. *See* DANGLING MODIFIERS

part of, on the *On the part of* is usually excess wordage. "By," "among," or "for" can be substituted with good results. "Heckling *on the part of* the crowd" can be cut to "heckling by the crowd" and improved at the same time.

party/person *Party* as a substitute for *person,* as in a question such as "Will the *party* who left a green coat on the plane please come to the ticket counter?" is a vulgarism. However, as long as there are long-distance telephone calls made person to person, there is little hope of escaping the operator's statement: "Your *party* is on the line."

parvenu/nouveau riche These two terms seem stilted and outdated in the United States today. Both are borrowed from French and mean a person who has suddenly risen to wealth but does not have the experience or background to enable him to conform to the customs of the class of society to which he now belongs.

pass away/pass on Euphemisms for "to die." Both should be avoided.

passel A fellow columnist was quoted as having written about "a passel of leftist thinkers corralled by Bertrand Russell," and the question was asked whether it was correct the use the word this way.

Passel is a variant of "parcel" and originated in regional Southern dialect. It has now acquired the broader meaning of a group or a fairly large number. It is a useful and colorful word in conversation and casual writing. It should be avoided in formal contexts.

pass-fail   In response to pressure for reform in grading systems, a number of colleges and universities initiated a limited form of *pass-fail* judgment of performance in academic courses. Under the *pass-fail* system, students are allowed to take certain courses with the understanding that they will not receive a letter or numeral grade but will instead receive academic credit if they complete the course satisfactorily. The result is that their point or grade average is not affected regardless of whether they pass or fail. One argument for it is that it enables a student to gain knowledge of certain fields in which he is not sure of his competence.

past history/past experience   Since both history and experience are products of the past, the use of *past* in these instances is redundant.

patent   The pronunciation PAT-'nt is standard for all noun and verb senses of this word. However, in the adjectival senses of "obvious" or "evident" ("This is a *patent* falsehood") the proper pronunciation is PAY-t'nt. This latter pronunciation is also standard for the botanical sense of "spreading out or open." In British speech PAY-t'nt is often, though not exclusively, heard in all senses of *patent*.

pathetic fallacy   This is the figure of speech in which human characteristics and emotions are attributed to inanimate objects. John Ruskin coined the name and a later writer, James Thurber, created our favorite example of the *pathetic fallacy* in a cartoon caption for *The New Yorker:* "It's a naïve domestic Burgundy without any breeding, but I think you'll be amused at its presumption."

pathos/bathos   *Pathos* is the quality in something seen or experienced that induces feelings of pity or sympathy. *Bathos* is excessive sentimentality, a sort of vulgarized *pathos.*

patio   One self-styled word expert, much given to flat pronouncements, decreed some years ago that "there is no 'pat' in *patio.*" His insistence was that *patio* must be pronounced PAH-tee-oh, in imitation of the Spanish PAH-tyoh. This is nonsense. There are two perfectly acceptable American pronunciations of *patio,* either PAT-ee-oh or PAH-tee-oh, with the former more widely heard.

patricide. *See* PARRICIDE/PATRICIDE

Patrick. *See* PADDY/PATRICK

patriot/patriotism A radio speaker, in an apparent attempt at an English accent, was heard to pronounce *patriotism* as PAH-trih-tism. He missed both the British version (which would have been PAT-rih-uh-tism) and the American (PAY-tree-uh-tism). Both Webster Second Edition (1934) and Funk & Wagnalls Unabridged (1913) recorded PAT-ree-ut and PAT-ree-uh-tism as acceptable alternate pronunciations. But, when this pronunciation is recorded at all today, it is identified as "chiefly British." Note, however, that there is a hamlet in southern Ohio, settled originally by Welsh immigrants, that still pronounces its name PAT-ree-ut.

patron As a fancy word for "regular customer," *patron* is used by snobbish restaurants and shops. It is stuffy and pretentious.

patsy This is slang for a person who is easily cheated, imposed upon, or otherwise victimized. It comes from the Italian "pazzo" meaning "fool" or "insane person."

pauper's field. *See* POTTER'S FIELD/PAUPER'S FIELD

peaceful/peaceable While some dictionaries make these two seem interchangeable, there is a distinction. *Peaceful* means "at peace, undisturbed by war or strife." *Peaceable* means "inclined toward or promoting peace," as in "He urged both nations to find a *peaceable* means of settling the dispute."

pea patch. *See* TEAR UP THE PEA PATCH

pecunious. *See* LOST POSITIVES

pedagogic/pedagogical These words, both meaning "pertaining to teaching," may be pronounced with either long or short "o" value for the third syllable: ped-uh-GOJ-ik or ped-uh-GOH-jik, and ped-uh-GOJ-ih-k'l or ped-uh-GOH-jih-k'l.

pedlock. *See* GRIDLOCK

peeler. *See* BOBBY

peer A "jury of his *peers*" and "*peer* group" (which is educational jargon) provide the most common uses of the word *peer*. A *peer* is an equal: someone in the same social, economic, or age group. It does not mean a person who is superior. The confusion on this score is that "peerless" does mean "superior" because it means that a person is without equal, literally without a *peer*.

peer group. *See* VOGUE WORDS

peeve *Peeve* is what linguists call a "back-formation" from the adjective "peevish," just as "enthuse" is a back-formation from "enthusiasm." *Peeve* is relatively new, though the adjective from which it is derived was in use before the time of Shakespeare. It is classed as informal rather than slang and is entirely acceptable in casual conversation and writing. It should still be avoided in formal writing and speaking.

pejoration. *See* MELIORATION

pell-mell/Pall-Mall There is no similarity between the meanings of these two phrases but they are frequently confused, probably because the British give them both the same pronunciation: PELL-MELL.

    Pall-mall was originally the name of a game—a sort of distant cousin of croquet—imported from Italy to London during the reign of Charles II. It became so popular with the upper crust that the alley in which it was played became a center of fashionable club life and *Pall-Mall* became a symbol of elegance, much like New York's Park Avenue.

    Pell-mell, on the other hand, denotes utmost confusion, headlong and disorderly haste.

penchant. *See* FETISH/PENCHANT

pendant/pendent/pending *Pendant* is a noun meaning "something that hangs from something else," often an item of jewelry hanging from a necklace. *Pendent* is the adjective form, meaning either "hanging" or "overhanging" or, in law, "undecided or remaining to be settled." In this latter sense, it is synonymous with *pending. See also* NOW PENDING.

pending. *See* NOW PENDING

penicillin Quite often dictionary editors, especially when recording pronunciations of technical or scientific words little used by the lay public, choose the one which should be right by the customary rules of pronunciation. Then, when the word comes into general use, the pronunciation favored by the mass of literate people may turn out to be something quite different from the one the experts chose.

    The classic case in point is *penicillin.* According to the word experts and, indeed, according to Sir Alexander Fleming, who discovered it, the drug should have been pronounced "peh-NISS-ih-lin." The lay public, however, was influenced by the similarity to "pencil" and called it peh-nih-SILL-in and so it has remained.

Pentagonese. *See* EUPHEMISM

penurious *Penurious* once meant "extremely poor" or "barren," but, while "penury" still means "extreme poverty," *penurious* has acquired a meaning of "miserly" or "stingy." This new meaning has supplanted the earlier meaning to a large degree.

people. *See* PERSONS/PEOPLE

people/peoples *People* is a collective noun which requires a plural verb and is used to refer to a single race or nation, as in "The *people* of America are united." When you speak of more than one of the nations of the world, the plural form may be *peoples:* "The *peoples* of the Western Alliance— French, British, German, and Americans alike—are united in their common beliefs."

people mover In an effort to help solve the problems of mass transit, various devices have been invented and labeled *people movers.* In all cases, they move along a fixed route and usually between two fixed points.

They range from mini-streetcars used to transport students from one campus to another to a conveyor belt for pedestrians, such as those seen in a few of the largest airports. In this sense, we have had *people movers* for a long time and called them "escalators."

pep pills. *See* DOWNERS/UPPERS

per *Per* means "for each" and is idiomatic in such expressions as "*per* mile," "*per* gallon," and "*per* person." In all other instances, *per* should be avoided, with the words "a," "by," or "in accordance with" (depending on the context) used instead.

A statement such as "Dues are $1 *per* each adult member of the household" is not only not idiomatic but ungrammatical, since the "each" is superfluous.

percale The preferred pronunciation is per-KALE and is the one most frequently heard in the Eastern United States. Per-KAL is, however, held also acceptable and is widely heard in the Middle and Far West.

percent/in care of, symbols for The *percent* symbol "%" is a figurative interpretation of the mathematical formula "x/100," expressing "by the hundred." It is a sign of laziness or ignorance for typists to use it in place of "c/o" when *in care of* is meant.

percent/percentage Both *percent* and *percentage* refer to a portion of the whole, whether it be large or small.

Percent is used with a definite figure. *Percentage* needs a qualifying adjective, such as "large" or "small" or "overwhelming." The number of the verb used depends on the object of the preposition "of." "Ten *percent* of the candy *is* chocolate," since "candy" is a singular noun; "Ten *percent* of the children *are* absent," since "children" is a plural. The same rule of thumb holds for *percentage* when it is followed by a prepositional phrase.

percolate A very common mispronunciation of *percolate* is PER-kyoo-layt and, of the device employed, PER-kyoo-lay-ter. Correct pronunciation calls for stress on the first syllable, with the second syllable the unstressed vowel or schwa sound: PER-kuh-layt and PER-kuh-lay-ter. Still more objectionable, however, is the adman's truncated form "perk" as in "fresh-perked."

per diem *Per diem* literally means "per day," and it is redundant to say or write, "a *per diem* allowance of $60 a day."

perfect/perfectly *Perfect* is viewed by many careful writers as one of the *uncomparable adjectives* (which see) and consequently not having comparative or superlative degrees, as in "more *perfect*" or "most *perfect.*" Others argue that the framers of our Constitution wrote of a desire "to form a more *perfect* union." The rebuttal to this is twofold: (1) that the usage of that time was not the same as today's, and (2) the comparison was to the union as it existed under the Articles of Confederation, which preceded the Constitution.

The Usage Panel approves "near-*perfect*" by 52 percent, with some of those approving expressing reluctance to do so. Many of those opposing its acceptance cited the analogy to "unique," which they feel is also an absolute.

Perfectly as an intensive, meaning "altogether," is also subject to some criticism but is widely used, as in "*perfectly* good." *See also* NEAR-PERFECT and MORE PERFECT.

perfume *Perfume* may be pronounced either PUR-fyoom or pur-FYOOM.

periodic/periodical *Periodic* and *periodical* are very similar, indeed overlapping, in meaning. Each means "occurring at regular intervals." However, *periodic* may have the special sense of occurring or appearing at irregular intervals. *Periodical* has special relevance to publication at regular intervals. In this sense it also is used as a noun, usually referring to a magazine or other publication that appears at regular, but not daily, intervals.

perk An article in a news magazine about congressional salaries and "various delightful extras" notes that "until a couple of years after World War

II, members of Congress were paid $10,000 per year and precious few *perks.*"

Perk, as used here, is shorthand for "perquisite" (pronounced PER-kwih-zit), which roughly equals what nonpoliticians call "fringe benefits." It is any sort of payment or benefit received in addition to basic salary.

permanence/permanency   Both are defined in dictionaries as "the state or quality of being permanent," with a second definition for *permanency* as "someone or something permanent." H. W. Fowler makes this point: "Writers whose feeling for distinctions is delicate will prefer *permanence* for the fact of abiding, and *permanency* for the quality or an embodiment of it: *We look forward to its* permanence; *The* permanency *of the orthodox marriage bonds.*"

permit   The accent falls on the second syllable of *permit* when it is used as a verb meaning "to allow or give permission to or for." When the word is used as a noun, the accent usually is placed on the first syllable. There has been, however, a noticeable increase in the number of radio and television reporters and commentators who accent the second syllable in both noun and verb. Dictionaries, for the most part, continue to make the distinction in pronunciation and it is a distinction worth preserving.

perpetrate/perpetuate   Only carelessness can cause confusion between these two words, but it happens frequently. *Perpetrate* means "to do something evil or criminal." Its noun form is a favorite of police forces everywhere in the United States: "The perpetrator took the money, raced from the bank, and ran down the street."

Perpetuate means "to cause to continue—to make perpetual."

per se   *Per se,* meaning "in or by itself," is a Latin phrase and in classical Latin was pronounced pur-SAY. However, the British and the legal fraternity have long pronounced it pur-SEE. Most American dictionaries give both pronunciations, indicating that either is acceptable, though most list the pur-SAY pronunciation first, indicating that it is preferable for general use.

persecute/prosecute   To *persecute* is to harass or to afflict unfairly; to *prosecute* is to charge and try under the law.

perseveration   *Perseveration* has appeared occasionally as a highfalutin synonym for "repetition." As such it is pretentious and unnecessarily confusing to the lay reader. Properly used, *perseveration* is a clinical term in psychology and psychiatry and refers to a patient's uncontrollable repetition of a word or phrase or his inability to control unwanted repetition of thoughts or images in the mind.

persnickety/pernickety   For many years the only form entered in dictionaries was *pernickety,* despite the fact that the most common spoken form was *persnickety.* (Both mean "too particular" or "fussy.") In fact, *persnickety* has been around for many decades in just as good use as *pernickety* but was ignored by dictionary editors.

In 1934 it was entered in the Webster Second Unabridged as a variant spelling. By the early 1950s it had been given its rightful place in the dictionaries and the most recent dictionaries now list *persnickety* as the preferred form, giving *pernickety* as a variant spelling. Slang.

person. *See* PARTY/PERSON

persona   *Persona* is a term recently borrowed from the jargon of psychology, meaning "the outer personality mask or façade assumed by one when facing others." Panelist Harold Schonberg calls it "nouveau and faddistic" and says that it "adds naught to our tongue." We agree. *See also* NONCE WORDS.

personality

USAGE PANEL QUESTION

Personality, in the sense of the aggregate of qualities that make a person an individual, is well established. In recent years, however, the term has been widely used, especially in show business, as a synonym for "notable" or "celebrity." Would you use *personality* in this sense?

In speech   Yes: 41%. No: 59%.
In writing   Yes: 26%. No: 74%.

ISAAC ASIMOV: "It's the illiteracy of agents. I also spit on 'He's a talent.' "
ALVIN BEAM: "And then there are 'fabulous personalities.' "
HAL BORLAND: "I suppose 'personality' is just as valid as 'name'—"He's a big name.' Get into that area and you find a number of odd ones—worthy, somebody, wheel, figure, big cheese, big shot, etc. The basic problem, it seems to me, is that virtually all of them have press-agent exaggeration, the old Madison Avenue fever-flush. A perfectly good word or expression is infected with false importance."
HEYWOOD HALE BROUN: "It may, however, have some use to describe people who show their emotional sores on talk shows."
RICHARD EDES HARRISON: "No, but I might slip."

ALEXANDER KENDRICK: "Not even ironically."

DWIGHT MACDONALD: "On same level with 'celeb.' "

EDWIN NEWMAN: "Yes—but sarcastically."

VERMONT ROYSTER: "Because there are some celebrities notable only in their personalities."

ELVIS STAHR, JR.: "Unless I am quoting or trying to be colloquial. Not seriously. It's cheap."

EARL UBELL: "I hate it because it implies more than 'celebrity' or 'notable.' It suggests a figure especially created for show biz like a wax doll for a tinsel show. If I used it, I would be sure that my reader or listener understood the full pejorative weight of this word."

When the question was put to the Usage Panel several years later, there was a drop of 7% in the number willing to accept it in speech, with a slightly smaller drop regarding writing.

USAGE PANEL QUESTION—SECOND EDITION

Personality, in the sense of the aggregate of qualities that make a person an individual ("Tom has a winning *personality*"), is long established. In recent years *personality* has been widely used as a synonym for "celebrity," which one of the ilk defines as a person "well-known for being well-known."

Would you use *personality* in this sense in speech? Yes: 34%. No: 66%.
In writing? Yes: 21%. No: 79%.

DAVE ANDERSON: "Yes, in the sense of a theatrical personality or sports personality."

ISAAC ASIMOV: "Nor do I refer to a person as 'a talent' or 'a property.' "

CHARLES BERLITZ: "It has a derisive and cynical sound as if set off by implied quotes."

BARRY BINGHAM, SR.: "It has become a part of standard speech, stemming from Hollywood and the TV networks."

BEN LUCIEN BURMAN: "I voted 'no' but I think in a very few years it will be universally accepted."

ALISTAIR COOKE: "I suffer from being called a 'television personality.' On the contrary, I am a human being."

ROBERT CROMIE: "Although I am attracted by the possibility that someone with a 'losing' personality could be called a non-celebrity it should be illegal to use any strange word without checking a good dictionary for the meaning."

FRANCES FRITCHMAN: "Once more into the breach—what's wrong with poor old 'celebrity'?"

PAUL HORGAN: "Show biz and P.R. vulgarity."

ROBERT LIPSYTE: "Personality is even better than celebrity for describing those talk-show guests who are not so much well-known as available to liven up the party with their . . . personality."

WADE MOSBY: " 'Personality,' as applied to certain radio performers, may not say exactly what it means, but neither does it say something that isn't meant. At one time, most of us rather arrogantly dismissed radio people as 'disk jockeys.' In defense of their calling, they described themselves as 'personalities.' For want of a better word, I'm willing to accept that appraisal, especially when some of the practitioners are among leaders of opinion in news, the arts, and, sometimes, in the sciences."

EDWIN NEWMAN: "Some people, for example, usually of no other distinction, are called television personalities."

MARGE PIERCY: "I would use it because it is more accurate than celebrity. Such people are generally in no sense celebrated; they exist, as do talk show hosts and guests, by virtue of seeming to be someone famous."

BERTON ROUECHÉ: "I think this usage goes back at least 60 years—and if it is popular now, it is a revival."

HAROLD SCHONBERG: "Can't see how it can be avoided. Luciano Pavarotti has a great deal of personality. Pavarotti is also an imposing personality. I'm afraid we're stuck with it, like it or not. I don't."

ERICH SEGAL: "This usage is already well established in European languages. I think the die is cast."

JACK SMITH: "It seems useful for a person who isn't quite a celebrity. But I don't like it."

JOSEPH VERGARA: "Seems O.K., as in 'He's not really an actor. He's a personality.' "

personnel   The substitution of *personnel* for "persons" is frequently found in Army statements of strength, capacities, and requirements, as in "The authorized strength of this unit has been increased by two *personnel.* "

Here is bureaucratic jargon at its most idiotic. Someone, thinking to make a routine statement more impressive, started using *personnel* when he should have used "persons" and has apparently persuaded other linguistic nitwits to follow suit.

Personnel means "employees" collectively. It can take a singular verb when it is viewed as a unit, as in "Our *personnel is* made up solely of white-collar workers," or a plural verb if the group is considered as individuals, as in "Our *personnel are* encouraged to make suggestions on safety procedures."

persons/people   The basic difference between *persons* and *people* is that *persons* is usually used when speaking of a number of people who can be counted and *people* is used when speaking of a large or uncounted number of individuals. Within these boundaries, *people* can sometimes be used instead of *persons* but *persons* cannot be substituted for *people*. For example, "There were twenty *persons* in the room" can be changed to "There were twenty *people* in the room." But it would be ridiculous to change "*People* were hurrying to catch the train" to "*Persons* were hurrying to catch the train."

People also has another sense which does not apply to *persons:* the members of a race or nation as a whole. For example, "The *people* of France." *See also* PEOPLE/PEOPLES.

perspective. *See* PROSPECTIVE/PERSPECTIVE

perspiration Ignorance or carelessness sometimes results in this word's being pronounced "prespiration."

peruse Too often *peruse* is used loosely as a synonym for "read." Its precise meaning is "to read very carefully, thoroughly, and completely."

petit/petty Once used synonymously, *petit* and *petty* both mean "small" or "minor." *Petit* is now confined primarily to legal language, as in "*petit* jury" (as opposed to "grand jury") and "*petit* larceny." Even here, "*petty* larceny" is more common outside the legal profession. The Old French spelling of *petit* is retained in "*petit* mal," a mild form of epilepsy (as opposed to "grand mal"); "*petit* point," embroidery done in small stitches; and "*petit* fours," tiny individually frosted cakes. All are pronounced PET-ee.

petrol British equivalent of the American "gas" or "gasoline."

pharmacomania. *See* MANIA

phase/faze A *phase* is a stage of transition or development and has a connotation of sequential change. Correctly used, it is not synonymous with "aspect," as in "There is another *phase* to the problem." Use "element" or "aspect" instead. Neither is it interchangeable with *faze,* which means "to disconcert" or "take aback."

phase in/phase out. *See* VOGUE WORDS

phenomenon/phenomena *Phenomenon* is the singular form. *Phenomena, the plural form, is sometimes erroneously used with a singular verb: "The phenomena of the show-business world is the success of So-and-so."* This results solely from ignorance. *See also* DATA/DATUM.

philanthropy Too often the broader meaning of a word is ignored, especially when a narrow meaning is widely used and accepted. Such was the case when a grammar school pupil's definition of *philanthropy* as a "love of mankind" was marked wrong by the teacher. It was the teacher's contention that the proper definition was "large amount of public gift giving."

The word comes from two Greek words, "philos" meaning "love" and "anthropos" meaning "mankind," so the child's definition is the basic one. The meaning "efforts to improve the well-being of mankind by charitable aid or donations" is an extended one.

philologist. *See* LEXICOGRAPHER/PHILOLOGIST

phobia/mania Both *phobia* and *mania* have a sense of strong emotion but beyond that they are opposite in meaning. A *phobia* is an unreasoning fear; a *mania* is a mad desire or enthusiasm for something.

The two most common *phobias* are claustrophobia, fear of being enclosed or crowded, and acrophobia, fear of heights. Among the many other phobias are: ambulophobia, dislike of walking; androphobia, hatred of men; arachnophobia, fear of spiders; aelurophobia, fear of cats; chronophobia, fear of time or clocks; cataphobia, fear of falling; demophobia, fear of crowds; erythrophobia, fear of blushing; and dentophobia, fear of dentists. *See also* MANIA.

phony While some dictionaries still insist that *phony* (meaning "not genuine" or "false") is slang, its use has become so widespread that it should certainly be considered acceptable in informal speech and writing. It can be used as either a noun or an adjective.

Photostat/photostat *Photostat* (capitalized) was coined in 1912 and originally applied only to the original Photostat machine and the copies made by it. Undoubtedly the owners of the trademark *Photostat* wish that popular usage were still limited that way. But, whether through failure to prosecute violators of their trademark or simply because of the popularity of the machine and its many imitators, the word *photostat* (with a small "p") is now part of the common tongue—a generic term.

The word "photostatic" is also part of the standard tongue. If the phrase "photostatic copy" is too cumbersome, use "photocopy." In informal memoranda, use the term that is universally accepted in the printing trade: simply "stat." Photostatic reproduction has been rendered nearly obsolete by the world-wide introduction of relatively low-cost, simple to operate copying machines pioneered by Xerox. Proprietors of the trade name "Xerox" have been as vigilant as the proprietors of *Photostat* were negligent. They insist, quite correctly, that the word "Xerox" must always appear with the initial "X" capitalized and, where appropriate, the copyright "bug" ©.

pianist   People with musical education tend to use the pronunciation PEE-uh-nist for this word but the majority of Americans say pee-AN-ist, probably because of the pronunciation of "piano," from which the word *pianist* is derived.

picnic/picnicking   In forming the principal parts of the verb *picnic,* there is a very good reason why a "k" is added to the present tense. If it were not there, people would not give the "k" sound to the "c." If it were misread as a soft "c," considerable confusion could result.

picture   *Picture* should be pronounced PIK-cher, not PITCH-er.

pidgin English   A blend of English words and Chinese syntax, *pidgin English* has long been a practical solution to the problem of communication between English-speaking traders and Chinese traders in ports of the Far East. (The word *pidgin* comes from the Chinese traders' mispronunciation of "business.") In these days of vastly expanding trade, however, and with English truly the international language of business, *pidgin* is less and less often heard.

    Where it is still in use, it sounds a lot like baby talk, since many short words are used to express the sense of a word not known to the natives. Thus "bishop" becomes "top-side piece-heaven pidgin man" and "belly-belong-me-walk-about" translates as "I'm hungry."

    There are many varieties of *pidgin English* and, for that matter, pidgin Spanish, pidgin French, and so on. In Mediterranean seaports a hybrid language containing elements of all the languages spoken in the area (Arabic, Turkish, Spanish, and others) is still spoken. It is known as Lingua Franca, literally the Frankish language. (The Franks were a Germanic tribe that ruled over most of Europe during the Middle Ages; Lingua Franca originally was the language through which the Muslims conducted business dealings with the Franks.) In Samoa and other Polynesian islands a fascinating language called "bêche-de-mer" is spoken. "Pour the coffee" becomes "capsize him coffee along cup." "Serve dinner" is "shoot him kai-kai." A Frenchman is "man-a-wee-wee" (man who says "oui-oui") and the butcher is "man belong bullamacow."

piecemeal   Washington newspaper correspondents, especially when appearing on informal talk shows, tend to accelerate the trend to convert non-verbs to verbs. "The department is trying to *piecemeal* the program" means that the department is not setting the program as a whole in operation or is holding back funds, giving only a little at a time. This has to be regarded as slang.

piedmont/Piedmont   *Piedmont,* which means quite literally "foot" (from the Latin "pes") "of the mountain" (from the Latin "mons") may be spelled either with a small or capital "p." With the small "p" it can be applied to any land area that lies at the foot of a mountain or mountain range. When spelled with a capital "P," it usually refers specifically either to Italy's Piedmont, a region in the northwest bordered by France and Switzerland, or the American Piedmont, which extends eastward from the Appalachians and Blue Ridge Mountains and northward from Alabama to New Jersey.

pier. *See* DOCK/PIER/WHARF

pig   Once a part of British underworld slang, *pig* as an insulting term for a police officer came into widespread use among anti-war protesters during the 1960s and 1970s. The acceleration of the feminist movement resulted in the widespread use of the phrase "male chauvinist *pig*" to describe a man who did not recognize equal rights or status for women.

pinch hit

USAGE PANEL QUESTION

Panelist SYDNEY J. HARRIS, commenting on the adaptation of sports terms to general use, writes: " '*Pinch hit*' is the worst offender—as used, for instance, to designate a substitute speaker. A pinch hitter in baseball is someone *better,* sent in to get a hit, not a mere substitute!"

Yet we commonly see statements in the press like "Richard Burton was unable to appear at last night's performance. His understudy, John Doe, *pinch hit* for him."

Do you feel that *pinch hit* should be accepted in such an instance? Yes: 70%. No: 30%.

Should we insist that *pinch hit* be reserved for occasions in which a comparable or superior performer (" . . . Richard Harris *pinch hit* for him") was substituted? Yes: 20%. No: 80%.

DAVE ANDERSON: "Not necessarily 'better' . . . sometimes a left-handed batter instead of a right-handed batter, or vice versa."

ISAAC ASIMOV: "Pinch hit is a nice, dramatic term. Let us not make invidious distinctions."

THOMAS S. BARBER: "I think a pinch hitter is one pressed into service *in an emergency*—regardless of his credentials."

JOHN BROOKS: "Pedantry. Besides, a pinch hitter isn't ordinarily better—only different—i.e. he bats left instead of right, or vice versa."

BEN LUCIEN BURMAN: "I'm sure I'm one of the oldest panelists and pinch hit has been around since I was in knee pants."

JOHN CIARDI: "His understudy substituted."

WILLARD R. ESPY: "This particular water has been over the dam long since. Outside of baseball, a pinch hitter is one who replaces another in time of need; superiority, or inferiority, has nothing to do with the matter."

FRANCES FRITCHMAN: "Dare one disagree with Sydney Harris? A pinch hitter in baseball is by no means always equal to or superior to the player in the line-up. There are many other reasons for the change."

RAY GANDOLF: "Let actors squabble over whether they are understudies or the more exalted 'stand-bys.' Pinch hitter is good enough for me."

PAUL HORGAN: "Popular usage has already won this."

JOHN K. HUTCHENS: "Perhaps as an old baseball fan, I think this phrase belongs *only* to baseball—not even for any other sport."

ELIZABETH JANEWAY: "The whole process of use has gone too far to make such a restriction successful."

WALTER KERR: "Otherwise, why borrow it?"

JAMES J. KILPATRICK: "Harris is correct, of course, on the precise meaning of 'pinch hitter.' Some years ago I fought to preserve the meaning, but the years pass and most of us get tired. I used to fight for the precise meaning of 'lion's share.' I gave up on that one, too. I continue to defend 'Hobson's choice' as meaning no choice at all, but I am being ground down by those who suppose that it means merely a hard choice. It is too late, I fear, to contend that 'pinch hitter' means something more than 'substitute.' Reluctantly, I vote no."

STANLEY KUNITZ: "The battle has already been lost. The fact of substitution is the relevant issue, not the value judgment."

ROBERT LIPSYTE: " 'Serious' writers over-use sports terms to score a point, but usually they strike out, distorting their own meaning and devaluing the precision of the sports term. I say, bench them for good."

JULES LOH: "Sydney is nit-picking."

DWIGHT MACDONALD: "Who but a baseball expert honors this distinction?"

WILLIAM McGUIRE: "We should try, and perhaps baseball fans, in their vigor, would help. Recruit Roger Angell."

WADE MOSBY: "Seems perfectly acceptable to me."

EDWIN NEWMAN: "Harris is right but it is too late to stop this use of pinch hit."

MARGE PIERCY: "For one thing, frequently a pinch hitter does not come through. What he is supposed to do is not even the majority of time what happens."

PETER S. PRESCOTT: "Splitting cummin [*sic*] seeds! The phrase should be left to the sports writers."

F. D. REEVE: "Jargon."

ANDY ROONEY: "Each of us should be allowed only a limited number of things like this to irritate us. I concede that Sydney is right but I'm not going to use up a place on my list by letting it annoy me."

BERTON ROUECHÉ: "Let's keep it in baseball."

VERMONT ROYSTER: "Sydney should know baseball better. Usually the pinch-hitter is thought to be better but the term is also used for any substitute. Useful word."

HAROLD SCHONBERG: "No, because 'pinch hit' in this usage has been around too long and is part of universal usage."

JACK SMITH: " 'Pinch hit' has long been part of the language. A pinch-hitter is not necessarily a *better* hitter but one who is thought to be more likely to get a hit in a particular situation."

ELVIS STAHR, JR.: "This is predicated on a shaky assumption. In baseball the pinch hitter is not necessarily someone 'better,' but rather someone more likely to carry out a very particular assignment in a very particular situation. In any case, it is O.K. for an understudy to pinch hit for an opera star."

HOWARD TAUBMAN: "Has Mr. Harris noticed the caliber and record of hitting ability of some of the pinch hitters sent up in recent years, say, by the Mets?"

HAROLD TAYLOR: "I wouldn't use pinch hit myself but it doesn't necessarily mean, when used outside baseball, that the substitute is better than the regular."

KARL V. TEETER: "Sydney Harris is not a baseball fan, it appears. A pinch hitter substitutes for *any* reason, including illness."

EDWARD TRIPP: "Isn't it a bit late to correct a nearly universal error?"

GEORGE WALD: "The 'substitute' sense is all that most of us know."

DOUGLAS WATT: "It's always useful in a pinch."

A.B.C. WHIPPLE: "Whatever its technical meaning, it has become accepted as 'substitute.' "

Ping-Pong. *See* RICOCHET WORDS

pinky   *Pinky,* also spelled *pinkie,* looks like a typical bit of nursery-age slang. So it comes as somewhat of a surprise to learn that it has been around a long time and that we originally borrowed it from the Dutch. Their word is "pinkje" and means the little finger. Dictionaries do not label it "slang"; most of them do not label it at all, indicating that it is acceptable; only *American Heritage* labels it 'informal."

pistol/automatic/revolver   A *pistol* can be either an *automatic* or a *revolver* but *automatic* and *revolver* are not synonymous. A *revolver* has a revolving cylinder which holds the cartridges; an *automatic* does not.

piteous/pitiable/pitiful   All three of these have the basic meaning of "arousing pity," but *piteous* means "deserving true pity or compassion." Both *pitiable* and *pitiful* mean "deserving disdainful pity" or "contemptible," while *pitiful* has an additional meaning of meager or insignificant, as in "A *pitiful* number of books in the school library."

pizza pie   This is a favorite redundancy of Americans. *Pizza* is an Italian pie made with tomato and cheese and other ingredients. So *pizza pie* is literally "pie pie."

pizzazz   "Vim," "vigor," "boldness," "energy," "vitality," and "flair" are all synonyms for the slang word *pizzazz* (which can also be spelled *pizazz*).

place names, adjectives from. *See* ALABAMAN/ALABAMIAN; CANTABRIGIAN; FORT WORTHERS/FORT WORTHIANS; LIVERPUDLIAN

place names, oddities among   *Oddities among* American *place names* can and do fill several books. The most nearly definitive is *American Place-Names* by George R. Stewart (Oxford University Press). A volume of the same name by Alfred H. Holt (T. Y. Crowell) is now unhappily out of print, but for anyone interested in odd pronunciations of place names it is worth seeking out in a library. Henry L. Mencken's *The American Language* (Alfred A. Knopf) includes much interesting material on the subject, including a marvelous list of names like Hog Eye, Black Ankle, Lick Skillet, and Nip and Tuck, all in Texas; Hot Coffee, Mississippi; Gizzard, Tennessee; Bowlegs, Oklahoma; and Peculiar, Missouri. But, as Mencken notes, "it was after the Plains and Rockies were crossed that the pioneers really spit on their hands and showed what they could do." In California alone there were Humbug Flat, Jackass Gulch, Red Dog, Lousy Level, and Hangtown, to say nothing of Chucklehead, Rat Trap, Gospel Swamp, Paint Pot, Poverty Hill, and Get-up-and-Git.

Other oddities include the fact that many Civil War battles are referred to by two different names, depending on the sympathies of the speaker. For example, Bull Run is the Northern term, Manassas the Southern.

Then, perhaps most peculiar of all is the fact that a number of rivers change names as they cross from one state to an adjoining state. The Yadkin River in North Carolina becomes the Pee Dee at the South Carolina line. The Catawba River in North Carolina becomes the Wateree in South Carolina but downstream a few miles. The Lumber River in North Carolina becomes the Little Pee Dee in South Carolina. And the White Marsh River in North Carolina becomes the Waccamaw River in South Carolina. Again, such a list could doubtless be expanded to fill a volume. The important thing to remember is to use the right name in the right place.

place names, pronunciation of   In the matter of *pronunciation of place names*, authorities generally agree that preference must be given to the pronunciation favored by residents of the area named, even though this may result in pronunciations rather remote from the strictly phonetic equivalents of the names involved. Thus, Louisiana is LOO-zee-an-uh to the native born, though outlanders would be inclined to say loo-EE-zee-an-uh. Other local or regional pronunciations are: Cairo, Illinois (KAY-roh, not KY-roh); New Orleans (noo-OR-luns, not noo-or-LEENZ); Baltimore (BOLL-ih-mer, not BALT-tih-more); Quincy (KWIN-zee in Massachusetts, but KWIN-see in Illinois); Rio Grande (REE-oh-grand in Texas but RY-oh-grand in Ohio); Palestine, Texas (pal-ess-TEEN, not pal-ess-TINE); Patriot, Ohio (PAT-ree-ot, not PAY-tree-ot); Missouri (mih-ZOOR-uh, not mih-ZOOR-ee); Thames (THAYMZ in Connecticut, TEMS in England); Berlin (BER-l'n in Connecticut, ber-LIN in Germany); Vienna (VY-en-uh in Illinois; VEE-en-uh in Austria); Arkansas (AR-ken-saw for the state, ar-KAN-zas for the river); Beaufort (BYOO-f'rt in South Carolina but BOH-f'rt in North Carolina); Pierre, South Dakota (PEER, not pee-AIR); Athens (AY-thens in New York but ATH-ens in Ohio and Greece); Calais (kuh-LAY in France, KAL-is in Maine); Calliope, Iowa (kal-ee-OHP, not kuh-LY-uh-pee); Castile, New York (kast-ILE, not kas-TEEL); Cecil, Arkansas (SEE-sil, not SESS-il); Cognac, North Carolina (KOG-nak, not KOH-nyak); Madrid (muh-DRID in Spain, MAD-rud in Maine and Iowa); Beatrice, Nebraska (bee-AT-riss, not BEE-uh-triss); and so on down a list that could be endless. The lesson to be drawn is the ancient one of "When in Rome, do as the Romans do." We don't suppose it's really a very serious error for you to tell a Bostonian that you are stopping over in "KWIN-see"—but he will recognize you instantly as a non-native.

plagiarism   Since the result of an author's or composer's work is a source of pride as well as income, the rights of ownership are jealously guarded and are protected by laws again *plagiarism*. *Plagiarism* is by definition the stealing of the writing or ideas of another and passing them off as one's own. Books usually carry a copyright notice as a defense against *plagiarism*. A typical notice might read: "All rights reserved. No part of this book may be used or reproduced in any manner whatsoever without written permission except in the case of brief quotations embodied in critical articles or reviews." The right to quote short excerpts from the work of another writer is generally recognized under a rather informal legal doctrine known as "fair use." No one has ever established conclusively just what a "short excerpt" is, but, generally speaking, anything under one hundred words (except poetry, for an entire poem may comprise fewer than one hundred words) may be quoted as long as credit is given to the author and publisher.

A somewhat light-hearted view of the matter is taken by folk singer Pete Seeger. Commenting on the common practice among composers of folk songs of borrowing snatches of tunes or lyrics from earlier songs, Seeger once remarked disarmingly that the practice had never bothered him because "*plagiarism* is basic to all cultures."

It is worth bearing in mind, though, that extensive borrowing, especially if coupled with an attempt to pass work of another off as one's own, will very likely lead to prosecution for *plagiarism.* That can be a messy and costly business indeed.

plan ahead A *redundancy* (which see), as is "advance planning."

plan to/try to/try and The phrases *plan to* come and *try to* come are classified as formal while *plan on* coming and *try and* come are acceptable in an informal context. It is worth noting that the formulation *try and* may be found even in the writings of such an esteemed author as Matthew Arnold.

plastic During the late 1960s, the adjective *plastic* acquired a new slang meaning of "phony" or "untrustworthy." A typical use is in the phrase *"plastic* hippie," which was defined for us as "a character who weekends in a phony beard and beads but is strictly establishment from Monday through Friday."

playwright A person who writes plays is a *playwright,* not a playwrite. The "wright" in this, as in "shipwright," means a person who constructs something.

pleasantly/pleasurably A reader raised a rather remarkable question: "Is there such a word as *pleasantly*?" Her reason was that, though she had been in the habit of using *pleasantly* in such expressions as *"pleasantly* surprised," she had been unpleasantly surprised to learn that the word was not entered in her dictionary. Should she, went the query, use *pleasurably* instead? We assured her that there is indeed such a word as *pleasantly* and that it had been omitted from the dictionary (*Webster's New World,* First Edition) only as a result of an editorial decision to omit adverbs regularly formed from adjectives by the addition of "-ly." We advised her that *pleasantly* was more appropriate in this context than the somewhat more stilted *pleasurably.*

NOTE: The Second Edition of *Webster's New World Dictionary* has altered its policy in such matters and does enter *pleasantly.*

please A reader notes that *please* is often used in the King James Bible in the sense of "give pleasure to" or "satisfy," but never as a form of request or as an indication of politeness. When, he asks, was it first used this way? Research indicates that, until after the time of Shakespeare, it appeared —in these senses—only as part of the literal translation of the French "s'il vous plait," "if it pleases you." However, shortly after the publication of the King James Bible and the death of Shakespeare—in 1622, to be precise —*please* in the senses used today appeared in print, according to the *OED.*

pled/pleaded As the past tense of the verb "plead," both *pleaded* and *pled* are acceptable today. *Pled* has the advantage of being shorter and easier to say.

In the courtroom, the accused must plead "guilty" or "not guilty" (or "nolo contendere," meaning "I do not wish to contend"). In general use, however, it is acceptable to "plead innocent" or, more commonly, "plead innocence."

plenteous/plentiful There is little if any difference between these two, which mean "having or yielding abundance," except that *plenteous* is less common and is more likely to be found in poetic contexts.

plenty As a noun, *plenty* is completely acceptable, as in "a land of *plenty*" or "*plenty* of food to feed ten people." The use of it as an adjective, as in "*plenty* money" is substandard. An "of" is needed. "*Plenty* tired" and similar adverbial uses of *plenty* are informal.

plotz *Plotz* is a Yiddish word meaning "to split, burst, or explode." It was brought to our attention as the result of a television show starring a chef and his delectable dishes. At the end of the program the announcer remarked that the onlookers were "already *plotzing*"—apparently ravenous for a share of the food.

It can also mean "to be aggravated beyond bearing or to be outraged," according to Leo Rosten's *Joys of Yiddish*.

plum *Plum* as a noun meaning pretty much the opposite of "lemon" is not new. If a person is awarded a position that he has mightily yearned for, his friends might well say, "Tom got a real *plum.*" When Henry Fonda's part in the one-man show about Clarence Darrow was referred to as a "*plum* role" it reflected the relatively recent development of the attributive use of nouns to modify other nouns.

plumber/sanitation engineer. *See* EUPHEMISM

plural forms, regular and irregular Plurals of nouns are regularly formed by the addition of "s" or "es": books, horses, Morrises, Joneses. Plurals of numbers may be formed by the addition of "s" or " 's": 707s or 707's. The first form is now more commonly seen, though formerly the " 's" was standard. The " 's" form is still to be preferred when confusion may result from the omission of the apostrophe, especially in forming the plurals of certain letters of the alphabet. Thus "as" and "is" are subject to misunderstanding that is easily avoided by the use of the apostrophe: "a's" and "i's."

A few irregular plurals ending in "en" have survived from Old English. Examples are: men, women, children, brethren, and oxen. One interesting oddity is the fact that the *plural form* of "woman" differs in pronunciation from the singular by a change in the first rather than the second syllable: WOOM-'n, singular, and WIMM-'n plural. It all began with the Old English "mann," meaning "human being." This was prefixed with "wif-" for "female." (That's the same "wif-," by the way, that gave us the word "wife.") So now we had "wifmann," which, in time, became "wimman" and eventually "woman," with the plural form "women." But the pronunciation WIMM-'n was carried over from the earlier phase when the plural of "wimman" was "wimmen."

The best solution to such problems is to consult a recent reliable dictionary. It will cite all irregular *plural forms*. If no example of the plural is given, you may count on it that the plural is regularly formed by the addition of a terminal "s" or "es."

plurality. *See* MAJORITY/PLURALITY

plurals of compound words and phrases   The formation of *plurals of compound words,* hyphenated phrases, and nonhyphenated phrases follows certain general rules. In a phrase such as "hole in one" the "s" is added to the first word: "holes in one." In hyphenated words such as "son-in-law" and "mother-in-law," the "s" is also added to the first word: "sons-in-law" and "mothers-in-law." When a word is written solid, as "teaspoonful" or "spoonful," it is now standard practice to add the "s" at the end of the word instead of inserting it, as used to be done, in the middle. So it is now "teaspoonfuls" rather than "teaspoonsful" as in old cookbooks.

Attorney general (which see) follows the rule for nonhyphenated phrases and in the plural is correctly "attorneys general."

plus/also   *Plus* cannot be used as a substitute for *also* as the first word of a sentence when the intent is to link the sentence with the one which precedes it. "*Plus,* he wanted to see for himself how bad conditions were" is illiterate. Some purists even object to *also* as the first word of such a sentence and prefer that it be connected to the previous sentence by "And *also.*"

plus/and   *Plus,* when used to introduce a prepositional phrase, does not have the weight or strength of *and,* and hence the prepositional phrase does not affect the number of the verb. The verb is still governed by the main subject of the sentence. "His intelligence *plus* his youth makes him a prime candidate for the job," while "His intelligence *and* his youth make him a prime candidate for the job."

pocketbook/wallet/purse   Today's ladies' *pocketbooks* could never fit into any conceivable pocket and don't look at all like books. Still, that is what the original *pocketbooks* did, back around 1800. They were men's *purses,* for the most part, containing compartments with hinged openings which were held together, when the *purse* was closed, by a clasp at the top. When open, the *purse* had something of the appearance of an open book. When closed, the *purse was* fitted into the owner's pocket.

The British suffer no such confusion. To them a *pocketbook* is a pocket diary or memorandum book. An Englishman keeps his money and credit cards in a *wallet* or *purse.*

Pocketbook and *purse* are synonymous to American women. *Wallet,* to both men and women, is a holder of paper money and credit cards.

pod   In addition to its meaning of "a seedcase for peas or beans," *pod* now also is applied to a large buslike vehicle which is used to carry airline passengers from an airline terminal to the plane. In some instances, it also serves as a waiting room and boarding ramp.

podium. *See* DAIS/PODIUM/LECTERN

pogonotomy   With the return of beards to fashion and with barbers becoming "hair stylists," the term *pogonotomy* (poh-goh-NOT-uh-mee) may come back into use. It is made up of two Greek words, "pogon," meaning "beard" and "-tomos," meaning "cutting." The man who decides to let his facial hair grow long is practicing pogonotrophy (po-goh-NOT-ruh-fee).

poinsettia   *Poinsettia* is properly pronounced poin-SET-ee-uh, not poin-SET-uh.

pointy   *Pointy* might be considered a slang or dialect variation of "pointed" but it is entered in *Webster's New World Dictionary,* Second Edition, without such designation. It is also entered in Merriam-Webster's Third International and Merriam's Seventh Collegiate in the sense of "coming to a point" or "having many points." Since neither the Third International nor the Collegiate gives levels of usage and since they have eliminated most labels like "slang" or "dialect," the fact that *pointy* is in these books does not necessarily mean that it is correct to use in all contexts.

However, two conclusions may be drawn from the evidence. Listing *pointy* in the Collegiate is an indication that Merriam's editors felt it has a relatively wide circulation among literate folk. More to the point is that the Third International quotes a phrase from A. J. Liebling, "A small merry-looking man with a pointy nose," as evidence for including the word. A. J. Liebling was one of the finest, most conscientious writers who ever graced the pages of *The New Yorker,* and *The New Yorker*'s standards of copyediting are among the highest in all publishing. What was good enough for Liebling is good enough for us.

You may hear the word used sarcastically and figuratively in the phrase *"pointy* little heads," implying a lack of brains or common sense. In this sense, *pointy* should be considered informal—but amusing.

poke. *See* BAG/SACK/POKE

polarize   What was once solely a scientific term has gained widespread usage in the fields of sociology and politics. Formerly it was used to mean "to create polar alignment of a physical property," but it now also means "to cause groups or forces to concentrate in two opposing positions." Controversies over the question of busing schoolchildren have *polarized* many a community in recent years, with each side vehemently—and sometimes violently—defending its stand. Developments in a political situation can *polarize* public opinion and, to a degree, the members of Congress.

policeman. *See* COP/OFFICER/POLICEMAN

politics is (are)   *Politics* is an unusual word in that it can be followed by either a singular or plural verb, depending on the context. It is correct to say that *"Politics is* the art of the possible" and also "Republican *politics are* distasteful to Democrats."

When the AP reported the sale of the Honolulu *Star-Bulletin* it concluded the story with this: "It has been dominant in circulation and advertising for many years. Its politics is Republican." That last sentence does look awkward but it is correct. A better version would have been "Politically, it has been Republican."

poor-mouth   To *poor-mouth* is to complain of or plead poverty. The use of it indicates a certain skepticism on the part of the speaker as to the validity of the complaint or plea. It is regional dialect.

pop. *See* SELTZER/SODA/POP/TONIC/SPARKLING WATER

pope's nose. *See* PARSON'S NOSE/POPE'S NOSE

pore. *See* POUR/PORE

porn/porno   With the controversy in recent years as to what constituted "obscenity," headline writers found the words "pornography" and "pornographic" much too long to fit into headlines easily and in the less-sedate papers they were shortened to *porn* and *porno*. *Porn* seems to be the abbreviation for the general term "pornography," while *porno* is used as a substitute for "pornographic" or to refer to a creator or distributor of pornography.

port/harbor While dictionaries indicate that these terms are synonymous, there is a slight distinction. All *ports* are *harbors* in that they provide a safe place to anchor. A *port,* however, must offer facilities for loading and unloading cargo or passengers. So all *harbors* are not *ports.* A *harbor* can be much smaller than a *port* and can be used only by privately owned boats. Commercial and naval vessels need *harbors* which qualify as *ports.*

portative/portable *Portative* exists—barely. It's a word with a long history, going back to 1450, according to the Oxford Dictionary. But it says nothing that *portable* doesn't say, so it has been obsolete for a long time, except as part of the phrase *"portative* organ," used to describe a small, *portable* organ.

portmanteau words. *See* BLEND WORDS/BRUNCH WORDS/PORTMANTEAU WORDS

positives, lost. *See* LOST POSITIVES

possessed When *possessed* is used to mean "owning" or "having" it is followed by the preposition "of": "He was *possessed of* a keen wit." When it is used to indicate an almost overwhelming influence or feeling, it is used with "by" or "with": *"possessed by* the devil" or *"possessed with* a desire to become rich and famous."

possessive, double The use of a *double possessive* as in "I might still have been none the wiser had not a friend of my wife's written in late January" may be frowned on by some purists but it is perfectly acceptable in informal writing.

As Porter Perrin points out in his *Writer's Guide and Index to English,* "Using both the 's and 'of' together is an English idiom of long and respectable standing . . . and usually has an informal flavor." Technically, the construction is known as a "double genitive."

possessive case The *possessive case,* sometimes also called the genitive, is usually expressed by the use of the apostrophe and "s" ("Bill's horse"). When the word being modified is a plural or a word of two syllables ending in a sibilant, it may form the possessive either by adding apostrophe and "s" ('s) or simply by adding the apostrophe: Morris's book or Morris' book. In Old English—an inflected language—possession was indicated by the word ending "es." Today's apostrophe and "s" ('s) simply shows the omission of the "e" from that inflectional ending.

possessive (for two names)   When writing or speaking of one thing owned by two persons, it is permissible to use the *possessive* for only one, as in "Don and Mary's Bar." When more than one item and separate ownership are involved, it is necessary to use two *possessives:* "We are taking Don's and Mary's autos."

possessive pronouns (agreement)   *Possessive pronouns* should always be in agreement with the number of the antecedent, but it is not uncommon to read statements such as "Today's college graduate has an advantage in that they have a greater choice." "Graduate" in this example is singular and "they" is plural. The simple solution is to make it "college graduates have an advantage." This is preferable because it avoids changing "they" to "he" and, as a result, eliminating females from the statement.

possible/probable   Many things are *possible,* even though not *probable.* If the sense is "in the realm of likelihood" (to any degree), the proper word is *probable.* If the sense is "capable of being achieved" (regardless of difficulty), the proper word is *possible.*

possibility. *See* ALTERNATIVE

post-. *See* PREFIXES AND SUFFIXES, WITH AND WITHOUT HYPHEN

post-box. *See* PILLAR-BOX/POST-BOX

postcard/postal card   There is a difference between the two terms, even though nobody but the greeting-card industry and the Postal Service seems to be aware of it. When you buy a preprinted card at the post office, you have bought a *postal card.* When you purchase a pretty picture card, that is a *postcard.*

postcard (as verb)   We mentioned in our column that "Matt Connolly of Washington *postcards* . . ." and were gently taken to task by some readers who could not imagine using *postcard* as a verb. However, the Merriam-Webster New International Second Edition (1934) enters *postcard* as both transitive and intransitive verb and defines it simply as "to write by postcard." So its acceptance as standard American is assured.

Post Office/Postal Service   You may still go to the post office (lower case) to buy stamps and mail letters and packages but the U.S. *Post Office* is no longer in existence. It is now the U.S. *Postal Service* (a government corporation) and should be referred to as such.

pot   A slang term for marijuana. Also called "grass" or "dope" or "Mary Jane." A "pothead" is one who smokes marijuana regularly.

pot shot   A curious and contradictory meaning of the phrase *pot shot* has recently crept into American dictionaries.

Pot shot originally meant a shot taken at game by a hunter in disregard of hunting rules and with only the desire to fill his cooking pot. It is a shot taken at easy range without giving the animal a sporting chance, the only intent being to kill. By extension, it came to mean a criticism of or verbal attack on a person. Webster's Second International defines *pot shot* as an "attack or attempt needing no special skill nor involving any difficulty." The Oxford Dictionary gives the "transferred use" of it as "a shot aimed at a person or animal that happens to be in easy range without giving any chance of self-defense."

Along with these meanings, Webster's Third International brings in the element of "random or sporadic manner" on the basis of several citations which are so interpreted by that book's editors. Although "random" contradicts the basic meaning of the word, the definition "random shot" has found its way into other dictionaries. Perhaps the editor who first wrote the word "random" was thinking of *pot shot* as analogous to "pot luck," which is far from the "sure thing" that *pot shot* is.

potter's field/pauper's field   The phrase *pauper's field* (for a burying place for indigent or unknown persons) is more readily understandable to the average American than *potter's field*. As a result, the term *pauper's field* has found its way into news reports on many occasions. However, the correct term is *potter's field* and here is why. The expression comes from the Bible (Matthew 27:7). Judas, repenting his betrayal of Christ, took his thirty pieces of silver to the temple, cast them before the chief priests, and hanged himself. The priests decided not to put the silver into the treasury because it was "the price of blood." (That's where we get the expression "blood money.") So they counseled among themselves and decided to use the money "to buy the potter's field, to bury strangers in."

pour/pore   Possibly because the first of these is more common, it is frequently misused when *pore* is required. A student does not *pour* over his books; he *pores* over them.

practicable/practical   Anything which is capable of being done is *practicable;* whether it is *practical* depends on other factors. It could be *practicable* to build a bridge across the river at a given point, yet not *practical* since it might receive little use.

practically/virtually Any distinction between *practically* and *virtually,* in the sense of "almost" or "as good as," is fast disappearing. There is one small area where *practically* remains preferable: when the meaning is "for all practical purposes."

praise. *See* COMMEND/PRAISE

pre-. *See* PREFIXES AND SUFFIXES, WITH AND WITHOUT HYPHEN

precede/proceed/procedure The confusion caused by these look-alike words is not one of meaning but of spelling. It is further complicated in that *proceed* drops one "e" in its noun form, *procedure.*

The phrase *"proceed to"* in the sense of going ahead and doing something is usually unnecessary and can be eliminated. "He then *proceeded* to go into great detail about his complaints" is better as "He then went into great detail. . . ."

precedence/precedents Dictionaries list two pronunciations for *precedence:* preh-SEE-denss and PRESS-ih-denss. However, *precedents* is also pronounced PRESS-ih-denss. To avoid confusion between the two words, the pronunciation of PRESS-ih-denss might be reserved for *precedents* and the pronunciation preh-SEE-denss given to *precedence.*

precipitate/precipitous

USAGE PANEL QUESTION

Precipitate is defined as "acting hastily, rashly, or impulsively." *Precipitous* is defined as "extremely steep." Yet an expression often heard is "He beat a *precipitous* retreat." Would you use *precipitous* in this context?
In writing   Yes: 7%. No: 93%.
In speech   Yes: 12%. No: 88%.

This question was put to the panel at the suggestion of one of its members who was concerned at what seemed to be a growing confusion between the two words. It is interesting to note that, despite the clear statement of the different meanings, a small percentage of the panel approved its use in writing and a slightly larger percentage approved *"precipitous* retreat" in speech. The validity of concern is illustrated by these facts and by the statement of one panelist that *"precipitous* retreat" is "a cliché in the making. I wouldn't really use it but accept it."

A far greater number of panelists, who felt the distinction should be maintained, offer facetious exceptions, including "Only if he climbed a cliff to get away," "I might if I were falling from the top of the Empire State Building," and "I suppose if Hannibal had been forced to retreat back over the Alps it might have been considered a 'precipitous retreat.' " Other panelists termed it "carelessness" or "ignorance." DAVIDSON TAYLOR commented: "This vulgar confusion of time and space annoys me sorely."

predicate Purists may argue that the verb *predicate* means "to affirm the quality or attributes of someone or something." However, in current American usage it often means "to base" and is used with "on" or "upon": "The governor of the state *predicates* his budget on the assumption that income will remain at a steady level."

predilection A sportscaster is reported to have remarked, "He is having a good game despite your preconceived *predilection* against him." The error here is that, since *predilection* means "preference," there can be no such thing as a *"predilection* against," only a *"predilection* for" or "in favor of." It is pronounced pred-ih-LEK-shun.

predominantly/predominately If you drop the prefixes and suffixes from these two words, you will recognize "dominant" as an adjective and "dominate" as a verb. Thus *predominant* is an adjective and *predominate* is a verb. From there on, however, confusion sets in for those who are not purists. *Webster's New World Dictionary* recognizes *predominate* as an adjective as well as a verb, which the *American Heritage Dictionary* does not. But *American Heritage,* along with most standard dictionaries, lists both *predominantly* and *predominately* as adverbial forms. For the purist, *predominantly* remains the choice as an adverb. It has a more logical evolution and falls better on the ear.

prefer *Prefer* is properly used in one of two ways. If the object of *prefer* is an infinitive, the infinitive is followed by "rather than" and a second infinitive, as in "I *prefer* to stay by the fire rather than to go out in the snow."

If the object of *prefer* is something other than an infinitive, "to" or "over" is used, as in "I *prefer* walking to riding" or "I *prefer* walking over riding."

preferable *Preferable* should be pronounced PREF-er-uh-b'l, not preh-FER-uh-b'l.

prefix A *prefix* is a word element added before a word or root in order to make a new word. "Infracaninophile" (friendship for the underdog) consists of the *prefix* "infra" and the word "caninophile."

prefixes and suffixes, with and without hyphen   For the guidance of newspaper copyeditors throughout the country, the Associated Press and the United Press International combined their efforts in compiling *The Associated Press Stylebook.* While in the past many newspapers had their own style manuals, we have found that the majority today use the AP style manual, sometimes with inserts to cover usages peculiar to a particular area.

The following general rules for *prefixes and suffixes* are given in that book.

all (prefix) hyphenated: All-Star

ante, anti (prefix) solid: antebellum, antiaircraft—except in proper noun usage: anti-American

bi (prefix) solid: biennial, bifocal

co (prefix) usually solid: copilot, coed, etc.

counter (prefix) solid: counterfoil, etc.

down (prefix and suffix) solid: downstroke, touchdown

electro (prefix) solid: electrolysis

ex (prefix) hyphenated: ex-champion

extra (prefix) solid: extraterritorial

fold (suffix) solid: twofold

goer (suffix) solid: churchgoer

in (prefix) solid: insufferable; (suffix) hyphenated: stand-in

infra (prefix) solid: infrared

inter (prefix) solid: interstate

intra (prefix) solid: intrastate, intramural

multi (prefix) solid: multimillion, multifaced

non (prefix) solid: nonpartisan, nonsupport

out (prefix) hyphenated: out-talk, out-box

over (prefix and suffix) solid: overcome, pushover

post (prefix) solid: postwar (but it is post-mortem)

pre (prefix) solid: predetermined, predawn

self (prefix) hyphenated: self-defense

semi (prefix) solid: semiannual

sub (prefix) solid: subzero

super (prefix) solid: superabundance, superman

trans (prefix) solid: transatlantic, transcontinental (but trans-Canada with proper name of country)

tri (prefix) solid: trifocal

ultra (prefix) solid: ultraviolet

un (prefix) solid: unshaven, unnecessary (but un-American with proper noun)

under (prefix) solid: underground, underdog, undersold

uni (prefix) solid: unicolor

wide (suffix) solid: worldwide, nationwide

NOTE: Curiously enough, the prefix *re-* (which see) is omitted from this list. And, as authors, we wish to protest any elimination of the hyphen in the word "co-author." We are "co-authors," NOT "coauthors." *See also* HYPHEN.

pregnant. *See* EXPECTING/EXPECTANT WITH/PREGNANT

prejudice   *Prejudice* is a preconceived viewpoint (a meaning which is obvious when one thinks of the verb "to prejudge"). Technically, it can be a favorable as well as an unfavorable viewpoint, but the most common usage is *"prejudice against."* If it is used in a non-pejorative sense, it is necessary to say *"prejudiced in favor of."*

prelude   *Prelude,* in the sense of a minor event prefatory to a more important occurrence, may be pronounced either PREL-yood or PREE-lood.

premiere/debut

USAGE PANEL QUESTION

Premiere, as a noun meaning the first performance of a motion picture, play, or TV show, is well established. Would you approve its use as a transitive verb—"Paramount *premiered Gatsby* in New York"?
Yes: 24%. No: 76%.
As an intransitive verb—*"Gatsby premiered* in New York"?
Yes: 25%. No: 75%.
A similar question arises regarding *debut* as a verb. Would you approve "Harper's will *debut* its fall line at the booksellers' convention"?
Yes: 9%. No: 91%.
How about "The new soprano *debuts* in February"?
Yes: 18%. No: 82%.

ISAAC ASIMOV: "I would prefer 'opened' but any attempt to counteract Hollywood illiteracy is a losing cause."
STEWART BEACH: "I think 'premiere' as a verb is barbarous, transitive or intransitive. The same is true of 'debut.' These are verbs wrenched from their respectable origins as nouns. They indicate a writer trying to be cute."
CHARLES BERLITZ: "Yes, in news reporting only."
HEYWOOD HALE BROUN: "No. It would be acceptable in a trade paper, not elsewhere. Publishers, whose English is epitomized by their jacket copy, will use it. I won't."
JOHN CIARDI: "I don't like these usages [*premiere*] but they are now estab-

lished and will not go away." *(Debut)*: "Not yet established. Can, therefore, be resisted."

GEROLD FRANK: "This is a sort of cablese or shorthand, which I think corrupts the language.""

NORMAN HOSS: " 'Premiere' is established theater cant. 'Debut' is striving to be cute."

JOHN K. HUTCHENS: "No. Only in *Variety,* which has its own rules."

HELEN L. KAUFMANN: "I deplore the tendency to use nouns as verbs. It doesn't enrich the language, is a short cut, a lazy way out."

ALEXANDER KENDRICK: "No. But this doesn't mean I am canceling my subscription to *Variety.*"

LAURENCE LAFORE: "Of course not."

PHYLLIS McGINLEY: "Frightful and vulgar!"

WRIGHT MORRIS: "Excellent examples of abusage 'making it' through usage."

WADE MOSBY *(Premiere)*: "Yes. It's handy, says it all and (I think) is generally understood." *(Debut)*: "I have trouble with the past tense of 'debut.' "

STANTON PECKHAM: "No. Should be left to the exclusive use of *Variety* and *Billboard.*"

ORVILLE PRESCOTT *(Premiere)*: "Vile." *(Debut)*: "Worse!"

LEO ROSTEN *(Premiere)*: "Yes, but not happily." *(Debut)*: "No."

RICHARD H. ROVERE *(Premiere)*: "Indifferent." *(Debut)*: "No."

VERMONT ROYSTER: "Well, accept it anyway. What can I do about it?"

HAROLD SCHONBERG: "Never. Cheap PR talk. *Variety.* Just *sounds* ugly and is ungrammatical."

ERICH SEGAL: "Mr. Shakespeare didn't hesitate to enrich our language by using nouns as verbs."

WALTER W. "RED" SMITH: "No. Nor 'hosted' nor 'guested' nor 'suited up' (as in sports) nor 'lettered in three sports.' "

HOWARD TAUBMAN: "In almost four decades of criticism, I never, I hope, committed that clumsiness."

BILL VAUGHAN: "No. And how about 'authored' for 'wrote'?"

DOUGLAS WATT: "No, but it sounds just right for Paramount and Gatsby, whoever he is; probably a new V.P. the company introduced there."

premises   "Premise," the singular form, means a basis for an argument or supposition. When used to refer to a piece of real estate, such as a building and the land on which it stands, it must be used in the plural, as in "Keep off the *premises.*" In this sense there is no such thing as "a premise."

An Ohio telephone company uses a sticker on records of homes and offices where the subscriber has installed equipment not obtained from the telephone company. It reads: "This premises has customer provided equipment." Whoever worded that sticker received only half the message.

preparatory to/before   In referring to the first of two successive actions, *preparatory* can be correctly used only if the one action leads to the other. It is not simply a synonym for *before*. *"Preparatory to* leaving for England, he sold his house and cars" is acceptable, but there must be an element of "in preparation for"; otherwise, *before* is preferred.

prepositional idiom   When grammarians speak of a *prepositional idiom* they mean simply that centuries of popular use have made one preposition appropriate in one phrase, another in another. For example, the United Nations Council could be said to agree "with" their leaders, "to" a proposal, and "on" a plan. In each case the guide to which preposition to use is a feeling for the right and proper one. This feeling is developed only through lifelong exposure to a language or by intense and careful study of it. That is why a *prepositional idiom* is such a problem for foreigners learning English and why failure to use the right preposition is one of the quickest ways to identify a foreign-born user of our native tongue.

preposition at end of sentence   One of the most durable holdovers from the dear, dead days of grammar "rules" is that one must never end a sentence with a preposition. Despite the fact that authorities as disparate as H. W. Fowler, Winston Churchill, and Morris Bishop have been making a mockery of this rule for more than half a century, there are still many millions of believers, as mail to our column amply attests. Every time we try to dispose of the foolish superstition, we receive a barrage of letters crying, "Outrage!" So let's take a look at the "rule" and its genesis.

During the eighteenth and nineteenth centuries many self-anointed grammarians worked to establish rules for the language. Since all were students of Latin, many of their efforts took the form of trying to fit English into the structural patterns of Latin, ignoring the fact that English is a very different language indeed. One of the favorite rules drawn from Latin is that a sentence must never end in a preposition. Why? Simply because such an arrangement almost never appears in classical Latin, where the sentence customarily ends with the verb.

The rulings of these grammarians, incidentally, were so effective that one of the greatest English writers, John Dryden, late in life went through all the prefaces to his plays, carefully moving prepositions from the ends of sentences and tucking them up ahead—with almost uniformly awkward results.

The truth is, as H. W. Fowler puts it, that this is "a cherished superstition [that exists] in spite of the incurable English instinct for putting them [prepositions] late . . . an important element in the flexibility of the language."

Winston Churchill's oft-quoted comment that the rule "is nonsense up with which I will not put" has spawned a host of imitators and set some writers to work seeing how many prepositions they can manage to put at a sentence's end. There's the celebrated query of a small child who asks, "What did you bring that book to me to be read to out of for?" And our old friend Morris Bishop, who managed to be both a distinguished authority on modern and classical languages and a notable light versifier, once created the following verse, whose final sentence ends with not one but seven prepositions: "I lately lost a preposition;/It hid, I thought, beneath my chair/And angrily I cried 'Perdition!/Up from out of in under there.'/ Correctness is my vade mecum,/And straggling phrases I abhor./And yet I wondered, 'What should he come/Up from out of in under for?' "

Another distinguished scholar, Lester M. Beattie, Emeritus Professor of English at Carnegie Tech, once wrote to us citing still another reason why the old "rule" should be honored in the breach rather than the observance. "In many such cases," he wrote, "the preposition should be regarded as an effectual part of the verb. I recently ran into this rather remarkable example: 'There was no hierarchy of importance among the various arts, because there was none of them with which serious men could dispense.' The author is not a pedant but a writer of some distinction mysteriously gone pedantic—Mark Van Doren. In the natural phrasing—'which serious men could dispense with'—the last word is not a preposition functionally. In effect it is the final unaccented syllable of a three-syllable verb, equivalent of 'ignore' or 'neglect.' The required space between 'dispense' and 'with' is deceptive. Van Doren's statement is something which I ran into or came across, not something into which I ran or across which I came." Those are pertinent words indeed, and we would like to believe that they represent the last word anyone need say about the matter of ending sentences with prepositions. But as long as writers as distinguished as Mark Van Doren can fall into the trap of clumsy avoidance of a nonexistent rule, we have to realize that battle to repeal that "cherished superstition" is far from won.

USAGE PANEL QUESTION

Many generations of schoolteachers warned against ending sentences with prepositions. Would you object to a sentence on the ground that it ended with a preposition?
Object: 20%. Do not object: 80%.

JULES BERGMAN: "There is often no substitute for a preposition to end a sentence with."
HEYWOOD HALE BROUN: "The object, after all, of purity is clarity and grace."

ANTHONY BURGESS: "It is natural for Germanic languages to use postposition for prepositions. It was doubtless the influence of Latin grammar that influenced schoolteachers who knew more Latin than German."

ABE BURROWS: "I think the rule is silly. It's left over from the days when verse ruled in literature. Generally if one ends a line of poetry with a preposition, he's ending with the short syllable of a foot, which is disaster. I seem to remember John Dryden being involved in this 'rule.' "

ELIZABETH JANEWAY: "The whole question is like infinitive-splitting, an area for pedantic nitpicking. Much better to casually split an infinitive or use a preposition to end a sentence with than arduously, ingeniously, and with great effort avoid doing so."

ORVILLE PRESCOTT: "More often than not prepositions end sentences awkwardly. However, in many instances they are natural, colloquial usage. To try to avoid them always means even more awkward circumlocutions."

PETER S. PRESCOTT: "This is dead forever, I hope. Churchill's comment killed the silly rule. Teachers generally don't try to write, but anyone who *does* knows that occasionally sentences will be ruined if terminal prepositions are forcibly bused to another neighborhood."

prerequisite   As an adjective, *prerequisite* means "required as a necessary condition beforehand" and is followed by the preposition *to.* When used as a noun it is followed by the preposition *for.* "Successful completion of a swimming course is *prerequisite to* the granting of a boat license" and "A life-saving certificate is a *prerequisite for* a job on the ferry boat." *See also* REQUIREMENT/REQUISITE/PREREQUISITE.

presage   Although *presage* can mean simply "to indicate in advance," its use should be confined to impending events of a dire or dangerous nature. It has an ominous connotation to it both as a verb ("to warn") and as a noun ("a warning").

prescribe/proscribe   Another pair of look-alike words which are sometimes confused. To *prescribe* is to dictate or to give medical directions. *Proscribe* means to outlaw or forbid.

presentation   Until recent years the pronunciation prez-en-TAY-shun was the only one listed as correct in such dictionaries as Funk & Wagnalls and Oxford. During the 1930s the pronunciation pree-zen-TAY-shun began to be widely used and was generally recorded as "acceptable but not preferred." Today at least two major dictionaries give pree-zen-TAY-shun first place and all others find it acceptable.

present incumbent   Since *incumbent* means one who holds office at the present time, *present incumbent* is redundant.

presently It is interesting to note that *presently* in the sense of "at the present time" is no newcomer to the language. In fact, the Oxford Dictionary traces it back to 1485 and notes that this was the original meaning of the word. However, the sense of "in the near future" soon became more popular, and when the Oxford Dictionary was published, the original sense of the word was labeled "now archaic or dialect."

USAGE PANEL QUESTION

How about *presently* for "now," as in "the temperature is *presently* 52 degrees"? Do you use *presently* in this sense in your own speech?
Yes: 16%. No: 84%.
In writing   Yes: 18%. No: 82%.

ISAAC ASIMOV: "What's wrong with 'at present'?"

W. H. AUDEN: "But possibly meaning 'immediately' is O.K."

STEWART BEACH: "It is utterly unnecessary to use 'presently' under any circumstances. It's pretentious. I can't imagine anyone except perhaps a sociology professor using it."

ALVIN BEAM: "Often the 'now,' too, can be struck out. I shudder at 'currently' as in 'He "currently" lives in New York.' "

ANTHONY BURGESS: "This is a bad Americanism. It kills a word."

ABE BURROWS: "I'd accept 'presently' if the line of dialogue were spoken by a dowager duchess about to have her last cup of tea."

WALT KELLY: " 'Presently' is a bastard word anyway. Some areas use it to mean 'in a little while.' "

HERMAN WOUK: "This is a barbarism like 'momentarily' and 'hopefully.' Let's fight it to the death."

presidential/President's In describing the activities of Lyndon Johnson's Inaugural Day, television reporters and commentators used the phrase "*presidential* daughters," which points up a fine distinction between *presidential* and *President's*. *Presidential* refers to the office of the Presidency and is correct when used in such phrases as "*presidential* papers" or "*presidential* authority." The daughters, however, did not come with the office and should be referred to as the "*President's* daughters."

prestigious

USAGE PANEL QUESTION

NOTE: The following question is one of a number put to the panel at the request of individual panelists. This one on *prestigious* was phrased by ALEX FAULKNER.

"It is almost impossible to read a newspaper nowadays without encountering *prestigious* in the sense of 'dazzling.' But *prestige* comes from the Latin *prestigia,* meaning jugglers' tricks, illusion—magic, in short—and my feeling has always been that *prestigious* should be reserved for something involving conjuring. Do members of the panel approve of its use for 'super'?"

Yes: 67%. No: 33%.

The majority of the panel, in voting approval of this use of *prestigious,* indicated that, as one stated, "most people connect it with prestige."

ISAAC ASIMOV: "I use it myself and *like* it."

HAL BORLAND: "If we are to stick to literal root meanings we are soon up to our ears in confusion . . . See 'pedigree,' literally 'foot of a crane.' "

HEYWOOD HALE BROUN: "Put prestigious in the same bag with 'image' and 'viable.' " (NOTE: He had suggested that such a bag be burned.)

JOHN CIARDI ("yes"): "As an acceptance of fact. I'd like to see the word recover its sense of 'dazzling trickery' but feel that hope is lost."

PAUL HORGAN: "Show-biz."

JOHN LEAR: "Here's one I never studied adequately; now that it has been brought to my attention, I like the old order."

RUSSELL LYNES: "I avoid it under any circumstances as pretentious and wishy-washy."

DWIGHT MACDONALD: "I use it for 'famous' (having prestige)—Never thought it meant 'dazzling'—nor was I aware of the interesting Latin derivation."

PHYLLIS MCGINLEY: "This has come to stay. Why fight it any longer? Evidently I am less a purist than I thought."

WRIGHT MORRIS: " 'Prestige' to 'prestigious' seems hard to fault, once it catches on."

ORVILLE PRESCOTT: "But 'prestige' has long since lost its association with magic. Today it means a favorable reputation. The adjective 'prestigious' is clumsy and pretentious."

PETER S. PRESCOTT: " 'Prestigious' to me means possessing that which is admired. Its Latin derivation is clearly long dead."

BERTON ROUECHÉ: "This is a vogue word and should be avoided like 'charisma.' "

ELVIS STAHR, JR.: "The word is one that has outgrown its root."

REX STOUT: "I don't approve of its use at all. It sounds bad."

BARBARA TUCHMAN: "I would not use 'prestigious' under any circumstances."

JUDITH VIORST: "Bah!"

HERMAN WOUK: " 'Prestigious' means having prestige or honor and is quite okay."

presume/assume Both *presume* and *assume* have an element of "take for granted," but *assume* is the milder of the two. To *assume* something is to suppose it to be a fact, with or without any basis for the belief. To *presume* means to "regard something as true because there is reason to do so and there is no evidence to the contrary."

A more common meaning for *presume* is to "take too much for granted" or to "act without reason or authority": "I would not *presume* to come for a week's visit without an invitation."

presumptive/presumptuous Two shades of meaning of *presume* (which see) are responsible for the difference in meaning of these two words. *Presumptive* means "based on reasonable likelihood," while *presumptuous* means "taking far too much for granted" or "arrogant."

pretense/pretext Both of these words come from the Latin and each has an element of false representation. *Pretext* means falsely claimed goal or reason. *Pretense* is a much broader term, which denotes action rather than statement, as in "He makes a *pretense* of being religious."

pretty good *Pretty,* in the sense of "fairly" or "somewhat," as in *pretty good,* was formerly labeled "colloquial" by the dictionaries. That meant that it was acceptable only in informal speech or writing. However, today it is acceptable on all levels of usage except the most formal.

prevail. *See* OBTAIN/PREVAIL

prevent Such formulations as *"prevent him* going" are substandard and should be changed to *"prevent his* going" or *"prevent him from* going."

preventive/preventative *Preventative* is not a correct word. The form does exist as a mistaken variant of *preventive.* It is what linguists call "an irregularly formed doublet" and should be avoided. It is listed in the Oxford English dictionaries and some American dictionaries but *preventive* is always given as the preferred form. The great English word expert

H. W. Fowler remarked that *"preventative* is a needless lengthening of an established word, due to oversight or caprice." Perhaps Americans have fallen into the habit of using *preventative* because of its similarity to "representative," but it represents a serious trend in American speech. The use of *preventative* for *preventive,* of "filtrate" for "filter," of "experimentalize" for "experiment," and of "finalize" for "end" seems to be part of a trend toward the elimination of simple, precise words in favor of flowery, pretentious gobbledegook.

principal/principle   Two commonly confused words in the English language are *principal* and *principle.*

One thing to remember is that *principle* is always a noun, never an adjective. It means "a standard of conduct," "an essential element," or "a general truth."

Principal is an adjective meaning "first in authority or importance." When used as a noun, as in *principals* of a play, *principal* of a school, or the *principal* of a loan, it is the shortened form of a phrase (*"principal* players," *"principal* teacher," and *"principal* sum").

A reader once suggested to us a way that everyone can keep this pair straight: if you can substitute "main" (which contains an "a"), use *principal* (which also contains an "a"). If you can substitute "rule" (which ends in "le"), use *principle* (which also ends in "le").

prioritize

USAGE PANEL QUESTION

"Priority" came into widespread use early in World War II when directors of the war effort found it necessary to assign priorities to the users of essential minerals, metals, fuels, and the like. Much more recently the verb *prioritize* made its appearance. *Newsweek* wrote of an executive who "expects his underlings to *prioritize* their work and their personal goals." Some critics find it unpalatable, to say the least. Panelist ROBERT LIPSYTE wrote: "A candidate for the school committee in our town used the word *'prioritize'* in a speech. Reluctantly I voted for her, then went home and worked in debasement."

Do you share Lipsyte's low regard for *prioritize?* Yes: 99%. No: 1%.

If your answer is "no," would you use it in writing of a serious nature? Yes: 1%. No: 99%.

WHITNEY BALLIETT: "I don't like the suffix 'ize,' although it seems permanently with us. Tacking it onto a word is like giving that word a pep pill. Cheap."

SAUL BELLOW: "Barbarous!"

ALTON BLAKESLEE: "New slang, lazy slang, and sounds affected."

HEYWOOD HALE BROUN: "It is, however, not surprising in the deliberations of a school committee."

BEN LUCIEN BURMAN: "Worse and worser."

JAMES MCGREGOR BURNS/JOAN SIMPSON BURNS: "It isn't even useful, as 'mirandize' is. There are many simpler ways of saying the same thing."

WILLARD R. ESPY: "Let us join in prioritizing the banishment of this horror."

GEROLD FRANK: "Izeing nouns in this fashion is an abomination."

ROBERT GOTTLIEB: "A real ugliness."

ELIZABETH HARDWICK: "Unnecessary, very poor usage and unjustified on the matter of clarity. I cannot see any usefulness equal to the atrocity."

SYDNEY J. HARRIS: "A perfect 'Haigism.' "

JOHN K. HUTCHENS: "A barbarism and a silly one at that."

E. J. KAHN, JR.: "I think all words ending in 'ize' should be outlawed, with the possible exception of 'anesthetize.' "

ROBERT LIPSYTE: "Lipsyte has told me, privately, that he has given up the battle against 'prioritize' as more and more politicians he otherwise respects—as well as educators, businessmen, etc.—use it. In fact, Lipsyte says: 'Among the word dragons to be slain, I prioritize "prioritize" very low.' "

ORVILLE PRESCOTT: "Abominable."

F. D. REEVE: " 'Ize' is a productive suffix (like '-wise'); people have fun and ease adding it to Latin-like words."

LEO ROSTEN: "Inexcusable. Anyone perpetrating 'prioritize' should be 'cemeterized.' "

HAROLD SCHONBERG: "Another barbarism, like most 'ize' constructions."

JACK SMITH: "It's here to stay but I don't have to like it."

WALLACE STEGNER: "Not in writing of *any* nature."

HAROLD TAYLOR: "My hate of it exceeds Lipsyte's."

DOUGLAS WATT: "Too awkward."

A.B.C. WHIPPLE: "Another lazy example of turning nouns into verbs."

HERMAN WOUK: "I would not use it in talking to the garbage man."

WILLIAM ZINSSER: "Very bad."

CHARLOTTE ZOLOTOW: "Robert, as always about language, is right! It's a *lazy, pretentious* substitute for real words."

priority. *See* VOGUE WORDS

prior to   *Prior to,* in the simple sense of "before," is stilted and affected in most instances, especially if what happened *prior to* something else was of short duration. If, however, you are speaking or writing about something of consequence and duration, it is proper to say, *"Prior to* becoming president of the university, he was head of the English Department." *See also* PREPARATORY TO/BEFORE.

probable. *See* POSSIBLE/PROBABLE

proceed/precede *Proceed* should be used in the figurative sense for "move forward" but not in the literal sense of "walk" or "travel" (as in "He *proceeded* from the dime store to the drugstore"). It means "to continue, especially after an interruption."

Precede means "to go before" and is not to be confused with *proceed.*

processes The pronunciation of this plural as if it ended in "eez" is standard in England and is widely heard in Canada. *Processes* was apparently first used in the United States by doctors and researchers in anatomy, since the 1934 Webster's labels it "Anat." Currently, however, the pronunciations PROSS-ess-eez and PROH-sess-eez are common enough to be recorded as fully acceptable by the original *American Heritage Dictionary* and the Merriam-Webster dictionaries.

prodigal Many people think that the word *prodigal* means "wandering" or "straying." It doesn't. It means "extravagant" or "wasteful." The error stems from the fact that many people know the word only through the New Testament story (Luke 15:11) of the *prodigal* son. He was the younger of two sons who took his share of his father's goods and "took his journey into a far country, and there wasted his substance with riotous living." It's the "wasting his substance" that earned him the label *prodigal,* but many people remember the long "journey into a far country" and mistakenly think that is what *prodigal* means.

professional There was a time when the only *professionals* were those who practiced law, medicine, or teaching, or were members of the clergy. Although *professional* is loosely used today to indicate a person highly skilled in his trade, whatever it may be, the word properly speaking means one who has mastered his profession—a liberal art or science requiring advanced study. A profession is the main activity of such a person and is also his or her means of earning a living. A means of living other than a profession is an occupation or trade.

prognosis. *See* DIAGONSIS/PROGNOSIS

program The preferred pronunciation for *program* is as spelled: PROH-gram. However, the pronunciation PROH-grum is also considered acceptable.

programed/programmed The verb *program* has suddenly acquired a variety of meanings and appears in print with ever-increasing frequency, but opinion is divided as to the spelling of its present and past participle forms.

Educators, who favor the single "m" *(programed* and *programing),* cite the "rule" for doubling consonants: If a word is not accented on the last syllable, the consonant need not be doubled and in American usage preferably is not doubled. So when they write of "*programed* instruction" it is with one "m."

Scientists, on the other hand, prefer to double the final consonant. Editors of such erudite publications as *Science* and *Scientific American* write of *programming.*

Dictionaries give both the single "m" and the double "m" forms as acceptable.

One argument for doubling the "m" is that it avoids the possibility of the mispronunciation "PROH-graymed." This would also lead to consistency on both sides of the ocean, for the British have used *programmed* in both scientific and educational contexts all along.

progress *Progress* is pronounced PROG-ress as a noun; pruh-GRESS as a verb.

promptness/promptitude Radio and television commentators, as well as politicians, sometimes use odd or unusual words to add interest to their remarks. One such commentator spoke of being pleased with the *promptitude* with which particular legislation was being prepared. It means precisely the same as "*promptness*" but you cannot fault it or its use. It has been in the language since before the time of Shakespeare and is a perfectly proper noun.

prone/supine It is impossible for a man to "lie *prone* on his back." *Prone* means "face downward." If he is lying on his back, he is *supine.*

pronouns, possessive. *See* POSSESSIVE PRONOUNS (AGREEMENT)

pronouns, reflexive and intensive. *See* SELF

pronunciation Pronunciation of English and American words presents no special problem to anyone familiar with the standard general dictionaries. With the exception of the Merriam-Webster Third International (1961), which uses a system of respelling that confuses even experts in phonetics, all American dictionaries respell words in various versions of what has become known as the Websterian or School Book method of pronunciation. This involves a few arbitrary symbols, the breve (˘), the macron (—), and the schwa (ə), the last a relatively new symbol used to indicate the unstressed vowel sound of the "u" in "circus," the "a" in "about," and so on.

Again excepting the Merriam-Webster Third International, which seems to have gone out of its way to make its pronunciations difficult for the dictionary user to fathom, all standard American lexicons incorporate a short key to pronunciation in immediate juxtaposition to the text, usually at the bottom of each page or of each right-hand page. Reference to this key will make the phonetic respellings (which usually follow the entry word) easy to understand.

Each dictionary usually contains a detailed article on pronunciation in the front pages. This can prove helpful, especially in clarifying pronunciations of foreign words borrowed into English. The earlier Merriam-Webster Second Edition (1934) has a remarkably fine article on pronunciation by John S. Kenyon, who later, with Thomas A. Knott, wrote the finest work yet to appear on the subject, *A Pronouncing Dictionary of American English.* In his article in Merriam-Webster II, Dr. Kenyon incorporates a remarkable table of variant pronunciations, showing how seven leading dictionaries (four American and three English) vary in recording the pronunciations of such common words as "abdomen," "accent," "acetic," and more than a thousand others. Although much of the material is now out of date, it remains a fascinating demonstration of how widely even professed "authorities" can differ among themselves.

Of the newer dictionaries, the original *American Heritage Dictionary* seems to us to contain the most helpful guidance to a dictionary user interested in pursuing the problems of pronunciation beyond the mere respelling given in the entry itself. In the Heritage front matter there are three articles bearing on pronunciation, one by Henry Lee Smith, Jr., one by Wayne O'Neil, and one by the managing editor, Norman Hoss. The last, contained in the overall "Guide to the Dictionary," seems to us most useful and informative.

In this *Harper Dictionary of Contemporary Usage,* we have not seen any need to treat pronunciations on whose propriety there is general consensus. The standard dictionaries, as we have noted, do that job remarkably well. However, there are a number of expressions that are so commonly mispronounced that we have entered them in regular alphabetical sequence with the other entries. There you will find such celebrated blunders as Dwight Eisenhower's pronunciation of "nuclear" as NOO-kyoo-ler, Gerald Ford's "executive" as ex-EK-uh-tiv, and the widely heard "chaise longue" as shays LOUNJ rather than shays LONG. Certain of these mispronunciations—those that have been so widely circulated that they threaten to replace the accepted pronunciations—must be guarded against. Hence their entry in this volume.

pronunciation, variations in Over the years we have had many thousands of letters from readers of our column complaining about what they consider to be egregious mispronunciations heard on radio and television. Very often they are right in so thinking. As a case in point, one reader reported that the newscaster on a network "flagship" station in New York City introduced the weatherman as the staff mee-ter-OL-uh-jist and the meteorologist proceeded to top the earlier mispronunciation by predicting VAIR-uh-b'l (for "variable") cloudiness. Such obvious mispronunciations can find no defenders.

However, the editors of the Merriam-Webster dictionaries, beginning with the Third International (1961), have been at some pains to record every conceivable variant pronunciation on the theory that whatever is is acceptable. One student of phonetics reported finding a phrase which, by following through all suggested permutations of pronunciation, could be pronounced 128 different ways "according to Webster." The simple word "forehead," about which one puzzled reader inquired, is given no fewer than eight pronunciations, including FAR-red and FOH-uh-red. Obviously no effort has been made to discriminate between what the educated speaker would consider proper and improper pronunciations.

In this volume we have recorded a considerable number of "proper pronunciations." The list is by no means exhaustive, for this is a dictionary of usage, not primarily of pronunciation. However, the words which we have phonetically respelled are words that have been of concern to our readers and hence, one may assume, to many literate speakers of our native tongue.

The pronunciations we indicate are those we believe to be the ones used by literate, educated, and careful speakers. They are not necessarily the only pronunciations that may be deemed "acceptable." To find these alternate pronunciations, we suggest consulting any of a number of dictionaries that are generally available. At the time of publication of this volume, we recommend for this purpose the original *American Heritage Dictionary, Webster's New World Dictionary,* Second College Edition, and the *Funk & Wagnalls Standard College Dictionary.*

proofreading marks. *See* CORRECTIONS IN MANUSCRIPT OR IN PRINTER'S PROOFS

propaganda Strictly speaking, *propaganda* means any means of obtaining support for a particular view or doctrine.

Propaganda originated as coinage of the Roman Catholic Church. It comes from the Latin phrase "Congregatio de *propaganda* fide," the Congregation for the Propagation of the Faith, and originally referred to the work of foreign missions.

In time *propaganda* alone came to mean any sort of organization, religious or secular, devoted to the spreading of particular doctrines. Then it became a name for the doctrines themselves, and now the term is chiefly used to refer to dogmas with which you do not agree.

The use of the word in a pejorative sense may have started with references to "German *propaganda*" during World War I. It seems unlikely that the trend will be reversed. *Propaganda* has become and will remain a semantically slanted word.

prophecy/prophesy The difference of one letter makes the difference between the noun and the verb. A *prophecy* (PROF-uh-see) is a noun meaning "a prediction." To *prophesy* (PROF-uh-sy) is to predict or foretell.

proportional/proportionate "In proportion" or "in due proportion" is the meaning of each of these words. Fastidious writers reserve *proportional* to refer to situations where a number of things are involved, as in the number of states involved in *"proportional* representation." *Proportionate* is then reserved for situations involving only two things, where each is *proportionate* to the other, as in "The number of books that can be printed in one month will be *proportionate* to the number of presses available at the time."

proportions/dimensions Any distinction between *proportions* and *dimensions,* in terms of size or extent, is rapidly vanishing and they are now used interchangeably. Originally, *proportions* had to deal with parts in relation to a whole, but something can now be "of huge *proportions*" without a direct comparison involved.

proscribe. *See* PRESCRIBE/PROSCRIBE

prosecute. *See* PERSECUTE/PROSECUTE

prospective/perspective *Prospective* is an adjective, formed from the noun "prospect," and means "expected" or "anticipated." *Perspective* is a noun and, aside from its technical meanings, is usually used to mean "impersonal point of view" or "coordinated outlook."

protagonist/antagonist Despite the seemingly parallel formation of these two words, they are not opposite sides of a coin.

A *protagonist* is the leading character in a play or any kind of drama, on stage or off. There is only one *protagonist;* "chief *protagonist*" is redundant; "the three *protagonists*" is impossible.

An *antagonist* is an opponent or adversary.

protective retaliation. *See* EUPHEMISM

protein The purists would have us pronounce *protein* with three syllables (PROH-tee-in), and some TV and radio commercial announcers try bravely to enunciate all three syllables. It is an uphill and losing battle, though, for the word is PROH-teen to the vast majority of the American public, lettered and unlettered alike, and so it will remain.

prototype   Since the Greek "protos" means "first," it is understandable that purists restrict the use of *prototype* to mean "the original model or example," or at least to "an early model or example for later ones." In current usage, *prototype* has come to mean a perfect example or ideal of a type. This extended use has not been completely accepted, however.

proved/proven   *Proven*, as the past participle of the verb "prove," is not recognized by some linguists. They insist that the past participle is *proved* only.

Actually, *proven* is the past participle of "preve," an early variant of the verb that existed only in Scotland after "prove" had taken over in England.

Many Americans have shown a preference for *proven*, as in "He has *proven* to be a valuable worker," and most current dictionaries list *proven* as having equal rank with *proved*, especially when used as an attributive adjective: a *proven* success.

provided/providing   Neither *provided* nor *providing* should be used if the word "if" will suffice. A simple possibility should be expressed through the use of "if." Where certain conditions or requirements are stated, either *provided* or *providing* (each followed by "that") is acceptable.

psychedelic   This is a word which has become familiar to the American people since the mid-1960s as a descriptive word for drugs, such as LSD, which are said to be "mind-expanding" or "consciousness-raising." It was coined from the Latin "psyche" (mind) and the Greek "delos" (clear or visible).

psyched up/out   Psyche (SY-kee), as a noun, has traditionally meant the human soul or spirit. In psychiatry, it refers to the mind as a functioning unit which governs feelings, emotions, and behavior.

Now we have a slang verb *psych*. Pronounced SIKE, it is used with *up* to mean "to be prepared mentally and emotionally," as in "It took me four days to get *psyched up* to have my tooth pulled." Used with *out*, it means "to disturb mentally or emotionally," as in "You completely *psyched* me *out* when you told me that."

pub. *See* SALOON

public-information officer/public-relations officer   Pentagonese euphemisms for "press agent." A top-ranking press agent is known in service terms as an "assistant secretary of defense for public affairs."

PUFA *PUFA* is an acronym, one of those words made from the initial letters of a long name. It is the simplest way to refer to those demons of the diet: poly-unsaturated fatty acids.

puffing. *See* EUPHEMISM

punctuation involving quotation marks A question that has perplexed many writers is the location of the period at the end of a sentence involving quotation marks. One reader wrote: "I am amazed to find in the textbooks that the period is always placed inside the final quotation mark without regard to logic but solely for the sake of appearance. To me it is ridiculous to end a sentence like this one with the period inside the quotation mark: The word you want is 'obstinate.' Or Pearl Buck wrote 'The Good Earth.' Can you cite an authority that says the logical method is acceptable?"

The answer is that, though all reason and logic favor putting the quotation mark before the period in the examples given, one would have to travel to England to find them so handled. Generations of American typesetters have insisted that the quotes always fall outside periods (commas, too, for that matter) regardless of the sense of the sentence. The theory is that the quotes help fill the small spot of white that would be left if the comma or period came outside the quote. To see the ridiculousness of this argument, you need only read a book or magazine printed in England. The eye quickly becomes used to quotation marks put where they logically belong and you soon become accustomed to that "small spot of white" that is supposed to be so bothersome. Realistically, however, matters are not likely to change. American printers have been handling copy this way for many decades and they aren't likely to change now just because a few voices are raised in a plea for logic and reason.

Incidentally, printers do permit logic to govern the placement of question marks and exclamation marks, when either one is part of a sentence that includes a quotation. For example: John Wilkes Booth shouted, "Sic semper tyrannis!" But: Did the doctor say, "Three times a day"?

puns and punning The *pun* or, more elegantly, paronomasia is a form of word play that has long intrigued writers. Shakespeare's clowns are forever dipping into *puns*. In our time such a wit as Peter DeVries is justly celebrated for inveterate *punning* along the order of "sibling revelry." Nonetheless, many hold punsters in low repute and the creation of a *pun* in conversation is often greeted with groans. To the punster, this denotes a grudging admiration for his remarkable talent. For the person doing the groaning, the motivation may be envy, if the *pun* is felicitously phrased, or pity, if the *pun* is awkward or far-fetched.

Still, *punning* flourishes among writers who delight in demonstrating that words are not only their tools but their playthings as well. James Boswell once noted that "no innocent species of wit or pleasantry should be suppressed; and a good pun may be admitted among the smaller excellencies of lively conversation." Curiously enough, many people attribute to Boswell's good friend Samuel Johnson the saying "He who would make a pun would pick a pocket." In fact, Johnson never made any such remark. It was John Dennis and what he actually said was: "A man who would make such a vile pun would not scruple to pick a pocket." The *pun* in question was vile, all right. In a pub one day a friend of Dennis named Purcell rang the bell for the "drawer" or waiter. When he failed to respond, Purcell rapped the table hard and asked Dennis what the table and the tavern had in common. The answer—and this is what caused Dennis to gag—was "Because there's no drawer in it."

pupil/student   *Pupil* has been defined as "a youth under the care of a teacher." Hence *pupil* is used to designate a child enrolled in the elementary grades. *Student* is the word to use to designate a person enrolled in secondary schools or colleges.

A *pupil* may also be a person studying one of the arts under the supervision of a master of that art. A *student* may also be a person pursuing independent study in a field in which he has a particular interest.

purist   As used in this dictionary, a *purist* is a person extremely fastidious about choice of words and grammatical constructions. While the term is not necessarily used pejoratively, it nonetheless denotes one who is exceedingly precise in the use of words.

purport   With the meaning of "to have the appearance of being," *purport* can be used to express a slight doubt without its user being openly skeptical: "The bank *purports* to be generous with small loans." Some linguists feel strongly that *purport* should never be used in the passive voice ("is *purported* to be"). The passive use is becoming more common, however, and may soon be accepted.

purposely/purposefully   *Purposely* means "intentionally." "The mayor was *purposely* absent last night." *Purposefully* has an element of being determined to reach an objective or goal. A man or woman acts *purposefully* when working overtime to meet a deadline.

purse. *See* POCKETBOOK/WALLET/PURSE

pusher   Slang for a person who sells illegal narcotic drugs to individual users, usually through personal contact or street trade. Shortened form of *drug pusher*.

put on/put down If someone is *"putting* you *on"* he is kidding you, mocking you, or playing you for a gullible fool. If he *"puts* you *down"* he is deprecating you or your opinions. Both are slang phrases.

Put-on and *put-down* are also used as nouns, the first in the sense of "an elaborate hoax," the second to mean "a belittling remark."

quality This noun is often used attributively (as an adjective), as in the phrase *"quality* education." Some people object to this but it is standard practice in English. In phrases such as "music teacher" the adjectival form would change the meaning. "Musical teacher" means something entirely different. *See also* NOUN MODIFIERS.

quartet. *See* TRIO/QUARTET/QUINTET

quasi/quasar We pronounce *quasi* in the classical Latin manner, with the "s" sounding like an "s." We applied the same principle to *quasar* when it came into popular use but we fear that we find ourselves in a minority today. Both Merriam-Webster and American Heritage dictionaries give KWAY-zar as the preferred pronunciation, though both also list KWAY-sar. Apparently the new breed of physicists who discovered these "quasi-stellar objects" are not as punctilious about pronunciation as we.

questionable/questioning Occasionally these two are confused even by journalists, as in the statement in a newspaper column: "A CBS News special 'The Football Scholars' cast a questionable eye on this unique aspect of higher education." The practice of granting football scholarships may be *questionable;* the eye of CBS should have been characterized as *questioning.*

quick/quickly Technically both forms are correctly used as adverbs.

A reader sent us the following quotation with a request for an opinion: "The messages from mind to mind may travel quick and slow but whether they travel quick or slow does not depend on the space; it depends on the spirit."

Many people mistakenly think that all adverbs end in "-ly" and so condemn such phrases as "Drive Slow." (See *slow/slowly.*) This is an error, since both "slow" and "slowly" are adverbs and the choice of which one to use depends chiefly on the context in which it appears.

In the case of *quick* and *quickly* the latter is more common, although the imperative "Come *quick!*" is often heard. In prose, such as the example given, the slightly more formal *quickly* and "slowly" are preferred.

quintet. *See* TRIO/QUARTET/QUINTET

quintuplet As to the pronunciation of this word, you will find widespread disagreement among authorities. All dictionaries edited before 1933 are quite definite that the only pronunciation permitted is KWIN-tuh-plit. At the time, of course, the word was almost never used outside medical circles—except that, around the turn of the century, someone built a few five-seater bicycles that were called *quintuplets.*

Then came the amazing birth of the Dionne *quintuplets* at Callander, Ontario, and suddenly the word *quintuplet* was on everyone's lips. Since dictionaries must record the pronunciations actually used by educated people, you'll find that today's dictionaries list as many as five different pronunciations, with kwin-TUP-lit being heard at least as commonly as KWIN-tuh-plit and KWIN-tyoo-plit, which are still preferred by purists.

quite a few *Quite a few* is an idiom which defies the laws of logic by using "few," which means "not many," to express the idea of "a lot." The late H. W. Fowler, in his *Dictionary of Modern English Usage,* collected a lot of these illogical idioms into a group which he called the "sturdy indefensibles." *Quite a few* is indeed sturdy; it shows no signs of being rooted out of the language.

quixotic Despite the fact that it is derived from the name of Cervantes' hero, Don Quixote, the adjective *quixotic* is English and its pronunciation is governed by English practices. Don Quixote is pronounced Don Kee-HOH-tee, which roughly approximates the Spanish original. The English adjective *quixotic* is pronounced kwix-OT-ik. An impractical dreamer, a chap carried away by romantic delusions and idealistic notions of chivalry and honor, is *quixotic.*

quiz *Quiz* originally was only a term for a brief and sometimes impromptu test given to students. It still has this meaning. Its use as a verb meaning "to question closely or in detail" is generally accepted, but its use as a noun synonymous with investigation ("Senate *quiz* brings results") is substandard.

quotation/quote *Quotation* is the preferred noun form and the one that should be used in formal contexts. However, *quote* as the colloquial noun form has been widely accepted for several decades and is now so recorded in the dictionaries. Note that there is nothing derogatory about the label "colloquial." It merely means "in a conversational tone" and is, in fact, the style used in most newspaper writing today.

quotation marks *Quotation marks* are the superscript signs (" and ') used to indicate matter directly quoted from the speech or writing of others; titles of short literary works; names of ships, trains, and planes; and words deliberately set apart from the context in order to direct special attention to them, sometimes for reasons of irony or double meaning. However, there is a breed of sign painters who seem to think that sprinkling quotation marks around words somehow adds importance to them. We have all seen signs reading "STRICTLY FRESH" EGGS and "GUARANTEED" USED CARS. To our minds the implication of such quotation marks is precisely the opposite of the sign painter's intention. We'd be doubtful about the freshness of eggs so labeled and would give that particular used-car dealer a wide berth. *See also* APOSTROPHE and PUNCTUATION INVOLVING QUOTATION MARKS.

q.v. This is the abbreviation for the Latin phrase "quod vide," meaning "which see." It is used as a means of cross reference, being placed in parentheses after the word or phrase involved.

"q" without "u" A "*q*" *without a* "*u*" is almost unknown in English. Unabridged dictionaries list some fifteen or twenty words beginning this way. Most of these, like Qattara, are proper names from Arabic or other Semitic languages. Others, like Qabbala (for Cabbala), are merely variant spellings. Then there is the oft-misspelled name of Australia's national airline QANTAS, an acronym for Queensland and Northern Territories Air Service.

A newspaper story out of Tangiers included the following statement: "As in the days of Hannibal, time meant little—the qsim, a span of time equal to five of our minutes, was the smallest unit known to the citizen dozing in a burnoose."

"Qsim" (presumably pronounced k-SIM) could be a very useful word, however. "I took only three qsims for my coffee break" doesn't sound nearly as bad as "fifteen minutes." And "Officer, I was only doing five miles a qsim" makes it sound as if you were only crawling.

R

rabbit. *See* WELSH RABBIT/RAREBIT

rabid *Rabid* literally means "afflicted with rabies," hence "raging mad." By extension it has come to mean "fanatical" but it should not be used where "enthusiastic" will suffice.

racist The growth of the civil-rights movement has made *racist* a common term for a person whose attitude, statements, and acts express or reflect discrimination on the basis of race. *See also* REVERSE RACISM/REVERSE DISCRIMINATION.

racket/racquet If you are British you use the spelling *racquet* to refer to the many-stringed bat used in tennis and badminton. If you are American, it's *racket.*

　　Racket, in the sense of "a scheme or business operated for the purpose of obtaining money illegally," is now accepted as informal. When it is used to mean any job or occupation (as in "What's your *racket*?") it is still considered slang by most dictionaries, although at least one dictionary considers that usage acceptable if it is meant humorously.

rack/wrack

USAGE PANEL QUESTION

A member of the panel comments: "It's a 'storm-wracked coast' and a 'pain-racked soldier,' but some insist that 'wrack' is interchangeable with 'rack.' " Do you agree?
Yes: 37%. No: 63%.
Would you write the phrase "wrack and ruin"?: 65%
or "rack and ruin"?: 35%.

BENJAMIN APPEL: "No. 'Wrack' is nineteenth century."

ISAAC ASIMOV: "Yes. But who needs the 'w.' "

SHERIDAN BAKER: "No. Unless the writer is *clearly* punning (against wrack) by using the instrument of torture—otherwise it just seems ignorant."

ALVIN BEAM: " 'Wrack' sounds a bit Shakespearean—on the antique side."

HAL BORLAND: "No. The rack was an instrument of torture, too."

HEYWOOD HALE BROUN: "I think of pain as racking one in the manner of Torquemada, and storms as wracking one as in shipwreck. I use the nautical version with ruin because it seems, to this grammarian, if not to the victim, more destructive than painful."

ALEX FAULKNER: "Frankly, I don't know. The Oxford defines 'wrack' as cast-up seaweed, so I favour 'wrack' for such nautical situations as 'storm-wracked coast,' but it says 'racking' is torture on the rack, so this seems more appropriate for 'pain-racked soldier.' In one edition I have *OED* gives both 'rack and ruin' and 'wrack and ruin'; so it looks as though one could take one's choice in this phrase, and I like the look of 'wrack.' "

THOMAS FLEMING: "I think 'wrack' is correct."

ELIZABETH JANEWAY: "Among those who say these are interchangeable is the *OED*. So it's O.K. with me to use either, but I'd write 'rack' myself."

ALEXANDER KENDRICK: "They're close but 'rack' to me always raises the image of a medieval torture instrument."

STANLEY KUNITZ: "Either way seems acceptable to me."

WRIGHT MORRIS: "Yes. Vide Webster."

PETER S. PRESCOTT: "Neither; the cliché is so dreadful we are spared the necessity of making a choice."

LEO ROSTEN: "I prefer 'wrack' by far, and resent the injustice to the eloquent 'w.' "

VERMONT ROYSTER: "I would write 'storm-wracked coast' but 'pain-racked soldier.' The first is literal, the second by analogy to the torture rack."

MARK SCHORER: "Doesn't 'rack' mostly have to do with the old torture bit, while 'wrack' is an early version of 'wreck'—quite different?"

HOWARD TAUBMAN: "I would try to find another—a fresh—phrase."

HAROLD TAYLOR: "I wouldn't use it at all. Ruin is enough, for God's sake."

BARBARA TUCHMAN: "I think the 'w' has just been dropped by custom though it probably belongs."

EARL UBELL: "Although 'rack' is an alternate to 'wrack,' the former derives from 'framework,' the latter from 'punish.' If one wishes to give the sense of being punished, or as if on a rack, then rack it; if one suggests destruction, then wrack it or wreck it."

JUDITH VIORST: "I've often wondered how the hell to use 'wrack.' "

HERMAN WOUK: "I wouldn't write either; they are very worn phrases."

radar. *See* ACRONYM

radical   In today's political terminology a *radical* is usually regarded as one sympathetic to leftist or revolutionary causes. In its precise sense *radical* signifies a person desirous of getting to the root of the matter, for the word comes from the Latin word for "root": "radix." *See also* ICONOCLAST/RADICAL.

radiosonde   *Radiosonde* is a radio device borne aloft, usually by balloon, whose purpose is to gather meteorological data for weather forecasting. It is a combination of *radio* and *sonde,* which is French for "sounding line." The final "e" is silent, so it is pronounced RAY-dee-oh-sond.

railroad/railway   *Railroad* and *railway* are both nouns but are often used attributively as adjectives. In years past the word *railway* was generally reserved for streetcar systems or other forms of rail transportation lighter than full-fledged *railroads* with locomotives and rolling stock. This distinction, which was never observed by the British, has gone by the board in America with the disappearance of our urban trolley-car systems, and today the two words are generally used interchangeably.

railroad, to In informal use, *railroad* as a verb has two meanings, both based, in a sense, on the speed and sureness with which trains are supposed to run. Important legislation being put through in a rush is said to have been *railroaded*. A person who is sent to prison after a speedy trial based on false charges is said to have been *railroaded*.

raise/rear Fifty years ago, the use of *raise* in the expression "born and *raised*" so infuriated the late Frank H. Vizetelly, then editor of the Funk & Wagnalls dictionaries, that he nearly exploded in his wrathful condemnation of the usage. "*Raised* should never be used in the sense of bringing human beings to maturity," he snorted. "It is a misuse common in the southern and western United States. Cattle are *raised*; human beings are brought up or, in an older phrase, reared."

Today, *raise* in the sense of "to bring up" or "to *rear*" is perfectly good usage and it matters not whether you are bringing up people or cattle.

raise/rise

USAGE PANEL QUESTION

A headline in *The New York Times* reads DELAY IN U.S. RAISES UPHELD BY SENATE. A panelist raises a question in this connection: "The noun for 'raise' in our style book was always 'rise' which purists pronounced 'rice.' So, in theory anyway, the underpaid rewrite man in those long-ago days was supposed to ask for a 'rice' in pay. Does anyone worry about this matter any longer?"
Yes: 7%. No: 93%.

ISAAC ASIMOV: "No! Good Lord!"

JOHN O. BARBOUR: "They can't get a rise out of me, and I can't get a raise out of them."

STEWART BEACH: "I have been in this business a good many years and I have never heard or seen 'rise' used for 'raise.' It is the accepted word in England but whether they say 'rice' or 'rise' I don't remember."

HEYWOOD HALE BROUN: "I'm pure, but I've never aspired to the hysterical purity of the *Times* style book."

BEN LUCIEN BURMAN: "The styles in the style book must have been taken from Godey's Ladies' Book."

ALEXANDER KENDRICK: "The trouble with the headline is that it makes you wonder what word was left out."

CLARK KINNAIRD: "A bad headline in either case. Much headline usage is ineffectual in describing the story or arousing a reader's interest."

LAURENCE LAFORE: "I wish people did, but they don't."

JOHN LEAR: "Some people do, but I do not."

EDWIN NEWMAN: "NBC had a man who did years ago. It stayed with me."

PETER S. PRESCOTT: "I had assumed that 'rise' in this sense was an Anglicism."

ROBERT SHERRILL: "There was actually such a style book? Sounds like Joe Miller's style book."

MIMS THOMASON: " 'Raise' is correct."

raison d'être   Since this French phrase means "reason for being" or "justification for existence," it should not be used as synonymous with the simple word "reason."

rambunctious   As an adjective meaning "wild and unruly" or "overexuberant," *rambunctious* is recorded in the *Oxford English Dictionary* as "U.S. slang, 1854." In variant forms, it goes back a lot farther than that, since etymologists have determined that it has origins in Latin. The most recent dictionaries have dropped the label "slang" and *rambunctious* is now accepted as standard English.

rang/rung   Either *rang* or *rung* used to be acceptable as the past tense of the verb "to ring" but the tendency today is to use only *rang* and restrict the use of *rung* to the past participle. The Third Edition of Webster's International Dictionary (Unabridged) still gives them both for the past tense, as did the Second Edition of that dictionary. More recent dictionaries give the past tense as *"rang,* sometimes *rung"* or label this use of *rung* as "rare." The original *American Heritage Dictionary* says flatly that *rung* as the past tense is "substandard."

   No such change has affected the verb "spring," the past tense of which may still be either "sprang" or "sprung."

rap   *Rap,* in the sense of participating in a group discussion, is common in informal speech today, having spread across the campuses of the United States in the late 1960s and early 1970s. In a more limited sense, it seems to have been established in Broadway slang in the 1930s. Damon Runyon (whose *Guys and Dolls* is something of a classic) used *rap* in the sense of "to speak to" or "to recognize" in this sentence written in 1932: "I wish Moose a hello and he never raps to me but only bows and takes my hat." Our theory (and it is just a theory) is that the current meaning is derived from the French "en rapport," meaning "in harmony with." People who are *rapping* are conversing, of course, but it is a special kind of conversation usually confined to topics about which they find themselves in agreement or harmony. *Rap* is also used as a noun meaning a lecture or talking-to: "He gave me this *rap* about the importance of acting responsibly." Another meaning is false conviction and *rap* is used here with "bum": "The defendant was given a bum *rap* and was sentenced to three years in prison without bail." *See also* VOGUE WORDS.

rape and other once-taboo words Today's metropolitan newspapers routinely print words that were strictly forbidden just a few years ago—words like "rape," "sodomy," and the names of various venereal diseases. Elmer Roessner, one-time editor of the *New York World Telegram* and later our editor at the Bell-McClure Syndicate, once reminisced for us about the changes in newspaper restrictions on some of these words.

" 'Rape' was long forbidden, except in references to 'The Rape of the Lock,' " he wrote. "The word used was 'assaulted,' while 'attacked' was reserved for being clobbered. I can remember, circa 1929, Jack Campbell, managing editor of the *Los Angeles Herald,* charging over to the city desk and shouting, 'Let's get this story straight, was this girl attacked or assaulted?' After getting clarification from me, the *Herald* came out with the headline L. A. SOCIETY GIRL ASSAULTED. If she had only been attacked, the story would have landed on page three.

"I was on the *World-Telegram* in the early 1930s when the words 'syphillis' and 'gonorrhea' first appeared in print in an American newspaper, outside of proper names of medical committees in *The New York Times.* Greta Palmer, women's page columnist, wrote about the need for frank understanding and, instead of calling them 'social diseases' as was the custom, came right out and said 'syphillis' and 'gonorrhea.'

"The rest of the staff sat around all day, waiting for God's thunderbolt to level Roy Howard's new six-story *World-Telegram* building.

"You may remember. It didn't happen."

Today, of course, newspapers and television use stories about various varieties of herpes, a "social disease" unheard of in Roessner's heyday, and euphemisms have long since been abandoned in reporting rape cases.

rarebit. *See* WELSH RABBIT/RAREBIT

rarely ever *Rarely* by itself means "seldom" and in formal speech or writing the seemingly nonsensical idiom *rarely ever* should not be used. Actually the idiom is a condensed form of *rarely if ever,* a phrase which would be acceptable in formal use. It is possible that *rarely ever* came into use by analogy with "hardly ever," which is itself standard English.

rasher Technically, a *rasher* is one thin slice of bacon (or sometimes ham) which is either broiled or fried. In practice, a *rasher* of bacon (a redundant but idiomatic expression) is several slices of bacon served as a side dish. If "a *rasher* of bacon" is listed on a restaurant menu, the number of pieces served is entirely up to the management.

rate, to   In the senses of "to deserve" or "to have influence or status," to *rate* has to be considered informal and not suitable for formal speech or writing.

rather   Although most dictionaries and usage books accept the idiom "had *rather* (do something)," it sounds quaint and old-fashioned. "Would *rather*" is the more common usage. *See also* KIND OF/RATHER/SOME-WHAT.

ratio. *See* MARGIN/SCORE

ration/ratio   Since both *ration* and *ratio* come from the Latin "ratio" (meaning "reasoning"), some people argue that both should be pronounced with a long "a": RAY-shun and RAY-shee-oh. In practice, however, either RASH-un or RAY-shun is acceptable for *ration,* with the former slightly preferred.

rattle, to   In the sense of "to disconcert" or "to unnerve," *rattle* is informal but not slang.

ravage. *See* RAVISH/RAVAGE

ravel/unravel   Usually the prefix "un-" changes the meaning of a word to the direct opposite. This is not the case with *ravel* and *unravel.* The Oxford Dictionary states that *ravel* has been in English since 1600 and means "to fray out, to unwind, to take to pieces, to disentangle." *Unravel* has much the same meaning and the two are interchangeable, except when *unravel* is used in the special sense of solving or clearing up a mystery or problem.

ravish/ravage   *Ravish* is sometimes mistakenly used when *ravage* is intended. To *ravish* is to abduct, rape, or "carry away with emotion, especially of joy." Buildings, towns, and forests cannot be *ravished.*

To *ravage* is to wreak great destruction or devastation. While there is an element of violence in the meanings of both words, they are not interchangeable.

re/in re   From the Latin word meaning "thing," *in re* or the shortened form, *re,* is used to mean "in the matter of" or "in regard to." *Re* is acceptable at the top of a business letter or memorandum to indicate the subject of the communication, or even in the body of such a letter or memorandum. It is standard in legal papers but it is pretentious in non-business or nonlegal situations.

re-   As a prefix meaning "again," *re-* sometimes is followed by a hyphen, sometimes not. If the word to which it is to be attached begins with an "e," a hyphen is called for: "*re-*enlist," "*re-*enter," "*re-*employed," for example. If the absence of a hyphen between the prefix and the word would result in the formation of a word with an entirely different meaning, the hyphen is needed to avoid confusion ("*re*cover"/"*re*-cover").

reaction   Once confined to the field of science where it meant a specific response to a specific stimulus, *reaction* is widely and loosely used to cover all varieties of responses, including feelings and opinions. Whenever possible, a more precise word is better: "attitude," "response," "reply," "opinion" are possibilities.

read   *Read* as a noun meaning "the act of reading" is a British expression that has become a bit of a vogue among "effete Eastern literary snobs." Statements such as "Tom's new novel is a smashing good *read*" flow freely in book-editor circles. Ironically, we first came across it in the rugged, rough-hewn prose of Brendan Behan's *Borstal Boy*. In recounting his literary discoveries while a pupil or inmate of Britain's Borstal Schools, Behan would again and again report that he found a newly discovered classic "a splendid read."

read his (her) rights. *See* MIRANDIZE

Reaganomics

USAGE PANEL QUESTION

Reaganomics has appeared in all the media as an omnibus designation for the monetary policies espoused by the Reagan administration. During the presidency of Richard Nixon, the economic policies of his administration were sometimes called "Nixonomics," a term now nearly forgotten.

In your view will *Reaganomics* merit a permanent place in our lexicons, like Roosevelt's "New Deal" and Truman's "Fair Deal"? Yes: 33%. No: 67%.

ISAAC ASIMOV: "Yes, as, I hope, a hissing and a byword."

THOMAS S. BARBER: "Too early to say, but I doubt it."

BARRY BINGHAM, SR.: "This too shall pass, just as Nixonomics did. Only when we have presidents with such convenient names can such inventions arise. There could not have been an 'Eisenhowernomics.' "

ALTON BLAKESLEE: "Yes, because of profound and enduring dislocations."

JOSEPH A. BRANDT: "Yes, unfortunately."

JOHN BROOKS: "A journalistic tag that will not survive the curious thing it describes."

ANTHONY BURGESS: "A good nonce word only."

BEN LUCIEN BURMAN: "It would be a sad day!"

JOAN SIMPSON BURNS: "The problem is that 'Reaganomics' is not a stable term. Reagan's policy switched so much. . . . No."

JOHN CIARDI: "The question a few years hence will probably be 'Reagan? . . . who was he?'"

WILLARD R. ESPY: " 'Reaganomics' is largely a media creation and often gives a faint stench of disapproval. If the President's economic policies succeed, 'Reaganomics' will indeed merit an honored place in our lexicon; if they fail, the word will still linger, largely as a term of opprobrium in editorials and political speeches."

GEROLD FRANK: "Too awkward a word—and I suspect Reagan will be a more transient phenomenon than we suspect."

FRANCES FRITCHMAN: "Clear, useful shorthand."

RAY GANDOLF: "The word will prevail if the policies prevail. I predict doom for both."

SYDNEY J. HARRIS: "No—the generic word is 'reactionary.' "

PAUL HORGAN: "Tacky journalism."

JOHN K. HUTCHENS: "Yes, I believe it will endure, simply because it has been used on such a large scale."

WALTER KERR: "When he goes, it goes."

JAMES J. KILPATRICK: " 'Reaganomics' is a nonce word. It will depart from our vocabularies on the same helicopter that one day will take Mr. Reagan from the White House. To find a permanent place in the language, new words must be susceptible to reasonably precise definitions. FDR's New Deal qualifies; so does Lyndon Johnson's Great Society, but if you asked a dozen political writers to define Truman's Fair Deal, Kennedy's New Frontier, Nixon's Nixonomics, or Reagan's Reaganomics, you would get a dozen definitions, none of them precise."

STANLEY KUNITZ: "It means something definite and has the right ring to it."

WILLIAM McGUIRE: " 'Fair Deal' has grown rather dim. 'Reaganomics' will fade, too, especially as its meaning gets blurred."

WADE MOSBY: "Yes, but perhaps in a derisive sense."

EDWIN NEWMAN: "Reagan's policies have changed. 'Reaganomics' is now harder to define."

MARGE PIERCY: "It is an extensive counter-revolution that has already had substantial impact on the lives of the poor, women, the elderly, Black people, and an equally strong impact on the lives of many other creatures who to their misfortune share the land, sea, and air with us."

ORVILLE PRESCOTT: "No, because it does not yet have a specific meaning. If Reagan continues to reverse his program the word will disappear."

PETER S. PRESCOTT: "No. A nonce word for sure."

LEO ROSTEN: "Since both monetarists and 'supply siders' support some parts of Reagan's policy, and rant against other parts, a word is needed (and appropriate) to label the aberrant credo."

VERMONT ROYSTER: " 'Shorthand' words of this kind can be useful temporarily but their usefulness passes. This one will vanish with Mr. Reagan."

ERICH SEGAL: "This is a question that history will decide."

JACK SMITH: "No, unless we sink into utter ruin and 'Reaganomics' becomes unforgettable."

ELVIS STAHR, JR.: " 'Reaganomics' was not a campaign slogan and is still not used by the President. It was coined by others but it is seen and heard every day and is already implanted in the language."

KARL V. TEETER: "Merit, no. Occupy, perhaps."

EDWARD TRIPP: "How long the term will last will doubtless depend on how long the conservative trend will last."

EARL UBELL: "Who knows?"

WILLIAM C. VERGARA: "Like similar media inventions, 'Reaganomics' is too imprecise for meaningful communication. It will probably disappear as the next wave of economic theory breaks on the political scene."

JUDITH VIORST: "The present administration *has* no monetary policy and it is possible that 'Reaganomics' may come to be a synonym for such a state of affairs."

GEORGE WALD: "No. Just a new bid for an old Hoover theme; trickle-down economics with 'prosperity just around the corner.' "

A.B.C. WHIPPLE: "Yes, because their effects may be longer lasting, alas."

WILLIAM ZINSSER: "Probably; too early to know."

real/really   The adjective *real* is often misused instead of the adverb *really,* as in "I feel *real* good" or "The hill is *real* steep." The correct usage is, of course, *"really* good" and *"really* steep." *Real* should be reserved for use as an adjective in the senses of "true, actual, or genuine," as in a *real* diamond, *real* people, or a *real* thrill.

real facts/true facts   It is possible to have some of the facts or all of the facts—but any fact is *real* and *true* by its very nature. Avoid the redundant *real fact* and *true fact.*

realistic/unrealistic   *Realistic* and *unrealistic* should be reserved for the sense of "based on facts or a situation as it really is," but they have become vogue words, with their meaning distorted in the process. *Realistic* is now used instead of "practical," "workable," "sensible," "wise," or "reasonable." The result is that whether something is *realistic* or *unrealistic* depends on your point of view. Precision in language would be better served if such usage of these words were abandoned and more exact words used.

Realtor/realty   In an effort to give more dignity to their members and to promote their organization, the National Association of Real Estate Boards coined and made a registered trademark of the term *Realtor.* As such it should be used only to refer to a member of the organization and should be capitalized. The Boston *Globe* reminds its staff that it should be used only in trade context and that in other contexts the term "real estate man" or similar label should be used. We feel it is a pretentious term and continue to call all in the trade—male or female—"real-estate agents."

Realtor should be pronounced REE-ul-tor, not REE-lih-tor, and *realty* is REE-ul-tee, not REE-lih-tee.

rear. *See* RAISE/REAR

reason is . . . that/because   A sentence beginning with "The *reason*" should be completed with a noun clause introduced by "that," as in "The *reason* she didn't come was *that* she had no transportation." Despite this, many thousands of people continue to speak and write, "The *reason* was . . . *because.* . . ." To be strictly accurate, a sentence should not contain both *reason* and *because.* If you want to use *because,* drop the *reason* and make it: "She did not come *because* she had no transportation."

reason why   There is no question that *the reason why* is a redundant expression and that the *why* is unnecessary. There is also no question that it is an established idiom in the American language.

Credit Alfred, Lord Tennyson for making this phrase a lasting part of the language. When he wrote, of the Six Hundred, "Theirs not to *reason why,* theirs but to do and die," he contributed a deathless phrase to the language. Granted that *reason* was used as a verb in this instance, *The Reason Why* was chosen as the title of a superb book by Cecil Woodham-Smith, still the best study of the ill-fated Crimean campaign. It has also served to impress the *reason why* idiom even more firmly into our language.

rebellion. *See* REVOLUTION/REBELLION/REVOLT

rebuff/repulse/repel/reject   A basic meaning is common to all four of these words: "to turn back or refuse to accept." Each has its own shade of meaning, however. To *rebuff* is to refuse bluntly or abruptly. To *repulse* is to reject with discourtesy or rudeness. To *repel* is to cause such distaste and disgust as to turn another away. (It has the added meanings of "to resist" or "to drive or force back.") To *reject* is not only "to refuse to accept" but "to refuse to use or believe." (It, too, has added meanings: "to discard or throw away" or "to deny love and care to," as in *rejected* child.) Some authorities argue that only *repel* has an element of "causing disgust," but in light of the meaning of *repulsive,* this is difficult to accept. Fowler's *Modern English Usage,* in a comparison of the adjectives *repellent* and *repulsive,* says *repellent* describes that which "keeps you at arm's length" and *repulsive* describes that "from which you recoil," and hence "the second is a much stronger word."

rebut/refute   *Rebut* and *refute* both mean to contradict, as a statement or accusation, but a *refutation* is more definitive than a *rebuttal* might be. To *refute* is to prove wrong; to *rebut* is to answer in contradiction, but not necessarily effectively enough to prove wrong.

recall. *See* REMEMBER/RECOLLECT/RECALL

recession. *See* DEPRESSION/RECESSION

recipe/receipt/Rx   *Recipe* is the common term for a cooking formula, but throughout New England and in rural areas in many other parts of the country you will still hear *receipt.*

Historically, both words come from the Latin "recipere," to receive. Although *recipe* appears to be closer to the Latin original, it actually developed later. According to the Oxford Dictionary *receipt* (or "receit") was well established in the language before 1700, while *recipe* in the sense of "ingredients and procedures for the making of a dish in cookery" did not appear until 1743. *Receipt* originally meant "that which has been received" and, since *receipts* are traditionally handed down from experienced to inexperienced cooks, these formulas are "received" by one from the other.

Receipt was formerly used to indicate a list of medical ingredients, later to be replaced by *recipe.* This helps to explain the *Rx* on prescription labels, the "R" being an abbreviation of *recipe* and the slant bar across the "R" supposed to represent the Roman god Jupiter, who, in addition to his other tasks, was the patron saint of medicine.

reckon   The traditional meanings of *reckon* are "to count or add up" and "to judge or consider," as in "Losses from the storm were *reckoned* to be more than one million dollars" and "I *reckon* John to be my best friend." In the sense of "guess" or "suppose," as in "I *reckon* it might rain tonight," it is informal or dialect.

reclusion   If a former political leader leaves the hectic life of Washington to return to his home town, it is perfectly proper to speak of "the friends who share his *reclusion.*"

Reclusion is a seldom-heard word, to be sure, but it has been part of the language for centuries. It is an extension of the noun "recluse," a person who withdraws from the world to live alone, as hermits do.

recollect. *See* REMEMBER/RECOLLECT/RECALL

record, new   A *record* is an achievement that surpasses previous accomplishments. There may be "previous" *records* but it is redundant to say *new record*.

records sales. *See* NOUN PLURALS, USED ATTRIBUTIVELY

recourse/resource/resort   These three nouns are sometimes confused, partly because they are similar in sound and partly because there are some instances in which one might be substituted for another.

Basically, a *resource* is something which is readily available to a person when he or she needs it; *recourse* is the act of turning to someone or something for aid (or the person or thing to which one turns); and *resort* is also a person or thing to which a person turns for aid. The latter is most frequently heard in the phrase "last *resort*" and has an element of finality that *recourse* does not have, since there may be several means of *recourse*. (The verb *resort* also has that element of finality.)

recurrence/reoccurence   Although *recurrence* is the more familiar of these two, there is such a word as *reoccurrence,* which has a slightly different meaning.

Reoccurrence means "a second happening," whereas *recurrence* has the sense (like the verb "recur") of happening repeatedly or periodically. So when the Soviet Union charged that U.S. planes had hit a Soviet ship in Vietnamese waters, the subhead on the story (as carried by one American newspaper) read: "Appropriate Measures Threatened by Soviets for Any Reoccurrence." If we grant that the Soviets meant to take stern measures if the incident occurred even once more, then the copyeditor was justified in selecting the more precise term *reoccurrence.*

red cap. *See* SKYCAP

red-letter day   Almanacs and calendars issued by religious organizations often have saints' days and holidays printed in red. Since these are days for special services, the phrase *red-letter day* has come to mean any very special day, especially one that brings luck.

redundancy   A *redundancy* is a phrase which includes words unnecessary to the meaning and which, as a result, repeats itself. A few such phrases have become idiomatic and are thus acceptable, as "mental telepathy," which survives despite the fact that "telepathy" means the communication of one mind with another by other than normal means.

For the most part, though, the deletion of repetitious words is desirable. The only possible justification of *redundancy* may be that many users think that it adds emphasis. The use of "cancel out" may seem to give a greater feeling of finality than "cancel." Most cases, however, simply reflect sloppy thinking or show illiteracy: "new innovation," "free gift," "old adage," "exact same," "hollow tube," and "revert back" are some such phrases.

It is possible to spread the *redundancy* throughout a sentence, as in this notice on a tax form: "By borough ordinance it is mandatory that you must file this form." The only cure for *redundancy* is deletion. In this case, delete "must."

red up   This phrase is a dialect version of "ready up," and has been heard throughout the country, especially in rural sections, for almost one hundred years. It is used in such statements as "We have to *red up* the living room before company comes." It is also spelled *redd up*.

refer/allude   To *refer* to someone or something is to mention directly with specific identification. To *allude* is to mention indirectly without specific identification.

refer back   A *redundancy* (which see). Since the prefix "re-" means "back," a second "back" is superfluous.

refute. *See* REBUT/REFUTE and CONFUTE/REFUTE

regard/regards to, (in/with)   *Regards,* a noun plural in form, is used only in the sense of good wishes or expression of affection, as in "Give my *regards to* your mother." *In regards to* is substandard; the correct form is *in regard to* or *with regard to*.

regardless/irregardless   *Regardless* requires the preposition "of." Possibly because of a need for emphasis, the word *irregardless* is used by some, but it is substandard. See Usage Panel Question at *irregardless*.

regime   In the strictest sense, a *regime* is a system of government, as in "democratic *regime*" or "totalitarian *regime*." In a less strict sense, it is used to refer to the period of time that a particular official is in office without any implication as to what kind of government is in power.

regional dialect. *See* DIALECT, REGIONAL

registered/enrolled   All voters are *registered* voters, since they have to take certain steps to be allowed to vote in general elections. In addition, a person may be an *enrolled* Democrat or Republican, allowing him or her to vote in the primaries of his or her party. But the phrase "*registered* Democrat (or Republican)" is inaccurate.

regretful/regrettable *Regretful* can only be applied to a person, since it means "full of regret." It does not mean "causing regret," which is the meaning of *regrettable*. *Regrettable* is the word to use to refer to a happening, condition, or situation.

rehabilitation In recent years the meaning of *rehabilitation* has been extended beyond its basic meaning of "reinstatement" or "restoration to former state or position with attendant privileges and rights." Now sociologists use it to mean treatment of a disabled or criminal person, through training or therapy, to achieve mental and physical health so that the person may lead a useful life.

reign/rein Despite the fact that they are pronounced alike, there is no similarity in meaning. *Reign* (as a verb) means "to rule or govern." *Rein* (also as a verb) means "to curb or restrain." *Reins* are the bridle straps used to control horses, and "to give full *rein* to" a horse is to allow him to run without restraint. "Tight *rein*" implies close control, since that is the result when a rider guides a horse by pulling back on the *reins.* When these expressions are used figuratively the spelling is always *rein.*

reiterate/iterate. *See* ITERATE/REITERATE

reject. *See* REBUFF/REPULSE/REPEL/REJECT

relate Normally *relate* means either "to tell the story of" or "to connect or associate or have a connection or association." In sociological jargon, which unfortunately spills over into the general language, *relate* has come to mean "to get along with or have common ideas or thoughts," as in "Having had a similar experience, he was able to *relate.*" All too often *relate* is the last word in such a statement. The least that should be done is to add an explanatory phrase, such as "to other victims of muggings."

relationship, meaningful. *See* MEANINGFUL

relative/relation A person having blood ties to another is a *relative* or a *relation,* but one is a *relative* or *relation* "of" the other, not "to." You should not say, "He is no *relation to* me" but ". . . no *relation of* mine." The preposition "to" should only be used when the wording is *related to* or "bears no *relation to.*" In the latter phrase, the meaning of *relation* is that of "connection with" rather than kinship.

relevant *Relevant,* in what Usage Panelist Charles Berlitz characterizes as "pseudo-political usage," has become a vogue word in other areas. Matters must be *relevant* or *meaningful* (which see) to be of any importance. Coming from the Latin word meaning "to bear upon," *relevant* simply means "having a bearing on or being related to the matter in hand." The trouble is that it is greatly overused and often misused. It is also misunderstood and mispronounced, as in the case of a young man who repeatedly spoke of "revalent" issues. *See also* VOGUE WORDS.

relocate/move   This is another business English borrowing from sociological gobbledegook. One no longer *moves* from Boston to New York, he *relocates* or is *relocated* from one place to the other. It is characteristic of the kind of mind that spawns these unnecessary additions to the vulgar tongue that it believes that any three-syllable word is by definition preferable to a monosyllable.

reluctant/reticent   A *reluctant* person is one who does not want to do something. A *reticent* person is one who does not wish to speak, especially one who is habitually silent or quiet.

remain. *See* LINKING VERBS

remand back   The presence of the prefix "re-" should be sufficient warning that "back" is not needed with *remand,* since "re-" itself means "back." To use "back" is to be guilty of a *redundancy* (which see). *Remand* alone means "to send back" or "to return." In legal use it means for a court to send a prisoner back to jail until his case has been investigated further or for a higher court to send a case back to a lower court for further consideration.

remember/recollect/recall   While all three words have a common meaning of "to bring to mind again," there is a slight distinction which should be observed. To *remember* can be to do so without any conscious effort; to *recollect* or to *recall* involves a deliberate effort to bring back to mind.

reminisce   *Reminisce* is what word experts call a "back-formation" from "reminiscence," a word that goes back in English to before Shakespeare's time. The language is full of such "back-formations" and, almost without exception, they are resisted by purists, who fight a delaying and futile battle to keep them out of the language. (A recent example is "enthuse," a back-formation from "enthusiasm," a word that is still barely tolerated by many purists.)

  Reminisce, when it first appeared in print in 1829, was considered to be "colloquial and jocose." This means that, in the view of British editors, *reminisce* was completely acceptable in conversation and informal writing and that it was originally used in joking fashion. Over the past century and a half it has acquired complete respectability and is now suitable for use on any level of speech or writing.

remnant   *Remnant,* a short length of fabric left when most of the bolt has been sold, is properly pronounced REM-nunt, not REM-uh-nunt, as all too often heard in the speech of tradespeople.

rendezvous   Both the singular and the plural forms of *rendezvous* are spelled the same but are pronounced differently. The singular is rahn-deh-VOO; the plural is rahn-deh-VOOS.

reparable/repairable/irreparable   Both *reparable* and *repairable* have the meaning of "capable of being mended, repaired, or remedied" but their usages differ slightly. *Repairable* is preferred in the literal sense: a chair is *repairable* rather than *reparable. Reparable* is more often used figuratively, especially in its negative form, *irreparable,* as in "The scandal did *irreparable* damage to his reputation."

   Repairable is pronounced reh-PARE-uh-b'l; *reparable* is pronounced REP-er-uh-b'l.

repast/meal   The meaning of *repast* as "food or nourishment" is now obsolete, and *repast* in the sense of "a meal" or "food eaten or provided at a meal" is on its way to join it. At best it is a stiff and pretentious term and should be eliminated in favor of *meal* or the name of a specific meal, such as "lunch," or "dinner."

repel. *See* REBUFF/REPULSE/REPEL/REJECT

repertoire/repertory   All the meanings of *repertoire* are common to *repertory* but *repertory* has some meanings exclusive to it. Both can mean the total of songs, plays, parts, operas, etc., which an actor, singer, or company is prepared to perform. However, *repertory* alone can mean the place where things are stored or the things which are so stored.

   "*Repertory* theater" is the term for a theater or company which presents a series of plays selected from its *repertoire* or *repertory* and announced in advance.

replete   *Replete* (followed by "with") means "having an abundance of." It does not mean "complete" and should not be used in that sense.

replica   Strictly speaking, a *replica* is a duplicate made by the original artist. Popular usage, however, has brought about acceptance of an extended meaning of "any duplicate or copy, even a scaled-down one."

republic. *See* DOMINION/REPUBLIC

repulse. *See* REBUFF/REPULSE/REPEL/REJECT

reputable *Reputable* should be pronounced REP-yuh-tuh-b'l, not reh-PYOOT-ih-b'l.

requirement/requisite/prerequisite While in most instances *requirement* and *requisite* are interchangeable, *requisite* seems to be a slightly stronger word. Purists may hold that *requirement* designates "a need" and *requisite* "a needed thing" but the distinction is difficult to establish, let alone maintain.

A more common word than *requisite* is *prerequisite,* a term familiar to college students who find that English 101 is a *prerequisite* for English 102.

reside/live *Reside* is a more formal (and, to some, more pretentious) word than *live,* but there should be no hesitancy about using it, especially when it is used to indicate place of residence in contrast to a place of employment: "He works in New York City but *resides* in Larchmont."

resin/rosin While *rosin* was once just a variant form of *resin,* each has its particular meaning today. *Resin* is the liquid of a tree; *rosin* is the solid distilled from the liquid.

resolution. *See* TABLE (A RESOLUTION)

resort. *See* RECOURSE/RESOURCE/RESORT

resource. *See* RECOURSE/RESOURCE/RESORT

respective/respectively There are times when *respective* or *respectively* are essential to clarity, but in most cases they are superfluous and the use of them is merely pretentious. One way to test the need for either of them is to eliminate the word and see if the sense of the sentence is affected.

When properly used, each provides a means of matching a list of two or more persons, places, or things with a parallel list of particulars. "Tom, Dick, and Harry had offices in Boston, London, and Philadelphia *respectively*" means that Tom's office was in Boston, Dick's office was in London, and Harry's office was in Philadelphia. "Alice and Joe will report Monday to their *respective* jobs as office manager and switchboard operator" means that Alice will be office manager and Joe will be switchboard operator. If the jobs are not named it is not necessary to say more than "Alice and Joe will report to their jobs on Monday"; there is no need to say "*respective* jobs."

responsible/caused Some people argue that only persons, not things or conditions, can be said to be *responsible,* in the sense of "causing," since only persons can be made to account for or make amends for anything.

This distinction is largely ignored in contemporary usage. The few who do observe it say that certain happenings or conditions *caused* or "resulted in," rather than "were *responsible* for."

restive/restless   In general, *restive* and *restless* are used interchangeably, with *restless* the more common word, but one can be *restless* for no particular reason. *Restive* people are people who are on the verge of rebelling against authority or who, at least, are unhappy about such authority affecting their lives.

restructure. *See* VOGUE WORDS

resume   *Resume,* despite the fact that it retains its French pronunciation (ray-zoo-MAY), has become thoroughly Americanized. It is now commonly written without the acute accent on the first and last "e's."

It is clearly impossible for anyone using a typewriter with a standard keyboard to type in accent marks. When a foreign word has been taken into English, as *resume* has been, it is correct to handle it as you would any other word, leaving off the accents. If the word has not yet become domesticated, it is well to underscore it or set it off with quotation marks. Thus: "chacun a son gout," meaning "everyone to his own taste." In this example, we have omitted two accent marks but the meaning is nonetheless clear and would be clear to anyone familiar with the original adage, even without the quotation marks.

See also VITAE/RESUME.

revenge. *See* AVENGE/REVENGE

reverend   *Reverend* is an adjective and should not be used as a noun, in the opinion of many careful users of English. It is incorrect to say "The Reverend will be here in a minute."

Its use as an adjective is governed by specific rules, the first of which is that it is not a title. It is wrong to refer to or address a minister as "Reverend Crawford." If he holds a Doctor of Divinity degree, he may be called "Dr. Crawford." If not, he should be referred to or addressed as "Mr. Crawford" or, in the case of Roman Catholic priests and some Episcopal priests, "Father Crawford," or, in some orders, "Father John."

When addressing a letter to a clergyman, write "The Reverend Thomas Smith" not just "Reverend Thomas Smith." When speaking or writing of two or more individual clergymen, it is proper to say "The Reverend Messrs. John Crawford, Thomas Smith, and William Jones."

Respect for the clergy and for the language dictate that *reverend* be used as an adjective only. When this happens, perhaps divinity students will be able to discard the doggerel verse long heard on divinity school campuses: "You may call me 'pal,' you may call me 'friend,'/But please don't call me 'Reverend.' "

A dissenting view: The foregoing reflects accurately the feeling of many, if not most, clergymen and of a clear majority of the usage consultants. However, a reasoned and perhaps persuasive dissent was filed by one of the readers of our column. It seems to us worthy of careful consideration.

"Some time ago [writes Jan Suter of Maumee, Ohio] you discussed in your column the use of 'Rev. Jones' in mentioning or addressing a clergyman. I was struck that you (along with the Vanderbilt and other etiquette books) give the Episcopal form as normative for all Protestant groups. My experience has been that the usage of careful and educated speakers in most congregations of Methodists, Baptists, and most smaller denominations is to call the minister a 'reverend.' The word is used as a noun and as a title before his last name.

"I have found that members of most Protestant congregations feel quite awkward in calling a minister 'Mr. Jones'; he's a reverend, not a minister. 'Bill' or 'Bill Jones' will do if the speaker knows him well or if Rev. Jones is informal. But 'Rev. William Jones' gets very fulsome, particularly when used for the fifth time in one conversation or when used to his face. 'Pastor Jones' is, in my experience, a strictly Lutheran dodge. (Maybe it's used in German Reformed circles, but I don't remember ever hearing it in Congregational, Presbyterian, Disciples or other Anglo-American Calvinist-descended groups.) Lots of clergy nowadays go after some doctorate or other, but 'Dr. Jones' doesn't help if he doesn't have some kind of doctorate, honorary or otherwise. And, in any case, the title that is needed is one that shows his standing as a religious man, not one that shows his academic achievements.

"The groups where a significant portion of the congregation is comfortable calling their leader 'Mr. Jones' includes many (if not most) Episcopal parishes, Unitarian churches of the more formal type (particularly around Boston where Unitarianism is Social Register), the Congregationalist congregations in urban areas (but not the more old-fashioned congregations), and no more than a smattering of the more socially ambitious congregations of other denominations.

"Baptist and Methodist ministers are taught in seminaries that they are 'Mr. Jones'—but that's only because lexicographical and etiquette-book standard setters have decreed that that's the 'right way.' My observation has been that not many Methodists, clergy or laity, are very comfortable with the Anglican usage.

"As to whether 'reverend' can be a noun: The *OED* lists 'reverend' as both adjective and substantive (noun). It gives a set of citations from 1608 to 1894 for the use of 'reverend' as a noun, including the philosopher Hume and the novelist Dickens. [NOTE: The citation from Dickens' *Martin Chuzzlewit* strikes us as worth quoting: "Those who had not attained to military honours were either doctors, professors or *reverends.* "]

"My impression is that 'Rev. Jones' is the usual preferred form among most Protestant congregations and that it has been the preferred form for at least 150 years. My opinion further is that attacks on the 'Rev. Jones' usage are mostly 20th century and stem from divisions of social class—upper-class Episcopalians and Unitarians trying to show that they are one up on the Baptists and Methodists whose customs are 'wrong.' . . . Since Roman and Orthodox Catholics are allowed by your authorities to determine the usage for their own titles—and so are Jews, Muslims, and other non-Christian groups—I fail to see why the Baptist custom cannot be given equal courtesy and recognition of grammatical and social correctness when it is applied to the Baptist clergy."

That's the end of the dissenting opinion, one which, as we noted earlier, is reasoned and perhaps persuasive.

reversal/reversion   The distinction between *reversal* and *reversion* is the same as that between the verbs from which they were formed: *reverse* and *revert.*

To *reverse* is "to put in an opposite direction." To *revert* is "to return to a former state, subject, opinion or practice." One can commit a *reversal* of position on an issue simply by announcing a change to a contrary position. One can commit a *reversion* of position only if he had changed his position once already. The position to which he reverts may not be a complete *reversal* but only slightly different.

reverse racism/reverse discrimination   The civil-rights movement to eliminate *racism* from the field of education and employment has resulted in the coinage of the phrase *reverse racism.* When colleges and employers adopted a policy of admitting or employing blacks, Chicanos, and other minority-group members in set ratio to the white students or employees, they were accused of *reverse racism* by white applicants who felt that qualifications of ability rather than race should govern such decisions. *Reverse discrimination* is now more widely used. *See also* RACIST.

revert (back)   A very common misuse of language is found in statements such as "If the committee does not spend the full amount, it will *revert back* to the general treasury of the club." This is clearly redundant.

Revert comes from the Latin "re-" meaning "back" and "vertere" meaning "to turn." "*Revert* to" (without "back") is sufficient.

revocable   *Revocable* should be pronounced REV-uh-kuh-b'l, not reh-VOHK-uh-b'l.

revolution/rebellion/revolt   A television news commentator, in referring to the Hungarian *revolt* of 1956, spoke of it as "the *revolution* that failed." He meant *rebellion*. A *revolution* succeeds. A *rebellion* fails. A *revolt* may or may not succeed.

revolver. *See* PISTOL/AUTOMATIC/REVOLVER

rhetoric   The basic meaning of *rhetoric* is "the art of speaking with eloquence and force" and this meaning has been extended to "artificial eloquence." During what were known as "the radical sixties," when mass demonstrations were taking place on campuses and elsewhere, *rhetoric* came to be used as a synonym for "inflammatory talk." *See also* VOGUE WORDS.

ricochet words   Echoic or reduplicative words, such as "hanky-panky," are also called *ricochet words* and are sometimes coined for humorous effect. Often the repetition of a sound tends to intensify the meaning of the root word. So it is with "hugger-mugger," which means "skullduggery," and which is thought to be a variation of "hoker-moker" from the Middle English "mokeren" ("to hoard or conceal"). Thus the meaning of secrecy or underhandedness is inherent in the root of the word and is strengthened by the repetition.

Other examples of *ricochet words* are: chitchat, harum-scarum, hoity-toity, Ping-Pong, hodge-podge, namby-pamby, boob tube, fiddle-faddle, hot shot, and super-duper.

Although "hugger-mugger" is standard English, most *ricochet words* are informal or slang and should not be used in formal writing or speech.

ride. *See* DRIVE/RIDE

right-of-way   The plural is *rights-of-way*, with the "s" added to the dominant noun, *right*.

rile   In the sense of "to anger or irritate," *rile* has long been considered as either "colloquial" or "dialect" by dictionary editors. Despite the fact that the *American Heritage Dictionary* states that it is "not necessarily inappropriate in formal writing," it should be considered informal at best.

Rio Grande River   A *redundancy* (which see). *Rio* means "river."

riot   *Riot* has many meanings, not all of them involving violence. The slang meaning of "a very funny person or thing" is not too far from the original meaning: debauched revels in which fun and games played a major role.

rip-off/rip off   A *rip-off* is cheating or a burglary. It's a *rip-off* if a purchase turns out to be of little value. It's also a *rip-off* when something is stolen, especially if the theft is accomplished by breaking and entering. When the phrase is used as a verb, there is no hyphen, as in "He told the police that his apartment had been *ripped off* and that his camera, his stereo, and other valuables were missing."

The origin of this phrase is only too obvious to anyone who has lived in crime-stricken sections of our major cities. In New York, the city we know best, drug addicts who perpetrate such thefts will often quite literally *rip off* the door of a flat to gain entrance, usually during the daytime hours when the occupant is at work. It is slang, of course, but colorful slang.

rise/arise/get up   In the sense of "to get out of bed in the morning," *arise* is the most formal of these three, with *rise* also falling in the formal category. *Get up* is the informal and most common usage.

road/street/avenue   A *road* was originally a way for passage of vehicles between one town and another. A *street* is a paved way in a town or city, usually with a walk for pedestrians on one or both sides. An *avenue* is a broad street (Park Avenue in New York City, for example), usually with a border of trees and with wide sidewalks. All three are loosely used, especially *avenue*, which real-estate promoters often apply to small, undistinguished streets in order to make their development sound elegant. All three words are standard English.

road up/road diversion   *Road up* is a British motoring term meaning that the road ahead is being repaired. In consequence, the driver may expect a sign reading *road diversion,* meaning "detour."

rob/steal   *Steal,* meaning "to take something illegally or unfairly," is seldom misused but *rob* has crept into headlines when *steal* is meant. The object of *rob* has to be a person, institution, or establishment (such as a bank or grocery store). In the process, the thief may *steal* money or groceries but he does not *rob* the money or groceries.

robbery/burglary/theft   A *robbery* occurs when one person takes the belongings of another person in the presence of the robbed one, either on the street or elsewhere, by use of threat, force, or violence. A *burglary* involves breaking and entering before stealing takes place. *Theft* is taking possession of valuables in an illegal manner, usually by stealth.

Both *robbery* and *theft* are used figuratively in an extended sense, as in "The cost of food these days is highway *robbery*" and "The candidate charged that the unfounded accusations constituted the *theft* of his good name."

robot   The mispronunciation "row-boat" is heard all too frequently. The correct pronunciation is ROH-but. It comes from the Czech "robota" meaning slave labor or drudgery and was made popular by Karel Capek's 1922 play *R.U.R.* ("Rossum's Universal Robots"), in which mechanical men did the work of human beings.

robust *Robust* may be pronounced either roh-BUST or ROH-bust.

rock hound An informal phrase for geologists and especially amateur geologists who collect specimens of rare rocks as a hobby.

rook *Rook* as a verb is standard English, not slang. It goes back to the time of Shakespeare and derives its meaning of "to swindle or cheat" from the thievishness of the bird of the same name.

rosin. *See* RESIN/ROSIN

round/around British and American usages differ in the case of these two words. The British have almost abandoned *around* as a variant of *round,* though not in such phrases as "*around* and about" and "all *around* us." They still resist the idea that the two words are interchangeable, insisting that a person goes *round* the world, sleeps *round* the clock, or works all year *round.* The theory presumably is that *round* means "circular"; the earth is *round,* clock hands travel in a circle, and the months pass in a rotating fashion, if only figuratively.

In the United States, *round* and *around* are interchangeable in informal use (but there is never an apostrophe in front of *round*).

In formal use, *around* is preferred in all standard meanings of the word (as "on all sides," "in a circle," or "traveling a circular route").

Around, in the sense of "about" or "approximately," is informal, as it is in the sense of "nearby." *See also* ALL-ROUND/ALL-AROUND.

roundabout British term for "traffic circle." Also for "merry-go-round."

route People like Army engineers, bus and plane dispatchers, and others professionally engaged in planning routes tend to pronounce *route* so that it rhymes with "out." Pronouncing it as if it were spelled "root" is, however, equally acceptable.

rubble Strictly speaking, *rubble* is rough fragments of rock or brick. It is a collective noun which can refer to a pile of such fragments or masonry made up of them. Buildings of stone or brick can be converted to *rubble* by earthquake or bombing, but to speak of a city being "smoldering *rubble*" or "flaming *rubble*" is nonsense. "Ruins" perhaps, but certainly not *rubble.*

run/manage/operate *Run*, in the sense of *manage* or *operate* a store or business, is informal and either *manage* or *operate* is preferable in formal contexts. One who *manages* a business is usually thought of as doing it on behalf of the owner, but one who *operates* a business is thought of as the owner, as well as the manager.

rung. *See* RANG/RUNG

Russia/Soviet Union Technically speaking, *Russia* is only one of the fifteen republics of the *Soviet Union* (Union of Soviet Socialist Republics), and its proper name is the Russian Soviet Federated Socialist Republic. Each of these republics has its own language, culture, and history, although the Russian language is becoming more common throughout the *Soviet Union*. As Markian M. Komichak of Pittsburgh wrote us, "Newsmen, journalists, college professors and historians in the West fail to see the distinction between the Soviet Union and Russia. The distinction lies in the difference between a whole and one of its parts."

It is a distinction which we try to observe when the occasion arises, but even dictionaries define *Russia* as "the name commonly applied to the Union of Soviet Socialist Republics."

Rx. *See* RECIPE/RECEIPT/RX

S

sack. *See* BAG/SACK/POKE

sack/get the sack A person who is *sacked* or who *gets the sack* is dismissed from his job. The expressions, more common in the United Kingdom than in the United States, are both considered informal. They are thought to have originated in the early days of the industrial revolution, when an itinerant mechanic would carry his tools with him in a sack. Thus the order *"get your sack"* meant "get ready to leave."

sadism *Sadism*, the procurement of pleasure through inflicting pain on others, may be pronounced either SAD-ism or SAYD-ism. Though the *American Heritage Dictionary* indicates a preference for the latter, we incline to favor the former.

Sahara The commonly heard expression *"Sahara* desert" is redundant, since *sahara* is simply the Arabic word for "desert." Say simply *Sahara* or *The Sahara.*

said The use of *said* to refer to a person or thing previously mentioned (*"said* attorney," *"said* bill of sale") is best restricted to business and legal contexts.

Saint/St. *Saint* is usually spelled in full in referring to a person canonized: *Saint* Matthew, *Saint* Agnes. In place names, it is customarily abbreviated *St.: St.* Louis, *St.* Paul.

salary increment Bureaucratic euphemism for "pay increase."

salmon/salmonella *Salmon,* the fish, is pronounced SAM-un, with the "l" silent. However, the "l" is articulated in the pronunciation of *salmonella,* a disease-causing bacterium commonly associated with food poisoning: sal-mon-EL-uh. There is no connection between the two, etymologically, since *salmonella* gets its name from its discoverer, an American veterinarian named Daniel Salmon.

saloon Among the many efforts of lawmakers to legislate morality, perhaps none was less successful than the pious resolve to "eliminate the corner *saloon,"* when Prohibition finally ended and the public drinking of liquor was again made legal. The *saloon* did not, of course, disappear. It's everywhere around us, disguised as "tavern," "club," "pub," "taproom," "cocktail lounge," or even "café." Still, in most states no pub dares call itself "saloon."

In New York State, for example, the Alcoholic Beverage Control Law of 1934 expressly forbids swinging doors on bars and adds, "It shall be against public policy to permit selling of alcoholic beverages . . . in such premises as were commonly known and referred to as *saloons.*" Two young New Yorkers, ignorant of this nicety in the law, opened a bar which they called "O'Neal's *Saloon.*" Soon they were put right by the authorities and changed the name to "O'Neal's Baloon," causing considerable distress to spelling purists but satisfying the law. Later on, the "B" on "Baloon" unaccountably was lost and the proprietors left the sign reading "O'Neal's aloon," noting that "it has a nice ring to it, if you slur it a bit." The law took no further action.

saloon/sunshine saloon In the U.S. a *saloon* is, as noted above, legally nonexistent but in actuality to be found under a variety of names in every city in the country. In Great Britain a *saloon* is pretty much the same as the automobile Americans call a sedan. A *saloon* with a slide-back roof is, rather charmingly, known as a *sunshine saloon.*

salute/salvo   A *salute,* militarily speaking, may be either a gesture of greeting or recognition or, more formally, the discharge of guns or cannon as a gesture of honor to a visiting dignitary. The origin of the latter custom goes back to the early days of fleet warfare when one ship would greet a friendly ship by discharging all its guns to indicate that it was, temporarily at least, disarmed. These simultaneous discharges of cannon are known as *salvos.* The words are, of course, etymologically related, both stemming eventually from the Latin "salus," health.

salvable/salvageable   *Salvable* and *salvageable* are both entirely correct in the sense of "capable of being salvaged," with the latter perhaps a bit more explicit and more often heard.

same, the   When *same* is used as a pronoun (usually preceded by *the*) its use should be confined to meaning "the identical" or "the equivalent," as in "Under the provisions of his will, each child will receive *the same.*"
   As a substitute for another pronoun, it is not considered good usage, outside of legal documents. "Please fill out the enclosed form and return *same* to me" should be changed to "Please fill out the enclosed form and return it to me."

same difference   Informal idioms in English often violate the rules of logic, as does the phrase *same difference.* In a discussion of which of two roads to take to another town, the verdict that "it's the same difference" would mean that the distance was about the same either way. This seemingly ridiculous idiom is well established in our popular tongue and, as long as it is used casually in conversation, there is no objection to it.

Sam Hill   *Sam Hill,* like "blazes," "heck," "Halifax," and many more, is simply a euphemism for "hell," one very popular with frontiersmen when they felt the need to clean up their language in the presence of ladies. It first appeared in print as long ago as 1839. We're told that Jim Hill, the legendary "empire builder" of the Great Northern Railroad, was so famous for his blasts of outrage when thwarted that Seattle papers carried a standing headline: JIM HILL MAD AS SAM HILL.

sample/example   A column reader objecting to our use of the word *sample* wrote: "More than fifty years ago I wrote on a high school English paper 'The following is a *sample.*' The teacher struck out the 's' in *sample* and replaced it with 'ex,' explaining 'A *sample* is a specimen; an *example* is an illustration.'" This distinction, if it ever had any validity, is long forgotten. Most dictionaries today define *sample* and *example* in terms of each other and indicate that, in many instances, they are interchangeable. Both, indeed, are derived from the same Latin word, "exemplum," which may be translated either as *sample* or as *example.*

sanguine English has several words with two quite contradictory meanings. "Cleave" means to split or separate, but also to cling to or stick fast together. "Ravel" may mean to separate fibers and also to tangle them. "Sanction" may mean permission and approval or a coercive punishment. One of the oddest of these two-faced words is *sanguine.* As one reader of our column wrote: "How can *sanguine* possibly mean such different things as "bloody" and "cheerful"? The "bloody" meaning is obvious, since the word is derived from the Latin "sanguis," meaning blood. The other meaning is based upon the medieval theory that a person's health depended on the dominance of one of four "humors." If the *sanguine* humor dominated, one would have a ruddy complexion and a cheerful disposition.

sank/sunk As the past tense of "sink," *sank* is considered preferable to *sunk,* but either is acceptable.

sartorial/sartorially QUERY: "The other day I noticed a well-dressed man downtown—well dressed except that he was wearing white socks with a dark suit. I remarked to my companion that the white socks were *sartorially* incorrect. Then I checked *sartorial* in the dictionary and found it defined as 'tailored.' Is it correct to use *sartorial* to describe the overall correctness of attire and not just the specific fit of a suit?"

REPLY: Entirely correct. Although *sartorial* (from the Latin "sartor," tailor) originally meant "concerned with tailors and their work," it has been extended in meaning. It may now properly be used to refer to any aspect of men's clothing from an individual item to the complete ensemble.

savings

USAGE PANEL QUESTION

From an advertisement: "Was $42.50. Now only $25.00. A *savings* of $17.50 over usual prices." Do you accept *savings* as a singular noun?
Yes: 28%. No: 72%.

SHANA ALEXANDER: "Yes . . . But only in ads . . . and I really don't accept advertising lingo."

BENJAMIN APPEL: "The 'savings' is both a singular noun and plural—in the sense of 17+ dollars."

ISAAC ASIMOV: "How about 'A saving of $17.50.' *Period.*"

STEWART BEACH: "I have already expressed my horror of 'savings' as a singular. My lowest example is 'Daylight Savings Time.' "

ALVIN BEAM: "Logical enough."

HAL BORLAND: "I wouldn't accept '*a* savings' either. It should read 'A saving of $17.50' . . . period."

ABE BURROWS: "Use 'saving' and put a period after $17.50."

STEPHEN H. FRITCHMAN: "Fire that copywriter!"

PAUL HORGAN: "No, but then language is not always logical."

HERBERT MITGANG: "Yes. The hell with the A & P!"

WRIGHT MORRIS: "This one is a lu-lu. Usage will continue to defy ear, eye and head."

PETER S. PRESCOTT: "Yes, by usage only."

MARK SCHORER: "Since all the rest is so cryptic, why not say only, 'Save $17.50'?"

EARL UBELL: "Advertisements and traffic signs are killing our language."

BILL VAUGHAN: "No. But, after all, it's ad-talk."

A.B.C. WHIPPLE: "Simply use 'saving'; kill 'over usual prices.' "

Because advertisers persist in using *savings* as a singular noun, we again asked the panel whether it has become acceptable. Here are the results:

USAGE PANEL QUESTION—SECOND EDITION

One often sees merchandise advertised at "a *savings*" of X dollars from the original price.

Would you use *savings* as a singular noun in speech? Yes: 22%. No: 78%. In writing? Yes: 10%. No: 90%.

HEYWOOD HALE BROUN: "It is a melancholy fact that every change you offer us is one in the direction of imprecision. Is there no hope for our language?"

FRANCES FRITCHMAN: "If I ever used this dreadful plural—and I may have —I *repent.*"

JOHN K. HUTCHENS: "Why not simply the singular noun 'saving'?"

ORVILLE PRESCOTT: "Reduction is the right word."

HAROLD SCHONBERG: "Yes—and so would 95% of all Americans."

DOLORES SIMON: "Yes, in informal writing."

JACK SMITH: "I have said 'savings,' I'm afraid, but I hate myself for it."

ELVIS STAHR, JR.: "Let us all strive mightily to eradicate this particular pestilence."

say   A book or bulletin may *say* something quite as well as a person. It's true, of course, that the primary meaning of *say* is to utter or speak, but its figurative extension to use by inanimate objects is centuries old. For example: "The Bible *says*. . . ."

say (used adverbially)   *Say* may be used *adverbially* in any context in the sense of "for example" ("any domestic animal, *say* the dog") or "nearly, about" ("He was traveling fast, *say* eighty miles per hour").

scan   *Scan* as a transitive verb has two diametrically opposed meanings and the one intended has to be made clear. It can mean either to look over in a perfunctory manner, as in "*scan* the headlines," or to go over very thoroughly. In scientific usage, the second meaning is more common, as is reflected in the term "brain-*scan*," a device for or method of monitoring the functioning of the brain.

scarcely   *Scarcely,* like *hardly* (which see), serves as a negative and should not be accompanied by another negative word. "With *scarcely* a sound, he crossed the room and left" but not "Without *scarcely* a sound. . . ."

scenario   During the exposure of the Watergate scandals there were many references to the *scenarios* for various activities and programs. This is a term which has been in use in the theater for a very long time, but the implication of it as a political term was that all the participants were acting in a predetermined fashion with carefully rehearsed lines, as actors do in the theater. *See also* ORCHESTRATE.

scene   *Scene,* which has always meant the place where something happens, now has an extended slang sense roughly equivalent to "situation," as in "With the two women arguing and the two men sulking it was a bad *scene.*" Used this way, *scene* does not mean that the people were making spectacles of themselves but simply that it was an unpleasant situation.

scheme   In the United States *scheme* has distinct connotations of sly conniving or underhanded business practice and intrigue. In Great Britain these derogatory implications are absent and *scheme* means simply "plan."

schlemiel. *See* YIDDISHISMS

schlep. *See* YIDDISHISMS

schlock   *Schlock* (pronounced SHLOK) is a Yiddishism used to describe any piece of inferior, cheaply made merchandise, from a bedroom suite (pronounced SUIT by those who sell *schlock*) to a trashy novel.

schmaltz. *See* YIDDISHISMS

schmooze *Schmooze* is a Yiddishism meaning to gossip idly as a way of passing the time. Noontime on Seventh Avenue in New York sees every street corner occupied by groups of dressmakers and suitmakers *schmoozing*. *Schmooze* should be used only in informal contexts.

schnook This is a Yiddish-American slang term for a person easily tricked: a very gullible, often stupid, person. *See also* YIDDISHISMS.

schnorrer. *See* YIDDISHISMS

schtick. *See* YIDDISHISMS

schwa The *schwa* (pronounced SHWAH) is the symbol resembling an upside-down "e" which appears in most new American dictionaries published since World War II. It represents the unstressed vowel sound in words like *a*bout, circ*u*s, and gall*o*p. In this dictionary we usually represent that sound by "uh," which is not quite as accurate as the *schwa* but is as close as we can come using the ordinary letters of the alphabet.

The *schwa* first appeared as one of the many symbols making up the International Phonetic Alphabet, which is widely used by teachers of speech and constitutes the most accurate method of transcribing the sounds we make in speech. Unfortunately, the considerable variety of symbols involved in the IPA makes it impractical for use in general dictionaries. Nonetheless, when Clarence Barnhart was editing the first major college dictionary of the post–World War II era, the *American College Dictionary*, he decided to use the *schwa* for the first time in a dictionary intended for the general reader. His reason was that it recorded the unstressed vowel sound more accurately than any of the various "Websterian" symbols that had previously been used. The *schwa* caught on quickly and now is used even in dictionaries for very young readers, like the Xerox-Ginn Beginning and Intermediate dictionaries, edited by the editors of this dictionary.

scissors (is/are) According to most dictionaries *scissors* is a plural noun which may be used with either a singular or plural verb. In other words, one may say either "The *scissors* is on the table" or "The *scissors* are on the table." We incline to favor the latter, if only because "The *scissors* is . . ." sounds more like a hiss than a rational statement.

score. *See* MARGIN/SCORE

Scotch woodcock Like *Welsh rabbit* (which see) this is a dish bearing no literal connection whatever to the actual bird called *woodcock.* It's simply a light dish of scrambled eggs, served on toast or crackers that have been spread with anchovy paste or anchovies. It is popular in the United Kingdom and is sometimes seen on American restaurant menus.

sculpt/sculpture   As verbs, *sculpt* and *sculpture* are equally acceptable.

scunner   *Scunner* is a Scottish dialect term meaning "intense dislike." One takes a *scunner* to another person. Though chiefly heard in the United Kingdom, it is not unknown in the United States. Indeed, your editor heard it first from the late Professor George Pierce Baker, founder of the Yale Department of Drama, who once said: "William, I took a *scunner* to Alexander Woollcott the first time I saw him—and have never had any reason to change my opinion."

search and destroy/search and clear. *See* EUPHEMISM

seasonal/seasonable   *Seasonal* applies to that which is affected by or controlled by the season of the year. *Seasonable* applies to that which is timely or appropriate to a particular season. A *seasonal* rise in profits is experienced by retail stores during the holiday season because of gift purchases; the rise in profits is *seasonal* because it tends to recur at the same season each year. High temperatures are *seasonable* in July and August in Ohio; freezing weather would not be.

seat of government. *See* CAPITAL/SEAT OF GOVERNMENT

secret tryst. *See* TRYST and REDUNDANCY

-sede. *See* -CEDE/-CEED/-SEDE

seed   *Seed* is an item of the jargon of sports, especially of tennis. It refers to the practice of scattering *(seeding)* the names of superior players in a tournament line-up in such a way as to guarantee that the top contestants won't face each other in the early matches. No sponsor of a tournament wants to risk having his stars cancel each other out of contention in the early rounds of play.

see if I can/can't   *See if I can't* in such expressions as "I'll *see if I can't* get the job done today" is illogical, for the intent of the speaker is that he will see if he *can* get the job done. However, the idiom is well established, almost to the point of rating with H. W. Fowler's "sturdy indefensibles," and must be accepted on the level of informal speech.

seem. *See* LINKING VERBS

seen *Seen* in such expressions as "I *seen* her yesterday" is wrong. At best it might be classed as a dialectal peculiarity; at worst as simply illiterate. Say rather: "I saw" or "I have *seen*."

seiche A *seiche* is described in this fashion by a native of Green Bay, Wisconsin: "On a perfectly calm day with not a ripple and the surface glassy, the water in the lake will gradually rise three or four feet, then gradually return to its former level. The cycle may be repeated several times and each cycle may take about ten minutes." In Green Bay the pronunciation of *seiche* is SEECH, rhyming with "peach" and "beach." However, the major dictionaries insist that *seiche* should be pronounced SAYSH. Nevertheless, we counseled the local residents to continue to use the prevailing local pronunciation because it is the pronunciation established in the region and anything else would sound false and affected for, as one native put it, "we're afraid to use the Webster pronunciation for fear of being thought queer." It seems to us that, in these days of omnipresent radio and TV, the language is in peril of becoming homogenized and of having all local color drained out of it by the bland and colorless announcers on the air and on the tube.

seldom. *See* ALMOST NEVER

self *Self* as a suffix forms intensive and reflexive pronouns: *myself, yourself, himself, herself, itself, ourselves, yourselves, themselves,* and *oneself.* Properly used to add emphasis ("She can do it *herself*") or to reflect back to the subject ("I hurt *myself*"), the *self* pronouns are sometimes susceptible to misuse, especially in the first person singular (see *me/I/myself* and *I*). When *self* is used as a prefix, it should be separated from the root word by a hyphen: "*self*-esteem."

self-addressed Occasionally a nit-picking correspondent will register a complaint like this one: "Your column mentions that answers will be sent if the reader encloses a *self-addressed* envelope. An envelope, being inanimate, is obviously incapable of addressing itself." The answer to this particular asininity is that the word *self* in such compounds may be considered either as the doer of the action or as the object thereof. In the former instance we have such a phrase as "self-appointed leader." In the latter case, *self-addressed.*

self-defeating. *See* COUNTERPRODUCTIVE/SELF-DEFEATING

self-deprecate/-depreciate. *See* DEPRECATE/DEPRECIATE

self-destruct *Self-destruct* as a verb was popularized during the 1960s by a television show named *Mission Impossible:* "In five seconds this tape will *self-destruct.*" However, it has been a part of space age jargon for a much longer time, though used mostly as an adjective in phrases like "*self-destruct* button." Here, in the words of a long-time space engineer, is the explanation: "Almost all missile guidance systems have two or more safety systems built in to protect populated areas from missiles, atmospheric probes, and so forth, which may have deviated from the planned path. One system can, in the early stages, be operated by the range officer. He simply presses a *destruct* button on his panel and an explosive charge in the 'bird' blows it to smithereens. When a longer-range 'bird' is being flown, it could wander off line while out of range of the launch site. Then a built-in sensor activates the explosive charge to destroy the 'bird.' This is known as the *self-destruct* button. Such systems are practically foolproof." That "practically" leaves us a bit shaken. In any event, *self-destruct* should be used only in technical contexts, unless used with deliberate jocosity—and that seems a trifle inappropriate under the circumstances.

seltzer/soda/pop/tonic/sparkling water *Seltzer,* sometimes called *seltzer water,* and *soda,* also called *club soda* or *soda water,* are virtually the same thing—a sparkling, flavorless, effervescent beverage, usually produced by charging plain water under pressure with carbon dioxide gas. The older name, *seltzer,* derives from the name of a town in Germany, Nieder Selters, where a similar naturally effervescent spring water was found. The terms *soda* and *soda water* do not appear in English until midway through the nineteenth century. They derive from the fact that early versions were made by adding bicarbonate of soda to water. In recent decades the term *club soda* has replaced *seltzer* in many parts of the U.S., though during the earlier years of the century plain *soda* for use in homes or clubs was usually bottled in siphon bottles and one asked for a siphon of *seltzer.*

With the repeal of Prohibition, bottlers of carbonated beverages found that they had a substantial market for what they soon labeled *sparkling water* or *soda.* The retreat from the word *seltzer* was doubtless influenced by widespread advertising of headache remedies with *seltzer* as part of their trade names. Obviously beverage manufacturers didn't care to associate the pleasures of party tippling with the horrors of the morning after, so the semantically infelicitous *seltzer* was doomed.

Flavored carbonated beverages are called *pop* in most areas of the U.S. However, in parts of New England and notably in the vicinity of Boston, such beverages as ginger ale and root beer are classified under the generic term *tonic.* So, if you hear a Bostonian suggest taking a few bottles of *tonic* along on a picnic, he's not talking about medicine, nor is he referring to the quinine water which is often called *tonic* by partisans of gin and *tonic.*

semantics. *See* VOGUE WORDS

semester/trimester A news dispatch about a college's plan to change from the conventional two-*semester* to a *trimester* academic year caused confusion in some minds. "Should that not be three-*semester* rather than *trimester?*" ran one query. The answer is "no" and the reason can be found in the Latin roots of the words involved. *"Semester"* is derived from the Latin words "sex," six, and "mensis," month, and originally meant a six-month or half-year period. It came in time to mean half a school year, not a literal six-month period. *Trimester* derives from the Latin "tres," three, and the same "mensis," and means a three-month period. In some schools the term is used literally; in others it simply means that the academic year is divided into three parts, each called a *trimester.*

semi-. *See* PREFIXES AND SUFFIXES, WITH AND WITHOUT HYPHEN

semicolon The primary function of the *semicolon* is to separate two independent elements of a sentence when they are not connected by a conjunction such as "and" or "but." Frequently these elements are closely related in concept: "Love is a lasting thing; flirtation is transitory." The *semicolon* may also be used to separate items in a long and complicated list: "Necessary to the completion of the task will be three autos, each seating six people; four armored weapons carriers, each manned by four soldiers; and an escort of motorcycles, each with an armed rider."

NOTE: *Semicolons* may also be used between two independent clauses when the second clause is introduced by "however," "moreover," or "nevertheless": "He had behaved badly; nevertheless I introduced him to my family."

semicolon, disappearance of QUERY: "What has happened to the *semicolon?* This item of punctuation is frequently omitted from printed matter. Where the *semicolon* should be used, commas are frequently thrown in. I correspond with an English professor; and he, too, is guilty of this error."

REPLY: One thing that has happened to the *semicolon* is that it is sometimes thrown in where it is neither wanted nor needed—and the last sentence of this query is a good example. Here we have an ordinary compound sentence: two complete statements linked by a coordinating conjunction, "and." In such cases the *semicolon* is superfluous. If the "and" were omitted, the *semicolon* would, of course, be the appropriate punctuation between the clauses. But never both "and" and the *semicolon.*

On the broader question, it's quite true that the *semicolon* seems to be vanishing. Perhaps the reason is to be found in the trend toward short, trenchant sentences starting in the 1920s with the prose of Hemingway and his followers and imitators. *Time* style, pioneered by Briton Hadden and Henry Luce, was responsible for some remarkably convoluted sentences (in Wolcott Gibbs's immortal phrase, "until backward reeled the mind") but it did emphasize "curt, clear, concise" sentences—and that would mean fewer *semicolons.* As one of our talented writer friends, the late Earl Schenck Miers, once remarked to us: "When I find I am writing into a *semicolon,* I know I'm in trouble—and that my reader will be in trouble, too. So I go back and start the sentence over, limiting it to one basic idea and holding the rest for separate expression in later sentences."

Miers was speaking particularly of the problem of writing succinct, readable prose for a broad audience including many young readers. But the precept he set forth is followed by the vast majority of writers for newspapers, magazines, and books today. Except for an occasional "think piece" on the editorial page, you will not find many *semicolons*—if any. So the gradual disappearance of the *semicolon* is only one aspect of the long-range trend away from formalism in virtually all media of communication and in the direction of more informal, colloquial means of expression.

seminal. *See* VOGUE WORDS

sensuous/sensual

USAGE PANEL QUESTION

Thanks to wide circulation of sex guides incorporating the word *sensuous* in their titles, the distinction between *sensual* (pertaining to the gratification of physical appetites, especially those of a sexual nature) and *sensuous* (pertaining to the senses, especially those involved in the appreciation of art, music, and poetry) seems to have been lost, at least temporarily. Do you regard the distinction between *sensual* and *sensuous* as worth retaining?

Yes: 82%. No: 18%.

ISAAC ASIMOV: "No. Why treat sexual perception as different from other senses? Victorianism."

HAL BORLAND: "Those I see use sexual, not sensual. There's no punch to sensual *or* sensuous. Let's keep them properly apart, even in bed."

HEYWOOD HALE BROUN: "There should be different words for listening to music and making love. We're confused enough."

WILLARD R. ESPY: "I still get a different sensation from a pretty girl than from a Beethoven symphony. Damn it, I *need* two words."

GEROLD FRANK: "The latter has always been a powerful word to me—the very feel of it is sensuous."

STEPHEN H. FRITCHMAN: "This misuse always makes me nauseated (*not* nauseous)."

S. I. HAYAKAWA: "Yes. But it's a tough fight!"

NORMAN HOSS: "It is gone."

JOHN K. HUTCHENS: "Let's not lose this one!"

ALEXANDER KENDRICK: "Yes. But it seems a hopeless cause."

WALTER LORD: "Hold that line!"

PHYLLIS McGINLEY: "Each time we blur the distinction, we cheapen the language."

WRIGHT MORRIS: "Yes, but I'm not hopeful."

ORVILLE PRESCOTT: "Yes, but a lost cause."

PETER S. PRESCOTT: "It must be retained! Are we really reduced to saying that Henry James has a masterful approach to sensual description? If so, we can no longer make ourselves understood."

VERMONT ROYSTER: "The mistaking of a sensuous person with a sensual one leads to some disappointments."

DANIEL SCHORR: "Many use 'sensuous' because they think they have found a euphemism for 'sensual.' "

ERICH SEGAL: "Yes, but there's little hope for purists."

CHARLES E. SILBERMAN: "Yes, but I doubt that the distinction can be restored."

BILL VAUGHAN: "Yes, but a losing cause."

DOUGLAS WATT: "It's probably too late for that."

HERMAN WOUK: "Yes, but a lost, lost cause."

sequence of tenses. *See* TENSES, SEQUENCE OF

set/sit *Set* is most commonly used as a transitive verb ("She *set* the table"), while *sit* is most commonly an intransitive verb ("He *sits* in the corner"). There are exceptions, however. A hen may *set* or *sit* upon her eggs and the sun *sets,* not *sits.*

set back This verb idiom is capable of two entirely different interpretations. The first and obvious meaning is to put back to an earlier point of time, as when one *sets back* the hands of a watch when changing time zones. But there is also the meaning of "hinder" and hence "delay." Thus a doctor might say that a patient's recovery was *set back* by his failure to respond to treatment—and thus the recovery would occur at a later time. There is certainly no logic in a single phrase being capable of two entirely opposite meanings—but then, no one ever successfully accused English of being logical.

sewer commission/pollution-control agency. *See* EUPHEMISM

sexism *Sexism* is widely used as a result of the growth of the Women's Liberation Movement. It is used to denote attitudes and practices based on prejudice because of sex alone, without regard to individual worth. *See also* FEMINIST and FEM LIB/FEMLIB.

sexism in language With the growth of the Women's Movement and the civil-rights movement a new interest developed in the way members of minority groups and all women were being treated in writing, especially in textbooks, news publications, and government documents. The result was a campaign to eliminate sexist as well as racist language wherever possible.

While any effort to legislate language on a broad scale is not only impossible but extremely unwise, the enforcement of the Civil Rights Act of 1964 by the Equal Employment Opportunity Commission has resulted in strict guidelines governing the language which can be used in help-wanted advertisements. Directives by the commission not only prohibit entirely the use of language which would "indicate a preference, limitation, specification or discrimination based on sex unless sex is a bona fide occupational qualification for the particular job involved" but also prohibit the use of words or phrases whose formulations indicate one sex or the other.

Thus synonyms have had to be found for such terms as "foreman," "draftsman," and "busboy." Help-wanted advertisements, which were formerly divided into separate columns of "Help Wanted—Male" and "Help Wanted—Female" are now combined in single columns headed "Help Wanted." "Girl Friday" has become "Girl/Man Friday." Employment agencies or companies which place the advertisements are legally responsible for any violation of the commission's directives, but responsible newspapers throughout the country refuse to accept advertising whose wording violates the guidelines of the commission.

So, to an extent, we have legislation of language, even though it be in a very special area.

The U.S. Department of Labor has revised its *Dictionary of Occupational Titles* with corrections in titles having sex and/or age connotations.

The latest revisions in the *DOT,* as it is called, include the following types of changes. Sex stereotyped language: with certain exceptions, language such as "man," "woman," or "lady" and suffixes that denote sex, such as "-ess," have been removed from Dictionary job titles and titles changed to neuter titles: e.g., "public relations man" changed to "public relations practitioner" or "shoe repairman" changed to "shoe repairer." Excepted titles include those (a) for which sex or age is a bona fide occupational requirement: e.g., the jobs of Leading Lady, Leading Man, and Juvenile and (b) whose titles have been fixed by legislation, international treaties, or other binding agreements, such as in the case of "master," "able seaman," and other marine occupational titles which are identified both by United States codes and international treaties, or "masseur" and "masseuse," whose sexual duality has been established by an administrative ruling. "Master" is to be eliminated, with the exception of job titles covered by legislation. "Yardmaster" has been changed to "yard manager." (NOTE: In church circles, the term "choir master" is being replaced by "choir director.")

Another government agency which has made official changes in the language it uses is the Bureau of the Census, which has changed the terms for 52 of its 441 work categories in an effort to eliminate sex stereotyping. Here are some examples:

OLD	NEW
credit men	credit and collection managers
newsboys	newspaper carriers and vendors
foremen	blue-collar worker supervisors
telephone linemen and splicers	telephone line installers and repairers
furnace men	furnace tenders
motormen	rail vehicle operators
fishermen	fishers
busboys	waiters' assistants
firemen	firefighters
chambermaids	lodging quarters cleaners
charwomen	building interior cleaners
airline stewardesses	flight attendants
laundresses	launderers
maids and servants	private household cleaners

The growing awareness of the extent to which choice of words may result in discrimination is found in the passage by state legislatures of general statutes which establish that existing laws which refer to "men" are applicable to women to the same degree. In the state of Connecticut, further efforts have been made to "sex-neutralize" the laws by writing new legislation in such a way as to use the forms "wo/man," "s/he," or at least "his/her" or "widow/widower." Pension laws are being amended to include the word "widower" as well as "widow."

Major book publishing firms, especially those which publish teaching materials, reference books, and nonfiction books, have issued guidelines for their authors and editors concerning avoidance of words which could result in stereotyping of both men and women. In some instances this is a matter of not assigning roles or characteristics to one particular sex. In others it is a matter of the form of the word used to describe a person, as in "firefighter" instead of "fireman." Scott, Foresman and Company, publishers of textbooks, was one of the first, with its "Guidelines for Improving the Image of Women in Textbooks."

A broader and more comprehensive manual was issued by McGraw-Hill Book Company, in which its objective was stated as "to show the role language has played in reinforcing inequality; and to indicate positive approaches toward providing fair, accurate, and balanced treatment of both sexes in our publications." These guidelines are intended primarily for use in teaching materials, reference works, and nonfiction works in general.

McGraw-Hill's "Guidelines for Equal Treatment of Sexes" was so enthusiastically received that it was entered in its entirety in the *Congressional Record*. It has been recently revised and expanded "to keep pace with a changing society" and now runs to 17 pages and incorporates many of the *DOT* designations.

The basic premise of the Guidelines is stated as "Men and women should be treated as individual people, not primarily as members of the opposite sex." Other recommendations include:

Using parallel language: parallel language should be used for women and men. Avoid the subtle stereotyping of women by roles. Women should be referred to as "ladies" only when men are referred to as "gentlemen." ("Husband and wife" rather than "man and wife.")

Titles: The same nomenclature should be used for the same job or position held by a man or a woman. Whenever possible, terms should be used which include both sexes.

Including women as participants: Women should be spoken of as participants in the world in their own right. Terms like "pioneer," "farmer," and "settler" should clearly include females as well as males. (Example: "Pioneer families moved west," not "Pioneers moved west, taking their wives and children with them.")

Describing women and men: Women and men should be treated with the same respect, dignity, and seriousness. . . . Although many of the inappropriate terms listed here . . . are being used less and less, they still appear occasionally and should be avoided.

NO	YES
the fair sex; the weaker sex	women
the girls or the ladies (when adult females are meant)	the women
girl, as in: I'll have my girl check that.	I'll have my secretary (or my assistant) check that. (Or use the person's name.)
lady used as a modifier, as in lady lawyer	lawyer

female-gender word forms, such as *authoress, poetess, Jewess*	*author, poet, Jew*
female-gender or diminutive word forms such as *suffragette, usherette, aviatrix*	*suffragist, usher, aviator* (or *pilot*)
libber	*feminist, liberationist*
co-ed (as a noun)	*student*
housewife	*homemaker*
career girl, career woman, cleaning lady, cleaning woman	Name the person's profession: *housekeeper, house cleaner, office cleaner.*

Avoiding "man" words: In references to humanity at large, gender-specific terms should be avoided whenever possible. The word "man," long used to denote all of humanity, perpetuates bias. The following alternatives are recommended.

mankind, man	*humanity, human beings, human race, people, men and women*
man's achievements	*human* achievements, *society's* achievements
manpower	*humanpower, human energy, workers, work force, personnel*
manhood	*adulthood, manhood, womanhood*
the average *man*	the average *person*

Choosing figures of speech: Figures of speech which are, or seem to be, sexist should be avoided. Expressions like "man in the street" are best reworded entirely rather than replaced with "man or woman in the street."

Using pronouns: The English language lacks a non-gender-specific singular personal pronoun. Although masculine pronouns have generally been used for reference to a hypothetical person or to humanity in general (in such constructions as "anyone . . . he" and "each child opened his book"), the following alternatives are recommended as preferable.

1. Recast to eliminate unnecessary gender-specific pronouns.
2. Use a plural form of the pronoun—a very simple solution and often the best.
3. Recast in the passive voice making sure there is no ambiguity.
4. Use "one" or "we."
5. Use a relative clause. (Example: "A mechanic who is checking the brakes must observe several precautions.")

6. Recast to substitute antecedent for the pronoun.
7. Use "he or she," or "his or her." (These expressions have passed easily into wide use.)

These guidelines have been incorporated into *The McGraw-Hill Style Manual: a Concise Guide for Writers and Editors,* edited by Marie M. Longyear, under the heading "Bias-Free Publishing," which also covers the proper use of terms applied to minority groups.

A more exhaustive treatment of the subject may be found in *The Handbook of Non-Sexist Writing for Writers, Editors and Speakers* by Casey Miller and Kate Swift (Lippincott & Crowell, New York).

Even *Roget's International Thesaurus* has eliminated words that are "biased, warped, twisted, swayed, jaundiced, closed, clannish, and cliquish." Sexist language has been changed so that "mankind" has become "humankind," "rich man" is now "rich person," and "countryman" is "country dweller."

The introduction to the McGraw-Hill guidelines states: "We realize that the language of literature cannot be prescribed." We agree, but we predict that changing social patterns will have an effect on the language, just as they have always had.

shake one's head "yes"   According to one column reader the expression "he *shook his head yes*" has appeared in print with increasing frequency. This blurs a useful, if modest, distinction because, as the same correspondent points out, if one can *shake his head "yes,"* there's no real reason why he can't nod his head "no." The careful writer will continue to observe the distinction and "nod" the head when signifying "yes," while *shaking the head* to signify "no."

shall/will   There once was a "rule" that one should use *shall* in the first person singular and plural ("I *shall*" and "we *shall*") to express simple futurity, and *will* in the second and third persons for the same purpose ("you *will*" and "he, she, it, or they *will*"). Precisely the reverse was to be used to express determination. This so-called "rule" is almost never observed today and may be said to have received its death blow when General Douglas MacArthur expressed his determination to recapture the Philippines not, as the rule would have it, by saying, "I *will* return," but with the flat statement "I *shall* return." Today, even among educated speakers, the prevailing tendency is to express simple futurity in all persons with *will* ("I *will,* you *will,* he *will,* etc."). Ohio-born James Thurber put it more colorfully: "Men who use '*shall*' west of the Appalachians are the kind who twirl canes and eat ladyfingers."

shambles

USAGE PANEL QUESTION

Panelist WALTER W. "RED" SMITH asks: "Has the panel yet considered 'shambles,' as in 'This living room is a shambles,' meaning that somebody has left Sunday's funny papers all over the floor? The other day I heard a space cadet on radio say that something or somebody had been reduced to a shamble. And he wasn't describing a gait." Would you accept "shamble" as used by the space cadet?

Yes: 22%. No: 78%.

ISAAC ASIMOV: "Of course not."

SHERIDAN BAKER: "Good grief!"

ALVIN BEAM: "I can scarcely imagine a modern writer's using 'shambles' as a term for a bloody battlefield. To the knowing he would sound archaic; to the non-knowing, flip."

BARRY BINGHAM, SR.: "Impossible usage."

HAL BORLAND: "A 'shamble' is a meat market when it isn't a lazy gait."

HEYWOOD HALE BROUN: " 'Shambles,' like funnies, come only in the plural."

ABE BURROWS: "I knew a lady who asked for 'a Kleenek' as the obvious singular of Kleenex."

PAUL HORGAN: "Not a matter of style—it's the actual meaning that is unclear."

JOHN K. HUTCHENS: "No—except as a kind of reaching for comic effect, and even then it wouldn't be so very funny."

HELEN L. KAUFMANN: "Strictly speaking, only a butcher can create a shambles."

ALEXANDER KENDRICK: "Not until a kudo is similarly accepted."

WADE MOSBY: "We had an editor who insisted that 'shambles' referred to a slaughterhouse, and wouldn't allow its use in any other context. That sort of thinking should be relegated to the slaughterhouse. Americans use it in terms of a general mess, and I certainly accept their word for it."

PETER S. PRESCOTT: "Out of ignorance, perhaps, but yes."

LEO ROSTEN: "No, but it's good as humor."

HAROLD SCHONBERG: "Yes, even though technically wrong."

CHARLES E. SILBERMAN: "I would reserve 'shambles' for greater disarray than simply leaving the newspapers lying around."

WALTER W. "RED" SMITH: "I won't hold still for any variety of 'shamble,' singular or plural, unless it means a butcher's block, a scene of blood and destruction, not just an untidy room or unruly lodge meeting."

LIONEL TRILLING: "The common use of 'shambles' is absurd enough!"

BILL VAUGHAN: "Neither 'shamble' nor 'shambles.' A shambles is an abattoir, it has to have blood."

A.B.C. WHIPPLE: "Even the plural 'shambles' is often misused."

HERMAN WOUK: "It has passed into the language as a counter word, a very worn one."

shanty Irish. *See* IRISH, BOG-TROTTING/LACE-CURTAIN/SHANTY

Shavian *Shavian* (pronounced SHAY-vee-un) is an adjective coined in the manner of "Shakespearian" and "Wagnerian" and means concerning or characteristic of the person or works of George Bernard Shaw. Unlike the two adjectives relating to Shakespeare and Wagner, however, *Shavian* was coined by the author himself. "Shawian," the logical adjective, apparently sounded awkward to this self-confessed genius, so he went to some pains to create his own adjective, inventing first the word "Shavius," as a Latinized form of "Shaw," and then deriving *Shavian* from it.

"she" as pronoun for ships Ships through all recorded history have been referred to in the feminine gender. One theory is that this results from the fact that to the sailor of old, embarked on voyages of a year or more in length, the ship was nearer and dearer than anything save his wife or mother. Less sentimental students of language, however, note that in many of the world's tongues, excluding English, all nouns have gender: masculine, feminine, or neuter. In the Romance languages, starting with the Latin "navis," the word for ship is invariably in the feminine gender. Thus seafaring men have for many centuries been accustomed to referring to their ships by using the feminine pronoun. So, even though English nouns do not have gender, the custom of referring to ships as *she* continues—occasionally with ludicrous results. Note this from a news story of a few years back: "Defense needs have given a new lease on life to two laid-up troop transports . . . the *General Robert E. Callan* and her sister ship, the *General Harry Taylor.*"

shelf-life. *See* VOGUE WORDS

sheveled. *See* ARCANE WORDS **and** LOST POSITIVES

shew/show *Shew* was the standard spelling of *show* in the eighteenth century, though the pronunciation then, as now, was SHOH. If it seems odd that the "ew" element should be pronounced "oh," give a thought to the word "sew," which still has that sound. By the end of the nineteenth century *shew* had virtually disappeared, except for its use by C. K. Scott-Moncrieff in his translation of Proust's *Remembrance of Things Past* and Shaw's use of it in his play *The Shewing-up of Blanco Posnet.*

ship/boat. *See* BOAT/SHIP

shoot deer in the balcony. *See* DEER IN THE BALCONY, SHOOT

shop (a store) The use of *shop* as a transitive verb ("We *shopped* Lazarus today") began during the 1930s when major department stores, like Macy's and Gimbels in New York, proudly boasted that "we will not be undersold." To make good on their boast, they employed comparison shoppers, who *shopped* the rival stores, reporting any prices that were lower than their own. Gradually what began as a special part of trade jargon crept over into the language spoken by the general public. While we would prefer that *shop* as a transitive verb be restricted to the jargon of the trade, we recognize that it is becoming more and more commonly used in the speech of literate Americans and hence must be considered acceptable in informal contexts.

short-lived/long-lived. *See* LIVED, LONG-/SHORT-

short-sighted *Short-sighted* in British usage has nothing to do with the American concept of lacking imagination or foresight. In British usage *short-sighted* simply means what Americans mean by "near-sighted."

should of/could of/would of These are common but illiterate mis-pronunciations of "should've," "could've," and "would've," which are perfectly acceptable informal contractions of "should have," "could have," and "would have." Occasionally, when we make this point, readers will accuse us of having tin ears, claiming that there is no such thing as *should of* and that we are actually hearing "should've." That this is patently untrue is illustrated by history's most famous instance of the use of *should of,* this by the famed fight manager, Joe Jacobs. One day in 1935 he left a hospital sickbed to attend a World Series game, only to see the team he had bet on go down to defeat. Asked to comment, Jacobs uttered the practically deathless line: "I *should of* stood in bed." *See also* STOOD/-STAYED.

show. *See* SHEW/SHOW

shower activity The advent on the television screen of wordy weather forecasters has resulted in the creation of many pompous phrases such as *shower activity* for what is simply "rain" or "showers." We once heard a report of "cloud activity."

shrink *Shrink* is slang for psychiatrist or psychoanalyst—and thoroughly detested by practitioners of both those medical specialties. The expression probably originated as "head shrinker," a derisory reference to efforts of psychiatrists to shrink or otherwise deflate the delusions of grandeur of some of their patients.

shuck   Show-business slang for a *put-on* (which see) or phony or elaborate hoax. According to one authority the imitation Beatles group called "The Monkees" was "nothing but a shuck."

Shut (hush) my mouth!   *Shut (or hush) my mouth* used to be a common expression of astonishment, especially among Southern blacks. The idea is that one is so surprised that he is, or should be, struck dumb. It should be considered dialect and not to be used in formal contexts.

shyster. *See* SNOLLYGOSTER

sibling   *Sibling* is a word voguish in the language of sociologists, psychiatrists, and other purveyors of specialized jargon. Actually it is a very old word, being traceable to Middle English and eventually to the Anglo-Saxon "sib," meaning kinship. In Middle English *sibling* meant any kind of relative, but in its current U.S. use it means children born at different times to the same parents. However, the *OED* extends *sibling* to "children having one or both parents in common," indicating that in England half-brothers and half-sisters also qualify as *siblings.* The term is perhaps most commonly heard in a phrase from the literature of psychiatry— "*sibling* rivalry." In our family we prefer to refer to this phenomenon by the more felicitous phrase coined by novelist Peter DeVries—"*sibling* revelry."

sic/c.q.   The expression *sic,* usually in parentheses *(sic)*, is used as a warning to the typesetter or typist to follow copy precisely, especially in cases where a spelling differs from the customary spelling: "Katharine *(sic)* Cornell." The expression *c.q.,* also in parentheses *(c.q.),* is similarly though less frequently used. *Sic* is the Latin word "thus" and is pronounced SIK. *C.q.* is a radio-telegraphy code symbol, designed to alert all listeners. It originally was short for "call to quarters." *Sic* is also used in quoted matter to show that a misspelling is in the original.

sick/ill   Some careful speakers make a distinction between *sick* and *ill,* using *sick* only to describe instances where the victim is physically nauseated, and *ill* in all other contexts. This distinction is still observed in England; indeed, the World Webster calls nausea the "dominant" meaning of *sick* in England. Curiously enough, this is based solely on what Fowler and Gowers call the "English love of euphemism which, shrinking from the blunt word *vomit,* has appropriated *sick* to that use, transferring its more general sense to *ill.*" So it would appear that this use of *ill* in lieu of *sick* is a nice-nellyism borrowed from England.

sick at/to one's stomach   Despite the complaints of a few purists that one cannot be *sick to one's stomach* but must be *sick at one's stomach,* both versions are perfectly acceptable idioms. Indeed, we suspect *sick to one's stomach* is rather more widely used. Both expressions should be considered informal.

sick-out   This is an item of labor-union jargon that describes the action or inaction of public servants who try to enforce their demands for increased pay by failing to appear for work, claiming sickness as the reason. The *sick-out* most seriously endangers the public weal when resorted to by firemen and policemen, but somehow we find the expression *sick-out* most irritating when used by schoolteachers, who, of all people, should have more respect for the language.

The tactic is used primarily by workers who are forbidden by law to go on strike. A *sick-out* by policemen is also called "blue flu."

sick with a temperature   An expression often found in personnel reports is "So-and-so is absent, *sick* at home *with a temperature.*" Strictly speaking, this is meaningless. A person running a fever has an abnormally high temperature. Certain other illnesses are characterized by abnormally low temperatures. But everybody "has a temperature" every day he is alive. Most of us alive and well have a temperature close to 98.6 degrees Fahrenheit. So we suggest that the phrase be changed to "at home sick with a fever" or, in the rare instance where it may be appropriate, "with a subnormal temperature."

sidious. *See* ARCANE WORDS

siege. *See* SPELLINGS, TRICKY

sierra   The word *sierra* (no capital) means a range of mountains which seem from a distance to have a saw-toothed outline. Thus, in referring to two or more of these ranges it is redundant to call them "sierra mountains"; the proper form is "the sierras."

silencer   *Silencer* is the British motoring equivalent for the U.S. "muffler."

silent letters   The question is often raised as to why there are so many *silent letters* in the spelling of English words: the "k" in "knife," the "g" in "gnat," and the "p" in "pneumonia," for example. In the words of one linguist, they act "as tombstones to mark the place where lie the unsightly remains of a dead and forgotten pronunciation." Various efforts have been made to rid the language of these unnecessary letters. The labors, largely unrewarded, of the simplified-spelling advocates are a case in point. Take "night" for example. We pronounce it "nite" and some people spell it that way, though dictionaries sternly refuse to sanction the spelling. However, the "gh," now silent, was once sounded as a guttural.

In like fashion all the silent "p's," "g's," and "k's" were originally pronounced. Since the written language has been formalized by centuries of tradition in millions of books, magazines, and newspapers, there's little likelihood that there will be any rapid changes in the printed forms of words like "knuckle," "psychology," and "knack." They will remain traps for the unwary and prime fodder for the folks who run spelling bees.

silly *Silly* is a good example of a word whose meaning has changed completely from its original sense. In Anglo-Saxon times a *silly* person was one who was blessed or innocent. Then it came to mean "happy" and "unworldly." Gradually the last element became dominant and the present meaning of *silly* as "foolish" or "absurd" developed. It has also developed still a newer sense of "senseless" or "dazed," as in "He slapped his opponent *silly.*"

simplistic *Simplistic* is an adjective formed from "simplism," which is a tendency to oversimplify, to make complicated problems unrealistically simple. However, it has recently enjoyed something of a vogue, especially among editorial writers, who view it as a ten-dollar version of "simple." As an example of misdirected editorial elegance, it is to be deplored.

since. *See* BECAUSE/FOR/SINCE/AS

sine die When a legislative group adjourns *sine die* ("without a day"), it simply is adjourning without setting any definite date for reconvening. In classical Latin, this would be pronounced SIN-eh DEE-ay. But, since most legislatures are dominated by lawyers, the British or "legal" Latin pronunciation is used: SY-neh DY-ee.

sine qua non *Sine qua non* (pronounced SIN-eh-kwah-NON and literally translated as "without which nothing") is properly used to mean an absolutely indispensable thing or condition, an absolute prerequisite. However, it is often used rather more loosely, as indicating something most desirable but not necessarily indispensable: "Dry martinis are the *sine qua non* of the successful business luncheon."

singer The pronunciation as SING-ger (holding on to the "g" longer than usual) is a regional pronunciation very common in the New York metropolitan area. Careful speakers avoid it.

single. *See* BACHELOR

singles bar/dating bar   The *singles bar* is a recent phenomenon of big cities, where many single men and women live with little opportunity for social life. A *dating bar* is a special kind of *singles bar. Time* magazine defined it thus: "What converts an ordinary bar into a dating bar is a weekend admission fee, a large welcome for single girls and a good neighborhood."

A *singles bar* is simply a bar which caters to single men and women, not necessarily charging admission.

Sino-   *Sino-* and *Chino-* are equally correct as combining forms meaning "of or pertaining to China." Thus one may speak or write of either "Sino-Soviet relations" or "Chino-Soviet relations."

sirup/syrup   At one time, not very many years ago, the Government Printing Office indicated a preference for the spelling *sirup,* as did several dictionaries, including the Merriam-Webster New International (1934). Apparently the preference for this spelling was related to the fact that English borrowed the word from the French "sirop." However, the manufacturers and bottlers of various brands of *syrups* were unpersuaded by the lexicographers and, without exception, continued to use the *syrup* spelling. Recent dictionaries, including Funk & Wagnalls and Merriam, have abandoned the losing battle and now indicate a preference for the *syrup* spelling.

sister-in-law   The plural of *sister-in-law* is *sisters-in-law. See also* PLURALS OF COMPOUND WORDS AND PHRASES.

sit. *See* SET/SIT

sixes and sevens, at   This informal expression meaning "all disorder and confusion" has a long history. It goes back to the early days of the ancient, if not honorable, sport of crap shooting. In medieval times dice had higher numbers than those used today, and it was possible to roll for a point of thirteen, a six and a seven. But it was a hard point to make and one that only a confused or distracted person was likely to attempt. Hence the present-day meaning.

skid road/skid row   *Skid road* and *skid row* are terms used to describe parts of cities, like the Bowery in New York City, primarily known as havens for drunken derelicts. The first such haven was in Seattle, Washington, and was so called because it was a *road* made out of greased logs over which lumbermen used to *skid* logs to the mills. When the expression was adopted in other parts of the nation to describe the section of town where men "on the skids" congregated, the *skid row* version was generally used. Both expressions are still classified slang.

skift This is a dialect term meaning "a small quantity" and is especially common in the expression "a *skift* of snow," meaning a light snowfall. Though *skift* is ignored by most general dictionaries, Mencken in *The American Language* records it as a "Kansas regionalism" and Harold Wentworth in his *American Dialect Dictionary* records its appearance in many parts of the country, from Maryland to Kansas. At least one column reader reports having heard it from Iowa to the state of Washington.

skilful/skillful *Skilful* is the preferred British spelling; *skillful* the preferred American spelling.

skycap *Skycaps* are baggage handlers at airports. The name, coined by analogy to the name of the railroad baggage handler, "red cap," is admissible in all appropriate contexts. Just for the record, railroad porters were first issued red caps to match the red carpet rolled out for passengers on the legendary Twentieth Century Limited.

skyjack

USAGE PANEL QUESTION

There has been considerable use on broadcasts and in the press of *skyjack* to designate the seizure by force of an aircraft while in flight. Granting the need for brevity in headline writing and on the air, do you regard this as a valuable addition to the language?
Yes: 75%. No: 25%.

SHANA ALEXANDER: "Very good."
ISAAC ASIMOV: "It sounds like *Time* magazine—but it's good anyway."
STEWART BEACH: "I think 'skyjack' is fine—a clear and specific word to cover a new crime."
CHARLES BERLITZ: "Okay to *skyjack,* but 'hijack' or 'highjack' would do just as well."
HAL BORLAND: " 'Skyjack' is a fad word coined for a purpose and probably will die. But it could live, so I vote 'yes.' "
ABE BURROWS: "I don't like 'skyjack.' It's too cute."
PAUL HORGAN: "Yes. Alas!"

JOHN K. HUTCHENS: "Yes. Not bad for a coined word."

ALEXANDER KENDRICK: "Yes. 'Skyjack' seems no worse than 'skycap.' "

STANLEY KUNITZ: "Yes. 'Skyjack' is an imaginative coinage."

WADE MOSBY: "Yes. 'Skyjack' is a fine, concise word."

PETER S. PRESCOTT: " 'Skyjack' is colorful and strong. I like it."

LEO ROSTEN: "Yes. 'Skyjack' is exact and inventive."

ROBERT SHERRILL: "Yes, but only for headlines."

WALTER W. "RED" SMITH: " 'Skyjack' hits the target exactly."

A.B.C. WHIPPLE: " 'Skyjack may not be 'a valuable addition to the language' but it is permissible and helpful when more colorful language is needed."

slacks/trousers   Despite the advertising claim of one maker of men's clothing that his firm makes "the preference *slack*," there is no such thing as a single *slack* any more than there is a single *trouser*. Both words exist only in the plural form: *slacks* and *trousers*.

slam/slammer   *Slam* and *slammer* are relatively new slang terms for "jail." A person in confinement is said to be "in the *slam*" or "in the *slammer*." The reference is apparently to the noise made by prison gates closing.

slander. *See* LIBEL/SLANDER

slang   *Slang* is casual language, more often met in speech than in writing, though writers of fiction often use *slang* expressions to create a mood or establish a character. *Slang* encompasses many borrowings from the special languages of such ethnic and professional segments of the general population as blacks, musicians, actors and other entertainers, prison inmates, teen-agers and, in recent years, technicians engaged in computer and other related electronics activities. By its very nature, *slang* is transitory and no element in our language goes out of date more quickly. A collection of teen-age *slang* that your editors made in the 1950s is utterly incomprehensible to the teen-ager of today. Expressions like "uptight" and "nitty-gritty"—popular borrowings from the Black *slang* of the 1960s—seem already sadly dated. *Slang* should not be confused with "colloquial" or, as labeled in this dictionary, informal expression. The latter forms a part of the language that is entirely appropriate in speech and in all save the most formal written contexts. As George Lyman Kittredge once noted: "I often write and always speak colloquial English." *Slang,* by contrast, is best avoided entirely in nonfiction writing and, except in the most casual contexts, in speech.

slithy. *See* BLEND WORDS/BRUNCH WORDS/PORTMANTEAU WORDS

USAGE PANEL QUESTION

On every highway in America one sees signs reading "Go *Slow*" or simply
"*Slow*." However, some people are of the opinion that they should read
"Go *Slowly*." Do you agree?
Yes: 18%. No: 82%.
In the following sentence would you use *slow* or *slowly*? "When you reach the
dirt road you will have to go *slow/slowly* if you don't want to break an
axle."
Slow: 37%. *Slowly*: 63%.

ISAAC ASIMOV: "Traffic signs use telegraphese. I would save every letter
possible in order to make what remains as large as possible."

SHERIDAN BAKER: " 'Slow' now seems O.K. for automotion."

JOHN O. BARBOUR: "Let's save money on the signs: SLO."

STEWART BEACH: "Only a pedant would mix grammatical accuracy with road
signs, which are designed to convey information so that he who is driving
at 60 mph can read and avoid an accident."

JULES BERGMAN: "Drivers would have to go too slow to read, 'go slowly' and
so increase accidents via lengthened recognition time."

CHARLES BERLITZ: "*Slow down* would be better and more to the point."

HAL BORLAND: "Split this hair and you must ban 'auto' and 'gas' and 'lube'
and God knows how many highway and street terms."

HEYWOOD HALE BROUN: "Yes. This is really an opinion influenced by the
wish to help sign painters get work."

ANTHONY BURGESS: "U.S. English, which accepts the ghost of German usage
(undoubtedly via Yiddish), can allow Hemingway to 'write good.' Let us
by all means save two letters worth of paint."

ABE BURROWS: "This may come as a shock to some people, but 'slow' is also
an adverb."

LEON EDEL: "Road signs should be as simple and direct as possible. 'Slowly'
would distract the illiterate."

WILLARD R. ESPY: " 'Slow' is an adverb. Correct in Shakespeare's time ('How
slow time goes . . .') and just as correct today."

ALEX FAULKNER: "So well-established that it would be rather pedantic to
answer YES!"

STEPHEN H. FRITCHMAN: "Safety demands the shorter, quicker-to-read
form."

RICHARD EDES HARRISON: " 'Slow,' O.K., 'Go Slow,' no. 'Slow down' even
better."

PAUL HORGAN: "Speed of apprehension dictates the shorter form in this context."

ALEXANDER KENDRICK: "Not as long as X-ing means 'crossing.' "

LAURENCE LAFORE: "Lost cause. 'Slow' is at least better than SLO."

JOHN LEAR: "I think simply 'slow' is best."

JULES LOH: "Neither . . . I'd say 'slow down.' "

RUSSELL LYNES: "I'd be more likely to say 'slow down.' "

HERBERT MITGANG: " 'Slow'—because it's read at 60 mph and the point is to catch the eye, not the grammarian."

WADE MOSBY: "Proponents are either rapid readers or slow drivers."

EDWIN NEWMAN: "I use 'slow' as I use 'fast'—I would not say 'go fastly.' "

ORVILLE PRESCOTT: "This is a lost cause, worthy but lost. I would use 'slowly' because I am an eccentric conservative in usage."

F. D. REEVE: "Both are O.K. adverbs (but not 'fastly' yet)."

LEO ROSTEN: "Yes, but signs are phrases, flexibly syntaxed." (# 2): "This is a sentence, hence adverbial use is mandatory."

BERTON ROUECHÉ: " 'Slowly,' though correct in this sense, sounds as wrong as 'badly.' "

RICHARD H. ROVERE: "No, but I'm not bothered by it."

VERMONT ROYSTER: "I consider either correct."

LEONARD SANDERS: "Safety first; grammatical considerations second."

DAVID SCHOENBRUN: "Bit of purism here, but what's wrong with being pure, if it is simple and graceful? I would only use 'go slow' to a friend living too fast!"

HAROLD SCHONBERG: "Both are accepted usage."

DANIEL SCHORR (voting for "slow" in the first case, "slowly" in the second): "Inconsistent, I admit. But I feel a difference between the imperative in a road signal and a complete sentence."

CHARLES E. SILBERMAN: "I have higher standards for myself than I do for road signs."

WALTER W. "RED" SMITH: "For highway signs 'slow' is perfect—clear, succinct, emphatic."

EARL UBELL: "Yes, but it is a lost cause."

BILL VAUGHAN: " 'Go slow' is convenient shorthand for clarity and brevity."

A.B.C. WHIPPLE: " 'Slow' . . . this is almost universally accepted today."

slow drawl A *redundancy* (which see). Delete "slow."

slud Irregular dialect past tense of *slide*, made famous by Jerome H. "Dizzy" Dean, celebrated pitcher for the St. Louis Cardinals "Gas House Gang" of the 1930s, later a noted baseball sportscaster: "Then he *slud* to third."

slum. *See* GHETTO/SLUM

slyboots   A *slyboots* is a crafty or cunning person or animal—especially one who pretends to be dull-witted or stupid. *Slyboots* is usually used in a lighthearted, joking fashion but, despite its appearance, is not slang but standard English.

small businessmen/small-business men   Here is a case where the hyphen (which see) is absolutely indispensable for clarity. Although *businessmen* is customarily written solid and *small business* written as two words, the sense of the expression is lost if conventional rules are followed. The meaning of the expression is not "diminutive businessmen" but "men who operate small businesses." Make it *small-business men.*

smarmy   *Smarmy* is a recent borrowing from British informal, currently enjoying a vogue among the literati. It means "unctuously flattering" or "sycophantically toadying." Back in Victorian times *smarm* was a sort of pomade used by dandies to slick down their hair. Then it came to mean the kind of fulsome flattery you might expect from chaps who slicked their hair that way.

smell. *See* LINKING VERBS

sneaked. *See* SNUCK

snob   *Snob,* though originally British university slang, is now standard and acceptable in any context. It means one who acts smugly superior to others.

snollygoster   *Snollygoster* is an item of regional dialect, made famous because it was used by President Harry S Truman as a derogatory label for a music critic who had adversely criticized his daughter's singing. Truman defined *snollygoster* as "a man born out of wedlock" but that is not its generally accepted meaning. H. L. Mencken reported that a *snollygoster* is a man who wants public office regardless of party, platform, or principles. Wentworth's *American Dialect Dictionary* says a *snollygoster* is the same thing as a "shyster" and Merriam defines him as "an unprincipled but shrewd person, especially a politician." Despite Truman's use of *snollygoster,* it is inappropriate in formal contexts.

snow job   Slang expression meaning the use of overwhelming flattery and cajolery to persuade a person to believe what is not necessarily true: "Representative Stratton complained that the Air Force gave him a *snow job* when he asked for information about the cheating scandal at the Air Force Academy."

snuck   *Snuck* as in "He *snuck* away after the movie" is a dialect variant of "sneaked," admissible only in informal contexts, usually as a bit of jocosity.

so. *See* THAT/SO

so/very   *So* as a substitute for *very* should be used only in informal speech or writing. A statement such as "I was *so* tired" is not acceptable in formal speech or writing unless it is followed by further explanation, such as "that I fell asleep during the lecture."

soap opera/soaps   A *soap opera* is a radio or television dramatic show characterized by domestic crises, sentimentality, misery, and cliff-hanger endings. The expressions *soap opera* and *soaps,* as they are called in the industry, should be regarded as informal. The name comes from the fact that in the early days of radio most of them were sponsored by soap makers.

so . . . as. *See* AS . . . AS/SO . . . AS

so-called   *So-called* is an expression often used to indicate irony, implying that the object or person so dubbed is likely to be unworthy of the label. "The *so-called* antiques were shunned by the experts." Note that quotation marks must not be used around the noun following *so-called.* You may use one or the other but not both. Thus, you could say "The 'antiques' were shunned . . ." but not "The *so-called* 'antiques' were shunned. . . ."

Social Registerite/Social Registrite   *Social Registrite* is wrong. *Social Registerite* is the correct label for a person listed in the *Social Register.* Note that capital letters are used on both words because Social Register is a trademark.

socked in   This is an item of aviation slang, meaning "closed down because of fog or other weather conditions." In the early days of aviation pilots had to rely on a conical sock hung from a mast for information about wind direction. This sock was usually placed atop the largest hangar. When fog hung heavily over the field, the sock was invisible and planes could neither take off nor land.

soda. *See* SELTZER/SODA/POP/TONIC/SPARKLING WATER

soldier of fortune. *See* MERCENARY/SOLDIER OF FORTUNE

solecism   A *solecism,* linguistically speaking, is an impropriety in usage or grammar. "Irregardless" is such a *solecism.* Other examples include a candidate's "We now realize that whomever is the next President . . ." and the statement of a famous actress that "I have been trodding the boards since childhood." Needless to say, examples of *solecisms* abound, and one of the prime functions of this dictionary is to expose and correct them.

solicitor. *See* BARRISTER/SOLICITOR

some/a   "*Some* woman came up to me and asked the way to the ferry boat" is an informal way of indicating that the woman was unknown or unidentified. Phrases such as "*some* woman" or "*some* man" should not be used in formal speech or writing or, for that matter, at any time by a careful user of the language. "A woman" or "a man" is sufficient; otherwise the person should be identified by name or description.

somebody/someone   Both *somebody* and *someone* require singular verbs, so logically the pronouns used with them should also be singular. "*Someone* (or *somebody*) has left his (or 'her' but not 'their') coffee cup on the edge of the counter." One solution is to make it simply "a coffee cup." *See also* PRONOUNS, AGREEMENT WITH ANTECEDENTS.

someplace else   *Someplace else* in expressions like "He was *someplace else* when it happened" was once scorned by grammarians as substandard and "somewhere else" prescribed in its place. Now, however, the expression *someplace else* is considered entirely acceptable, especially in informal contexts.

something   *Something* should be pronounced SUM-thing, not SUM-thun or SUM-pun. Careful articulation of the "-ing" word endings remains a mark of the careful speaker.

somewhat. *See* KIND OF/RATHER/SOMEWHAT

song. *See* ANTHEM/SONG

son-in-law   The plural of *son-in-law* is *sons-in-law. See also* PLURALS OF COMPOUND WORDS AND PHRASES.

sophisticated   During the 1920s and 1930s *sophisticated* was used chiefly to describe people with a high quotient of worldly wisdom and urbanity —the likes of Cole Porter, Fred Astaire, and Dorothy Parker. Since World War II a new scientific application has evolved, and today one speaks of highly *sophisticated* computers and *sophisticated* weapons systems, when describing devices that are complicated in design and advanced in form. Both senses of *sophisticated* are standard English.

sort of a. *See* KIND OF A/SORT OF A

sound. *See* LINKING VERBS

Soviet Union. *See* RUSSIA/SOVIET UNION

spanner British name for the kind of nonadjustable wrench used on octagonal nuts. The monkey wrench is called "wrench" in England as well as America.

sparkling water. *See* SELTZER/SODA/POP/TONIC/SPARKLING WATER

spatial/spacial *Spatial* (not *spacial*) is the preferred adjectival form of *space.* It takes that form because it is derived directly from the Latin word for *space,* "spatium," while the noun *space* came into English by way of French, "espace."

spattsey. *See* SPUTTSEY/SPATTSEY

spayed/spaded When a female animal has been "altered" by the excision of the ovaries, she is said to have been *spayed* (past tense of *spay*). However, owing to the process of folk etymology by which people tend to confuse an unfamiliar word with a familiar one, one often hears that an animal has been *spaded.* This is, at best, a dialect variation, at worst an illiteracy.

speak to/speak with Both *to* and *with* are perfectly acceptable with *speak.* The slight shade of difference between the two is simply that *speak with* connotes conversation, while *speak to* may be monologue, as when a sergeant *speaks to* a duty detail or a senator *speaks to* a subject.

special/specially. *See* ESPECIAL/ESPECIALLY/SPECIAL/SPECIALLY

species/specie *Species,* referring to a fundamental category of organism, has the same form in the singular and the plural: "This *species* of frog is nearing extinction" and "Many *species* of waterfowl were observed on the trip."

Specie means "coin," usually gold or silver. It is not the singular form of *species,* despite its use in that sense by some semi-literate "word mechanics."

spectators. *See* AUDIENCE/SPECTATORS/CONGREGATION

spell *Spell* as a verb meaning "to relieve a person of his duty by replacing him for a short while" is standard English, not slang. *Spell* as a noun (a *spell* of weather, a *spell* of sickness) is well established in American English but is still regarded as informal.

spelling, variations in "Baksheesh, for the love of Allah" is the plaintive plea of beggars throughout the Middle East. "Baksheesh," the tourist soon learns, means "alms" or "handouts." But when he comes to write this down in his diary, he finds that the dictionary makers give him no fewer than four different ways to spell this word: "baksheesh," "backsheesh," "bakshish," and "backshish." If his evening meal includes the regional specialty "shish kebab," he'll find that the dictionary editors haven't been able to make up their minds on how that should be spelled, either. "Kebab," "cabob," and "kabob"—any of these spellings will pass muster in one or another of our dictionaries.

How can it be that editors cannot agree among themselves on the correct spelling of more than fifteen hundred words, according to a recent study? Why can't they decide once and for all how to spell such simple words as "advisor," "traveler," "taboo," "bazar," and "caffeine"? Simply because today's dictionaries do not attempt to prescribe which spelling is right and which is wrong. Their job is to record actual spellings as used in books, magazines, and newspapers. If enough reputable publications spell these words "adviser," "traveller," "tabu," "bazaar," and "caffein," the dictionaries must record these as acceptable variant spellings. So the ultimate decision on how to spell such words is the guidance given by a reputable dictionary. Note, however, that the fact that "adviser" precedes "advisor" in the dictionary does not necessarily mean that it is the preferred spelling. If the entry reads "adviser, advisor"—with the two words separated only by a comma, that signifies that the editors think them equally usable. If the entry reads "adviser. Also advisor" that means that, in the judgment of the editors, "adviser" is definitely the preferred spelling.

spellings, tricky Here is one editor's list of words which are most frequently misspelled in print: "accommodate, affidavit, diphtheria, embarrass, harass, inoculate, precede, supersede, and siege." As a challenge, he dictated the list to a group of 172 schoolteachers. Only three could claim a perfect score.

spell out in detail This is a redundancy. Say either "spell out" or "detail" (as a verb). A related phrase, "to outline in detail," is, on the other hand, a contradiction.

spent/passed

USAGE PANEL QUESTION

Usage Panelist EARL UBELL sends this note: "The New York *Herald Tribune* copy desk would feverishly cross out 'spent' in such phrases as 'spent the time watching the birds' and replace it with 'passed.' 'Passed' always seemed a little highfalutin, but I was dutiful. I wonder what our panel would say." Do you agree with the copy-desk verdict?
Yes: 7%. No: 93%.

SHANA ALEXANDER: "I hear a shade of difference of meaning. 'Passed' suggests the subject was bored, was expectant, was waiting for something. 'Spent' is neutral."

ISAAC ASIMOV: "I see nothing wrong in 'spent.' "

HAL BORLAND: "Nit-picking, common to all copy desks. I know. I've been a copyeditor."

HEYWOOD HALE BROUN: "There is some deep reference to the work ethic here but it's not germane, thank God."

BEN LUCIEN BURMAN: "As an old copy-desk hand myself, 90% of 'em should be placed opposite novel copyreaders; then let them fight and hopefully end up like the Killkenny cats."

ABE BURROWS: "It seems to me that 'passed the time' implies inactivity. Whereas 'spent' sounds fairly active. I imagine the copy desk was protecting the reporter's job and expense account."

THOMAS FLEMING: " 'Spent' is fresher, more colloquial."

STEPHEN H. FRITCHMAN: "The words mean two quite distinguishable things, both correct in their contexts."

JOHN K. HUTCHENS: "No—because one *does* spend time watching birds, and well spent, too."

ALEXANDER KENDRICK: "No. Not in these days of planned and packaged leisure."

WALTER KERR: "No . . . and I worked there."

LAURENCE LAFORE: "No. This is a silly sort of perfectionism."

STANTON PECKHAM: "Newspaper copy desks are staffed by idiots. When I wrote 'the *Berengaria* had charisma,' mine changed it to 'real class.' "

LEO ROSTEN: "I spend some time (actively) and pass some time (comatose)."

DAVID SCHOENBRUN: " 'Spent the time' has become accepted usage. 'Passed the time' is certainly better."

WALTER W. "RED" SMITH: "On the *Trib* I learned to avoid 'spent' lest it be changed to 'passed.' I was told the rule was made by the Queen Mother, who took 'spent' to mean sexually exhausted or relieved. I may have been misinformed and do not wish to slander Helen Rogers Reid."

spick-and-span   *Spick-and-span* is an expression that has been part of the language since before the time of Shakespeare. It was first used by ship-builders. A *spik* was a spike and a *span* was a chip or shaving. So anything *spick-and-span* was sparkling fresh. (A trademarked version of it, "Spic-and-Span," has been the name of a household cleaner for years.) Despite its honorable origin *spick-and-span* is generally regarded as close to slang.

When Samuel Johnson was putting together his dictionary, he noted with irritation that writers of the eminence of Dean Swift and Samuel Butler had used it. But that couldn't make him like it. "Spick-and-span," he growled, "is a low word."

spiral   To *spiral* is to move either up or down in a circular motion or fashion. It has acquired a new meaning, not accepted by all writers, of "to rise continuously, especially at a rapid rate," as in "The report showed prices to be *spiraling* while employment remained at the same level." Purists will continue to defend its use in such phrases as "leaves *spiraling* to the ground."

spizzerinctum   *Spizzerinctum* is an obsolescent, if not obsolete, slang expression meaning "vigor, energy, and enthusiasm." As St. Clair McKelway noted back in the 1930s: "*Spizzerinctum* . . . was a word that was popular in some of the older and snappier circles along the Eastern Seaboard."

splanch   This is a particularly revolting bit of real-estate agents' jargon. It's a blend of "split level" and "ranch." We once saw—so help us!—an advertisement for a "Colonial *splanch.*"

split   This word, both as a noun and as a verb, has many meanings, but during the 1960s it acquired a new slang usage as a verb meaning "to go away," "to leave or depart." It became so widely used that the Air Force included it in a glossary of terms that would probably not be known to former prisoners of war returning from Vietnam.

split infinitive. *See* INFINITIVE, SPLIT

spoke   *Spoke* is an archaic past participle of "speak." *Spoken* is the form used today ("often spoken [not *spoke*] of as very talented"). *Spoke* is found today in the British expression *bespoke,* "made-to-order" or "custom-made," as in "*bespoke* dinner jacket." *Spoke* is also the simple past tense of "speak": "I *spoke* to the boss."

spoonerisms   A *spoonerism* is the accidental transposition of sounds in a spoken sentence. The most famous *spoonerism* in recent American history is the utterance of a radio announcer, reputedly Harry Von Zell: "From the White House in Washington, we bring you the President of the United States, Mr. Hoobert Heever." A somewhat similar slip of the tongue was committed by Usage Panelist Lowell Thomas, who, in a wartime broadcast, referred to British cabinet minister Sir Stafford Cripps as "Sir Stifford Crapps."

Spoonerisms get their name from the Rev. William A. Spooner, for many years the warden of New College, Oxford. After performing one wedding ceremony, Spooner is reported to have advised the groom: "It is now kisstomary to cuss the bride." The affliction was apparently contagious, for one of the ushers in his church was heard to say: "Let me sew you to your sheet." This was after he had queried a somewhat startled parishioner in these words: "Marden me, Padam, aren't you occupewing the wrong pie."

On another occasion the good doctor, irked that one of his pupils had failed to appear at one of the history lectures he gave, chided him for having "hissed my mystery lecture." And there was another celebrated occasion when he startled clergy and laity alike by announcing that the next hymn would be "When Kinquering Congs Their Titles Take." He even survived what must have seemed in the Victorian Era a shocking lack of respect for royalty when he referred to "our dear old queen" as "our queer old dean."

Incidentally, though certainly the most celebrated, Spooner was by no means the first or last victim of such transpositions. Grammarians have a name for them, "metathesis" (pronounced meh-TATH-eh-sis), a word derived from the Greek term for "to place differently." For instance our "bird" was "bridd" in Old English and "clasp" was earlier "clapse."

In our own experience we have heard the London *Sunday Times* referred to as the "Londay *Sundon Times,*" "overweight wives" as "overwite waves," a show called *Bewitched* as *We Bitched*, and Ben Grauer's introduction of Carrie Chapman Catt: "We are deepful greatly that you could be here today."

Two more examples to wind this up with one swell foop are "blushing crow" for "crushing blow" and Spooner's own thoughtful assurance that "the Lord is indeed a shoving leopard."

spoonful (plural of). *See* PLURALS OF COMPOUND WORDS AND PHRASES

sputtsey/spattsey *Sputtsey* and *spattsey* are regional dialect names for the common English sparrow. The words are especially common in Pittsburgh, Milwaukee, and other cities with a large percentage of residents of German descent. They seem to be corruptions of the German "Spatz," pronounced "shpahts."

square one   When one reaches an impasse in a project or fails completely to achieve a goal, the advice is usually "go back to *square one,*" meaning to start all over again. This phrase originated with an early children's board game, probably Uncle Wiggily, in which the players move along a path of numbered squares according to instructions given on cards which are dealt or drawn in turn.

A variation of this phrase is "back to the drawing board," which originated in the field of engineering design but owes its popularity as a catch phrase to a celebrated Peter Arno cartoon that appeared in *The New Yorker* a few decades ago. The test flight of a small propeller plane ends disastrously in a cloud of smoke. As rescue ambulances race to the scene, one figure turns away, shrugging his shoulders and saying: "Well, back to the old drawing board again!"

Square one is not to be confused with "ground zero" (which see).

squawk. *See* BLEND WORDS/BRUNCH WORDS/PORTMANTEAU WORDS

squeegee   *Squeegee,* the word for a T-shaped device with a rubber blade most commonly used to wipe water from newly washed windows, is—despite its casual appearance and sound—standard English, suitable in any context. It's probably an intensive form of "squeeze" and, as those who have used it know, somewhat onomatopoetic.

squoze   *Squoze* is a dialect variation of "squeezed." We met it first in the proud boast of the holder of the world's record for squeezing oranges: two dozen in two minutes. "I never *squoze* oranges in my life, except maybe one or two for breakfast," said the champion, radiating modesty. According to Wentworth's *American Dialect Dictionary, squoze* has been common in the dialect of country folks from Virginia to Arkansas ever since the late 1800s. It is, of course, substandard.

St. *See* SAINT/ST.

staffer

USAGE PANEL QUESTION

Panelist BILL VAUGHAN asks: "Is anyone else irritated by the word 'staffer,' meaning a member of the staff?"
Yes: 77%. No: 23%.

ISAAC ASIMOV: "No. I never heard the word but I think it serves a purpose. I would use it in speech or writing."

JOHN O. BARBOUR: "Yes. I find it demeaning."

STEWART BEACH: "I believe this is an old *Time* coinage. I don't like it and would never use it in either speech or writing."

HAL BORLAND: "Yes. Would staffers accept 'crewers,' members of a crew?"

HEYWOOD HALE BROUN: "Yes. It's a jaunty word and I hate jauntiness. It is one with 'newshawk' or 'gal Friday.' "

JAMES MACGREGOR BURNS: "Yes. But I think it is here to stay. (I might use it in speech.)"

NORMAN HOSS: "No, in speech. And I seldom have occasion to write on any level other than 'colloq.' "

ELIZABETH JANEWAY: "Not pretty, but handy in rapid speech. I would not write it."

PHYLLIS MCGINLEY: "No. Not if it's used in an office."

WADE MOSBY: "No. I regard it as purely a newspaper term. I would use it in speech."

STANTON PECKHAM: "Yes. Bad Press Club jargon."

FRANCIS ROBINSON: "Yes, emphatically."

VERMONT ROYSTER: "No. A useful word that saves words."

WALTER W. "RED" SMITH: "I don't mind it in speech."

ELVIS STAHR, JR.: "Yes, in speech; no, in writing."

BILL VAUGHAN: "Yes. How can I say otherwise?"

HERMAN WOUK: "Yes! I might use it in writing to characterize the speech of a bureaucratic dolt."

stagflation   This is a creation of economists, invented to indicate a condition in which a stagnant economy is combined with rising unemployment and growing inflation.

The Barnhart *Dictionary of New Words* labels it "British" and gives citations dating back to 1971. Like many terms used by economists it is not completely understood by the general public; indeed, it is mistrusted by many. It is subject to varying interpretations, as are *recession* and *depression* (see *depression/recession*).

stairs, pair of   This is a regional dialect variation of "flight of stairs." It appeared in a news story in a Pittsburgh paper thus: "Police said they then fled up a *pair of stairs,* dropping a bag containing $800 as they ran." *Pair of stairs* is substandard.

stall   To *stall* in the sense of "to act in a delaying fashion" is primarily informal, but it is accepted in certain phrases for both informal and formal writing. "To *stall* for time," "to *stall* off creditors," and "*stalling* tactics" are examples of common usage.

stanch/staunch   Originally *stanch* meant "stop the flow of blood," while *staunch* meant "firm and steadfast." The words have quite different origins, *stanch* coming from a Latin verb meaning "to stop or stand," and *staunch* from an Old French word meaning "firm or strong." However, through centuries of use or misuse, the two spellings became interchangeable, and now either may be used for either meaning. However, we incline still to prefer *stanch* as meaning "to stop the flow of blood" and *staunch* in the sense of "standing fast and true."

standee. *See* -EE, SUFFIX

stand for office *Stand for office* is the British equivalent of the American "run for office."

stash *Stash* is both noun and verb. As a verb it means "to hide something, to put away articles of value so that they cannot be readily found." As a noun, it means "the place where such articles are hidden." *Stash* was first considered an item of regional dialect, perhaps of hobo or underworld jargon, and is so recorded in Wentworth's *American Dialect Dictionary*. He reports first recording it in 1929 and cites this example in a remark heard in the Ozarks of northwest Arkansas: "Billy, he done *stashed* the jug in the brush and now the danged ol' fool cain't find hit." However, a Pittsburgh reader reports her belief that it is far older and that her mother and grandmother had used it all their lives. "It did not necessarily refer to anything illegal," she adds, "but rather to anything hoarded away for future use. Since these people were very close to the Pennsylvania Dutch (German) folks, perhaps the word stems from their speech." Perhaps—but most linguists prefer to think that *stash* is a blend of "store" and "cache."

state. *See* COMMONWEALTH/STATE

state of the art

USAGE PANEL QUESTION

State of the art has become a very voguish expression. We hear discussions of the *"state of the art* of TV journalism" and, though one might cavil at the use of "art" in relation to TV journalism, the construction seems otherwise acceptable. But *state of the art* as an adjectival phrase occurs with increasing frequency. The president of Amtrak announces that long-line service will be improved by the addition of *"state of the art"* equipment." A maker of cast-iron stoves announces "From the State of Vermont Comes the *State of the Art."* Presumably the expression is a shortened form of "highest (or finest) *state of the art."*

state of the art

Would you use *state of the art* in writing? Yes: 25%. No: 75%.
In speech? Yes: 23%. No: 77%.

ISAAC ASIMOV: "Yes, but in the strict sense."

WHITNEY BALLIETT: "Horrible."

BARRY BINGHAM, SR.: "Pure voguishness. The phrase is not needed for any useful purpose."

JOHN BROOKS: " 'State of the art' is a contribution to the language of our time."

HEYWOOD HALE BROUN: "No. But then I don't use 'creative' to describe advertising."

JOHN CIARDI: "Yes, but warily, if at all."

ROBERT CROMIE: "Fifty states are enough."

WILLARD R. ESPY: "As an adjectival phrase—never. Nor as an ellipsis; why expect a reader to assume that 'highest' is implied before a phrase like 'state of the art equipment'? But it is unexceptionable to say (assuming it is no lie) that 'laser weapons are impractical in the present state of the art'!"

RAY GANDOLF: "It's meaningless. I've heard it used to describe the current state of the art and the debased state of the art as well as the highest."

PETE HAMILL: "It's advertising copy language and too goddamned vague."

PAUL HORGAN: "Phony grandeur."

JOHN K. HUTCHENS: "Yes, but only when it relates to art in its esthetic, traditional sense."

ELIZABETH JANEWAY: "I wouldn't use it myself but I have heard it used unexceptionably, in, for instance, discussing the technical expertise of a company doing research on biogenetics. A pretty limited acceptable area of use, I agree!"

JAMES J. KILPATRICK: "The use of 'state of the art,' except in a technical sense, is so much jargon. It obscures, rather than clarifies, meaning."

IRVING KOLODIN: "Only in specific technical cases—electronics, for example."

STANLEY KUNITZ: "Not for me—too voguish. But I accept it from others."

JULES LOH: "I restrict it to the limited sense of technical development."

WILLIAM McGUIRE: "No. Has become a cliché in academic jargon, including University Press editors."

EDWIN NEWMAN: "This is typical. A useful phrase is made boring by too much use."

MARGE PIERCY: "Ironically only."

ANDY ROONEY: "Some words and phrases are tired old clichés the first time they're used. (I guess it might be called a tired new cliché.)"

LEO ROSTEN: "No. 'State of the art' refers to a body of unscientific knowledge. Its size is irrelevant."

VERMONT ROYSTER: "In writing, this is one more example of decline in the state of the art."

HAROLD SCHONBERG: "It's not new. The phrase came from the audio industry to describe the most advanced equipment available. (I remember it from the fifties.) If Vermont wants to make a pun out of it, O.K. But it's not a very good one."

ERICH SEGAL: "It's gibberish."

JACK SMITH: "No. No. At this point in time, I'm already sick of it."

ELVIS STAHR, JR.: "I can, I think, accept it as descriptive of a degree of development in a general field, e.g.: 'We're dealing here with state-of-the-art electronics' (rather than 'this is a state-of-the-art computer')."

WALLACE STEGNER: "Possibly. It's a fashionable variant of 'up-to-date,' I suppose. But less precise."

KARL V. TEETER: "Source is scholarly inquiry: a state of the art paper."

EDWARD TRIPP: "You don't make it clear whether the question applies to noun, adjective, or both. In fast-moving technologies, such as electronics, the noun phrase can be reasonably specific and therefore useful. The adjective is false and clumsy."

BARBARA TUCHMAN: "Not as an adjective. I might use it as a noun."

DOUGLAS WATT: "In any case, it would demand hyphens when used as an adjective. But *no;* NEVER!"

stationary/stationery Fowler's *Modern English Usage* gives a clue to be remembered by those who tend to confuse these two words. *Stationery,* the noun, comes from the word "stationer," "one who has a station in a market for the sale of books, as distinguished from an itinerant vendor." *Stationary,* of course, is an adjective meaning "not moving."

status *Status* may be pronounced either STAY-tus or STAT-us. Earlier in this century, dictionaries indicated a decided preference for STAY-tus, with the Funk & Wagnalls Unabridged (1913) accepting only this pronunciation and the Merriam-Webster Unabridged (1934) indicating a preference for it. However, Kenyon and Knott's *Pronouncing Dictionary of American English* (1944) records both pronunciations as equally acceptable and all other authorities now follow suit.

statutory rape. *See* FORCIBLE RAPE/STATUTORY RAPE

staunch. *See* STANCH/STAUNCH

stay. *See* LINKING VERBS

stayed. *See* STOOD/STAYED

steal. *See* ROB/STEAL

stem to stern   When one studies a matter *stem to stern,* he examines it in full detail throughout its entire length. The expression is borrowed from sailor talk and is roughly equivalent to "from bow to stern." The *stem* of a boat is the member to which the ship's sides are joined at the prow, but it's loosely used as a synonym for "bow." The expression is appropriate in all contexts.

stepmother/stepfather/stepchild   A *stepmother* or *stepfather* is a person who married one's parent after the death or divorce of the other parent. A *stepchild* in Chaucer's time was an orphaned child, but the term has long since been extended in meaning to the child of one's husband or wife by a former marriage.

Stillson wrench   This is a trademark for a pipe wrench invented in 1869 by Daniel Stillson. Like all trademarks, its initial letter should be capitalized whether used in full, as *Stillson wrench* or, less formally, as *Stillson.*

stink   *Stink* in its primary sense of "to give off a powerful and unpleasant odor" is perfectly acceptable in any context, though some people object to *stink* as vulgar. These are the same people who prefer "abdomen" to "belly." In actuality, *stink* is a word with a much longer and more honorable history than many of the genteel euphemisms, like "odor" and "aroma," that may be considered preferable in polite society. *Stink* in the sense of "being of poor quality" ("This car *stinks*") or as a noun meaning "outrage" or "protest" ("He raised quite a *stink* about police corruption") is considered slang.

St. John   *St. John* as a British given name is pronounced SIN-jin. The late New York *World* once imported an English theater critic named *St. John* Ervine. He shuddered at hearing the colonials call him "Saint John" but smiled benignly (as benignly as any critic could) on hearing SIN-jin.

stoned   Before the great increase in drug use in the 1960s, *stoned* was interpreted as "intoxicated to the point of insensibility." The agent, of course, was alcohol. Now the agent may be marijuana or another drug. It is slang.

stonewall   *Stonewall* as a verb, derived from the famous feats of Civil War General Thomas Jonathan "Stonewall" Jackson, surfaced during the Watergate affair in the early 1970s. Apparently a borrowing from the language of advertising-agency executives, of whom there were several on the Nixon staff, it means "to refuse adamantly any form of cooperation." In one conversation with Mr. Nixon, John Dean, speaking of another aide,

Gordon Strachan, said: "Strachan is as tough as nails. He can go in and *stonewall* and say, 'I don't know anything about what you're talking about.' He has already done it twice, you know, in interviews." *Stonewall* should be considered jargon and inappropriate for use in any formal contexts, except perhaps as a bit of jocosity.

It is perhaps worth mentioning that *stonewall* is a term common in the jargon of cricket. According to the *Oxford English Dictionary*, it means "to block balls persistently; to play solely on the defensive." It is also common in Australian political slang, where it is used synonymously with the American "filibuster"—that is, to delay parliamentary business with lengthy speeches.

stood/stayed   The use of *stood* in place of the more formal *stayed* (as in the classic complaint of a losing gambler "I should of *stood* in bed") is generally believed to be a Yiddishism, perhaps because its most celebrated utterance was the one cited above from the lips of fight promoter Joe Jacobs. However, correspondents assure us that the formulation was well established as long ago as the turn of the century in the speech of Pennsylvania Dutch (German) farm folk. It must, under any circumstances, be regarded—however amusing it may be—as substandard. *See also* SHOULD OF/COULD OF/WOULD OF.

stop by   *Stop by* in the sense of make a brief visit or to "drop in" on a person is perfectly acceptable informal English. Most dictionaries have ignored this casual colloquial expression, but the Merriam-Webster Third International not only saw fit to enter it (as they very properly should) but chose to illustrate it with a citation from the work of a celebrated ex-brothel madam, Polly Adler. From her book *A House Is Not a Home,* the Merriam editors chose this: ". . . suggested that she *stop by* that evening to talk things over." Merriam draws the curtain on just what "things" were discussed.

stop to think   The expression "when you *stop to think* about it" brought criticism from a column reader who contended that "thinking is a continuous process," so one could not literally *stop to think.* This complaint runs directly into the fact that *stop to think* is a well-established idiom and actually means "stop and give special thought to one particular point." So the expression is entirely acceptable in informal contexts.

straight   *Straight* in the sense of "consecutive" ("five *straight* games") has met with some criticism from purists—none of it, in our view, justified. Indeed, this sense of *straight,* in reference to an unbroken sequence of playing cards, has been in use at least since Sir Edmond Hoyle compiled his famous book on card games in the eighteenth century. It currently has a slang sense of not using drugs or alcohol.

straitjacket/straitlaced   *Strait* as an adjective means "restricting" or "confining," a meaning which is embodied in *straitjacket* or *straitlaced*. Although dictionaries do enter "straightjacket" and "straightlaced" as alternate spellings, this is probably the result of persistent errors on the part of writers. The preferred spellings, then, are *straitjacket* and *strait-laced*.

strangled (to death)   *Strangle* in its literal sense means to kill by choking or suffocation. The words "to death" are unnecessary and redundant.

stratum/strata   *Stratum,* like *datum,* is a Latin word whose last syllable becomes "a" in the plural. However, many people unfamiliar with Latin believe *strata* to be the singular and use "stratas" for the plural form. Those who use the word should at least recognize that *stratum* is the singular, as in "each (every) *stratum* of society is. . . ." While the Anglicized *stratums* is recognized by dictionaries as a possible plural, "stratas" defies all laws of logic and language and is completely unacceptable. *See also* DATA/DATUM.

street. *See* ROAD/STREET/AVENUE

strided/strode   The following appeared in a news story in *The New York Times:* " 'Just a few,' she said impatiently, then strided into a drawing room." This led panelist Alex Faulkner to ask whether *strided* was an obscure Americanism. Obviously it is not—merely an error by an obscure *Times* man, for not long thereafter Theodore Bernstein in the *Times* house organ *Winners and Sinners* reprinted the blunder with this succinct comment: "The past tense of *stride* is *strode.*"

stroking. *See* EUPHEMISM

structure   *Structure* as a transitive verb ("He *structured* the agenda for maximum efficiency") is newly voguish in the sense of "construct" or "organize." It's a borrowing from the jargon of sociologists, a group that has probably done more calculated harm to the English language than any other scholarly or quasi-scholarly group. *Structure* is very popular with people who use words like "crunch," "thrust," and "seminal." Such people are best avoided. *See also* VOGUE WORDS.

student. *See* PUPIL/STUDENT

stupid. *See* DUMB

sub-. *See* PREFIXES AND SUFFIXES, WITH AND WITHOUT HYPHEN

subjunctive mood   The *subjunctive mood* of verbs is used to express hypothesis, supposition, contingency. "If I *were* king," "If wishes *were* horses, beggars would ride," "If 'ifs' and 'ands' *were* pots and pans, there would be no need for tinkers," and "If it *be* God's will" are all examples of the *subjunctive mood*—and you don't hear or read the subjunctive much any more. Nowadays the way language is used by educated, literate speakers and writers is the final criterion and, by this standard, the subjunctive is today just about dead. The only time you are likely to run into it—save in the most formal writing, such as state papers—is in instances where there is very serious doubt of the fulfillment of the "if" clause or when the condition is contrary to fact, as in the famous song from *Fiddler on the Roof:* "If I *were* [not *was*] a rich man." Nowadays you will almost invariably hear and read the indicative rather than the subjunctive. As Porter Perrin remarked: "Today the subjunctive is a trait of style rather than of grammar and is used by writers chiefly to set their language a little apart from everyday usage."

submarine. *See* GRINDER/HERO/HOAGIE/SUBMARINE

submariner   The men who man submarines are called sub-muh-REE-ners, not sub-MAR-ih-ners.

subsequent/subsequent to/subsequently   These words offer three different ways of referring to an event which follows an earlier one. In the case of an announcement which followed a convention, it is possible to say "a *subsequent* announcement," "an announcement *subsequent to* the convention," or "an announcment made *subsequently.*"

substance abuse. *See* CONTROLLED SUBSTANCE

such a   *Such a,* when used to modify a noun and followed by a clause introduced by "that," is accepted, as in "There was *such a* crowd at the game that we left early." Used as an intensive without a "that" clause, it is not acceptable in formal writing or speech. "We had *such a* good time" is better as "We had a very good time" or "We enjoyed ourselves very much."

Phrases such as "no *such a* thing" are illiterate. Make it "no *such* thing."

sudden death/sudden victory   *Sudden death* periods in various sports are periods which occur after the regular playing time has ended with the contesting teams tied. The first team to score wins the game. The expression is not new. Indeed, gamblers have long used it to describe the final single throw of the dice or flip of the coin. However, it is a relatively new development in professional football and led one televised sportscaster to invent what he considered a more acceptable term. However, in the words of Usage Panelist "Red" Smith: "The protesting ear rejects Curt Gowdy's Nice Nellie euphemism 'sudden victory.' " So do we.

suffer. *See* SUSTAIN (INJURY/LOSS)

suffer (from/with) *Suffer from* is the preferred construction when speaking of a disease, illness, disability, or shortcoming. *Suffer with* is not ungrammatical, when speaking of an immediate or temporary condition of the body, but *suffer from* is more common.

sufficient enough There is no need to describe anything as *sufficient enough,* as in "The available money was not *sufficient enough* to cover the costs." Either *sufficient* or *enough* but not both.

suffix A *suffix* is a word element added after the stem or root of a word to make a new word. "Friendship" consists of the word "friend" plus the *suffix* "-ship." *See also* INFIX and PREFIX.

suffragette/suffragist The suffix "ette" is often used to mean imitation or substitute, as in "flannelette" and "leatherette." Many feminists feel that when the suffix is applied as in *suffragette* it conveys a belittling effect.

Historically, the "ette" ending was given to the word *suffragist* in England to deride those women demanding the right to vote. Suffragist, according to the *OED,* predates *suffragette* by more than 60 years (1822). It is defined as "an advocate of the extension of the political franchise, especially (since about 1885) to women."

suite/suit The correct pronunciation of *suite* is SWEET. However, in the furniture trade the pronunciation SOOT (the same as for "suit") is very commonly heard, especially in shops specializing in what the trade privately calls *borax* (which see) and *schlock* (which see) merchandise. The fact that the pronunciation SOOT is widely heard does not make it acceptable in literate speech.

sump British automotive equivalent for the American "crankcase."

sums/numbers QUERY: "A newspaper reports that 'entertaining vast *sums* of people is a problem.' Is this correct?"

COMMENT: No. The idioms are "*sums* of money" and "*numbers* of people."

sunshine saloon. *See* SALOON/SUNSHINE SALOON

super-. *See* PREFIXES AND SUFFIXES, WITH AND WITHOUT HYPHEN

super-duper. *See* RICOCHET WORDS

superhighway. *See* TURNPIKE/THRUWAY/PARKWAY/HIGHWAY/ FREEWAY/SUPERHIGHWAY

superior/inferior The preposition "to" is used after both *superior* and *inferior.*

supersede. *See* SPELLINGS, TRICKY

supine. *See* PRONE/SUPINE

supper. *See* DINNER/SUPPER/LUNCH

suppose. *See* GUESS/SUPPOSE

surface. *See* VOGUE WORDS

surgery/operation *Surgery* in the U.S. may be either the act of removal or repair of parts of the body by operative methods or the room or area of a hospital in which such *operations* are performed ("She had *surgery* for removal of a benign tumor" or "The doctor is now in *surgery*"). In the United Kingdom, *surgery* usually means simply "the doctor's office" and "The doctor is in *surgery*" means simply that he's in his office.

surprise/astonish Dictionaries today regard these verbs as synonymous, differing solely in the intensity of *surprise* expressed. *Surprise* may indicate a relatively mild reaction to an unexpected revelation, while *astonish* implies a revelation so remarkable that the observer is truly shocked. In earlier times a deeper distinction was observed by purists, with *surprise* being restricted to its etymological meaning of being caught unawares. This is the source of perhaps the oldest lexicographical legend, a tale that has been told about every dictionary editor from Robert Cawdrey (1604) to Noah Webster. It goes like this. IRATE WIFE, finding editor in the arms of the downstairs maid: "What ARE you doing? I am surprised!" EDITOR: "Not so. I am the one who is surprised. You are astonished." As noted above, this distinction, like the downstairs maid, is nowadays seldom observed.

surreptitious entry/breaking and entering. *See* EUPHEMISM

surveillance/surveil *Surveillance,* a noun meaning "observation of a person or premises, especially in connection with a crime," may be pronounced either sur-VAYL-unss or sur-VAYL-yunss. A verb *surveil* has been coined, as a back-formation from *surveillance.* It seems limited in use to the jargon of law-enforcement officers, the chaps whose world seems to be exclusively peopled by "perpetrators" whom they must *surveil*. We see no reason why the word should attain any wider circulation. "Keep watch over" or "keep under *surveillance*" seems entirely adequate.

survey   *Survey* as a verb meaning "to subject to general inspection" ("*survey* the field for possible competitors") and, in the technical sense, "to measure land to determine its boundaries" is well established as standard English. However, *survey* also has a special meaning limited, as far as we know, to use by the United States Navy, though other armed services may also use it. In this use, *survey* is an abbreviation of "Report of Survey" —an official report detailing the circumstances concerning loss, damage, or destruction of property. This report serves as authorization for dropping the property from the official records and disposing of it. In Navy parlance, then, a piece of property, from a battleship to a typewriter, cannot be disposed of until it has been *surveyed*.

survey in depth. *See* VOGUE WORDS

suspicion/suspect   The use of *suspicion* in the sense of *suspect* ("I *suspicion* she is right") is fairly common in some regional dialects, notably in the Ozarks and some parts of West Virginia and Kentucky. It is acceptable in the United States only as an item of informal or dialect speech, though it is still considered standard English in the United Kingdom.

sustain (injury/loss)   Because *sustain* has a basic meaning of "endure," many writers have reservations about its indiscriminate use as a synonym for "suffer," "receive," or "undergo." If *injuries* are fatal, they argue, the victim has hardly *sustained* them. If *losses* result in bankruptcy, the loser has hardly *sustained* them.

swan, I   The expression "Well, *I swan*" is an item of antique slang or dialect meaning "I swear" and dating back at least as far as the Revolution. It is thought to be a borrowing from a British dialect expression, "I's wan," meaning "I'll warrant."

swoop, one fell   *One fell swoop* is a common enough idiom—some might call it a cliché—and originally meant one fierce, sudden onslaught, such as a hawk might make swooping down on a small defenseless animal. The *fell* comes from the Anglo-Saxon "fel," meaning cruel or furious, from which we also get "felon," a person guilty of a serious crime. Today it simply means "all at once," as "He collapsed the house of cards with *one fell swoop.*" The expression also sometimes is heard in the spoonerism version "one swell foop." *See also* SPOONERISMS.

swum/swam/swim *Swum* is the correct form of the past participle of the verb to *swim* ("He has *swum* for hours"). It is also occasionally heard as the past tense of *swim* ("He *swum* across the creek"). However, this is now regarded as dialect or archaic and inappropriate in literate speech or writing.

synergistic *Synergistic* is a word voguish in the vocabulary of advertising copywriters, who regard it as an elegant synonym for "working together." Actually, *synergistic*—a word borrowed from the language of medicine—refers to two ingredients, each powerful in itself, which in combination exert much more power than the sum of their individual forces. The Seidlitz powders of old were *synergistic*. Each of the two powders when dissolved in water had some therapeutic value. When they were combined, you had both sparkling effervescence and a vastly more powerful cathartic. *See also* VOGUE WORDS.

synonyms, discrimination of This is a term used in lexicography to describe the method by which the various different shades of meaning in a group of *synonyms* is shown. For example, a dictionary will enter and define "sycophant." It will then note that the words "toady" and "flatterer" have somewhat the same meaning as "sycophant" (that is, they are *synonyms*). The better dictionaries will then proceed to *discriminate* the subtle shades of meaning that account for the differences between the three words.

syrup. *See* SIRUP/SYRUP

table (a resolution) *Tabling a resolution* or proposition in Great Britain means presenting it for discussion and eventual action. In the U.S. it means precisely the opposite—to postpone it, perhaps permanently. Both expressions are technical and formal.

take a scunner to. *See* SCUNNER

takeover This is an item from business English. Originally British but now commonly heard in the U.S., it refers to a financial or stock manipulation by which one firm takes over control of another.

talk the hind leg off a donkey This colorful British expression vividly describes a person afflicted with logorrhea or logomania, an abnormally incessant talker. It parallels the American frontier expression "talking a blue streak" or the even more common "talking his/her head off."

talk to/talk with In ordinary conversation today, these expressions are practically interchangeable. However, there is a subtle difference which a good speaker will want to observe. If you *talk to* a person or group it is a one-sided affair. If you *talk with* a person, he or she will contribute as much or nearly as much to the conversation as you do. There are exceptions, of course. If the boss says he wants to *talk with* you—watch out.

tap/tap water These are British expressions, not unknown in the U.S. A *tap* is the same thing as a "faucet." Its most common appearance in the U.S. is in the expression "beer on *tap,*" although *tap water* is commonly heard.

taproom. *See* SALOON

tarmac *Tarmac* is British for what Americans call the "apron" in front of an airplane hangar. It is a contraction of *tar* and *macadam,* referring to the materials originally used to create the surface.

tarnal *Tarnal* is a regional dialect version of "eternal," used by older generations to avoid profanity. It is still in use today, passed down from one generation to another.

taste. *See* LINKING VERBS

taut ship/tight ship In nautical terminology, a *taut ship* is one whose crew is well disciplined and whose efficiency rating is high. Presumably it comes from the days of sailing vessels, when lines drawn taut would be a sign of a shipshape craft and crew.

In the extended or figurative sense of "well-organized and well-run," the phrase acquired a variant: *tight ship.* Either is acceptable for general use, but when referring to a vessel, *taut ship* is still preferable.

tavern. *See* SALOON

teach. *See* LEARN/TEACH

tear up the pea patch A *pea patch,* in the sense of a small garden, is an old expression especially common in the South. To *tear up the pea patch* means "to go on a rampage" or "to upset the apple cart." The expression was popularized some years ago—at least in the East—by a well-known sports writer, Red Barber, who announced the Brooklyn Dodgers games in the days when there still were Brooklyn Dodgers. Barber used to liven up his play-by-play narrative with expressions like *tearing up the pea patch* and "sitting in the catbird seat," which meant sitting pretty—like a batter with three balls and no strikes.

teaspoonsful/teaspoonfuls Old-time cookbooks often used the *teaspoonsful* form. However, the forming of plurals of compound words by adding the "s" at the end of the word *(teaspoonfuls)* has now become standard practice.

temperature. *See* SICK WITH A TEMPERATURE

tenses, sequence of The "rule" governing *sequence of tenses* in a sentence is "When the verb in the main clause of a sentence is in past or past perfect tense, the verb in the subordinate clause should also be in past or past perfect tense."

The exception to this rule is when the subordinate clause refers to a continuing situation or condition. If you say, "I told him that I had been employed at the factory," it means that you are no longer employed there. On the other hand, "I told him that I am employed at the factory" makes it clear that you still have a job.

An example of how ridiculous the strict application of the rule can be appeared in a cutline in *The New York Times:* "Dr. Frederick J. Dockstader, director, at the Museum of the American Indian. Dr. Dockstader defended the institution. He said it did not now have adequate income." The insertion of "now" is awkward. It would have been better to delete "now" and change "did" to "does."

tenure/academic tenure *Tenure* is defined as "the period of holding something," but in academic circles it is said that a professor has *tenure* after five years. One reader contended that the professor had *tenure* during those five years and that "permanent *tenure*" would be more accurate in this instance.

The problem is that *tenure* involves a right. Under English law of centuries ago, *tenure* meant the right to hold something, usually land, under certain terms and conditions. Since most old English leaseholds were limited as to the number of years or lives they covered, the word also came to mean the time a *tenure* was in effect. It also became applied to officeholding, and today we speak of a politician's actions "during his *tenure* in office."

In each of these cases the right to hold land or office was clearly defined. Not so in the case of a teacher or professor until the principle of *academic tenure* was established, through bitter struggle, to protect a member of a faculty from indiscriminate and often unfair firing. However, with that fight won and the right to keep a teaching job established (in the absence of proven serious misconduct or incompetence), the phrase *academic tenure* has been shortened to *tenure*.

terrible/terribly/terrifying   Properly speaking, something that is *terrible* strikes terror into the heart of the observer or listener. Orson Welles's famous broadcast about the Martian invasion—a broadcast that caused widespread panic—was truly a *terrible* broadcast, even though it was performed all too brilliantly.

In informal speech, however, *terrible* has acquired the meaning of "very bad," as in "Doesn't she look *terrible*?" or "What a day I've had. I really feel *terrible*." *Terribly* is now an informal synonym for "very," as in "*terribly* sad," and *terrifying* is used in the sense of "causing terror."

thankfully/fortunately   *Thankful* is invariably defined as meaning "grateful" and it does not lose that meaning in its adverbial form. Nor does it acquire the meaning of "fortunate." Sentences such as "*Thankfully* the gasoline lasted until we reached a service station" are wrong and reflect a growing tendency to misuse words ending in "-ful" and -fully" (see *meaningful* and *hopefully*). Only persons can behave *thankfully* (expressing gratitude).

thank you kindly   This is a quaint but nonsensical phrase. What the speaker who uses it really means is "thank you for being so kind." It may also stem from use of "kindly" in such a request as "Would you kindly do so-and-so?"

"Thank you very much" is a better form to use than *thank you kindly*.

thank you much

USAGE PANEL QUESTION

The expression *thank you much* seems to be enjoying a vogue. Grammatically it is quite as defensible as "thank you very much" but to some ears the expression seems mannered, even ugly. Would you use *thank you much*?

In speech   Yes: 23%. No: 77%.
In writing   Yes: 11%. No: 89%.

BENJAMIN APPEL: "No. My ear agrees!"
SHERIDAN BAKER: "No, but my friends do."

STEWART BEACH: "No. I often say or write in a letter 'Thanks a lot' which I believe is just as grammatically O.K."

ALVIN BEAM: "No, but I have no objection to it."

HEYWOOD HALE BROUN: "Genuine gratitude should fuel a 'very.' This seems the kind of phrase used by magazine executives as a verbal tip for an expense-account lunch, and in those circumstances may be enough."

ANTHONY BURGESS: "As you say, no reason why not (German influence again?) but the rhythm seems wrong. (Carroll uses it in 'The Walrus and the Carpenter'—'They thanked him much for that.')"

BEN LUCIEN BURMAN: "Appalling, thank you much!"

ABE BURROWS: "No. Ugly indeed."

JOHN CIARDI: "No. I don't loathe this usage. I prefer 'many thanks.' "

ROBERT CRICHTON: "Not much!"

PAUL HORGAN: "No. I've been spared exposure to this."

CLARK KINNAIRD: "In speech, 'thank you very much,' or 'thank you much,' or simply 'thank you' gets all its warmth (if any is intended) from the intonation and the accompanying expression of the speaker. In writing, it can only convey warmth and sincerity with words clarifying the reason for the 'thank you.' 'Very' and 'much' are superfluous in either case."

LAURENCE LAFORE: "It is dialect Midwestern—but it seems to me rather engaging. In writing I should use it only in quotation marks—but then I can't think when I should have occasion to write 'Thank you' at all except in quotation marks."

JULES LOH: "Yes. But 'thank you muchly' (also in vogue)? No thank you much."

WRIGHT MORRIS: "No [in speech], yes [in writing] to characterize an offensive type—quickly!"

ORVILLE PRESCOTT: "No, because it offends the ear."

BERTON ROUECHÉ: "Yes, when I get used to it."

LEONARD SANDERS: "In Texas, the vogue is 'thank you now.' "

DAVID SCHOENBRUN: "No. I would not use it but it does not offend me."

ERICH SEGAL: "Are we discussing what is 'beautiful' or what we consider to be 'correct'? I don't think we should adjudicate the beauty or ugliness of a phrase. Our task is tough enough."

ROBERT SHERRILL: "No, but I don't find it offensive."

ELVIS STAHR, JR.: "No. It's rather graceless in most situations."

BILL VAUGHAN: "No. Sounds like airline hostess cuteness."

A.B.C. WHIPPLE: "No. Not much."

that/so The use of *that* as an adverb, as in "It's not *that* important," was once found chiefly in regional dialects. Expressions like "I'm *that* frightened that I can't sleep" are still commonly heard in the dialect of country folk.

However, the use of *that* in place of *so* has become so common and appears so often in reputable magazines and newspapers that it must be accepted. Most dictionaries enter this use without any special label such as "colloquial" or "informal," and thus indicate its acceptance as standard use. *See also* NOT THAT MUCH.

that/which

USAGE PANEL QUESTION

Panelist HAROLD SCHONBERG questions whether a distinction can be drawn between "The book *that* I read last night" and "The book *which* I read last night." The grammatical "rule" is that *which* should be used to introduce nonrestrictive clauses ("Those ideals, *which* we respect so highly, are now in peril") and *that* should be used to introduce restrictive clauses ("The book *that* I read last night was amusing"). Do you regard these distinctions as worth preserving?
Yes: 62%. No: 38%.
Do you observe the distinctions in your own speech?   Yes: 55%. No: 45%.
In your writing   Yes: 68%. No: 32%.

SHERIDAN BAKER: "I hold rigorously to 'which' as non-restrictive only, except in a series of restrictions, where 'thats' seem awkward. 'The book which he liked, which she hated, and which no one could put down.' But I always drop the restrictive 'that' where possible: 'The book I read. . . .' "

STEWART BEACH: "The distinction between using 'which' and 'that' seems to me a grammarian's dream whose night has passed. Some people may know by instinct which to use. I confess that I don't stop to think when I'm speaking whether I am about to utter a nonrestrictive or a restrictive clause, though I sometimes do in writing. In that case, though, I usually select the one that sounds best—or better."

ALVIN BEAM: "Yes, but as a copyeditor, I would strike the word 'that' out in each of these examples. The 'thats' are quite unnecessary."

CHARLES BERLITZ: "Insistence on this distinction is stultifying and not linguistically logical—cf. German, Dutch, the Scandinavian and other languages related to English."

HAL BORLAND: "I long ago forgot the actual difference, so I rely on my ear. Only occasionally does the wrong use annoy me in another writer's work. Euphony is my guide."

JOHN BROOKS: "Not only should the distinction be retained, it's a key to good English usage."

HEYWOOD HALE BROUN: "Rules of grammar which don't contribute to clarity can be thrown out with the classroom chalk stubs."

JOHN CIARDI: "Yes, but in this case, I prefer 'The book I read last night.' "

ALEX FAULKNER: "I think I would say, 'The book I read last night.' "

THOMAS FLEMING: "Most of the time."

PAUL HORGAN: "Not consistently, I'm afraid."

NORMAN HOSS: "Yes . . . only because of being inoculated by Fowler via Harold Ross."

JOHN K. HUTCHENS: "But 'that' is not at all necessary in this usage. Why bother with an extra word?"

ALEXANDER KENDRICK: "They are worth preserving, but no one is doing it."

WALTER LORD: "Yes. In writing, I've always felt that the *comma* was what determined the matter. No comma = restrictive; comma = nonrestrictive."

RUSSELL LYNES: "No. Why not 'the book I read last night'?"

PHYLLIS McGINLEY: "I usually just say 'the book I read last night.' "

WADE MOSBY: "Only if I can remember the difference. Perry C. Hill, the chairman of the Milwaukee *Journal*'s style committee and an editorial writer of vast persuasive powers, recently retired. At his retirement party, the chief editorial writer, John Reddin, said: 'Perry for years has been explaining to me the difference between "that" and "which," and I never did get it straight.' Now that we no longer have Perry to kick around, John and I will have to continue flying by the seats of our pants. 'That' and/or 'which' are well worn in this struggle."

EDWIN NEWMAN: "I try to. I try to."

PETER S. PRESCOTT: "I feel guilty about the loss of any distinction, but this one, more than any other, has caused me trouble. I operate on instinct and am sometimes totally confused as to which I want."

F. D. REEVE: "Follow usage, not a 'rule.' "

LEO ROSTEN: "Even Fowler gets fouled up on this."

BERTON ROUECHÉ: "I try."

VERMONT ROYSTER: "Yes, but I often use neither; simply 'the book I read last night.' "

HARRISON SALISBURY: "I don't understand them—never did."

ROBERT SHERRILL: "Not always."

CHARLES E. SILBERMAN: "I try—but not always successfully!"

ELVIS STAHR, JR.: "I often use neither, I'm afraid. I'd say, usually, 'The book I read last night.' "

HAROLD TAYLOR: "Yes, although I don't usually notice. I seem to remember using 'which' a lot more than 'that.' "

BARBARA TUCHMAN: "They would be worth preserving if only one could make the distinction more comprehensible. I have never been able to apply the rule because (as in your examples) I can't see any difference in the restrictive nature of the two clauses—so I always end up going by sound. I wish a good clear rule could be evolved."

that's for sure/certain/real Until the mid-1940s, people would say "that's sure" or "that's certain," but in recent years the phrases have become *that's for sure* and *that's for certain.* Another example is *that's for real.* The use of the preposition "for" to intensify but not alter the meaning of the word following it has become widespread. This may be acceptable on an informal or slang level of speech but it is surely to be avoided in formal speech and especially in formal writing.

the, pronunciation of The simplest rule is to say THEE (long "e") before vowels ("*the* open road") and THUH (short "e") before consonants ("*the* high school"). There are some parts of the country, notably the South, where the short "e" pronunciation is often heard before vowels as well.

the above. *See* ABOVE

theater/theatre The American spelling preference is *theater,* the British *theatre.* However, when New York's legitimate theaters were built, the stage was much under British influence, so many of the houses have the "-re" spelling in their names. When writing of the *theater* in general, it is best to use the "-er" spelling. If referring to a specific *theater,* it is best to check to see which ending is proper.

theft. *See* ROBBERY/BURGLARY/THEFT

therapy/treatment The redundant phrase "both therapy and treatment" is sometimes used by persons who think of *therapy* only in terms of "physical *therapy.*" *Therapy* simply means "treatment of any mental or physical disease or disability by medical or physical means." The term does not usually include surgery. *See also* REDUNDANCY.

Third World Sometimes capitalized, sometimes not, this phrase is used to designate the underdeveloped or emergent countries of the world, particularly those in Africa and Asia. The reasoning behind this term is that the Old World is made up of Europe, Russia, China, India, and the long-established nations of North Africa; the New World is made up of North America and some of the Latin American countries. And the Third World is made up of new nations, independent of either the "old" or the "new" and resisting the influence of both the so-called free world and the communist world.

this/that/these/those (in place of articles) The substitution of a demonstrative pronoun such as *this* for an article, as in "I once knew *this* woman who loved to ski," is at best an informal usage. A better wording would be "a woman who loved to ski." *See also* SOME/A.

this (these) kind (kinds) A very common but nonetheless irritating error on the part of even educated persons is the use of *these kind* when speaking of more than one kind of things. If there are a number of things, all of one kind, the proper usage is *this kind*. If the things are of several different kinds, the proper usage is *these kinds*. *These kind* is sloppy and wrong.

It may seem elementary but we would like to underscore the fact that *this* and *these* are demonstrative pronouns and must agree in number with the noun to which each refers, in this case *kind*.

though. *See* ALTHOUGH/THOUGH and IF/WHETHER/THOUGH

thousand/thousands The use of *thousand* is governed by the same rule as that for "hundred" and "million." When the number of *thousands* is given, as in "fifteen *thousand* tons," the form is singular. If the number is not given, the phrase is simply *"thousands* of tons."

thrust. *See* VOGUE WORDS

thruway. *See* TURNPIKE/THRUWAY/PARKWAY/HIGHWAY/FREE-WAY/SUPERHIGHWAY

thus

USAGE PANEL QUESTION

Panelist JAMES MACGREGOR BURNS writes: "As a working author, I have trouble with the following problem: I want to illustrate a general point with an example, but find that saying 'for example' each time is heavy and formal. Thus I find myself using the word 'thus' instead. It is apt and unpretentious, though doubtless wrong. Example: 'Roosevelt enjoyed royalty; thus he often invited Princess Martha to tea.' Or 'We were able to get a plane nonstop from New York to L.A.; thus we avoided stops in Chicago and Denver.'. . . We badly need a short word for 'for example' and I nominate 'thus.' "
Would you, as a writer, agree?   Yes: 53%. No: 47%.
Would you, as a writer, prefer a still less formal word such as "so"?   Yes: 72%. No: 28%.

ISAAC ASIMOV: "Good Lord! 'Thus' has the faint aroma of 'therefore' while 'so' says it just right."
STEWART BEACH: " 'Thus' seems to me a stuffy and academic usage. It is rarely if ever necessary to use 'for example.' In the second sentence you *can't* use it. But I have always avoided 'thus' and 'so.' "
CHARLES BERLITZ: "Yes, for a variation."

HAL BORLAND: "Neither example seems apt. I agree to the need, but not to 'thus.' 'So' is far better."

JOSEPH A. BRANDT: " 'For example' has a nice geometric quality I'd prefer to keep."

HEYWOOD HALE BROUN: " 'So' is more than informal, it's sloppy."

BEN LUCIEN BURMAN: "This seems haywire, to me. 'Thus' does not seem to me to mean 'for example' no matter how you stretch your imagination."

JOHN CIARDI: "Neither. 'For example,' like 'he said,' in dialogue functions almost as a punctuation. The reader registers it and passes it over. I don't object to 'thus,' but I have no objection to any number of 'for examples.' "

ROBERT CROMIE: "I'm on the fence. How about 'hence'?"

RICHARD EDES HARRISON: "I prefer 'so' to avoid overdoing 'thus.' "

S. I. HAYAKAWA: "The first use of 'thus' could mean 'for example' or 'therefore.' The second use does not mean 'for example' at all, but 'thus.' "

PAUL HORGAN: "I don't find the need urgent. Mostly one can delete 'for example' or 'thus,' etc."

JOHN K. HUTCHENS: "I would use 'thus' but use 'so' as well, to avoid repetition."

WALT KELLY: "Well, I don't care for either of the examples. 'Thus,' to me, means 'by so doing' or 'as a result,' NOT 'for example.' "

ALEXANDER KENDRICK: "I question the example—only royalty can properly *enjoy* royalty. But applaud the usage."

WALTER KERR: " 'Thus' is O.K., but I prefer 'so.' "

LAURENCE LAFORE: "I dislike 'thus' anyway; and in these cases a colon, or even a semicolon, would serve the purpose."

WALTER LORD: "What's the matter with 'hence'?"

RUSSELL LYNES: "Your first 'thus' should be 'therefore'; the second should be 'in this manner.' What's the matter with 'for example'?" 'So' is possible, but not in all cases."

HENRY W. MALONE: "Why not use all three and also revise the sentence to avoid the need?"

JESSICA MITFORD: "Your first 'thus' should be omitted altogether; the second doesn't mean 'for example,' it means 'consequently.' The use of 'so' depends on the context."

HERBERT MITGANG: "In the cadence of a paragraph of exposition, 'for example,' 'so,' and 'thus' all are different. It is best illustrated in fiction. A stuffy character might say 'thus' to be in character but he would not use 'so,' which would be more colloquial. Has it occurred that 'for example' can be cut out often, just giving the example?"

WRIGHT MORRIS: "Why not 'inviting' and 'avoiding'? 'So' is better than 'thus' but not a solution."

EDWIN NEWMAN: "It seems to me the need in these examples could be met by 'and.' "

PETER S. PRESCOTT: " 'Thus' is, as the writer says, clearly wrong. I think the problem should be solved by restructuring the sentence. Also, there are synonyms that this writer seems not to have tried."

LEO ROSTEN: "A colon works, or a mixture of words—'that is why,' 'therefore,' 'and so.'. . ."

RICHARD H. ROVERE: "I'd accept 'stop' in most cases."

LEONARD SANDERS: "My experience has been that most of the 'work' in 'working author' involves finding ways to avoid repetitious phrases. But one that calls attention to the 'work' detracts from the effect. To my ear, 'thus' is such a word."

HAROLD SCHONBERG: "I also use 'therefore,' 'so'—lots of ways to get out of it. But there is nothing wrong with 'thus.' "

DANIEL SCHORR: "I don't prefer 'so,' but would use it when it seemed right."

HOWARD TAUBMAN: "Why does one need any word or phrase? Why not just go ahead and give the example?"

BARBARA TUCHMAN: "I see no need whatever for a rule to govern this usage. Let a writer make his own choice according to his style. Personally, I would take out those semicolons (which should be reserved for use where indispensable) and in the first case, change 'thus' to 'and'; in the second, delete 'we avoided' and substitute 'avoiding.' "

WILLIAM C. VERGARA: "I sympathize with the author! Science writers are always on the lookout for a new 'for example.' I've used 'thus,' 'so,' 'consider this,' 'imagine,' 'one method is to,' and heaven knows whatever else. Also, 'to illustrate.' "

JUDITH VIORST: "Prefer 'so,' depending on formality of context."

GEORGE WALD: " 'Hence,' sometimes 'too.' Use both. 'So' is useful too."

CHARLOTTE ZOLOTOW: "In most instances the 'so' or 'thus' is implied. I'd suggest a dash, just to separate statement from example."

thusly The nonstandard *thusly* must have been coined by someone who thought that all adverbs have to end in "-ly" or who thought *thusly* was a little more "elegant" than just "thus." In any event it is an abomination. "Thus" is stuffy enough for all normal purposes. *See also* FIRSTLY/ THUSLY.

tick *Tick* has two British meanings which are relatively unfamiliar in the U.S. In England one *ticks* off items on a list, where an American would "check" them off. Also in Great Britain one buys *on tick,* where an American would buy "on credit" or "on a charge account."

ticket-of-leave *Ticket-of-leave* is the British equivalent of "parole." The expression is a very old one, according to the *OED,* dating back at least to 1732. A *ticket-of-leave* man is a paroled convict.

t.i.d. *See* B.I.D./T.I.D./RX

tight/tightly *Tight* is both an adjective and an adverb and, as an adverb, can be used synonymously with *tightly.* In posting a notice to users of a steam valve to shut it off properly you could write either, "Turn the valve off *tight*" or "Turn the valve off *tightly.*" Since the instruction is one on which safe operation of the equipment depends, we favor "Turn the valve off *tight*" to make the point as quickly and as effectively as possible. *See also* SLOW/SLOWLY.

tights *Tights,* as the name for a woman's knitted under and outer garment, was standard American just a few years ago, though the fashion seems to have been outmoded by pantyhose. However, the British use *tights* as the name for what Americans call *pantyhose.* Professional dancers on both sides of the Atlantic wear dancing *tights* when they are not wearing the all-over leotard.

tight ship. *See* TAUT SHIP/TIGHT SHIP

tilde The wavy line over the middle consonant in such Spanish words as "piñon," "cañon," and "señor" is used to indicate the sound of "ny." It is pronounced TIL-duh.

till/until/'til/'till Many people are not aware that the word *till* exists and that it is equally acceptable as and interchangeable with *until.* Some writers who do know this still prefer to use *until,* rather than *till,* at the beginning of a sentence. Most people who say *till* think they are using a contraction of *until,* which sometimes appears in writing as *'til* and is acceptable only in informal writing.

The formation *'till* is a bastard word and is substandard.

tilt at windmills This is a colorful figure of speech which means to pursue a course foredoomed to frustration and failure. The allusion is to Cervantes' hero, Don Quixote, who, accompanied by his faithful manservant, Sancho Panza, roamed the countryside and tilted at a group of windmills with his lance under the delusion that they were giants.

timbromania. *See* MANIA

Time!/Time, gentlemen, please! *Time!* or, in full, *Time, gentlemen, please!* is the ancient cry of the British publican warning that the time is at hand when his pub must be closed. Despite the "gentlemen," the stricture applies equally to ladies.

tin/tinned food/tin-opener   The English grocer does not stock canned goods but *tinned food*. One opens a *tin* of peas, obviously, with a *tin-opener*.

tiny little detail   A *redundancy* (which see). A *detail* is essentially small and neither adjective is needed. Use of the phrase "every detail" or "last detail" will convey any sense of completeness intended.

tithesis. *See* LOST POSITIVES

to be   The rule that the verb *to be* must be followed by the same case that precedes it was applied to English by grammarians schooled in Latin, where the rule works every time. English, however, is an unruly language, ever-changing and ever-growing. For this reason, even though strict purists say that you must say, "It is I," most of us find that the sentence is stilted and unnatural. In conversation, even among literate and educated people, you will hear, "It's me."

That is the exception to the rule. Everywhere except in the third person singular, the verb *to be* is followed by the same case that precedes it.

to be, omission of   New residents of cities such as Pittsburgh and Milwaukee frequently write to comment on the practice by many residents of these places of omitting the verb *to be* in such phrases as "my carpet needs cleaned" and "my hair needs washed." *See also* ELLIPTICAL ILLITERACIES.

tolic   *Tolic* is a very old regional dialect word which means much the same as "whole kit and caboodle." Harold Wentworth in his *American Dialect Dictionary* reports having heard it in 1922 from a ninety-three-year-old woman in Danbury, Connecticut, whose descendants had also adopted it. He found it in phrases like "the whole kit and *tolic* of you." A Pittsburgh woman tells us that it is still in use in her family, as in "There's an awful *tolic* of dishes to be washed."

tomato   Probably no pronunciation in our American language is more argued about than that of the simple vegetable, the *tomato*. Most ordinary Americans say tuh-MAY-toh and regard the pronunciation tuh-MAH-toh as affected, though many New Englanders and Southerners pronounce it that way from childhood. (We have heard New England farmers speak of it as a tuh-MATT-er, which is obviously a dialect pronunciation.) Merriam's Third International Dictionary (Unabridged) lists what appear to be six variant pronunciations. Two criteria for deciding which to use are offered to us, partly in jest. An advertising man of our acquaintance says:

"*Tomato* should be pronounced tuh-MAH-toh in institutional campaigns but tuh-MAY-toh for hard-sell campaigns." A Milwaukee reader reports: "It's a tuh-MAY-toh unless they are more than thirty-nine cents a pound. Above that price it's a tuh-MAH-toh." At today's prices the dividing line has to be higher.

tomfoolery   *Tomfoolery* seems to be a very casual word but it is listed in the dictionaries without any restriction on its use. It has a long history in the English language, though not a very humane one. In medieval times it was considered great sport to watch the antics of insane people in asylums such as Bedlam in London. The nicknames "Tom o' Bedlam" and "Tom Fool" were often used for male inmates who were favorites of the audience. Over the centuries the word *tomfoolery* evolved—eventually acquiring the relatively innocuous meaning it has today: "foolish behavior" or "nonsense."

tomorrow is (will be)   The use of the present tense in sentences with the word *tomorrow,* while seemingly illogical, is firmly rooted in our English idiom. We hear "*Tomorrow* the Colts play the Packers." "*Tomorrow is* Sunday" is far more common than "*Tomorrow will be* Sunday."

tonic. *See* SELTZER/SODA/POP/TONIC/SPARKLING WATER

too/very   The prejudice against the use of *too* in the sense of *very* dies hard. Today it is listed in all standard dictionaries as perfectly correct usage. It usually appears with "not," as in *not too good/not too bright* (which see).

All sorts of logical arguments can be given to show that we don't need another synonym for *very* and that, even if we did, *too* would be an illogical word to use. But our language does not always follow the rules of logic. The fact is that many people of education and breeding do use such expressions as "not doing *too* badly." Winston Churchill is on record as using the phrase "not *too* good." So *too* in this sense has to be considered standard English, though it is not recommended for a sermon, state paper, or any other formal speech or writing.

torch   *Torch,* in addition to the customary senses, has a special British meaning of "flashlight."

total   *Total,* as a verb meaning to destroy totally, is a fairly recent item of U.S. slang: "Tom *totaled* his car in the crash."

to the manner born. *See* MANNER BORN, TO THE

track record

USAGE PANEL QUESTION

Panelist "RED" SMITH, commenting in his column on what fellow panelist ROBERT LIPSYTE christened "sportspeak," noted that many expressions like "go to bat for" have been useful to individuals writing or speaking about matters that have nothing to do with baseball and, in most cases, the meaning is entirely clear. "But," he added, "some widely popular examples of sportspeak are barbarisms whose use should be a misdemeanor, if not a capital offense." An example he cites is *track record* in expressions like "In the matter of civil rights, the governor's *track record* is not very good." Mr. Smith noted that humans don't have *track records,* while horses, greyhounds, and racing cars do. A *track record,* properly used, refers to the fastest time made on a certain track over a specified distance.

Do you agree with Mr. Smith that such imprecise use of sports terms should be considered "a misdemeanor, if not a capital offense"?

In speech? Yes: 41%. No: 59%.
In writing? Yes: 51%. No: 49%.

ISAAC ASIMOV: "The point is that the word 'track' is unnecessary. Leave it out, make no other change, and all is well."

WHITNEY BALLIETT: "Something that 'comes in from left field' connotes oddness, mysteriousness, and has taken on a quite different meaning from the sports usage. Better not to shut the door completely—although many sports terms have become dreadful clichés: 'You're out,' 'Who's on first?' etc."

BARRY BINGHAM, SR.: "I dislike differing with the late, illustrious 'Red' Smith, but find no objection to a reference to a person's 'track record,' not to indicate his best speed but his general level of performance."

JOSEPH A. BRANDT: "No. A mile runner who breaks a world record has a good record and can prove it."

HEYWOOD HALE BROUN: "Nations should not be run by 'game plans.' "

ANTHONY BURGESS: "The effect of U.S. idioms of this kind is highly parochial. Also they've become a real problem to outsiders listening to U.S. political speeches."

JAMES MacGREGOR BURNS: "I believe there is much gain in carrying over expressions from one field to another and little harm in adaptation and survival of the fittest!"

ROBERT CROMIE: "I think it's too colorful and concise and useful *not* to use."

WILLARD E. ESPY: " 'Red' Smith, bless his memory, was being puritanical here. 'Track record' is perhaps objectionable as a cliché, or even a redundancy, but not as a metaphor."

ALEX FAULKNER: "A capital offense, perhaps, in serious writing but a jolly good way to perk up a light-hearted piece."

RAY GANDOLF: "It grieves me to disagree with 'Red' Smith. He knew much more about horse racing than I do and was quite properly upset by the misuse of 'track record.' But I find sports expressions, including 'track record,' generally more interesting and colorful than similar borrowings from other walks of life. I would much rather begin life 'with two strikes against me' than come from 'a disadvantaged neighborhood.' "

ROBERT GOTTLIEB: "I think this is acceptable if used in speech and in informal writing. It's not the accuracy of such phrases that counts, but whether they enrich or impoverish the language; I don't see any harm being done here."

ELIZABETH HARDWICK: "I don't mind 'track record' although it inclines the speaker in the direction of the mixed metaphor. I believe the extension of 'go to bat' is amusing and valuable."

JOHN K. HUTCHENS: "I agree with 'Red Smith' on all counts on this one."

DIANE JOHNSON: "Yes, especially by government officials."

JAMES K. KILPATRICK: "Metaphors that come from the world of sports have an indispensable place in both speech and writing. The peril for those of us who cover politics is not misuse but hackneyed use: front runner, dark horse, high hurdles, throw in the towel, and so on."

STANLEY KUNITZ: " 'Track' is superfluous. Delete it."

ROBERT LIPSYTE: "Lipsyte, the father of sportspeak, slides with his spikes up when he hears speakers use sports phrases to, at once, vivify and obscure their message. It's a trick to divert us, to confuse us—and when sports phrases are used in military and political contexts, it's often an attempt to victimize us."

JULES LOH: "I must disagree with the late Master on this one. Metaphors are not to be taken literally to begin with, so a slight imprecision in the transfer would seem to be tolerable."

WILLIAM MCGUIRE: " 'Go to bat' seems O.K. in colloquial usage. 'Track record' strikes me as less acceptable."

EDWIN NEWMAN: " 'Track record' in the usage you cite is like 'ground rules.' The 'track' and the 'ground' can be omitted."

F. D. REEVE: "Rebarbative jargon."

VERMONT ROYSTER: "This is no more a capital offense than saying that the QE2 *sailed* from New York."

DAVID SCHOENBRUN: "Human beings do follow or run on tracks both literally in track events, and figuratively. I tend to be tolerant of new speech expressions, but a purist in writing."

HAROLD SCHONBERG: "It's been with us for too long and has, I think, established itself."

JACK SMITH: " 'Track record' has been virtually replaced by 'record,' which would be enough. Why would a Justice of the Supreme Court need a track record? How about 'ballpark estimate'?"

ELVIS STAHR, JR.: "To me, 'track record,' in a figurative sense, suggests that there have been a good many undertakings along a certain line. It has become useful as a succinct way of highlighting past performances."

WALLACE STEGNER: "Of all our activities, sports are the most colloquial. Deny sportsmen this privilege and they aren't themselves any more. They are entitled to their technical jargon as computer science is."

EDWARD TRIPP: "I have little use for speakers who try to prove themselves 'in the know,' 'hip,' forceful, lively, or colorful by using words of any sort without bothering to find out what they mean. 'Track record,' moreover, is not only wrong but a redundancy; it means nothing in this context that 'record' doesn't mean."

BARBARA TUCHMAN: "I feel foolish taking issue with 'Red' Smith, but is not the whole sports activity of running and its variations called 'track'? I don't see why a person cannot have a 'track record'—seems quite acceptable."

EARL UBELL: "I have a problem regarding the use of sports words and metaphors; they tend to make us think about serious things in the same terms as games and sports, which have little to do with human beings confronting reality. President Nixon was known for his reliance on football concepts with unhappy results. Was it he that used the phrase 'when the going gets tough, the tough get going' as prelude to the Ellsberg break-in? I cannot imagine a more terrible mixture than sports thinking and foreign policy."

JOSEPH VERGARA: " 'Track record,' for some reason, doesn't bother me. 'Ball park figure' does. What sense does that make?"

DOUGLAS WATT: " 'Track record' has become a cliché, long since in need of being retired."

A.B.C. WHIPPLE: "I guess it's a matter of taste. 'Track record' doesn't jar my ear the way 'mirandize' and 'prioritize' do."

CHARLOTTE ZOLOTOW: "No, but they are tough on some of us non-sport types."

trade mark/trademark   *Trade mark* originally appeared in the language as two words. It was, quite literally, the mark used by one member of a trade to differentiate his product from his competitor's product. With the passage of time, the phrase was joined by a hyphen, especially in expressions like "*trade-marked* merchandise." For the past several decades, however, the tendency has been very strong to write it solid *(trademark)* whether it is used as a noun or as a verb. Curiously enough, the closely related expression "trade name" is still given as two words in all reference sources consulted. A *trademark* is, in the U.S., a name or symbol registered with the U.S. Patent Office (though it is not a patent in itself) and is legally restricted in use to the products of a single manufacturer.

Coca-Cola and Xerox are *trademarks* and should always be spelled with initial capital letters. Owners of *trademarks* zealously strive to protect their rights to the exclusive use of their *trademarks,* lest they fall into the public domain and become *generic words* (which see).

trans-. *See* PREFIXES AND SUFFIXES, WITH AND WITHOUT HYPHEN

transitive/intransitive Many otherwise literate folk have difficulty in differentiating between the *transitive* and *intransitive* forms of verbs, in part because a very great many verbs have both *transitive* and *intransitive* senses. Put briefly and simply, a *transitive* verb is one that needs a direct object to complete its meaning: "He hit the ball'—"hit" is the *transitive* verb and "ball" is the direct object. An *intransitive* verb is one that does not require an object: "He hit in the clean-up position"—"hit" in this instance does not require a direct object to complete its meaning.

That seems simple enough, but we can testify, on the basis of a quarter of a century of dictionary editing, that most staff editors on such works still do not comprehend the difference and the ones who are most adamant that they do know the difference are usually the ones who bungle the definitions and mix *transitive* and *intransitive* senses indiscriminately.

translucent. *See* OPAQUE/TRANSLUCENT

transpire

USAGE PANEL QUESTION

Years ago this problem was set before the *Information, Please* panel: "It's a dark night in a lonely mansion on the moors. The master of the house, who believes he is alone, hears sudden loud moans from a third-floor room. Racing up the stairs, he throws open the attic door. What transpires?" After a brief pause, John Kieran answered: "He does." Would you regard this sense of *transpire*—virtually synonymous with "perspire" —as obsolete?
Yes: 77%. No: 23%.
If your answer is "no," would you use it in speech?   Yes: 25%. No: 75%.
In writing   Yes: 23%. No: 77%.

BENJAMIN APPEL: "A good pun, though!"
ISAAC ASIMOV: "Transpiration applies to the stomata of leaves, actually."
SHERIDAN BAKER: "I think the word is now useless, both pretentious and inaccurate in its newer sense of 'happens.' "
STEWART BEACH: "We have few John Kierans in our nation and he was

probably alone in knowing that 'transpire' is a synonym of 'perspire.' I didn't. I think that meaning should be labeled obsolete."

SAUL BELLOW: "Kieran was speaking French—'to transpire' does not mean 'to happen.' It is a subtle word and its subtlety should be protected."

BARRY BINGHAM, SR.: "I find Kieran's answer delightfully witty, but I can't really regard his usage of 'transpire' as a viable current synonym for 'perspire.' "

HAL BORLAND: "In this sense the word is not only wrong but pretentious. It has a clear and needed biological meaning in science."

HEYWOOD HALE BROUN: "One wonders, as in all such cases of 'dictionary' usage, what is wrong with a simple word like 'happens.' "

ABE BURROWS: "I'm afraid the original meaning of 'transpire' has been lost forever. The wrong meaning has triumphed in stuffy circles. I think the word should be dropped from the language. 'Happen' happens to be a very good word."

JOHN CIARDI: "I will use anything that serves. If an obsolete sense serves, I will use that."

LEON EDEL: "It's really French: *transpirer.*"

RICHARD EDES HARRISON: "A useful verb in botany."

LAURENCE LAFORE: " 'Transpire' in the metaphorical sense of 'leak out' seems to me acceptable. But it is not acceptable as a synonym for 'happen.' "

JULES LOH: "But I like the gag—and approve in that sense."

LEO ROSTEN: " 'Transpires' for 'happens' is tantamount to lifting your pinkie while drinking tea."

DAVID SCHOENBRUN: "The only true meaning of 'transpire' is 'to breathe through,' thus a synonym for 'perspire.' Alas, hardly anyone knows that 'any more.' "

WALTER W. "RED" SMITH: "Say it's *virtually* obsolete."

EARL UBELL: "In botany, cell physiology, O.K."

trash barrel/ecological receptacle. *See* EUPHEMISM

tread. *See* TROD/TREAD/TRODDEN

treatment. *See* THERAPY/TREATMENT

tri-. *See* PREFIXES AND SUFFIXES, WITH AND WITHOUT HYPHEN

trimester. *See* SEMESTER/TRIMESTER

trio/quartet/quintet These three terms for musical groups have been converted by some journalists to refer to three, four, or five persons, regardless of whether they are related to each other in any way.

trip *Trip* is a slang word whose special meaning originated in the use of hallucinogenic drugs. The time spent under the influence of such a drug could be either a "good *trip*" or a "bad *trip*" depending on one's reaction to the drug.

Then it came to be applied to any experience similar in that it involved a degree of delusion. An "ego *trip*" means an experience which inflates the ego. "Being chairman of the committee is a real ego *trip* for him." A "guilt *trip*" is a reaction involving unwarranted guilt. "She told me that I would be profiting from another's misfortune but I wouldn't buy that guilt *trip*."

tripos A British term, *tripos* means, at Cambridge University, England, any of the examinations given for a B.A. degree with honors ("honours" in England).

Tripos originally was the three-legged stool on which a graduate would sit during the commencement ceremonies and dispute in bantering doggerel with the degree candidates. Later the verse created by the *tripos* wits was published and, for reasons now obscure, the list of candidates qualified for the honors degree in mathematics was printed on the back of the sheet. Thus the name of the three-legged stool finally became the name of the examination itself.

trod/tread/trodden There is a curious misconception that *trod* is a variant form of "to *tread*," reflected in such statements as "The actress is now *trodding* the boards in Cincinnati." A *New York Times* article on Antarctica says "a shipload of tourists will trod on land that has been reserved for the select few." One of our favorite Broadway actresses was quoted as saying, "I'll never forget that 'Dolly' response. I don't care how hardboiled or cynical you may be or how many years you've been trodding the boards—something like that strikes home."

Trod has only two possible uses: as the past tense and alternate past participle of the verb *tread*. (The other alternate past participle is *trodden*.) John Paul Jones didn't say, "Don't trod on me."

trolley *Trolley* in the U.S. refers to the obsolescent if not quite obsolete means of mass transportation also called "streetcar." In England a *trolley* is more likely to be a tea wagon.

troop/troops/troupe/trooper The difference between the uses of *troop* in the singular and plural forms is a verbal oddity that can be explained not on any ground of logic but only as a matter of accepted usage.

A *troop* (singular) is always a collection of people, usually men and usually organized for military purposes. This idea of a group goes back to its Latin predecessor "troppus" meaning "a flock." In the plural *(troops)* it is used as if in reference to the individual soldiers. Thus 100,000 *troops* does not mean, as you might logically expect it to mean, "100,000 groups of soldiers" but simply "100,000 soldiers."

The use of *troop* to mean "a company of actors" is now archaic. The preferred form for this meaning is *troupe.*

Trooper may be used to refer to a cavalryman (or his horse), a paratrooper, a mounted policeman, or any state policeman.

true facts To use *true* with *facts* is to create a *redundancy* (which see). Nothing is a *fact* unless it is *true.*

try and/try to The idiom *try and,* in such expressions as "*try and* stop me" has long been criticized as being illogical, which indeed it is. The meaning of the expression is clearly "*try to* stop me." But, as we have noted elsewhere, the only consistent aspect of language is its inconsistency, a premise that we may in this instance extend to its illogicality. In any event, despite the protests of purists, *try and* has met with acceptance by usage authorities ever since the first edition of Fowler's *Modern English Usage,* in which he noted that "while *try to* do can always be substituted, *try and* do has a shade of meaning that justifies its existence. . . . It is an idiom that should not be discountenanced, but used when it comes natural." So *try and* is entirely acceptable in informal contexts but is to be avoided in formal speech or writing.

tryst *Tryst,* meaning a secret meeting between lovers, is a word which has long been loved by headline writers, though it may not be used as frequently now as it used to be. It is seldom heard in speech. The phrase "secret *tryst*" is a *redundancy* (which see) and as such is nonsense. *Tryst* may be pronounced with either a long or short "i."

tsar/tzar. *See* CZAR/TSAR/TZAR

tsimmis/tsimmes These are variant spellings for a borrowing from Yiddish which has gained a fair degree of currency in recent years, especially in show-business circles. It originally meant a stew, whether of vegetables or fruit. As borrowed into English it may mean either a prolonged, complicated affair or, more commonly, a troublesome argument or confrontation.

tuck *Tuck* is British slang for a substantial meal, especially one with a variety of special dishes, rather on the order of high tea.

turf accountant This is one of the relatively rare instances when the British have adopted an expression that reeks of phony elegance as contrasted with the American version. (It's usually the other way around.)

Anyhow, the *turf accountant* is nothing more than the chap with whom you put down your bets on horse races. In America he's called a "bookie" or, rarely, a "bookmaker."

turnpike/thruway/parkway/highway/freeway/superhighway

Highway is the oldest of all these terms for roads and still has the basic meaning of "a main road which connects towns and cities." It is a general term which includes all the others.

A *parkway* is a special kind of *highway* in that it is bordered by or divided by trees, bushes, and grass. With the higher-speed cars came the *superhighways:* the *turnpike, thruway,* and *freeway.*

Turnpikes and *thruways* are usually toll roads, as was the original road from which present-day *turnpikes* got their name. The "pike" was, in olden days, a pole mounted on a vertical post so as to bar movement along a road. When a toll was paid, the pike was turned and the traveler passed along on his way. The name *thruway,* for much the same kind of road as a *turnpike,* is attributed to the man who sponsored the bill which authorized the building of the New York State Thruway, State Assembly-man Abbot Low Moffat. Roads leading out of New York City at that time were *parkways* and not really suited to fast-moving through traffic. Moffat sought a name which would express the primary purpose of the road he was proposing—a two-way express artery uninterrupted by grade crossings. He took "thoroughfare," modified it to "throughway," shortened that to *thruway,* and named the new highways. *Thruways* and *turnpikes* are really the same. There is little difference when you leave the New York State Thruway and find yourself on the Connecticut Turnpike, just different lights and differently labeled toll booths. A *freeway* is still another *superhighway,* so named because no tolls are collected. *Turnpike, thruway, parkway, highway, freeway,* and *superhighway* are now all standard English.

turophile *Turophile* is a word which has just recently made it into the pages of the unabridged dictionaries and one which Clifton Fadiman is credited with coining. It means "a connoisseur or fancier of cheese" and comes quite logically from two Greek words: "tyros" for "cheese" and "philos" for "loving."

twice as many . . . as/than The editor of a major newspaper wrote us: "I was distressed to find two misuses of exactly the same nature in a recent issue of our newspaper. In both cases the expression used was *'twice as many . . . . than.'* " The clippings showed that the stories bore different by-lines. One stated: "Kentucky issued *twice as many* strip-mining per-mits in the first three months of 1974 *than* during the same period in 1973." The other story contained the phrase "*twice as many* prospective starters *than* Churchill Downs can accommodate in a single line-up." Obviously the formulation in each instance should be *twice as many . . . as.*

The editor commented: "I have an uneasy suspicion that it may be attributable to some television personality whose words are unquestionably echoed by many Americans."

two-bit Used only in informal speech and writing, *two-bit* has an extended meaning of "cheap or tawdry" or "inferior or worthless." It gets its meaning from *two-bits,* the slang term given the United States quarter when it was coined. In the Southwest United States several generations ago Mexican currency was used interchangeably with local coinage and the "real" (pronounced RAY-ahl), a coin worth about 12½ cents, was called a "bit." "Bit" was originally British slang for any small coin.

two-faced words. *See* SANGUINE

twofer Theatrical slang for a cut-rate ticket, so called because they formerly were sold at the price of two for *(twofer)* one.

two times two is/are Preferred usage is "*two times two is* four," not "*two times two are* four." If there is any logic there, it is that a phrase such as "the result of" is understood to precede the statement. Some linguists, while noting that the singular verb is more widely used, insist that "*two times two are* four" is not wrong and must also be accepted.

ultra-. *See* PREFIXES AND SUFFIXES, WITH AND WITHOUT HYPHEN

un-. *See* PREFIXES AND SUFFIXES, WITH AND WITHOUT HYPHEN

unabridged. *See* ABRIDGED/UNABRIDGED

unalienable/inalienable *Unalienable* is familiar to all from studying the Declaration of Independence: "We hold these Truths to be self-evident, that all Men are created equal, that they are endowed by their Creator with certain unalienable Rights, that among these are Life, Liberty, and the Pursuit of Happiness." Today, however, the dictionaries which do list *unalienable* (and at least one no longer does) label it "archaic" and give *inalienable* as the accepted form.

So *unalienable* joins *more perfect* (which see) among the words which our founding fathers chose but which are no longer part of the living language.

unauthorized trespassing A *redundancy* (which see). "Unauthorized presence," yes. *Unauthorized trespassing,* no. *Trespassing* alone is sufficient.

unaware. *See* OBLIVIOUS/UNAWARE

unbeknownst/unbeknown The *Oxford English Dictionary* records *unbeknownst* as appearing before 1850 but labels it "vulgar and dialectal." This seems curious, for the word sounds more quaint and formal than "vulgar." Over the years, however, it has gradually been emerging into accepted status. By 1934 Webster was content to drop the "vulgar" label and indicate merely that it was most often heard in regional dialects. At the same time, *unbeknown* became the more common form and current dictionaries give both forms (*unbeknown* preferred) without any restriction on use. It means simply "unknown" or "without one's knowledge" and is usually followed by "to."

uncomparable To identify adjectives which are absolutes, such as "unique" and "eternal," linguists now use the term "incomparable" to indicate that these adjectives are not subject to comparison by the use of "more" and "most," or "-er" and "-est."

"Incomparable" has the more common meaning of "matchless" or "unequaled" and, in view of this, it would seem logical that *uncomparable* would be a better word to apply to adjectives which are absolutes. But, despite the fact that all dictionaries, especially unabridged ones, devote pages to words with the prefix "un-," it is necessary to go back to the minute type in which Merriam's Second International (Unabridged) lists all the "un-" words which it does not define to find *uncomparable*. We would like to see it revived just as an appropriate descriptive for the absolutes and so use it in this volume.

under. *See* OVER/UNDER

under-. *See* PREFIXES AND SUFFIXES, WITH AND WITHOUT HYPHEN

underclass

USAGE PANEL QUESTION

Sociologists and writers of a sociological bent have long shown a propensity for creating new labels for conditions which may indeed be new or may merely be existing conditions dramatized by the new labels. About 30 years ago A. C. Spectorsky coined "exurbia" to describe semi-rural areas beyond the suburbs of large cities where his "exurbanites" lived the lush life. Those words are now fading memories but each age brings new words and one such is *underclass,* created by Ken Auletta. According to *The New Yorker,* which originally published the work, his book is "a portrait of nine million people in the United States who have been cut off from society by poverty."

Would you regard *underclass* as still another euphemism for "poor," like "underprivileged" and "disadvantaged"? Yes: 49%. No: 51%.

Do you feel that *underclass* is a valuable addition to the lexicon of words dealing with society's problems? Yes: 41%. No: 59%.

ISAAC ASIMOV: " 'Poor' is 'poor' however many syllables you add. As for 'underclass,' that will surely go the way of 'underworld,' which is strictly 1920s now."

BARRY BINGHAM, SR.: " 'Underclass' has a special ring to it that is not quite the same as 'poor' or 'underprivileged.' I believe it is here to stay."

JOHN BROOKS: "I dislike it for reasons other than those suggested in the first question."

ANTHONY BURGESS: "A superogatory word."

BEN LUCIEN BURMAN: "Emphatically NO."

JOAN SIMPSON BURNS: "Yes, but it wasn't created by Ken Auletta. It has been around for a long time. 'Underclass' is perhaps a better term than 'underprivileged' or 'disadvantaged,' since those last two words apply as well to people who are not poor."

JOHN CIARDI: "Seems to be a fad word. 'Underprivileged' and 'disadvantaged' do the job."

WILLARD R. ESPY: "Though my answer is 'yes,' 'underclass' does have a nuance of meaning all its own. It presumes, as I read it, that the poverty of one section of our citizenry is unalterable without a revolutionary change in our society. 'Underprivileged,' 'disadvantaged,' and certainly 'poor' carry no such negative freight. Advantages can be made available to the disadvantaged, and privileges to the underprivileged. Since 'underclass' reveals a point of view, it is a useful word, however much one may disagree with its thesis."

FRANCES FRITCHMAN: "*Not* a euphemism—an accurate term describing a newly recognized fact about our society."

RAY GANDOLF: " 'Poor' is a euphemism for 'underclass,' which is an accurate, pungent, damning word."

JOHN K. HUTCHENS: "No. I don't see that it effectively replaces 'poor,' 'underprivileged,' and, especially, 'disadvantaged.' "

ELIZABETH JANEWAY: "I'm not crazy about this word but what Auletta appears to be describing exists in society (or, rather, on its margins) and has for a long time. Marx spoke of the *'Lumpenproletariat'* and I would vote for 'underclass' over that. . . . Indeed, Auletta seems to be describing not simply the 'poorest of the poor' but a group of people who do have a characteristic similarity in that they are all seen as being outside society; and who have developed the quality of being marginal, of not fitting, almost as a positive condition. Not, I hasten to say, a *chosen* condition. . . . It is a terrible phenomenon. Whether 'underclass' is the best name I don't know, but the phenomenon deserves to be recognized. To say nothing of being dealt with!"

WALTER KERR: "It doesn't of itself express a new shade of meaning."

JAMES J. KILPATRICK: "I can't see that 'underclass' adds anything useful to the euphemisms for 'poor' that already abound. The word smells of the academic lamp. It has none of the vivid imagery of 'underdog.' "

JULES LOH: "The word has a derogatory ring which I would not like to see applied to the poor."

DWIGHT MACDONALD: "Not the same thing at all. A permanent phenomenon."

WADE MOSBY: "We *have* acquired an 'underclass' of persons who sleep in boxes and never seem to be able to cope."

MARGE PIERCY: " 'Underclass' serves no purpose not better served by 'poor people,' or, if you like Marxist resonances, *'Lumpenproletariat.'* I prefer simply 'the poor,' whom we have always with us, apparently, under new euphemisms."

PETER S. PRESCOTT: "Auletta makes it clear that not all of the 'underclass' are poor—street hustlers, for instance. The 'underclass' comprises those who, because of unshakable poverty or chronic antisocial behavior, have become a burden or threat to the community at large. The distinction between it and 'poor' is important. Are you sure Auletta created the word? I seem to remember hearing it before." (NOTE: Edwin Newman remembers using it long before.)

ANDY ROONEY: "I don't have much feeling about it. If it's an addition, it isn't a very valuable one."

LEO ROSTEN: "Not all of the poor belong to the 'underclass.' "

BERTON ROUECHÉ: "I think it describes a new (in the U.S.A.) class—the class below the poor—a permanent underdog."

VERMONT ROYSTER: "The word is not a euphemism for 'poor.' It is a good descriptive term for the group—found in every society—which cannot, for whatever reason, participate in the society in the fullest sense."

HAROLD SCHONBERG: "We just *hate* the term 'lower class' in our supposedly egalitarian society. So we have to find *something,* don't we?"

I. F. STONE: "I think it started with Myrdal."

HOWARD TAUBMAN: "Euphemism or synonym, 'underclass,' it seems to me, is as useful a word as upper class."

EDWARD TRIPP: " 'Underclass' is presumably inspired by 'lower class' but implies not merely on a lower level but underneath, with other classes on top, holding it down. This is a real distinction, at least in theory. The 'under' in 'underprivileged' merely suggests 'meagerly,' as in 'under-fed.' "

BARBARA TUCHMAN: "I understand it as something more than poor—a class without a stake in (and without respect for) our society."

WILLIAM C. VERGARA: "Needless inventions like 'underclass' appear in books primarily for dramatic effect. If we accept 'underclass,' will we soon have —heaven forbid—'overclass'?"

GEORGE WALD (re euphemism for "poor," etc.): "No." (re valuable addition): "Yes, because it institutionalizes unemployment and poverty. After a few years of unemployment one ceases to be officially recognized as unemployed; the condition, now permanent, needs another designation. See Robert McNamara's *Marginal Men*—persons for whom the marketplace has no use or place."

underground press/alternate press   What may have started out as the *underground press* certainly is no longer that, and even the people who publish such newspapers prefer the term *alternate press.* In the beginning, some of the newspapers were truly underground in the sense that they were published in defiance of rules and regulations, especially at Army installations and on university campuses, where the distribution of "unauthorized" papers was forbidden. Today such papers are sold by vendors on street corners, in some newsstands, and even by mail subscription.

Essentially, they are a medium for the expression of opposition to or criticism of the established order of life in the United States and elsewhere. Many of them are still published by staffs of volunteers, but a few have grown to imitate the newspapers which they had criticized and have paid editorial and advertising staffs. *See also* COUNTER-CULTURE.

under way/weigh. *See* WEIGH/WAY

underwhelm

USAGE PANEL QUESTION

A word that enjoyed some recent popularity is *underwhelm,* meaning to create a reaction of indifference, to fail to rouse enthusiasm. For example, *Time* reported that "Rockefeller's long, prepared speeches . . . often underwhelm his audiences." Do you regard this as a useful addition to the language?

Yes: 25%. No: 75%.
Would you use *underwhelm* in your own conversation?   Yes: 28%. No: 72%.
In writing   Yes: 20%. No: 80%.

ISAAC ASIMOV: "I would use it, but not very often."

SHERIDAN BAKER: "I enjoy it as the writer's witty innovation. As a permanent fixture, I would no longer enjoy its wit, and it would seem a brainless offense against meaning."

STEWART BEACH: "It seems to me a vogue word that will die of its own silliness. It is only cute."

HAL BORLAND: "Cute, a quip, but not really needed."

JOHN BROOKS: "A joke word that is, alas, quite unfunny."

HEYWOOD HALE BROUN: "It's as cute as 'couth' and as useful."

JAMES MACGREGOR BURNS: "It is a comic perversion allowable for that effect."

JOHN CIARDI: "Clearly a joke word. Etymologically unsound, but to the point. The language will not be schooled out of its own illogic, which is idiom."

PAUL HORGAN: "Wretched 'cuteness' to it."

NORMAN HOSS: "Such nonce words are good only once, then they become clichés."

JOHN K. HUTCHENS: "An agreeable new one, for occasional comic use, like 'couth' or 'gruntled.' "

ELIZABETH JANEWAY: "It is strictly *Time*-ese, as far as I'm concerned, and *Time*-ese is apt to be sticky."

HELEN L. KAUFMANN: "It's not a bad word, no reason for not using it, but new to me, so I withhold judgment."

ALEXANDER KENDRICK: "No. *Time*, as always, will heal this wound, too."

WALTER KERR: "No. It's a joke, and tired now."

CLARK KINNAIRD: "No. *Time*'s made-words underwhelm me."

STANLEY KUNITZ: "No. Too cute."

LAURENCE LAFORE: "Ingenious slang."

JULES LOH: "Faddish. A bit arch."

WALTER LORD: "Yes, but only when trying to be funny."

RUSSELL LYNES: "Only as a rather limp attempt at humor."

EUGENE MCCARTHY: "Underwhelm should not be used often—or to describe a poor speech. It should be used as a positive word—for negative effect."

PHYLLIS MCGINLEY: "I've never encountered it. Is it supposed to be funny?"

JESSICA MITFORD: "No. See also 'gruntled' vs. 'disgruntled'—a ponderous joke."

HERBERT MITGANG: "Just for laughs—till it becomes a cliché."

WADE MOSBY: "I regard it as a fad word, a one-time humorous switch that is becoming a cliché."

EDWIN NEWMAN: "Only used humorously."

STANTON PECKHAM: "It's overused even facetiously so that it is no longer effective or amusing."

ORVILLE PRESCOTT: "Yes. Nice, light, humorous."

PETER S. PRESCOTT: "I'm astonished: I thought it was just a joke, good for only one use."

LEO ROSTEN: "No. It was a cute Kaufmanism."

BERTON ROUECHÉ: "No. This is a good example of smart-ass striving."

HAROLD SCHONBERG: "[I don't use it] because it has now become trite."

MARK SCHORER: "No . . . only humorously."

DANIEL SCHORR: "Yes, humorously."

WALTER W. "RED" SMITH: "I think I coined this. When Vince Lombardi went to Green Bay, I wrote that the Packers were a soft-bitten team that had overwhelmed one opponent, underwhelmed 10, and whelmed one."

EARL UBELL: "Yes, but fun, but the fun will soon go with overuse."

BILL VAUGHAN: "No. Trendy (also bad), like 'boggles the mind.' "

DOUGLAS WATT: "Quite possibly, since it makes a clear point and represents no corruption of root."

unflappable   Regarded as slang or informal by those dictionaries which enter it, *unflappable* means "imperturbable," "calm," or "not easily excited or upset."

The word "flap" started in England as meaning an air-raid alarm and in the 1950s acquired a slang meaning that caught on quickly in both England and the United States. A "flap" was consternation, frenzied excitement, or confusion. More often than not, the flap turned out to be much ado about nothing.

The term *unflappable* became widely used in the early 1960s, applied to British Prime Minister Harold Macmillan, who seemed able to maintain unshakable calm no matter what dangers threatened his steadily eroding empire. "Mac the Unflappable" was his nickname, and there is no evidence that this rather disrespectful label ever caused him to flap either. *See also* FLAP/FLAPPABLE.

uni-. *See* PREFIXES AND SUFFIXES, WITH AND WITHOUT HYPHEN

unique

USAGE PANEL QUESTION

Unique is regarded by grammarians as one of the "absolute" adjectives, one not possessing a comparative or superlative form. Yet one often sees expressions like "a rather *unique* apartment" and "a most *unique* occasion." Would you approve such expressions?

In writing   Yes: 11%. No: 89%.
In casual speech   Yes: 24%. No: 76%.

MICHAEL J. ARLEN: "No. It's dumb."

ISAAC ASIMOV: "No. I am a slight perfectionist in this respect. (Joke.)"

W. H. AUDEN: "No. Do, do use 'perfect.' "

SAUL BELLOW: "In speech, I'd tolerate it."

JULES BERGMAN: "The mass of words spoken over the radio, TV—books, and the unbelievable events of our era have already left 'unique' by the wayside. Its strength has ebbed."

BARRY BINGHAM, SR.: "Why spoil a highly specific and exact word by stretching it all out of shape?"

HAL BORLAND: "This practice is inexcusable in anyone with even a high school education."

HEYWOOD HALE BROUN: "No. Muddying of exact meaning makes communication even more difficult."

ANTHONY BURGESS: "No. The word must not be weakened into a comparative. It has a unique meaning."

ABE BURROWS: "This comes from the weakening of a great and useful word. Or perhaps I should say a 'most divine' word and 'most perfect.' "

JOHN CIARDI: "No. Not while 'distinctive' is so readily available."

ROBERT CRICHTON: "Yes. No one means 'unique' uniquely any more."

ROBERT CROMIE: "No. 'Unique' means *one* with no rivals and nothing comparable."

GEROLD FRANK: "No—but perhaps permissible in casual speech."

JOHN K. HUTCHENS: "In casual speech—yes—but a bit uneasily."

WALT KELLY: "No. This sort of thing, softening the precise, is useful in comic writing when you want to show the speaker to be a boob."

IRVING KOLODIN: "No. This is an abuse of 'unique,' which is degraded to 'unusual' or 'uncommon.' "

ROBERT LIPSYTE: "No. You lose the word."

RUSSELL LYNES: "Yes—grudgingly."

DWIGHT MACDONALD: "Etymology makes this un-possible."

DAVID MCCORD: "What corpse is ever 'a trifle dead'?"

HERBERT MITGANG: "No. Too basic."

EDWIN NEWMAN: "No. I deliver unwelcome lectures on this subject to colleagues and have discussed it on the air."

ORVILLE PRESCOTT: "An indefensible outrage!"

PETER S. PRESCOTT: "Never, because it is meaningless."

BERTON ROUECHÉ: "I think we should oppose anything that diminishes the language by destroying a word."

VERMONT ROYSTER: "Is it unique or isn't it? Or is it rather unusual, different, or impressive?"

LEONARD SANDERS: "Each time a word is misused, its value is diminished to some extent, and the language has lost that degree of clarity."

FRANK SULLIVAN: " 'Most unique' is wrong but the radio and television announcers use it so much that I suppose it's pedantic to hold out against it. It's 'in.' "

HOWARD TAUBMAN: "No. Only the other day a good writer spoke of 'the most perfect.' Like 'unique,' can there be anything more than perfect?"

DAVIDSON TAYLOR: "No. It is not comparable."

EARL UBELL: "Let's hold out for the meaning of this unique word."

unisex *Unisex* describes styles, especially of clothing, suitable for members of both sexes. Originally a British term, it acquired some nonce popularity in the U.S. as a general label for equalization of the sexes in sports as well as fashion.

universal. *See* ADJECTIVES, UNCOMPARABLE

unknown Only if absolutely no one knows a fact is it *unknown,* unless it is modified by a phrase, as in *"unknown* to the authorities." Thus "an *unknown* man" is more likely to be an "unidentified man" and an *"unknown* destination" is more likely to be an "undisclosed destination."

unless and until *Unless and until* is a cliché phrase which is used primarily for emphasis in negative statements, as in "You will not be allowed to leave this house *unless and until* you have straightened up your room and made your bed." Obviously either "unless" or "until" could be omitted and the result would be the same. *See also* IF AND WHEN and WHEN, AS, AND IF.

unloosen. *See* LOOSEN/UNLOOSEN

unravel. *See* RAVEL/UNRAVEL

unrealistic. *See* REALISTIC/UNREALISTIC

Un-rules for News Writers Ray Erwin, who some years ago used to write a column for the newspaper trade magazine *Editor & Publisher,* once gave us these "Un-rules for News Writers," which we cherish.

1. Don't use no double negative.
2. Make each pronoun agree with their antecedent.
3. Join clauses good, like a conjunction should.
4. About them sentence fragments.
5. When dangling, watch your participles.

6. Verbs has to agree with their subjects.
7. Just between you and I, case is important too.
8. Don't write run-on sentences they are hard to read.
9. Don't use commas, which aren't necessary.
10. Try to not ever split infinitives.
11. It's important to use your apostrophe's correctly.
12. Proofread your writing to see if you any words out.
13. Correct spelling is esential.

until. *See* TILL/UNTIL/'TIL/'TILL

up   One of the leading desk dictionaries devotes a full column to more than forty definitions of the simple word *up*. It is one of the most versatile words you will find in the English language. It functions as adverb, preposition, adjective, transitive verb, and intransitive verb.

Far too many times, however, it is used when it is completely unnecessary, as in "wash *up* the dishes," "make *up* the bed," "clean *up* the house," and "fix *up* the car." These uses are commonplace in our day-to-day speech and probably do no harm but, however harmless in conversation, these superfluous *ups* should be avoided in formal speech and writing.

USAGE PANEL QUESTION

"So-and-so wants to *up* the ante" and "proposals to *up* the tariff quotas" both appeared recently in a single issue of a major newspaper. Would you use *up* as synonymous with "raise"?

In writing   Yes: 24%. No: 76%.
In speech   Yes: 62%. No: 38%.

SHERIDAN BAKER: "Yes, but *only* with 'ante,' the idiom of poker."

STEWART BEACH: "This use of 'up' has a long history. Not elegant but graphic. No objection."

HAL BORLAND: "No more than I would say, 'He downed the price by a dollar.'"

HEYWOOD HALE BROUN: "Excusable only in headlines where letter count is a problem."

ABE BURROWS: "'Up the ante' is the whole phrase. Upping anything else makes no point."

JOHN CIARDI: "Not as a rule, but 'up the ante' is sacred poker idiom."

ALEX FAULKNER: "No. But maybe humorously."

STEPHEN H. FRITCHMAN: "'Up' is not a verb here."

ALEXANDER KENDRICK: "'Up' as a verb is bad enough. What about 'up' as a noun? Or at least 'up-and-up'? For some reason, the British say 'up-and-up' to indicate improvement, thus, 'His health was on the up-and-up,' or the stockmarket was. In the U.S. it means bona fide or 'legit.' "

CLARK KINNAIRD: "No. This usage has come from headline writers."

ORVILLE PRESCOTT: "Yes [in speech] but only with 'ante' as poker players have used it for generations."

PETER S. PRESCOTT: "Dreadful, just dreadful."

VERMONT ROYSTER: "In 'up the ante,' yes; the whole phrase is a common poker term. 'Up the quotas,' no."

LEONARD SANDERS: "This apparently is another contribution to the language from lazy headline writers."

ROBERT SHERRILL: "No. I don't dislike it. I just don't use it."

BILL VAUGHAN: "No, except this ['up the ante'] is almost an idiom."

uppers. *See* DOWNERS/UPPERS

uptight

USAGE PANEL QUESTION

Panelist JOSEPH A. BRANDT writes: "The increasing use of 'uptight' for 'tense' annoys me. What does the panel think?" Do you use *uptight* in casual conversation?
Yes: 43%. No: 57%.
Do you use it in writing?   Yes: 20%. No: 80%.

ISAAC ASIMOV: "Yes. Rather a colorful phrase."

W. H. AUDEN: "Surely 'uptight' now means 'square.' "

ALVIN BEAM: "Yes . . . I'm beginning to in conversation and may soon in writing. (The usage has never 'annoyed' me—but has always interested me. I think it quite expressive.)"

CHARLES BERLITZ: "No. It will enter the language eventually or (hopefully) vanish like all cant, jargon, and secret recognition languages of certain groups."

JOHN BROOKS: "It's a vogue word that is useful if used very sparingly."

BEN LUCIEN BURMAN: "No. It makes me 'nauseous'!"

ABE BURROWS: "I like this in speech. It's better than 'tense.' In writing, I would only use it in dialogue."

JOHN CIARDI: "Yes, when I am reflecting casual conversation. No, when writing in my own voice."

THOMAS FLEMING: "Yes. With four teenagers in the house, I've stopped shuddering."

STEPHEN H. FRITCHMAN: "It is a vivid neologism which has some use, but which I rather hope won't last."

RICHARD EDES HARRISON: "No. Not yet!"

JOHN K. HUTCHENS: "Yes. I don't think it will be with us long, but at the moment it serves."

ELIZABETH JANEWAY: "I think it's a damned good word. Why is Mr. Brandt so uptight? Anyway, it isn't exactly synonymous with 'tense.' There's a pejorative overtone in 'uptight.' It pertains to continuing characteristics more than 'tense'—or it does to me."

WALTER KERR: "I have used it, but only lightly—when being deliberately slangy. It will pass—but has a certain humor just now."

RUSSELL LYNES: "No. But I rather like it in the young."

DWIGHT MACDONALD: " 'Up tight'—is it one word?—is broader than 'tense.' I think it a useful neologism."

HENRY W. MALONE: "No . . . but in casual conversation with students I accept it."

WRIGHT MORRIS: "In writing, when called for. This is topical vernacular until another 'annoying' term takes its place."

DANIEL PATRICK MOYNIHAN: "No. When heard in speech, I would form an impression."

ORVILLE PRESCOTT: "Absurd jargon. 'Tense,' 'nervous,' or 'worried,' or a dozen other words are better."

PETER S. PRESCOTT: "It's more than tense: it suggests a life-style and set of attitudes. It's useful, a good addition. 'He's uptight' about something doesn't mean he's 'tense' about it—it means that he has made up his mind, is not open to suggestions; it can *also* mean that he's 'nervous.' Note that it has long been used as an insult: 'Don't be so uptight . . . you're uptight about it.' "

HAROLD SCHONBERG: "Yes . . . in writing, once in a while, but very seldom."

MARK SCHORER: "No one uses it to mean 'tense.' The younger people (younger than I, I mean) who use it constantly mean something much more complicated—tied up in some unhinted attitude, stuck in a dogma, or even a pose, constricted in preconceptions—in other words, *not open.* But these can be the least 'tense' people one knows—the stolid, contented, utterly smug *bores.*"

ELVIS STAHR, JR.: " 'Uptight' is a new word which has greater meaning and richer connotations—*by far*—than does 'tense' or any *other* established word. I *welcome* 'uptight' to the language—it has no substitute. It enriches."

DAVIDSON TAYLOR: "Yes. It means far more than 'tense.' It means 'hard up against it.' "

BARBARA TUCHMAN: "Yes, in conversation; no, in writing."

BILL VAUGHAN: "No. This too shall pass. In speech, it depends on the speaker's age."

JUDITH VIORST: "Yes, but only sardonically. In speech, it depends entirely on the age of the speaker."

T. HARRY WILLIAMS: "No. I shudder when I hear it from an older person —who is, I think, trying to demonstrate that he is also young. I put up with it from the young because I assume they don't know any better."

HERMAN WOUK: "Another bit of banal shorthand. One uses it when tired or hurried."

CHARLOTTE ZOLOTOW: "Yes, it is more vivid than 'tense.' It wouldn't make me uptight at all to hear it."

When *uptight* was put to the Usage Panel for the second time, the great majority of the members felt that it has survived very well and a number even stated that it is a useful word.

USAGE PANEL QUESTION—SECOND EDITION

Uptight in the sense of tense or nervous was much in vogue at the time of publication of the First Edition of this dictionary. Nearly one-half of the panelists said they would use *uptight* in casual conversation, though only one in five would use it in writing.

Do you find *uptight* a word in considerable current use? Yes: 79%. No: 21%.

Would you regard *uptight* as already obsolescent? Yes: 16%. No: 84%.

BARRY BINGHAM, SR.: "Perhaps 'uptight' is not as widely used as it was five or ten years ago, but it is still a standard part of the vocabulary of Americans under 30. It is a sharp, compact word."

DAVID H. BRADLEY: "Yes (in current use). I wouldn't use it, however."

JOHN BROOKS: "No—and yet 'uptight' is to a degree a useful word. It happens also to be a particularly nauseating one."

HEYWOOD HALE BROUN: "It doesn't, as the world now stands, seem a likely candidate for obsolescence."

WILLARD R. ESPY: "Though I would not be likely to use 'uptight' in writing, I consider it a useful addition to the language."

FRANCES FRITCHMAN: "It is a vividly descriptive and useful word—for oral use, not written."

RAY GANDOLF: "I don't think my vote means much here. The people I hang out with are all as nervous as a cat on a hot tin roof."

DWIGHT MACDONALD: "Seems a useful slang term."

MARGE PIERCY: "People still use it, but it is mostly a generational word and passing."

PETER S. PRESCOTT: "I rather like this word—very expressive."

F. D. REEVE: "It means more than tense or nervous; it specifies an attitude."

JACK SMITH: "Uptight, like rip off, is handy and might survive."

ELVIS STAHR, JR. "I've lived to regret my heresy in the First Edition. Uptight just doesn't wear well."

HAROLD TAYLOR: "Except for myself and a few others, people use it regularly."

WILLIAM ZINSSER: "Very good word. I accept it at all levels."

us/we   When a personal pronoun is used before a noun, some people have a marked tendency to use the nominative case regardless of the structure of the sentence, as in "none of *we* girls." Obviously the phrase "*we* girls" is the object of the preposition "of" and should be "*us* girls." A simple test to determine whether nominative or objective case should be used is to eliminate the noun. No one would ever say "none of *we.*"

used car. *See* EUPHEMISM

vacillation. *See* AMBIVALENCE/VACILLATION

vacuum   While most authorities prefer VAK-yoo-um as the proper pronunciation for *vacuum,* the pronunciation VAK-yoom is so widely used by literate, educated people that most up-to-date dictionaries accept it as perfectly permissible. The *World Webster* (college edition) notes that this pronunciation is especially common when *vacuum* is used as an attributive in phrases like "*vacuum* cleaner."

varsity   An effort to maintain the pure meaning of *varsity* used to be made every year by a venerable gentleman named Tufts, who, as a master at Phillips Exeter Academy, would deliver a lecture at the beginning of the football season to remind the students that Exeter, being a preparatory school, did not have a *varsity* but a "school team." "Since *varsity* is a contraction of 'university,' " he would declaim, "its use should be limited to college and university teams." Even those many years ago the students ignored the distinction. Today's dictionaries define *varsity* as "the main team of a college, university or school" so Mr. Tufts's battle is completely lost. The British, however, still use *varsity* solely as a contraction of "university."

vase VAHS is the British pronunciation and perfectly acceptable in the speech of a native of Britain. For an American to use it, however, is a mark of affectation. Say rather: VAYSS or VAYZ.

vehicle *Vehicle* should be pronounced VEE-ih-k'l, not vee-HIK-ul. The "h" should be silent and the accent on the first, not the second, syllable.

verb. sap./verb. sat./verbum sap./verbum sat. These are variant clipped forms of the Latin expression *verbum sapienti sat est,* "a word to the wise is sufficient." The expression is appropriate in scholarly, literary, or other formal contexts but sounds a bit condescending elsewhere.

verbal. *See* ORAL/VERBAL

verbomania. *See* MANIA

verbs ending in -en. *See* -EN, VERBS ENDING IN

verge British term for the shoulder of a highway or lesser road. In some American states, among them Ohio, this shoulder is called a "berm."

vernissage This is a word from the world of art which has come to mean "preview." It is a word very much in vogue in art circles. Literally it means "varnishing day" and refers to an old custom of reserving the day prior to the opening of an exhibit for the painter's use in touching up or varnishing items in his exhibit. Soon the custom developed of inviting a few friends in, and now it usually means a reception on the afternoon or evening of the day before the formal opening of an exhibit.

vert. *See* LOST POSITIVES

very. *See* TOO/VERY and MIGHTY/VERY

very pleased (interested)/very much pleased (interested) There is a grammatical theory that *very,* as an intensive, should modify only adjectives which indicate quality, not verbs which indicate action. On this ground some purists object to "*very pleased,*" arguing that *pleased* is a participle or verbal adjective. (They apply the same arguments against *very interested.*)

    The distinction between adjectives and participles was never very pronounced and is rather an artificial distinction. In any event, the use of *very pleased* and *very interested* is certainly common in the speech and writing of well-educated people today. The formulation *very much pleased* and *very much interested* is still preferred in formal writing.

very truly yours/yours truly/yours very truly All three forms of what is called a "complimentary close" are acceptable, although some secretaries report having been taught that anything other than *very truly yours* is grammatically incorrect. There is no basis for such teaching.

viable *Viable* really means "capable of living, as a newborn infant reaching a stage of development that will permit it to survive." It has become a *vogue word* (which see), especially in the phrase "*viable* alternative," and the evidence shows that the users of it are not aware of its meaning but think that it means simply "workable" or "sensible." Since it comes from the Latin word for "life," it is to be hoped that some precision will come to be exercised in its use. "Workable?" Maybe, but with the distinction that something *viable* also be capable of continued existence and success. In other words, capable of surviving.

Otherwise *viable* will go the way of *burgeon* (which see), which used to mean "to bud" before the word mechanics took over and decided that it actually should mean "to mushroom."

vicious circle/vicious cycle While *vicious cycle* may seem an amusing play on words, *vicious circle* is the proper idiom for a situation in which the solution to one problem creates new problems which in turn bring back the original problem and make it more difficult to solve. Thus the matter goes full *circle*, returning to its beginning. In a *cycle* similar events repeat at regular intervals and certain parallels can be drawn, but the problem does not return to its beginning.

victuals. *See* VITTLES/VICTUALS

vigorish *Vigorish* looks like an adjective but it is a noun from the slang of the gambling world. It is the percentage of a bet which is held out by the bookmaker. It can also mean the excessive interest charged by a loan shark. We have heard it used to refer to the commission or profit on a business deal, especially one which is shady or risky.

virtually. *See* PRACTICALLY/VIRTUALLY

vitae/resume *Vitae* as a synonym for *resume* is an abbreviated form of "curriculum vitae," a Latin phrase which literally means "the running, course, or career of one's life." In its entirety it is a formal and stiff phrase, but to abbreviate it seems a bit gauche. To top it all, we had a query from a secretary as to whether "vita" is not the singular. For the record, the singular would be "curriculum vitae" and the plural is "curricula vitae," which is ridiculous since the summary of only one life is involved.

It is better to use the simple word *resume,* with or without the acute accents over the first and final "e's."

vittles/victuals The word *victuals,* meaning any kind of food provisions, is pronounced VIT-t'ls, which has led to the erroneous spelling *vittles.* In the nineteenth century, when the word was more common in America than it is today, such humorists as Petroleum V. Nasby and Bill Nye used to affect all sorts of deliberate misspellings in an effort to represent what they considered to be the dialects of farmers and frontiersmen. One of the favorite misspellings of this school of humor was *vittles* for *victuals* and, since the word is seldom seen in print today, some people simply don't know the correct spelling. It is not dialect, however; it is listed (*victuals,* that is) as standard in all dictionaries.

vituperous/vituperative *Vituperous* is a seldom seen but perfectly good variant of *vituperative,* meaning "given to strong and wordy abuse." It has one small advantage: it has one fewer syllable.

vociferous/voracious The temptation to use big words without really knowing what they mean can have amusing results. A Wisconsin teacher informed us that the parent of one of his pupils told him "ever since childhood I have been a *vociferous* reader." What he meant, of course, was *voracious,* meaning "insatiable." It comes from the Latin "vorare" meaning "to devour." *Vociferous,* meaning "loud or noisy in expressing opinions," comes from the Latin "vociferari," "to cry out," which in turn comes from "vox," meaning "voice."

vogue words *Vogue words* and phrases are words or expressions that suddenly and inexplicably crop up repeatedly in speeches of bureaucrats, comments of columnists—particularly those of the political type—and in hundreds of radio and television broadcasts. A prime example of a *vogue word* is "charisma," which achieved a remarkable vogue during the years of the John F. Kennedy administration—a period often referred to by another *vogue word,* "Camelot." These instant contemporary clichés soon become debased by overuse and lose their initial sparkle and freshness. Within a year or two of its resuscitation (for it had been in the small type of dictionaries all along), "charisma" was being defined by at least one national magazine as synonymous with "star quality."

Other *vogue words* of the recent past would include "thrust," "credit crunch," "zap," and "rap." One of our column readers was moved to comment by integrating a few of the more abused of these *vogue words* and phrases into a few "meaningful" paragraphs, which "hopefully" will make their own point.

"Seldom has there been such a *dynamic escalation* of the language," he writes. "This snappy new *rhetoric* supplies *meaningful guidelines. On balance* it is inevitable that a *confrontation* occurs between the reading public and those *knowledgeable* scribes whose *expertise* in *semantics* has earned them a *consensus.* There is a tiresome repetition of *disarray, dé-*

tente, ambivalent, structure and *restructure.* On the public platform it is the speaker's *considered judgment* that a *survey in depth* be made, *basically* so that he may *face up to the facts,* although facing the facts at the *eyeball-to-eyeball* level is more effective.

"To get his ideas across, he must set up a *meaningful dialogue* to *communicate* with his audience when direct talk would do the business. Readers are fed liberal doses of *erode* and *minuscule,* to say nothing of *expertise.* Nevertheless, as more of this gibberish *surfaces* and speakers and writers are exposed to it, they are inspired to fresh *conceptual creativity,* pounce enthusiastically on the new-fangled expressions—and work them to death." All of this, may we add, in an effort to *optimize their advantage* over other speakers and writers.

At the peak of their popularity *vogue words* seem to be omnipresent, but just as suddenly they seem faded, dated—in a word, out of *vogue.* The name comes from a definition of sorts supplied by H. W. Fowler who, in *Modern English Usage,* described them as "words owing their *vogue* to the joy of showing one has acquired them." Some *vogue words* are commented upon in this dictionary in their proper alphabetical order. What follows is a sort of omnium gatherum of some of the *vogue words* that have come to our attention during the past few decades. You will note that most of them are obsolescent if not already obsolete. But fret not, the word polishers in government and in the news media are already polishing up a new crop of *vogue words* to brighten our prose for a moment and then to bore us until they drop entirely out of sight.

Here they are: input, output, hangup, freak out, flap, camp, kitsch, watershed, bench mark, overview, empathy, infrastructure, phase (in and out), ongoing, seminal, in depth, feedback, escalate (we were once startled to read that the New York City police threatened to "escalate their slowdown"), relevant, generation gap, clout, biodegradable, interface, parameter, ingroup, outgroup, peer group, synergy and synergistic, and longuette. The last, in case it escaped you, was a word coined in the late 1960s to describe the "midi" dress which was supposed to "obsolete" the mini. It had a shelf-life (ah, there!) shorter than the style itself—and that was only a month or two. In the 1980s *upscale, awesome* (which see), and *state of the art* (which see) were voguish.

Eventually, and perhaps sooner, all of these briefly popular words and phrases will go into the limbo reserved for the *vogue words* of yesteryear, joining such *vogue words* of the past as "boondoggle" and "priority."

voyeur Originally a French word, *voyeur* means a person who derives pleasure from secretly observing others—a Peeping Tom. But it can also be used as a synonym for "observer," as in "American anthropologists insist on being participant observers (not simply *voyeurs*) when they go into the field." The point is that many American anthropologists (for example, Margaret Mead in her classic *Coming of Age in Samoa*) actually live the lives of their subjects, while others (Desmond Morris, British author of *The Naked Ape,* for example) merely observe and comment.

vulgar   *Vulgar,* as used in this dictionary, may have one of two meanings. It may simply mean common, as distinguished from language used by educated, literate folk. As an example, see *relocate/move. Vulgar* may also, of course, have the meaning of bawdy, coarse, and offensive to many. The word "obscene" is not used in this connection because the authors do not believe that any word can be, in and of itself, "obscene." Incidentally, *vulgar* in either of the senses noted above is far removed from its original meaning, which simply was "to be associated with the masses of common people," as in Shakespeare's "the *vulgar* sort of marketmen."

waffle, to   *Waffle,* in the sense of speaking or writing in a vague or indecisive fashion, is a term recently borrowed from British English and briefly in vogue in the higher echelons of the Washington bureaucratic set.

It is a very stylish way of referring to the kind of prose in which bureaucrats have excelled for decades, if not for centuries: weighty, seemingly portentous prose that actually says little or nothing. Norman W. Schur, in his admirable book *British Self-Taught* (Macmillan), quotes a British parliamentarian as defining *waffling* as "the art of that which is superficially profound."

wait on/wait for   As Usage Panelist Wade Mosby puts it: "I was brought up believing *wait on* meant to serve in some capacity. But the sportscasting fraternity seems to have adopted it as a synonym for 'expect.' 'He's right down there waitin' on that pass.' " While this expression is common in regional dialect, it is better to say *wait for.* The only time *wait on* is correct is when a waiter or waitress *waits on* you. *Wait for* in the sense of "await the arrival of" is the only proper usage in standard English.

However, the dialect *wait on* is firmly entrenched in folk speech throughout our Southern states. Harold Wentworth in his authoritative *American Dialect Dictionary* lists more than fifty examples of its use, ranging in time from 1871 to the present day and in territory from southeastern Pennsylvania to the Gulf of Mexico.

wallet. *See* POCKETBOOK/WALLET/PURSE

want/wish *Want* and *wish* are synonymous, as most dictionaries point out. The difference in their use is chiefly one of level of use, and the selection of the appropriate one depends on the context of the sentence. *Wish* is decidedly more formal and is especially appropriate when the thing desired is remote, as in "I *wish* for eternal salvation." On the informal level, though, *want* is the word more common in such statements as "I *want* a little peace and quiet around the house."

want out (in) "I *want out*" instead of "I want to get out" is a regional expression heard most commonly in the Middle West. It is used literally in terms of physical departure but also figuratively, in the sense of "to be free of involvement," as in "He said he was tired of their marriage and *wanted out.*"

　　Want in is a similar phrase, if less common: "Open the door; I *want in.*"

war/car/par/far QUERY: "If *car* is pronounced like *par* and *far*, why isn't *war* pronounced to rhyme with all three?"

　　ANSWER: Partly because English and American pronunciations follow no simple and orderly rules. Since our language is a fusion of languages, drawing from Latin, Greek, French, German, the Scandinavian languages, and a host of other sources, it is never possible to say with certainty that one word will sound like another simply because it is spelled in like fashion.

War Department/Defense Department. *See* EUPHEMISM

warm/warmly When Charlie Chaplin returned to the United States after a long absence, newspaper headlines stated that CLASSIC COMIC NOW FEELS MORE WARMLY TOWARD AMERICA, and the question arose as to whether it should be *warm* or *warmly*.

　　In this case the idiom runs contrary to the way it does in the case of *bad/badly* (which see). Technically, "feel" is a linking verb and is followed by the adjectival form, hence "I feel bad" is preferred to "I feel badly." In the case of *warm* and *warmly*, however, other elements enter in. "I feel *warm*" means that my body temperature is higher than usual. "I feel *warmly*" means that I have feelings of cordiality or affection.

warmth. *See* COOLTH/WARMTH

warping/warpage *Warping* and *warpage*, though similar in appearance and actually derived from the same etymological roots, have very different meanings. *Warping* refers to the fact of becoming bent, as in "The book's covers are *warping.*" *Warpage* refers to the charge made for *warping* (that is, hauling) ships.

Watergate language A phenomenon much commented on during the period beginning in 1973 and ending with Richard Nixon's resignation as President, when newspapers focused daily attention on the revelations of corruption, both political and linguistic, of the conversations taped at the White House, was the extraordinary lack of literacy displayed by the defendants in the various inquiries and criminal actions. Panelist Barry Bingham, Sr., chairman of the board of the Louisville *Courier-Journal* wrote us at the time, as follows:

"Dear William and Mary: As our most valued watchdogs of the English language, you have been observing the Watergate hearings on TV as a demonstration of current usage in Washington's Bureau-Land. Whatever one may think about the testimony politically, it seems guaranteed to chill the marrow of the listener who cares about precision in speech.

"John Mitchell [Richard Nixon's Attorney-General] has furnished the most devastating barrage of cliché phrases, each repeated endlessly. He can never mention a subject, it is always 'subject matter.' The phrase 'in the area of' modifies countless statements. For instance, he does not say that he first met Nixon in about 1966 but 'in the area of 1966.' Nobody ever joins a group or committee, he 'comes aboard.' The incorrect use of 'media' to designate one newspaper or one television station is endemic. Nothing is said to have happened 'then' but 'in that time frame.'

"The main tendency of this government jargon is to use several words where one would do the job satisfactorily. The other and more disturbing tendency is to eliminate the precise word and substitute the imprecise. Perhaps lawyers have sometimes consciously employed such devices for fuzzing up the meaning of language in a deliberate effort to avoid committing themselves too clearly. I don't believe that is the motive which governs the Watergate testimony. It seems to be a national trend toward the unclear, the imprecise, the vague and the equivocal.

"The Watergate hearings will be heard by many millions of Americans, and I believe that this lame and degenerated language used so persistently will appeal to many people as sophisticated, insider talk, and therefore worthy of imitation."

As we told Mr. Bingham at the time, we did not entirely share his belief that the language of those testifying would act as a pernicious influence on speech habits of the general American public. Rather we felt dismayed at the realization that, thanks in part to the low level of language affected by the advertising industry (from which White House aides Haldeman, Ehrlichman, Magruder, and many other of the defendants came), their debased speech might actually represent patterns already widespread throughout the country. We noted further the appalling fact that virtually everyone involved in the whole messy affair was at least a college graduate, with most of them holding graduate degrees in law. What this says about the level of literacy in our institutions of higher learning must give anyone who cares about the language a bad case of the wimwams.

Precisely because so much of the testimony at the hearings and the conversations recorded on the Nixon White House tapes were fraught with solecisms and sheer illiteracies, we doubt if many of the expressions will survive save as horrible examples of language gone astray or, more aptly, torn asunder. Nonetheless, here are a few, for the record:

At this point in time (translation: now)
At that point in time (translation: then)
 Stroke (translation: soothe or cajole a potential troublemaker)
Go the hangout road (translation: tell the truth)
Launder the money (translation: pass illegal campaign contributions through foreign banks so that donor's identity is hidden)
 Plumber (translation: undercover political espionage agent)
 Operation (translation: tapping phoes and burglarizing offices of a political opponent)
Stonewall (translation: flatly refuse to cooperate even with duly constituted authority
Go public (translation: make a statement via TV to the public).
 NOTE: As this edition goes to press, the phrases marked above by asterisks are still appearing regularly in the press.

The list could be endlessly extended, but, as noted above, we scarcely believe that much of it will survive except as horrendous reminders of a time when our language as well as our nation's fortunes were at their nadir. Of the language on the presidential tapes, little need be said except that it contributed the memorable "(expletive deleted)" to the language. Although, as one critic noted, "the tapes are crammed with dull metaphors that scream the absence of thought," very few of them are worth recording. Characteristic are Nixon's description of Judge Sirica as "the big white knight who is clean as a hound's tooth" and the musing about whether Attorney General Mitchell as a sacrificial lamb would appease the grand jury: ". . . if they get a hell of a big fish, that is going to take a lot of the fire out of this thing."

Finally, it may be salutary to recall the words of panelist "Red" Smith, who sent us a few suggestions about redefining standard English words in light of the scandals. " 'Overzealous,' " he wrote, "might now be used to describe zealots who break, enter, lie, suborn perjury, obstruct justice and bribe judges. 'Patriotic' might now apply to Vice Presidents who steal. And 'inoperative' simply means 'a damn lie.' "

water has passed under the bridge, a lot of This tired expression has been used so often that it may best be avoided in favor of the simple statement that "a lot of time has passed" or "that happened a long time ago." *See also* CLICHÉ.

watershed A *watershed*, technically, is a "ridge or stretch of high land, dividing areas drained by different rivers or river systems," as defined by *Webster's New World Dictionary*, but it has acquired a very voguish meaning among bureaucrats and those who chronicle bureaucratic activities. A *watershed*, as they use the word, means a critically important boundary or, as some of them would have it, a vitally important "point in time." Like such other vogue expressions as "crunch," "thrust," and "bench mark," *watershed* is not likely to have a very long life in this special extended sense. In any event, it should be avoided as pretentious and unnecessary.

way. *See* WEIGH/WAY

way/ways, long. *See* LONG WAY/LONG WAYS

we. *See* US/WE

we, editorial What has come to be known as the *editorial we* originated in newspaper offices where phrases such as "*we* believe," "*we* endorse," or "*we* support" were used to indicate that the opinions expressed in the editorial columns of the papers represented the collective judgment of the editors and, as such, the policy of the paper. For a while the *editorial we* broke out of the editorial offices and was used by writers who thought it immodest to say "I" and politicians who thought it gave their statements more weight. Writers have for the most part abandoned the practice but old politicians never change. Younger ones have no such illusions.

weasel words The Society of Weasel Word Watchers, an informal and completely unorganized society, was created by Carroll Carroll in the early 1970s through his column in *Variety*, the show-business magazine, in which he zeroed in on television advertising.

He defined a *weasel word* as "a description given by advertising people to that key word in a piece of copy that takes the responsibility out of the most exaggerated claim." As an example, he noted the dishwasher detergent that "leaves glasses virtually spotless." If you think that means without spots, you are wrong. It means practically without spots or with some spots. So, in point of fact, what the ad says is that your glasses will not be completely clean if you use this particular detergent. Another example is the remedy for "simple nervous tension." How do you define "simple"?

Many of our readers became members of the Society of Weasel Word Watchers, that gallant band of long-suffering radio and television listeners with the common goal of exposing deliberately deceitful advertising claims, among them Mrs. Isabelle R. Young of Teaneck, New Jersey.

"My pet peeve," she wrote, "is the oh-so-scientific statistics presented with such fanfare that the listener is unaware that the information is absurdly incomplete and, hence, meaningless. Example: 'Four out of five dentists surveyed recommend Blah-and-Blah for their patients who chew gum.' Surveyed by whom? Perhaps by the manufacturer's 6-year-old daughter gathering material for Show-and-Tell? How many doctors were surveyed? All five witch doctors in Upper and Lower Slobovia? What was the form of their recommendation? Did they say 'Oh, well, if you must chew gum, we suppose that Blah-and-Blah is the least harmful'? This simply is not using the language to convey truth. It is flimflam. It comes perilously close to being *gobbledegook*" (which see).

It is a commentary on our continued misuse of the language that the phrase *weasel word* was coined around the turn of the century. Back in 1904 one commentator referred to the Democratic party's noncommittal platform as "filled with *weasel words.*"

But it was President Theodore Roosevelt who gave the expression its greatest popularity. In 1916 he denounced some government communiqués for being full of *weasel words.* "When a weasel sucks eggs," he snorted, "the meat is sucked out of the egg. If you use one *weasel word* after another there is nothing left of the other. You can have 'universal training' or you can have 'voluntary training' but when you use the word 'voluntary' to qualify the word 'universal,' you are using a *weasel word.* It has sucked the meaning out of 'universal.' The two words flatly contradict each other." Theodore Roosevelt is long gone—but the *weasel word* is with us still. *See also* EUPHEMISMS and WATERGATE LANGUAGE.

we'd of/we'd have   The substitution of *of* for *have* in such statements as "*We'd of* said that the bottom would drop out of the market" is a speech pattern which is defended by people who say that what sounds like *of* is actually a slurring of *have* or *'ve.* We have seen abundant evidence in the informal correspondence of semi-educated writers that they actually write *of* as well as say it. It is, of course, illiterate.

weigh/way   "*Weighing* anchor" merely means hauling it up, so that a ship may sail from the spot where it has been moored. This has led to some confusion among sailors, many of whom use the phrase "under *weigh*" to indicate that their boats or ships are in motion. Once a ship gains headway she is "under *way.*"

The nautical use of *weigh* can be traced to its early Anglo-Saxon origin in the word "wegan," which meant "to carry, bear, or move." The concept of lifting or balancing objects in the hands to determine their weight came later and represents a somewhat more sophisticated sense of the original word.

welsh/welsher   Pejorative terms based on race, religion, nationality, or color should be avoided at all times except when recording a direct quotation from someone using them. Words that particularly strike home to the editors of this book, both of whom have ancestral ties to Wales, are the verb to *welsh* and the noun *welsher*. Dictionaries define *welsh* as meaning "to cheat on a bet" and the image of a Welshman as dishonest is given to small children through the nursery rhyme "Taffy was a Welshman, Taffy was a thief . . ." "Taffy," incidentally, is the generic name for Welshmen, a corruption of David, the name of the patron saint of Wales.

There is some difference of opinion as to whether Taffy deserves the label of "thief." The Welshman has shared for centuries with the Scotsman a reputation of being a canny trader, one who may even resort to subterfuge to get the better part of a bargain. This is not an uncommon trait or even a bad one. Our own Yankee traders are legendary for trickery and even Abe Lincoln is remembered as one of the canniest horse traders of his time.

In Britain during the eighteenth and early nineteenth centuries the term *welsher* became common in the argot of racing bettors to describe a person who made a bet and then reneged on it. The term was definitely a derogatory racial term but it received wide circulation and, eventually, was shortened into the verb form as we know it today.

Patriotic Welshmen will tell you that the *welshers* were actually British gamblers, who, when they were unable to pay their losses, fled to Wales to avoid their debts and thus gave the Welsh a bad name. *See also* **DEROGATORY TERMS.**

Welsh rabbit/rarebit   *Welsh rabbit* is a dish made of melted cheese, milk or cream or sometimes ale, and served on toast or crackers. Over the years it has been altered by lovers of Elegant English to *Welsh rarebit,* but the ever-proper Harvard Club of New York lists on its menu "Assorted *Rabbits: Welsh* (plain); Golden Buck (poached egg); Long Island (egg yolk) and Yorkshire (poached egg and bacon)." *See also* **SCOTCH WOODCOCK.**

This is how the question was put to our panelists:

USAGE PANEL QUESTION

H. W. Fowler in the "True and False Etymology" article in his celebrated *Modern English Usage* wrote: "Welsh rarebit is stupid and wrong." American cookbooks and American supermarket shelves display an overwhelming preference for "rarebit."

Would you use "rarebit" in speech: Yes: 56%. No: 44%.

In writing? Yes: 55%. No: 45%.
Would you defend "rabbit" (and Fowler) to the end? Yes: 26%. No: 74%.

ISAAC ASIMOV: "Not that I ever particularly use the expression or hear it used but 'rarebit' is an affectation of would-be literates."

BARRY BINGHAM, SR.: "For once I cannot fully agree with the estimable Fowler."

ALTON BLAKESLEE: " 'Rarebit' is classy—'rabbit' is not."

HEYWOOD HALE BROUN: "Who dares quarrel with Fowler?"

ANTHONY BURGESS: "I married into Wales, which has real rabbits. My in-laws rightly said 'rarebit.' "

BEN LUCIEN BURMAN: "I love Welsh rabbit. But Welsh 'rarebit' gives me the stomachache."

ROBERT CROMIE: "In response to Fowler I cry: Hare! Hare!"

WILLARD R. ESPY: "The common use of 'rarebit' is gentrification, I suppose —unless the writers of cookbooks fear that their readers will miss the joke, and insist on having a real rabbit."

ALEX FAULKNER: "For once I part company with H. W. Fowler. He is right, of course, to regard 'rarebit' as a corruption of 'rabbit,' the first usage of the latter being recorded by the O.E.D. as 1725, but with 'rarebit' cropping up as early as 1785. Surely this is simply a case of evolution of the language and, since now most people speak of 'Welsh rarebit' (as does the *Times Cookery Book* and most others), and since there is no rabbit in this delightful concoction anyway, it seems to me that it would be merely puristic to go on insisting on 'rabbit.' "

PAUL HORGAN: "Yes (to rabbit), more fun."

ELIZABETH JANEWAY: "Fowler Forever."

WALTER KERR: "No matter who's right, the world now marches to 'rarebit.' "

STANLEY KUNITZ: "My inglorious compromise would be to write 'rarebit' but to pronounce 'rabbit.' "

HERBERT MITGANG: "I'll eat 'rarebit' but not 'rabbit,' which, I suspect, is why 'rarebit' is on the menu."

MARGE PIERCY: "I think this is a change easily understood and quite rational. 'Welsh rabbit' contains no meat. So labeled, it will put off vegetarians and disappoint carnivores."

VERMONT ROYSTER: "The dish has no connection whatever with a rabbit— but it is a 'rare bit'—and an excellent one!"

HAROLD SCHONBERG: "Let's not be didactic or stubborn. 'Rarebit' is used all over the place, 'rabbit' almost never."

DOLORES SIMON: "We are trying hard, at least in Harper cookbooks, to ban 'rarebit.' "

ELVIS STAHR, JR.: "Not even at the outset. Fowler was just misguided for once."

HAROLD TAYLOR: "It's a British/Fowler judgement, not American."

KARL V. TEETER: " 'Rarebit' is a folk etymology and a snotty one but in the end it is usage, not Fowler, that carries the day."

BARBARA TUCHMAN: " 'Rabbit' may be correct, but as melted cheese it strikes me as much less appropriate than 'rarebit' and to insist on it seems one of those pedantries intended to make the user look erudite."

JOSEPH VERGARA: "It's a shame to lose the playfulness of 'Welsh rabbit.' Restaurants prefer 'rarebit' because it sounds elegant and can carry a higher price."

JUDITH VIORST: "It's not worth the fight."

A.B.C. WHIPPLE: "Another case of ignorance. 'Rabbit' of course comes from the days when cheese was the closest a Welshman could come to a rabbit."

Westminster   There is a common tendency to insert an extra syllable in *Westminster,* making it into "Westminister." This reflects a confusion of the words "minster" and "minister." A "minister" is a member of the clergy; a "minster" is a church building or cathedral.

The proper name for the cathedral where British monarchs are crowned is not *Westminster* Cathedral; it is *Westminster* Abbey. Actually the name *Westminster* Abbey is redundant but it has a basis in history. *Westminster* is the name of the borough of London in which the cathedral as well as the Houses of Parliament is located. It was originally a monastery occupied by Benedictine monks, hence the name "Abbey."

"wh," words beginning with   American people, from the lowest to the highest, tend to leave the "h" sound out of words beginning with "wh" and "White House" becomes "Wite House." The slurring of such words is deplorable. Perhaps if speakers would remember that the sound spelled "wh" is actually "hw," they would be more aware of the need to articulate it properly. (Anyone who doesn't believe that "wh" is really "hw" should try saying a few "wh" words aloud and listening closely. The lips do indeed articulate the "h" before the "w.") There are one or two exceptions to the "hw" sound for "wh," exceptions which indicate even more clearly the mistake that is made when the "h" is slurred or omitted. These are "who" and "whole." In both of these words the "w" has disappeared from pronunciation, leaving only the "h."

WHAM   This is one of the most unfortunate of the acronyms created by our federal government and is included here primarily as an illustration of why it is important to consider the result when giving titles to programs or organizations.

WHAM was created during the Vietnam War to designate the program designed, we were told, to "*W*in the *H*earts *A*nd *M*inds" of the Vietnamese people. The program as implemented was later discredited as having lived up to the acronym far too well. In any event, it was surely the least felicitous coinage since the famous CINCUS (Commander in

Chief U.S.) which the Navy hastily abandoned right after Pearl Harbor. A close runner-up for the Least Felicitous Acronym Award would, of course, be Mr. Nixon's Committee to Re-Elect the President (CREEP). *See also* ACRONYM.

wharf. *See* DOCK/PIER/WHARF

when, as, and if Like "unless and until," *when, as, and if* is used for emphasis, but both phrases are clichés, so tired and worn that they should be avoided.

whereabouts Generally *whereabouts* as a noun takes a singular verb, for it is usually used to refer to the location of one person or thing. Some people seem to think that because it ends in "s" it requires a plural verb. This is true only when you are speaking of the location of more than one person or thing, providing it is possible that they are in different locations. If you speak of the *whereabouts* of "the woman and her companion" it is likely that they are in the same place and the singular verb is called for.

whether. *See* IF/WHETHER/THOUGH

whether or not

USAGE PANEL QUESTION

Panelist CLARK KINNAIRD questions the propriety of *whether or not,* contending that *or not* is unnecessary. Do you agree?
Yes: 56%. No: 44%.

SHERIDAN BAKER: "Yes. But it's still acceptable, for rhetorical emphasis."
HEYWOOD HALE BROUN: "Yes. Although I like the variation 'or no' to give a feeling of the indecision the phrase implies."
JAMES MACGREGOR BURNS: "No. 'Whether' by itself has a somewhat different use."
PAUL HORGAN: "No. Implied is 'whether yes or no.'"
NORMAN HOSS: "No. Redundancy is essential to language, one of its most valuable rhetorical tools."
HELEN L. KAUFMANN: "No. A sometimes thing. It all depends."
ALEXANDER KENDRICK: "No. I'd rather have my druthers."
WALTER KERR: "No. At least optional."
CLARK KINNAIRD: "Yes, naturally."
STANLEY KUNITZ: "Usually unnecessary, but there are occasions when the negative emphasis of 'or not' may be desirable."

LAURENCE LAFORE: "Yes, generally; but it is sometimes necessary to write: 'whether . . . or not.' "

RUSSELL LYNES: "No. The 'or not' may be unnecessary but it is not necessarily a solecism."

F. D. REEVE: " 'Whether' presents alternatives, as Hamlet reminds us; 'or not' is still one of them."

LEO ROSTEN: "No. Does he wince at 'If, perhaps'?"

RICHARD H. ROVERE: "Yes, with certain exceptions."

VERMONT ROYSTER: "Yes, but I sometimes use it, whether or not correct."

DANIEL SCHORR: "No. What's wrong with a bit of emphasis?"

ERICH SEGAL: "Many languages (e.g., Latin) distinguish among interrogatory methods which expect negative or positive replies."

ROBERT SHERRILL: "Unnecessary, yes; but sometimes it gives the desired emphasis."

ELVIS STAHR, JR.: "Yes; it seems to me to add no clarity, just verbiage."

DAVIDSON TAYLOR: "No. 'Whether his mother would let him or no.' "

LIONEL TRILLING: "No. It's an established and idiomatic phrase; also the more traditional: 'whether or no.' "

BARBARA TUCHMAN: "Strictly speaking, it is unnecessary but not objectionable."

HERMAN WOUK: "Common usage has made this redundant noise a most intelligible one."

whisky/whiskey   By custom and tradition, the preferred British spelling is *whisky*. This practice carries over to Scotch and Canadian whiskies. Thus you find White Horse *Whisky* and Canadian Club *Whisky*. The Irish, never too happy about following British custom, thumb their noses at those folks across the Irish Sea and spell the word *whiskey*. Thus you see Bushmills Irish *Whiskey*. All American brands follow the lead of Ireland and use the *whiskey* spelling.

white paper   A *white paper* is simply a government publication setting forth the official position on a specific question. Such papers, by the very nature of the auspices under which they are issued, usually picture the government as blameless.

whole new ball game. *See* BALL GAME, WHOLE NEW

wholly. *See* COMPLETELY/WHOLLY

who/whom/whoever/whomever   The confusion arising from the use and misuse of *whom* and, in like fashion, *whomever* seems unending. Not long ago one writer on matters linguistic seriously proposed that *whom* be banished from the language, presumably in large part to ease his pain at seeing it so often misused. His suggestion was not exactly a new one.

Back in 1928 the Oxford Dictionary noted that "*whom* is no longer current in natural colloquial speech" and there is evidence that Noah Webster was on record as favoring the elimination of this objective case form of the pronoun *who*.

Whom seems to sound natural today only when immediately following a preposition: "The boy to *whom* I threw the ball cast it to the ground." When *who* or *whom* appears before the verb, in what C. C. Fries called "subject territory," the instinct is to use the subjective, or nominative, case *(who* or *whoever)* rather than the objective *(whom* or *whomever),* even though a precisionist in language use could diagram the sentence and prove that the objective form is required.

A further complication arises with the blind use of *whom* following the preposition "to" in the notion that the objective case is always needed as object of the preposition, while actually the entire clause is the object. Here's an example—from *Fortune* magazine: "They rent it to whomever needs it." This should have read: ". . . to *whoever* needs it," since the pronoun must be subject of the verb "needs." Other examples of mistaken use of *who* and *whom* appear in these citations from the house organ of the Louisville *Courier-Journal:* "DeMotte said he repeatedly asked Hunt *who* he was working for." Make it *whom,* which is object of the preposition "for." "He spoke of catcher Carlton Fisk, *whom* he felt had a chance for. . . ." The words "he felt" are parenthetical. Read it: "Fisk, *who* had a chance. . . ."

Obviously the complications involving *whom* and *whomever* seem endless. Our files contain hundreds of examples of the misuse and abuse of these words. Our feeling, after years of contemplation of the sorry scene, is that a distinction may be drawn here between formal and informal, with precision in the use of the pronouns demanded in formal contexts ("The man *whom* you marry . . .") but a casual approach taken in informal contexts, like the name of a now-departed TV show, *Who Do You Trust?*

For a long time *The New Yorker* used to run items like "*Whom* did you say is coming?" under the standing head "The Omnipotent Whom." We once mentioned to Hobart Weekes, then managing editor of the magazine, that we hadn't seen any such items in recent years. He nodded sadly and said, "We had to give it up. We found that almost nobody knew what was wrong with them."

who's/whose   The similarity of pronunciation of these two words can lead to ridiculous mistakes, as on the part of an advertising writer who described the leading players in the movie *Paper Moon* as portraying "A slick con man and a 9-year-old whose even slicker." *Who's,* of course, is a contraction of "who is"; *whose* is the possessive form of the pronoun "who."

whose

A generation of prescriptive grammarians decreed that *whose* could be used only in reference to human beings, not to animals or inanimate objects. Thus: "The lad *whose* dog had lost its collar" and "the dog the collar of which had been lost." Do you feel that this distinction retains any merit?
Yes: 20%. No: 80%.
Should it be buried for good?   Yes: 77%. No: 23%.

STEWART BEACH: "While I know all about the feeling of the prescriptive grammarians, we have no word in English which is a synonym of 'whose.' "

BARRY BINGHAM, SR.: "It is just too awkward to be obliged to say 'the dog the collar of which has been lost.' "

HAL BORLAND: "Sheer nonsense. But an English publisher changed the title of my book, *The Dog Who Came to Stay* to *The Dog* Which *Came to Stay.*

JOHN BROOKS: "Yes . . . but the second example sentence is preposterous and could be rephrased."

A. B. GUTHRIE, JR.: "Why not use 'that' for the dog?"

HELEN L. KAUFMANN: "In science, there is no such thing as an inanimate object. And a dog = a person. 'Who' for both, say I."

LAURENCE LAFORE: " 'Whose' seems to me unsuitable, even comical, in reference to inanimate objects. But O.K. for dogs."

JESSICA MITFORD: "Animals, O.K., inanimate, no."

PETER S. PRESCOTT: "Perhaps not, but my editors try to make me use 'who' in connection with non-human beings: I wrote the monster which and they changed it to the monster who. *That* is illiterate."

DAVID SCHOENBRUN: "Grammar should not impose awkward style construction."

BARBARA TUCHMAN: "In this case I would use 'the dog whose . . .' because the alternative is so awkward. In general, this problem brings up what is involved in being a *writer:* one has to know when *not* to be bound by a 'prescriptive rule.' "

HERMAN WOUK: "Yes. On inanimate objects, surely."

wiblic. *See* EUPHEMISM

wife. *See* MAN AND WIFE

will. *See* SHALL/WILL

wind screen British automotive equivalent of the American "windshield."

wing British equivalent of the American automobile's "fender."

-wise

USAGE PANEL QUESTION

As a suffix, *-wise*, indicating manner or characteristic of the root word (as "clockwise") has a long and honorable history. In recent decades, and especially in business jargon, *wise* has been widely used in the sense of "with reference to" or "concerning" (as "saleswise," "weatherwise," and the like). Would you accept "Performancewise, the new man proved a failure"?

In writing   Yes: 6%. No: 94%.
In casual speech   Yes: 18%. No: 82%.

SHANA ALEXANDER: "Yes, but only for style . . . to mock the awful new jargon . . . or for fun, as "Funwise, this ballot is a gas.""

CLEVELAND AMORY: "No. I've gotten so I don't even like 'otherwise.' ""

MICHAEL J. ARLEN: "I hate these '-wise' suffixes, but I guess the alternative is: 'In terms of performance, the new man—etc.' That's okay in writing but I think it's unrealistic to expect people to *say* all that—and I don't think the rules of usage should require people to be unrealistic."

ISAAC ASIMOV: "Jocularwise, such usage may suit."

SHERIDAN BAKER: "Only in jest, where it works beautifully."

JOHN O. BARBOUR: "No wise."

JULES BERGMAN: "Mechanization, technology, and pace of events make it certain that '-wise' is here to stay, as ungrammatical and vague as such terms are."

BARRY BINGHAM, SR.: " 'Clockwise' is an entirely different sort of word, indicating a direction in a graphic way. 'Performancewise' is a useless vulgarism."

HAL BORLAND: "There's no reason businessmen can't speak English, too."

JOHN BROOKS: "In speech—yes—only if used jocularly."

ANTHONY BURGESS: " '-wise' only seems to work well with nouns of Germanic origin."

BEN LUCIEN BURMAN: "Awkward. Too much of a mouthful or penful. As difficult to write or pronounce as some of the German names of sausages."

ABE BURROWS: "This is, for me, a matter of taste. I accept 'weatherwise,' 'clockwise.' I don't like 'performancewise' and 'saleswise,' etc.—they don't sound pretty."

JOHN CIARDI: "What's wrong with 'The new man performed badly'?"

ROBERT CROMIE: "UGH."

WALTER CRONKITE: "A very valuable, meaningful mutation."

THOMAS FLEMING: "Madison Avenue argot should be limited to Madison Avenue."

GEROLD FRANK: "NO!"

A. B. GUTHRIE, JR.: "Are you kidding?"

RICHARD EDES HARRISON: "I try not to overlook it for comic effect."

WAKEMAN HARTLEY: "I find it irritating—but practical. It's a good short cut."

GEOFFREY HELLMAN: "Only as a joke."

PAUL HORGAN: "False and vulgar cleverness, always to be avoided."

JOHN K. HUTCHENS: "No—unless it's used for comic reasons, or as jargon, as in *Variety.*"

WALT KELLY: "This, also, is useful to delineate a pretentious slog. It is my hope that such malaproperties will continue to flourish, or I will be out of material."

ALEXANDER KENDRICK: "The only trouble is overkill. It's time to put an end to '-wise,' repetitionwise."

WALTER KERR: "S. J. Perelman had an actor say 'catharsis-wise' and that should have ended it once and for all."

CLARK KINNAIRD: "They are not wise in using it as a bobtail compound, unless they are weatherwise animals or birds."

LAURENCE LAFORE: "Yes—if clearly intended as a mockery."

ROBERT LIPSYTE: "Not even in business writing or speech."

WALTER LORD: "Usage-wise, I abhor it."

DWIGHT MACDONALD: "Yes, but not in this use ('performancewise') because too grotesque looking. Would have said 'no' five years ago, but think it's time-wise to say 'yes.' It *is* a gain in conciseness and neatness."

DAVID McCORD: "Summerwise, one swallow is insufficient. This random use, which may be defended grammatically, is both affected and silly. Glasswise, you have poured me enough."

PHYLLIS McGINLEY: "The people I know use the suffix 'wise' only as a joke."

DANIEL PATRICK MOYNIHAN: "Fear, usagewise, I am like almost unique."

EDWIN NEWMAN: "A horror."

ORVILLE PRESCOTT: "In speech—yes—reluctantly."

FRANCIS ROBINSON: "In the same class with 'contact' as a verb."

HARRISON SALISBURY: "Utter abomination. Blame the Pentagon—source of worse jargon than even the schoolteachers!"

LEONARD SANDERS: "If a single word as apt as 'clockwise' is added to the language, the fad will be worth enduring."

DAVID SCHOENBRUN: "Deliberate vulgarity. My favorite, from Johnny Carson, is 'He's a clever man—I mean wisewise.' "

MARK SCHORER: "Only if the speaker means to be funny."

DANIEL SCHORR: "Only humorously intended."

CHARLES E. SILBERMAN: "No. I feel strongly about this one!"

WALTER W. "RED" SMITH: "Grammarwise, it is an abomination."

ELVIS STAHR, JR.: "If not overdone, this one can enhance the communication and conciseness of English."

DAVIDSON TAYLOR: "A poor way to make adverbs. Hope it dies."

LIONEL TRILLING: "This is a peculiarly revolting locution, even though one can recognize its usefulness—it is perhaps cruel to expect people nowadays to say, 'In respect to performance' or 'In point of performance.' One reason for the repulsiveness of the form is that it violates the meaning of '-wise'—i.e., in the way of, in the fashion of, or, simply, *like*. 'Clockwise' means 'as a clock's hands move,' 'crabwise' means 'the way a crab walks,' etc."

EARL UBELL: "No. Other '-wise' words will succeed depending on how they appeal to the ear."

JUDITH VIORST: "No. I'm afraid my standards are impure and utterly subjective. Some things simply make me wince; others I feel comfortable with —and that's that. I love splitting infinitives, for instance, but 'performancewise' gives me pains in my stomach."

HERMAN WOUK: "I wouldn't even use it in character dialogue, unless the aim were crude caricature."

wish. *See* WANT/WISH

wish I was/wish I were According to the rule books, "I *wish I were*" is the correct form, since the situation is contrary to fact and the *subjunctive* (which see) is used to express supposition and possibility rather than actual fact. However, the subjunctive is seldom used in American English today, though it is common in most European languages. "I *wish I were*" is always best in formal speech and writing. Its use in speech and writing is an indication of care and respect for the niceties of our native tongue. But *was* is much more common in informal speech and writing, as in "I *wish I was* in Dixie. . . ."

without fear of contradiction This expression has been so often used, especially by political orators, that it has become a cliché to be avoided except in deliberate parodies of stump speeches and Rotarian oratory. *See also* CLICHÉ.

wok *Wok* is a word which may have been known to gourmet cooks for some time but it has only been since our relations with China have improved that it has received general circulation. It is the basic Chinese cooking utensil: a wide, shallow metal bowl which sits on a separate base over the source of heat. We saw enormous *woks* when we were allowed in the kitchen of a Chinese restaurant many years ago but did not know their name.

The *wok* burst on the American scene so suddenly that when we gave some as Christmas gifts in 1972 no one knew what they were, let alone what to do with them. The word was not in any American dictionary, even the unabridged. But *woks* and *wok* cookbooks are now in the housewares departments of thousands of stores.

woman. *See* LADY/WOMAN

Women's Liberation Movement. *See* FEMINIST, FEM LIB/FEMLIB, SEXISM, and SEXISM IN LANGUAGE

wop This is one of a number of pejorative terms based on race, religion, nationality, and color—all of which should be avoided at all times except when recording a direct quotation. Originally a term of praise and commendation, it has become so corrupted that it is deeply resented by people of Italian descent.

Usage Panelist Charles Berlitz, the language expert, commented: "It is odd that Italian-Americans object so to the epithet 'wop.' Apparently they don't realize that originally it was a term of high praise. It's derived from 'guappo,' an Italian dialect word meaning strong and handsome. When Italian immigrant laborers were coming in great numbers to this country in the nineteenth century, they were often represented by 'padrones,' who would place them in jobs for a fee. The biggest and strongest were described as 'guappos' and they drew the best jobs."

Wop, however, has lost its original meaning and has become a word that would best be banished from the language.

worsen This is one of the few words left in English that are formed with the suffix "-en" to indicate a gradual change in condition. Other such verbs are "darken," "deepen," and "lengthen." Early on in World War II, *worsen* enjoyed a vogue among the voice-of-doom broadcasters, who delighted in pointing out the rapidly *worsening* situations in all parts of the globe.

would of. *See* SHOULD OF/COULD OF/WOULD OF

wreak/wreck/wrought The phrase *wreak havoc* becomes *wreck havoc* on occasion. A report of a tornado contained the following: "The tornado struck without warning after about ten minutes of rain. In seconds it had *wrecked havoc* and gone."

Wreck havoc is both wrong and redundant. *Havoc* is "great destruction, as resulting from wars or hurricanes" and *wreck,* of course, means "to destroy or damage badly."

Wreak, a relatively unfamiliar word, comes from the Anglo-Saxon "wrecan," and means "to inflict or deliver a damaging blow." Thus *wreak havoc* is the proper phrase in the case of widespread destruction.

Wrought havoc instead of *wreaked havoc* is also sometimes seen in print. A writer of such a phrase is probably influenced by the Biblical quotation "What hath God wrought!" (Numbers 23:23), which Samuel F. B. Morse used for the first telegraph message he sent to his partner, Alfred Vail, from Washington to Baltimore in 1844. *Wrought* is an alternate past tense or past participle of "work" and can mean "created," but the idiom remains *"wreak havoc."*

wright/write A *wright* is a craftsman or workman such as a mill*wright*, ship*wright*, or wheel*wright*. In the case of play*wright*, the word *write* has no connection, even though writing is the craft he or she practices.

write. *See* ADVISE/INFORM/WRITE

X (as symbol for "unknown" and as signature) *X* has at least two functions in standard English. It may serve as a *symbol* for an unknown quantity: "Her comprehension of abstract art is *X.*" Likewise *X* may legally serve as the *signature* of an illiterate person.

X (sounded as "Z") Some years ago a reader of our column complained about words like "xylophone," spelled with an initial *x* but pronounced as though spelled with an initial *z*. We took the matter up with the late Joshua Whatmough, then chairman of the Department of Linguistics at Harvard. Here is what he told us: "In English the letter 'x' appears initially only in words borrowed from the Greek, as in the words 'xylophone' and 'xenophobe.' In modern English, the letter 'x' is generally pronounced 'z' when it comes at the beginning of a word, 'ks' after an accented vowel ('exit,' 'exigent,' and 'execute'), and 'gz' before an accented vowel ('exonerate' and 'examine')."

Xanadu *Xanadu,* a word you will not find in most dictionaries, has appeared in magazine articles and real-estate advertising as a sort of elegant synonym for "paradise." Example: "The Road to Xanadu—Fleeing Manhattan for Morocco and Spain." *Xanadu* is the invention of two English writers, Samuel Purchas and Samuel Taylor Coleridge, and originally referred to the legendary home of Kubla Khan: "In Xanadu did Kubla Khan/A stately pleasure dome decree:/Where Alph, the sacred river ran/Through caverns measureless to man/Down to a sunless sea." We're not at all sure that we approve this conversion of *Xanadu* into an adman's vision of his dream home—but perhaps that may be considered poetic license.

Xerox. *see* PHOTOSTAT/PHOTOSTAT

Xmas *Xmas* is widely considered to be department-store shorthand for "Christmas" and hence looked down on by many careful users of the language. This is, however, far from the truth, which is that *Xmas* has been part of the language at least since 1555. The "X" in *Xmas* is the Greek letter *X*, transliterated as "Kh" and representing the Greek "Khristos," meaning Christ. However, the prejudice against *Xmas* is so widespread that its use may best be confined to informal contexts.

Yankee Strictly speaking, *Yankee* is a suitable label only for natives of the New England states. However, throughout the world, *Yankee* is used as a catch word to refer to all inhabitants or natives of the United States. Efforts have been made to coin a more appropriate word but without success. A glance at three of the candidates will explain why. They were "Unisians," "Unitedstatesians," and "Columbards."

yay/yea (big) (small) Expressions like *yay big* and *yay small* have achieved considerable currency, especially in the casual speech of members of the scientific fraternity. The expressions are invariably accompanied by a gesture of the hands to indicate the size of the object described, much like the gesture used by fishermen to show the size of the fish that got away. *Yay,* sometimes spelled *yea,* thus proves itself a remarkably versatile word, one which can mean either. overwhelmingly large or not very big. As Humpty Dumpty said in *Through the Looking-Glass:* "When I use a word, it means just what I choose it to mean—neither more nor less." It appears that Humpty Dumpty and some of our scientists may have quite a bit in common—*yay* much, so to speak. Nonetheless, the use of *yay* and *yea* should be confined to informal contexts.

ye *Ye,* as in *Ye* Olde Tea Shoppe, is usually pronounced YEE, but the correct pronunciation is the same as for "the"—THEE or, if unstressed, THUH. The confusion arose from the medieval printers' practice of substituting the letter "y" for the runic letter called "thorn," which was the symbol used in Old and Middle English to indicate the sound now expressed by "th."

yesterday, want it "He *wants it yesterday*" is a fairly commonplace business expression, meaning simply that someone—usually a boss or customer—is so insistent on prompt service that it's almost as though he expects delivery before the order is even placed. The expression is suitable only in informal contexts.

Yiddishisms   Among the most notable and lively contributions to contemporary American English have been the borrowings from Yiddish, itself a blend of High German and Hebrew. Many *Yiddishisms* (for example "chutzpah") are given individual entry in this dictionary. Here are a few, most of them popularized by radio and television comedians who carried them over from their own apprenticeship in the Yiddish theater and, more recently and importantly, in the theaters of the so-called Borscht Belt, a group of resort hotels in New York's Catskill Mountains catering almost exclusively to vacationing Jews from New York City. A staple of each day's menus was a beet soup known as "borscht." Hence, "Borscht Circuit" or "Borscht Belt."

Among the borrowings are: schlemiel, schmaltz, chutzpah, kitsch, schnook, schtick, dreck, schlep, klutz, and schnorrer. A "schlemiel" is an unlucky bungler, a perennial patsy. His name comes from Shelumiel, an Old Testament leader of the tribe of Simeon. While other leaders won their battles, he lost them all. "Schmaltz" is literally melted fat, usually chicken fat, but now connotes excessive sentimentality. "Chutzpah" is nerve, brass, or gall. "Kitsch" describes anything of poor quality but wide popularity, like the poetry of Edgar Guest. A "schnook" is a sucker, a dupe. One's "schtick" is one's trademark, like Groucho Marx's mustache or Jack Benny's stinginess. "Dreck," also spelled "drek," is simply trash, junk, or, in the clothing trade, a poorly made garment. To "schlep" something is to move it from one place to another, usually clumsily and with difficulty. A "klutz" is a very dull or clumsy person. In fact, "klutz" comes from the German "klotz," meaning clod or blockhead. And a "schnorrer" is a parasite, a leech, and sometimes an outright beggar. As one Yiddish comedian put it, a "schnorrer" is the fellow who goes through a revolving door on your push.

All of these *Yiddishisms*, lively and colorful though they may be, are best restricted to use in informal contexts.

yoke   *Yoke* is the Baltimore underworld slang term for "mug," that is, to seize a person unawares with robbery as a motive. It was originally sailor slang and came from the practice of catching a sailor from behind by the yoke of his tightly fitted collar. Then, by twisting his neckerchief, the mugger (or *yoker*) would quickly have him under control. Crooks who did this were sometimes called "jumper jacks"—the latter word an obvious allusion to "Jack Tar," the sailor's nickname. In his *American Language,* H. L. Mencken—a lifelong Baltimorean—says, "It is called 'mugging' in New York, but *yoking* in most other places." But our research indicates that precisely the opposite is true: this sense of *yoke* is virtually unknown outside of Baltimore.

you know   The use of *you know* as a bit of verbal punctuation has become very common, especially among young and relatively inarticulate people. It's a painful experience to have to listen to these young people punctuating every sentence with two or three *you knows*—and seeming blissfully unaware of what they are saying or the fact that the repetition bores any intelligent listener to extinction. One wonders what would happen if the offenders were forced to listen to tapes of their own *you know* statements, repeated again and again and again. That, in W. S. Gilbert's phrase, would indeed be a punishment that fits the crime.

young/younger/youngest   News item: "Searchers scoured the area where the *youngest* of the two missing pupils was seen last." *Younger,* not *youngest,* is called for here. The superlative form of the adjective *(youngest)* should be used only when three or more persons or objects are involved.

yours truly/yours very truly. *See* VERY TRULY YOURS/YOURS TRULY/YOURS VERY TRULY

zap. *See* VOGUE WORDS

zero   The numeral *zero* is seldom so called any more, except when weather reports give the temperature as "approaching *zero*". Nowadays *zero* is most often articulated as "oh." Thus Highway 101 is One-Oh-One. A variant, closer to *zero* but not quite the same thing, is the increasingly heard *zip* (which see). *Zero* also is heard as a substitute for "no," as in "*zero* population growth." *See also* GROUND ZERO.

zip/ZIP codes   Increasingly popular with broadcasters as a sort of voguish slang substitute for "zero" is *zip,* as in "The Mets blanked the Braves five -*zip*" or "Chances of precipitation today are *zip.*" We suspect that part of the reason for its increasing popularity is the stress placed on ZIP codes by the Postal Service, though there is really no connection between the two. The ZIP in ZIP codes is a rather strained acronym for Zone Improvement Program—a phrase that surpasses even routine bureaucratic phrasing for sheer bafflement.

zoomania. *See* MANIA

Epilogue

Quite a few years ago the late Bruce Bliven wrote an apologia for his life as a crusading copyreader. It appeared (date unknown) in the old *Saturday Evening Post.*

We quoted it to our panelists and asked them if they felt that we should remain active in what one panelist has called "the conspiracy to save the language."

Here is Mr. Bliven's statement:

I Give Up My Crusade

This is to serve notice on the world that I give up the crusade. For 40 years I worked on the copy desks of newspapers and magazines, trying to straighten out the grammar of the great American public, and, in particular, six of the most common faults.

My success has been about that of most reformers. Things have been getting steadily worse.

As every copyreader knows, six of the most common faults are these:

Using "data" as a singular noun. (The data is readily available.)

Using "contact" as a verb. (I'll contact you tomorrow.)

Confusing "like" and "as." (Just go on acting like you did before.)

Comparing "unique." (His collection of coins is rather unique.)

Using "providing" for "provided." (He will come, providing he is able.)

Using "literally" for "figuratively." (I was literally burned up at what he said.)

It is perfectly clear that the American people in their collective unconscious wisdom are changing the language. They have every right to do it. I can't stop it. This has been going on as long as there has been a language, with fussbudgets like me being dragged, kicking and screaming, at the tail of the procession.

NOTE: Members of the Usage Panel, to the contrary, endorse the need for a "conspiracy to save the language," while, at the same time, accepting additions and changes that are valid and will last.

JOHN BROOKS: "Now more than in Bruce Bliven's time. I have ample confidence in the language's propensity to change as needed; Our job is to screen out the bad changes and let only the valuable ones stand."

HEYWOOD HALE BROUN: "As ADA, the Defense Department's computer language, looms over us, let's toast each other in proper English. As Logan Pearsall Smith put it, 'When they can no longer sustain me with oysters and sips of champagne, I will say with my last breath, You cannot be too fastidious.' "

ANTHONY BURGESS: "But the fight is not going to be won. We must be purists in our own writing as long as we can care."

BEN LUCIEN BURMAN: "Of course the language must continue to change and grow but we must stand guard twenty-four hours a day to protect it from the attacks of the Mechanical Age, which has no respect for beauty or tradition. If we fail, the panelists for the next Dictionary of Usage will be computers."

ROBERT CROMIE: "There is hope for the English language if we can persuade politicians, economists, and admen to use some *other* language."

WILLARD R. ESPY: "The most interesting point about the six no-nos on which Bruce Bliven gave up after 40 years is that they are still no-nos 50 years later."

GEROLD FRANK: "Let's try to maintain the purity of the language as best we can, because it is being bastardized whether we like it or not."

FRANCES FRITCHMAN: "We are not just quaint antiquarians opposing progress. What we are really fighting for is clarity, accuracy, exactitude— qualities never more needed than now!"

ELIZABETH HARDWICK: "I am sure that what follows is not news to you but I will state it anyway. I feel a great many of the barbarisms are an expression of distrust of simple language, a fear that the simple old words are not refined enough. 'Person' does not seem to many as 'educated' as 'individual.' 'Area' seems more up-to-date than 'place' and so on. 'Overly' is preferred to 'very.' Bureaucratic, Latinate words are preferred to old root words of common speech. All of this depresses me. On the other hand I love new coinages from 'street language' when they are imaginative and fresh. I like 'split' for going away quickly and even 'splitsville' for divorce, even though the latter is already passé. I have a word new to me recently that intrigues me—'booked' for leaving. 'I got fed up and I booked.' I cannot figure out the origin and I daresay this 'booking' is a passing fancy.

I put all of this down for you to give a general picture of my feelings about language as I hear it."

DIANE JOHNSON: "Probably all the pet crusades will fail. 'Lay' will surely replace 'lie.' I see no hope for some other changing forms; but the jargon will perhaps die away. I think it is proper to constitute a conservative force, a resistance, though, to make sure that only the most inevitable get through."

JAMES J. KILPATRICK: "I surrendered a few years ago on 'to contact,' but I will keep fighting on the others."

STANLEY KUNITZ: "Yes, except for 'contact' in its colloquial usage, which offends me less than it used to. The reason for wanting to 'save the language' is that one believes in the possibility of a language that saves."

JULES LOH: "Mr. Bliven's six most common faults must indeed continue to be protested, along with dozens more, and, yes, your panel must never give up its conspiracy to save the language. I am proud to be one of the conspirators.

"We must also find a way to attend to other problems which seem to me to be growing apace, the effusion of jargon. Bloated language has always been with us, but, today, with more and more television channels, more word processors hatching all over the place, more duplicating machines to serve as manure spreaders, the babblers have so much greater opportunity. In Mr. Bliven's day, the grandiose spoutings of bureaucrats, technocrats, and abstract academics could be tracked down and stomped on, or at least humiliated, one at a time. The problem now, as one editor put it, is like duck shooting: Every time you pause to reload, a whole flock gets by.

"We need more conspirators."

ORVILLE PRESCOTT: "Bliven's points are all still valid. To object to these lamentable usages is a lost cause, but a glorious lost cause like that of the Stuarts."

F. D. REEVE: "What *else* can an old poet do?"

VERMONT ROYSTER: "What I deplore is the debasement of the language, whether from violation of the simple and logical rules of grammar or from using good, useful words wrongly. In both cases, the fault is ignorance. In both cases the consequence is a breakdown in communication. Not only are all subtleties and shades of meaning lost, but in some cases there is actual misunderstanding between writer and reader, the writer intending one meaning, the reader receiving another. This occurs no matter whether it is the writer or the reader who is using the language wrongly."

DAVID SCHOENBRUN: "A living language must be tolerant of change, at first in speech, then, cautiously, in writing. The only thing that doesn't change is something that is dead. English is a wonderfully flexible instrument and should not be made rigid by purists. But each change should be carefully examined before acceptance. Does it create a better image? Improve understanding? Not offend aesthetics or brutalize grammar and diction?"

HAROLD SCHONBERG: "We've always had bad and sloppy language and will continue to have. But what is disturbing is that people supposed to be educated—degree holders, scientists, government officials, even professional writers—are misusing language more and more. The very ones supposed to uphold standards are beginning to be the worst offenders, and that seems to me to be unprecedented. We are in for a bad time."

ERICH SEGAL: "The battle has been lost on 'data,' 'contact,' and 'literally.' I think we should continue to fight the misuse of the other examples, which are less firmly entrenched."

ELVIS STAHR, JR.: "Evolution of the language must go on, of course, but retrogression is not progression and degradation is not enrichment."

WALLACE STEGNER: "I think you can't keep untrained dogs from rushing and pulling. I think further that somebody has to hang onto the leash."

HAROLD TAYLOR: "I'm especially worried about the state of writing and reading in the schools and colleges. The students just coast along and are not often aware of what it means to write well or to use words with precision of meaning. The most promising movement in improving the situation is the one which makes *all* the teachers, not merely the remedial and writing crowd, responsible for the quality of student writing."

KARL V. TEETER: "It is good writing and convincing speech that will 'save the language,' not pontification."

EVAN W. THOMAS: "I might take a more relaxed view but the confusion between 'like' and 'as' is the spark that makes me feel strongly about *all* the miserable examples."

EARL UBELL: "I sometimes feel as Bruce Bliven does when someone says 'I am nauseous' rather than the correct 'I am nauseated.' But I have to learn to hold my tongue because if I make the correction, no matter how gently, my respondent responds with a grimace that says 'Pedant! Elitist! Nit-

Picker!' and worse. I guess the road to preservation of the language in understandable form is doing one's best to do things right and, when in a position to edit, to correct the wrong. Otherwise, keep your friends."

JOSEPH VERGARA: "It's obvious that lots of busy people really care. For no pay they took time out to study and answer the questionnaires. As long as talented users of the language feel this strongly about the state of the language, we have nothing to fear. The language will continue to absorb, reject, change, gather, and grow. It's good to know that the Morrises and their team of literary watchdogs will be on the lookout against pretentiousness, ignorance, and poor taste. Happy to be on the team."

HERMAN WOUK: "Nobody has to 'save' English. It is extraordinarily supple and vigorous. The thing is to distinguish between mutations and excrescences. That is worth doing."

Bibliography

This is a selective listing of books referred to in the course of writing and editing this dictionary. As will be obvious to any reader of the dictionary, many more books were referred to from time to time during the years of manuscript preparation. One function of this bibliography is to give the student of language specific titles and publishing information on works that are somewhat casually referred to in the text, for example *AHD* for American Heritage Dictionary of the English Language, or "Fowler" for H. W. Fowler: Dictionary of Modern English Usage.

Ash, Rev. John: *Dictionary of the English Language*, London, 1775.

Barnhart, Clarence: *New Century Cyclopedia of Names*, Englewood Cliffs, N.J., Prentice-Hall.

Barnhart, Clarence, et al. (eds.): *Barnhart Dictionary of New English Since 1963*, New York, Harper & Row.

Bartlett, John: *Familiar Quotations* (14th ed.), Boston, Little, Brown.

Bender, James F.: *NBC Handbook of Pronunciation*, New York, Crowell.

Bernstein, Theodore M.: *The Careful Writer*, New York, Atheneum.

Berry, Lester V., and Van Den Bark, Melvin: *American Thesaurus of Slang*, New York, Crowell.

Bloomfield, Leonard: *Language*, New York, Holt, Rinehart & Winston.

Bohle, Bruce: *Home Book of American Quotations*, New York, Dodd, Mead.

Brewer, E. Cobham: *Brewer's Dictionary of Phrase and Fable*, New York, Harper & Row.

Burchfield, R. W. (ed.): *Supplements to the Oxford English Dictionary*, Oxford, Oxford University Press.

Colby, Frank O.: *American Pronouncing Dictionary*, New York, Crowell.

Colby, Frank O.: *Practical Handbook of Better English*, New York, Grosset & Dunlap.

Copperud, Roy: *Words on Paper*, New York, Hawthorn Books.

Craigie, Sir William A.: *Dictionary of American English*, Chicago, University of Chicago Press.

Cummings, Parke: *Dictionary of Baseball*, Cranbury, N.J., A. S. Barnes.

Follett, Wilson: *Modern American Usage*, New York, Hill & Wang.

Fowler, Henry W.: *Dictionary of Modern English Usage* (also revised ed., Sir Ernest Gower, ed.), Oxford, Oxford University Press.

Fries, Charles C.: *American English Grammar*, Englewood Cliffs, N.J., Prentice-Hall.

Funk & Wagnalls Dictionaries: *New Standard* (1913); *Standard College* (1966), New York, Funk & Wagnalls.

Goldin, Hyman E.: *Dictionary of American Underworld Lingo*, New York, Twayne.

Greet, W. Cabell: *World Words*, New York, Columbia University Press.

Guralnik, David B. (ed.): *Webster's New World Dictionary of the American Language,* 1st ed. (1953); 2nd ed. (1970), New York, World.

Hart, James D.: *Oxford Companion to American Literature,* New York, Oxford University Press.

Harvey, Sir Paul: *Oxford Companion to English Literature,* New York, Oxford University Press.

Johnson, Samuel: *Dictionary of the English Language* (4th ed.), London, 1770.

Kenyon, John S., and Knott, Thomas A.: *Pronouncing Dictionary of American English,* Springfield, Mass., G. & C. Merriam.

Longyear, Marie M. (ed.): *The McGraw-Hill Style Manual: A Concise Guide for Writers and Editors,* New York.

Mankiewicz, Frank: *Perfectly Clear,* New York, Quadrangle Books.

Manual of Style, A (13th ed.), Chicago, University of Chicago Press.

Marckwardt, Albert H., and Walcott, Fred: *Facts About Current English Usage,* Englewood Cliffs, N.J., Prentice-Hall.

Mathews, Mitford: *Dictionary of Americanisms,* Chicago, University of Chicago Press.

Mencken, H(enry) L(ouis): *The American Language* (plus *Supplements One* and *Two*), New York, Knopf.

Miller, Casey, and Swift, Kate: *The Handbook of Nonsexist Writing for Writers, Editors and Speakers,* New York, Lippincott & Crowell.

Morris, William: *Your Heritage of Words,* New York, Dell.

Morris, William (ed.): *American Heritage Dictionary of the English Language* (Original Edition), Boston, Houghton Mifflin.

Morris, William (ed.): *Words: The New Dictionary,* New York, Grosset & Dunlap.

Morris, William and Mary: *Dictionary of Word and Phrase Origins,* volumes I, II and III, New York, Harper & Row.

Naiman, Arthur: *Word Processing Buyers' Guide,* New York, McGraw-Hill.

Neaman, Judith S., and Silver, Carole G.: *Kind Words: A Thesaurus of Euphemisms,* New York, Facts on File.

Newman, Edwin: *A Civil Tongue,* New York, Bobbs-Merrill.

Newman, Edwin: *Strictly Speaking,* New York, Bobbs-Merrill.

Onions, C. T. (ed.): *Shorter Oxford English Dictionary,* New York, Oxford University Press.

Parrott, Thomas Marc (ed.): *Shakespeare: Plays and Sonnets,* New York, Scribners.

Partridge, Eric: *Dictionary of Slang and Unconventional English,* New York, Macmillan.

Partridge, Eric: *Usage and Abusage,* New York, Harper & Row.

Perrin, Porter G.: *Writer's Guide and Index to English,* Glenview, Ill., Scott, Foresman.

Perrin, Porter G., and Smith, George H.: *Perrin-Smith Handbook of Current English,* Glenview, Ill., Scott, Foresman.

Rank, Hugh (ed.): *Language and Public Policy,* Urbana, Ill., National Council of Teachers of English.

Rosten, Leo: *Joys of Yiddish,* New York, McGraw-Hill.

Schur, Norman W.: *British Self-Taught with Comments in American,* New York, Macmillan.

Smith, Eldon C.: *Dictionary of American Family Names,* New York, Harper & Row.

Spencer, Donald D.: *Computer Dictionary for Everyone,* New York, Charles Scribner's Sons.

Stewart, George R.: *American Place Names,* New York, Oxford University Press.

Strunk, William, Jr., and White, E. B.: *Elements of Style,* New York, Macmillan.

U.S. Government Printing Office: *Style Manual,* Washington, D.C.

Webster, Noah: *An American Dictionary of the English Language* (1828 ed.), New York, Johnson Reprint.

Webster's Dictionaries: *Second International* (1934); *Fifth Collegiate (1936); Third International* (1961); *Seventh Collegiate* (1963), Springfield, Mass., G. & C. Merriam.

Wentworth, Harold: *American Dialect Dictionary,* New York, Crowell.

Wentworth, Harold, and Flexner, Stuart Berg: *Dictionary of American Slang,* New York, Crowell.

Williams, Nick (ed.): *Los Angeles Times Style Guide,* Los Angeles.

Winkler, G. P. (ed.): *Associated Press Stylebook,* New York.

Winship, Tom (ed.): *Boston Globe Stylebook,* Boston.

Zinsser, William: *On Writing Well,* New York, Harper & Row.

Zinsser, William: *Writing with a Word Processor,* New York, Harper & Row.

NOTE: Research has also involved daily monitoring of the print and electronic media, including *The New York Times,* the *Hartford Courant,* the *Wall Street Journal, Greenwich Time,* and the Boston *Globe,* as well as the news and information programs of the three major radio and television networks and those of Cable News Network, Public Broadcasting System, and National Public Radio.

ABOUT THE AUTHORS

WILLIAM MORRIS is one of the world's best-known authorities on the English language. With his late wife, Mary, he wrote the internationally syndicated daily newspaper column, "Words, Wit and Wisdom," for more than thirty years. In his distinguished career as a lexicographer, William Morris was also editor-in-chief of the original, widely-hailed *American Heritage Dictionary of the English Language*. Together, William and Mary Morris wrote more than a dozen books, including the *Morris Dictionary of Word and Phrase Origins*.